||| || || ||||||| || |||||| |||||| || | |||| ||||| |||

⊲ **W9-BPM-518**

3.4 FIELD DEFINITION   81
   3.4.1 The DFHMDF Macro   81
3.5 RESULTS OF MAP ASSEMBLY   86
   3.5.1 How Maps Are Stored   86
TEST YOUR UNDERSTANDING   116
   Questions and Exercises   116

4   Programming Techniques for Terminal I/O Operations   117

4.1 SIMPLE TERMINAL I/O WITHOUT USING MAPS   118
   4.1.1 The SEND Command   118
   4.1.2 The RECEIVE Command   120
   4.1.3 Setting Up Your Error-Handler Routine   121
   4.1.4 HANDLE CONDITION Command   122
   4.1.5 Terminating the Task   123
   4.1.6 Data Structures: Which Options Should You
       Choose?   123
   4.1.7 An Optional Topic: Terminal I/O Using the Linkage
       Section   123
4.2 USING MAP I/O COMMANDS   129
   4.2.1 SEND MAP Command Format   129
   4.2.2 RECEIVE MAP Command   136
4.3 PROGRAMMING CONSIDERATIONS FOR MAP I/O   137
   4.3.1 Error Handling   137
   4.3.2 The Attention Identifier   143
   4.3.3 Other Programming Considerations   146
TEST YOUR UNDERSTANDING   149
   Questions and Exercises   149

5   Communication Between Program Modules   151

5.1 PSEUDOCONVERSATIONAL DESIGN   151
   5.1.1 Conversational vs. Pseudoconversational
       Programming   151
5.2 THE RETURN COMMAND   155
   5.2.1 Format and Function of the RETURN Command 155
5.3 THE XCTL COMMAND   158
   5.3.1 Format and Function of the XCTL Command   158
5.4 THE LINK COMMAND   159
   5.4.1 Format and Function of the LINK Command   159
5.5 PROGRAMMING CONSIDERATIONS   160
   5.5.1 Possible Error Situations   160
   5.5.2 Maintaining Control over Your Application 161
   5.5.3 A Warning about DFHCOMMAREA Length   162

5.6 OTHER METHODS FOR PASSING DATA BETWEEN
   PROGRAMS   164
   5.6.1 Common Work Area   164
   5.6.2 Transaction Work Area   165
   5.6.3 Terminal Control Table User Area   165
   5.6.4 Accessing the CWA, TWA, and TCTUA   165
   5.6.5 Which Areas to Use?   166
   5.6.6 More about the ASSIGN Command   166
5.7 STORING DATA IN PROGRAM FORM   167
   5.7.1 LOAD under Mainframe CICS   167
   5.7.2 LOAD under CICS OS/2 1.20   168
5.8 STARTING NEW TASKS FROM AN APPLICATION
   PROGRAM   168
   5.8.1 START and RETRIEVE   168
5.9 SUBPROGRAMS   170
   5.9.1 The COBOL CALL Statement   170
5.10 USEFUL INFORMATION PROVIDED BY THE CICS
   SYSTEM   171
   5.10.1 The EXEC Interface Block   171
   5.10.2 CICS 1.7 and Above: Options on ASSIGN
       Command   174
   5.10.3 Time and Date Commands   175
5.11 SAMPLE APPLICATION PROGRAMS   176
   5.11.1 A Menu Program   176
TEST YOUR UNDERSTANDING   193
   Questions and Exercises   193

6   Indexed File I/O and Related Topics   195

6.1 INTRODUCTION TO VSAM AND ACCESS METHOD
   SERVICES   196
   6.1.1 Brief Review of Indexed File Concepts   196
   6.1.2 Introduction to Access Method Services Utilities
       (IDCAMS)   202
6.2 CONCEPTS OF ONLINE INDEXED FILE PROCESSING   208
   6.2.1 Relationship between Files and CICS   208
   6.2.2 Sharing Files among Applications in a CICS System   209
6.3 PROGRAMMING TECHNIQUES FOR INDEXED FILE I/O   210
   6.3.1 I/O Commands for VSAM KSDS Files   210
   6.3.2 Commands for File Browsing   233
6.4 CHANGES TO CICS VSAM FILE PROCESSING   262
   6.4.1 File Opening Procedures   262
   6.4.2 More Application Programming Changes   263
TEST YOUR UNDERSTANDING   264
   Questions and Exercises   264

CICS COMMAND LEVEL PROGRAMMING

SECOND EDITION

ALIDA JATICH

JOHN WILEY & SONS, INC.

New York • **Chichester** • **Brisbane** • **Toronto** • **Singapore**

To Sammy
and our other little friends

This publication is designed to provide accurate and authoritative information in regard to the subject matter covered. It is sold with the understanding that the publisher is not engaged in rendering legal, accounting, or other professional service. If legal advice or other expert assistance is required, the services of a competent professional person should be sought. FROM A DECLARATION OF PRINCIPLES JOINTLY ADOPTED BY A COMMITTEE OF THE AMERICAN BAR ASSOCIATION AND A COMMITTEE OF PUBLISHERS.

Copyright 1991 © by John Wiley & Sons, Inc.

Library of Congress Cataloging-in-Publication Data

Jatich, Alida
    CICS command level programming / by Alida Jatich. -- 2nd ed.
      p.   cm.
    Includes bibliographical references and index.
    ISBN 0-471-52861-7 (alk. paper). -- ISBN 0-471-52862-5 (pbk. :
alk. paper)
    1. On-line data processing. 2. CICS (Computer system)
3. Electronic digital computers--Programming. 4. COBOL (Computer
program language) I. Title.
QA76.55J38 1991
005.4'3--dc20   90-27513
                                                        CIP

Printed in the United States of America

      10 9 8 7

Contents

Preface to the Second Edition   xiii

Preface to the First Edition   xvii

Acknowledgments   xxi

**1   Overview of CICS from the Application Programmer's
      Standpoint**   1

1.1 WHAT A CICS ONLINE SYSTEM ACTUALLY DOES   1
    1.1.1 Online Processing: What It Is, Why It Is Used   1
    1.1.2 Software Capabilities Needed for Online Processing   6
    1.1.3 Relationship between Applications Programs and
          CICS, and between CICS and the Operating
          System   7
1.2 CICS PROGRAMS, MAPS, AND LANGUAGE
    TRANSLATION: WHAT THE CICS LANGUAGE
    FACILITIES PROVIDE   7
    1.2.1 Online I/O Accesses: How They Differ from Batch
          Usage   7
    1.2.2 CICS Command Format   10
    1.2.3 What the Command Translator Does with Your
          Program   12
    1.2.4 Command Level and Macro Level   13

1.2.5 Maps: What They Are and How They Are Created   22
1.2.6 Making Compiled Programs and Maps Available to
    the CICS System   33
1.3 STRUCTURE OF CICS   34
    1.3.1 CICS Tables   34
    1.3.2 Programs within CICS   37
    1.3.3 Mainframe CICS Architecture under CICS 3.1 and
        Later   43
    1.3.4 Resource Definition Online (RDO)   45
    1.3.5 The CEDA Transaction   46
TEST YOUR UNDERSTANDING   47
    Questions and Exercises   47

2 Terminal Device Concepts   **48**

2.1 TERMINALS   48
    2.1.1 What Is a Terminal?   48
2.2 KEYBOARD FUNCTIONS   49
    2.2.1 Transmission of Data to Mainframe   49
2.3 CRT SCREEN FUNCTIONS   50
    2.3.1 Need for Formatting   50
    2.3.2 Data Streams: How CICS Communicates with Your
        Terminal   50
    2.3.3 Use of Cursor Position in Online Applications   53
    2.3.4 Use of Field Attributes in Online Applications   53
    2.3.5 Modified Data Tag: What It Is, How It Works   56
    2.3.6 Field Length Indicator   58
    2.3.7 Other Types of Terminal I/O   59
    2.3.8 Other Types of Terminal Devices   59
TEST YOUR UNDERSTANDING   61
    Questions and Exercises   61

**3 Programming Techniques for Mapping the Terminal
Screen**   **62**

3.1 SETTING UP A SCREEN LAYOUT   62
    3.1.1 Preparing Sample Screens   62
    3.1.2 Sample Online Application   64
    3.1.3 Which Level of Basic Mapping Support Is
        Available?   76
    3.1.4 Basic Mapping Support Macros   77
3.2 MAP SET DEFINITION   77
    3.2.1 The DFHMSD Macro   77
3.3 MAP DEFINITION   81
    3.3.1 The DFHMDI Macro   81

7   **Temporary Storage**   267

7.1 THE ROLE OF TEMPORARY STORAGE IN A CICS
      APPLICATION   267
      7.1.1 Need for Temporary Storage   267
      7.1.2 How Temporary Storage is Allocated and Used   269
7.2 PROGRAMMING TECHNIQUES   271
      7.2.1 I/O Commands for Reading, Writing, and Deleting
              Temporary Storage   271
      7.2.2 Programming Recommendations   274
      7.2.3 Sample Program: Customer Record Change
              Processor   275
TEST YOUR UNDERSTANDING   286
      Questions and Exercises   286

8   **Sequential File I/O in CICS Programs**   287

8.1 SEQUENTIAL I/O CONCEPTS   287
      8.1.1 Uses for Sequential I/O under CICS   287
      8.1.2 Transient Data Queue Concepts   288
      8.1.3 Logging and Journaling Concepts   291
8.2 PROGRAMMING TECHNIQUES FOR SEQUENTIAL I/O
      OPERATIONS   293
      8.2.1 Transient Data I/O Commands   293
      8.2.2 Commands for Writing Journal Records   294
      8.2.3 Appearance of Journal File Contents   297
      8.2.4 Programming Techniques for Tasks Using Protected
              Resources   298
TEST YOUR UNDERSTANDING   302
      Questions and Exercises   302

9   **Testing Methods for CICS Applications**   303

9.1 PLANNING FOR A VALID TEST   304
      9.1.1 Creating a Test Plan   304
      9.1.2 Creating Good Test Data   306
      9.1.3 System Capacity   306
9.2 WHAT TO DO IF AN APPLICATION BEGINS LOOPING   306
      9.2.1 Breaking Out of a Loop   306
9.3 USING EXECUTION DIAGNOSTIC FACILITY   307
      9.3.1 What Is EDF?   307
      9.3.2 How to Run Your Application under EDF   308
      9.3.3 Features Available under EDF   309
      9.3.4 Using EDF Instead of a Memory Dump   315
      9.3.5 Temporary Storage Browse   316
      9.3.6 CECI and CECS   317

9.4 USING THE ANIMATOR FOR DEBUGGING UNDER OS/2   318
    9.4.1 What Animated Debugging Is All About   318
    9.4.2 Compiling Programs to Run under Animator   318
    9.4.3 Telling CICS OS/2 to Use Animator   319
    9.4.4 Running a Program with Animator   320
TEST YOUR UNDERSTANDING   326
    Questions and Exercises   326

10 Troubleshooting Program ABENDs   **327**

10.1 USING DUMPS   328
    10.1.1 Dump Concepts   328
    10.1.2 Step-by-Step Method for Reading Mainframe
         ABEND Dumps   329
    10.1.3 ABEND Codes for CICS Application Programs   350
    10.1.4 Storage Violation Dumps   352
    10.1.5 CICS Commands to Create Dumps   354
10.2 TRACE TABLE   356
    10.2.1 Relating Trace Table Entries to CICS Control
         Functions   356
    10.2.2 Finding Useful Information in Trace Table   357
TEST YOUR UNDERSTANDING   359
    Questions and Exercises   359

11 Advanced Topics: Screen Handling and Printing   **397**

11.1 ADVANCED BASIC MAPPING SUPPORT: PAGING AND
    MULTIPLE MAPS   397
    11.1.1 How Paging Works; What Are Its Limitations   397
    11.1.2 Coding a Set of Maps to Occupy the Same Screen   399
    11.1.3 I/O commands for Building and Sending Pages
         Composed of One or More Maps per Screen   402
    11.1.4 Partition Sets: A Brief Discussion   406
11.2 PRINTING UNDER CICS   408
    11.2.1 Using CICS Printing Terminals   408
    11.2.2 Accessing JES from CICS: Description   412
    11.2.3 JES Spooling Commands   413
11.3 ADVANCED BASIC MAPPING SUPPORT: TEXT AND
    MESSAGE DATA   415
    11.3.1 Text Processing: How It Works; When to Use It   415
    11.3.2 Output Commands for Sending Text   415
    11.3.3 Message Routing   416
TEST YOUR UNDERSTANDING   417
    Questions and Exercises   417

12 Advanced Topics: Interfacing 418

12.1 ACCESSING DL/I SEGMENTS FROM A CICS PROGRAM 418
    12.1.1 DL/I—CICS Concepts 418
    12.1.2 DL/I Program Setup 419
    12.1.3 Using DL/I I/O Commands 420
12.2 INTERSYSTEM COMMUNICATION AND
MULTIREGION OPERATION 421
    12.2.1 Description of ISC and MRO 421
    12.2.2 LUTYPE 6.2 (APPC) 422
    12.2.3 Types of Distributed Processing 423
    12.2.4 The CRTE Transaction 424
    12.2.5 Introduction to Commands for LUTYPE6.2 (APPC) 425
TEST YOUR UNDERSTANDING 428
    Questions and Exercises 428

13 More About Application Design 429

13.1 APPLICATION SECURITY 429
    13.1.1 Password Protection During Sign-on 429
    13.1.2 File Backup Procedures 431
13.2 SUGGESTIONS FOR EFFICIENT DESIGN 432
    13.2.1 Working Set 432
    13.2.2 Quasi-Reentrance 433
    13.2.3 Simulated versus Real BMS Paging 433
    13.2.4 Minimizing Data Transmission 433
    13.2.5 When to Use Linkage Section I/O Areas 434
13.3 DOCUMENTING YOUR APPLICATION 434
    13.3.1 Writing Skills 434
    13.3.2 Technical Documentation for Programmers 434
    13.3.3 User Documentation 437
13.4 SYSTEM INTEGRITY IN MULTI-CPU CICS
INSTALLATIONS 438
    13.4.1 Precautions for Multi-CPU Processing 438
TEST YOUR UNDERSTANDING 440
    Questions and Exercises 440

14 CICS OS/2 441

14.1 CICS IN THE OS/2 ENVIRONMENT 441
    14.1.1 What is OS/2? 441
    14.1.2 Installing CICS OS/2 443
    14.1.3 CICS OS/2 in the OS/2 Environment 446
    14.1.4 Advantages and Disadvantages 446

14.2 WHAT IS SUPPORTED UNDER CICS OS/2 AND WHAT
    IS NOT   447
    14.2.1 Mainframe EXEC CICS Command Set   447
    14.3.2 Access to Presentation Manager: Icing on the Cake   448
14.3 OS/2 FILE HANDLING AS IT APPLIES TO CICS   448
    14.3.1 OS/2 vs. Mainframe Design Philosophy   448
    14.3.2 Program Libraries   449
    14.3.3 VSAM Files   449
    14.3.4 The OS/2 Printer   449
    14.3.5 Sequential Files   450
    14.3.6 SQL-Based Databases   450
14.4 TRANSLATING PROGRAMS AND MAPS   450
    14.4.1 Command Files   450
    14.4.2 Compilation with Micro Focus Workbench   452
    14.4.3 An Installation Glitch   455
14.5 CICS STARTUP AND SHUTDOWN   456
    14.5.1 CICS Startup   456
    14.5.2 CICS Shutdown   461
14.6 CICS SYSTEM DEFINITION TABLES   462
    14.6.1 The CEDA Transaction   462
    14.6.2 Table Contents   463
14.7 CICS SYSTEM UTILITY COMMANDS   475
    14.7.1 Determining System Status   475
    14.7.2 Signon and Signoff   477
14.8 Multiuser CICS OS/2   477
    14.8.1 3151 ASCII Terminals   477
14.9 INTERSYSTEM COMMUNICATIONS WITH CICS OS/2   478
    14.9.1 Available Communications Features   478
    14.9.2 Distributed Program Link (DPL)   478
    14.9.3 More about ASCII vs. EBCDIC   479
14.10 SUMMARY   479
    14.10.1 CICS OS/2 Application Development Steps   479
TEST YOUR UNDERSTANDING   480
    Questions and Exercises   480

15 SQL-Based Databases   **481**

15.1 SQL CONCEPTS   481
    15.1.1 Relational Database   481
    15.1.2 Data Definition and Data Manipulation   484
    15.1.3 Definition of SQL Terminology   484
    15.1.4 Database Design Principles   487
15.2 OS/2 EXTENDED EDITION DATABASE MANAGER   492
    15.2.1 Where Database Manager Keeps Its Data   492
    15.2.2 Installation and Setup   493

15.2.3 What Query Manager Can Do   493
15.2.4 Precompiler and Bind   494
15.2.5 Compiler Directives   496
15.2.6 Security   496
15.3 DATABASE DEFINITION   497
15.3.1 Defining a Database   497
15.3.2 Defining Tables   499
15.3.3 Defining Indexes   501
15.3.4 Defining Views   501
15.3.5 Sample "One-Time" Program to Create a Database   502
15.4 DATABASE MANIPULATION   502
15.4.1 SELECT Command (with a Unique Key)   502
15.4.2 INSERT Command   504
15.4.3 UPDATE Command   505
15.4.4 DELETE Command   506
15.4.5 SELECTing for More than One Record: CURSOR   506
15.4.6 More Complex SELECTs   507
15.4.7 Sample Programs   508
TEST YOUR UNDERSTANDING   580
Questions and Exercises   580

Appendix   **581**

MAINFRAME PROGRAM COMPILATION AND MAP
ASSEMBLY   581
Parameters and JCL   581
Command Files for OS/2 Systems   586
THE SYSTEM PROGRAMMER'S EYE VIEW   586
CEMT Commands   586
Extended Recovery Facility (XRF)   591
System Programming Interface   591
SOURCES OF ADDITIONAL INFORMATION   592
IBM Manuals for Mainframe CICS Programmers   592
Books and Manuals for CICS OS/2 Programmers   593

List of Figures   **595**

Index   **599**

Preface to the Second Edition

CICS was written over twenty years ago, and it continues to grow, both in capabilities and in the number of users. The original version of CICS became available as a program product in 1969. It ran in only 256K and contained most of the macro-level applications programming interface. CICS began as a way to interface many terminals with applications in one CICS region on one CPU. This was needed to avoid having applications programs concern themselves with the minutiae of handling I/O for varying numbers of terminals. Function shipping, the earliest form of inter-systems communications, became available with CICS/VS 1.4 in 1978. Over the years, CICS has evolved into a "network operating system" for handling data communications in large networks made up of mainframes and smaller systems. CICS is also the primary communications handler for providing access to SQL-based databases on mainframe systems.

Updates to major IBM software products are issued in the form of new versions (major updates) or new releases (minor updates). For example, the current release for MVS/ESA sites is called CICS/ESA Version 3 Release 1.1. When a new version or release is issued, IBM lets its customers know how much longer prior releases will be supported. This support involves problem resolution as well as interfaces with other IBM software and hardware products. Most installations try to update their software within a reasonable amount of time so that this support will not be lost. In the case of CICS, IBM may be expected to support the newest release and the most recent prior release, and to set a date to discontinue support for the second most recent prior release.

The content of each new release is governed by two sources: customer requests and the marketing needs of IBM. User group input figures prominently. IBM, of course, adds new software features to interface with hardware and software being added to its product lines. It also drops software features that support old hardware and software products that have been replaced by newer products. For example, BTAM support is being dropped because lBM wants its customer base to take advantage of the additional features offered by VTAM, and because it is uneconomical for IBM to support obsolete telecommunications access methods. On the other hand, IBM is expanding CICS intercommunication capabilities to encourage attachment of mainframes to other devices in IBM's product lines. Certain other general trends may be noted. The use of VSAM, DL/I, and SQL-based databases is being encouraged at the expense of other forms of data set organization. Recoverability and "uptime" are being improved. More and more CICS management functions, such as table changes, can be done interactively and without having to shut down the system. Greater use is being made of 31-bit extended addressing, available in MVS/XA and MVS/ESA environments.

Versions of CICS are now available for MVS, MVS/XA, MVS/ESA, DOS/VSE, VM, and OS/2 systems. CICS is a strategic part of IBM's SAA (Systems Application Architecture) strategy. The goal of SAA is to provide a common interface across many hardware platforms for both users and applications programmers. This means that we may eventually see versions of CICS for all of IBM's computers. The internals will differ, but the application programming interfaces will remain substantially the same. Regardless of hardware platform, the resulting applications can be made to have a consistent "look and feel" from the user's point of view. In this way, it will be possible to network computers of various sizes and types without having to retrain programmers and users for each type.

At present, CICS/ESA 3.1 is the most powerful version of CICS. It is available only for sites running the MVS/ESA operating system. These are the largest mainframe sites. With this release, more system resources have been placed above the 16-megabyte address boundary for virtual storage constraint relief. The entire internal architecture of CICS has been redesigned for this release. Installation, tuning, and debugging are easier. Database recovery has been improved. On the other hand, some functionality has been removed. CICS/ESA no longer supports BTAM, TCAM ACB, COBOL macro level, or PL/I macro level. 3.1 will be the last release to support assembler macro level programs, access to CICS control blocks, or CICS internal signon security. In a nutshell, IBM wants customers to stop tweaking the system control blocks, but they will provide other interfaces which will give the same functionality without using release-dependent code.

For MVS/XA sites, the current release is CICS/MVS 2.1.1. This release supports data tables. This means that small VSAM files that are accessed frequently can be kept in virtual memory for faster online access. The applications programming interface changed very little between CICS 1.7 and CICS 2.1.1. The main difference, introduced with release 2.1, involved mirrored processing for fault tolerance. For DOS/VSE sites, and for MVS sites that are not ESA or XA sites, the current release of CICS is still 1.7. For VM sites, a version of CICS is available which is a subset of mainframe CICS, intended primarily for program development. Of course, sites that run DOS/VSE or MVS as guest operating systems under VM can run other versions of CICS under the guest operating system.

Now for the new part: running CICS on a microcomputer. Version 1.10 of CICS OS/2 was announced early in 1989, but it lacked many commands present in mainframe CICS. Version 1.20, introduced in spring 1990, has almost everything found in mainframe CICS, with a few "extras" besides. Basic mapping support (BMS) is somewhat limited in its implementation under CICS OS/2, which supports the minimum function set. On the other hand, CICS OS/2 lets you access all of the features on the OS/2 machine from your application. There is no artificial division between privileges allowed for "batch" (background) or "online" (interactive) programs. For instance, you could use Presentation Manager calls in a CICS OS/2 application, to create your own graphical user interface in place of text-based BMS.

A PS/2 or other OS/2 machine running CICS OS/2 can be used in place of a terminal. It can be used for those online applications which would benefit from splitting the processing work load between the mainframe and the workstation. It can be used for applications which need to use the graphics adapter, mouse, or other capabilities of the OS/2 machine. It can be used as a network node supporting four users: one on its own monitor and keyboard, and three on 3151 ASCII text-only terminals connected to serial ports. Probably the most common use of CICS OS/2 will be as a workstation for developing and testing programs to be ported to a mainframe. This provides great advantages for the following reasons: the programmer is not held up by downtime or by slow mainframe response or turnaround, the programmer cannot crash the mainframe by testing faulty programs on the OS/2 workstation, and the programmer can be made responsible for setting up his or her own CICS table entries for testing on the OS/2 machine. On a mainframe, since many people share the same test resources, it's customary to assign this duty to a systems programmer. This, of course, is slower. With CICS OS/2 as a test platform, the systems programmer would need to get involved only when putting applications into production.

If you wonder, "How compatible is CICS OS/2 with mainframe CICS?" you should be aware that there is no separate application programmer's reference manual for CICS OS/2. You simply buy the CICS 2.1.1 book and use that! You can use a COBOL compiler, such as Micro Focus, which can be set up to match mainframe COBOL or VS COBOL II, by using the correct compiler directives. CICS OS/2 has its own VSAM support. The only real difference from mainframe VSAM is the fact that it exists just within CICS, so that you set it up with file control table entries rather than with IDCAMS. Finally, the SQL commands that work with CICS and OS/2 EE 1.2 are compatible with mainframe DB2 SQL commands.

The examples in this book have been updated to match IBM's SAA CUA (common user access) standards for designing user access screens. This makes programming somewhat more complex, but provides a consistent "look and feel" across all of the online applications in your installation.

The sample CICS OS/2 programs in this book are available on diskette from the author for $50.00. Please specify 5¼" or 3½" diskettes. Send check or money order to:

Alida M. Jatich
Cogito Corp.
3835 West 56th Place
Chicago, IL 60629

ALIDA M. JATICH

Chicago, Illinois
May 1991

Preface to the First Edition

This book is intended for batch programmers who wish to learn to design and code online applications using command level CICS. The first eight chapters cover what one needs to know in order to begin writing simple CICS applications. Some background is provided concerning the work that the CICS system and the terminal network actually do. This is intended to help you understand the purpose of each CICS command and make a wise choice whenever CICS offers several ways to accomplish a given task. Guidelines concerning CICS applications design are also presented so that you will know how to begin putting the CICS commands together into useful programs and systems.

The next four chapters cover some of the other features and tools that form part of an experienced CICS programmer's repertoire. Various programming methods that provide greater security, efficiency, or user convenience are described, together with their advantages and disadvantages. Software aids for testing and troubleshooting are also described in detail.

The philosophy behind this book is one of simplicity. Whenever there are several possible methods for accomplishing something, suggest using the simplest method, unless there is a sound reason to do otherwise. As one might suppose, this philosophy was developed during many hours of maintenance programming on both batch and online systems.

It may take time to become accustomed to the concepts involved in online programming. After the first few chapters, you might find it useful to set up a few test data sets and to use the sample programs in the book as a model to write a few simple online transactions. Testing the transactions, possibly with the aid of the debugging tools described in this book, will show you first-hand what CICS is all about. There is no substitute for hands-on experience; therefore, specific machine exercises are suggested in the book. Whether or not it is possible to carry out the machine exercises immediately, the exercises should be studied carefully. They are intended to get you to think about design issues beyond those discussed in the text.

Anyone who has tried to learn CICS from the IBM manuals is likely to have encountered some problems. Information is scattered throughout many separate volumes, some of which may not be easy to obtain. The writing in most IBM manuals is complex, partly because the writer of each IBM manual assumes that you already know a considerable amount of background information about many topics and that you are only using the manual as a reference book. The CICS Application Programmer's Reference Manual (Command Level) assumes that you know how terminal devices work and how they are used in a typical application. It assumes that you know something about how the CICS system functions and how it accesses programs, files, and terminal devices. It assumes that you are familiar with online applications design conventions.

This book, on the other hand, only assumes that you can write batch COBOL applications and that you can read and understand simple OS/VS or DOS/VS JCL. It covers, in one volume, what you need to know to put up a simple CICS application, including some hard-to-find knowledge acquired through research and painful trial-and-error. Simple language is used to make this book readable and understandable. You will be given a framework of concepts presented in a logical order, instead of a collection of seemingly unrelated facts. Since you will observe how each part relates to the whole system, you should be able to retain at least twice as much knowledge if you read this book as you would if you try to teach yourself from IBM reference manuals. However, readers who are curious about certain specialized topics that might not concern most CICS applications programmers will find a list of sources of additional information at the end of the book.

This book places special emphasis on terminal devices: how they work, how they relate to the rest of the system, and how they are used in actual applications. Many batch programmers are unfamiliar with terminals and have had little opportunity to observe typical online programs in use. In order to use any I/O device effectively, one has to know something about how it works. Programmers who do not understand how terminals function and how they are connected to the system tend to write CICS programs that never quite work. Having had to maintain and/or rewrite some of these myself, I have tried to alleviate that problem in the first few chapters.

In keeping with this emphasis on terminal devices, basic mapping support (BMS) will be introduced early in the book. Maps are an enormously powerful and widely used tool for terminal access. Since sample applications in the book are intended to resemble real applications, the examples will use some maps and will show the roles that maps play within the CICS system. You will also be introduced to sequential and indexed file access using VSAM, since VSAM forms the cornerstone of so many CICS applications. My goal is to make the sample programs in the book so similar to actual programs that you will be able to copy them and use them as starting points when designing production online applications.

Finally, we will be looking at CICS applications from the user's point of view. An application must make sense to the user, and it must give correct results. It must not waste the user's time with slow response or with excessive keying. If it requires security features, these must not interfere with legitimate work activities. I believe that a project is successful only if the user is happy with the results.

Notice: This book was completed just as CICS Version 1 Release 6 was coming out. Not everything that IBM eventually intends to make available with Release 6 was on hand when the book was being written, and very few sites were actually using Release 6. Before using some of the newest features of CICS, you may wish to obtain the newest copies of the applicable IBM manuals to determine whether any changes have just been made to those features.

ALIDA JATICH

Chicago, Illinois
October 1984

Acknowledgments

Thanks to the following people: Phil Nowak, for collecting information, for coding programs, for setting up my computer hardware and keeping it working, and for helping me to stay on schedule; Dan Kapp, for advising me about what should be included in the book; Carl Moore, for offering encouragement; Jim Gallichio, Jim Egerton, and the rest of the team at Management Data Communications, Inc., for providing technical assistance and a good service bureau environment for running the sample programs used in the first edition; Mike Bouros, for reviewing the first edition for technical accuracy; Ken Jones at Blue Cross and Blue Shield of Illinois, for technical assistance; Henry Werner, Ian Webb, John Gridley, and many others at IBM, for providing software and technical assistance; and Mike McCandless, Steve Soskin, Howard Hinman, Mike Fidel, Larry Simmons, and Alan Thomas at Micro Focus, for providing software and technical assistance.

AJ

1

Overview of CICS from the Application Programmer's Standpoint

This chapter will tell you what CICS is and what it can do. It will show how the CICS teleprocessing software relates to the computer and its operating system. It will explain what the CICS language translators do and how to use them. Finally, it will describe the purpose of some of the modules within CICS software.

1.1 WHAT A CICS ONLINE SYSTEM ACTUALLY DOES

1.1.1 Online Processing: What It Is, Why It Is Used

You are probably quite familiar with batch systems, in which user departments fill out input documents for a large number of similar processing tasks, collect them, submit them for data entry, and schedule them to be run at a certain time each day, week, or month. An individual processing task might be something like checking a file to see whether a part description record is present and adding it if it is not, or updating some files to indicate that a shipment has arrived and has been warehoused at a certain location. However, you might not be so familiar with online systems.

Figure 1.1 shows how a simple online application might look to the termi-

1

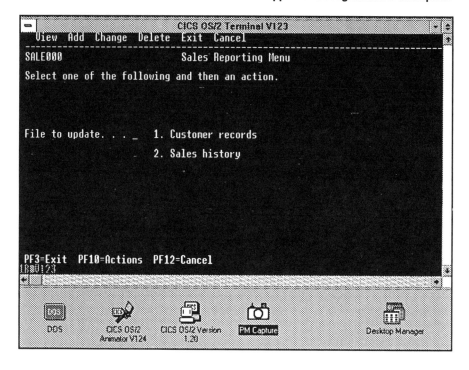

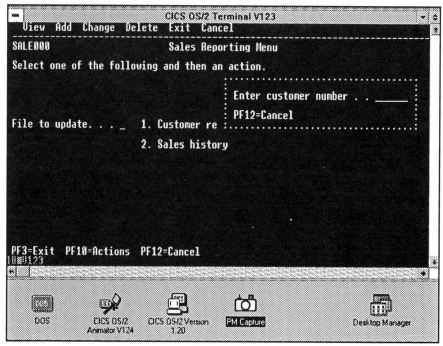

FIGURE 1.1   Screen displays of maps used in sample programs.

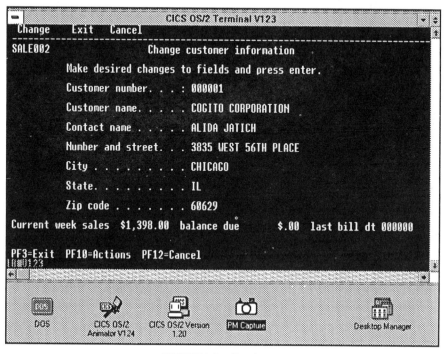

FIGURE 1.1 *(Continued)*

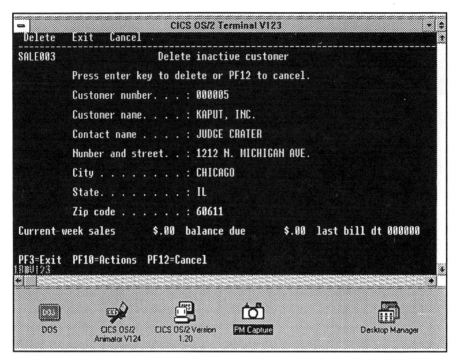

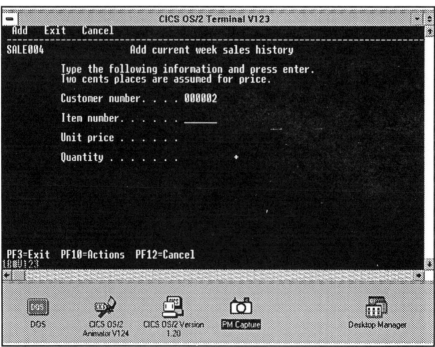

FIGURE 1.1   *(Continued)*

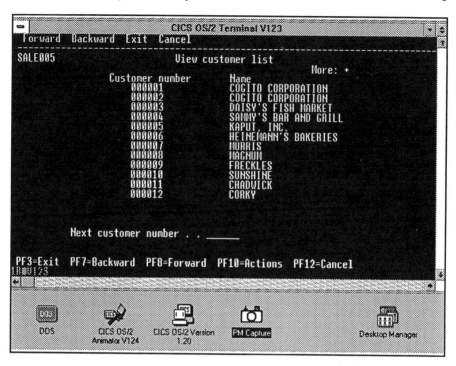

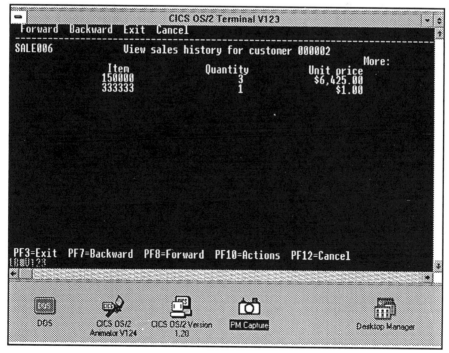

FIGURE 1.1 *(Continued)*

nal user. These examples were run on a CICS OS/2 system. Screen images on mainframe terminals will look slightly different. Menu screens allow the user to choose what action to perform, and to choose what objects to perform that action against. The user needs to know what customer, vendor, employee, product, part, or other entity is involved, but not how the files or databases are structured. After choices are made on the menu, other screens appear on the user's terminal that allow the selected data to be entered. When the first action has been performed successfully, the program will let the user choose a new action. If anything goes wrong, the program will display an error message to the user. CICS is a software package that allows programs of this type to be written and executed. **In other words, the CICS system allows terminal users to access programs to perform online processing.**

In what ways does online processing differ from batch processing? **Online processing allows someone to use a terminal to perform only one action, or one group of related actions, at a time, without having to wait for a large number of tasks to be collected for a scheduled run.** For instance, if a customer reserves a seat on an airplane, or a patient receives some medication, or a vendor delivers a shipment of fuel, the appropriate files can be updated at once so that they reflect what has just taken place. The sooner these updates are posted to the files, the less chance there is for mistakes to occur, such as giving medication to the patient twice or assigning the customer's seat reservation to someone else.

Online processing also makes it possible to see the results of a single task promptly. The terminal user can update files or databases and can determine whether the results are satisfactory without having to wait for a stack of reports to be printed and shipped to his or her office. If the user makes an error, the terminal can give any feedback needed to correct the situation with only a few seconds' delay. This saves time for the terminal user. Let us look at what is needed to perform online processing.

1.1.2   Software Capabilities Needed for Online Processing

Online processing requires terminal devices, together with software that can determine whether each terminal device is ready to send or receive data. Online processing also requires application programs that can interpret and use this data. If many terminal devices are attached to the same computer system, and if they are all being used at once to perform different types of tasks, software is needed that will monitor each terminal to determine which resources each terminal user will need.

Suppose a terminal user types a **transaction identification code** on a terminal screen. A transaction code is somewhat like a job name in that it identifies one or more programs to be run on behalf of the user. Entering a transaction code constitutes a request to begin a task. To fulfill this request, the software must do the following things:

1. It must find and load the programs needed to perform that task.
2. It must associate those programs with the correct terminal, so that replies can be sent back to the terminal from which the transaction was requested.
3. It must start the execution of the first program needed for that task.
4. It must allocate execution time between the new task and any others that might be running at the same time.
5. It must provide each task with the storage and file accesses it needs.
6. It must free system resources after the work is done.
7. It must provide for file security and integrity.

If you are reasonably familiar with any version of MVS, DOS/VSE, VM, OS/2, or any other operating system, you will know that an operating system loads programs, allocates resources, and services all input and output requests coming from the programs that it loads. CICS is a software product that performs these functions for online programs, just as DOS/VSE or MVS does for batch programs. This means in effect that CICS is a subordinate operating system. CICS runs as a program under the control of MVS or another operating system, and applications programs run under the control of CICS.

1.1.3 Relationship between Applications Programs and CICS, and between CICS and the Operating System

Whenever an online program needs to do I/O, it issues a command to CICS. CICS fulfills this command at the proper time by requesting whatever services it needs from the operating system. This process is shown in Figure 1.2. CICS I/O commands of this type, embedded in a COBOL, assembler language, or PL/I online program, differ in format from batch COBOL, assembler language, C, or PL/I I/O statements. In fact, since all I/O requests must go through CICS, rather than directly through the operating system, in a mainframe environment the CICS programmer is restricted from using batch I/O statements. This leads to our next topic, which involves CICS online applications programs and how they relate to the CICS software.

1.2 CICS PROGRAMS, MAPS, AND LANGUAGE TRANSLATION: WHAT THE CICS LANGUAGE FACILITIES PROVIDE

1.2.1 Online I/O Accesses: How They Differ from Batch Usage

When you write a CICS program, you substitute CICS commands for certain batch statements. For example, instead of COBOL FDs (file de-

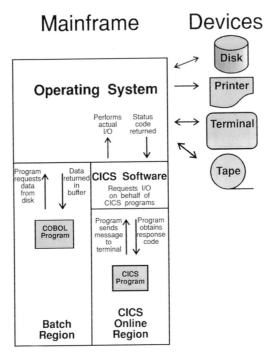

FIGURE 1.2 Relationship of CICS to system environment (chart).

scriptions) and the like, you will simply define record layouts in working storage or in the linkage section (01-levels or the equivalent) to hold data set records. These are exactly the same as the record descriptions that you now use, except for the fact that they are not placed in the file section.

The vast majority of CICS command level programs are written in COBOL, although there are some installations that use assembler language, PL/I, RPG (under DOS/VSE), C/370 (under CICS/ESA 3.1) or C (under OS/2) for this purpose. Because of this, we will emphasize CICS COBOL programs in this book.

You do not need JCL for a CICS application program, even though it uses files. This is because the files do not "belong" to your application, but to the CICS system as a whole. Your program ordinarily does not need to open or close the files that it uses; the CICS system provides methods for opening datasets manually or automatically before your online applications are loaded. So where is the JCL? When the CICS system is loaded into a partition or region at system startup time, a **CICS startup job** is used. The startup job contains DD cards or DLBL and EXTENT statements for files that the CICS system needs. These are the same as the DD cards or other JCL that you would use to run batch programs that access the same files. For VSAM files used by application programs, you might not even need to do that. You can just define them with full dataset names in the **file control table (FCT)**—a table which belongs to CICS. When CICS begins running, it tells the operating system to allocate the files referenced in the FCT. As an applications programmer, you will need to be concerned about this only when you are setting up a new file. In that case, you or the systems programmer will make the FCT entries or JCL changes.

A CICS program contains no SELECT statements or the like. Information describing physical data set characteristics is stored and maintained by CICS in system tables. There is one FCT entry for each MVS DDNAME or DOS/VSE file name. As you will see in the next example, whenever your program accesses a file, it uses the file name or DDNAME. A CICS program contains no data set description statements at all. This means that the configuration of a data set can often be changed without affecting the program.

A CICS application should not attempt to execute a COBOL STOP RUN or GOBACK statement. Reliable sources indicate that executing STOP RUN in CICS programs using older versions of COBOL will cause the entire CICS region to terminate instantly with no messages and without performing its normal shutdown activities. The author has resisted the temptation to try this, and so should you. It is correct to place a GOBACK statement in the program somewhere where it will never be executed, in order to avoid getting a compiler diagnostic message. Even under VS COBOL II, good programming practice requires that the actual exit from a CICS application program be done with a CICS command. A mainframe CICS program will always use CICS I/O commands, never COBOL or PL/I I/O statements, nor C library routines, nor assembler language I/O macros. Here is a typical CICS command:

```
EXEC CICS WRITE
     FROM(your-work-area)
     LENGTH(ws-rec-length-field)
     DATASET("ddname")
     RIDFLD(ws-record-key-field)
     END-EXEC.
```

Notice that the record is written from a formatted work area that you must specify, and that the command refers to the MVS DDNAME (or its DOS/VSE counterpart) directly. This differs from COBOL usage, which allows you to assign the DDNAME to a COBOL internal file name. File commands will be covered in more detail in Chapter 6.

Most CICS programs access just a few file records. Most of these file accesses are by record key. You may be accustomed to batch programs that typically process an entire file sequentially, with one or more processing loops to handle the repetitive activities. One of the few CICS programs that needs to loop through many records is a file browse, which is the sequential processing of a group of records, usually for display to the terminal user.

1.2.2   CICS Command Format

The form of CICS that this book covers is known as **command level**. It makes use of **CICS commands,** which all follow the same format. Let's examine a typical CICS command:

```
EXEC CICS READ
      INTO(data-area)
      UPDATE
      LENGTH(data-area)
      DATASET(name)
      RIDFLD (ws-record-key-field)
      END-EXEC
```

This example shows a typical CICS I/O command; in this instance, a random-access read for update. It differs from COBOL and other batch I/O statements you may be accustomed to using. All CICS commands follow a syntax similar to that shown above.

When we discuss CICS command syntax in this book, we will stay reasonably close to the format used in standard manuals and data processing texts. A vertical line appearing between options indicates that a choice is offered. Curved brackets signify required parameters; if several possible choices appear, one of them must be selected. Square brackets signify optional parameters. Lowercase words are to be replaced by appropriate literals, data names, program names, and so forth. Later in the book, we will discuss these conventions more.

All CICS commands begin with the words EXEC CICS. The EXEC CICS is followed by one or two words indicating the command type; in this case, READ. This is followed in turn by a list of keyword parameters that can be presented in any order (for example, the word DATASET above). If a keyword parameter needs an argument value, such as the data set name, this value appears in parentheses after the keyword parameter. Each CICS command is terminated with an ending delimiter, which for commands used within a COBOL program should be specified as END-EXEC. The period following the END-EXEC is optional, and may be omitted if, for instance, you wish to avoid terminating a COBOL IF-statement prematurely. You can place several parameters on one line or place each on a separate line.

CICS command formats are identical for COBOL, assembler language, C, and PL/I, except for the ending delimiter, which is a semicolon in PL/I, and which is omitted in assembler language. In the C language, a null character is used to delimit the end of a character string. The CICS translator does not recognize this. When coding in C, do not interrupt a line in a CICS command with a comma or period followed by a space. This book will show all commands with the COBOL delimiter of END-EXEC. As we discuss each CICS command, we will specify what set of parameters needs to be given for each activity we wish to perform, and what form the required arguments should take. **Do not use the character strings "CICS," "EXEC," "END-EXEC," "DLI," "DFH," or "FAA" as names or as parts of names in your program. Similarly, never begin a transaction ID with the letter C, and never begin a program, map, or map set name with DFH. These names are reserved for IBM-supplied software, and are to be used similarly to COBOL "reserved words."**

An interesting aside: DFH is the prefix used for CICS system data names in the mainframe environment. People often ask "What does DFH mean? Is it someone's initials?" According to some IBMers, DFH does not stand for anything, but was a random combination of letters chosen so as to keep data names from conflicting with anything else. Under CICS OS/2, the prefix is FAA.

Argument values can be specified in several different ways, depending on what is required for the command. Examples of arguments will be presented when each command is discussed. Here are the options:

Data-value: Use the name of a character field, PIC X(—), or use the name of a half-word binary field, PIC S9(4) COMP, or use the name of a full-word binary field, PIC S9(8) COMP, depending on what that argument needs.

Data-area: Use any of the above, or use the name of any elementary or group data item that would be appropriate for the command.

Pointer-value: In older versions of COBOL, use the name of a BLL cell or the name of another data item that contains a value moved from a BLL cell. In VS COBOL II, use the name of a pointer data item. A BLL cell is a **base locator for linkage:** an address value used for providing addressability into fields in the linkage section.

Pointer-ref: Use the name of a USAGE IS POINTER data item or BLL cell.

Name: Use a nonnumeric literal, which is a character string in quotation marks. "Name" is used for supplying DDNAMEs, program names, and the like. The name must be left-justified and blank-filled to the maximum length. Instead of a nonnumeric literal, you may use the name of a COBOL data field of the appropriate length.

Label: Use a COBOL paragraph or section name.

Hhmmss: Use a numeric literal (without quotation marks), or a
                      PIC S9(7) COMP-3 field, containing a time-of-day ex-
                      pressed in the format 0HHMMSS+.

1.2.3   What the Command Translator Does with Your Program

A command level program is compiled in two stages. The appendix
contains sample CICS compile JCL for command level COBOL applications; your systems programmer may provide slightly different JCL at your
site. Under OS/2, .CMD files take the place of JCL. CICSTCL.CMD, supplied with CICS OS/2, handles translation, compilation, and linking of a
CICS COBOL application program. See Figure 1.3.

The first compilation step puts the source code through the COBOL
version of the CICS command translator. Different command translators
are used for CICS programs written in other languages. This translator
adds certain CICS system work areas to your program's data definitions,
and replaces each CICS command with a COBOL subprogram CALL statement. This CALL is to a subprogram called DFHEI1, which is actually a
part of CICS. Just as with any other COBOL subprogram CALL, arguments
are passed, although in this case the arguments include bit patterns that
ordinarily do not show up on a printed listing. Notice that the command

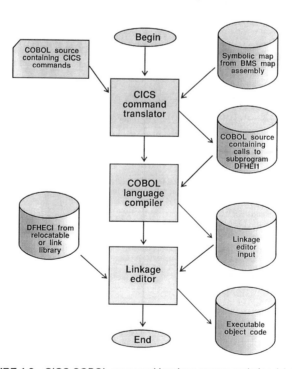

FIGURE 1.3   CICS COBOL command level program translation (chart).

translator comments out your original source code before inserting the CALL statement; for example:

```
* EXEC CICS
*       HANDLE CONDITION
*       MAPFAIL (SEND-NEW-MAP)
*       ERROR (GENERAL-ERR-HANDLER)
*       END-EXEC.
MOVE "          " TO DFHEIVO CALL "DFHEI1"
USING DFHEIVO GO TO
SEND-NEW-MAP GENERAL-ERR-HANDLER DEPENDING ON DFHEIGDI.
```

The command translator also inserts a working storage area called DFHEIVAR, which contains fields for passing the arguments to CICS in each subprogram CALL. In the linkage section, it inserts another area called DFHEIBLK, the EXEC interface block, which the CICS system uses to pass information back to your application about the results of each CALL.

The second part of the compile job puts this translated source through the same language compiler that you normally use for your batch programs. The subprogram calls are compiled along with the other COBOL source statements in the program. If you've ever compiled a batch program with embedded subprogram CALL statements, this works in much the same way.

After both of these job steps are complete, the object is link-edited in the normal manner, using IEWL or another linkage editor, depending on your environment. The linkage editor links your program together with other modules. For example, in a mainframe environment, your program is linked with the CICS command level interface module, DFHECI. Depending upon your operating environment, the executable module is then stored in a core image library, load library, or .DLL available to the CICS system. See Figure 1.4.

Additional steps for DB2 database access: If your mainframe command level CICS program uses SQL commands to access DB2 databases, you will need to run a separate DB2 precompiler step to translate the SQL commands. The DB2 precompiler will be your first job step, before the command level CICS translator step. At the end of your job, you will also need to run a BIND step to create a new DB2 application plan. The application plan tells DB2 how to satisfy your application's SQL commands efficiently at run time, given the current structure of your databases.

1.2.4 Command Level and Macro Level

You may hear of a type of CICS known as **macro level**. Your mainframe installation may have some older programs written in it. Newer applications are being written in command level, because command level is much simpler to use, because command level allows you to do practically everything that macro level allows, and because IBM no longer supports

```
CICS/VS COMMAND LANGUAGE TRANSLATOR VERSION 1.5                    TIME 02.24 DATE 4 OCT 83

          CBL XOPTS (LANGLVL(2),CICS)                                  00000100

  LINE            SOURCE LISTING

 00001              IDENTIFICATION DIVISION.                           00000200
 00002              PROGRAM-ID.  SALEINIT.                             00000300
 00003              AUTHOR.  ALIDA JATICH AND PHIL NOWAK.              00000700
 00004              ***************************************************** 00000400
 00005          *     SALEINIT.  MENU FORMATTER.                     *  00000500
 00006          *     SALEINIT SENDS A FRESH COPY OF THE SALES REPORTING MENU  *
 00007          *     TO THE USER'S TERMINAL SCREEN.  IT THEN EXECUTES A RETURN *
 00008          *     TO TRANSID SALO.  SALO IS ASSOCIATED WITH THE MENU SCREEN *
 00009          *     PROCESSOR, SALEP000.                           *
 00010              ***************************************************** 00000600
 00011              ENVIRONMENT DIVISION.                              00000800
 00012              DATA DIVISION.                                     00000900
 00013              WORKING-STORAGE SECTION.                           00001000
 00014              PROCEDURE DIVISION.                                00001100
 00015              MAIN-ROUTINE.                                      00001200
 00016                  EXEC CICS SEND                                 00001300
 00017                      MAP ('SALE000')                           00001400
 00018                      MAPSET ('MSALE00')                         00001500
 00019                      MAPONLY                                    00001600
 00020                      ERASE                                      00001700
 00021                      END-EXEC.                                  00001800
 00022                  EXEC CICS RETURN                               00001900
 00023                      TRANSID ('SALO')                          00002000
 00024                      END-EXEC.                                  00002100
 00025                  GOBACK.                                        00002200


CICS/VS COMMAND LANGUAGE TRANSLATOR VERSION 1.5                    TIME 02.24 DATE 4 OCT 83

*OPTIONS IN EFFECT*      APOST, NODEBUG, FLAGW, LANGLVL(2), LIST, NONUM, OPT, SEQ, SPACE1, NOXREF, CICS

NO MESSAGES PRODUCED BY TRANSLATOR.

TRANSLATION TIME:-   0.00 MINS.
```

FIGURE 1.4   Sample CICS COBOL command level program compilation.

```
PP 5740-CB1 RELEASE 2.3 + PTF 8 - UP13477          IBM OS/VS COBOL   JULY 24, 1976

        1                        2.25.01      OCT  4,1983

   00001          IDENTIFICATION DIVISION.                                   00000200
   00002          PROGRAM-ID.  SALEINIT.                                     00000300
   00003          AUTHOR.  ALIDA JATICH AND PHIL NOWAK.                      00000700
   00004          *********************************************************  00000400
   00005          *    SALEINIT.  MENU FORMATTER.                        *   00000500
   00006          *    SALEINIT SENDS A FRESH COPY OF THE SALES REPORTING MENU  *
   00007          *    TO THE USER'S TERMINAL SCREEN.  IT THEN EXECUTES A RETURN *
   00008          *    TO TRANSID SALO.  SALO IS ASSOCIATED WITH THE MENU SCREEN *
   00009          *    PROCESSOR, SALEP000.                              *
   00010          *********************************************************  00000600
   00011          ENVIRONMENT DIVISION.                                      00000800
   00012          DATA DIVISION.                                             00000900
   00013          WORKING-STORAGE SECTION.                                   00001000
   00014          COPY DFHEIVAR.
   00015 C        01  DFHEIV.                                                04000000
   00016 C            02  DFHEIV0   PICTURE X(26).                           08000000
   00017 C            02  DFHEIV1   PICTURE X(8).                            12000000
   00018 C            02  DFHEIV2   PICTURE X(8).                            16000000
   00019 C            02  DFHEIV3   PICTURE X(8).                            20000000
   00020 C            02  DFHEIV4   PICTURE X(6).                            24000000
   00021 C            02  DFHEIV5   PICTURE X(4).                            28000000
   00022 C            02  DFHEIV6   PICTURE X(4).                            32000000
   00023 C            02  DFHEIV7   PICTURE X(2).                            36000000
   00024 C            02  DFHEIV8   PICTURE X(2).                            40000000
   00025 C            02  DFHEIV9   PICTURE X(1).                            44000000
   00026 C            02  DFHEIV10  PICTURE S9(7) USAGE COMPUTATIONAL-3.     48000000
   00027 C            02  DFHEIV11  PICTURE S9(4) USAGE COMPUTATIONAL.       52000000
   00028 C            02  DFHEIV12  PICTURE S9(4) USAGE COMPUTATIONAL.       56000000
   00029 C            02  DFHEIV13  PICTURE S9(4) USAGE COMPUTATIONAL.       60000000
   00030 C            02  DFHEIV14  PICTURE S9(4) USAGE COMPUTATIONAL.       64000000
   00031 C            02  DFHEIV15  PICTURE S9(4) USAGE COMPUTATIONAL.       68000000
   00032 C            02  DFHEIV16  PICTURE S9(9) USAGE COMPUTATIONAL.       72000000
   00033 C            02  DFHEIV17  PICTURE X(4).                            76000000
   00034 C            02  DFHEIV18  PICTURE X(4).                            80000000
   00035 C            02  DFHEIV19  PICTURE X(4).                            84000000
   00036 C            02  DFHEIV97  PICTURE S9(7) USAGE COMPUTATIONAL-3 VALUE ZERO.88000000
   00037 C            02  DFHEIV98  PICTURE S9(4) USAGE COMPUTATIONAL VALUE ZERO.  92000000
   00038 C            02  DFHEIV99  PICTURE X(1)  VALUE SPACE.               96000000
   00039          LINKAGE SECTION.
   00040          COPY DFHEIBLK REPLACING EIBLK BY DFHEIBLK.
   00041 C        *    EIBLK EXEC INTERFACE BLOCK                            02000000
   00042 C        01  DFHEIBLK.                                              04000000
   00043 C        *        EIBTIME       TIME IN OHHMMSS FORMAT              06000000
   00044 C            02 EIBTIME         PICTURE S9(7) USAGE COMPUTATIONAL-3.08000000
   00045 C        *        EIBDATE       DATE IN 00YYDDD FORMAT              10000000
   00046 C            02 EIBDATE         PICTURE S9(7) USAGE COMPUTATIONAL-3.12000000
   00047 C        *        EIBTRNID      TRANSACTION IDENTIFIER              14000000
   00048 C            02 EIBTRNID        PICTURE X(4).                       16000000
   00049 C        *        EIBTASKN      TASK NUMBER                         18000000
   00050 C            02 EIBTASKN        PICTURE S9(7) USAGE COMPUTATIONAL-3.20000000
   00051 C        *        EIBTRMID      TERMINAL IDENTIFIER                 22000000
   00052 C            02 EIBTRMID        PICTURE X(4).                       24000000
   00053 C        *        DFHEIGDI      RESERVED                            26000000
   00054 C            02 DFHEIGDI        PICTURE S9(4) USAGE COMPUTATIONAL.  28000000
```

FIGURE 1.4 *(Continued)*

```
    2                      2.25.01      OCT  4,1983

00055 C    ✦         EIBCPOSN    CURSOR POSITION                     30000000
00056 C        02 EIBCPOSN    PICTURE S9(4) USAGE COMPUTATIONAL.     32000000
00057 C    ✦         EIBCALEN    COMMAREA LENGTH                     34000000
00058 C        02 EIBCALEN    PICTURE S9(4) USAGE COMPUTATIONAL.     36000000
00059 C    ✦         EIBAID      ATTENTION IDENTIFIER                38000000
00060 C        02 EIBAID      PICTURE X(1).                          40000000
00061 C    ✦         EIBFN       FUNCTION CODE                       42000000
00062 C        02 EIBFN       PICTURE X(2).                          44000000
00063 C    ✦         EIBRCODE    RESPONSE CODE                       46000000
00064 C        02 EIBRCODE    PICTURE X(6).                          48000000
00065 C    ✦         EIBDS       DATASET NAME                        50000000
00066 C        02 EIBDS       PICTURE X(8).                          52000000
00067 C    ✦         EIBREQID    REQUEST IDENTIFIER                  54000000
00068 C        02 EIBREQID    PICTURE X(8).                          56000000
00069 C    ✦         EIBRSRCE    RESOURCE NAME                       58000000
00070 C        02 EIBRSRCE    PICTURE X(8).                          60000000
00071 C    ✦         EIBSYNC     SYNCPOINT REQUIRED                  62000000
00072 C        02 EIBSYNC     PICTURE X.                             64000000
00073 C    ✦         EIBFREE     TERMINAL FREE REQUIRED              66000000
00074 C        02 EIBFREE     PICTURE X.                             68000000
00075 C    ✦         EIBRECV     DATA RECEIVE REQUIRED               70000000
00076 C        02 EIBRECV     PICTURE X.                             73000000
00077 C    ✦         EIBSEND     RESERVED                            76000000
00078 C        02 EIBSEND     PICTURE X.                             79000000
00079 C    ✦         EIBATT      ATTACH DATA EXISTS                  82000000
00080 C        02 EIBATT      PICTURE X.                             85000000
00081 C    ✦         EIBEOC      GOTTEN DATA IS COMPLETE             88000000
00082 C        02 EIBEOC      PICTURE X.                             91000000
00083 C    ✦         EIBFMH      GOTTEN DATA CONTAINS FMH            94000000
00084 C        02 EIBFMH      PICTURE X.                             97000000
00085       01  DFHCOMMAREA PICTURE X(1).
00086       01  DFHBLLSLOT1 PICTURE X(1).
00087       01  DFHBLLSLOT2 PICTURE X(1).
00088       PROCEDURE DIVISION USING DFHEIBLK DFHCOMMAREA.
00089         SERVICE RELOAD DFHEIBLK.                               00001100
00090       MAIN-ROUTINE.                                           00001200
00091      ✦    EXEC CICS SEND
00092      ✦               MAP ('SALE000')
00093      ✦               MAPSET ('MSALE00')
00094      ✦               MAPONLY
00095      ✦               ERASE
00096      ✦               END-EXEC.
00097           MOVE 'SALE000' TO DFHEIV1 MOVE 'MSALE00' TO DFHEIV2 MOVE '  00001300
00098      -        '  TO DFHEIV0 CALL 'DFHEI1' USING DFHEIV0
00099           DFHEIV1 DFHEIV99 DFHEIV98 DFHEIV2.
00100
00101
00102
00103      ✦    EXEC CICS RETURN
00104      ✦               TRANSID ('SALO')
00105      ✦               END-EXEC.
00106           MOVE 'SALO' TO DFHEIV5 MOVE '        ' TO DFHEIV0 CALL 'DFH00001900
00107      -    'EI1' USING DFHEIV0 DFHEIV5.
00108
00109           GOBACK.                                             00002200
```

FIGURE 1.4 *(Continued)*

3   SALEINIT   2.25.01   OCT 4,1983

INTRNL NAME	LVL	SOURCE NAME	BASE	DISPL	INTRNL NAME	DEFINITION	USAGE
DNM=1-051	01	DFHEIV	BL=1	000	DNM=1-051	DS 0CL106	GROUP
DNM=1-070	02	DFHEIV0	BL=1	000	DNM=1-070	DS 26C	DISP
DNM=1-087	02	DFHEIV1	BL=1	01A	DNM=1-087	DS 8C	DISP
DNM=1-104	02	DFHEIV2	BL=1	022	DNM=1-104	DS 8C	DISP
DNM=1-121	02	DFHEIV3	BL=1	02A	DNM=1-121	DS 8C	DISP
DNM=1-138	02	DFHEIV4	BL=1	032	DNM=1-138	DS 6C	DISP
DNM=1-155	02	DFHEIV5	BL=1	038	DNM=1-155	DS 4C	DISP
DNM=1-172	02	DFHEIV6	BL=1	03C	DNM=1-172	DS 4C	DISP
DNM=1-189	02	DFHEIV7	BL=1	040	DNM=1-189	DS 2C	DISP
DNM=1-206	02	DFHEIV8	BL=1	042	DNM=1-206	DS 2C	DISP
DNM=1-223	02	DFHEIV9	BL=1	044	DNM=1-223	DS 1C	DISP
DNM=1-240	02	DFHEIV10	BL=1	045	DNM=1-240	DS 4P	COMP-3
DNM=1-258	02	DFHEIV11	BL=1	049	DNM=1-258	DS 2C	COMP
DNM=1-276	02	DFHEIV12	BL=1	04B	DNM=1-276	DS 2C	COMP
DNM=1-294	02	DFHEIV13	BL=1	04D	DNM=1-294	DS 2C	COMP
DNM=1-312	02	DFHEIV14	BL=1	04F	DNM=1-312	DS 2C	COMP
DNM=1-330	02	DFHEIV15	BL=1	051	DNM=1-330	DS 2C	COMP
DNM=1-348	02	DFHEIV16	BL=1	053	DNM=1-348	DS 4C	COMP
DNM=1-366	02	DFHEIV17	BL=1	057	DNM=1-366	DS 4C	DISP
DNM=1-384	02	DFHEIV18	BL=1	05B	DNM=1-384	DS 4C	DISP
DNM=1-402	02	DFHEIV19	BL=1	05F	DNM=1-402	DS 4C	DISP
DNM=1-420	02	DFHEIV97	BL=1	063	DNM=1-420	DS 4P	COMP-3
DNM=1-438	02	DFHEIV98	BL=1	067	DNM=1-438	DS 2C	COMP
DNM=1-456	02	DFHEIV99	BL=1	069	DNM=1-456	DS 1C	DISP
DNM=1-474	01	DFHEIBLK	BLL=3	000	DNM=1-474	DS 0CL66	GROUP
DNM=2-000	02	EIBTIME	BLL=3	000	DNM=2-000	DS 4P	COMP-3
DNM=2-017	02	EIBDATE	BLL=3	004	DNM=2-017	DS 4P	COMP-3
DNM=2-034	02	EIBTRNID	BLL=3	008	DNM=2-034	DS 4C	DISP
DNM=2-052	02	EIBTASKN	BLL=3	00C	DNM=2-052	DS 4P	COMP-3
DNM=2-073	02	EIBTRMID	BLL=3	010	DNM=2-073	DS 4C	DISP
DNM=2-091	02	DFHEIGDI	BLL=3	014	DNM=2-091	DS 2C	COMP
DNM=2-109	02	EIBCPOSN	BLL=3	016	DNM=2-109	DS 2C	COMP
DNM=2-127	02	EIBCALEN	BLL=3	018	DNM=2-127	DS 2C	COMP
DNM=2-145	02	EIBAID	BLL=3	01A	DNM=2-145	DS 1C	DISP
DNM=2-161	02	EIBFN	BLL=3	01B	DNM=2-161	DS 2C	DISP
DNM=2-176	02	EIBRCODE	BLL=3	01D	DNM=2-176	DS 6C	DISP
DNM=2-194	02	EIBDS	BLL=3	023	DNM=2-194	DS 8C	DISP
DNM=2-209	02	EIBREQID	BLL=3	02B	DNM=2-209	DS 8C	DISP
DNM=2-227	02	EIBRSRCE	BLL=3	033	DNM=2-227	DS 8C	DISP
DNM=2-245	02	EIBSYNC	BLL=3	03B	DNM=2-245	DS 1C	DISP
DNM=2-262	02	EIBFREE	BLL=3	03C	DNM=2-262	DS 1C	DISP
DNM=2-282	02	EIBRECV	BLL=3	03D	DNM=2-282	DS 1C	DISP
DNM=2-299	02	EIBSEND	BLL=3	03E	DNM=2-299	DS 1C	DISP
DNM=2-316	02	EIBATT	BLL=3	03F	DNM=2-316	DS 1C	DISP
DNM=2-332	02	EIBEOC	BLL=3	040	DNM=2-332	DS 1C	DISP
DNM=2-348	02	EIBFMH	BLL=3	041	DNM=2-348	DS 1C	DISP
DNM=2-364	01	DFHCOMMAREA	BLL=4	000	DNM=2-364	DS 1C	DISP
DNM=2-385	01	DFHBLLSLOT1	BLL=5	000	DNM=2-385	DS 1C	DISP
DNM=2-406	01	DFHBLLSLOT2	BLL=6	000	DNM=2-406	DS 1C	DISP

FIGURE 1.4   *(Continued)*

```
SALEINIT        2.25.01        OCT  4,1983


                MEMORY MAP

        TGT                     00110

SAVE AREA                       00110
SWITCH                          00158
TALLY                           0015C
SORT SAVE                       00160
ENTRY-SAVE                      00164
SORT CORE SIZE                  00168
RET CODE                        0016C
SORT RET                        0016E
WORKING CELLS                   00170
SORT FILE SIZE                  002A0
SORT MODE SIZE                  002A4
PGT-VN TBL                      002A8
TGT-VN TBL                      002AC
RESERVED                        002B0
LENGTH OF VN TBL                002B4      5        SALEINIT        2.25.01        OCT  4,1983
LABEL RET                       002B6
RESERVED                        002B7
DBG R14SAVE                     002B8
COBOL INDICATOR                 002BC             PFMCTL CELLS              00334
A(INIT1)                        002C0             PFMSAV CELLS              00334
DEBUG TABLE PTR                 002C4             VN CELLS                  00334
SUBCOM ITR                      002C8             SAVE AREA =2              00334
SORT-MESSAGE                    002CC             SAVE AREA =3              00334
SYSOUT DDNAME                   002D4             XSASW CELLS               00334
RESERVED                        002D5             XSA CELLS                 00334
COBOL ID                        002D6             PARAM CELLS               00334
COMPILED POINTER                002D8             RPTSAV AREA               00346
COUNT TABLE ADDRESS             002DC             CHECKPT CTR               00348
RESERVED                        002E0
DBG R11SAVE                     002E8      LITERAL POOL (HEX)
COUNT CHAIN ADDRESS             002EC
PRBL1 CELL PTR                  002E0      00368 (LIT+0)     E2C1D3C5  F0F0F0D4  E2C1D3C5  F0F01EC4  D0000400  00000005
RESERVED                        002F4      00386 (LIT+24)    62040000  20E2C1D3  F00E0880  0C040CC0  1000
TA LENGTH                       002F5
RESERVED                        002FC
PCS LIT PTR                     00304                  PGT                      00350
DEBUGGING                       00308
CD FOR INITIAL INPUT            0030C             OVERFLOW CELLS            00350
OVERFLOW CELLS                  00310             VIRTUAL CELLS             00350
BL CELLS                        00310             PROCEDURE NAME CELLS      00360
DECBADR CELLS                   00314             GENERATED NAME CELLS      00360
FIB CELLS                       00314             DCB ADDRESS CELLS         00364
TEMP STORAGE                    00318             VNI CELLS                 00364
TEMP STORAGE-2                  00318             LITERALS                  00368
TEMP STORAGE-3                  00318             DISPLAY LITERALS          00392
TEMP STORAGE-4                  0031B
BLL CELLS                       00318
VLC CELLS                       00334      REGISTER ASSIGNMENT
SBL CELLS                       00334
INDEX CELLS                     00334         REG 6    BL =1
SUBADR CELLS                    00334
ONCTL CELLS                     00334      WORKING-STORAGE STARTS AT LOCATION 000A0 FOR A LENGTH OF 0006C.
```

FIGURE 1.4   *(Continued)*

```
     6        SALEINIT      2.25.01      OCT  4,1983


                                   CONDENSED LISTING

    88      ENTRY      000392           89      SERVICE      0003AA           97      MOVE      0003AA
    97      MOVE       0003B4           97      MOVE         0003BE           98      CALL      0003CE
   106      MOVE       000418          106      MOVE         00041E          106      CALL      00042E
   109      GOBACK     000460


     7        SALEINIT      2.25.01      OCT  4,1983

*STATISTICS*    SOURCE RECORDS =    109    DATA DIVISION STATEMENTS =    49    PROCEDURE DIVISION STATEMENTS =     9
*OPTIONS IN EFFECT*     SIZE =  131072  BUF =   16384  LINECNT = 57  SPACE1, FIAGW,   SEQ,   SOURCE
*OPTIONS IN EFFECT*       DMAP, NOPMAP,   CLIST,   SUPMAP, NOXREF,   SXREF,   LOAD, NODECK, APOST, NOTRUNC, NOFLOW
*OPTIONS IN EFFECT*     NOTERM, NONUM, NOBATCH, NONAME, COMPILE=01, NOSTATE, NORESIDENT, NODYNAM,   LIB, NOSYNTAX
*OPTIONS IN EFFECT*     NOOPTIMIZE, NOSYMDMP, NOTEST,    VERB,   ZWB, SYST, NOENDJCB, NOLVL
*OPTIONS IN EFFECT*     NOLST , NOFDECK,NOCDECK, LCOL2,  L120,   DUMP ,   ADV , NCFRINT,
*OPTIONS IN EFFECT*     NOCOUNT, NOVBSUM, NOVBREF, LANGLVL(2)
```

FIGURE 1.4 *(Continued)*

```
      8          SALEINIT        2.25.01       OCT  4,1983


                                               CROSS-REFERENCE DICTIONARY


 DATA NAMES                            DEFN     REFERENCE


 DFHBLLSLOT1                           000086
 DFHBLLSLOT2                           000087
 DFHCCMMAREA                           000085
 DFHE1BLK                              000042
 DFHE1GDI                              000054
 DFHE1V                                000015
 DFHE1V0                               000016     000097    000098    000106
 DFHE1V1                               000017     000097    000098
 DFHE1V10                              000026
 DFHE1V11                              000027
 DFHE1V12                              000028
 DFHE1V13                              000029
 DFHE1V14                              000030
 DFHE1V15                              000031
 DFHE1V16                              000032
 DFHE1V17                              000033
 DFHE1V18                              000034
 DFHE1V19                              000035
 DFHE1V2                               000018     000097    000098
 DFHE1V3                               000019
 DFHE1V4                               000020
 DFHE1V5                               000021     000106
 DFHE1V6                               000022
 DFHE1V7                               000023
 DFHE1V8                               000024
 DFHE1V9                               000025
 DFHE1V97                              000036
 DFHE1V98                              000037     000098
 DFHE1V99                              000038     000098
 EIBAID                                000060
 EIBATI                                000080
 EIBCALEN                              000058
 EIBCPOSN                              000056
 EIBDATE                               000046
 EIBDS                                 000066
 EIBECC                                000082
 EIBFMH                                000084
 EIBFN                                 000062
 EIBFREE                               000074
 EIBRCODE                              000064
 EIBRECV                               000076
 EIBREQID                              000068
 EIBRSRCE                              000070
 EIBSEND                               000078
 EIBSYNC                               000072
 EIBTASKN                              000050
 EIBTIME                               000044
 EIBTRMID                              000052
 EIBTRNID                              000048



      9          SALEINIT        2.25.01       OCT  4,1983


 PROCEDURE NAMES                       DEFN     REFERENCE


 MAIN-ROUTINE                          000090
```

FIGURE 1.4   *(Continued)*

```
F64-LEVEL LINKAGE EDITOR OPTIONS SPECIFIED XREF,LIST,MAP
        DEFAULT OPTION(S) USED -  SIZE=(196608,65536)
IEW0000      INCLUDE SYSLIB(DFHEC1)                                              50000000
```

CROSS REFERENCE TABLE

```
CONTROL SECTION                        ENTRY

   NAME    ORIGIN  LENGTH                 NAME    LOCATION     NAME   LOCATION     NAME   LOCATION     NAME   LOCATION
 DFHEC1      00      18
                                        DFHCBLI       4      DFHE11        A     DLZEIO1        A    DLZEIO2       A
                                        DLZEIO3       A      DLZEIO4       A     DFHAICBA      14
 SALEINIT    18      546
 ILBOCOMO*   560     16D
                                        IlBOCOM      560
 ILBOSRV *   6D0     4A4
                                        ILEOSRVO     6DA      ILEOSR5      6DA    ILEOSR3       6DA    ILEOSR       6DA
                                        ILLOSRV1     6DE      ILBOSTP1     6DE    ILFOST        6E2    ILECSTPO     6E2
 ILBOBEG *   B78     188
                                        I1BOBEGO     E7A
 ILBOMSG *   D00     100
                                        I1BOMSGO     D02


 LOCATION  REFERS TO SYMBOL  IN CONTROL SECTION          LOCATION  REFERS TO SYMBOL  IN CONTROL SECTION
    368         ILBOSRVO        ILBOSRV                     36C         ILBOSR5         ILBOSRV
    370         DFHE11          DFHEC1                      374         ILBOSRV1        ILBOSRV
    2E0         ILBOCOMO        ILBOCOMO                    A5C         ILBOCOR         ILBOCOMO
    A70         ILBOSTIC        $UNRESOLVED (6)             A60         ILBOCMMO        $UNRESOLVED (W)
    A64         ILBOFEGO        ILBOBEG                     A68         ILBOMSGO        ILBOMSG
    A6C         ILBOSND2        $UNRESOLVED (W)             CB8         ILBOPRMO        $UNRESOLVED (6)

 ENTRY ADDRESS        18

 TOTAL LENGTH        E00
 ****SALEINIT  NOW REPLACED IN DATA SET
 AUTHORIZATION CODE IS         0.
```

FIGURE 1.4 (Continued)

the use of macro level code in the newer releases of CICS. In fact, to take advantage of some valuable features in current CICS releases, it is necessary to convert your programs to use command level code.

Macro level instruction formats are somewhat different, resembling assembler language macro calls. A different language translator is used, so the two types of CICS should not be mixed in a COBOL program. The programmer is responsible for obtaining necessary storage and for putting correct values into address pointers. If you will have to maintain or convert any old macro level programs in the future, you will probably find it easier to learn after you have some command level experience. This book will not cover the writing of macro level programs. However, there are a few macros which are not part of the macro level interface. You will be learning how to use them in order to form CICS maps.

1.2.5   Maps: What They Are and How They Are Created

A map is a screen format, which a COBOL programmer can think of as an FD for the terminal screen, although there is much more to it than that. A map must be coded and assembled before any CICS application programs that use it are compiled. Why is this so? If you have used a copy library before, you know that the storage layouts and record formats used by your program must be available in the copy library before you compile. Your CICS program will contain one or more map layouts from the copy library in this manner.

Examine Figure 1.5, the map assembly diagram, and notice the way in which it relates to Figure 1.3, the command level program translation diagram. Also see Figure 1.6. Maps are also assembled in two sep-

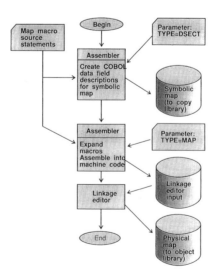

FIGURE 1.5   Map assembly (chart).

```
ADDR1 ADDR2  STMT   SOURCE STATEMENT                              ASM 0201 01.57 10/04/83

          1 MSALE00  DFHMSD TYPE=MAP,                                         X00000200
                            TERM=3270,                                        X00000300
                            LANG=COBOL,                                       X00000400
                            MODE=INOUT,                                       X00000500
                            TIOAPFX=YES,                                      X00000600
                            CTRL=(FREEKB,FRSET)                                00000800
          2+* DEFAULT TAKEN: (NOT STORAGE=AUTO)               @BCAD311 03228500
          3 SALE000  DFHMDI SIZE=(24,80)                                      00000900
          4+         PUNCH '     01  SALE000I.'               @FA26388 05670000
          5+         PUNCH '         02  FILLER PIC X(12).'   @BC6D00T 05780000
          6 SOTRAN   DFHMDF LENGTH=04,                                        X00001000
                            POS=(01,01),                                      X00001100
                            ATTRB=(ASKIP,NORM,FSET),                          X00001200
                            INITIAL='SALO'                                    00001300
          7+         PUNCH '         02  SOTRANL   COMP PIC S9(4). ' @ECC5E01 06180000
          8+         PUNCH '         02  SOTRANF   PICTURE X.'       @FCC5E01 06200000
          9+         PUNCH '         02  SOTRANI   PIC X(4).'        @ECC5E01 06290000
         10          DFHMDF LENGTH=43,                                        X00001400
                            POS=(01,30),                                      X00001500
                            ATTRB=(ASKIP,NORM),                               X00001600
                            INITIAL='SALES REPORTING MENU'                    00001700
         11          DFHMDF LENGTH=43,                                        X00001400
                            POS=(05,19),                                      X00001500
                            ATTRB=(ASKIP,NORM),                               X00001600
                            INITIAL='ADD A NEW CUSTOMER ------------------- FF1'    00002100
         12          DFHMDF LENGTH=43,                                        X00001800
                            POS=(07,19),                                      X00001900
                            INITIAL='CHANGE CUSTOMER DATA ----------------- FF2'    00002100
         13          DFHMDF LENGTH=43,                                        X00002200
                            POS=(09,19),                                      X00002300
                            INITIAL='DELETE INACTIVE CUSTOMER ------------- FF3'    00002100
         14          DFHMDF LENGTH=43,                                        X00002200
                            POS=(11,19),                                      X00002300
                            INITIAL='ENTER CURRENT WEEK SALES ------------- PF4'    00002100
         15          DFHMDF LENGTH=43,                                        X00002200
                            POS=(13,19),                                      X00002300
                            INITIAL='VIEW CUSTOMER LIST ------------------- PF5'    00002100
         16          DFHMDF LENGTH=43,                                        X00002200
                            POS=(15,19),                                      X00002300
                            INITIAL='VIEW CURRENT WEEK SALES -------------- FF6'    00002100
         17          DFHMDF LENGTH=43,                                        X00002200
                            POS=(17,19),                                      X00002300
                            INITIAL='EXIT TRANSACTION --------------------- FA1'    00002100
         18          DFHMDF LENGTH=16,                                        X00003900
                            POS=(18,30),                                      X00004000
                            INITIAL='CUSTOMER NUMBER:'                        00004100
         19 SOCUST   DFHMDF LENGTH=06,                                        X00003500
                            POS=(18,47),                                      X00003600
                            ATTRB=(IC,NUM),                                   X00001200
                            INITIAL='_____'                                  00003800
         20+         PUNCH '         02  SOCUSTL   COMP PIC S9(4). ' @ECC5E01 06180000
         21+         PUNCH '         02  SOCUSTF   PICTURE X.'       @ECC5E01 06200000
         22+         PUNCH '         02  SOCUSTI   PIC X(6).'        @ECC5E01 06290000
         23          DFHMDF LENGTH=01,                                        X00004400
                            POS=(18,54)
```

FIGURE 1.6   Sample CICS map assembly.

```
                                                          ASM 0201  02.58  01/14/84

25+          PUNCH '             03 SOCUSTA     PICTURE X.'       aBCD5E01 62280000
26+          PUNCH '           C2  SOCUSTI  PIC X(6).'            aBCD5E01 62940000
27           DFHMDF LENGTH=C1,                                             XC0004400
               POS=(18,54)
28           DFHMDF LENGTH=44,                                             XC0002200
               POS=(21,19),                                                XC0002300
               INITIAL='ENTER CUSTOMER NUMBER AND PRESS FUNCTION KEY'      00002100
29 SCERR     DFHMDF LENGTH=78,                                             XC0005200
               POS=(24,C1),                                                XC0005300
               ATTRB=(ASKIP,BRT)                                           C0005400
30+          PUNCH '           C2  SOERRL     COMP  PIC  S9(4). '  aBCD5E01 61860000
31+          PUNCH '           C2  SOERRF     PICTURE X.'          aBCD5E01 61980000
32+          PUNCH '           C2  FILLER REDEFINES SOERRF.'       aBCD5E01 62220000
33+          PUNCH '             03 SOERRA     PICTURE X.'         aBCD5E01 62280000
34+          PUNCH '           C2  SOERRI  PIC X(78).'             aBCD5E01 62940000
35           DFHMSD TYPE=FINAL                                             C0031400
36+          PUNCH '       01  SALEOOOD REDEFINES SALEOOOI.'       aRA26388 68400000
37+          PUNCH '           C2  FILLER PIC X(12).'              aBC6DOOT 68560000
38+          PUNCH '           C2  FILLER PICTURE X(3).'           aBCD5E01 72080000
39+          PUNCH '           C2  SOTRANO  PIC X(4).'             *73120000
  +                                                               aBCD5E01 73200000
40+          PUNCH '           C2  FILLER PICTURE X(3).'           aBCD5E01 72080000
41+          PUNCH '           C2  SOCUSTO  PIC X(6).'             *73120000
  +                                                               aBCD5E01 73200000
42+          PUNCH '           C2  FILLER PICTURE X(3).'           aBCD5E01 72080000
43+          PUNCH '           C2  SOERRO  PIC X(78).'             *73120000
  +                                                               aBCD5E01 73200000
44           END                                                           00031500
```

FIGURE 1.6 (Continued)

ASSEMBLER DIAGNOSTICS AND STATISTICS

ASM 0201 01.57 10/04/83   PAGE   3

NO STATEMENTS FLAGGED IN THIS ASSEMBLY
HIGHEST SEVERITY WAS   0
OPTIONS FOR THIS ASSEMBLY
 ALIGN, ALOGIC, BUFSIZE(STD), DECK, ESD, FLAG(0), LINECOUNT(55), LIST, NOMCALL, YFLAG, WORKSIZE(2097152)
 NOMLOGIC, NONUMBER, NOOBJECT, NORENT, RLD, NOSYM, NOLIBMAC, NOTERMINAL, NOTEST, XREF(SHORT)
 SYSPARM(DSECT)
WORK FILE BUFFER SIZE/NUMBER =19066/ 1
TOTAL RECORDS READ FROM SYSTEM INPUT   54
TOTAL RECORDS READ FROM SYSTEM LIBRARY 3838
TOTAL RECORDS PUNCHED   22
TOTAL RECORDS PRINTED   97

DATA SET UTILITY - GENERATE   PAGE 0001

PROCESSING ENDED AT EOD

EXTERNAL SYMBOL DICTIONARY

ASM 0201 01.56 10/04/83   PAGE   1

SYMBOL TYPE ID ADDR LENGTH LDID
  PC   0001 000000 00024A

FIGURE 1.6 *(Continued)*

```
LOC   OBJECT CODE   ADDR1 ADDR2  STMT   SOURCE STATEMENT                                    ASM 0201 01.56 10/04/83

                                    1  MSALE00  DFHMSD  TYPE=MAP,                                                         X00000200
                                                        TERM=3270,                                                       X00000300
                                                        LANG=COBOL,                                                      X00000400
                                                        MODE=INOUT,                                                      X00000500
                                                        TIOAPFX=YES,                                                     X00000600
                                                        CTRL=(FREEKB,FRSET)                                              X00000800
                                    2+* DEFAULT TAKEN: (NOT STORAGE=AUTO)                          @BCAD311   03228000
000000                              3+*************************************************************************   04610000
000000 D4E2C1D3C5F0F0F040           4+MSALE00  DS   0D             MAP SE1 ORIGIN                                04660000
000008 00                           5+          DC   CL8'MSALE00'   MAP SE1 NAME                                 04710000
000009 40                           6+          DC   AL1(DFHBM801)  OVEPFLCW TRAILER LENGTH                      04720000
00000A 4040                         7+          DC   X'40'          VERSION 1.4   OF CICS          @BCA5E01      04730000
                                    8+          DC   CL2'  '        LDC MNEMONIC                   @BC85D1L      04780000
                                    9+*************************************************************************   05270000

00000C                             11  SALE000  DFHMDI  SIZE=(24,80)                                             00000900
00000C                             12+*************************************************************************   04700000
00000C 00000000                    13+SALE000  DS   0C             MAP ORIGIN                     @BA26388      04750000
000010 00000000                    14+          DC   AL4(0)         MAP CHAIN ADDRESS                            04770000
000014 E2C1D3C5F0F0F040            15+          DC   AL4(0)         MAP DATA ADDRESS               @BA26388      04780000
00001C 023A                        16+          DC   CL8'SALE000'   MAP NAME                                     04790000
000020 008C                        17+          DC   AL2(DFHBM101)  MAP LENGTH                                   04800000
000022 0068                        18+          DC   AL2(DFHBM601)  MAP SPECIFICATION LENGTH                     04810000
000024 0237                        19+          DC   AL2(DFHBM201)  INPUT WORK AREA LENGTH                       04820000
000024 C0                          20+          DC   AL2(DFHBM301)  OUTPUT WORK AREA LENGTH        @BC9D30A      04830000
000025 C3                          21+          DC   AL1(192)       MAP DESCRIPTOR FLAG BYTE                     04840000
000026 057F                        22+          DC   CL1'C'         3270 WRITE CONTROL CHARACTER                 04850000
000028 00                          23+          DC   AL2(DFHBM401)  3270 CURSOR POSITION                         04860000
000029 18                          24+          DC   AL1(0)         MAP MARGIN                                   04870000
00002A 50                          25+          DC   AL1(24)        MAP LENGTH - NUMBER OF LINES                 04800000
00002B FF                          26+          DC   AL1(80)        MAP WIDTH - NUMBER OF COLUMNS                04800000
00002C FE                          27+          DC   AL1(255)       MAP STARTING LINE NUMBER                     04910000
00002D 00                          28+          DC   AL1(254)       MAP STARTING COLUMN NUMBER                   04910000
00002E 00                          29+          DC   AL1(DFHBM701)  MAP INDICATOR                                04920000
00002F 00                          30+          DC   AL1(0)         TYPE REQUEST BYTE TWO                        04930000
000030 00                          31+          DC   AL1(0)         TYPE REQUEST BYTE THREE                      04940000
000031 00                          32+          DC   AL1(0)         TYPE REQUEST BYTE FOUR                       04950000
000032 0000                        33+          DC   AL2(0)         TYPE REQUEST BYTE FIVE                       04960000
000034 00                          34+          DC   AL2(0)         REQUEST1 CURSOR POSITION                     04970000
000035 00                          35+          DC   AL1(0)         REQUEST1 WRITE CONTROL CHARACTER             04980000
                                   36+          DC   AL1(0)         RESERVED                                     04990000
                                   37+*************************************************************************   05000000

                                   39  SOTRAN   DFHMDF  LENGTH=04,                                               X00001000
                                                        POS=(01,01),                                            X00001100
                                                        ATTRB=(ASKIP,NORM,FSET),                                X00001200
                                                        INITIAL='SALO'                                            00001300
000036                             40+*************************************************************************   03640000
000036 0000                        41+SOTRAN   DS   0C             FIELD NAME                                   03650000
000038 0004                        42+          DC   AL2(0)         FIELD PAGE POSITION                          03670000
                                   43+          DC   AL2(4)         FIELD LENGTH                                 03680000
```

FIGURE 1.6 *(Continued)*

```
LOC    OBJECT CODE      ADDR1 ADDR2  STMT  SOURCE STATEMENT                                          ASM C201 01.56 10/04/83

00003A 03                                 44+      DC    AL1(3)                     FIELD DESCRIPTOR FLAG BYTE    a 03690000
00003E F1                                 45+      DC    CL1'1'                     FIELD ATTRIBUTE                 03700000
00003C 0000                               46+      DC    AL2(0)                     FIELD POSITION                 03710000
00003E E2C113F0                           47+      DC    CL4'SALO'                  DEFAULT MAP DATA       aEA54765 03730000
                                          48+*●●●●●●●●●●●●●●●●●●●●●●●●●●●●●●●●●●●●●●●●●●●●●●●●●●●●●●●●●●●●●●●●●●● 03750000

                                          50       DFHMDF LENGTH=43,                                            X00001400
                                                          POS=(01,30),                                         X00001500
                                                          ATTRB=(ASKIP,NORM),                                  X00001600
                                                          INITIAL='SALES REPORTING MENU'                        00001700
                                          51+*●●●●●●●●●●●●●●●●●●●●●●●●●●●●●●●●●●●●●●●●●●●●●●●●●●●●●●●●●●●●●●●●●●● 03640000
000042 0000                               52+      DS    0C                         FIELD NAME               a 03650000
000042 002B                               53+      DC    AL2(0)                     FIELD PAGE POSITION      a 03670000
000046 02                                 54+      DC    AL2(43)                    FIELD LENGTH               03680000
000047 F0                                 55+      DC    AL1(2)                     FIELD DESCRIPTOR FLAG BYTE a 03690000
000048 001D                               56+      DC    CL1'0'                     FIELD ATTRIBUTE            a 03700000
00004A E2C1D3C5E240D9C5                   57+      DC    AL2(29)                    FIELD POSITION            a 03710000
U00052 D7D6E9E3C9D5C740                   58+      DC    CL43'SALES REPORTING MENU' DEFAULT MAP DATA         X03730000
                                          +                      aEA54765                                      03730000
                                          59+*●●●●●●●●●●●●●●●●●●●●●●●●●●●●●●●●●●●●●●●●●●●●●●●●●●●●●●●●●●●●●●●●●●● 03750000

                                          61       DFHMDF LENGTH=43,                                            X00001400
                                                          POS=(05,19),                                         X00001500
                                                          ATTRB=(ASKIP,NORM),                                  X00001600
                                                          INITIAL='ADD A NEW CUSTOMER ----------------- FF1'    00002100
                                          62+*●●●●●●●●●●●●●●●●●●●●●●●●●●●●●●●●●●●●●●●●●●●●●●●●●●●●●●●●●●●●●●●●●●● 03640000
000075 0000                               63+      DS    0C                         FIELD NAME               a 03650000
000075 002B                               64+      DC    AL2(0)                     FIELD PAGE POSITION      a 03670000
000079 02                                 65+      DC    AL2(43)                    FIELD LENGTH               03680000
00007A F0                                 66+      DC    AL1(2)                     FIELD DESCRIPTOR FLAG BYTE a 03690000
00007B 0152                               67+      DC    CL1'0'                     FIELD ATTRIBUTE            a 03700000
00007D C1C4C440C140D5C5                   68+      DC    AL2(338)                   FIELD POSITION            a 03710000
000085 E640C73E4E2E3D6D4                  69+      DC    CL43'ADD A NEW CUSTOMER --------------- FF1' DEFAULX03730000
                                          +          T MAP DATA            aEA54765                            03730000
                                          70+*●●●●●●●●●●●●●●●●●●●●●●●●●●●●●●●●●●●●●●●●●●●●●●●●●●●●●●●●●●●●●●●●●●● 03750000

                                          72       DFHMDF LENGTH=43,                                            X00001800
                                                          POS=(07,19),                                         X00001900
                                                          INITIAL='CHANGE CUSTOMER DATA ----------- FF2'        00002100
                                          73+*●●●●●●●●●●●●●●●●●●●●●●●●●●●●●●●●●●●●●●●●●●●●●●●●●●●●●●●●●●●●●●●●●●● 03640000
0000A8 0000                               74+      DS    0C                         FIELD NAME               a 03650000
0000A8 002B                               75+      DC    AL2(0)                     FIELD PAGE POSITION      a 03670000
0000AA 02                                 76+      DC    AL2(43)                    FIELD LENGTH               03680000
U000AC 02                                 77+      DC    AL1(2)                     FIELD DESCRIPTOR FLAG BYTE a 03690000
0000AD F0                                 78+      DC    CL1'0'                     FIELD ATTRIBUTE            a 03700000
0000AE 01F2                               79+      DC    AL2(498)                   FIELD POSITION            a 03710000
0000E0 C3C8C1D5C7C540C3                   80+      DC    CL43'CHANGE CUSTOMER DATA ----------- FF2' DEFAULX03730000
0000E8 E4E2E3D6D4CSD940                   +          T MAP DATA            aEA54765                            03730000
                                          81+*●●●●●●●●●●●●●●●●●●●●●●●●●●●●●●●●●●●●●●●●●●●●●●●●●●●●●●●●●●●●●●●●●●● 03750000
```

FIGURE 1.6 (Continued)

27

```
LOC      OBJECT CODE       ADDR1 ADDR2  STMT  SOURCE STATEMENT

                                         83          DFHMDF LENGTH=3,                                                      X00002200
                                                            POS=(09,19),                                                  X00002300
                                                            INITIAL='DELETE INACTIVE CUSTOMER ------------- PF3'           00002100
                                        84+*****************************************************************************  03640000
0000DB                                  85+        DS    0C                         FIELD NAME                         @   03650000
0000DE  0000                            86+        DC    AL2(0)                     FIELD PAGE POSITION                @   03670000
0000DD  002B                            87+        DC    AL2(43)                    FIELD LENGTH                       @   03680000
0000DF  02                              88+        DC    AL1(2)                     FIELD DESCRIPTOR FLAG BYTE         @   03690000
0000E0  F0                              89+        DC    CL1'0'                     FIELD ATTRIBUTE                    @   03700000
0000E1  0292                            90+        DC    AL2(658)                   FIELD POSITION                     @   03710000
0000E3  C4C5D3C5E3C540C9                91+        DC    CL43'DELETE INACTIVE CUSTOMER ------------- PF3' DEFAULX03730000
0000EF  D5C1C3E3C9E5C540                                                                        @BA54765
                                        92+*****************************************************************************  03750000


                                         94          DFHMDF LENGTH=3,                                                      X00002200
                                                            POS=(11,19),                                                  X00002300
                                                            INITIAL='ENTER CURRENT WEEK SALES ------------ PF4'            00002100
                                        95+*****************************************************************************  03640000
00010E                                  96+        DS    0C                         FIELD NAME                         @   03650000
00010E  0000                            97+        DC    AL2(0)                     FIELD PAGE POSITION                @   03670000
000110  002B                            98+        DC    AL2(43)                    FIELD LENGTH                       @   03680000
000112  02                              99+        DC    AL1(2)                     FIELD DESCRIPTOR FLAG BYTE         @   03690000
000113  F0                             100+        DC    CL1'0'                     FIELD ATTRIBUTE                    @   03700000
000114  0332                           101+        DC    AL2(818)                   FIELD POSITION                     @   03710000
000116  C5D5E3C5D940C3E4               102+        DC    CL43'ENTER CURRENT WEEK SALES ------------ PF4' DEFAULX03730000
00011E  D9D9C5D5E340E6C5                                                                        @BA54765
                                       103+*****************************************************************************  03750000


                                        105          DFHMDF LENGTH=3,                                                      X00002200
                                                            POS=(13,19),                                                  X00002300
                                                            INITIAL='VIEW CUSTOMER LIS1 ------------------ PF5'            00002100
                                       106+*****************************************************************************  03640000
000141                                 107+        DS    0C                         FIELD NAME                         @   03650000
000141  0000                           108+        DC    AL2(0)                     FIELD PAGE POSITION                @   03670000
000143  002B                           109+        DC    AL2(43)                    FIELD LENGTH                       @   03680000
000145  02                             110+        DC    AL1(2)                     FIELD DESCRIPTOR FLAG BYTE         @   03690000
000146  F0                             111+        DC    CL1'0'                     FIELD ATTRIBUTE                    @   03700000
000147  03D2                           112+        DC    AL2(978)                   FIELD POSITION                     @   03710000
000149  E5C9C5E640C3E4E2               113+        DC    CL43'VIEW CUSTOMER LIST ------------------ PF5' DEFAULX03730000
000151  E3D6D4C5D940D3C9                                                                        @BA54765
                                       114+*****************************************************************************  03750000


                                        116          DFHMDF LENGTH=3,                                                      X00002200
                                                            POS=(15,19),                                                  X00002300
                                                            INITIAL='VIEW CURRENT WEEK SALES ------------- PF6'            00002100
                                       117+*****************************************************************************  03640000
000174                                 118+        DS    0C                         FIELD NAME                         @   03650000
000174  0000                           119+        DC    AL2(0)                     FIELD PAGE POSITION                @   03650000
000176  002B                           120+        DC    AL2(43)                    FIELD LENGTH                       @   03660000
```

FIGURE 1.6 *(Continued)*

28

```
LOC      OBJECT CODE      ADDR1 ADDR2   STMT   SOURCE STATEMENT                                    ASM 0201 01.56 10/04/83

000178 02                             121+      DC    AL1(2)              FIELD DESCRIPTOR FLAG BYTE        @ 03690000
000179 F0                             122+      DC    CL1'0'              FIELD ATTRIBUTE                   @ 03700000
00017A 0472                           123+      DC    AL2(1138)           FIELD POSITION                    @ 03710000
00017C E5C9C5E40C3E4D9                124+      DC    CL43'VIEW CURRENT WEEK SALES --------- PF6' DEFAULTX03730000
000184 D9C5D5E340E6C5C5                      *        T MAP DATA       @EA54765                            @* 03750000
                                      125+*ccccccccccccccccccccccccccccccccccccccccccccccccccccccccccccccccccc

127                                   DFHMDF LENGTH=43,                                                   X00002200
                                             POS=(17,19),                                                X00002300
                                             INITIAL='EXIT TRANSACTION ----------------- FA1'             00002100
                                      128+*ccccccccccccccccccccccccccccccccccccccccccccccccccccccccccccccccccc
0001A7                                129+      DS    0C                  FIELD NAME                        @ 03640000
0001A7 0000                           130+      DC    AL2(0)              FIELD PAGE POSITION               @ 03650000
0001A9 002B                           131+      DC    AL2(43)             FIELD LENGTH                      @ 03680000
0001AB 02                             132+      DC    AL1(2)              FIELD DESCRIPTOR FLAG BYTE        @ 03690000
0001AC F0                             133+      DC    CL1'0'              FIELD ATTRIBUTE                   @ 03700000
0001AD 0512                           134+      DC    AL2(1298)           FIELD POSITION                    @ 03710000
0001AF C5E7C9E340E3D9C1               135+      DC    CL43'EXIT TRANSACTION ----------------- FA1' DEFAULTX03730000
0001B7 D5E2C1C3E3C9D6D5                      *        T MAP DATA       @EA54765                            @* 03750000
                                      136+*ccccccccccccccccccccccccccccccccccccccccccccccccccccccccccccccccccc

138                                   DFHMDF LENGTH=16,                                                   X00003900
                                             POS=(18,30),                                                X00004000
                                             INITIAL='CUSTOMER NUMBER:'                                   00004100
                                      139+*ccccccccccccccccccccccccccccccccccccccccccccccccccccccccccccccccccc
0001DA                                140+      DS    0C                  FIELD NAME                        @ 03640000
0001DA 0000                           141+      DC    AL2(0)              FIELD PAGE POSITION               @ 03650000
0001DC 0010                           142+      DC    AL2(16)             FIELD LENGTH                      @ 03680000
0001DE 02                             143+      DC    AL1(2)              FIELD DESCRIPTOR FLAG BYTE        @ 03690000
0001DF F0                             144+      DC    CL1'0'              FIELD ATTRIBUTE                   @ 03700000
0001E0 056D                           145+      DC    AL2(1389)           FIELD POSITION                    @ 03710000
0001E2 C3E4E2E3D6D4C5D9               146+      DC    CL16'CUSTOMER NUMBER:' DEFAULT MAP DATA   @EA54765   @* 03730000
0001EA 40D5E4D4C2C5D97A                                                                                      03750000
                                      147+*ccccccccccccccccccccccccccccccccccccccccccccccccccccccccccccccccccc

149 SOCUST                            DFHMDF LENGTH=06,                                                   X00003500
                                             POS=(18,47),                                                X00003600
                                             ATTRB=(IC,NUM),                                             X00001200
                                             INITIAL='......'                                            00003000
                                      150+*ccccccccccccccccccccccccccccccccccccccccccccccccccccccccccccccccccc
0001F2                                151+*SOCUST DS  0C                  FIELD NAME                        @ 03640000
0001F2 0000                           152+      DC    AL2(0)              FIELD PAGE POSITION               @ 03650000
0001F4 0006                           153+      DC    AL2(6)              FIELD LENGTH                      @ 03680000
0001F6 0F                             154+      DC    AL1(15)             FIELD DESCRIPTOR FLAG BYTE        @ 03690000
0001F7 50                             155+      DC    CL1'&'              FIELD ATTRIBUTE                   @ 03700000
0001F8 057E                           156+      DC    AL2(1406)           FIELD POSITION                    @ 03710000
0001FA 6D6D6D6D6D6D                   157+      DC    CL6'......'  .      DEFAULT MAP DATA       @EA54765   @* 03730000
                                      158+*ccccccccccccccccccccccccccccccccccccccccccccccccccccccccccccccccccc  03750000
```

FIGURE 1.6 (Continued)

29

```
LOC    OBJECT CODE    ADDR1 ADDR2  STMT   SOURCE STATEMENT                                    ASM 0201 02.57 C1/14/E4

                                    160        DFHMDF LENGTH=C1,                                              XC004400
                                                      POS=(18,54)                                            38520000
                                    161+*****************************************************************    385RCC00
                                    162+       DC    AL2(C)            FIELD NAME                             38700000
000200  0000                        163+       DC    AL2(1)            FIELD PAGE POSITION                    3R760000
000202  0001                        164+       DC    AL1(0)            FIELD LENGTH                           38820000
000204  00                          165+       DC    AL1(0)            FIELD DESCRIPTOR FLAG BYTE             38880000
000205  FO                          166+       DC    CL1'0'            FIELD ATTRIBUTE                        36940000
000206  0585                        167+       DC    AL2(1413)         FIELD POSITION                         40560000
                                    168+*****************************************************************

                                    170        DFHMDF LENGTH=44,                                              XC002200
                                                      POS=(21,19),                                            XC002300
                                                      INITIAL='ENTER CUSTOMER NUMBER AND PRESS FUNCTION KEY'  C0002100
                                    171+*****************************************************************    38520000
                                    172+       DS    OC                FIELD NAME                             385R0000
000208  0000                        173+       DC    AL2(0)            FIELD PAGE POSITION                    36700000
00020A  002C                        174+       DC    AL2(44)           FIELD LENGTH                           3R760000
00020C  02                          175+       DC    ALI(2)            FIELD DESCRIPTOR FLAG BYTE             28820000
00020D  FO                          176+       DC    CL1'0'            FIELD ATTRIBUTE                         38880000
00020E  0652                        177+       DC    AL2(1618)         FIELD POSITION                         38940000
000210  C5D5E3C5C940C3E4            178+       CL44'ENTER CUSTOMER NUMBER AND PRESS FUNCTION KEY' CEFAUX      4C440000
000218  E2E3D604C5D94CD5                             @RA54765                                                 40560000
                                    179+*****************************************************************

000230                              1R1  SCERP DFHMDF LENGTH=7B,                                              XC005200
                                                      POS=(74,C1),                                            YC005300
                                                      ATPB=(ASKIF,PRT)                                        C0005400
                                    182+*****************************************************************    38520000
                                    183+SCERR  DS    OC                FIELD NAME                             3R56C000
00023C  0C00                        184+       DC    AL2(01)           FIELD PAGE POSITION                    36700000
00023E  004E                        185+       DC    AL2(7F)           FIELD LENGTH                           3R760000
000240  01                          186+       DC    ALI(1)            FIELD DESCRIPTOR FLAG BYTE             38820000
000241  F8                          187+       DC    CL1'8'            FIELD ATTRIBUTE                         38880000
000242  0730                        188+       DC    AL2(IR40)         FIELD POSITION                         36940000
                                    189+*****************************************************************    40560000

                                    191        DFHMSD TYPE=FINAL                                              C0031400
                                    192+*****************************************************************    48440000
00008C                              193+DFHBM601 EQU   14C               MAP SPECIFICATION LENGTH             4R860000
00068                               194+DFHBM201 EQU   104               INPUT WORK AREA LENGTH               48930000
00237                               195+DFHBM301 EQU   567               OUTPUT WORK AREA LENGTH              49000000
0057F                               196+DFHBM401 EQU   14C7              CURSOR POSITION                       49070000
00000                               197+DFHBM701 EQU   0                 MAP INDICATOR                        49280000
                                    198+*                                END OF MAP                           49350000
000244  FFFF                        199+DFHBM501 EQU   2XLI'FF'          END OF MAP                           49420000
00246                               200+DFHBM101 EQU   DFHBM01-SALECOO-0 MAP LENGTH                 @BA71362  49490000
00000                               201+DFHBM801 EQU   0                 OVERFLOW TRAILER LEN.      @BCAD311  49630000
000246  FFFFFFFF                    202+       DC    4X'FF'            END OF MAPSET                @BCAD311  49700000
```

FIGURE 1.6 (Continued)

203+◊◊◊*◊◊◊◊ 05280000

205 END 00031500

CROSS-REFERENCE ASM 0201 01.56 10/04/83

SYMBOL	LEN	VALUE	DEFN	REFERENCES
DFHBM101	00001	0000023A	00200	00017
DFHBM201	00001	00000068	00194	00019
DFHBM301	00001	00000237	00195	00020
DFHBM401	00001	0000057F	00196	00023
DFHBM501	00001	00000246	00199	00200
DFHBM601	00001	0000008C	00193	00018
DFHBM701	00001	00000000	00197	00029
DFHBM801	00001	00000000	00201	00006
SALE000	00001	0000000C	00013	00200

ASSEMBLER DIAGNOSTICS AND STATISTICS ASM 0201 01.56 10/04/83

```
NO STATEMENTS FLAGGED IN THIS ASSEMBLY
HIGHEST SEVERITY WAS    0
OPTIONS FOR THIS ASSEMBLY
  ALIGN, ALOGIC, BUFSIZE(STD), DECK, ESD, FLAG(0), LINECOUNT(55), LIST, NOMCALL, YFLAG, WORKSIZE(2097152)
  NOMLOGIC, NONUMBER, NOOBJECT, NORENT, RLD, NOSTMT, NOLIPMAC, NOTERMINAL, NOTEST, XREF(SHORT)
  SYSPARM(MAP)
WORK FILE BUFFER SIZE/NUMBER =19066/ 1
TOTAL RECORDS READ FROM SYSTEM INPUT       54
TOTAL RECORDS READ FROM SYSTEM LIBRARY   3838
TOTAL RECORDS PUNCHED                      13
TOTAL RECORDS PRINTED                     288
```

FIGURE 1.6 (Continued)

```
F64-LEVEL LINKAGE EDITOR OPTIONS SPECIFIED LIST,XREF,1E1
         DEFAULT OPTION(S) USED -  SIZE=(196608,65536)


                              CROSS REFERENCE TABLE

CONTROL SECTION              ENTRY
   NAME    ORIGIN  LENGTH         NAME  LOCATION   NAME  LOCATION   NAME  LOCATION   NAME  LOCATION   NAME  LOCATION
$PRIVATE     00     24A

ENTRY ADDRESS        00

TOTAL LENGTH        250
****MSALE00   NOW REPLACED IN DATA SET
AUTHORIZATION CODE IS      0.
```

FIGURE 1.6 *(Continued)*

arate stages. Observe that the first stage of map assembly writes a copy book or source member out to a source statement library. This is the part that acts somewhat like an FD for the terminal screen. When your CICS program is compiled, it must include this copy book, called a **symbolic map**, in its working storage or linkage section. Symbolic map copy library members may be stored in a partitioned data set maintained under TSO/SPF, or placed in ICCF library members, or kept in any other source statement library maintenance facility available at your site. Map definition works much the same way under CICS OS/2 as on a mainframe: you keep map layout copy members in the appropriate subdirectory.

How will you use this symbolic map within your program? You will use this area as an I/O area for sending and receiving terminal data that pertains to certain fields. How does the map assembly software "know" which fields on the screen your program will need to access? You specify those fields by providing each of them with a *field name* when you code your map macros. Fields on the map that are not named behave like COBOL FILLER for the terminal screen: your program cannot change their contents because they are not included in the symbolic map. Unnamed fields are used for constant data such as headers and captions.

The second stage of the map assembly takes the same source data and expands each map and field definition macro into assembler language data definitions. These data definitions are assembled in the normal manner and are stored on the core image library or load library as an object program containing only data definitions, not object code. This object program is called a **physical map**. The CICS software, at run time, refers to this map object program for information whenever your command level program sends or receives that map. The physical map tells CICS how to format the map data, and what constant fields should be displayed on the screen. Maps will be covered in more detail in Chapter 3.

1.2.6   Making Compiled Programs and Maps Available to the CICS System

You must name your programs and maps to make them available to the CICS system. A program name may contain up to eight characters. Every map must be assigned to a **map set**, which identifies a nonexecutable load module containing one or more physical maps. A map set name may contain up to seven characters. The eighth position in a map set name is reserved for CICS internal use as a flag indicating device type. (You might use this if you have to support several different terminal types.) Even though this flag is typically blank, you must keep the eighth position free for this use.

Every site should adopt standards or conventions for naming programs, maps, map sets, and transactions. Since terminal users enter four-digit transaction codes in order to bring up an application on a terminal, these transaction codes should have some mnemonic resemblance to the application name. Payroll maintenance could be PAYR, sales reporting could be SALE, and so forth. Some CICS installations name programs and maps by attaching a suffix to the particular transaction code with which the programs are associated. For instance, if two maps and three programs are needed in order to execute the SALE transaction, the two map sets could be named MSALE01 and MSALE02, and the three programs could be named SALEP001, SALEP002, and SALEP003. A consistent naming scheme helps identify "stray" programs that have become obsolete and are no longer used by any transactions. In large CICS installations, obsolete programs often clutter the CICS libraries and tables because no one is certain that they are useless and can be deleted.

CICS uses internal tables to keep track of all of its resources and activities. These tables are loaded into memory when CICS is started up. One of these tables tells CICS where to find object programs and physical maps. Whenever a program or map is compiled or assembled, mainframe CICS must be told that a new copy of the program or map object code is in the load library at a particular address. There are two ways this can take place. If CICS is brought down and then started up again, the tables will be reloaded into memory with the updated disc addresses of the programs. However, bringing CICS down may disrupt normal activities. Instead, the CEMT SET PROGRAM NEWCOPY master terminal command can be used to load the appropriate disc address. A discussion of CEMT is in the appendix.

1.3   STRUCTURE OF CICS

1.3.1   CICS Tables

CICS is a *table-driven system*. The tables tell CICS what work it must do, what programs, files, storage, and terminals it may use, what priorities it must observe, and what users may access the system. Certain of these tables may need to be updated when you write a new CICS application. Here are some that you may need to know about:

Data Conversion Table (CVT):   This table applies only to CICS OS/2 when used to communicate with mainframes. OS/2 is an ASCII-based environment, while mainframes are an EBCDIC-based environment. What do you do when you want to pass data back and forth? In order to translate a record, you need to be able to specify which parts of it are character,

Workstation Set Up (WSU):   Like the CVT, the WSU exists only on the OS/2 side. You can use it to set up your key assignments and screen colors.

You or your systems programmer will put new entries into these tables for your new transaction codes, programs and maps, terminal devices, and data sets, so that you can make use of these resources under CICS. Mainframe table updates may be done as a batch job when CICS is not running. Preferably, much of this work may be done through the IBM-supplied CEDA online transaction, which first became available with mainframe CICS 1.6. The systems programmer will need to know what programs go with what transactions, what programming language was used for each module, what file definition parameters you used, and so forth, in order to construct the table entries. See Figures 1.7 through 1.12.

1.3.2 Programs within CICS

The CICS run-time software supplied by IBM is composed of a number of modules. **In mainframe releases prior to 3.1, the CICS run-time modules are known as control programs or management modules.** Each of the CICS tables that we discussed is used by one or more control program. For instance, the **terminal control table** is used by the terminal management modules, which scan the network looking for devices with transactions or data to send. The terminal management modules also take care of transmissions from your program and from the CICS system to terminal devices.

The program control table is used by the **task control program,** which initiates all requested tasks and which sets up a task control area for each new task. The processing program table is used by the **program control program,** which obtains and loads needed object modules for programs and maps. The file control table is used by the **file control program**, which passes indexed and direct file I/O requests to and from the access method software.

The **transient data program** deals with I/O requests against sequential files, known as *queues*. Information about such queues is kept in the **destination control table.** The **temporary storage program** creates work areas that are used for communication between CICS programs and applications. These work areas may be in memory or on disc. There is also a management module called the **storage control program,** which obtains virtual storage allocations needed by your application program and by other management modules. The **interval control program** provides timing facilities needed by CICS. This module is used to start transactions at a later time, for example. Other management modules include the **dump control program,** which provides memory dumps, the **dynamic transaction backout program,** which backs out incomplete transactions if a program terminates abnormally, and **basic mapping support,** which formats your terminal I/O.

```
          DFHPPT TYPE=INITIAL,SUFFIX=AJ
* SYSTEM ENTRIES
          DFHPPT TYPE=ENTRY,PROGRAM=DFHNEP,PGMLANG=ASSEMBLER,               +
                 PGMSTAT=ENABLED,RELOAD=NO,RES=NO,RSL=0
          DFHPPT TYPE=ENTRY,PROGRAM=DFHPEP,PGMLANG=ASSEMBLER,               +
                 PGMSTAT=ENABLED,RELOAD=NO,RES=YES,RSL=0
          DFHPPT TYPE=ENTRY,PROGRAM=DFHRTY,PGMLANG=ASSEMBLER,               +
                 PGMSTAT=ENABLED,RELOAD=NO,RES=YES,RSL=0
          DFHPPT TYPE=ENTRY,PROGRAM=DFHTEPT,PGMLANG=ASSEMBLER,              +
                 PGMSTAT=ENABLED,RELOAD=NO,RES=YES,RSL=0
          DFHPPT TYPE=ENTRY,PROGRAM=DFHUAKP,PGMLANG=ASSEMBLER,              +
                 PGMSTAT=ENABLED,RELOAD=NO,RES=NO,RSL=0
          DFHPPT TYPE=GROUP,FN=(AKP,AUTOSTAT,BACKOUT,BMS,CONSOLE,EDF,       +
                 FE,HARDCOPY,INQUIRESET,INTERPRETER,ISC,JOURNAL,            +
                 MASTTERM,MSWITCH,MVS,OPENCLSE,OPERATORS,RDO,RESEND,        +
                 RESPLOG,RMI,SIGNON,STANDARD,TIME,VTAM,VTAMPRT)
          DFHPPT TYPE=ENTRY,PROGRAM=DFHPLTAJ,PGMLANG=ASSEMBLER,             +
                 PGMSTAT=ENABLED,RELOAD=NO,RES=NO,RSL=0
          DFHPPT TYPE=ENTRY,PROGRAM=DFHPLTA1,PGMLANG=ASSEMBLER,             +
                 PGMSTAT=ENABLED,RELOAD=NO,RES=NO,RSL=0
          DFHPPT TYPE=ENTRY,PROGRAM=DFHXLTAJ,PGMLANG=ASSEMBLER,             +
                 PGMSTAT=ENABLED,RELOAD=NO,RES=NO,RSL=0
* APPLICATION ENTRIES
          DFHPPT TYPE=ENTRY,PROGRAM=EXAMP000,PGMLANG=COBOL,                 +
                 PGMSTAT=ENABLED,RELOAD=NO,RES=NO,RSL=0
          DFHPPT TYPE=ENTRY,PROGRAM=EXAMP001,PGMLANG=COBOL,                 +
                 PGMSTAT=ENABLED,RELOAD=NO,RES=NO,RSL=0
          DFHPPT TYPE=ENTRY,PROGRAM=EXAMP002,PGMLANG=COBOL,                 +
                 PGMSTAT=ENABLED,RELOAD=NO,RES=NO,RSL=0
          DFHPPT TYPE=ENTRY,PROGRAM=EXAMP003,PGMLANG=COBOL,                 +
                 PGMSTAT=ENABLED,RELOAD=NO,RES=NO,RSL=0
          DFHPPT TYPE=ENTRY,PROGRAM=SALEINIT,PGMLANG=COBOL,                 +
                 PGMSTAT=ENABLED,RELOAD=NO,RES=NO,RSL=0
          DFHPPT TYPE=ENTRY,PROGRAM=SALEP000,PGMLANG=COBOL,                 +
                 PGMSTAT=ENABLED,RELOAD=NO,RES=NO,RSL=0
          DFHPPT TYPE=ENTRY,PROGRAM=SALEP001,PGMLANG=COBOL,                 +
                 PGMSTAT=ENABLED,RELOAD=NO,RES=NO,RSL=0
          DFHPPT TYPE=ENTRY,PROGRAM=SALEP002,PGMLANG=COBOL,                 +
                 PGMSTAT=ENABLED,RELOAD=NO,RES=NO,RSL=0
          DFHPPT TYPE=ENTRY,PROGRAM=SALEP003,PGMLANG=COBOL,                 +
                 PGMSTAT=ENABLED,RELOAD=NO,RES=NO,RSL=0
          DFHPPT TYPE=ENTRY,PROGRAM=SALEP004,PGMLANG=COBOL,                 +
                 PGMSTAT=ENABLED,RELOAD=NO,RES=NO,RSL=0
          DFHPPT TYPE=ENTRY,PROGRAM=SALEP005,PGMLANG=COBOL,                 +
                 PGMSTAT=ENABLED,RELOAD=NO,RES=NO,RSL=0
          DFHPPT TYPE=ENTRY,PROGRAM=SALEP006,PGMLANG=COBOL,                 +
                 PGMSTAT=ENABLED,RELOAD=NO,RES=NO,RSL=0
          DFHPPT TYPE=ENTRY,PROGRAM=STUBPGM,PGMLANG=COBOL,                  +
                 PGMSTAT=ENABLED,RELOAD=NO,RES=NO,RSL=0
          DFHPPT TYPE=ENTRY,PROGRAM=STUBPG2,PGMLANG=COBOL,                  +
                 PGMSTAT=ENABLED,RELOAD=NO,RES=NO,RSL=0
          DFHPPT TYPE=ENTRY,MAPSET=MCUST00,PGMLANG=ASSEMBLER,               +
                 PGMSTAT=ENABLED,RELOAD=NO,RES=NO,RSL=0
          DFHPPT TYPE=ENTRY,MAPSET=MSALE00,PGMLANG=ASSEMBLER,               +
                 PGMSTAT=ENABLED,RELOAD=NO,RES=NO,RSL=0
          DFHPPT TYPE=ENTRY,MAPSET=MSALE01,PGMLANG=ASSEMBLER,               +
                 PGMSTAT=ENABLED,RELOAD=NO,RES=NO,RSL=0
          DFHPPT TYPE=ENTRY,MAPSET=MSALE02,PGMLANG=ASSEMBLER,               +
                 PGMSTAT=ENABLED,RELOAD=NO,RES=NO,RSL=0
          DFHPPT TYPE=ENTRY,MAPSET=MSALE03,PGMLANG=ASSEMBLER,               +
                 PGMSTAT=ENABLED,RELOAD=NO,RES=NO,RSL=0
          DFHPPT TYPE=ENTRY,MAPSET=MSALE04,PGMLANG=ASSEMBLER,               +
                 PGMSTAT=ENABLED,RELOAD=NO,RES=NO,RSL=0
          DFHPPT TYPE=ENTRY,MAPSET=MSALE05,PGMLANG=ASSEMBLER,               +
                 PGMSTAT=ENABLED,RELOAD=NO,RES=NO,RSL=0
          DFHPPT TYPE=ENTRY,MAPSET=MSALE06,PGMLANG=ASSEMBLER,               +
                 PGMSTAT=ENABLED,RELOAD=NO,RES=NO,RSL=0
*
          DFHPPT TYPE=FINAL
          END
```

FIGURE 1.7   Sample CICS table definition: PPT (processing program table).

```
DFHSIT TYPE=CSECT,
       SUFFIX=AJ,            TABLE SUFFIX                               +
       ABDUMP=NO,            SYSTEM DUMP FOR ASRB ABENDS                +
       AKPFREQ=200,          ACTIVITY KEYPOINT FREQUENCY                +
       ALT=NO,               APPLICATION LOAD TABLE                     +
       AMXT=25,              ACTIVE MAXIMUM TASKS                       +
       APPLID=DBDCCICS,      VTAM APPLICATION IDENTIFIER                +
       AUTINST=(100,DFHZATDX,000000,099000), AUTOINSTALL               +
       AUXTR=OFF,            AUXILIARY TRACE                            +
       BFP=YES,              BUILT-IN FUNCTIONS PROGRAM                 +
       BMS=(FULL,COLD,ALIGN,NODDS), BASIC MAPPING SUPPORT              +
       CICSSVC=216,          CICS TYPE 2 SVC                            +
       CLSDSTP=NOTIFY,       VTAM CLSDST PASS NOTIFICATION              +
       CMXT=(,,,,,,,,,),     CLASS MAX TRANS                            +
       COBOL2=YES,           COBOL II                                   +
       DATFORM=MMDDYY,       EXTERNAL DATE DISPLAY FORMAT               +
       DBP=1$,               DYNAMIC TRANSACTION BACKOUT PROGRAM        +
       DBUFSZ=500,           DYNAMIC BUFFER SIZE FOR DTB                +
       DCT=(AJ,COLD),        DESTINATION CONTROL TABLE                  +
       DDIR=,                DDIR LIST                                  +
       DIP=NO,               BATCH DATA INTERCHANGE PROGRAM             +
       DLDBRC=NO,            DATA BASE RECOVERY CONTROL                 +
       DLI=NO,               DL/I DATA BASES IN USE                     +
       DLIOLIM=,             DL/I DATA BASE MAX IO ERRORS               +
       DLIRLM=NO,            IMS/VS RESOURCE LOCK MANAGER               +
       DLLPA=NO,             IMS/VS MODULES FROM LINK PACK AREA         +
       DLMON=NO,             DL/I DATA BASE MONITORING                  +
       DLTHRED=,             DL/I INTERFACE THREAD NUMBER               +
       DLXCPVR=NO,           PAGE FIX ISAM/OSAM BUFFERS                 +
       DMBPL=0,              DL/I DATA MANAGEMENT BLOCK POOL SIZE       +
       DTB=MAIN,             DTB DYNAMIC BUFFER SPILL                   +
       DUMP=FORMAT,          TYPE OF DUMP FOR CICS ABEND                +
       DUMPDS=AUTO,          DUMP DATA SET DETERMINATION                +
       ENQPL=0,              IMS/VS ENQ CONTROL BLOCK SPACE             +
       EXEC=YES,             COMMAND LEVEL SUPPORT                      +
       EXITS=YES,            USER EXIT INTERFACE                        +
       EXTSEC=NO,            EXTERNAL SECURITY MANAGER                  +
       FCT=AJ,               FILE CONTROL TABLE                         +
       FLDSEP='/',           TERMINAL INPUT END-OF-FIELD                +
       FLDSTRT=' ',          FIELD-NAME-START CHARACTER                 +
       GMTEXT='WELCOME TO CICS/VS', GOOD MORNING TEXT                  +
       GMTRAN=CSGM,          GOOD MORNING TRANSACTION                   +
       GRPLIST=DBDCLIST,     RDO GROUP LIST                             +
       ICP=,                 INTERVAL CONTROL PROGRAM START             +
       ICV=1000,             REGION EXIT TIME INTERVAL                  +
       ICVR=5000,            RUNAWAY TASK TIME INTERVAL                 +
       ICVS=20000,           SYSTEM STALL TIME INTERVAL                 +
       ICVTSD=100,           TERMINAL SCAN DELAY INTERVAL               +
       IOCP=1,               TASK CNTRL WAITS FOR DASD I/O              +
       IRCSTRT=YES,          IRC START AT SYSTEM INITIALIZATION         +
       ISC=YES,              INTERSYSTEM COMMUNICATION SUPPORT          +
       JCT=AJ,               JOURNAL CONTROL TABLE                      +
       LGNMSG=NO,            VTAM LOGON DATA AVAIL TO APPLICATION       +
       LPA=YES,              MANAGEMENT MODULES FROM LINK PACK          +
       MAXSMIR=999,          MAXIMUM SUSPENDED MIRROR TASKS             +
       MCT=NO,               MONITOR CONTROL TABLE                      +
       MONITOR=,             MONITORING CLASSES                         +
       MROBTCH=1,            MRO BATCHING                               +
       MROLRM=NO,            MRO LONG-RUNNING MIRROR                    +
       MSGLVL=1,             GENERATION OF MESSAGES TO CONSOLE          +
       MXT=40,               MAXIMUM TASKS                              +
       NLT=AJ,               NUCLEUS LOAD TABLE                         +
       OPNDLIM=10,           OPEN/CLOSE DESTINATION REQUEST LIMIT       +
       OSCOR=160000,         OPERATING SYSTEM STORAGE                   +
       PCDUMP=NO,            SYSTEM DUMP FOR ASRA ABENDS                +
       PCT=AJ,               PROGRAM CONTROL TABLE                      +
       PDIR=,                PDIR LIST                                  +
       PGCHAIN=X/,           BMS TERMINAL PAGE-CHAIN COMMAND            +
       PGCOPY=C/,            BMS COPY OUTPUT COMMAND                    +
```

FIGURE 1.8   Sample CICS table definition: SIT (system initialization table).

```
          PGPURGE=T/,            BMS TERMINAL PAGE-PURGE COMMAND      +
          PGRET=P/,              BMS TERMINAL PAGE-RETRIEVAL COMMAND  +
          PGSIZE=2048,           CICS VIRTUAL STORAGE PAGE SIZE       +
          PISCHD=NO,             PROGRAM ISOLATION SCHEDULING         +
          PLI=NO,                PL/I PROGRAM SUPPORT                 +
          PLISHRE=NO,            PL/I SHARED LIBRARY SUPPORT          +
          PLTPI=AJ,              PROGRAM LIST TABLE AT INITIALIZATION +
          PLTSD=A1,              PROGRAM LIST TABLE AT TERMINATION    +
          PPT=AJ,                PROGRAM PROCESSING TABLE             +
          PRGDLAY=0010,          BMS PURGE DELAY TIME INTERVAL        +
          PRINT=PA1,             PRINT CONTENTS OF 3270 SCREEN KEY    +
          PSBCHK=NO,             DL/I SECURITY CHECKING               +
          PSBPL=,                PROGRAM SPECIFICATION BLOCK POOL SIZE+
          RAMAX=256,             I/O AREA ALLOCATED FOR RECEIVE ANY   +
          RAPOOL=2,              FIXED RPL'S FOR VTAM RECEIVE ANY     +
          SCS=16384,             STORAGE CUSHION                      +
          SIMODS=(A1,B1,C1,D1,E1,F1,G1,H1,I1,J1), SYS INIT OVERLAY+
          SPOOL=NO,              SYSTEM SPOOLING INTERFACE SUPPORT    +
          SRBSVC=215,            CICS TYPE 6 SVC                      +
          SRT=AJ,                SYSTEM RECOVERY TABLE                +
          START=AUTO,            TYPE START                          +
          STARTER=YES,           PERMIT USE OF STARTER SYSTEM MODULES +
          SVD=NO,                STORAGE VIOLATION DUMP/RECOVERY      +
          SYSIDNT=CICS,          CICS SYSTEM PRIVATE NAME             +
          TBEXITS=(,,,),         TRANSACTION BACKOUT PROGRAMS         +
          TCAM=NO,               TCAM SUPPORT                         +
          TCP=NO,                TERMINAL CONTROL PROGRAM             +
          TCT=AJ,                TERMINAL CONTROL TABLE               +
          TD=(3,3),              INTRAPARTITION TRANSIENT DATA        +
          TRACE=(2000,ON),       TRACE TABLE                         +
          TRAP=OFF,              FE GLOBAL TRAP EXIT                  +
          TS=(,3,3),             TEMPORARY STORAGE                    +
          TSMGSET=50,            TEMPORARY STORAGE MESSAGE SET        +
          TST=AJ,                TEMPORARY STORAGE TABLE              +
          VSP=YES,               MVS SUBTASKING                       +
          VTAM=YES,              VTAM ACCESS METHOD                   +
          WRKAREA=3584,          COMMON WORK AREA                     +
          XDCT=NO,               EXT SEC FOR TRANSIENT DATA           +
          XFCT=NO,               EXT SEC FOR FILE CONTROL             +
          XJCT=NO,               EXT SEC FOR JOURNAL CONTROL          +
          XLT=AJ,                TRANSACTION LIST TABLE               +
          XPCT=NO,               EXT SEC FOR STARTED TRANSACTIONS     +
          XPPT=NO,               EXT SEC FOR PROGRAM ENTRIES          +
          XPSB=NO,               EXT SEC FOR PSB ENTRIES              +
          XRF=NO,                EXTENDED RECOVERY FACILITY           +
          XTRAN=NO,              EXT SEC FOR TRANSACTIONS             +
          XTST=NO,               EXT SEC FOR TEMPORARY STORAGE        +
          ZCP=(S$,HPO)           ZCP MODULES VTAM HIGH PERF OPTION
      END DFHSITBA
```

FIGURE 1.8 *(Continued)*

```
          DFHPCT TYPE=INITIAL,SUFFIX=AJ
* SYSTEM ENTRIES
          DFHPCT TYPE=GROUP,FN=(AKP,AUTOSTAT,BMS,CONSOLE,EDF,FE,         +
               HARDCOPY,INTERPRETER,ISC,JOURNAL,MASTTERM,MSWITCH,        +
               MVS,NUMERICS,OPENCLSE,OPERATORS,RDO,RESEND,RESPLOG,       +
               RMI,SIGNON,STANDARD,TIME,VTAM,VTAMPRT)
* APPLICATION ENTRIES
          DFHPCT TYPE=ENTRY,TRANSID=EX00,PROGRAM=EXAMP000,               +
               ANTICPG=NO,DTB=YES,DTIMOUT=0010,DUMP=YES,EXTSEC=NO,       +
               INBFMH=NO,JFILEID=NO,LOGREC=NO,NEPCLAS=000,RAQ=NO,        +
               RESTART=NO,RSL=0,RSLC=NO,RTIMOUT=NO,                      +
               SCRNSZE=DEFAULT,SPURGE=NO,TCLASS=NO,TRACE=YES,            +
               TRANSEC=01,TRNPRTY=001,TRNSTAT=ENABLED,TWASIZE=0
          DFHPCT TYPE=ENTRY,TRANSID=EX01,PROGRAM=EXAMP001,               +
               ANTICPG=NO,DTB=YES,DTIMOUT=0010,DUMP=YES,EXTSEC=NO,       +
```

FIGURE 1.9 Sample CICS table definition: PCT (program control table).

```
                INBFMH=NO,JFILEID=NO,LOGREC=NO,NEPCLAS=000,RAQ=NO,          +
                RESTART=NO,RSL=0,RSLC=NO,RTIMOUT=NO,                        +
                SCRNSZE=DEFAULT,SPURGE=NO,TCLASS=NO,TRACE=YES,              +
                TRANSEC=01,TRNPRTY=001,TRNSTAT=ENABLED,TWASIZE=0
        DFHPCT TYPE=ENTRY,TRANSID=EX03,PROGRAM=EXAMP003,                    +
                ANTICPG=NO,DTB=YES,DTIMOUT=0010,DUMP=YES,EXTSEC=NO,         +
                INBFMH=NO,JFILEID=NO,LOGREC=NO,NEPCLAS=000,RAQ=NO,          +
                RESTART=NO,RSL=0,RSLC=NO,RTIMOUT=NO,                        +
                SCRNSZE=DEFAULT,SPURGE=NO,TCLASS=NO,TRACE=YES,              +
                TRANSEC=01,TRNPRTY=001,TRNSTAT=ENABLED,TWASIZE=0
        DFHPCT TYPE=ENTRY,TRANSID=SALE,PROGRAM=SALEINIT,                    +
                ANTICPG=NO,DTB=YES,DTIMOUT=0010,DUMP=YES,EXTSEC=NO,         +
                INBFMH=NO,JFILEID=NO,LOGREC=NO,NEPCLAS=000,RAQ=NO,          +
                RESTART=NO,RSL=0,RSLC=NO,RTIMOUT=NO,                        +
                SCRNSZE=DEFAULT,SPURGE=NO,TCLASS=NO,TRACE=YES,              +
                TRANSEC=01,TRNPRTY=001,TRNSTAT=ENABLED,TWASIZE=0
        DFHPCT TYPE=ENTRY,TRANSID=SAL1,PROGRAM=SALEP001,                    +
                ANTICPG=NO,DTB=YES,DTIMOUT=0010,DUMP=YES,EXTSEC=NO,         +
                INBFMH=NO,JFILEID=NO,LOGREC=NO,NEPCLAS=000,RAQ=NO,          +
                RESTART=NO,RSL=0,RSLC=NO,RTIMOUT=NO,                        +
                SCRNSZE=DEFAULT,SPURGE=NO,TCLASS=NO,TRACE=YES,              +
                TRANSEC=01,TRNPRTY=001,TRNSTAT=ENABLED,TWASIZE=0
        DFHPCT TYPE=ENTRY,TRANSID=SAL2,PROGRAM=SALEP002,                    +
                ANTICPG=NO,DTB=YES,DTIMOUT=0010,DUMP=YES,EXTSEC=NO,         +
                INBFMH=NO,JFILEID=NO,LOGREC=NO,NEPCLAS=000,RAQ=NO,          +
                RESTART=NO,RSL=0,RSLC=NO,RTIMOUT=NO,                        +
                SCRNSZE=DEFAULT,SPURGE=NO,TCLASS=NO,TRACE=YES,              +
                TRANSEC=01,TRNPRTY=001,TRNSTAT=ENABLED,TWASIZE=0
        DFHPCT TYPE=ENTRY,TRANSID=SAL3,PROGRAM=SALEP003,                    +
                ANTICPG=NO,DTB=YES,DTIMOUT=0010,DUMP=YES,EXTSEC=NO,         +
                INBFMH=NO,JFILEID=NO,LOGREC=NO,NEPCLAS=000,RAQ=NO,          +
                RESTART=NO,RSL=0,RSLC=NO,RTIMOUT=NO,                        +
                SCRNSZE=DEFAULT,SPURGE=NO,TCLASS=NO,TRACE=YES,              +
                TRANSEC=01,TRNPRTY=001,TRNSTAT=ENABLED,TWASIZE=0
        DFHPCT TYPE=ENTRY,TRANSID=SAL4,PROGRAM=SALEP004,                    +
                ANTICPG=NO,DTB=YES,DTIMOUT=0010,DUMP=YES,EXTSEC=NO,         +
                INBFMH=NO,JFILEID=NO,LOGREC=NO,NEPCLAS=000,RAQ=NO,          +
                RESTART=NO,RSL=0,RSLC=NO,RTIMOUT=NO,                        +
                SCRNSZE=DEFAULT,SPURGE=NO,TCLASS=NO,TRACE=YES,              +
                TRANSEC=01,TRNPRTY=001,TRNSTAT=ENABLED,TWASIZE=0
        DFHPCT TYPE=ENTRY,TRANSID=SAL5,PROGRAM=SALEP005,                    +
                ANTICPG=NO,DTB=YES,DTIMOUT=0010,DUMP=YES,EXTSEC=NO,         +
                INBFMH=NO,JFILEID=NO,LOGREC=NO,NEPCLAS=000,RAQ=NO,          +
                RESTART=NO,RSL=0,RSLC=NO,RTIMOUT=NO,                        +
                SCRNSZE=DEFAULT,SPURGE=NO,TCLASS=NO,TRACE=YES,              +
                TRANSEC=01,TRNPRTY=001,TRNSTAT=ENABLED,TWASIZE=0
        DFHPCT TYPE=ENTRY,TRANSID=SAL6,PROGRAM=SALEP006,                    +
                ANTICPG=NO,DTB=YES,DTIMOUT=0010,DUMP=YES,EXTSEC=NO,         +
                INBFMH=NO,JFILEID=NO,LOGREC=NO,NEPCLAS=000,RAQ=NO,          +
                RESTART=NO,RSL=0,RSLC=NO,RTIMOUT=NO,                        +
                SCRNSZE=DEFAULT,SPURGE=NO,TCLASS=NO,TRACE=YES,              +
                TRANSEC=01,TRNPRTY=001,TRNSTAT=ENABLED,TWASIZE=0
        DFHPCT TYPE=ENTRY,TRANSID=STB2,PROGRAM=STUBPG2,                     +
                ANTICPG=NO,DTB=YES,DTIMOUT=0010,DUMP=YES,EXTSEC=NO,         +
                INBFMH=NO,JFILEID=NO,LOGREC=NO,NEPCLAS=000,RAQ=NO,          +
                RESTART=NO,RSL=0,RSLC=NO,RTIMOUT=NO,                        +
                SCRNSZE=DEFAULT,SPURGE=NO,TCLASS=NO,TRACE=YES,              +
                TRANSEC=01,TRNPRTY=001,TRNSTAT=ENABLED,TWASIZE=0
        DFHPCT TYPE=ENTRY,TRANSID=STUB,PROGRAM=STUBPGM,                     +
                ANTICPG=NO,DTB=YES,DTIMOUT=0010,DUMP=YES,EXTSEC=NO,         +
                INBFMH=NO,JFILEID=NO,LOGREC=NO,NEPCLAS=000,RAQ=NO,          +
                RESTART=NO,RSL=0,RSLC=NO,RTIMOUT=NO,                        +
                SCRNSZE=DEFAULT,SPURGE=NO,TCLASS=NO,TRACE=YES,              +
                TRANSEC=01,TRNPRTY=001,TRNSTAT=ENABLED,TWASIZE=0
*

        DFHPCT TYPE=FINAL
        END
```

FIGURE 1.9 *(Continued)*

```
        DFHFCT TYPE=INITIAL,SUFFIX=AJ
* SYSTEM ENTRIES
        DFHFCT TYPE=DATASET,                                        +
            DATASET=DFHCSD,                                         +
            ACCMETH=VSAM,                                           +
            BUFND=3,                                                +
            BUFNI=2,                                                +
            DISP=SHR,                                               +
            DSNSHR=ALL,                                             +
            FILSTAT=(ENABLED,CLOSED),                               +
            JID=NO,                                                 +
            LOG=NO,                                                 +
            LSRPOOL=1,                                              +
            RECFORM=(VARIABLE,BLOCKED),                             +
            RSL=0,                                                  +
            SERVREQ=(ADD,BROWSE,DELETE,READ,UPDATE),                +
            STRNO=2
* APPLICATION ENTRIES
        DFHFCT TYPE=DATASET,                                        +
            DATASET=CUSTMST,                                        +
            ACCMETH=VSAM,                                           +
            BUFND=3,                                                +
            BUFNI=2,                                                +
            DISP=SHR,                                               +
            DSNSHR=ALL,                                             +
            FILSTAT=(ENABLED,CLOSED),                               +
            JID=02,                                                 +
            JREQ=(RU,WN,WU),                                        +
            LOG=NO,                                                 +
            LSRPOOL=1,                                              +
            RECFORM=(VARIABLE,BLOCKED),                             +
            RSL=0,                                                  +
            SERVREQ=(ADD,BROWSE,DELETE,READ,UPDATE),                +
            STRNO=2
        DFHFCT TYPE=DATASET,                                        +
            DATASET=LINEITM,                                        +
            ACCMETH=VSAM,                                           +
            BUFND=3,                                                +
            BUFNI=2,                                                +
            DISP=SHR,                                               +
            DSNSHR=ALL,                                             +
            FILSTAT=(ENABLED,CLOSED),                               +
            JID=02,                                                 +
            JREQ=(RU,WN,WU),                                        +
            LOG=NO,                                                 +
            LSRPOOL=1,                                              +
            RECFORM=(VARIABLE,BLOCKED),                             +
            RSL=0,                                                  +
            SERVREQ=(ADD,BROWSE,DELETE,READ,UPDATE),                +
            STRNO=2
* LOCAL SHARED RESOURCES POOL
        DFHFCT TYPE=SHRCTL,                                         +
            BUFFERS=(2048(15),4096(30),16384(10)),                  +
            KEYLEN=25,LSRPOOL=1,STRNO=6
*
        DFHFCT TYPE=FINAL
        END
```

FIGURE 1.10   Sample CICS table definition: FCT (file control table).

```
            DFHDCT TYPE=INITIAL,SUFFIX=AJ
*  SYSTEM ENTRIES
            DFHDCT TYPE=SDSCI,BLKSIZE=1024,BUFNO=2,DSCNAME=DFHSTM,          +
                   RECFORM=VARBLK,TYPEFLE=OUTPUT
            DFHDCT TYPE=SDSCI,BLKSIZE=1024,BUFNO=2,DSCNAME=DFHSTN,          +
                   RECFORM=VARBLK,TYPEFLE=OUTPUT
            DFHDCT TYPE=SDSCI,BLKSIZE=136,BUFNO=1,DSCNAME=LOGUSR,           +
                   RECSIZE=132,RECFORM=VARUNB,TYPEFLE=OUTPUT
            DFHDCT TYPE=SDSCI,BLKSIZE=136,BUFNO=1,DSCNAME=MSGUSR,           +
                   RECSIZE=132,RECFORM=VARUNB,TYPEFLE=OUTPUT
            DFHDCT TYPE=SDSCI,BLKSIZE=137,BUFNO=1,DSCNAME=PLIMSG,           +
                   RECSIZE=133,RECFORM=VARUNB,TYPEFLE=OUTPUT
            DFHDCT TYPE=SDSCI,BLKSIZE=450,BUFNO=1,DSCNAME=LNITEM,           +
                   RECSIZE=45,RECFORM=FIXBLK,TYPEFLE=OUTPUT
            DFHDCT TYPE=EXTRA,DESTID=LMSG,DSCNAME=LNITEM
            DFHDCT TYPE=EXTRA,DESTID=CPLI,DSCNAME=PLIMSG
            DFHDCT TYPE=EXTRA,DESTID=CSSL,DSCNAME=MSGUSR
            DFHDCT TYPE=EXTRA,DESTID=CSSM,DSCNAME=DFHSTM,OPEN=DEFERRED
            DFHDCT TYPE=EXTRA,DESTID=CSSN,DSCNAME=DFHSTN,OPEN=DEFERRED
            DFHDCT TYPE=INDIRECT,DESTID=CADL,INDDEST=CSSL
            DFHDCT TYPE=INDIRECT,DESTID=CPLD,INDDEST=CPLI
            DFHDCT TYPE=INDIRECT,DESTID=CSCS,INDDEST=CSSL
            DFHDCT TYPE=INDIRECT,DESTID=CSDL,INDDEST=CSSL
            DFHDCT TYPE=INDIRECT,DESTID=CSFL,INDDEST=CSSL
            DFHDCT TYPE=INDIRECT,DESTID=CSML,INDDEST=CSSL
            DFHDCT TYPE=INDIRECT,DESTID=CSMT,INDDEST=CSSL
            DFHDCT TYPE=INDIRECT,DESTID=CSTL,INDDEST=CSSL
*
            DFHDCT TYPE=FINAL
            END
```

FIGURE 1.11 Sample CICS table definition: DCT (destination control table).

```
            DFHJCT TYPE=INITIAL,SUFFIX=AJ
*  SYSTEM ENTRIES
            DFHJCT TYPE=ENTRY,JFILEID=SYSTEM,BUFSIZE=32000,BUFSUV=16000,    +
                   JTYPE=DISK2,JOUROPT=(CRUCIAL,INPUT,RETRY),               +
                   OPEN=INITIAL
*  APPLICATION ENTRIES
            DFHJCT TYPE=ENTRY,JFILEID=02,BUFSIZE=32000,BUFSUV=16000,        +
                   JTYPE=DISK1,JOUROPT=(CRUCIAL,INPUT,PAUSE),               +
                   OPEN=INITIAL
*
            DFHJCT TYPE=FINAL
            END
```

FIGURE 1.12 Sample CICS table definition: JCT (journal control table).

1.3.3 Mainframe CICS Architecture under CICS 3.1 and Later

Much of the code in CICS online modules has been rewritten for CICS/ESA 3.1. The code has been divided into the main CICS control module, which is called the CICS **kernel,** and various **domains**. Here is a list of the domains which exist under 3.1:

- Application ("old" CICS control program code, not yet migrated to new architecture)
- Dispatcher (replaces task control)
- Domain manager (initiates and terminates the other domains)

- Dump (generates memory dumps)
- Global catalog (resources shared between active and backup systems)
- Kernel (coordinates the relationship between the other domains)
- Loader (handles dynamic storage compression)
- Local catalog (resources used on active or backup system)
- Lock manager (resource sharing)
- Message (diagnostics)
- Monitoring (keeps track of performance)
- Parameter (handles system initialization parameters)
- Statistics (statistics at system shutdown, resource counts)
- Storage manager (allows storage allocation above 16 megabyte line)
- Timer (replaces interval control)
- Trace (table entries for debugging)

Communications between domains follow standard protocols known as **gateways**. At this time, many of the functions which service the requests of applications programs are still in the application domain. In later releases, they will be moved into domains of their own. Why is mainframe CICS being rewritten? This is being done to improve reliability and to make better use of extended addressing available on larger mainframes. For more information about CICS/ESA architecture, see the CICS/ESA Processing Overview or the appropriate CICS/ESA release guide.

All command level CICS commands cause the EXEC interface program to be executed at run time. The EXEC interface program examines each subroutine call and puts it into a form that the other CICS modules can use. It stores information about the progress of its activities in a work area called the **EXEC interface block,** which your program can examine if necessary. We observed that the CICS language translator automatically includes a work area for this purpose in your program.

If you are a command level programmer, many of the activities of the control programs will be transparent to you. You will encounter them if you ever need to read the trace table in a memory dump. However, it is important for you to realize that these control programs are generated with specific features at CICS system time. If you intend to use a resource or feature supported by CICS that has never before been used at your site, such as a large-screen terminal, or a new DL/I or DB2 data base, or certain recovery facilities, the feature may not work properly until the appropriate management modules have been generated. Every service that an application is permitted to request from CICS is specified in parameters during sysgen. This even includes such commonly used features as VSAM file support.

Although you might not need to concern yourself at this point with details of what each module actually does, there are a few things that you should know. First of all, whenever your program issues a CICS command, control is ordinarily taken away from your program and given to the appropriate module within CICS. The control program may call another CICS module or perform some I/O, but execution of your own program is usually suspended until the control program has finished its work. While your program is waiting, CICS runs other application programs. This resembles the behavior of an operating system.

Online I/O uses more resources than does batch I/O. Several CICS modules become involved in each I/O operation. Your program must wait while the EXEC interface program reformats your command, the storage control program obtains a work area, the file control program or other program sets up the I/O request, the access method program performs the I/O, and so forth. There are more steps here than in batch I/O processing. What does this mean to you? Any unnecessary file I/O in an online system will make the online programs run longer and will make the terminal user wait longer. CICS is best used only for file processing applications that can benefit from user interaction. Any other file processing should be run in a batch region or partition, where it will have less impact upon online programs running at the same time.

1.3.4 Resource Definition Online (RDO)

Before CICS release 1.6, whenever CICS table entries needed to be changed, it was necessary to bring the system down and to run a batch macro assembly job to install the new table entries. Interactive resource definition was introduced in 1.6 and has been expanded in subsequent mainframe releases. Depending on the release, transactions, programs, BMS mapsets and partitionsets, VTAM terminals and sessions, and datasets can be defined while CICS is running. (BTAM is not supported under RDO; IBM is encouraging its customers to convert from BTAM to VTAM.) **Under CICS OS/2, all CICS table entries are made through interactive RDO screens, not with batch macro assembly jobs.**

On a mainframe, terminal control table entries can be created in three ways: by a batch job, by interactive commands using the CEDA transaction, or automatically at signon time by CICS and VTAM. If your installation supports a large number of terminals, and if some of these terminals rarely sign on to your CICS region, it wastes virtual storage to fill the TCT with entries for seldom-used resources. Instead, it is preferable to make permanent entries only for those terminals that are used constantly, and to allow the other TCT entries to be built automatically under the AUTOINSTALL option. New entries may be built as they are needed from VTAM table entries and from other CICS information, and dropped at end of session. CICS can even gather some information from the terminal devices during the logon procedure through the SNA QUERY function.

CICS resource definition is ordinarily the duty of the systems programming staff. It would take hundreds of pages to cover everything that a systems programmer would want to know about the many options involved in defining CICS resources; this is beyond the scope of a book intended for applications programmers. However, all CICS applications programmers should have some idea of the range of new features that are available. For more on the topic of mainframe CEDA, see the IBM manual, *Resource Definition (Online)*. CEDA under CICS OS/2 is covered in more detail in the CICS OS/2 System and Application Guide.

1.3.5   The CEDA Transaction

CEDA is the IBM-supplied transaction that provides for online resource definition. When CEDA is used to define a resource, it places the definition on a file known as the **CSD (CICS System Definition).** During CICS initialization, existing information in the CSD is used to build table entries such as PCT, PPT, and TCT entries. New table entries defined with CEDA commands can be placed in the CICS tables while CICS is running by using the CEDA INSTALL command.

Each resource on the CSD is assigned a group name. To put a terminal into the CICS tables when CICS is running, all existing terminals in its group are taken out of service using CEMT commands. Then, CEDA DEFINE commands are used to describe the new terminal. A CEDA INSTALL command is used to build the new CICS table entries. Finally, CEMT (master terminal commands) can be used to make the new terminal, and others in its group, available to CICS once again. This applies to other resources also; CEMT commands should be used to lock out all of the resources in the group until installation is complete.

Groups on the CSD are, in turn, members of **group lists.** These lists are used at CICS system initialization time to indicate which CSD entries should become available during CICS startup.

In mainframe CICS, the systems programmer ordinarily maintains the CICS tables. The options present on the CEDA screens will vary with the release of CICS. They are described in the Resource Definition (Online) manual for the appropriate release of CICS. In the OS/2 environment, the applications programmer is likely to be responsible for using CEDA to update his or her own CICS tables during program development. The CICS OS/2 CEDA screens are somewhat different from the mainframe screens, and will be shown later in the chapter on CICS OS/2.

TEST YOUR UNDERSTANDING

Questions and Exercises

1. CICS software includes language translation facilities for programs and maps. Describe the steps involved in using these facilities to assemble a map and to compile a program.
2. CICS also provides online system software under which applications programs are run. What role does this CICS software play in relation to the operating system and to your program?
3. How does CICS keep track of system resources?
4. What do you have to tell CICS about your resources if you want to use them under CICS?
5. What are some of the modules that make up CICS?
6. What is the relationship among a transaction, a task, and a program?

2

Terminal Device Concepts

The main purpose of CICS is to make it convenient to use terminal devices to access data. We will begin by discussing the devices themselves: how they work, how they are connected to the mainframe, what information needs to be passed to and from the terminals, and what features they offer to the applications programmer. In this chapter, we will describe the way a terminal might be used in a simple program. In Chapters 3 and 4, we will follow up by showing the actual coding needed to work with terminals.

2.1 TERMINALS

2.1.1 What Is a Terminal?

To most computer users, a terminal is a keyboard and CRT screen that is somehow attached to a computer. For our purposes, however, we need a broader definition of the term. To an online programmer, a terminal is any device that can communicate with a computer by using any of IBM's telecommunications access methods or protocols. In other words, anything at all that can send or receive data streams in a suitable format is a terminal. Terminal devices can involve keyboards, CRT screens, printers, point-of-sale devices, banking devices, and computers of every size and description. By far the most common type of terminal used under CICS is the 3270-series keyboard and screen, together with personal computers in 3270 emulation mode and various 3270-compatible non-IBM devices. This type of device will be discussed in some detail here. Many other terminal devices that have keyboards and CRT screens behave like 3270-type devices, or can be programmed to do so, although not all of these include the full range of 3270 special features.

A CICS OS/2 workstation is not usually attached to a mainframe in 3270 emulation mode (also known as LU 2). It is usually connected by means of another method known as LU 6.2, which recognizes the fact that the workstation has more processing capabilities than does a 3270 workstation. The CICS OS/2 workstation in turn can have several terminals. These can be logical terminals, which are shown as windows on the OS/2 screen, or separate ASCII physical terminal devices.

2.2 KEYBOARD FUNCTIONS

2.2.1 Transmission of Data to Mainframe

The 3270-type terminal consists of a keyboard, a screen, and certain logic and storage facilities. If you have worked with one before, you know that if you press any letter or numeral keys, the characters will show up on the screen, but nothing will be sent to the computer until certain "special" keys are pressed. These "special" keys (for example, ENTER, PA1, PA2, CLEAR, PF1, PF2, and so forth) are sometimes called **attention keys.** Pressing an attention key signals the mainframe that the terminal is ready to give some data back to the mainframe. Teleprocessing access method software, most commonly VTAM, installed along with CICS, examines the status of each piece of 3270-type terminal hardware regularly to determine whether an attention key has been pressed. This process retrieves input from terminal users. Certain types of terminal devices are interrupt driven, but that does not affect your application programming under CICS. You will not need to write any polling or interrupt routines yourself.

When ENTER or a PF key is pressed, whatever data has been entered on the screen goes back to the mainframe, together with a signal identifying which attention key was pressed. This signal is called an **attention identifier** or **AID.** However, when a PA key is pressed, a signal identifying the attention key goes back to the mainframe, but no data from the screen goes with it. A PA key might be useful for signaling your application program that the terminal user wants to ignore whatever is on the screen and wants to be sent a menu display or wants to terminate processing. The CLEAR key can also be used for this purpose; CLEAR is similar to the PA keys, but it also erases whatever is showing on the screen.

2.3 CRT SCREEN FUNCTIONS

2.3.1 Need for Formatting

Everything that is intended to appear on a terminal screen must be formatted in some manner. When your program sends data to the terminal
device, where on the screen should the data appear? When a terminal user
enters data, where should he or she be guided to position the data so that
the system will recognize it? Obviously, each element of data that arrives
at the terminal must be accompanied by information telling the device
where on the screen the data should go. This type of information fulfills a
function similar to that of carriage controls and tab settings on a typewriter
or printer terminal.

2.3.2 Data Streams: How CICS Communicates with Your Terminal

When you write batch programs that generate printed reports, you generate
each report line separately, with control characters for skips and page ejects
in between as needed. A terminal screen is *not* treated as a series of
fixed-length records. Instead, it is treated as a series of character fields
separated by positioning information. Let's take as an example a 3270-type
terminal with a screen 24 by 80 characters. The character positions on the
screen are laid out in the manner shown in Figure 2.1. Note that the first

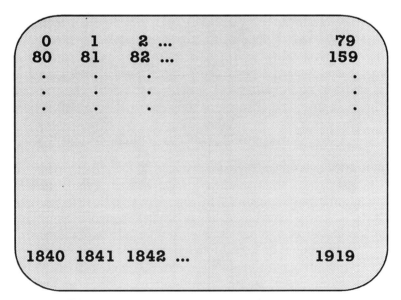

FIGURE 2.1   Screen addresses on a typical 3270 device.

position is located zero in the upper left-hand corner, and that position 80 is directly below it, and that position 1919 is in the lower right-hand corner.

Suppose you want to make the terminal look as it does in Figure 2.2. To get the screen to look this way, the mainframe could send instructions to the terminal device to clear the screen, to tab to location 420 to display in high intensity the message "**FILE IN USE—TRY LATER,**" and to tab to location 1860 to display the message "PRESS ENTER TO RETURN TO MENU" in normal intensity. Such a series of instructions, making use of the correct formatting and control characters, is called a **native-mode 3270 data stream.**

Notice that CICS need not send an 80-character row 24 times in order to fill up the terminal screen. Since most of the screen contains no data, this would waste transmission time. The entire screen can be erased with one brief instruction. The "set buffer address" instruction, which is hex "11' followed by a half-word screen address, functions as a skip instruction. It indicates the next screen address into which new information should be inserted. CICS uses this instruction to skip all unaffected parts of the screen. Although you, as a programmer, need not code native-mode 3270 data streams, you do have control over what pieces of data should be sent and received.

If you did have to code your own data streams, you would have to know exactly what type and model of terminal your program will be accessing. You would have to hard-code all of the display field locations into your program, together with all of the constant information such as captions and headers. Doing this would involve lengthy coding, which would have to be

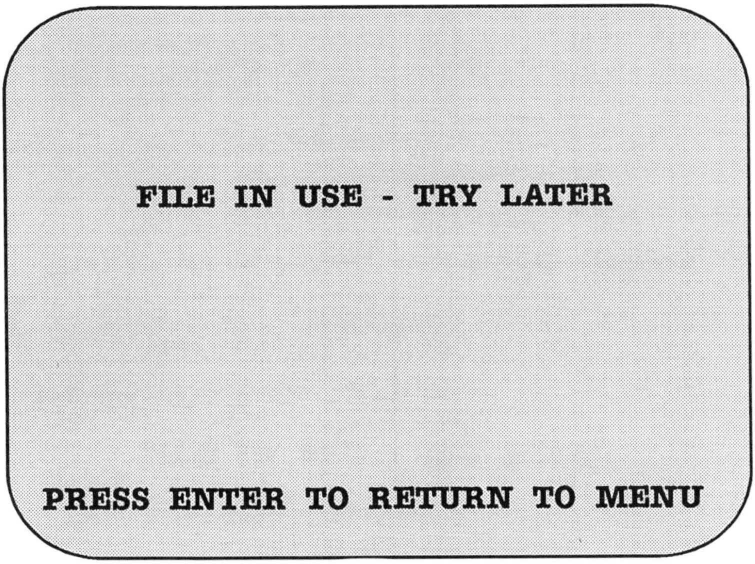

FIGURE 2.2 Sample screen display.

changed every time anyone wanted anything different on the screen. In practice, screen formats tend to be revised often, making format changes an error-prone nuisance unless some software is available to help with the work.

Whenever your program accepts input from a terminal device, this input also arrives in the form of a terminal data stream. This data stream contains only those fields that have been "tagged" as having been modified (keyed or rekeyed) by the user. If you had to write code to interpret such data streams, your code would have to be able to search through each data stream for field locations to determine which fields on the screen were included in the transmission and which were omitted. Here again, this type of coding is difficult to do and restricts your program to using one device type and one screen format. Obviously, we want to be able to make our programs as independent of format and device changes as possible.

One of the reasons CICS is used is the fact that it builds and interprets terminal data streams for a variety of different device types, largely through the use of **basic mapping support (BMS)**. Knowing how terminal data streams work will help you to understand what CICS is doing and how CICS commands work. Later, this knowledge will help you to optimize your programming so as to cause CICS to transmit no more data than is necessary. However, you will not have to look at or work with native-mode 3270 data streams directly. CICS BMS provides an interlace between your program and the terminal device, so that the fields your program uses can be made available to your program in a formatted work area (see Figure 2.3).

Now we will discuss some of the features available on 3270-type devices, and how typical CICS applications make use of them.

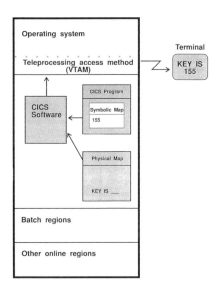

FIGURE 2.3   Relationship of terminal to computer.

2.3.3   Use of Cursor Position in Online Applications

Terminals that consist of a keyboard and a screen require a **cursor**. A cursor is simply the address into which the next character being entered will go. If you have worked with any type of CRT terminal, you will know that a **cursor indicator** is normally on the screen to show you the cursor's position in relation to the other data on the screen. Of course, only one cursor position can exist for a given terminal at a time.

The cursor position is a tool you can use to help the terminal operator enter data in the right places on the screen with minimum effort. When your program presents a display to the terminal user, the cursor position should be the first character of the first field in which you want the user to enter data. To encourage the terminal user to correct errors, for instance, you may want your program to move the cursor to the start of the first incorrect field before redisplaying the screen to the user.

In the next chapters, you will see that when you define a map, you can specify where the cursor will appear when the map is displayed. When the map is sent to a terminal, the cursor will be at the beginning of whichever field you chose when you defined the map. However, you can override this default cursor position with code in your CICS application program, before your program actually sends the map.

How does CICS tell the terminal what its initial cursor position is supposed to be? When CICS sends a data stream to a terminal, it includes a hex "13' (insert cursor) instruction in the appropriate position within the data stream. Once the information reaches the terminal screen, however, cursor movement is controlled by operator action and by *field attributes.*

2.3.4   Use of Field Attributes in Online Applications

On a 3270-type terminal device, different fields on the display screen can be made to behave in different ways. For instance, in a typical application, the user will be permitted to key data into some fields, but not into others. The keyboard will lock up if any attempt is made to key into a field that is defined as display only. Some fields on the screen go into an alpha shift mode when the terminal user begins to enter them, while others go into a numeric shift mode. Some fields are displayed with normal intensity, and some with high intensity. Some do not display data that is keyed into them at all. On color terminals, including computers with color CRTs running in 3270 emulation mode, you can set different colors for different fields. It is even possible to select some fields with a light pen, on some devices equipped for that purpose.

Figure 2.4 shows a screen from a sample application, with a display that allows a terminal user to add a new name and address to a file. The screen contains a transaction ID in the upper left-hand corner, a header, five fields

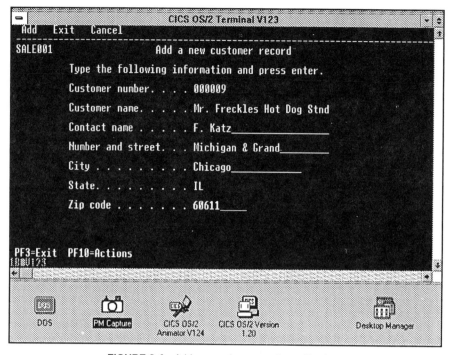

FIGURE 2.4 Add screen from sample application.

to be entered (each with a brief caption), and a field at the bottom for error messages.

Let's discuss some features that would be useful to implement in such an application. We do not want to allow the user to type on any part of the display screen except for the five fields that are intended for data entry. In fact, we want to make the user's cursor skip over all *non*enterable fields. If we do this, the cursor will automatically move to the next enterable field as soon as the previous enterable field has been filled up (or the skip key has been pressed). This saves time and keystrokes.

We also want to take over some of the shift key effort, so that the user need not hold the shift key under most circumstances. The terminal should be in numeric mode when entering the ZIP code, and should be in alpha mode for the rest of the fields. The alpha shift will be a default shift setting, which will not, for instance, keep the user from pressing the numeric shift key to enter a house number in the address field.

Finally, if the user makes a mistake, we would like to be able to redisplay the same screen, but with an error message on the last line. This error message should be in high-intensity display mode to attract user attention.

How can a terminal "know" whether a particular field should be user-enterable or not, numeric or alpha, bright or normal intensity, or whatever? It "knows" because the character position just before each field on the screen, called the **attribute byte,** contains this information in its individual bit settings. You do not have to set the bits yourself. When you code the map macro for an individual field, you will specify the attribute characteristics you want. The map macro assembly software will reserve this byte for you and will put the right bits in it. These initial attribute settings are stored in the physical map.

Will you want your CICS program to be able to change the attribute of a field at run time? If the map was set up to allow your program to access the data in that field, your program will also be able to access the attribute byte connected with the field. An attribute byte, among other things, accompanies each field in the symbolic map that you copy into your program. Your program can put new values into any of the attribute bytes in the symbolic map. When you send the map to the terminal, BMS will include these new attribute values in the data stream sent to the terminal, preceding them with hex "1D" (start field) to indicate that they represent attribute values. The data characters for each field follow the attribute value for that field.

You can, in other words, specify one set of field attribute characteristics when you code a map. These became default characteristics. You can change these attribute characteristics later when your program sends the map display to the terminal. This enables you, for instance, to light up a field in high intensity if that field contains an error, when redisplaying the screen.

What about **nondisplay fields?** Why would anyone want to use those? Sometimes someone wishes to accept data from the terminal user, without letting anyone read it over his or her shoulder. This is useful for password fields. Data in nondisplay fields remains in the screen buffer storage belonging to the terminal device, but does not show up on the screen itself.

It is important to notice that each attribute byte takes up a full character position on the screen. It is impossible to enter or display anything in a position occupied by an attribute byte. This turns out to provide a useful feature to the application programmer: better control of cursor movement.

It is common practice to define a one-byte dummy field just after the end of each enterable field. These are called **stopper bytes** or **skip bytes**. Stopper bytes are defined with protected (keyboard lock) attributes. Skip bytes are defined with autoskip attributes, as nonenterable fields generally should be. How do they work? Any attempt to key into the attribute of a skip byte causes the cursor to skip automatically to the next enterable field. (Keying into a stopper byte, similarly, causes the keyboard to lock until the RESET key is pressed.) No data can be keyed into a skip byte, a stopper byte, or its attribute. This stops the user from keying too much data. Since any data that is not keyed in an enterable field is ignored by the system, the terminal user needs skip or stopper bytes to tell him or her how much data the program will accept without truncation. See Figure 2.5.

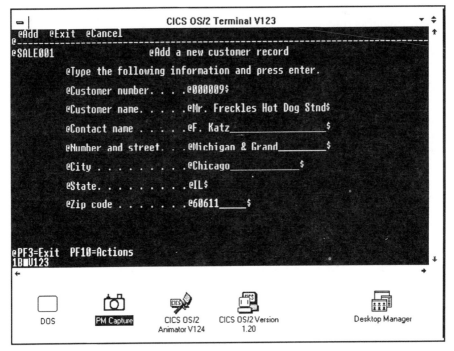

FIGURE 2.5 Add screen with attributes and stopper/skip bytes visible.

Look at the CITY, STATE, and ZIP line in the illustration. The CITY and STATE fields are not followed by skip bytes because there already happens to be another field following each of them. For instance, the CITY field is followed by the label for the STATE field, which has its own attribute byte. Skip bytes need to be specified only for fields that are not immediately followed by other fields.

Attribute information is stored as a bit pattern within each attribute byte. These combinations are translatable into EBCDIC (on mainframe) or ASCII (under OS/2) characters. However, there are only eight bits, which is not enough room for some of the features that exist on newer terminal devices. Such things as color, underlining, reverse video, and so forth are expressed as **extended attribute** settings. These are sent in the 3270-compatible data stream, as are "ordinary" attribute bytes, but they do *not* take up another position on the terminal screen.

2.3.5 Modified Data Tag: What It Is, How It Works

When we discussed the manner in which a terminal communicates with a mainframe, we mentioned that only certain portions of the screen contents are transmitted, not the entire 1,920 (or however many) characters that appear on the screen. Let us explore how this works and how you can control what is transmitted.

As you may remember, we mentioned that whenever any 3270-type terminal transmits data back to the mainframe, it sends only the contents of those fields that are "tagged" as having been modified by the terminal operator. What exactly does this mean?

The 3270-type device keeps a switch called a **modified data tag** associated with each field. It is part of the attribute byte stored in the terminal buffer. This is what tells the device whether or not to bother transmitting the data from that field. The modified data tag is turned on whenever the terminal user enters data in the field. In other words, when the terminal device is about to transmit data back to the mainframe, it examines the fields in its storage buffer, and only those fields whose modified data tags are turned on will be included in the transmission. When the data appears in the formatted work area in your program, only those fields whose modified data tags were turned on will contain data. The other fields will contain low-values.

If you want a certain field to be included in the next input transmission regardless of whether or not it was actually updated by the terminal user, you can preset the modified data tag "on" when you send the map to the user terminal. One way to do this is by making the field attribute on the map "premodified" or FSET, as we shall see later. One of the bits in every attribute byte indicates whether the modified data tag for that field should be turned on when it is sent to the terminal. Notice that if FSET is specified for a field which is also autoskip, your program will be able to access the data coming back from the terminal, even though the terminal user will not be able to modify that field.

Turning off modified data tags may make your program more efficient by reducing the number of bytes to be transmitted, but there is a price to be paid. If only a few fields are coming back from the terminal, the values of all of the other fields not included in the transmission must be obtained from somewhere else, as is shown in Figure 2.6. Some other CICS facility must be used to retain these values. This makes your program somewhat more complex. It is worthwhile to turn off modified data tags to reduce transmission time if you are dealing with a screen that contains many fields, and if the user can be expected to enter data into only a few of them. On the other hand, if the terminal user is supposed to enter data in all of the fields on a particular screen, then it might make sense to leave all of the fields FSET so that the modified data tags always stay on. Similarly, if you are using a field on a terminal screen to pass a few characters of data from one program to another, you would FSET that field.

It is important to realize that if your *program* (as opposed to the terminal user) puts a new data value into a field being sent to the terminal, this action will not affect that field's modified data tag. Just because the new field data is visible on the terminal screen does not mean that the modified

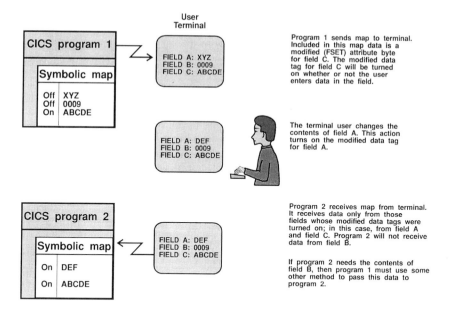

FIGURE 2.6   How the modified data tag affects the data that a program receives.

data tag is on. In other words, when the data comes back to your program, those fields might not be included in the data stream. If you want your program to turn on the modified data tag for that field, your program must change the *attribute* for that field to an FSET attribute.

What turns a modified data tag OFF? This depends upon what options were taken in the map set definition macro, which we will discuss in Chapter 3. If you always want to know whether the user keyed into a particular field, you may choose to reset (turn off) the modified data tags whenever the display is sent back to the terminal. The only exceptions will be those fields being given FSET attributes. This means that the modified data tags will be off unless the user has just entered data in the field or unless the field is being given an FSET attribute. If you do not choose to reset the modified data tags, then once they are turned on, they stay on.

2.3.6   Field Length Indicator

When your program is examining fields coming back from a terminal, there may be times when you want your program to be able to tell how much of a field was actually keyed by the terminal user. In the example, there is a nine-digit ZIP code. Suppose we have the following require-ments: If nine digits were entered, accept the data in the field "as is." If five digits were entered, perform a routine that looks up the other four digits on an indexed data set. If any other number of digits was entered, accept it if the address is non-USA; otherwise send an error message. How could we fulfill such requirements without examining each character in the ZIP code field one by one?

The program receiving the data must check the field length indicator for the ZIP code field. Where can your program find this indicator? Every field in your program's formatted map work area is accompanied by a field length indicator. The map assembly software provides this for you. When your CICS program accepts map data from a terminal, CICS puts a binary field length value into each of these half-word field length indicators. These binary values tell your program exactly how many characters the terminal user keyed into each field. A field length will be zero whenever the terminal operator did not enter anything in the field, or whenever the operator pressed the ERASE EOF key at the start of that field.

The field length half-word has one other purpose in a typical application. When your command-level program sends a map display back to the terminal, it can move binary -1 to the field length indicator of any field in the map work area. Then, if the map is sent with the CURSOR option, a command will be generated to place the cursor in the first character of that field when the map display appears on the screen. (Naturally, you can specify only one place for the cursor to be at any one time. If you specify more than one cursor location using this method, all but the first one will be ignored.) This procedure will be demonstrated in Chapter 4.

2.3.7 Other Types of Terminal I/O

CICS offers several methods besides maps for performing terminal I/O. There is a facility for sending and receiving text streams for word processing and text editing applications. There are some facilities for interchanging data between separate computer systems. There is also a facility for sending messages to terminals and for receiving messages from terminals without using maps. No field formatting is provided when this method is used. The entire message is treated as one long field with one default attribute byte applying to the entire field. Because no provision is made for guiding the terminal user to enter data in the correct format, this facility should be used only for simple and brief messages and for I/O against device types that do their own formatting or that are not supported by BMS.

2.3.8 Other Types of Terminal Devices

You may have some non-3270 devices in your installation, such as line printers, TWX, banking devices, retail scanners, and non-3270 CRT terminals. CICS supports a wide variety of these devices in such a way that the commands needed for sending and receiving messages and maps are substantially the same for these devices as for 3270 terminals. If you choose to use BMS for those device types that are supported under BMS, all device-dependent control characters will be inserted into the terminal data streams automatically.

However, not all device types are supported under BMS. If that is the case, or if you have some other reason for not using basic mapping support, you may have to deal with certain device-dependent features. For example, for TWX output, you will have to put carriage returns and line feeds into your message, and for banking devices, you might specify PASSBK in the SEND command for output that is to be printed in a customer's passbook.

Although basic mapping support provides access to many device types, not all features supported under BMS are meaningful for all device types. For example, attribute bytes are generated automatically by BMS, but they are ignored and are treated as blanks whenever a map is used with a non-3270-compatible device. In general, if your program tries to use a feature that is not implemented on a particular terminal device, BMS just ignores that feature. From your point of view as an application programmer, you will use the same commands for map I/O and the same macros for map definitions for all device types.

A microcomputer is often used as a 3270-compatible device. Several manufacturers offer circuit boards, software, modems, and so forth that allow PCs to mimic 3270 devices. As far as CICS is concerned, such a device is the same as any other 3270. This means that most of the processing power of the desktop computer remains untapped. On the other hand, if you are running CICS OS/2 on a microcomputer, you can use the microcomputer to do more editing and formatting locally, while passing data back and forth to the mainframe. This lets you share the processing effort between the mainframe and the microcomputer. The monitor and keyboard of the OS/2 machine itself becomes the user's terminal. You can define one or more logical terminals, each occupying a window on the OS/2 machine's display. Only one window, the selected window, will be active at a time, so that the keyboard is associated with the active window.

The next chapter will present a subset of basic mapping support, which will let you set up simple screen formats resembling those used in actual systems. In Chapter 4, you will learn how to use these maps to access terminal devices from your programs.

TEST YOUR UNDERSTANDING

Questions and Exercises

1. Describe what happens when the PF1 key is pressed. How does this differ from what happens when the PA1 key is pressed?
2. What is a modified data tag, and how does use of modified data tags help to reduce the amount of data transferred from the terminal to your program?
3. What are attribute bytes? What field characteristics do attribute bytes define?
4. What advantages are provided by use of basic mapping support? What would you have to do if basic mapping support did not exist?

3

Programming Techniques for Mapping the Terminal Screen

In this chapter, we will show you how to design terminal screen layouts, and how to code basic mapping support maps that implement your screen design. We will approach the subject by showing you how to determine the user's screen design requirements for an online system. After that, we will discuss the tools that can be used to satisfy those requirements.

3.1 SETTING UP A SCREEN LAYOUT

3.1.1 Preparing Sample Screens

A good way to begin designing a system is to find out what output the user wants to see. If you are designing a batch system, the user might tell you what reports to produce, how often they should come out, and what fields they should show. You probably would have to spend some time with the user to find out exactly what is wanted. You might draw some sample reports on layout forms to help the user to visualize the completed output. Later, you can use these diagrams as a guide to help you design the programs and files that the new system will require.

When you design an online system, or the online programs in a mixed online and batch system, you may find it helpful to create screen layouts on paper in the same way that you would ordinarily use report layouts.

You can prepare sample screens on standard screen layout forms or on sheets of graph paper that contain the correct number of rows and columns, generally 24 x 80. Alternatively, you can use a text editor or word processor on your computer to create a data file with 24 records of 80 characters each. If you do this, you might want to add "ruler lines" at the top and bottom to make it easier to define the columns. **Once you have prepared a set of screen formats, you should show them to the terminal users.** Allow the users to take some time to think about the application, and then sit down with them to hear what they have to say about what data should be shown on each screen, and what functions should be available for selection when a given screen is visible. Make whatever changes are necessary to help the users to feel comfortable using the application. Update your sample layouts to reflect these changes, so that they can be used as an aid in setting up the basic mapping support macros to produce the screens.

Typical User Preferences. Terminal users ordinarily want to see these characteristics in an online application:

1. Consistent screen design. All screens in an application should have standard positions for headers, error message fields, user instruction fields, data fields, and so forth. Line 22 on every screen could be set aside for error messages, for instance. Function keys should be assigned in a consistent manner. If PF3 is used to exit from the current screen, then it should serve this purpose on every screen.

In the past, there was no preferred way to set up these things. Each CICS shop commonly had its own standards. If a particular shop had no written standards, the systems designer had no better choice than to duplicate the design conventions of old screens the terminal users were accustomed to using. If the shop also had applications purchased from outside vendors, then each one would have its own design conventions. This made it difficult for terminal users to switch from one application to another.

IBM recommends that all of its customers follow a set of standards for user interface design. This set of standards is called **Common User Access** or **CUA. CUA is a part of IBM's Systems Application Architecture** strategy. Many screens accompanying IBM-supplied software are being redesigned to comply with these standards. CUA has two levels: basic and advanced. The basic interface standards, which apply to text-mode terminals such as 3270-compatible terminals or anything used with BMS, are covered in a book called *SAA CUA Basic Interface Design Guide.* The advanced interface standards, which apply to graphics-mode workstations such as those supporting Presentation Manager applications, are covered in a book called *SAA CUA Advanced Interface Design Guide.* While it is certainly possible to write a graphics-mode Presentation Manager front end to a CICS application running under CICS OS/2, this level of complexity is beyond the scope of this book. Examples shown here will be limited to text mode, following the basic guidelines only.

A minor disclaimer: In this book, we will not try to cover all of the "bells and whistles" in CUA, even at the basic level. This is because the primary purpose of this book is to introduce you to CICS. To do this, the examples have to be kept very simple. To show all of the recommended features of CUA as would be done in a complete application would make the examples too long and too confusing. Once you become more familiar with CICS, I recommend studying the more complex sample applications in the Basic Interface Design Guide.

2. Instructional messages and captions. Screens need text information which tells the user what can be done at each step. Each field needs a meaningful label. Each screen should have one or more comment lines to tell the user which function keys to use. For example, the user should always be able to terminate the operation and exit from the current screen, without updating any files, by pressing PF3. CUA indicates that function key information should go at the bottom of the screen.

You must determine what user responses should be accepted by your application. Your screens must guide the user in providing correct responses. Fields found to contain errors should be highlighted with a bright attribute or by changing the color, depending on your display device. Your programs must display an informative error message to reject any responses other than the correct ones. Avoid allowing your application to "bomb" because someone pressed the wrong attention key or because someone entered invalid data or no data at all. If a program fails often in this way, or if errors are hard to correct, terminal users may become apprehensive about using the application.

3. Field placement. The typical data entry screen contains a list of fields. In what order should these fields be presented? Fields that are entered or updated most often should be placed closest to the top of the screen. Keystrokes are wasted when it is necessary to tab through a large number of fields on each screen to get to a desired field. Related fields should be grouped together. If the terminal user is entering data from a source document, the order of the fields on the screen(s) should match the order of the fields that are actually used on the source document, and the captions should match if possible. Remember that the cursor will move through each field from left to right along each line before moving down to the next line.

3.1.2 Sample Online Application

You may be wondering, "Where do I begin?" Let's look at an existing CICS application that uses several screens. Most CICS applications start with an initial menu screen that allows the user to choose a variety of transaction screens. Large CICS applications may contain several levels of submenus between the main menu and the transactions. Figures 3.1 through 3.8 show a simplified online sales reporting system that has only one menu screen. A terminal user may obtain this menu by signing on to CICS and then by typing SALE on the upper left corner of a blank screen and pressing ENTER. The purpose of a menu is to describe what choices are available in terms the user understands.

Under CUA, menu options are presented to the user in **object-action** form. The objects are listed in the central part of the menu (known as the **work area**) and the actions are listed in an **action bar** on the top line of the menu. The user selects an object by typing a number associated with that item, or by checking it off by typing a slash in the selection field next to it.

```
****************************************************************************
*       MSALE00: main menu map - Alida Jatich and Phil Nowak              *
****************************************************************************
*            TITLE 'MSALE00 - MAIN MENU MAP - ALIDA JATICH AND PHIL NOWAK'
MSALE00 DFHMSD TYPE=&SYSPARM,                                              *
               MODE=INOUT,                                                 *
               CTRL=FREEKB,                                                *
               LANG=COBOL,                                                 *
               TIOAPFX=YES,                                                *
               MAPATTS=(COLOR,HILIGHT),                                    *
               DSATTS=(COLOR,HILIGHT),                                     *
               COLOR=WHITE
SALE000 DFHMDI SIZE=(24,80)
SOVIEW  DFHMDF POS=(01,02),LENGTH=05,ATTRB=UNPROT,COLOR=YELLOW,            *
               INITIAL=' View'
SOADD   DFHMDF POS=(01,08),LENGTH=04,ATTRB=UNPROT,COLOR=WHITE,             *
               INITIAL=' Add'
SOCHG   DFHMDF POS=(01,13),LENGTH=07,ATTRB=UNPROT,COLOR=WHITE,             *
               INITIAL=' Change'
SODLT   DFHMDF POS=(01,21),LENGTH=07,ATTRB=UNPROT,COLOR=WHITE,             *
               INITIAL=' Delete'
SOEXIT  DFHMDF POS=(01,29),LENGTH=05,ATTRB=UNPROT,COLOR=WHITE,             *
               INITIAL=' Exit'
SOCAN   DFHMDF POS=(01,35),LENGTH=07,ATTRB=UNPROT,COLOR=WHITE,             *
               INITIAL=' Cancel'
        DFHMDF POS=(02,01),LENGTH=78,COLOR=BLUE,                          *
               INITIAL='------------------------------------------------*
               ------------------------------'
SOPANID DFHMDF POS=(03,01),LENGTH=07,INITIAL='SALE000',COLOR=BLUE,         *
               ATTRB=(ASKIP,FSET)
        DFHMDF POS=(03,30),LENGTH=20,INITIAL='Sales Reporting Menu',      *
               COLOR=BLUE
        DFHMDF POS=(05,01),LENGTH=70,ATTRB=ASKIP,COLOR=GREEN,             *
               INITIAL='Select one of the following and then an action.*
               '
        DFHMDF POS=(11,01),LENGTH=19,ATTRB=ASKIP,COLOR=GREEN,             *
               INITIAL='File to update. . .'
SOSEL1  DFHMDF POS=(11,21),LENGTH=01,ATTRB=(UNPROT,BRT,FSET,NUM,IC),       *
               COLOR=TURQUOISE,INITIAL='_'
        DFHMDF POS=(11,23),LENGTH=01,ATTRB=ASKIP
        DFHMDF POS=(11,25),LENGTH=20,ATTRB=ASKIP,COLOR=WHITE,             *
               INITIAL='1. Customer records'
        DFHMDF POS=(13,25),LENGTH=20,ATTRB=ASKIP,COLOR=WHITE,             *
               INITIAL='2. Sales history'
SOMSG   DFHMDF POS=(22,01),LENGTH=79,INITIAL=' '
SOKEYS  DFHMDF POS=(24,01),LENGTH=79,COLOR=BLUE,                          *
               INITIAL='PF3=Exit  PF10=Actions  PF12=Cancel'
        DFHMSD TYPE=FINAL
        END
```

FIGURE 3.1 Source code for map SALE000.

```
*********************************************************************
*        MCUST00: customer popup - Alida Jatich and Phil Nowak      *
*********************************************************************
*         TITLE 'MCUST00-CUSTOMER POPUP MAP-ALIDA JATICH & PHIL NOWAK'
MCUST00  DFHMSD TYPE=&SYSPARM,                                        *
                MODE=INOUT,                                           *
                CTRL=FREEKB,                                          *
                LANG=COBOL,                                           *
                TIOAPFX=YES,                                          *
                MAPATTS=(COLOR,HILIGHT),                              *
                DSATTS=(COLOR,HILIGHT),                               *
                COLOR=BLUE
CUST000  DFHMDI SIZE=(24,80)
         DFHMDF POS=(06,40),LENGTH=36,COLOR=BLUE,                     *
                INITIAL='.................................'
         DFHMDF POS=(07,40),LENGTH=1,COLOR=BLUE,INITIAL=':'
         DFHMDF POS=(07,75),LENGTH=1,COLOR=BLUE,INITIAL=':'
         DFHMDF POS=(08,40),LENGTH=1,COLOR=BLUE,INITIAL=':'
         DFHMDF POS=(08,42),LENGTH=25,COLOR=GREEN,                    *
                INITIAL='Enter customer number . .'
COCUST   DFHMDF POS=(08,68),LENGTH=06,COLOR=TURQUOISE,                *
                ATTRB=(UNPROT,NUM,IC),INITIAL='_____'
         DFHMDF POS=(08,75),LENGTH=1,COLOR=BLUE,INITIAL=':'
         DFHMDF POS=(09,40),LENGTH=1,COLOR=BLUE,INITIAL=':'
         DFHMDF POS=(09,75),LENGTH=1,COLOR=BLUE,INITIAL=':'
         DFHMDF POS=(10,40),LENGTH=1,COLOR=BLUE,INITIAL=':'
COKEYS   DFHMDF POS=(10,42),LENGTH=32,COLOR=BLUE,INITIAL='PF12=Cancel'
         DFHMDF POS=(10,75),LENGTH=1,COLOR=BLUE,INITIAL=':'
         DFHMDF POS=(11,40),LENGTH=36,COLOR=BLUE,                     *
                INITIAL=':................................:'
COMSG    DFHMDF POS=(22,01),LENGTH=79,INITIAL=' ',COLOR=WHITE
         DFHMSD TYPE=FINAL
         END
```

FIGURE 3.2   Source code for map CUST000.

```
*********************************************************************
*      MSALE01: add a new customer record - Alida Jatich & Phil Nowak  *
*********************************************************************
*         TITLE 'MSALE01 - ADD A NEW CUSTOMER - A. JATICH & P. NOWAK'
MSALE01  DFHMSD TYPE=&SYSPARM,                                        *
                MODE=INOUT,                                           *
                CTRL=(FREEKB),                                        *
                LANG=COBOL,                                           *
                TIOAPFX=YES,                                          *
                MAPATTS=(COLOR,HILIGHT),                              *
                DSATTS=(COLOR,HILIGHT),                               *
                COLOR=WHITE
SALE001  DFHMDI SIZE=(24,80)
S1PROC   DFHMDF POS=(01,01),LENGTH=04,ATTRB=UNPROT,COLOR=YELLOW,      *
                INITIAL=' Add'
S1EXIT   DFHMDF POS=(01,07),LENGTH=05,ATTRB=UNPROT,COLOR=WHITE,       *
                INITIAL=' Exit'
S1CAN    DFHMDF POS=(01,14),LENGTH=07,ATTRB=UNPROT,COLOR=WHITE,       *
                INITIAL=' Cancel'
         DFHMDF POS=(02,01),LENGTH=78,ATTRB=ASKIP,COLOR=BLUE,         *
                INITIAL='----------------------------------------------------*
                --------------------------------'
S1PANID  DFHMDF POS=(03,01),LENGTH=07,INITIAL='SALE001',              *
                ATTRB=(ASKIP,FSET),COLOR=BLUE
         DFHMDF POS=(03,27),LENGTH=25,INITIAL='Add a new customer recor*
                d',ATTRB=ASKIP,COLOR=BLUE
S1INSTR  DFHMDF POS=(05,11),LENGTH=60,ATTRB=ASKIP,COLOR=GREEN,        *
                INITIAL='Type the following information and press enter.*
                '
         DFHMDF POS=(07,11),LENGTH=22,COLOR=GREEN,                    *
                INITIAL='Customer number. . . .'
```

FIGURE 3.3   Source code for map SALE001.

```
S1CUST    DFHMDF POS=(07,34),LENGTH=06,ATTRB=(UNPROT,NUM,FSET,IC),       *
          COLOR=TURQUOISE,INITIAL='_____'
          DFHMDF POS=(07,41),LENGTH=01,ATTRB=ASKIP
          DFHMDF POS=(09,11),LENGTH=22,COLOR=GREEN,                       *
          INITIAL='Customer name. . . . .'
S1NAME    DFHMDF POS=(09,34),LENGTH=25,ATTRB=UNPROT,                      *
          COLOR=TURQUOISE,INITIAL='_____'
          DFHMDF POS=(09,60),LENGTH=01,ATTRB=ASKIP
          DFHMDF POS=(11,11),LENGTH=22,COLOR=GREEN,                       *
          INITIAL='Contact name . . . . .'
S1CNTCT   DFHMDF POS=(11,34),LENGTH=25,ATTRB=UNPROT,                      *
          COLOR=TURQUOISE,INITIAL='_____'
          DFHMDF POS=(11,60),LENGTH=01,ATTRB=ASKIP
          DFHMDF POS=(13,11),LENGTH=22,COLOR=GREEN,                       *
          INITIAL='Number and street. . .'
S1ADDR    DFHMDF POS=(13,34),LENGTH=25,ATTRB=UNPROT,                      *
          COLOR=TURQUOISE,INITIAL='_____'
          DFHMDF POS=(13,60),LENGTH=01,ATTRB=ASKIP
          DFHMDF POS=(15,11),LENGTH=22,COLOR=GREEN,                       *
          INITIAL='City . . . . . . . . .'
S1CITY    DFHMDF POS=(15,34),LENGTH=20,ATTRB=UNPROT,                      *
          COLOR=TURQUOISE,INITIAL='_____'
          DFHMDF POS=(15,55),LENGTH=01,ATTRB=ASKIP
          DFHMDF POS=(17,11),LENGTH=22,COLOR=GREEN,                       *
          INITIAL='State. . . . . . . . .'
S1STATE   DFHMDF POS=(17,34),LENGTH=02,ATTRB=UNPROT,                      *
          COLOR=TURQUOISE,INITIAL='__'
          DFHMDF POS=(17,37),LENGTH=01,ATTRB=ASKIP
          DFHMDF POS=(19,11),LENGTH=22,COLOR=GREEN,                       *
          INITIAL='Zip code . . . . . . .'
S1ZIP     DFHMDF POS=(19,34),LENGTH=10,ATTRB=UNPROT,                      *
          COLOR=TURQUOISE,INITIAL='_____'
*THIS STOPPER BYTE WILL NOT SKIP TO THE NEXT FIELD.
          DFHMDF POS=(19,45),LENGTH=01,ATTRB=PROT
S1MSG     DFHMDF POS=(22,01),LENGTH=79,INITIAL=' '
S1KEYS    DFHMDF POS=(24,01),LENGTH=79,ATTRB=ASKIP,COLOR=BLUE,            *
          INITIAL='PF3=Exit   PF10=Actions'
          DFHMSD TYPE=FINAL
          END
```

FIGURE 3.3 *(Continued)*

```
********************************************************************
*      MSALE02: change customer data - Alida Jatich & Phil Nowak    *
********************************************************************
*         TITLE 'MSALE02 - CHANGE CUSTOMER DATA - A. JATICH & P. NOWAK'
MSALE02   DFHMSD TYPE=&SYSPARM,                                           *
          MODE=INOUT,                                                     *
          CTRL=(FREEKB),                                                  *
          LANG=COBOL,                                                     *
          TIOAPFX=YES,                                                    *
          MAPATTS=(COLOR,HILIGHT),                                        *
          DSATTS=(COLOR,HILIGHT),                                         *
          COLOR=WHITE
SALE002   DFHMDI SIZE=(24,80)
S2PROC    DFHMDF POS=(01,01),LENGTH=08,ATTRB=UNPROT,COLOR=YELLOW,         *
          INITIAL=' Change'
S2EXIT    DFHMDF POS=(01,11),LENGTH=05,ATTRB=UNPROT,COLOR=WHITE,          *
          INITIAL=' Exit'
S2CAN     DFHMDF POS=(01,18),LENGTH=07,ATTRB=UNPROT,COLOR=WHITE,          *
          INITIAL=' Cancel'
          DFHMDF POS=(02,01),LENGTH=78,ATTRB=ASKIP,COLOR=BLUE,            *
          INITIAL='-------------------------------------------------*
          -----------------------------'
S2PANID   DFHMDF POS=(03,01),LENGTH=07,INITIAL='SALE002',                 *
          ATTRB=(ASKIP,FSET),COLOR=BLUE
          DFHMDF POS=(03,26),LENGTH=27,INITIAL='Change customer informat*
```

FIGURE 3.4 Source code for map SALE002.

```
               ion',ATTRB=ASKIP,COLOR=BLUE
               DFHMDF POS=(05,41),LENGTH=01,ATTRB=ASKIP
S2INSTR   DFHMDF POS=(05,11),LENGTH=60,ATTRB=ASKIP,COLOR=GREEN
               DFHMDF POS=(07,11),LENGTH=22,COLOR=GREEN,                          *
               INITIAL='Customer number. . . :'
S2CUST    DFHMDF POS=(07,34),LENGTH=06,ATTRB=(UNPROT,FSET),                       *
               COLOR=TURQUOISE,INITIAL=' '
               DFHMDF POS=(09,11),LENGTH=22,COLOR=GREEN,                          *
               INITIAL='Customer name. . . . .'
S2NAME    DFHMDF POS=(09,34),LENGTH=25,ATTRB=(UNPROT,IC),                         *
               COLOR=TURQUOISE,INITIAL=' '
               DFHMDF POS=(09,60),LENGTH=01,ATTRB=ASKIP
               DFHMDF POS=(11,11),LENGTH=22,COLOR=GREEN,                          *
               INITIAL='Contact name . . . . .'
S2CNTCT   DFHMDF POS=(11,34),LENGTH=25,ATTRB=UNPROT,                              *
               COLOR=TURQUOISE,INITIAL=' '
               DFHMDF POS=(11,60),LENGTH=01,ATTRB=ASKIP
               DFHMDF POS=(13,11),LENGTH=22,COLOR=GREEN,                          *
               INITIAL='Number and street. . .'
S2ADDR    DFHMDF POS=(13,34),LENGTH=25,ATTRB=UNPROT,                              *
               COLOR=TURQUOISE,INITIAL=' '
               DFHMDF POS=(13,60),LENGTH=01,ATTRB=ASKIP
               DFHMDF POS=(15,11),LENGTH=22,COLOR=GREEN,                          *
               INITIAL='City . . . . . . . . .'
S2CITY    DFHMDF POS=(15,34),LENGTH=20,ATTRB=UNPROT,                              *
               COLOR=TURQUOISE,INITIAL=' '
               DFHMDF POS=(15,55),LENGTH=01,ATTRB=ASKIP
               DFHMDF POS=(17,11),LENGTH=22,COLOR=GREEN,                          *
               INITIAL='State. . . . . . . . .'
S2STATE   DFHMDF POS=(17,34),LENGTH=02,ATTRB=UNPROT,                              *
               COLOR=TURQUOISE,INITIAL=' '
               DFHMDF POS=(17,37),LENGTH=01,ATTRB=ASKIP
               DFHMDF POS=(19,11),LENGTH=22,COLOR=GREEN,                          *
               INITIAL='Zip code . . . . . . .'
S2ZIP     DFHMDF POS=(19,34),LENGTH=10,ATTRB=UNPROT,                              *
               COLOR=TURQUOISE,INITIAL='      -     '
*THIS STOPPER BYTE WILL NOT SKIP TO THE NEXT FIELD.
               DFHMDF POS=(19,45),LENGTH=01,ATTRB=PROT
*DISPLAY-ONLY FIELDS FOLLOW....
               DFHMDF POS=(21,01),LENGTH=18,COLOR=BLUE,INITIAL='Current week *
               sales'
S2SALES   DFHMDF POS=(21,20),LENGTH=11,COLOR=BLUE,PICOUT='$$$,$$$.99-'
               DFHMDF POS=(21,32),LENGTH=11,COLOR=BLUE,INITIAL='balance due'
S2BAL     DFHMDF POS=(21,44),LENGTH=11,COLOR=BLUE,PICOUT='$$$,$$$.99-'
               DFHMDF POS=(21,56),LENGTH=12,COLOR=BLUE,INITIAL='last bill dt'
S2BDATE   DFHMDF POS=(21,69),LENGTH=08,COLOR=BLUE,PICOUT='XX/XX/XX'
S2MSG     DFHMDF POS=(22,01),LENGTH=79,INITIAL=' '
S2KEYS    DFHMDF POS=(24,01),LENGTH=79,ATTRB=ASKIP,COLOR=BLUE,                    *
               INITIAL='PF3=Exit  PF10=Actions  PF12=Cancel'
               DFHMSD TYPE=FINAL
               END
```

FIGURE 3.4   *(Continued)*

```
***********************************************************************
*        MSALE03: delete customer record - Alida Jatich & Phil Nowak      *
***********************************************************************
*          TITLE 'MSALE03 - DELETE CUSTOMER RECORD-A. JATICH & P. NOWAK'
MSALE03  DFHMSD TYPE=&SYSPARM,                                            *
                MODE=INOUT,                                               *
                CTRL=(FREEKB),                                            *
                LANG=COBOL,                                               *
                TIOAPFX=YES,                                              *
                MAPATTS=(COLOR,HILIGHT),                                  *
                DSATTS=(COLOR,HILIGHT),                                   *
                COLOR=WHITE
SALE003  DFHMDI SIZE=(24,80)
S3DEL    DFHMDF POS=(01,01),LENGTH=07,ATTRB=(UNPROT,IC),                  *
                COLOR=YELLOW,INITIAL=' Delete'
S3EXIT   DFHMDF POS=(01,10),LENGTH=05,ATTRB=UNPROT,COLOR=WHITE,           *
                INITIAL=' Exit'
S3CAN    DFHMDF POS=(01,17),LENGTH=07,ATTRB=UNPROT,COLOR=WHITE,           *
                INITIAL=' Cancel'
         DFHMDF POS=(02,01),LENGTH=78,ATTRB=ASKIP,COLOR=BLUE,             *
                INITIAL='---------------------------------------------*
                -------------------------------'
S3PANID  DFHMDF POS=(03,01),LENGTH=07,INITIAL='SALE003',                 *
                ATTRB=(ASKIP,FSET),COLOR=BLUE
         DFHMDF POS=(03,27),LENGTH=24,INITIAL='Delete inactive customer*
                ',ATTRB=ASKIP,COLOR=BLUE
S3INSTR  DFHMDF POS=(05,11),LENGTH=60,ATTRB=ASKIP,COLOR=GREEN
         DFHMDF POS=(07,11),LENGTH=22,COLOR=GREEN,                       *
                INITIAL='Customer number. . . :'
S3CUST   DFHMDF POS=(07,34),LENGTH=06,ATTRB=(UNPROT,IC,NUM,FSET),         *
                COLOR=TURQUOISE,INITIAL=' '
         DFHMDF POS=(09,11),LENGTH=22,COLOR=GREEN,                       *
                INITIAL='Customer name. . . . :'
S3NAME   DFHMDF POS=(09,34),LENGTH=25,ATTRB=ASKIP,                       *
                COLOR=TURQUOISE,INITIAL=' '
         DFHMDF POS=(11,11),LENGTH=22,COLOR=GREEN,                       *
                INITIAL='Contact name . . . . :'
S3CNTCT  DFHMDF POS=(11,34),LENGTH=25,ATTRB=ASKIP,                       *
                COLOR=TURQUOISE,INITIAL=' '
         DFHMDF POS=(13,11),LENGTH=22,COLOR=GREEN,                       *
                INITIAL='Number and street. . :'
S3ADDR   DFHMDF POS=(13,34),LENGTH=25,ATTRB=ASKIP,                       *
                COLOR=TURQUOISE,INITIAL=' '
         DFHMDF POS=(15,11),LENGTH=22,COLOR=GREEN,                       *
                INITIAL='City . . . . . . . . :'
S3CITY   DFHMDF POS=(15,34),LENGTH=20,ATTRB=ASKIP,                       *
                COLOR=TURQUOISE,INITIAL=' '
         DFHMDF POS=(17,11),LENGTH=22,COLOR=GREEN,                       *
                INITIAL='State. . . . . . . . :'
S3STATE  DFHMDF POS=(17,34),LENGTH=02,ATTRB=ASKIP,                       *
                COLOR=TURQUOISE,INITIAL=' '
         DFHMDF POS=(19,11),LENGTH=22,COLOR=GREEN,                       *
                INITIAL='Zip code . . . . . . :'
S3ZIP    DFHMDF POS=(19,34),LENGTH=10,ATTRB=ASKIP,                       *
                COLOR=TURQUOISE,INITIAL='         -      '
*SALES HISTORY FIELDS FOLLOW....
         DFHMDF POS=(21,01),LENGTH=18,COLOR=BLUE,INITIAL='Current week *
                sales'
S3SALES  DFHMDF POS=(21,20),LENGTH=11,COLOR=BLUE,PICOUT='$$$,$$$.99-'
         DFHMDF POS=(21,32),LENGTH=11,COLOR=BLUE,INITIAL='balance due'
S3BAL    DFHMDF POS=(21,44),LENGTH=11,COLOR=BLUE,PICOUT='$$$,$$$.99-'
         DFHMDF POS=(21,56),LENGTH=12,COLOR=BLUE,INITIAL='last bill dt'
S3BDATE  DFHMDF POS=(21,69),LENGTH=08,COLOR=BLUE,PICOUT='XX/XX/XX'
S3MSG    DFHMDF POS=(22,01),LENGTH=79,INITIAL=' '
S3KEYS   DFHMDF POS=(24,01),LENGTH=79,ATTRB=ASKIP,COLOR=BLUE,            *
                INITIAL='PF3=Exit   PF10=Actions   PF12=Cancel'
         DFHMSD TYPE=FINAL
         END
```

FIGURE 3.5   Source code for map SALE003.

```
***********************************************************************
*       MSALE04: add current week sales history record                *
*       Alida Jatich and Phil Nowak                                   *
***********************************************************************
*          TITLE 'MSALE04 - ADD CURRENT WEEK SALES HISTORY RECORD'
MSALE04   DFHMSD TYPE=&SYSPARM,                                        *
                 MODE=INOUT,                                           *
                 CTRL=(FREEKB),                                        *
                 LANG=COBOL,                                           *
                 TIOAPFX=YES,                                          *
                 MAPATTS=(COLOR,HILIGHT),                              *
                 DSATTS=(COLOR,HILIGHT),                               *
                 COLOR=WHITE
SALE004   DFHMDI SIZE=(24,80)
S4ADD     DFHMDF POS=(01,01),LENGTH=04,ATTRB=UNPROT,COLOR=YELLOW,      *
                 INITIAL=' Add'
S4EXIT    DFHMDF POS=(01,07),LENGTH=05,ATTRB=UNPROT,COLOR=WHITE,       *
                 INITIAL=' Exit'
S4CAN     DFHMDF POS=(01,14),LENGTH=07,ATTRB=UNPROT,COLOR=WHITE,       *
                 INITIAL=' Cancel'
          DFHMDF POS=(02,01),LENGTH=78,ATTRB=ASKIP,COLOR=BLUE,         *
                 INITIAL='----------------------------------------------*
                 -------------------------------'
S4PANID   DFHMDF POS=(03,01),LENGTH=07,INITIAL='SALE004',              *
                 ATTRB=(ASKIP,FSET),COLOR=BLUE
          DFHMDF POS=(03,24),LENGTH=31,INITIAL='Add current week sales h*
                 istory',ATTRB=ASKIP,COLOR=BLUE
S4INSTR   DFHMDF POS=(05,11),LENGTH=60,ATTRB=ASKIP,COLOR=GREEN,        *
                 INITIAL='Type the following information and press enter.*
                 '
S4INST2   DFHMDF POS=(06,11),LENGTH=60,ATTRB=ASKIP,COLOR=GREEN,        *
                 INITIAL='Two cents places are assumed for price.'
          DFHMDF POS=(08,11),LENGTH=22,COLOR=GREEN,                    *
                 INITIAL='Customer number. . . .'
S4CUST    DFHMDF POS=(08,34),LENGTH=06,ATTRB=(UNPROT,NUM,IC,FSET),     *
                 COLOR=TURQUOISE,INITIAL='_____'
          DFHMDF POS=(08,41),LENGTH=01,ATTRB=ASKIP
          DFHMDF POS=(10,11),LENGTH=22,COLOR=GREEN,                    *
                 INITIAL='Item number. . . . . .'
S4ITEM    DFHMDF POS=(10,34),LENGTH=06,ATTRB=(UNPROT,NUM),             *
                 COLOR=TURQUOISE,JUSTIFY=(RIGHT,ZERO),PICIN='999999',  *
                 INITIAL='_____'
          DFHMDF POS=(10,41),LENGTH=01,ATTRB=ASKIP
          DFHMDF POS=(12,11),LENGTH=22,COLOR=GREEN,                    *
                 INITIAL='Unit price . . . . . .'
S4UNITP   DFHMDF POS=(12,34),LENGTH=06,ATTRB=(UNPROT,NUM),             *
                 COLOR=TURQUOISE,JUSTIFY=(RIGHT,ZERO),PICIN='9999V99'
          DFHMDF POS=(12,41),LENGTH=01,ATTRB=ASKIP
          DFHMDF POS=(14,11),LENGTH=22,COLOR=GREEN,                    *
                 INITIAL='Quantity . . . . . . .'
S4QTY     DFHMDF POS=(14,34),LENGTH=06,ATTRB=(UNPROT,NUM),             *
                 COLOR=TURQUOISE,JUSTIFY=(RIGHT,ZERO),PICIN='999999'
          DFHMDF POS=(14,41),LENGTH=01,ATTRB=ASKIP
S4SIGN    DFHMDF POS=(14,43),LENGTH=01,ATTRB=UNPROT,COLOR=TURQUOISE,   *
                 INITIAL='+'
*THIS STOPPER BYTE WILL NOT SKIP TO THE NEXT FIELD.
          DFHMDF POS=(14,45),LENGTH=01,ATTRB=PROT
S4MSG     DFHMDF POS=(22,01),LENGTH=79,INITIAL=' '
S4KEYS    DFHMDF POS=(24,01),LENGTH=79,ATTRB=ASKIP,COLOR=BLUE,         *
                 INITIAL='PF3=Exit  PF10=Actions  PF12=Cancel'
          DFHMSD TYPE=FINAL
          END
```

FIGURE 3.6 Source code for map SALE004.

```
*****************************************************************
*       MSALE05: view customer list                            *
*       Alida Jatich and Phil Nowak                            *
*****************************************************************
*          TITLE 'MSALE05 - VIEW CUSTOMER LIST - A. JATICH & P. NOWAK'
MSALE05  DFHMSD TYPE=&SYSPARM,                                  *
                MODE=INOUT,                                     *
                CTRL=(FREEKB),                                  *
                LANG=COBOL,                                     *
                TIOAPFX=YES,                                    *
                MAPATTS=(COLOR,HILIGHT),                        *
                DSATTS=(COLOR,HILIGHT),                         *
                COLOR=WHITE
SALE005  DFHMDI SIZE=(24,80)
S5FWD    DFHMDF POS=(01,01),LENGTH=08,ATTRB=UNPROT,COLOR=YELLOW, *
                INITIAL=' Forward'
S5BKW    DFHMDF POS=(01,10),LENGTH=09,ATTRB=UNPROT,COLOR=WHITE,  *
                INITIAL=' Backward'
S5EXIT   DFHMDF POS=(01,20),LENGTH=05,ATTRB=UNPROT,COLOR=WHITE,  *
                INITIAL=' Exit'
S5CAN    DFHMDF POS=(01,26),LENGTH=07,ATTRB=UNPROT,COLOR=WHITE,  *
                INITIAL=' Cancel'
         DFHMDF POS=(02,01),LENGTH=78,ATTRB=ASKIP,COLOR=BLUE,    *
                INITIAL='--------------------------------------------------*
                -------------------------------'
S5PANID  DFHMDF POS=(03,01),LENGTH=07,INITIAL='SALE005',         *
                ATTRB=(ASKIP,FSET),COLOR=BLUE
         DFHMDF POS=(03,30),LENGTH=18,INITIAL='View customer list', *
                ATTRB=ASKIP,COLOR=BLUE
         DFHMDF POS=(04,55),LENGTH=5,ATTRB=ASKIP,COLOR=WHITE,     *
                INITIAL='More:'
S5PLUS   DFHMDF POS=(04,61),LENGTH=1,ATTRB=(ASKIP,FSET),COLOR=WHITE
S5MINUS  DFHMDF POS=(04,63),LENGTH=1,ATTRB=(ASKIP,FSET),COLOR=WHITE
         DFHMDF POS=(05,18),LENGTH=15,ATTRB=ASKIP,COLOR=GREEN,    *
                INITIAL='Customer number'
         DFHMDF POS=(05,40),LENGTH=4,ATTRB=ASKIP,COLOR=GREEN,     *
                INITIAL='Name'
S5CST01  DFHMDF POS=(06,22),LENGTH=06,ATTRB=ASKIP,COLOR=GREEN
S5NAM01  DFHMDF POS=(06,40),LENGTH=25,ATTRB=ASKIP,COLOR=GREEN
S5CST02  DFHMDF POS=(07,22),LENGTH=06,ATTRB=ASKIP,COLOR=GREEN
S5NAM02  DFHMDF POS=(07,40),LENGTH=25,ATTRB=ASKIP,COLOR=GREEN
S5CST03  DFHMDF POS=(08,22),LENGTH=06,ATTRB=ASKIP,COLOR=GREEN
S5NAM03  DFHMDF POS=(08,40),LENGTH=25,ATTRB=ASKIP,COLOR=GREEN
S5CST04  DFHMDF POS=(09,22),LENGTH=06,ATTRB=ASKIP,COLOR=GREEN
S5NAM04  DFHMDF POS=(09,40),LENGTH=25,ATTRB=ASKIP,COLOR=GREEN
S5CST05  DFHMDF POS=(10,22),LENGTH=06,ATTRB=ASKIP,COLOR=GREEN
S5NAM05  DFHMDF POS=(10,40),LENGTH=25,ATTRB=ASKIP,COLOR=GREEN
S5CST06  DFHMDF POS=(11,22),LENGTH=06,ATTRB=ASKIP,COLOR=GREEN
S5NAM06  DFHMDF POS=(11,40),LENGTH=25,ATTRB=ASKIP,COLOR=GREEN
S5CST07  DFHMDF POS=(12,22),LENGTH=06,ATTRB=ASKIP,COLOR=GREEN
S5NAM07  DFHMDF POS=(12,40),LENGTH=25,ATTRB=ASKIP,COLOR=GREEN
S5CST08  DFHMDF POS=(13,22),LENGTH=06,ATTRB=ASKIP,COLOR=GREEN
S5NAM08  DFHMDF POS=(13,40),LENGTH=25,ATTRB=ASKIP,COLOR=GREEN
S5CST09  DFHMDF POS=(14,22),LENGTH=06,ATTRB=ASKIP,COLOR=GREEN
S5NAM09  DFHMDF POS=(14,40),LENGTH=25,ATTRB=ASKIP,COLOR=GREEN
S5CST10  DFHMDF POS=(15,22),LENGTH=06,ATTRB=ASKIP,COLOR=GREEN
S5NAM10  DFHMDF POS=(15,40),LENGTH=25,ATTRB=ASKIP,COLOR=GREEN
S5CST11  DFHMDF POS=(16,22),LENGTH=06,ATTRB=ASKIP,COLOR=GREEN
S5NAM11  DFHMDF POS=(16,40),LENGTH=25,ATTRB=ASKIP,COLOR=GREEN
S5CST12  DFHMDF POS=(17,22),LENGTH=06,ATTRB=ASKIP,COLOR=GREEN
S5NAM12  DFHMDF POS=(17,40),LENGTH=25,ATTRB=ASKIP,COLOR=GREEN
         DFHMDF POS=(21,11),LENGTH=24,COLOR=GREEN,               *
                INITIAL='Next customer number . .'
S5CUST   DFHMDF POS=(21,36),LENGTH=06,ATTRB=(UNPROT,NUM,IC,FSET), *
                COLOR=TURQUOISE,INITIAL='_____'
*THIS STOPPER BYTE WILL NOT SKIP TO THE NEXT FIELD.
         DFHMDF POS=(21,43),LENGTH=01,ATTRB=PROT
S5MSG    DFHMDF POS=(22,01),LENGTH=79,INITIAL=' '
S5KEYS   DFHMDF POS=(24,01),LENGTH=79,ATTRB=ASKIP,COLOR=BLUE,     *
                INITIAL='PF3=Exit  PF7=Backward  PF8=Forward  PF10=Actio*
                ns  PF12=Cancel'
         DFHMSD TYPE=FINAL
         END
```

FIGURE 3.7 Source code for map SALE005.

```
********************************************************************
*       MSALE06: view sales for one customer                      *
*       Alida Jatich and Phil Nowak                               *
********************************************************************
*          TITLE 'MSALE06 - VIEW CUSTOMER SALES - A. JATICH & P. NOWAK'
MSALE06 DFHMSD TYPE=&SYSPARM,                                      *
               MODE=INOUT,                                         *
               CTRL=(FREEKB),                                      *
               LANG=COBOL,                                         *
               TIOAPFX=YES,                                        *
               MAPATTS=(COLOR,HILIGHT),                            *
               DSATTS=(COLOR,HILIGHT),                             *
               COLOR=WHITE
SALE006 DFHMDI SIZE=(24,80)
S6FWD   DFHMDF POS=(01,01),LENGTH=08,ATTRB=UNPROT,COLOR=YELLOW,    *
               INITIAL=' Forward'
S6BKW   DFHMDF POS=(01,10),LENGTH=09,ATTRB=UNPROT,COLOR=WHITE,     *
               INITIAL=' Backward'
S6EXIT  DFHMDF POS=(01,20),LENGTH=05,ATTRB=UNPROT,COLOR=WHITE,     *
               INITIAL=' Exit'
S6CAN   DFHMDF POS=(01,26),LENGTH=07,ATTRB=UNPROT,COLOR=WHITE,     *
               INITIAL=' Cancel'
        DFHMDF POS=(02,01),LENGTH=78,ATTRB=ASKIP,COLOR=BLUE,       *
               INITIAL='----------------------------------------------*
               -------------------------------'
S6PANID DFHMDF POS=(03,01),LENGTH=07,INITIAL='SALE006',            *
               ATTRB=(ASKIP,FSET),COLOR=BLUE
        DFHMDF POS=(03,21),LENGTH=31,ATTRB=ASKIP,COLOR=BLUE,       *
               INITIAL='View sales history for customer'
S6CUST  DFHMDF POS=(03,53),LENGTH=06,ATTRB=(UNPROT,NUM,IC,FSET),   *
               COLOR=TURQUOISE,INITIAL='_____'
*THIS STOPPER BYTE WILL NOT SKIP TO THE NEXT FIELD.
        DFHMDF POS=(03,60),LENGTH=01,ATTRB=PROT
        DFHMDF POS=(04,65),LENGTH=5,ATTRB=ASKIP,COLOR=WHITE,       *
               INITIAL='More:'
S6PLUS  DFHMDF POS=(04,71),LENGTH=1,ATTRB=(ASKIP,FSET),COLOR=WHITE
S6MINUS DFHMDF POS=(04,73),LENGTH=1,ATTRB=(ASKIP,FSET),COLOR=WHITE
        DFHMDF POS=(05,18),LENGTH=04,COLOR=GREEN,INITIAL='Item'
        DFHMDF POS=(05,36),LENGTH=08,COLOR=GREEN,INITIAL='Quantity'
        DFHMDF POS=(05,55),LENGTH=10,COLOR=GREEN,INITIAL='Unit price'
S6ITM01 DFHMDF POS=(06,17),LENGTH=06,COLOR=TURQUOISE
S6QTY01 DFHMDF POS=(06,36),LENGTH=08,COLOR=TURQUOISE,PICOUT='ZZZ,ZZ9-'
S6PRC01 DFHMDF POS=(06,55),LENGTH=10,COLOR=TURQUOISE,PICOUT='$$$,$$$.9*
               9'
S6ITM02 DFHMDF POS=(07,17),LENGTH=06,COLOR=TURQUOISE
S6QTY02 DFHMDF POS=(07,36),LENGTH=08,COLOR=TURQUOISE,PICOUT='ZZZ,ZZ9-'
S6PRC02 DFHMDF POS=(07,55),LENGTH=10,COLOR=TURQUOISE,PICOUT='$$$,$$$.9*
               9'
S6ITM03 DFHMDF POS=(08,17),LENGTH=06,COLOR=TURQUOISE
S6QTY03 DFHMDF POS=(08,36),LENGTH=08,COLOR=TURQUOISE,PICOUT='ZZZ,ZZ9-'
S6PRC03 DFHMDF POS=(08,55),LENGTH=10,COLOR=TURQUOISE,PICOUT='$$$,$$$.9*
               9'
S6ITM04 DFHMDF POS=(09,17),LENGTH=06,COLOR=TURQUOISE
S6QTY04 DFHMDF POS=(09,36),LENGTH=08,COLOR=TURQUOISE,PICOUT='ZZZ,ZZ9-'
S6PRC04 DFHMDF POS=(09,55),LENGTH=10,COLOR=TURQUOISE,PICOUT='$$$,$$$.9*
               9'
S6ITM05 DFHMDF POS=(10,17),LENGTH=06,COLOR=TURQUOISE
S6QTY05 DFHMDF POS=(10,36),LENGTH=08,COLOR=TURQUOISE,PICOUT='ZZZ,ZZ9-'
S6PRC05 DFHMDF POS=(10,55),LENGTH=10,COLOR=TURQUOISE,PICOUT='$$$,$$$.9*
               9'
S6ITM06 DFHMDF POS=(11,17),LENGTH=06,COLOR=TURQUOISE
S6QTY06 DFHMDF POS=(11,36),LENGTH=08,COLOR=TURQUOISE,PICOUT='ZZZ,ZZ9-'
S6PRC06 DFHMDF POS=(11,55),LENGTH=10,COLOR=TURQUOISE,PICOUT='$$$,$$$.9*
               9'
S6ITM07 DFHMDF POS=(12,17),LENGTH=06,COLOR=TURQUOISE
S6QTY07 DFHMDF POS=(12,36),LENGTH=08,COLOR=TURQUOISE,PICOUT='ZZZ,ZZ9-'
S6PRC07 DFHMDF POS=(12,55),LENGTH=10,COLOR=TURQUOISE,PICOUT='$$$,$$$.9*
               9'
S6ITM08 DFHMDF POS=(13,17),LENGTH=06,COLOR=TURQUOISE
S6QTY08 DFHMDF POS=(13,36),LENGTH=08,COLOR=TURQUOISE,PICOUT='ZZZ,ZZ9-'
```

FIGURE 3.8   Source code for map SALE006.

```
S6PRC08  DFHMDF POS=(13,55),LENGTH=10,COLOR=TURQUOISE,PICOUT='$$$,$$$.9*
               9'
S6ITM09  DFHMDF POS=(14,17),LENGTH=06,COLOR=TURQUOISE
S6QTY09  DFHMDF POS=(14,36),LENGTH=08,COLOR=TURQUOISE,PICOUT='ZZZ,ZZ9-'
S6PRC09  DFHMDF POS=(14,55),LENGTH=10,COLOR=TURQUOISE,PICOUT='$$$,$$$.9*
               9'
S6ITM10  DFHMDF POS=(15,17),LENGTH=06,COLOR=TURQUOISE
S6QTY10  DFHMDF POS=(15,36),LENGTH=08,COLOR=TURQUOISE,PICOUT='ZZZ,ZZ9-'
S6PRC10  DFHMDF POS=(15,55),LENGTH=10,COLOR=TURQUOISE,PICOUT='$$$,$$$.9*
               9'
S6ITM11  DFHMDF POS=(16,17),LENGTH=06,COLOR=TURQUOISE
S6QTY11  DFHMDF POS=(16,36),LENGTH=08,COLOR=TURQUOISE,PICOUT='ZZZ,ZZ9-'
S6PRC11  DFHMDF POS=(16,55),LENGTH=10,COLOR=TURQUOISE,PICOUT='$$$,$$$.9*
               9'
S6ITM12  DFHMDF POS=(17,17),LENGTH=06,COLOR=TURQUOISE
S6QTY12  DFHMDF POS=(17,36),LENGTH=08,COLOR=TURQUOISE,PICOUT='ZZZ,ZZ9-'
S6PRC12  DFHMDF POS=(17,55),LENGTH=10,COLOR=TURQUOISE,PICOUT='$$$,$$$.9*
               9'
S6ITM13  DFHMDF POS=(18,17),LENGTH=06,COLOR=TURQUOISE
S6QTY13  DFHMDF POS=(18,36),LENGTH=08,COLOR=TURQUOISE,PICOUT='ZZZ,ZZ9-'
S6PRC13  DFHMDF POS=(18,55),LENGTH=10,COLOR=TURQUOISE,PICOUT='$$$,$$$.9*
               9'
S6ITM14  DFHMDF POS=(19,17),LENGTH=06,COLOR=TURQUOISE
S6QTY14  DFHMDF POS=(19,36),LENGTH=08,COLOR=TURQUOISE,PICOUT='ZZZ,ZZ9-'
S6PRC14  DFHMDF POS=(19,55),LENGTH=10,COLOR=TURQUOISE,PICOUT='$$$,$$$.9*
               9'
S6ITM15  DFHMDF POS=(20,17),LENGTH=06,COLOR=TURQUOISE
S6QTY15  DFHMDF POS=(20,36),LENGTH=08,COLOR=TURQUOISE,PICOUT='ZZZ,ZZ9-'
S6PRC15  DFHMDF POS=(20,55),LENGTH=10,COLOR=TURQUOISE,PICOUT='$$$,$$$.9*
               9'
S6ITM16  DFHMDF POS=(21,17),LENGTH=06,COLOR=TURQUOISE
S6QTY16  DFHMDF POS=(21,36),LENGTH=08,COLOR=TURQUOISE,PICOUT='ZZZ,ZZ9-'
S6PRC16  DFHMDF POS=(21,55),LENGTH=10,COLOR=TURQUOISE,PICOUT='$$$,$$$.9*
               9'
S6MSG    DFHMDF POS=(22,01),LENGTH=79,INITIAL=' '
S6KEYS   DFHMDF POS=(24,01),LENGTH=79,ATTRB=ASKIP,COLOR=BLUE,          *
               INITIAL='PF3=Exit  PF7=Backward  PF8=Forward  PF10=Actio*
               ns  PF12=Cancel'
         DFHMSD TYPE=FINAL
         END
```

FIGURE 3.8   *(Continued)*

The user selects an action by moving the cursor to the appropriate action field on the action bar, or by using a function key which is defined to invoke that same action.

In a more complex application, there will probably be too many actions on some of the screens to fit them all into the action bar at the top of the screen. In that case, selecting a "main" action from the action bar will cause a **pull-down menu** to appear immediately below the selected action. This is simply a boxed list showing "lower-level" actions. The user would then choose one of those. Our examples do not show this because we want to keep things simple. However, we do show a **popup**. The BMS and CICS code that you would use to show a pull-down menu is similar to what is used for a popup in the examples. Popups containing help information can be provided using similar logic. Help popups should be shown whenever the user presses the F1 key or moves the cursor to the Help option on the action bar. SAA CUA standards strongly recommend that programmers provide help screen information.

Starting from the top of the screen, the CUA standards indicate the following:

- Action bar.
- Dividing line.
- Line(s) for screen ID and title.
- Work area (main body of screen); this may contain a scrollable area.
- Message area (for sending error and other messages to the user).
- Command area (for those applications which accept typed commands).
- Description of function key assignments.

In our sample application, suppose the terminal user wants to sign up a new customer. The user keys the numeral 1 for "Customer records," tabs the cursor to "Add" on the action bar, and presses the enter key. A popup menu appears, so that the user can enter the new customer number being assigned to that customer. When the user presses the enter key again, another screen comes up, labeled "Add a new customer record." This screen allows the user to enter customer address information. When these items are entered, the user may press the enter key to put the new record on the file. If the user decides against making the update, he or she can press PF3 or select the "Cancel" action bar choice to return to the main menu. Similar screens allow the user to change existing customer records or delete inactive customers (those with no recent sales). To reflect the fact that the new customer rented some computer time, the user keys the numeral 2 for "Sales history," tabs the cursor to "Add" on the action bar, and presses the enter key. The next screen allows entry of item, quantity, and rate fields that eventually will appear in line items in the customer's invoice.

A customer list can be obtained by keying the numeral 1 for "Customer records," tabbing the cursor to "View" on the action bar, and pressing the enter key. The user can enter a starting customer number in the popup menu if desired. Otherwise, the display screen will start with the first record on the customer file. The "View customer list" screen contains the customer number and name extracted from each customer record. Twelve customers are shown at a time on this screen. The user can use PF7 and PF8 to move backward or forward in the customer file.

Let's look back at the menu screen, as was shown earlier in Figure 1.1. There is only one field in which the user can enter data on this screen: the selection field. This field must be followed by a skip byte to prevent the user from entering too many characters in the field. Notice also that there is a space between the caption "File to update . . . " and the actual selection field. This allows room for the attribute byte.

Some CICS applications have been written with the four- digit transaction code shown in the first four character positions on the screen after the beginning attribute byte (in other words, in the upper left corner). In the last chapter, we mentioned that the information coming from the terminal to the computer is in the form of a data stream. If the transaction code is in the upper left corner, it will be the first four data characters being sent in the data stream. If the CICS system has not already been given a transaction code to tell it what program to execute next, it will assume that the first four data characters in the stream are its transaction code. It will look up the transaction code in the PCT to determine what program to execute for this terminal. On the other hand, if a program is already running at this terminal, and the program tells CICS what transaction to use next, then CICS will ignore the transaction code on the screen.

Controlling application flow using this method has some drawbacks. First of all, if you allow the user to key something else in the transaction code field, the user might pick a code that doesn't exist in the system or that would inappropriately break the flow of work in the application. However, some installations deliberately choose to provide that level of freedom to the terminal user. Second, when using this method, you can't use the communications area (DFHCOMMAREA) to pass data to the next task, because CICS won't know ahead of time what the next transaction will be. (We will discuss the DFHCOMMAREA later on.) Third, placing the transaction code in the upper left corner of the screen interferes with the use of the top row of the screen for the action bar required by the CUA standards. In the BMS screen examples here, we will not be placing the transaction ID on the map.

If you have written batch report programs, you probably have included a program number or other report number in the page headers. If a user has any questions or complaints about the report or its contents, he or she can use the report number to let you know which report is being discussed. Other programmers might use the report number to locate documentation or to determine what program creates the report. Similarly, if you are designing online screens, you might consider putting a panel ID on each screen. Under the CUA standards, this would go in the upper left corner of the main portion of the screen, just under the action bar. The panel ID may be the map set name, the map name, or some other user-defined name.

We will want to keep at least one FSET field on each screen. What happens if there are no FSET fields? If the terminal user does not happen to enter any data in fields on the screen, but simply presses one of the attention keys, the CICS program will receive a data stream that does not look like a valid map, because its data length is zero. A MAPFAIL error condition will be triggered. Making one field FSET forces the terminal to send some actual data, which makes the data stream recognizable as a map to the CICS system.

3.1.3   Which Level of Basic Mapping Support is Available?

Under versions of mainframe CICS starting with 1.6 and later, it is possible to generate three different levels of basic mapping support. (Under CICS OS/2, as of release 1.20, only the minimum level is supported.) Higher levels of support permit you to do more things, but use more resources. You should ask your systems programmer which level of BMS has been generated at your site. If only 3270-compatible terminals are being used at a site, then minimum function BMS might provide you all the capabilities that you need. Minimum function BMS will support a terminal that uses the extended data stream option, which means that there is room in the data stream for extra device control options such as color, blink, and inverse video, mandatory fill checking, and so forth. These extra options (called *extended attributes*) are ignored if the terminal is not set up to use them.

If terminals other than 3270s or MS-DOS and OS/2 workstations are being used at a site, then standard function BMS must be generated. Standard function BMS also supports more powerful printer commands, BMS text processing, and several new features such as support for model 8775 terminal "split-screen" processing. This allows parts of a physical terminal screen to be treated as separate logical terminal screens that can be given separate I/O commands from the same application program. Some of these options will be covered in a later chapter.

Standard function BMS allows the use of **trigger fields,** if the terminal device supports this feature. A trigger field is a field that transmits data to the mainframe if the terminal user modifies it and then tries to move the cursor out of the field. Only the attention identifier and the data value in the trigger field itself are sent to the mainframe, not the data on the entire screen.

Full function BMS supports **BMS paging**, which will be discussed later. It also allows the use of the IBM-supplied CMSG transaction, which enables a terminal user to send messages to other terminals or terminal users. It permits message routing, which means that your application program can send maps to many terminals.

In this chapter, we will focus on features that are supported in minimum function BMS. We will assume that the user's terminal is an ordinary text-mode 3270-series device (or microcomputer running 3270 terminal emulation) with a screen containing 24 rows and 80 columns. Because of the growing use of microcomputer workstations, we will assume color support exists. The simplest way to map this screen is with a single 24 x 80 map defined as INOUT. This means that one BMS map will occupy the entire screen, and that the same map can be used for both input and output. Other BMS facilities allow you to place several small maps on a terminal screen, or to design multiple-page maps, but we will discuss the simpler cases first.

3.1.4 Basic Mapping Support Macros

To define a BMS map, we use three macros: DFHMSD, DFHMDI, and DFHMDF. These are coded as mainframe assembler language macros. Each macro begins with a label field (optional for DFHMDF), and contains an operation (DFHMSD, DFHMDI, or DFHMDF) followed by a series of keyword parameters. A BMS macro is continued to a following line by placing any character in column 72 and then by continuing the next line in column 16.

What happens if you are defining BMS maps on a PS/2 under CICS OS/2? You use the same macro syntax, because the BMS translator provided with CICS OS/2 emulates the mainframe version.

DFHMSD stands for "map set definition." What is a map set? A map set is a group of maps that are intended to be loaded into main memory together. If you just want to load one map into memory at a time, which is the usual case, you still must use the DFHMSD macro, but you place only one map in the map set.

Why would you want to load several maps into memory together? This would make sense only if the maps were all intended to be used together for some purpose. Several small maps can be used instead of one large map to cover a terminal screen, especially if some of the data is formatted in a repetitive manner. A series of maps can also be used to build up a report that may be sent to a small printer connected as a CICS terminal.

DFHMDI is the macro used to define an individual map within a map set. The label field in the DFHMSD macro specifies the name of the entire set of maps that is to be loaded, while the label field in the DFHMDI macro specifies the name of the individual map within the map set. **DFHMDF is used to define fields within a map.** We already discussed the fact that only those DFHMDF macros that contain labels may be referenced in a CICS application program. Unlabeled DFHMDF macros are similar to COBOL "FILLER," in that they are used to set up headers, captions, and other constant data on the screen.

3.2 MAP SET DEFINITION

3.2.1 The DFHMSD Macro

The DFHMSD macro allows you to set certain parameters that apply to the entire map set. Some of these parameters could be omitted here, and could instead be specified separately for each map, using the DFHMDI macro. The TYPE parameter, however, must go in the DFHMSD macro, because it tells the assembler what output to produce. TYPE=MAP causes a physical map to be produced, and TYPE=DSECT causes a symbolic map to be produced. In many installations, TYPE=$SYSPARM is specified. The JCL stream assembles the map twice, replacing $SYSPARM first with MAP and then with DSECT to produce the two types of map output from the same map macro source code. **A DFHMSD macro with TYPE = FINAL is placed at the end of the map set source code to tell the assembler that there are no more source lines to process for that map set. This should be followed by an END statement to eliminate a warning return code.**

Here are some other DFHMSD parameters that are needed in the application. Descriptions of DFHMSD parameters are shown under boldfaced headings. Descriptions of parameter argument list options are shown under lightfaced headings.

MODE=(IN,OUT,INOUT)

This parameter tells the assembler to include in the map all of the fields that are needed for input, for output, or both. If you specify MODE = INOUT, the symbolic map will contain an input map, whose name is suffixed with I, and an output map, whose name is suffixed with O. The output map is redefined over the same area occupied by the input map. Ordinarily, you will need to use each map for both purposes. The same map can be used by more than one program within your application. One program can use the map as an output map to send data to a terminal, while the next program in the application can use the same map as an input map to receive data back from the same terminal. There is an exception to this: You could define a map MODE = OUT if the map is being used only to send data to a printer.

CTRL=(argument list)

This allows you to specify several options that pertain to 3270-series devices. The CTRL parameter can be used in either the DFHMSD macro or the DFHMDI macro, or both. Argument values used in the DFHMDI macro for an individual map override the argument values used in the DFHMSD macro for the map set. Argument values should be placed in parentheses after the equal sign. Here are your choices:

FREEKB

This unlocks the user's keyboard each time a map is sent. Ordinarily you should specify FREEKB, because otherwise you would have to unlock the keyboard each time from your program.

FRSET

This clears all modified data tags on fields being written to the terminal. The only exceptions are fields currently being given modified attributes by your program. On the next input from the terminal, the only fields that will be included in the data stream will be those that were just given modified attributes by your program or that have just been modified by the terminal user. If FRSET is not specified, then whenever a modified data tag is set on, it will stay on. If you want to turn modified data tags off so that your program sees only the data that was modified in the most recent transmission, you would specify FRSET here. This was discussed in Section 2.3.5.

ALARM

If the terminal has an audible alarm, this argument will cause it to sound when the map is displayed. CUA recommends using this for error display screens, or for anything requiring immediate attention from the operator. However, the audible alarm should not be overused. If the alarm sounds unnecessarily, terminal operators will be tempted to turn off the beep completely.

PRINT

This is needed only if your application program will be sending some output to a 3270-compatible printer. It causes actual printing to begin when the map is sent.

Incidentally, some mainframe 3270-type terminals are equipped with a print key that sends a screen image directly to a 3287-type printer attached to the same controller. This is a purely local activity that does not involve transmission of data between the terminal and the mainframe. The CICS system has no knowledge of or control over the use of this feature.

LANG=

This tells the assembler how to make up the DSECT; for instance, whether to use COBOL statements, assembler language statements, or PL/I statements. For a COBOL program, specify LANG=COBOL.

TIOAPFX=YES

This tells the assembler to include a prefix in the DSECT that the CICS system will use for control purposes. TIOAPFX=YES is required in command-level CICS COBOL programs.

BASE=(name)

This parameter tells the map translator to build the symbolic map copy member as a *redefinition* of another COBOL 01-level data field whose name you specify in the (name) argument. You must make sure that the data area is long enough to hold the symbolic map data. If there is more than one map in a map set, using BASE will cause all of the maps in the map set to be redefined over the same area.

TERM=

Omitting the TERM parameter, or coding TERM=ALL, causes BMS to create a map that is intended for 3270 devices but that will still work for other device types. The map set name suffix will be blank, which means that the map set name will appear to have seven characters. However, if you are using only 80-column 3270 terminals, specifying 3270-2 will create a smaller and more efficient map.

Since minimum function BMS supports only 3270-1 40-column display terminals (which are obsolete) and 3270-2 80-column display terminals, you will not need this parameter under minimum function BMS unless you want to make up two different versions of your map set to use on terminals with two different screen sizes. If you do this, the map set names will be suffixed with L and with M, respectively. They must also be represented this way when they are cataloged in the assembly JCL. In order to cause CICS to look for the suffixed version, your systems programmer will specify SCRNSZE=ALTERNATE in the PCT entry for the transaction, or alternatively will specify the suffix in the TCT entry for the terminal.

Under standard and full function BMS, the TERM = parameter is used to optimize performance with certain other device types. If a non-3270 device type is specified, the map set name in the JCL and the PPT must also be given the correct device-dependent suffix. Remember that we said that almost any I/O device can be used as a terminal. The TERM parameter even allows the use of banking devices, tape drives, disk drives, or card reader/line printer.

MAPATTS and DSATTS

Extended attribute bytes are additional bytes inserted into the 3270 data stream, which take advantage of special features, such as color, which are available on certain terminal devices. These bytes are present in the symbolic map and in the 3270 data stream. Unlike ordinary attribute bytes, they do not take up a character position on the menu. Under CICS/VS 1.7 and later, an extended attribute byte can be placed in BMS maps for those terminals which have a feature allowing display fields to be outlined. Data names for these "outline" extended attribute bytes are suffixed with "U" in the symbolic map.

How do you tell CICS which extended attribute bytes, if any, you want to include in your symbolic map? In the DFHMSD and DFHMDI macros, you can now specify the MAPATTS and DSATTS options. Arguments specified with these options tell CICS which extended features to use. Available choices are COLOR, HILIGHT, OUTLINE, PS, SOSI, TRANSP, and VALIDN.

The MAPATTS option controls which extended attributes will be included in the physical map. The DSATTS option controls which extended attributes will be included in the symbolic map, so that your CICS program can change their contents from their initial values.

For mainframe releases of CICS prior to 1.7, the EXTATT = (YES, NO, MAPONLY) was used to tell BMS whether to provide for extended attributes. If EXTATT = MAPONLY is specified, then the extended features will apply only to the default data on the physical map, and not to the symbolic map copied into your application program. This means that you can set up default extended attribute features using BMS map macros, but that you will not be able to modify these features from your program. If EXTATT = YES is specified, you can set up these features using BMS map macros, and then modify them later from your application program. EXTATT=NO is specified if these features are not being used.

3.3 MAP DEFINITION

3.3.1 The DFHMDI Macro

The DFHMDI macro is used to describe individual maps within a map set. In our main menu example, we want to specify that the map is to occupy the entire terminal screen. To do this, we specify SIZE = (24 x 80). If all of the parameters that have been specified at the map set level are satisfactory and do not need to be overridden, nothing else needs to be specified in the DFHMDI macro.

3.4 FIELD DEFINITION

3.4.1 The DFHMDF Macro

The DFHMDF macro is used to define each field within a map. Remember that screen addresses start at location zero in the upper left corner and increase from left to right, and then from top to bottom. Screen address 80 is directly under screen address 0. If fields or their attributes overlap, the map assembly will fail, and an MNOTE diagnostic error message will appear on the output listing. Versions of CICS starting with release 6 allow DFHMDF macros to be coded in any order, as long as no overlap occurs.

The DFHMDF macro, like the other BMS macros, is used with keyword parameters. Here are the ones that are used most often:

POS = (row,column) or POS = screen address

This parameter tells basic mapping support where to position the field. The address can be expressed as an offset from screen location zero, but it is much simpler to use the row and column. However, you should be aware that the first row is row 1, not row 0, and that the first column is column 1, not column 0. **Notice that you should specify the position of the attribute byte that appears just before each field, not the position of the field itself.** For example, if you want a screen title to begin in row 3, column 20, you should specify POS=(3, 19).

LENGTH = number

This parameter tells BMS how long the actual data in the field is permitted to be. The length parameter excludes the attribute byte. A field must never be so long that it "wraps" from one line on the screen to the next, nor may it continue from the bottom of the screen to the top.

INITIAL = "literal"

INITIAL allows you to specify what each field on the map will contain when it is sent to the terminal. If the field is labeled, you may override this value in your program if desired. The INITIAL value is built into the physical map, not the symbolic map (DSECT). This means that the map data fields copied into your program will not contain value clauses.

ATTRB =(argument list)

This parameter allows you to specify various combinations of attribute settings. Each argument actually refers to bit settings within the attribute byte. The attribute settings should appear in parentheses after the equals sign. What happens if you do not specify attribute arguments for a field? If you do not specify any attributes at all, the default will be ASKIP and NORM (autoskip and normal intensity). This is likely to be what you want for captions and headers. If you do specify some attribute arguments, but you do not specify protection or intensity, the default will be UNPROT and NORM (unprotected and normal intensity).

UNPROT

This setting allows the user to key data into the field.

PROT

This setting causes the keyboard to lock if the user tries to key any data into the field. This can annoy the terminal user. In most cases, it is better to specify ASKIP to prevent the user from keying into the wrong parts of the screen.

ASKIP

This setting is a combination of the bit settings for protected and for numeric shift. It causes the cursor to skip to the next unprotected field whenever the terminal user attempts to key data into the field. Incidentally, whenever a screen position contains an attribute byte, it behaves as though it were an autoskip byte. It is not possible to key anything into a 3270 attribute byte field.

NUM

This setting causes the field to behave in two different ways depending upon whether the keyboard numeric lock feature is installed at your site. If the keyboard numeric lock feature is not present, then the NUM attribute setting causes the user terminal to behave as though its numeric shift key were pressed. Even if the attribute of a field is NUM, it is possible to hold down the alpha shift key to enter alphabetic data into this field. It is necessary for the application program to make sure that data coming into each field is numeric. Note that the NUM setting does not create a numeric picture clause; you use PICIN or PICOUT to do that.

On the other hand, if the keyboard numeric lock feature is installed, then it is possible to enter only the digits 0 through 9, the decimal point, the minus sign, and the DUP key in a field specified as having a NUM attribute.

BRT

This setting causes the field to be displayed in high intensity. This feature is useful for error messages or for highlighting fields that contain errors. For devices that support a light pen, a BRT field may be made light pen detectable by specifying DET as well as specifying BRT.

NORM

This setting causes the field to be displayed in normal intensity, and with no provision for selector pen detection.

DRK

This setting keeps the field from being displayed at all. It will still take up the same number of screen positions, but these screen positions will appear blank. This is useful for the entry of passwords. Messages on the screen can also be "stored" in nondisplay fields, and can be "lit up" later by changing their attribute bytes to NORM or BRT. A DRK field is not detectable by a light pen.

DET

This setting makes it possible to use a light pen to detect this field, provided that the terminal is equipped with a light pen, and provided that the first character in the data field contains a blank, question mark, "greater than" symbol, or ampersand. How do light pen fields behave? If the field begins with a blank or with an ampersand, the field is **immediately detectable.** The act of selecting this field with a light pen will cause transmission. In other words, the selector pen will behave as an attention key. When this happens, the first character of the field is changed to hexadecimal FF, and the rest of the field is set to hexadecimal 00 (nulls). The data stream from the terminal will contain only the attention identifier indicating that a light pen was used, and the contents of the one field that was selected.

On the other hand, if the field begins with a question mark or a "greater than" symbol, then nothing will be transmitted from the field until an attention key is pressed. The act of selecting this field with a light pen will change the first character from a question mark to a "greater than" symbol. Repeated selection of the same field will switch the first character back and forth between the two values. This is useful for situations in which the terminal user will be making many choices on the same screen. When the user does press an attention key that transmits data back to the mainframe, all modified data on the screen will be included in the data stream. This means that all fields selected with the light pen will be included.

IC

This setting causes the initial cursor position to be at the beginning of this field when the map is sent to the user, unless this setting is overridden in your application program. It is important to know that the IC argument is specified along with the ATTRB parameter, but that the IC setting is not really part of the attribute byte setting for the field.

FSET

This setting causes the modified data tag for this field to be set on whenever the map is used for output to a terminal. The next time your program receives data from the terminal, this field will be included in the data stream whether or not the user modified the data in the field. As we discussed before, there should be at least one FSET field on each map.

GRPNAME=(name)

If several fields are specified as having the same group name, then when the symbolic map (DSECT) is assembled, these fields will be built as elementary items within the same group item. This allows your application program to update or move all of the elementary items at once.

OCCURS=

This parameter causes the field to be repeated the desired number of times in the physical map and in the symbolic map (DSECT). If the map is being prepared for a COBOL program, the symbolic map field will be prepared with a COBOL OCCURS clause. You can use a subscript to access the desired occurrence, or you can modify the symbolic map in your source library (before copying it into your program) to add an INDEXED BY clause. The GRPNAME and the OCCURS clauses are mutually exclusive. This means the map macro assembler will not allow you to use the GRPNAME and the OCCURS clauses on the same field. What does this mean to you? Look back once again at the customer list screen shown in Figure 1.1. On it you will need to work with a repeating group item containing customer number and customer name. If you specify OCCURS = 12, then you cannot specify a GRPNAME for customer number and for customer name. One way to handle this situation is to define a 79-character field on each line, with the attribute byte in the first column. You can then format each line in the application program and move the data to each screen line as a unit. **Alternatively, once you have copied a map DSECT into your program, you can append your own COBOL redefinition to it.** This is done with map set MSALE05 in the sample application shown in this book. Using a redefinition often helps you to work with repeating fields more conveniently.

JUSTIFY=(LEFT|RIGHT,BLANK|ZERO)

This operand allows the choice of right or left justification of partially entered fields, and blank or zero padding in the unused portions remaining. The default settings are LEFT, BLANK for alphanumeric fields and RIGHT, ZERO for numeric fields. These default settings are practical for most situations, so you probably will not need to use this operand.

PICIN=(picture)

This operand lets you specify a picture clause that will be used when the map assembler builds the input version of the symbolic map entry for this field. This is the field name suffixed with the letter I. Suppose you are coding a map to be used in a COBOL program, and you specify PICIN="9999V99'. When your program reads numeric map data from that field, it will assume two decimal places.

PICOUT=(picture)

This operand lets you specify a picture clause that will be used when the map assembler builds the output version of the symbolic map entry for this field. This is the field name suffixed with the letter O. PICIN and PICOUT can be specified for the same field in an INOUT map. Remember that in an INOUT map, the output version of the map is redefined over the same area as the input version. This means that the PICIN and PICOUT information will be used to build two definitions of the same field.

How do you use PICOUT? Suppose you wanted to put a dollars field on the screen. You can use COBOL's editing routines by specifying PICOUT="$$,$$$.99'. When you place numeric data in this field, the decimal point and comma will be inserted, and leading zeros will be replaced with a single floating dollar sign.

COLOR=

If you have specified MAPATTS=COLOR in DFHMSD, you can use this parameter to specify any of the colors your terminal device supports, such as WHITE, GREEN, etc.

Now we are ready to put all of this information together to produce maps for the screens needed by the sample programs.

3.5 RESULTS OF MAP ASSEMBLY

3.5.1 How Maps Are Stored

After you have run your map assembly job (or CICSMAP.CMD command file, in the case of CICS OS/2), the physical map output (CSECT on a mainframe) should be in a run-time library, and the symbolic map or DSECT output should be in a source statement library. You can look at the symbolic map to familiarize yourself with the features that it offers you. Figures 3.9 through 3.19 show the copy library used in the sample system, including the record format and the symbolic maps. Once the map is in the source statement library, you can change names and make various modifications, as long as you do not change the field lengths and positions in any way. However, you should know that you will have to make the modifications all over again if you make changes and reassemble your map. You should probably make changes only to create something that BMS does not provide, such as indexes or repeating group items.

The format of the copy statement that places the symbolic map work area in your program will vary with the version of compiler and the type of source library maintenance utilities at your site. In many sites, the copy statement will contain the input map name, followed by the map set name. The input portion of your map will be identified with your map name, suffixed with I:

```
01 mapnameI COPY mapsetn.
```

Each *named* data field within your map will also be identified by the name you assigned to it in the DFHMDF macro, suffixed with I. Any PICIN that you specified will appear in the PICTURE clause here. In these fields, you can find the actual data that you have read from a terminal device. For each field, there will also be a half-word binary (two-byte) **length indicator,** suffixed with L. This length indicator will tell you how much of the

```
01  WS-COMMAREA.
    05  WS-COMM-PREV-MAP          PIC X(8)          VALUE SPACES.
    05  WS-COMM-OBJECT            PIC X(8)          VALUE SPACES.
    05  WS-COMM-ACTION            PIC X(8)          VALUE SPACES.
    05  WS-COMM-KEY.
        10  WS-COMM-CUST-NO       PIC X(6).
        10  WS-COMM-DATE          PIC S9(7) COMP-3.
        10  WS-COMM-TIME          PIC S9(7) COMP-3.
        10  WS-COMM-ITEM-CODE     PIC X(6).
    05  WS-COMM-NEXT-KEY.
        10  WS-COMM-NEXT-CUST-NO
                                  PIC X(6).
        10  WS-COMM-NEXT-DATE     PIC S9(7) COMP-3.
        10  WS-COMM-NEXT-TIME     PIC S9(7) COMP-3.
        10  WS-COMM-NEXT-ITEM-CODE
                                  PIC X(6).
    05  WS-COMM-COUNTER           PIC S9(8) COMP VALUE +0.
*
01  WS-EXPECTED-EIBCALEN          PIC S9(4) COMP VALUE +68.
*
01  CUSTMST-REC.
    05  CUST-VSAM-KEY.
        10  CUST-NO               PIC X(6).
    05  CUST-NAME                 PIC X(25).
    05  CUST-CONTACT              PIC X(25).
    05  CUST-STREET-ADDRESS       PIC X(25).
    05  CUST-CITY                 PIC X(20).
    05  CUST-STATE                PIC XX.
    05  CUST-ZIP.
        10  CUST-ZIP-5            PIC X(5).
        10  FILLER               PIC X(5).
    05  CUST-LAST-BILL-DATE.
        10  CUST-BILL-YY          PIC 99.
        10  CUST-BILL-MM          PIC 99.
        10  CUST-BILL-DD          PIC 99.
    05  CUST-LAST-BILL-BAL-DUE    PIC S9(5)V99.
    05  CUST-CURR-WK-SALES        PIC S9(5)V99.
    05  FILLER                    PIC X(17).
```

FIGURE 3.9   Copy library members used in the sample system (record formats).

field was actually keyed by the terminal user. If your map is specified as INOUT, you can use this length indicator to change the cursor position when the map is sent back to the user terminal, by moving -1 to the length indicator of the appropriate field and specifying CURSOR on the SEND MAP instruction. Finally, the input portion of your map contains a **flag byte** for each field, suffixed with F. The flag byte is defined over the **attribute byte** position, which is suffixed with A. When you are using the map for input of terminal data, the flag byte will ordinarily contain hexadecimal 00. However, it will contain hexadecimal 80 if the terminal user pressed the ERASE EOF key within the field.

```
*    MSALE00  Mapset.  Date - 01/03/91   Time - 23:08:44
 01  SALE000I.
     02   FILLER      PIC X(12).
     02   SOVIEWL     PIC S9(4) COMP.
     02   SOVIEWF     PIC X.
     02   FILLER REDEFINES SOVIEWF.
     03   SOVIEWA     PIC X.
     02   FILLER      PIC X(0002).
     02   SOVIEWI     PIC X(0005).
     02   SOADDL      PIC S9(4) COMP.
     02   SOADDF      PIC X.
     02   FILLER REDEFINES SOADDF.
     03   SOADDA      PIC X.
     02   FILLER      PIC X(0002).
     02   SOADDI      PIC X(0004).
     02   SOCHGL      PIC S9(4) COMP.
     02   SOCHGF      PIC X.
     02   FILLER REDEFINES SOCHGF.
     03   SOCHGA      PIC X.
     02   FILLER      PIC X(0002).
     02   SOCHGI      PIC X(0007).
     02   SODLTL      PIC S9(4) COMP.
     02   SODLTF      PIC X.
     02   FILLER REDEFINES SODLTF.
     03   SODLTA      PIC X.
     02   FILLER      PIC X(0002).
     02   SODLTI      PIC X(0007).
     02   SOEXITL     PIC S9(4) COMP.
     02   SOEXITF     PIC X.
     02   FILLER REDEFINES SOEXITF.
     03   SOEXITA     PIC X.
     02   FILLER      PIC X(0002).
     02   SOEXITI     PIC X(0005).
     02   SOCANL      PIC S9(4) COMP.
     02   SOCANF      PIC X.
     02   FILLER REDEFINES SOCANF.
     03   SOCANA      PIC X.
     02   FILLER      PIC X(0002).
     02   SOCANI      PIC X(0007).
     02   SOPANIDL    PIC S9(4) COMP.
     02   SOPANIDF    PIC X.
     02   FILLER REDEFINES SOPANIDF.
     03   SOPANIDA    PIC X.
     02   FILLER      PIC X(0002).
     02   SOPANIDI    PIC X(0007).
     02   SOSEL1L     PIC S9(4) COMP.
     02   SOSEL1F     PIC X.
     02   FILLER REDEFINES SOSEL1F.
     03   SOSEL1A     PIC X.
     02   FILLER      PIC X(0002).
     02   SOSEL1I     PIC X(0001).
     02   SOMSGL      PIC S9(4) COMP.
     02   SOMSGF      PIC X.
     02   FILLER REDEFINES SOMSGF.
     03   SOMSGA      PIC X.
     02   FILLER      PIC X(0002).
     02   SOMSGI      PIC X(0079).
     02   SOKEYSL     PIC S9(4) COMP.
     02   SOKEYSF     PIC X.
     02   FILLER REDEFINES SOKEYSF.
     03   SOKEYSA     PIC X.
     02   FILLER      PIC X(0002).
     02   SOKEYSI     PIC X(0079).
 01  SALE000O REDEFINES SALE000I.
     02   FILLER      PIC X(12).
     02   FILLER      PIC X(3).
     02   SOVIEWC     PIC X.
     02   SOVIEWH     PIC X.
     02   SOVIEWO     PIC X(0005).
     02   FILLER      PIC X(3).
```

FIGURE 3.10   Symbolic map SALE000, as it appears in the copy library.

```
02    SOADDC     PIC X.
02    SOADDH     PIC X.
02    SOADDO     PIC X(0004).
02    FILLER     PIC X(3).
02    SOCHGC     PIC X.
02    SOCHGH     PIC X.
02    SOCHGO     PIC X(0007).
02    FILLER     PIC X(3).
02    SODLTC     PIC X.
02    SODLTH     PIC X.
02    SODLTO     PIC X(0007).
02    FILLER     PIC X(3).
02    SOEXITC    PIC X.
02    SOEXITH    PIC X.
02    SOEXITO    PIC X(0005).
02    FILLER     PIC X(3).
02    SOCANC     PIC X.
02    SOCANH     PIC X.
02    SOCANO     PIC X(0007).
02    FILLER     PIC X(3).
02    SOPANIDC   PIC X.
02    SOPANIDH   PIC X.
02    SOPANIDO   PIC X(0007).
02    FILLER     PIC X(3).
02    SOSEL1C    PIC X.
02    SOSEL1H    PIC X.
02    SOSEL1O    PIC X(0001).
02    FILLER     PIC X(3).
02    SOMSGC     PIC X.
02    SOMSGH     PIC X.
02    SOMSGO     PIC X(0079).
02    FILLER     PIC X(3).
02    SOKEYSC    PIC X.
02    SOKEYSH    PIC X.
02    SOKEYSO    PIC X(0079).
```

FIGURE 3.10   *(Continued)*

The output portion of your map will be identified with your map name, suffixed with the letter O. Each named data field within your map will be identified by the name you assigned to it in the DFHMDF macro, suffixed with the letter O. Any PICOUT that you specified will appear in the PICTURE clause here. Data placed in output fields will be sent to the user's terminal, after COBOL PICOUT edits have been implemented. There is an exception to this: If you set the first byte of any field in the symbolic map to hexadecimal 00 (nulls), BMS will ignore it and will not include the field in the terminal data stream. Whatever is in the terminal user's screen buffer will remain there in that case.

Although the attribute bytes are defined within the input portion of the symbolic map, you will be using them to send new attribute byte settings to the user terminal. Here again, if you place hexadecimal nulls in an attribute field in your program, BMS will allow the existing attribute setting at the user's terminal to remain in effect.

```
*    MCUST00  Mapset.  Date - 01/03/91   Time - 23:10:33
 01  CUST000I.
     02   FILLER    PIC X(12).
     02   COCUSTL   PIC S9(4) COMP.
     02   COCUSTF   PIC X.
     02   FILLER REDEFINES COCUSTF.
      03  COCUSTA   PIC X.
     02   FILLER    PIC X(0002).
     02   COCUSTI   PIC X(0006).
     02   COKEYSL   PIC S9(4) COMP.
     02   COKEYSF   PIC X.
     02   FILLER REDEFINES COKEYSF.
      03  COKEYSA   PIC X.
     02   FILLER    PIC X(0002).
     02   COKEYSI   PIC X(0032).
     02   COMSGL    PIC S9(4) COMP.
     02   COMSGF    PIC X.
     02   FILLER REDEFINES COMSGF.
      03  COMSGA    PIC X.
     02   FILLER    PIC X(0002).
     02   COMSGI    PIC X(0079).
 01  CUST000O REDEFINES CUST000I.
     02   FILLER    PIC X(12).
     02   FILLER    PIC X(3).
     02   COCUSTC   PIC X.
     02   COCUSTH   PIC X.
     02   COCUSTO   PIC X(0006).
     02   FILLER    PIC X(3).
     02   COKEYSC   PIC X.
     02   COKEYSH   PIC X.
     02   COKEYSO   PIC X(0032).
     02   FILLER    PIC X(3).
     02   COMSGC    PIC X.
     02   COMSGH    PIC X.
     02   COMSGO    PIC X(0079).
```

FIGURE 3.11   Symbolic map CUST000.

```
*    MSALE01  Mapset.  Date - 01/03/91   Time - 23:09:00
 01  SALE001I.
     02   FILLER    PIC X(12).
     02   S1PROCL   PIC S9(4) COMP.
     02   S1PROCF   PIC X.
     02   FILLER REDEFINES S1PROCF.
      03  S1PROCA   PIC X.
     02   FILLER    PIC X(0002).
     02   S1PROCI   PIC X(0004).
     02   S1EXITL   PIC S9(4) COMP.
     02   S1EXITF   PIC X.
     02   FILLER REDEFINES S1EXITF.
      03  S1EXITA   PIC X.
     02   FILLER    PIC X(0002).
     02   S1EXITI   PIC X(0005).
     02   S1CANL    PIC S9(4) COMP.
     02   S1CANF    PIC X.
     02   FILLER REDEFINES S1CANF.
      03  S1CANA    PIC X.
     02   FILLER    PIC X(0002).
     02   S1CANI    PIC X(0007).
     02   S1PANIDL  PIC S9(4) COMP.
     02   S1PANIDF  PIC X.
     02   FILLER REDEFINES S1PANIDF.
      03  S1PANIDA  PIC X.
     02   FILLER    PIC X(0002).
     02   S1PANIDI  PIC X(0007).
     02   S1INSTRL  PIC S9(4) COMP.
     02   S1INSTRF  PIC X.
```

FIGURE 3.12   Symbolic map SALE001.

```
        02   FILLER REDEFINES S1INSTRF.
         03  S1INSTRA  PIC X.
        02   FILLER    PIC X(0002).
        02   S1INSTRI  PIC X(0060).
        02   S1CUSTL   PIC S9(4) COMP.
        02   S1CUSTF   PIC X.
        02   FILLER REDEFINES S1CUSTF.
         03  S1CUSTA   PIC X.
        02   FILLER    PIC X(0002).
        02   S1CUSTI   PIC X(0006).
        02   S1NAMEL   PIC S9(4) COMP.
        02   S1NAMEF   PIC X.
        02   FILLER REDEFINES S1NAMEF.
         03  S1NAMEA   PIC X.
        02   FILLER    PIC X(0002).
        02   S1NAMEI   PIC X(0025).
        02   S1CNTCTL  PIC S9(4) COMP.
        02   S1CNTCTF  PIC X.
        02   FILLER REDEFINES S1CNTCTF.
         03  S1CNTCTA  PIC X.
        02   FILLER    PIC X(0002).
        02   S1CNTCTI  PIC X(0025).
        02   S1ADDRL   PIC S9(4) COMP.
        02   S1ADDRF   PIC X.
        02   FILLER REDEFINES S1ADDRF.
         03  S1ADDRA   PIC X.
        02   FILLER    PIC X(0002).
        02   S1ADDRI   PIC X(0025).
        02   S1CITYL   PIC S9(4) COMP.
        02   S1CITYF   PIC X.
        02   FILLER REDEFINES S1CITYF.
         03  S1CITYA   PIC X.
        02   FILLER    PIC X(0002).
        02   S1CITYI   PIC X(0020).
        02   S1STATEL  PIC S9(4) COMP.
        02   S1STATEF  PIC X.
        02   FILLER REDEFINES S1STATEF.
         03  S1STATEA  PIC X.
        02   FILLER    PIC X(0002).
        02   S1STATEI  PIC X(0002).
        02   S1ZIPL    PIC S9(4) COMP.
        02   S1ZIPF    PIC X.
        02   FILLER REDEFINES S1ZIPF.
         03  S1ZIPA    PIC X.
        02   FILLER    PIC X(0002).
        02   S1ZIPI    PIC X(0010).
        02   S1MSGL    PIC S9(4) COMP.
        02   S1MSGF    PIC X.
        02   FILLER REDEFINES S1MSGF.
         03  S1MSGA    PIC X.
        02   FILLER    PIC X(0002).
        02   S1MSGI    PIC X(0079).
        02   S1KEYSL   PIC S9(4) COMP.
        02   S1KEYSF   PIC X.
        02   FILLER REDEFINES S1KEYSF.
         03  S1KEYSA   PIC X.
        02   FILLER    PIC X(0002).
        02   S1KEYSI   PIC X(0079).
 01  SALE001O REDEFINES SALE001I.
        02   FILLER    PIC X(12).
        02   FILLER    PIC X(3).
        02   S1PROCC   PIC X.
        02   S1PROCH   PIC X.
        02   S1PROCO   PIC X(0004).
        02   FILLER    PIC X(3).
        02   S1EXITC   PIC X.
        02   S1EXITH   PIC X.
        02   S1EXITO   PIC X(0005).
        02   FILLER    PIC X(3).
        02   S1CANC    PIC X.
```

FIGURE 3.12   *(Continued)*

```
02   S1CANH    PIC X.
02   S1CANO    PIC X(0007).
02   FILLER    PIC X(3).
02   S1PANIDC  PIC X.
02   S1PANIDH  PIC X.
02   S1PANIDO  PIC X(0007).
02   FILLER    PIC X(3).
02   S1INSTRC  PIC X.
02   S1INSTRH  PIC X.
02   S1INSTRO  PIC X(0060).
02   FILLER    PIC X(3).
02   S1CUSTC   PIC X.
02   S1CUSTH   PIC X.
02   S1CUSTO   PIC X(0006).
02   FILLER    PIC X(3).
02   S1NAMEC   PIC X.
02   S1NAMEH   PIC X.
02   S1NAMEO   PIC X(0025).
02   FILLER    PIC X(3).
02   S1CNTCTC  PIC X.
02   S1CNTCTH  PIC X.
02   S1CNTCTO  PIC X(0025).
02   FILLER    PIC X(3).
02   S1ADDRC   PIC X.
02   S1ADDRH   PIC X.
02   S1ADDRO   PIC X(0025).
02   FILLER    PIC X(3).
02   S1CITYC   PIC X.
02   S1CITYH   PIC X.
02   S1CITYO   PIC X(0020).
02   FILLER    PIC X(3).
02   S1STATEC  PIC X.
02   S1STATEH  PIC X.
02   S1STATEO  PIC X(0002).
02   FILLER    PIC X(3).
02   S1ZIPC    PIC X.
02   S1ZIPH    PIC X.
02   S1ZIPO    PIC X(0010).
02   FILLER    PIC X(3).
02   S1MSGC    PIC X.
02   S1MSGH    PIC X.
02   S1MSGO    PIC X(0079).
02   FILLER    PIC X(3).
02   S1KEYSC   PIC X.
02   S1KEYSH   PIC X.
02   S1KEYSO   PIC X(0079).
```

FIGURE 3.12   *(Continued)*

```
*    MSALE02  Mapset.  Date - 01/03/91   Time - 23:09:15
01  SALE002I.
    02   FILLER    PIC X(12).
    02   S2PROCL   PIC S9(4) COMP.
    02   S2PROCF   PIC X.
    02   FILLER REDEFINES S2PROCF.
     03  S2PROCA   PIC X.
    02   FILLER    PIC X(0002).
    02   S2PROCI   PIC X(0008).
    02   S2EXITL   PIC S9(4) COMP.
    02   S2EXITF   PIC X.
    02   FILLER REDEFINES S2EXITF.
     03  S2EXITA   PIC X.
    02   FILLER    PIC X(0002).
    02   S2EXITI   PIC X(0005).
    02   S2CANL    PIC S9(4) COMP.
    02   S2CANF    PIC X.
    02   FILLER REDEFINES S2CANF.
     03  S2CANA    PIC X.
```

FIGURE 3.13   Symbolic map SALE002.

```
02   FILLER    PIC X(0002).
02   S2CANI    PIC X(0007).
02   S2PANIDL  PIC S9(4) COMP.
02   S2PANIDF  PIC X.
02   FILLER REDEFINES S2PANIDF.
 03  S2PANIDA  PIC X.
02   FILLER    PIC X(0002).
02   S2PANIDI  PIC X(0007).
02   S2INSTRL  PIC S9(4) COMP.
02   S2INSTRF  PIC X.
02   FILLER REDEFINES S2INSTRF.
 03  S2INSTRA  PIC X.
02   FILLER    PIC X(0002).
02   S2INSTRI  PIC X(0060).
02   S2CUSTL   PIC S9(4) COMP.
02   S2CUSTF   PIC X.
02   FILLER REDEFINES S2CUSTF.
 03  S2CUSTA   PIC X.
02   FILLER    PIC X(0002).
02   S2CUSTI   PIC X(0006).
02   S2NAMEL   PIC S9(4) COMP.
02   S2NAMEF   PIC X.
02   FILLER REDEFINES S2NAMEF.
 03  S2NAMEA   PIC X.
02   FILLER    PIC X(0002).
02   S2NAMEI   PIC X(0025).
02   S2CNTCTL  PIC S9(4) COMP.
02   S2CNTCTF  PIC X.
02   FILLER REDEFINES S2CNTCTF.
 03  S2CNTCTA  PIC X.
02   FILLER    PIC X(0002).
02   S2CNTCTI  PIC X(0025).
02   S2ADDRL   PIC S9(4) COMP.
02   S2ADDRF   PIC X.
02   FILLER REDEFINES S2ADDRF.
 03  S2ADDRA   PIC X.
02   FILLER    PIC X(0002).
02   S2ADDRI   PIC X(0025).
02   S2CITYL   PIC S9(4) COMP.
02   S2CITYF   PIC X.
02   FILLER REDEFINES S2CITYF.
 03  S2CITYA   PIC X.
02   FILLER    PIC X(0002).
02   S2CITYI   PIC X(0020).
02   S2STATEL  PIC S9(4) COMP.
02   S2STATEF  PIC X.
02   FILLER REDEFINES S2STATEF.
 03  S2STATEA  PIC X.
02   FILLER    PIC X(0002).
02   S2STATEI  PIC X(0002).
02   S2ZIPL    PIC S9(4) COMP.
02   S2ZIPF    PIC X.
02   FILLER REDEFINES S2ZIPF.
 03  S2ZIPA    PIC X.
02   FILLER    PIC X(0002).
02   S2ZIPI    PIC X(0010).
02   S2SALESL  PIC S9(4) COMP.
02   S2SALESF  PIC X.
02   FILLER REDEFINES S2SALESF.
 03  S2SALESA  PIC X.
02   FILLER    PIC X(0002).
02   S2SALESI  PIC X(0011).
02   S2BALL    PIC S9(4) COMP.
02   S2BALF    PIC X.
02   FILLER REDEFINES S2BALF.
 03  S2BALA    PIC X.
02   FILLER    PIC X(0002).
02   S2BALI    PIC X(0011).
02   S2BDATEL  PIC S9(4) COMP.
02   S2BDATEF  PIC X.
```

FIGURE 3.13 *(Continued)*

```
    02   FILLER REDEFINES S2BDATEF.
     03  S2BDATEA  PIC X.
    02   FILLER    PIC X(0002).
    02   S2BDATEI  PIC X(0008).
    02   S2MSGL    PIC S9(4) COMP.
    02   S2MSGF    PIC X.
    02   FILLER REDEFINES S2MSGF.
     03  S2MSGA    PIC X.
    02   FILLER    PIC X(0002).
    02   S2MSGI    PIC X(0079).
    02   S2KEYSL   PIC S9(4) COMP.
    02   S2KEYSF   PIC X.
    02   FILLER REDEFINES S2KEYSF.
     03  S2KEYSA   PIC X.
    02   FILLER    PIC X(0002).
    02   S2KEYSI   PIC X(0079).
01  SALE002O REDEFINES SALE002I.
    02   FILLER    PIC X(12).
    02   FILLER    PIC X(3).
    02   S2PROCC   PIC X.
    02   S2PROCH   PIC X.
    02   S2PROCO   PIC X(0008).
    02   FILLER    PIC X(3).
    02   S2EXITC   PIC X.
    02   S2EXITH   PIC X.
    02   S2EXITO   PIC X(0005).
    02   FILLER    PIC X(3).
    02   S2CANC    PIC X.
    02   S2CANH    PIC X.
    02   S2CANO    PIC X(0007).
    02   FILLER    PIC X(3).
    02   S2PANIDC  PIC X.
    02   S2PANIDH  PIC X.
    02   S2PANIDO  PIC X(0007).
    02   FILLER    PIC X(3).
    02   S2INSTRC  PIC X.
    02   S2INSTRH  PIC X.
    02   S2INSTRO  PIC X(0060).
    02   FILLER    PIC X(3).
    02   S2CUSTC   PIC X.
    02   S2CUSTH   PIC X.
    02   S2CUSTO   PIC X(0006).
    02   FILLER    PIC X(3).
    02   S2NAMEC   PIC X.
    02   S2NAMEH   PIC X.
    02   S2NAMEO   PIC X(0025).
    02   FILLER    PIC X(3).
    02   S2CNTCTC  PIC X.
    02   S2CNTCTH  PIC X.
    02   S2CNTCTO  PIC X(0025).
    02   FILLER    PIC X(3).
    02   S2ADDRC   PIC X.
    02   S2ADDRH   PIC X.
    02   S2ADDRO   PIC X(0025).
    02   FILLER    PIC X(3).
    02   S2CITYC   PIC X.
    02   S2CITYH   PIC X.
    02   S2CITYO   PIC X(0020).
    02   FILLER    PIC X(3).
    02   S2STATEC  PIC X.
    02   S2STATEH  PIC X.
    02   S2STATEO  PIC X(0002).
    02   FILLER    PIC X(3).
    02   S2ZIPC    PIC X.
    02   S2ZIPH    PIC X.
    02   S2ZIPO    PIC X(0010).
    02   FILLER    PIC X(3).
    02   S2SALESC  PIC X.
    02   S2SALESH  PIC X.
    02   S2SALESO  PIC $$$,$$$.99-.
```

FIGURE 3.13   *(Continued)*

```
02   FILLER    PIC X(3).
02   S2BALC    PIC X.
02   S2BALH    PIC X.
02   S2BALO    PIC $$$,$$$.99-.
02   FILLER    PIC X(3).
02   S2BDATEC  PIC X.
02   S2BDATEH  PIC X.
02   S2BDATEO  PIC XX/XX/XX.
02   FILLER    PIC X(3).
02   S2MSGC    PIC X.
02   S2MSGH    PIC X.
02   S2MSGO    PIC X(0079).
02   FILLER    PIC X(3).
02   S2KEYSC   PIC X.
02   S2KEYSH   PIC X.
02   S2KEYSO   PIC X(0079).
```

FIGURE 3.13 *(Continued)*

```
*    MSALE03  Mapset.  Date - 01/03/91   Time - 23:09:31
01   SALE003I.
     02   FILLER    PIC X(12).
     02   S3DELL    PIC S9(4) COMP.
     02   S3DELF    PIC X.
     02   FILLER REDEFINES S3DELF.
      03  S3DELA    PIC X.
     02   FILLER    PIC X(0002).
     02   S3DELI    PIC X(0007).
     02   S3EXITL   PIC S9(4) COMP.
     02   S3EXITF   PIC X.
     02   FILLER REDEFINES S3EXITF.
      03  S3EXITA   PIC X.
     02   FILLER    PIC X(0002).
     02   S3EXITI   PIC X(0005).
     02   S3CANL    PIC S9(4) COMP.
     02   S3CANF    PIC X.
     02   FILLER REDEFINES S3CANF.
      03  S3CANA    PIC X.
     02   FILLER    PIC X(0002).
     02   S3CANI    PIC X(0007).
     02   S3PANIDL  PIC S9(4) COMP.
     02   S3PANIDF  PIC X.
     02   FILLER REDEFINES S3PANIDF.
      03  S3PANIDA  PIC X.
     02   FILLER    PIC X(0002).
     02   S3PANIDI  PIC X(0007).
     02   S3INSTRL  PIC S9(4) COMP.
     02   S3INSTRF  PIC X.
     02   FILLER REDEFINES S3INSTRF.
      03  S3INSTRA  PIC X.
     02   FILLER    PIC X(0002).
     02   S3INSTRI  PIC X(0060).
     02   S3CUSTL   PIC S9(4) COMP.
     02   S3CUSTF   PIC X.
     02   FILLER REDEFINES S3CUSTF.
      03  S3CUSTA   PIC X.
     02   FILLER    PIC X(0002).
     02   S3CUSTI   PIC X(0006).
     02   S3NAMEL   PIC S9(4) COMP.
     02   S3NAMEF   PIC X.
     02   FILLER REDEFINES S3NAMEF.
      03  S3NAMEA   PIC X.
     02   FILLER    PIC X(0002).
     02   S3NAMEI   PIC X(0025).
     02   S3CNTCTL  PIC S9(4) COMP.
     02   S3CNTCTF  PIC X.
     02   FILLER REDEFINES S3CNTCTF.
```

FIGURE 3.14 Symbolic map SALE003.

```
    03  S3CNTCTA  PIC X.
    02  FILLER    PIC X(0002).
    02  S3CNTCTI  PIC X(0025).
    02  S3ADDRL   PIC S9(4) COMP.
    02  S3ADDRF   PIC X.
    02  FILLER REDEFINES S3ADDRF.
    03  S3ADDRA   PIC X.
    02  FILLER    PIC X(0002).
    02  S3ADDRI   PIC X(0025).
    02  S3CITYL   PIC S9(4) COMP.
    02  S3CITYF   PIC X.
    02  FILLER REDEFINES S3CITYF.
    03  S3CITYA   PIC X.
    02  FILLER    PIC X(0002).
    02  S3CITYI   PIC X(0020).
    02  S3STATEL  PIC S9(4) COMP.
    02  S3STATEF  PIC X.
    02  FILLER REDEFINES S3STATEF.
    03  S3STATEA  PIC X.
    02  FILLER    PIC X(0002).
    02  S3STATEI  PIC X(0002).
    02  S3ZIPL    PIC S9(4) COMP.
    02  S3ZIPF    PIC X.
    02  FILLER REDEFINES S3ZIPF.
    03  S3ZIPA    PIC X.
    02  FILLER    PIC X(0002).
    02  S3ZIPI    PIC X(0010).
    02  S3SALESL  PIC S9(4) COMP.
    02  S3SALESF  PIC X.
    02  FILLER REDEFINES S3SALESF.
    03  S3SALESA  PIC X.
    02  FILLER    PIC X(0002).
    02  S3SALESI  PIC X(0011).
    02  S3BALL    PIC S9(4) COMP.
    02  S3BALF    PIC X.
    02  FILLER REDEFINES S3BALF.
    03  S3BALA    PIC X.
    02  FILLER    PIC X(0002).
    02  S3BALI    PIC X(0011).
    02  S3BDATEL  PIC S9(4) COMP.
    02  S3BDATEF  PIC X.
    02  FILLER REDEFINES S3BDATEF.
    03  S3BDATEA  PIC X.
    02  FILLER    PIC X(0002).
    02  S3BDATEI  PIC X(0008).
    02  S3MSGL    PIC S9(4) COMP.
    02  S3MSGF    PIC X.
    02  FILLER REDEFINES S3MSGF.
    03  S3MSGA    PIC X.
    02  FILLER    PIC X(0002).
    02  S3MSGI    PIC X(0079).
    02  S3KEYSL   PIC S9(4) COMP.
    02  S3KEYSF   PIC X.
    02  FILLER REDEFINES S3KEYSF.
    03  S3KEYSA   PIC X.
    02  FILLER    PIC X(0002).
    02  S3KEYSI   PIC X(0079).
01  SALE0030 REDEFINES SALE003I.
    02  FILLER    PIC X(12).
    02  FILLER    PIC X(3).
    02  S3DELC    PIC X.
    02  S3DELH    PIC X.
    02  S3DELO    PIC X(0007).
    02  FILLER    PIC X(3).
    02  S3EXITC   PIC X.
    02  S3EXITH   PIC X.
    02  S3EXITO   PIC X(0005).
    02  FILLER    PIC X(3).
    02  S3CANC    PIC X.
    02  S3CANH    PIC X.
```

FIGURE 3.14 *(Continued)*

```
      02   S3CANO     PIC X(0007).
      02   FILLER     PIC X(3).
      02   S3PANIDC   PIC X.
      02   S3PANIDH   PIC X.
      02   S3PANIDO   PIC X(0007).
      02   FILLER     PIC X(3).
      02   S3INSTRC   PIC X.
      02   S3INSTRH   PIC X.
      02   S3INSTRO   PIC X(0060).
      02   FILLER     PIC X(3).
      02   S3CUSTC    PIC X.
      02   S3CUSTH    PIC X.
      02   S3CUSTO    PIC X(0006).
      02   FILLER     PIC X(3).
      02   S3NAMEC    PIC X.
      02   S3NAMEH    PIC X.
      02   S3NAMEO    PIC X(0025).
      02   FILLER     PIC X(3).
      02   S3CNTCTC   PIC X.
      02   S3CNTCTH   PIC X.
      02   S3CNTCTO   PIC X(0025).
      02   FILLER     PIC X(3).
      02   S3ADDRC    PIC X.
      02   S3ADDRH    PIC X.
      02   S3ADDRO    PIC X(0025).
      02   FILLER     PIC X(3).
      02   S3CITYC    PIC X.
      02   S3CITYH    PIC X.
      02   S3CITYO    PIC X(0020).
      02   FILLER     PIC X(3).
      02   S3STATEC   PIC X.
      02   S3STATEH   PIC X.
      02   S3STATEO   PIC X(0002).
      02   FILLER     PIC X(3).
      02   S3ZIPC     PIC X.
      02   S3ZIPH     PIC X.
      02   S3ZIPO     PIC X(0010).
      02   FILLER     PIC X(3).
      02   S3SALESC   PIC X.
      02   S3SALESH   PIC X.
      02   S3SALESO   PIC $$$,$$$.99-.
      02   FILLER     PIC X(3).
      02   S3BALC     PIC X.
      02   S3BALH     PIC X.
      02   S3BALO     PIC $$$,$$$.99-.
      02   FILLER     PIC X(3).
      02   S3BDATEC   PIC X.
      02   S3BDATEH   PIC X.
      02   S3BDATEO   PIC XX/XX/XX.
      02   FILLER     PIC X(3).
      02   S3MSGC     PIC X.
      02   S3MSGH     PIC X.
      02   S3MSGO     PIC X(0079).
      02   FILLER     PIC X(3).
      02   S3KEYSC    PIC X.
      02   S3KEYSH    PIC X.
      02   S3KEYSO    PIC X(0079).
```

FIGURE 3.14   *(Continued)*

```
*    MSALE04  Mapset.  Date - 01/03/91   Time - 23:09:47
 01  SALE004I.
      02   FILLER     PIC X(12).
      02   S4ADDL     PIC S9(4) COMP.
      02   S4ADDF     PIC X.
      02   FILLER REDEFINES S4ADDF.
       03  S4ADDA     PIC X.
```

FIGURE 3.15   Symbolic map SALE004.

```
02    FILLER      PIC X(0002).
02    S4ADDI      PIC X(0004).
02    S4EXITL     PIC S9(4) COMP.
02    S4EXITF     PIC X.
02    FILLER REDEFINES S4EXITF.
 03   S4EXITA     PIC X.
02    FILLER      PIC X(0002).
02    S4EXITI     PIC X(0005).
02    S4CANL      PIC S9(4) COMP.
02    S4CANF      PIC X.
02    FILLER REDEFINES S4CANF.
 03   S4CANA      PIC X.
02    FILLER      PIC X(0002).
02    S4CANI      PIC X(0007).
02    S4PANIDL    PIC S9(4) COMP.
02    S4PANIDF    PIC X.
02    FILLER REDEFINES S4PANIDF.
 03   S4PANIDA    PIC X.
02    FILLER      PIC X(0002).
02    S4PANIDI    PIC X(0007).
02    S4INSTRL    PIC S9(4) COMP.
02    S4INSTRF    PIC X.
02    FILLER REDEFINES S4INSTRF.
 03   S4INSTRA    PIC X.
02    FILLER      PIC X(0002).
02    S4INSTRI    PIC X(0060).
02    S4INST2L    PIC S9(4) COMP.
02    S4INST2F    PIC X.
02    FILLER REDEFINES S4INST2F.
 03   S4INST2A    PIC X.
02    FILLER      PIC X(0002).
02    S4INST2I    PIC X(0060).
02    S4CUSTL     PIC S9(4) COMP.
02    S4CUSTF     PIC X.
02    FILLER REDEFINES S4CUSTF.
 03   S4CUSTA     PIC X.
02    FILLER      PIC X(0002).
02    S4CUSTI     PIC X(0006).
02    S4ITEML     PIC S9(4) COMP.
02    S4ITEMF     PIC X.
02    FILLER REDEFINES S4ITEMF.
 03   S4ITEMA     PIC X.
02    FILLER      PIC X(0002).
02    S4ITEMI     PIC 999999.
02    S4UNITPL    PIC S9(4) COMP.
02    S4UNITPF    PIC X.
02    FILLER REDEFINES S4UNITPF.
 03   S4UNITPA    PIC X.
02    FILLER      PIC X(0002).
02    S4UNITPI    PIC 9999V99.
02    S4QTYL      PIC S9(4) COMP.
02    S4QTYF      PIC X.
02    FILLER REDEFINES S4QTYF.
 03   S4QTYA      PIC X.
02    FILLER      PIC X(0002).
02    S4QTYI      PIC 999999.
02    S4SIGNL     PIC S9(4) COMP.
02    S4SIGNF     PIC X.
02    FILLER REDEFINES S4SIGNF.
 03   S4SIGNA     PIC X.
02    FILLER      PIC X(0002).
02    S4SIGNI     PIC X(0001).
02    S4MSGL      PIC S9(4) COMP.
02    S4MSGF      PIC X.
02    FILLER REDEFINES S4MSGF.
 03   S4MSGA      PIC X.
02    FILLER      PIC X(0002).
02    S4MSGI      PIC X(0079).
02    S4KEYSL     PIC S9(4) COMP.
02    S4KEYSF     PIC X.
```

FIGURE 3.15 *(Continued)*

```
      02   FILLER REDEFINES S4KEYSF.
      03   S4KEYSA    PIC X.
      02   FILLER     PIC X(0002).
      02   S4KEYSI    PIC X(0079).
  01  SALE0040 REDEFINES SALE004I.
      02   FILLER     PIC X(12).
      02   FILLER     PIC X(3).
      02   S4ADDC     PIC X.
      02   S4ADDH     PIC X.
      02   S4ADDO     PIC X(0004).
      02   FILLER     PIC X(3).
      02   S4EXITC    PIC X.
      02   S4EXITH    PIC X.
      02   S4EXITO    PIC X(0005).
      02   FILLER     PIC X(3).
      02   S4CANC     PIC X.
      02   S4CANH     PIC X.
      02   S4CANO     PIC X(0007).
      02   FILLER     PIC X(3).
      02   S4PANIDC   PIC X.
      02   S4PANIDH   PIC X.
      02   S4PANIDO   PIC X(0007).
      02   FILLER     PIC X(3).
      02   S4INSTRC   PIC X.
      02   S4INSTRH   PIC X.
      02   S4INSTRO   PIC X(0060).
      02   FILLER     PIC X(3).
      02   S4INST2C   PIC X.
      02   S4INST2H   PIC X.
      02   S4INST2O   PIC X(0060).
      02   FILLER     PIC X(3).
      02   S4CUSTC    PIC X.
      02   S4CUSTH    PIC X.
      02   S4CUSTO    PIC X(0006).
      02   FILLER     PIC X(3).
      02   S4ITEMC    PIC X.
      02   S4ITEMH    PIC X.
      02   S4ITEMO    PIC X(0006).
      02   FILLER     PIC X(3).
      02   S4UNITPC   PIC X.
      02   S4UNITPH   PIC X.
      02   S4UNITPO   PIC X(0006).
      02   FILLER     PIC X(3).
      02   S4QTYC     PIC X.
      02   S4QTYH     PIC X.
      02   S4QTYO     PIC X(0006).
      02   FILLER     PIC X(3).
      02   S4SIGNC    PIC X.
      02   S4SIGNH    PIC X.
      02   S4SIGNO    PIC X(0001).
      02   FILLER     PIC X(3).
      02   S4MSGC     PIC X.
      02   S4MSGH     PIC X.
      02   S4MSGO     PIC X(0079).
      02   FILLER     PIC X(3).
      02   S4KEYSC    PIC X.
      02   S4KEYSH    PIC X.
      02   S4KEYSO    PIC X(0079).
```

FIGURE 3.15 *(Continued)*

```
*     MSALE05  Mapset.  Date - 01/03/91   Time - 23:10:02
 01   SALE005I.
      02    FILLER      PIC X(12).
      02    S5FWDL      PIC S9(4) COMP.
      02    S5FWDF      PIC X.
      02    FILLER REDEFINES S5FWDF.
       03   S5FWDA      PIC X.
      02    FILLER      PIC X(0002).
      02    S5FWDI      PIC X(0008).
      02    S5BKWL      PIC S9(4) COMP.
      02    S5BKWF      PIC X.
      02    FILLER REDEFINES S5BKWF.
       03   S5BKWA      PIC X.
      02    FILLER      PIC X(0002).
      02    S5BKWI      PIC X(0009).
      02    S5EXITL     PIC S9(4) COMP.
      02    S5EXITF     PIC X.
      02    FILLER REDEFINES S5EXITF.
       03   S5EXITA     PIC X.
      02    FILLER      PIC X(0002).
      02    S5EXITI     PIC X(0005).
      02    S5CANL      PIC S9(4) COMP.
      02    S5CANF      PIC X.
      02    FILLER REDEFINES S5CANF.
       03   S5CANA      PIC X.
      02    FILLER      PIC X(0002).
      02    S5CANI      PIC X(0007).
      02    S5PANIDL    PIC S9(4) COMP.
      02    S5PANIDF    PIC X.
      02    FILLER REDEFINES S5PANIDF.
       03   S5PANIDA    PIC X.
      02    FILLER      PIC X(0002).
      02    S5PANIDI    PIC X(0007).
      02    S5PLUSL     PIC S9(4) COMP.
      02    S5PLUSF     PIC X.
      02    FILLER REDEFINES S5PLUSF.
       03   S5PLUSA     PIC X.
      02    FILLER      PIC X(0002).
      02    S5PLUSI     PIC X(0001).
      02    S5MINUSL    PIC S9(4) COMP.
      02    S5MINUSF    PIC X.
      02    FILLER REDEFINES S5MINUSF.
       03   S5MINUSA    PIC X.
      02    FILLER      PIC X(0002).
      02    S5MINUSI    PIC X(0001).
      02    S5CST01L    PIC S9(4) COMP.
      02    S5CST01F    PIC X.
      02    FILLER REDEFINES S5CST01F.
       03   S5CST01A    PIC X.
      02    FILLER      PIC X(0002).
      02    S5CST01I    PIC X(0006).
      02    S5NAM01L    PIC S9(4) COMP.
      02    S5NAM01F    PIC X.
      02    FILLER REDEFINES S5NAM01F.
       03   S5NAM01A    PIC X.
      02    FILLER      PIC X(0002).
      02    S5NAM01I    PIC X(0025).
      02    S5CST02L    PIC S9(4) COMP.
      02    S5CST02F    PIC X.
      02    FILLER REDEFINES S5CST02F.
       03   S5CST02A    PIC X.
      02    FILLER      PIC X(0002).
      02    S5CST02I    PIC X(0006).
      02    S5NAM02L    PIC S9(4) COMP.
      02    S5NAM02F    PIC X.
      02    FILLER REDEFINES S5NAM02F.
       03   S5NAM02A    PIC X.
      02    FILLER      PIC X(0002).
      02    S5NAM02I    PIC X(0025).
      02    S5CST03L    PIC S9(4) COMP.
```

FIGURE 3.16 Symbolic map SALE005.

```
02   S5CST03F  PIC X.
02   FILLER REDEFINES S5CST03F.
 03  S5CST03A  PIC X.
02   FILLER    PIC X(0002).
02   S5CST03I  PIC X(0006).
02   S5NAM03L  PIC S9(4) COMP.
02   S5NAM03F  PIC X.
02   FILLER REDEFINES S5NAM03F.
 03  S5NAM03A  PIC X.
02   FILLER    PIC X(0002).
02   S5NAM03I  PIC X(0025).
02   S5CST04L  PIC S9(4) COMP.
02   S5CST04F  PIC X.
02   FILLER REDEFINES S5CST04F.
 03  S5CST04A  PIC X.
02   FILLER    PIC X(0002).
02   S5CST04I  PIC X(0006).
02   S5NAM04L  PIC S9(4) COMP.
02   S5NAM04F  PIC X.
02   FILLER REDEFINES S5NAM04F.
 03  S5NAM04A  PIC X.
02   FILLER    PIC X(0002).
02   S5NAM04I  PIC X(0025).
02   S5CST05L  PIC S9(4) COMP.
02   S5CST05F  PIC X.
02   FILLER REDEFINES S5CST05F.
 03  S5CST05A  PIC X.
02   FILLER    PIC X(0002).
02   S5CST05I  PIC X(0006).
02   S5NAM05L  PIC S9(4) COMP.
02   S5NAM05F  PIC X.
02   FILLER REDEFINES S5NAM05F.
 03  S5NAM05A  PIC X.
02   FILLER    PIC X(0002).
02   S5NAM05I  PIC X(0025).
02   S5CST06L  PIC S9(4) COMP.
02   S5CST06F  PIC X.
02   FILLER REDEFINES S5CST06F.
 03  S5CST06A  PIC X.
02   FILLER    PIC X(0002).
02   S5CST06I  PIC X(0006).
02   S5NAM06L  PIC S9(4) COMP.
02   S5NAM06F  PIC X.
02   FILLER REDEFINES S5NAM06F.
 03  S5NAM06A  PIC X.
02   FILLER    PIC X(0002).
02   S5NAM06I  PIC X(0025).
02   S5CST07L  PIC S9(4) COMP.
02   S5CST07F  PIC X.
02   FILLER REDEFINES S5CST07F.
 03  S5CST07A  PIC X.
02   FILLER    PIC X(0002).
02   S5CST07I  PIC X(0006).
02   S5NAM07L  PIC S9(4) COMP.
02   S5NAM07F  PIC X.
02   FILLER REDEFINES S5NAM07F.
 03  S5NAM07A  PIC X.
02   FILLER    PIC X(0002).
02   S5NAM07I  PIC X(0025).
02   S5CST08L  PIC S9(4) COMP.
02   S5CST08F  PIC X.
02   FILLER REDEFINES S5CST08F.
 03  S5CST08A  PIC X.
02   FILLER    PIC X(0002).
02   S5CST08I  PIC X(0006).
02   S5NAM08L  PIC S9(4) COMP.
02   S5NAM08F  PIC X.
02   FILLER REDEFINES S5NAM08F.
 03  S5NAM08A  PIC X.
02   FILLER    PIC X(0002).
```

FIGURE 3.16 *(Continued)*

```
        02    S5NAM08I   PIC X(0025).
        02    S5CST09L   PIC S9(4) COMP.
        02    S5CST09F   PIC X.
        02    FILLER REDEFINES S5CST09F.
        03    S5CST09A   PIC X.
        02    FILLER     PIC X(0002).
        02    S5CST09I   PIC X(0006).
        02    S5NAM09L   PIC S9(4) COMP.
        02    S5NAM09F   PIC X.
        02    FILLER REDEFINES S5NAM09F.
        03    S5NAM09A   PIC X.
        02    FILLER     PIC X(0002).
        02    S5NAM09I   PIC X(0025).
        02    S5CST10L   PIC S9(4) COMP.
        02    S5CST10F   PIC X.
        02    FILLER REDEFINES S5CST10F.
        03    S5CST10A   PIC X.
        02    FILLER     PIC X(0002).
        02    S5CST10I   PIC X(0006).
        02    S5NAM10L   PIC S9(4) COMP.
        02    S5NAM10F   PIC X.
        02    FILLER REDEFINES S5NAM10F.
        03    S5NAM10A   PIC X.
        02    FILLER     PIC X(0002).
        02    S5NAM10I   PIC X(0025).
        02    S5CST11L   PIC S9(4) COMP.
        02    S5CST11F   PIC X.
        02    FILLER REDEFINES S5CST11F.
        03    S5CST11A   PIC X.
        02    FILLER     PIC X(0002).
        02    S5CST11I   PIC X(0006).
        02    S5NAM11L   PIC S9(4) COMP.
        02    S5NAM11F   PIC X.
        02    FILLER REDEFINES S5NAM11F.
        03    S5NAM11A   PIC X.
        02    FILLER     PIC X(0002).
        02    S5NAM11I   PIC X(0025).
        02    S5CST12L   PIC S9(4) COMP.
        02    S5CST12F   PIC X.
        02    FILLER REDEFINES S5CST12F.
        03    S5CST12A   PIC X.
        02    FILLER     PIC X(0002).
        02    S5CST12I   PIC X(0006).
        02    S5NAM12L   PIC S9(4) COMP.
        02    S5NAM12F   PIC X.
        02    FILLER REDEFINES S5NAM12F.
        03    S5NAM12A   PIC X.
        02    FILLER     PIC X(0002).
        02    S5NAM12I   PIC X(0025).
        02    S5CUSTL    PIC S9(4) COMP.
        02    S5CUSTF    PIC X.
        02    FILLER REDEFINES S5CUSTF.
        03    S5CUSTA    PIC X.
        02    FILLER     PIC X(0002).
        02    S5CUSTI    PIC X(0006).
        02    S5MSGL     PIC S9(4) COMP.
        02    S5MSGF     PIC X.
        02    FILLER REDEFINES S5MSGF.
        03    S5MSGA     PIC X.
        02    FILLER     PIC X(0002).
        02    S5MSGI     PIC X(0079).
        02    S5KEYSL    PIC S9(4) COMP.
        02    S5KEYSF    PIC X.
        02    FILLER REDEFINES S5KEYSF.
        03    S5KEYSA    PIC X.
        02    FILLER     PIC X(0002).
        02    S5KEYSI    PIC X(0079).
    01  SALE0050 REDEFINES SALE005I.
        02    FILLER     PIC X(12).
        02    FILLER     PIC X(3).
```

FIGURE 3.16   *(Continued)*

```
02   S5FWDC      PIC X.
02   S5FWDH      PIC X.
02   S5FWDO      PIC X(0008).
02   FILLER      PIC X(3).
02   S5BKWC      PIC X.
02   S5BKWH      PIC X.
02   S5BKWO      PIC X(0009).
02   FILLER      PIC X(3).
02   S5EXITC     PIC X.
02   S5EXITH     PIC X.
02   S5EXITO     PIC X(0005).
02   FILLER      PIC X(3).
02   S5CANC      PIC X.
02   S5CANH      PIC X.
02   S5CANO      PIC X(0007).
02   FILLER      PIC X(3).
02   S5PANIDC    PIC X.
02   S5PANIDH    PIC X.
02   S5PANIDO    PIC X(0007).
02   FILLER      PIC X(3).
02   S5PLUSC     PIC X.
02   S5PLUSH     PIC X.
02   S5PLUSO     PIC X(0001).
02   FILLER      PIC X(3).
02   S5MINUSC    PIC X.
02   S5MINUSH    PIC X.
02   S5MINUSO    PIC X(0001).
02   FILLER      PIC X(3).
02   S5CST01C    PIC X.
02   S5CST01H    PIC X.
02   S5CST01O    PIC X(0006).
02   FILLER      PIC X(3).
02   S5NAM01C    PIC X.
02   S5NAM01H    PIC X.
02   S5NAM01O    PIC X(0025).
02   FILLER      PIC X(3).
02   S5CST02C    PIC X.
02   S5CST02H    PIC X.
02   S5CST02O    PIC X(0006).
02   FILLER      PIC X(3).
02   S5NAM02C    PIC X.
02   S5NAM02H    PIC X.
02   S5NAM02O    PIC X(0025).
02   FILLER      PIC X(3).
02   S5CST03C    PIC X.
02   S5CST03H    PIC X.
02   S5CST03O    PIC X(0006).
02   FILLER      PIC X(3).
02   S5NAM03C    PIC X.
02   S5NAM03H    PIC X.
02   S5NAM03O    PIC X(0025).
02   FILLER      PIC X(3).
02   S5CST04C    PIC X.
02   S5CST04H    PIC X.
02   S5CST04O    PIC X(0006).
02   FILLER      PIC X(3).
02   S5NAM04C    PIC X.
02   S5NAM04H    PIC X.
02   S5NAM04O    PIC X(0025).
02   FILLER      PIC X(3).
02   S5CST05C    PIC X.
02   S5CST05H    PIC X.
02   S5CST05O    PIC X(0006).
02   FILLER      PIC X(3).
02   S5NAM05C    PIC X.
02   S5NAM05H    PIC X.
02   S5NAM05O    PIC X(0025).
02   FILLER      PIC X(3).
02   S5CST06C    PIC X.
02   S5CST06H    PIC X.
```

FIGURE 3.16   *(Continued)*

```
02   S5CST060   PIC X(0006).
02   FILLER     PIC X(3).
02   S5NAM06C   PIC X.
02   S5NAM06H   PIC X.
02   S5NAM060   PIC X(0025).
02   FILLER     PIC X(3).
02   S5CST07C   PIC X.
02   S5CST07H   PIC X.
02   S5CST070   PIC X(0006).
02   FILLER     PIC X(3).
02   S5NAM07C   PIC X.
02   S5NAM07H   PIC X.
02   S5NAM070   PIC X(0025).
02   FILLER     PIC X(3).
02   S5CST08C   PIC X.
02   S5CST08H   PIC X.
02   S5CST080   PIC X(0006).
02   FILLER     PIC X(3).
02   S5NAM08C   PIC X.
02   S5NAM08H   PIC X.
02   S5NAM080   PIC X(0025).
02   FILLER     PIC X(3).
02   S5CST09C   PIC X.
02   S5CST09H   PIC X.
02   S5CST090   PIC X(0006).
02   FILLER     PIC X(3).
02   S5NAM09C   PIC X.
02   S5NAM09H   PIC X.
02   S5NAM090   PIC X(0025).
02   FILLER     PIC X(3).
02   S5CST10C   PIC X.
02   S5CST10H   PIC X.
02   S5CST100   PIC X(0006).
02   FILLER     PIC X(3).
02   S5NAM10C   PIC X.
02   S5NAM10H   PIC X.
02   S5NAM100   PIC X(0025).
02   FILLER     PIC X(3).
02   S5CST11C   PIC X.
02   S5CST11H   PIC X.
02   S5CST110   PIC X(0006).
02   FILLER     PIC X(3).
02   S5NAM11C   PIC X.
02   S5NAM11H   PIC X.
02   S5NAM110   PIC X(0025).
02   FILLER     PIC X(3).
02   S5CST12C   PIC X.
02   S5CST12H   PIC X.
02   S5CST120   PIC X(0006).
02   ¯ILLER     PIC X(3).
02   S5NAM12C   PIC X.
02   S5NAM12H   PIC X.
02   S5NAM120   PIC X(0025).
02   FILLER     PIC X(3).
02   S5CUSTC    PIC X.
02   S5CUSTH    PIC X.
02   S5CUSTO    PIC X(0006).
02   FILLER     PIC X(3).
02   S5MSGC     PIC X.
02   S5MSGH     PIC X.
02   S5MSGO     PIC X(0079).
02   FILLER     PIC X(3).
02   S5KEYSC    PIC X.
02   S5KEYSH    PIC X.
02   S5KEYSO    PIC X(0079).
```

FIGURE 3.16   *(Continued)*

```
*     MSALE06  Mapset.   Date - 01/03/91   Time - 23:10:17
  01  SALE006I.
      02   FILLER     PIC X(12).
      02   S6FWDL     PIC S9(4) COMP.
      02   S6FWDF     PIC X.
      02   FILLER REDEFINES S6FWDF.
       03  S6FWDA     PIC X.
      02   FILLER     PIC X(0002).
      02   S6FWDI     PIC X(0008).
      02   S6BKWL     PIC S9(4) COMP.
      02   S6BKWF     PIC X.
      02   FILLER REDEFINES S6BKWF.
       03  S6BKWA     PIC X.
      02   FILLER     PIC X(0002).
      02   S6BKWI     PIC X(0009).
      02   S6EXITL    PIC S9(4) COMP.
      02   S6EXITF    PIC X.
      02   FILLER REDEFINES S6EXITF.
       03  S6EXITA    PIC X.
      02   FILLER     PIC X(0002).
      02   S6EXITI    PIC X(0005).
      02   S6CANL     PIC S9(4) COMP.
      02   S6CANF     PIC X.
      02   FILLER REDEFINES S6CANF.
       03  S6CANA     PIC X.
      02   FILLER     PIC X(0002).
      02   S6CANI     PIC X(0007).
      02   S6PANIDL   PIC S9(4) COMP.
      02   S6PANIDF   PIC X.
      02   FILLER REDEFINES S6PANIDF.
       03  S6PANIDA   PIC X.
      02   FILLER     PIC X(0002).
      02   S6PANIDI   PIC X(0007).
      02   S6CUSTL    PIC S9(4) COMP.
      02   S6CUSTF    PIC X.
      02   FILLER REDEFINES S6CUSTF.
       03  S6CUSTA    PIC X.
      02   FILLER     PIC X(0002).
      02   S6CUSTI    PIC X(0006).
      02   S6PLUSL    PIC S9(4) COMP.
      02   S6PLUSF    PIC X.
      02   FILLER REDEFINES S6PLUSF.
       03  S6PLUSA    PIC X.
      02   FILLER     PIC X(0002).
      02   S6PLUSI    PIC X(0001).
      02   S6MINUSL   PIC S9(4) COMP.
      02   S6MINUSF   PIC X.
      02   FILLER REDEFINES S6MINUSF.
       03  S6MINUSA   PIC X.
      02   FILLER     PIC X(0002).
      02   S6MINUSI   PIC X(0001).
      02   S6ITM01L   PIC S9(4) COMP.
      02   S6ITM01F   PIC X.
      02   FILLER REDEFINES S6ITM01F.
       03  S6ITM01A   PIC X.
      02   FILLER     PIC X(0002).
      02   S6ITM01I   PIC X(0006).
      02   S6QTY01L   PIC S9(4) COMP.
      02   S6QTY01F   PIC X.
      02   FILLER REDEFINES S6QTY01F.
       03  S6QTY01A   PIC X.
      02   FILLER     PIC X(0002).
      02   S6QTY01I   PIC X(0008).
      02   S6PRC01L   PIC S9(4) COMP.
      02   S6PRC01F   PIC X.
      02   FILLER REDEFINES S6PRC01F.
       03  S6PRC01A   PIC X.
      02   FILLER     PIC X(0002).
      02   S6PRC01I   PIC X(0010).
      02   S6ITM02L   PIC S9(4) COMP.
```

FIGURE 3.17 *Symbolic map SALE006.*

```
02   S6ITM02F  PIC X.
02   FILLER REDEFINES S6ITM02F.
 03   S6ITM02A  PIC X.
02   FILLER     PIC X(0002).
02   S6ITM02I  PIC X(0006).
02   S6QTY02L  PIC S9(4) COMP.
02   S6QTY02F  PIC X.
02   FILLER REDEFINES S6QTY02F.
 03   S6QTY02A  PIC X.
02   FILLER     PIC X(0002).
02   S6QTY02I  PIC X(0008).
02   S6PRC02L  PIC S9(4) COMP.
02   S6PRC02F  PIC X.
02   FILLER REDEFINES S6PRC02F.
 03   S6PRC02A  PIC X.
02   FILLER     PIC X(0002).
02   S6PRC02I  PIC X(0010).
02   S6ITM03L  PIC S9(4) COMP.
02   S6ITM03F  PIC X.
02   FILLER REDEFINES S6ITM03F.
 03   S6ITM03A  PIC X.
02   FILLER     PIC X(0002).
02   S6ITM03I  PIC X(0006).
02   S6QTY03L  PIC S9(4) COMP.
02   S6QTY03F  PIC X.
02   FILLER REDEFINES S6QTY03F.
 03   S6QTY03A  PIC X.
02   FILLER     PIC X(0002).
02   S6QTY03I  PIC X(0008).
02   S6PRC03L  PIC S9(4) COMP.
02   S6PRC03F  PIC X.
02   FILLER REDEFINES S6PRC03F.
 03   S6PRC03A  PIC X.
02   FILLER     PIC X(0002).
02   S6PRC03I  PIC X(0010).
02   S6ITM04L  PIC S9(4) COMP.
02   S6ITM04F  PIC X.
02   FILLER REDEFINES S6ITM04F.
 03   S6ITM04A  PIC X.
02   FILLER     PIC X(0002).
02   S6ITM04I  PIC X(0006).
02   S6QTY04L  PIC S9(4) COMP.
02   S6QTY04F  PIC X.
02   FILLER REDEFINES S6QTY04F.
 03   S6QTY04A  PIC X.
02   FILLER     PIC X(0002).
02   S6QTY04I  PIC X(0008).
02   S6PRC04L  PIC S9(4) COMP.
02   S6PRC04F  PIC X.
02   FILLER REDEFINES S6PRC04F.
 03   S6PRC04A  PIC X.
02   FILLER     PIC X(0002).
02   S6PRC04I  PIC X(0010).
02   S6ITM05L  PIC S9(4) COMP.
02   S6ITM05F  PIC X.
02   FILLER REDEFINES S6ITM05F.
 03   S6ITM05A  PIC X.
02   FILLER     PIC X(0002).
02   S6ITM05I  PIC X(0006).
02   S6QTY05L  PIC S9(4) COMP.
02   S6QTY05F  PIC X.
02   FILLER REDEFINES S6QTY05F.
 03   S6QTY05A  PIC X.
02   FILLER     PIC X(0002).
02   S6QTY05I  PIC X(0008).
02   S6PRC05L  PIC S9(4) COMP.
02   S6PRC05F  PIC X.
02   FILLER REDEFINES S6PRC05F.
 03   S6PRC05A  PIC X.
02   FILLER     PIC X(0002).
```

FIGURE 3.17   *(Continued)*

```
02    S6PRC05I   PIC X(0010).
02    S6ITM06L   PIC S9(4) COMP.
02    S6ITM06F   PIC X.
02    FILLER REDEFINES S6ITM06F.
 03   S6ITM06A   PIC X.
02    FILLER     PIC X(0002).
02    S6ITM06I   PIC X(0006).
02    S6QTY06L   PIC S9(4) COMP.
02    S6QTY06F   PIC X.
02    FILLER REDEFINES S6QTY06F.
 03   S6QTY06A   PIC X.
02    FILLER     PIC X(0002).
02    S6QTY06I   PIC X(0008).
02    S6PRC06L   PIC S9(4) COMP.
02    S6PRC06F   PIC X.
02    FILLER REDEFINES S6PRC06F.
 03   S6PRC06A   PIC X.
02    FILLER     PIC X(0002).
02    S6PRC06I   PIC X(0010).
02    S6ITM07L   PIC S9(4) COMP.
02    S6ITM07F   PIC X.
02    FILLER REDEFINES S6ITM07F.
 03   S6ITM07A   PIC X.
02    FILLER     PIC X(0002).
02    S6ITM07I   PIC X(0006).
02    S6QTY07L   PIC S9(4) COMP.
02    S6QTY07F   PIC X.
02    FILLER REDEFINES S6QTY07F.
 03   S6QTY07A   PIC X.
02    FILLER     PIC X(0002).
02    S6QTY07I   PIC X(0008).
02    S6PRC07L   PIC S9(4) COMP.
02    S6PRC07F   PIC X.
02    FILLER REDEFINES S6PRC07F.
 03   S6PRC07A   PIC X.
02    FILLER     PIC X(0002).
02    S6PRC07I   PIC X(0010).
02    S6ITM08L   PIC S9(4) COMP.
02    S6ITM08F   PIC X.
02    FILLER REDEFINES S6ITM08F.
 03   S6ITM08A   PIC X.
02    FILLER     PIC X(0002).
02    S6ITM08I   PIC X(0006).
02    S6QTY08L   PIC S9(4) COMP.
02    S6QTY08F   PIC X.
02    FILLER REDEFINES S6QTY08F.
 03   S6QTY08A   PIC X.
02    FILLER     PIC X(0002).
02    S6QTY08I   PIC X(0008).
02    S6PRC08L   PIC S9(4) COMP.
02    S6PRC08F   PIC X.
02    FILLER REDEFINES S6PRC08F.
 03   S6PRC08A   PIC X.
02    FILLER     PIC X(0002).
02    S6PRC08I   PIC X(0010).
02    S6ITM09L   PIC S9(4) COMP.
02    S6ITM09F   PIC X.
02    FILLER REDEFINES S6ITM09F.
 03   S6ITM09A   PIC X.
02    FILLER     PIC X(0002).
02    S6ITM09I   PIC X(0006).
02    S6QTY09L   PIC S9(4) COMP.
02    S6QTY09F   PIC X.
02    FILLER REDEFINES S6QTY09F.
 03   S6QTY09A   PIC X.
02    FILLER     PIC X(0002).
02    S6QTY09I   PIC X(0008).
02    S6PRC09L   PIC S9(4) COMP.
02    S6PRC09F   PIC X.
02    FILLER REDEFINES S6PRC09F.
```

FIGURE 3.17 *(Continued)*

```
03  S6PRC09A  PIC X.
02  FILLER    PIC X(0002).
02  S6PRC09I  PIC X(0010).
02  S6ITM10L  PIC S9(4) COMP.
02  S6ITM10F  PIC X.
02  FILLER REDEFINES S6ITM10F.
 03  S6ITM10A  PIC X.
02  FILLER    PIC X(0002).
02  S6ITM10I  PIC X(0006).
02  S6QTY10L  PIC S9(4) COMP.
02  S6QTY10F  PIC X.
02  FILLER REDEFINES S6QTY10F.
 03  S6QTY10A  PIC X.
02  FILLER    PIC X(0002).
02  S6QTY10I  PIC X(0008).
02  S6PRC10L  PIC S9(4) COMP.
02  S6PRC10F  PIC X.
02  FILLER REDEFINES S6PRC10F.
 03  S6PRC10A  PIC X.
02  FILLER    PIC X(0002).
02  S6PRC10I  PIC X(0010).
02  S6ITM11L  PIC S9(4) COMP.
02  S6ITM11F  PIC X.
02  FILLER REDEFINES S6ITM11F.
 03  S6ITM11A  PIC X.
02  FILLER    PIC X(0002).
02  S6ITM11I  PIC X(0006).
02  S6QTY11L  PIC S9(4) COMP.
02  S6QTY11F  PIC X.
02  FILLER REDEFINES S6QTY11F.
 03  S6QTY11A  PIC X.
02  FILLER    PIC X(0002).
02  S6QTY11I  PIC X(0008).
02  S6PRC11L  PIC S9(4) COMP.
02  S6PRC11F  PIC X.
02  FILLER REDEFINES S6PRC11F.
 03  S6PRC11A  PIC X.
02  FILLER    PIC X(0002).
02  S6PRC11I  PIC X(0010).
02  S6ITM12L  PIC S9(4) COMP.
02  S6ITM12F  PIC X.
02  FILLER REDEFINES S6ITM12F.
 03  S6ITM12A  PIC X.
02  FILLER    PIC X(0002).
02  S6ITM12I  PIC X(0006).
02  S6QTY12L  PIC S9(4) COMP.
02  S6QTY12F  PIC X.
02  FILLER REDEFINES S6QTY12F.
 03  S6QTY12A  PIC X.
02  FILLER    PIC X(0002).
02  S6QTY12I  PIC X(0008).
02  S6PRC12L  PIC S9(4) COMP.
02  S6PRC12F  PIC X.
02  FILLER REDEFINES S6PRC12F.
 03  S6PRC12A  PIC X.
02  FILLER    PIC X(0002).
02  S6PRC12I  PIC X(0010).
02  S6ITM13L  PIC S9(4) COMP.
02  S6ITM13F  PIC X.
02  FILLER REDEFINES S6ITM13F.
 03  S6ITM13A  PIC X.
02  FILLER    PIC X(0002).
02  S6ITM13I  PIC X(0006).
02  S6QTY13L  PIC S9(4) COMP.
02  S6QTY13F  PIC X.
02  FILLER REDEFINES S6QTY13F.
 03  S6QTY13A  PIC X.
02  FILLER    PIC X(0002).
02  S6QTY13I  PIC X(0008).
02  S6PRC13L  PIC S9(4) COMP.
```

FIGURE 3.17 *(Continued)*

```
02   S6PRC13F   PIC X.
02   FILLER REDEFINES S6PRC13F.
 03  S6PRC13A   PIC X.
02   FILLER     PIC X(0002).
02   S6PRC13I   PIC X(0010).
02   S6ITM14L   PIC S9(4) COMP.
02   S6ITM14F   PIC X.
02   FILLER REDEFINES S6ITM14F.
 03  S6ITM14A   PIC X.
02   FILLER     PIC X(0002).
02   S6ITM14I   PIC X(0006).
02   S6QTY14L   PIC S9(4) COMP.
02   S6QTY14F   PIC X.
02   FILLER REDEFINES S6QTY14F.
 03  S6QTY14A   PIC X.
02   FILLER     PIC X(0002).
02   S6QTY14I   PIC X(0008).
02   S6PRC14L   PIC S9(4) COMP.
02   S6PRC14F   PIC X.
02   FILLER REDEFINES S6PRC14F.
 03  S6PRC14A   PIC X.
02   FILLER     PIC X(0002).
02   S6PRC14I   PIC X(0010).
02   S6ITM15L   PIC S9(4) COMP.
02   S6ITM15F   PIC X.
02   FILLER REDEFINES S6ITM15F.
 03  S6ITM15A   PIC X.
02   FILLER     PIC X(0002).
02   S6ITM15I   PIC X(0006).
02   S6QTY15L   PIC S9(4) COMP.
02   S6QTY15F   PIC X.
02   FILLER REDEFINES S6QTY15F.
 03  S6QTY15A   PIC X.
02   FILLER     PIC X(0002).
02   S6QTY15I   PIC X(0008).
02   S6PRC15L   PIC S9(4) COMP.
02   S6PRC15F   PIC X.
02   FILLER REDEFINES S6PRC15F.
 03  S6PRC15A   PIC X.
02   FILLER     PIC X(0002).
02   S6PRC15I   PIC X(0010).
02   S6ITM16L   PIC S9(4) COMP.
02   S6ITM16F   PIC X.
02   FILLER REDEFINES S6ITM16F.
 03  S6ITM16A   PIC X.
02   FILLER     PIC X(0002).
02   S6ITM16I   PIC X(0006).
02   S6QTY16L   PIC S9(4) COMP.
02   S6QTY16F   PIC X.
02   FILLER REDEFINES S6QTY16F.
 03  S6QTY16A   PIC X.
02   FILLER     PIC X(0002).
02   S6QTY16I   PIC X(0008).
02   S6PRC16L   PIC S9(4) COMP.
02   S6PRC16F   PIC X.
02   FILLER REDEFINES S6PRC16F.
 03  S6PRC16A   PIC X.
02   FILLER     PIC X(0002).
02   S6PRC16I   PIC X(0010).
02   S6MSGL     PIC S9(4) COMP.
02   S6MSGF     PIC X.
02   FILLER REDEFINES S6MSGF.
 03  S6MSGA     PIC X.
02   FILLER     PIC X(0002).
02   S6MSGI     PIC X(0079).
02   S6KEYSL    PIC S9(4) COMP.
02   S6KEYSF    PIC X.
02   FILLER REDEFINES S6KEYSF.
 03  S6KEYSA    PIC X.
02   FILLER     PIC X(0002).
```

FIGURE 3.17 *(Continued)*

```
       02    S6KEYSI   PIC X(0079).
01  SALE0060 REDEFINES SALE006I.
       02    FILLER    PIC X(12).
       02    FILLER    PIC X(3).
       02    S6FWDC    PIC X.
       02    S6FWDH    PIC X.
       02    S6FWDO    PIC X(0008).
       02    FILLER    PIC X(3).
       02    S6BKWC    PIC X.
       02    S6BKWH    PIC X.
       02    S6BKWO    PIC X(0009).
       02    FILLER    PIC X(3).
       02    S6EXITC   PIC X.
       02    S6EXITH   PIC X.
       02    S6EXITO   PIC X(0005).
       02    FILLER    PIC X(3).
       02    S6CANC    PIC X.
       02    S6CANH    PIC X.
       02    S6CANO    PIC X(0007).
       02    FILLER    PIC X(3).
       02    S6PANIDC  PIC X.
       02    S6PANIDH  PIC X.
       02    S6PANIDO  PIC X(0007).
       02    FILLER    PIC X(3).
       02    S6CUSTC   PIC X.
       02    S6CUSTH   PIC X.
       02    S6CUSTO   PIC X(0006).
       02    FILLER    PIC X(3).
       02    S6PLUSC   PIC X.
       02    S6PLUSH   PIC X.
       02    S6PLUSO   PIC X(0001).
       02    FILLER    PIC X(3).
       02    S6MINUSC  PIC X.
       02    S6MINUSH  PIC X.
       02    S6MINUSO  PIC X(0001).
       02    FILLER    PIC X(3).
       02    S6ITM01C  PIC X.
       02    S6ITM01H  PIC X.
       02    S6ITM01O  PIC X(0006).
       02    FILLER    PIC X(3).
       02    S6QTY01C  PIC X.
       02    S6QTY01H  PIC X.
       02    S6QTY01O  PIC ZZZ,ZZ9-.
       02    FILLER    PIC X(3).
       02    S6PRC01C  PIC X.
       02    S6PRC01H  PIC X.
       02    S6PRC01O  PIC $$$,$$$.99.
       02    FILLER    PIC X(3).
       02    S6ITM02C  PIC X.
       02    S6ITM02H  PIC X.
       02    S6ITM02O  PIC X(0006).
       02    FILLER    PIC X(3).
       02    S6QTY02C  PIC X.
       02    S6QTY02H  PIC X.
       02    S6QTY02O  PIC ZZZ,ZZ9-.
       02    FILLER    PIC X(3).
       02    S6PRC02C  PIC X.
       02    S6PRC02H  PIC X.
       02    S6PRC02O  PIC $$$,$$$.99.
       02    FILLER    PIC X(3).
       02    S6ITM03C  PIC X.
       02    S6ITM03H  PIC X.
       02    S6ITM03O  PIC X(0006).
       02    FILLER    PIC X(3).
       02    S6QTY03C  PIC X.
       02    S6QTY03H  PIC X.
       02    S6QTY03O  PIC ZZZ,ZZ9-.
       02    FILLER    PIC X(3).
       02    S6PRC03C  PIC X.
       02    S6PRC03H  PIC X.
```

FIGURE 3.17 *(Continued)*

```
02   S6PRCO30   PIC $$$,$$$.99.
02   FILLER     PIC X(3).
02   S6ITM04C   PIC X.
02   S6ITM04H   PIC X.
02   S6ITM040   PIC X(0006).
02   FILLER     PIC X(3).
02   S6QTY04C   PIC X.
02   S6QTY04H   PIC X.
02   S6QTY040   PIC ZZZ,ZZ9-.
02   FILLER     PIC X(3).
02   S6PRC04C   PIC X.
02   S6PRC04H   PIC X.
02   S6PRC040   PIC $$$,$$$.99.
02   FILLER     PIC X(3).
02   S6ITM05C   PIC X.
02   S6ITM05H   PIC X.
02   S6ITM050   PIC X(0006).
02   FILLER     PIC X(3).
02   S6QTY05C   PIC X.
02   S6QTY05H   PIC X.
02   S6QTY050   PIC ZZZ,ZZ9-.
02   FILLER     PIC X(3).
02   S6PRC05C   PIC X.
02   S6PRC05H   PIC X.
02   S6PRC050   PIC $$$,$$$.99.
02   FILLER     PIC X(3).
02   S6ITM06C   PIC X.
02   S6ITM06H   PIC X.
02   S6ITM060   PIC X(0006).
02   FILLER     PIC X(3).
02   S6QTY06C   PIC X.
02   S6QTY06H   PIC X.
02   S6QTY060   PIC ZZZ,ZZ9-.
02   FILLER     PIC X(3).
02   S6PRC06C   PIC X.
02   S6PRC06H   PIC X.
02   S6PRC060   PIC $$$,$$$.99.
02   FILLER     PIC X(3).
02   S6ITM07C   PIC X.
02   S6ITM07H   PIC X.
02   S6ITM070   PIC X(0006).
02   FILLER     PIC X(3).
02   S6QTY07C   PIC X.
02   S6QTY07H   PIC X.
02   S6QTY070   PIC ZZZ,ZZ9-.
02   FILLER     PIC X(3).
02   S6PRC07C   PIC X.
02   S6PRC07H   PIC X.
02   S6PRC070   PIC $$$,$$$.99.
02   FILLER     PIC X(3).
02   S6ITM08C   PIC X.
02   S6ITM08H   PIC X.
02   S6ITM080   PIC X(0006).
02   FILLER     PIC X(3).
02   S6QTY08C   PIC X.
02   S6QTY08H   PIC X.
02   S6QTY080   PIC ZZZ,ZZ9-.
02   FILLER     PIC X(3).
02   S6PRC08C   PIC X.
02   S6PRC08H   PIC X.
02   S6PRC080   PIC $$$,$$$.99.
02   FILLER     PIC X(3).
02   S6ITM09C   PIC X.
02   S6ITM09H   PIC X.
02   S6ITM090   PIC X(0006).
02   FILLER     PIC X(3).
02   S6QTY09C   PIC X.
02   S6QTY09H   PIC X.
02   S6QTY090   PIC ZZZ,ZZ9-.
02   FILLER     PIC X(3).
```

FIGURE 3.17 *(Continued)*

```
02   S6PRC09C   PIC X.
02   S6PRC09H   PIC X.
02   S6PRC09O   PIC $$$,$$$.99.
02   FILLER     PIC X(3).
02   S6ITM10C   PIC X.
02   S6ITM10H   PIC X.
02   S6ITM10O   PIC X(0006).
02   FILLER     PIC X(3).
02   S6QTY10C   PIC X.
02   S6QTY10H   PIC X.
02   S6QTY10O   PIC ZZZ,ZZ9-.
02   FILLER     PIC X(3).
02   S6PRC10C   PIC X.
02   S6PRC10H   PIC X.
02   S6PRC10O   PIC $$$,$$$.99.
02   FILLER     PIC X(3).
02   S6ITM11C   PIC X.
02   S6ITM11H   PIC X.
02   S6ITM11O   PIC X(0006).
02   FILLER     PIC X(3).
02   S6QTY11C   PIC X.
02   S6QTY11H   PIC X.
02   S6QTY11O   PIC ZZZ,ZZ9-.
02   FILLER     PIC X(3).
02   S6PRC11C   PIC X.
02   S6PRC11H   PIC X.
02   S6PRC11O   PIC $$$,$$$.99.
02   FILLER     PIC X(3).
02   S6ITM12C   PIC X.
02   S6ITM12H   PIC X.
02   S6ITM12O   PIC X(0006).
02   FILLER     PIC X(3).
02   S6QTY12C   PIC X.
02   S6QTY12H   PIC X.
02   S6QTY12O   PIC ZZZ,ZZ9-.
02   FILLER     PIC X(3).
02   S6PRC12C   PIC X.
02   S6PRC12H   PIC X.
02   S6PRC12O   PIC $$$,$$$.99.
02   FILLER     PIC X(3).
02   S6ITM13C   PIC X.
02   S6ITM13H   PIC X.
02   S6ITM13O   PIC X(0006).
02   FILLER     PIC X(3).
02   S6QTY13C   PIC X.
02   S6QTY13H   PIC X.
02   S6QTY13O   PIC ZZZ,ZZ9-.
02   FILLER     PIC X(3).
02   S6PRC13C   PIC X.
02   S6PRC13H   PIC X.
02   S6PRC13O   PIC $$$,$$$.99.
02   FILLER     PIC X(3).
02   S6ITM14C   PIC X.
02   S6ITM14H   PIC X.
02   S6ITM14O   PIC X(0006).
02   FILLER     PIC X(3).
02   S6QTY14C   PIC X.
02   S6QTY14H   PIC X.
02   S6QTY14O   PIC ZZZ,ZZ9-.
02   FILLER     PIC X(3).
02   S6PRC14C   PIC X.
02   S6PRC14H   PIC X.
02   S6PRC14O   PIC $$$,$$$.99.
02   FILLER     PIC X(3).
02   S6ITM15C   PIC X.
02   S6ITM15H   PIC X.
02   S6ITM15O   PIC X(0006).
02   FILLER     PIC X(3).
02   S6QTY15C   PIC X.
02   S6QTY15H   PIC X.
```

FIGURE 3.17 *(Continued)*

```
02    S6QTY15O   PIC ZZZ,ZZ9-.
02    FILLER     PIC X(3).
02    S6PRC15C   PIC X.
02    S6PRC15H   PIC X.
02    S6PRC15O   PIC $$$,$$$.99.
02    FILLER     PIC X(3).
02    S6ITM16C   PIC X.
02    S6ITM16H   PIC X.
02    S6ITM16O   PIC X(0006).
02    FILLER     PIC X(3).
02    S6QTY16C   PIC X.
02    S6QTY16H   PIC X.
02    S6QTY16O   PIC ZZZ,ZZ9-.
02    FILLER     PIC X(3).
02    S6PRC16C   PIC X.
02    S6PRC16H   PIC X.
02    S6PRC16O   PIC $$$,$$$.99.
02    FILLER     PIC X(3).
02    S6MSGC     PIC X.
02    S6MSGH     PIC X.
02    S6MSGO     PIC X(0079).
02    FILLER     PIC X(3).
02    S6KEYSC    PIC X.
02    S6KEYSH    PIC X.
02    S6KEYSO    PIC X(0079).
```

FIGURE 3.17 *(Continued)*

```
*******************************************************************
*   CONTROL BLOCK NAME= DFHBMSCA                                  *
*                                                                *
*   NAME OF MATCHING ASSEMBLER CONTROL BLOCK = NONE              *
*                                                                *
*   DESCRIPTIVE NAME = 3270 ATTRIBUTE VALUES                     *
*                                                                *
*   COPYRIGHT        =              5688-101                     *
*                               COPYRIGHT = NONE                 *
*                                                                *
*   STATUS        RELEASE 1.2                                    *
*                                                                *
*   FUNCTION = Provides the values for 3270 attribute bytes *
*      use by the BMS support in CICS OS/2                       *
*                                                                *
*                                                                *
*******************************************************************
01       DFHBMSCA.
 02      DFHBMPEM   PICTURE X    VALUE IS  X'19'.
 02      DFHBMPNL   PICTURE X    VALUE IS  X'13'.
 02      DFHBMASK   PICTURE X    VALUE IS  '0'.
 02      DFHBMUNP   PICTURE X    VALUE IS  ' '.
 02      DFHBMUNN   PICTURE X    VALUE IS  '&'.
 02      DFHBMPRO   PICTURE X    VALUE IS  '-'.
 02      DFHBMBRY   PICTURE X    VALUE IS  'H'.
 02      DFHBMDAR   PICTURE X    VALUE IS  ''.
 02      DFHBMFSE   PICTURE X    VALUE IS  'A'.
 02      DFHBMPRF   PICTURE X    VALUE IS  '/'.
 02      DFHBMASF   PICTURE X    VALUE IS  '1'.
 02      DFHBMASB   PICTURE X    VALUE IS  '8'.
 02      DFHBMPSO   PICTURE X    VALUE IS  X'1E'.
 02      DFHBMPSI   PICTURE X    VALUE IS  X'1F'.
 02      DFHBMEOF   PICTURE X    VALUE IS  X'80'.
 02      DFHCOLOR   PICTURE X    VALUE IS  X'42'.
 02      DFHPS      PICTURE X    VALUE IS  'C'.
 02      DFHHLT     PICTURE X    VALUE IS  X'41'.
 02      DFH3270    PICTURE X    VALUE IS  X'C0'.
```

FIGURE 3.18 IBM-supplied partial table of attribute byte values and table of attention identifier values.

```
        02   DFHVAL     PICTURE X    VALUE IS 'A'.
        02   DFHOUTLN   PICTURE X    VALUE IS X'C2'.
        02   DFHALL     PICTURE X    VALUE IS X'00'.
        02   DFHDFT     PICTURE X    VALUE IS X'FF'.
        02   DFHDFCOL   PICTURE X    VALUE IS X'00'.
        02   DFHBLUE    PICTURE X    VALUE IS '1'.
        02   DFHRED     PICTURE X    VALUE IS '2'.
        02   DFHPINK    PICTURE X    VALUE IS '3'.
        02   DFHGREEN   PICTURE X    VALUE IS '4'.
        02   DFHTURQ    PICTURE X    VALUE IS '5'.
        02   DFHYELLO   PICTURE X    VALUE IS '6'.
        02   DFHNEUTR   PICTURE X    VALUE IS '7'.
        02   DFHBASE    PICTURE X    VALUE IS X'00'.
        02   DFHDFHI    PICTURE X    VALUE IS X'00'.
        02   DFHBLINK   PICTURE X    VALUE IS '1'.
        02   DFHREVRS   PICTURE X    VALUE IS '2'.
        02   DFHUNDLN   PICTURE X    VALUE IS '4'.
        02   DFHUNNOD   PICTURE X    VALUE IS '('.
        02   DFHUNIMD   PICTURE X    VALUE IS 'I'.
        02   DFHUNNUM   PICTURE X    VALUE IS 'J'.
        02   DFHUNINT   PICTURE X    VALUE IS 'R'.
        02   DFHUNNON   PICTURE X    VALUE IS ')'.
        02   DFHPROTI   PICTURE X    VALUE IS 'Y'.
        02   DFHPROTN   PICTURE X    VALUE IS '%'.
        02   DFHDFFR    PICTURE X    VALUE IS X'00'.
        02   DFHUNDER   PICTURE X    VALUE IS X'01'.
        02   DFHRIGHT   PICTURE X    VALUE IS X'02'.
        02   DFHOVER    PICTURE X    VALUE IS X'04'.
        02   DFHLEFT    PICTURE X    VALUE IS X'08'.
        02   DFHBOX     PICTURE X    VALUE IS X'0F'.
        02   DFHSOSI    PICTURE X    VALUE IS X'01'.
RC0650  02   DFHSA      PICTURE X    VALUE IS X'1F'.
```

FIGURE 3.18   *(Continued)*

```
    01  CICS-ATTRIBUTE-BYTES.
    * UNPROTECTED USER ENTRY FIELDS THAT ARE NOT FSET
        05  ALP-REG-UNM-UNP        PIC X    VALUE SPACE.
        05  ALP-DET-UNM-UNP        PIC X    VALUE 'D'.
        05  ALP-BRT-UNM-UNP        PIC X    VALUE 'H'.
        05  ALP-DRK-UNM-UNP        PIC X    VALUE ' '.
        05  NUM-REG-UNM-UNP        PIC X    VALUE '&'.
        05  NUM-DET-UNM-UNP        PIC X    VALUE 'M'.
        05  NUM-BRT-UNM-UNP        PIC X    VALUE 'Q'.
        05  NUM-DRK-UNM-UNP        PIC X    VALUE '*'.
    * UNPROTECTED USER ENTRY FIELDS THAT ARE FSET (PREMODIFIED)
        05  ALP-REG-MOD-UNP        PIC X    VALUE 'A'.
        05  ALP-DET-MOD-UNP        PIC X    VALUE 'E'.
        05  ALP-BRT-MOD-UNP        PIC X    VALUE 'I'.
        05  ALP-DRK-MOD-UNP        PIC X    VALUE '('.
        05  NUM-REG-MOD-UNP        PIC X    VALUE 'J'.
        05  NUM-DET-MOD-UNP        PIC X    VALUE 'N'.
        05  NUM-BRT-MOD-UNP        PIC X    VALUE 'R'.
        05  NUM-DRK-MOD-UNP        PIC X    VALUE ')'.
    * PROTECTED NUMERIC FIELDS (AUTOSKIP)
        05  NUM-REG-UNM-PRO        PIC X    VALUE '0'.
        05  NUM-DET-UNM-PRO        PIC X    VALUE '4'.
        05  NUM-BRT-UNM-PRO        PIC X    VALUE '8'.
        05  NUM-DRK-UNM-PRO        PIC X    VALUE '@'.
        05  NUM-REG-MOD-PRO        PIC X    VALUE '1'.
```

FIGURE 3.19   Table of attribute byte values.

```
      05  NUM-DET-MOD-PRO          PIC X     VALUE '5'.
      05  NUM-BRT-MOD-PRO          PIC X     VALUE '9'.
      05  NUM-DRK-MOD-PRO          PIC X     VALUE QUOTE.
 *  PROTECTED ALPHA FIELDS (KEYBOARD LOCK)
      05  ALP-REG-UNM-PRO          PIC X     VALUE '-'.
      05  ALP-DET-UNM-PRO          PIC X     VALUE 'U'.
      05  ALP-BRT-UNM-PRO          PIC X     VALUE 'Y'.
      05  ALP-DRK-UNM-PRO          PIC X     VALUE '%'.
      05  ALP-REG-MOD-PRO          PIC X     VALUE '/'.
      05  ALP-DET-MOD-PRO          PIC X     VALUE 'V'.
      05  ALP-BRT-MOD-PRO          PIC X     VALUE 'Z'.
      05  ALP-DRK-MOD-PRO          PIC X     VALUE '_'.
```

FIGURE 3.19 *(Continued)*

If you are using the extended data stream option, then several other suffixed fields will appear here: H suffix for highlighting, P suffix for the programmed symbol set to be used, V suffix for type of validation processing to be used, and C for color. If you place values in these fields other than hex nulls, those fields will appear in the data stream being sent to the terminal. Meaningful values for these fields are present in the IBM-supplied copy library member, DFHBMSCA.

DFHBMSCA contains various settings that can be used for regular attribute field values as well. However, it does not contain every possible combination. If you find that you need some other attribute value, the COBOL area in Figure 3.18 contains all possible settings. You can place it in a copy library member and include it in your programs. Alternatively, you can specify the EBCDIC characters that you need directly in your program by using display literals, for example:

```
MOVE "I' TO SOCUSTA.
```

TEST YOUR UNDERSTANDING

Questions and Exercises

1. Describe the steps that you would go through if you were asked design terminal screens for a new online application.

2. Describe the purpose of the DFHMSD, DFHMDI, and DFHMDF macros.

3. How does FRSET affect modified data tags? How does FSET affect modified data tags? In which macros may these parameters be specified?

4. What data is transmitted from fields that contain low-values or hex nulls?

5. How do you specify a DFHMDF field length? How do you specify a DFHMDF field position?

6. What is the difference between a symbolic map (TYPE=DSECT) and a physical map (TYPE=MAP)? Where is each stored, and what does each contain?

7. Describe a way to change the cursor position on a map being sent to a terminal user.

8. Code a small map called STUBMAP. Assume it is to be used for testing purposes. Place the following fields on it (the first field must be in the upper left corner, and the other fields may be wherever you choose, as long as they are in order):

Field name:	Contents:
STUBTRN	Must be FSET to allow it to be read by the mainframe at all times. Initial value should be STUB. Do not allow user input.
Unlabeled field	Initial value should be "SAMPLE MAP FOR TESTING CICS PROGRAMS".
Unlabeled field	Initial value should be "50 CHARS. ALPHA INPUT:"
STUBF1	Field should be 50 bytes. Allow user input. Initial cursor position should be at the beginning of this field. Follow with a skip byte.
Unlabeled field	Initial value should be, "7 DIGITS NUMERIC INPUT:"
STUBF2	Field should be numeric, 7 bytes, followed by a skip byte.
Unlabeled field	Initial value should be, "DATA RECEIVED WAS:"
STUBF3	Field should be 50 bytes, autoskip.
STUBF4	Field should be 7 bytes, autoskip.

9. Suppose, for security reasons, you do not want to allow the terminal user to see the transaction codes on the maps. How could STUBMAP be changed to keep the user from seeing the transaction code in the upper left corner?

4

Programming Techniques for Terminal I/O Operations

In this chapter, we will begin showing you some very simple CICS programs that contain I/O commands for sending data to terminals and for receiving data from terminals. We will discuss the terminal I/O commands themselves and other CICS commands and data structures that play a role in the programs. We will show you what to do in order to make sure that the I/O took place successfully. Finally, we will show you how to interpret the data that your program receives from a terminal.

Throughout the chapter, we will examine the issue of which CICS options to use when the same things can be accomplished several ways. Some programmers are tempted to use difficult coding tricks, not because any optimization is actually needed, but because they want to show how well they know CICS. Even if you learn how to exercise every feature of CICS, that does not guarantee that you will be able to write a good CICS application. A good CICS application is likely to use only a small subset of the features that CICS offers. This is because elegant design, simplicity, and brevity usually provide more efficiency advantages than do difficult coding maneuvers. We will discuss which situations might require which techniques.

4.1 SIMPLE TERMINAL I/O WITHOUT USING MAPS

4.1.1 The SEND Command

In the last chapter, we mentioned that it is possible to do terminal I/O without using maps. You may recall that we suggested that maps be used whenever possible, unless the messages are very simple and brief, because maps make it so much easier to guide the user in the correct entry of data. Terminal I/O that does not involve maps may be useful for testing purposes or for writing a few message lines to a printer. Figure 4.1 is a program stub written for testing purposes that simply echoes the message it received, plus an additional message. To run STUBPGM, a PCT entry must be created for the transaction STUB, referring to the program STUBPGM. In a mainframe environment (but not under OS/2), a PPT entry

```
IDENTIFICATION DIVISION.
PROGRAM-ID. STUBPGM.
AUTHOR. ALIDA M. JATICH AND PHIL NOWAK.
*********************************************************************
* STUBPGM RECEIVES A MESSAGE FROM THE USER'S TERMINAL. IF THE      *
* USER ENTERED TOO MUCH DATA, MAKING THE MESSAGE LONGER THAN       *
* EXPECTED, STUBPGM WILL SEND AN ERROR MESSAGE BACK TO THE         *
* USER'S TERMINAL. OTHERWISE, STUBPGM WILL ECHO THE USER'S         *
* ORIGINAL MESSAGE BACK TO THE TERMINAL.                           *
*********************************************************************
ENVIRONMENT DIVISION.
DATA DIVISION.
WORKING-STORAGE SECTION.
77  EXPECTED-MESSAGE-LENGTH      PIC S9(4) COMP VALUE +24.
01  INPUT-MESSAGE-FIELD.
    05  TRAN-CODE                PIC XXXX        VALUE SPACES.
    05  INPUT-MESSAGE-VAR        PIC X(20)       VALUE SPACES.
01  OUTPUT-MESSAGE-FIELD.
    05  FILLER                   PIC X(34)       VALUE
' MESSAGE RECEIVED BY STUBPGM WAS: '.
    05  OUTPUT-MESSAGE-VAR       PIC X(20)       VALUE SPACES.
01  BAD-NEWS.
    05  FILLER                   PIC X(36)       VALUE
' STUBPGM TERMINAL INPUT WAS TOO LONG'.
01  CICS-RESPONSE1               PIC S9(8) COMP VALUE +0.
PROCEDURE DIVISION.
MAIN-PROG.
    EXEC CICS RECEIVE
              INTO (INPUT-MESSAGE-FIELD)
              RESP (CICS-RESPONSE1)
              LENGTH (EXPECTED-MESSAGE-LENGTH)
              END-EXEC.
    IF CICS-RESPONSE1 = DFHRESP(LENGERR)
        EXEC CICS SEND
                  FROM (BAD-NEWS)
                  END-EXEC
    ELSE
        MOVE INPUT-MESSAGE-VAR TO OUTPUT-MESSAGE-VAR
        EXEC CICS SEND
                  FROM (OUTPUT-MESSAGE-FIELD)
                  END-EXEC
    END-IF.
    EXEC CICS RETURN
              END-EXEC.
    GOBACK.
```

FIGURE 4.1 STUBPGM source code.

must be created for the program STUBPGM. STUBPGM uses the SEND, RECEIVE, and RETURN commands. We will concern ourselves first with the SEND command, which is quite simple:

```
EXEC CICS SEND
FROM (data-area)
LENGTH (data-value)
ERASE
END-EXEC.
```

To code the SEND command, you simply place the name of the field containing your message in parentheses following FROM, and you place the length in bytes of the field in parentheses following LENGTH. You can use a numeric literal for the field length, or you can use a COBOL COMP data item. In many commands, the LENGTH can be omitted if you are using VS COBOL II.

There are some minor differences in coding CICS commands if you have a VS COBOL II compiler at your site. The use of this compiler is recommended because it offers ANSI-standard features that makes writing structured programs easier. VS COBOL II Version 3.0 supports the full 1985 ANSI COBOL standard. Under MVS/XA or MVS/ESA, VS COBOL II automatically makes use of 31-bit extended addressing mode, which allows access to virtual storage above the 16-megabyte line. VS COBOL II interfaces with CICS command-level in a more convenient manner. Upgrading to the new compiler will eventually become necessary as support for older compilers is withdrawn. Only command-level CICS, not macro-level CICS, may be used in programs being compiled under VS COBOL II. If a VS COBOL II compiler is available in your installation, there are many advantages to using it, both in terms of CICS and in terms of structured programming. Find out what is available to you. For example, if you are using the Micro Focus COBOL compiler under OS/2, then you can use compiler directives to make the compiler compatible with VS COBOL II. (You also need to use the COBOL2 directive for the translator step.)

How does this affect the SEND and RECEIVE commands? VS COBOL II has a LENGTH special register which automatically supplies the length of your working-storage or linkage section data area for CICS commands that refer to a data area in a FROM or INTO parameter. Under VS COBOL II, then, you can often omit the LENGTH parameter from CICS commands, unless you want to send or receive data of a length different from that of your working storage or linkage section data area.

What happens when the SEND command is executed? The CICS system will build a data stream from your message, and will send it to the terminal. How does CICS "know" which terminal should get the message? If a particular terminal began by requesting a task, CICS considers the terminal to be "attached" to that task. CICS will send all of the task's messages to that same terminal, unless told otherwise. Where on the user's terminal screen will the message appear? The message will appear on the screen starting at the current cursor location, unless the ERASE option was specified. In that case, the screen will be cleared and the cursor returned to the upper left corner. See Figure 4.2. Incidentally, it is possible to insert native-mode 3270 data stream bit patterns into the message being sent to the terminal, if you feel like doing your work the hard way. Under ordinary circumstances, this is not recommended. See Figure 4.1.

4.1.2   The RECEIVE Command

The RECEIVE command has a few more options:

```
EXEC CICS RECEIVE
{INTO (data-area)|SET (pointer-ref)}
LENGTH (data-area)
[MAXLENGTH (data-value)]
[NOTRUNCATE]
END-EXEC.
```

On its first execution within a task, the RECEIVE command takes data that the CICS terminal control program has *already* received from the terminal device and makes this data available to your program. Remember

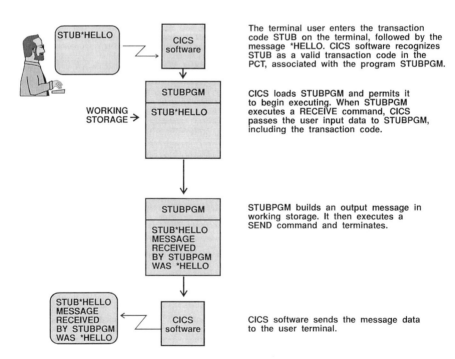

The terminal user enters the transaction code STUB on the terminal, followed by the message *HELLO. CICS software recognizes STUB as a valid transaction code in the PCT, associated with the program STUBPGM.

CICS loads STUBPGM and permits it to begin executing. When STUBPGM executes a RECEIVE command, CICS passes the user input data to STUBPGM, including the transaction code.

STUBPGM builds an output message in working storage. It then executes a SEND command and terminates.

CICS software sends the message data to the user terminal.

FIGURE 4.2   How STUBPGM works.

that, under CICS, terminal control is active at all times, so that CICS can pick up messages intended for later use by your program even before your program is loaded. If the first part of the data is a four-character transaction code that was used to start the transaction, this transaction code will be made available to your program also. If any task executes the RECEIVE command more than once, CICS will determine whether additional data has arrived from the terminal and will pass along whatever data it finds to your task. If there is none, your task will wait.

In Figure 4.1, we have chosen to read the terminal message into a *working storage field*. We have used the INTO (data-area) option to provide the name of the working storage field into which we wanted the data to go. Our other choice would have been to read the message into a *linkage section field* with a BLL pointer (base locator for linkage). This is done by using the SET (pointer-ref) option to specify the BLL pointer associated with the linkage section field, as shown in the next section.

In this example, the LENGTH (data-area) option serves two purposes. We use it to tell CICS how long a message we were prepared to receive. CICS uses the LENGTH parameter field to pass back to the program the actual length of message data received. Remember that, in our example, we are receiving the data into a fixed-length working storage field. When CICS receives the data from the user, it checks the length of the data against the LENGTH parameter you specify. If the data is too long, CICS tells your program that the LENGERR condition has been invoked. Otherwise, CICS will place the actual length of the received data into the LENGTH parameter field.

4.1.3 Setting Up Your Error-Handler Routine

Whenever you use a CICS command in your program, you should think about what you want the program to do if the command fails to deliver the expected results. There may be many possible exceptional conditions, and you might not want to handle all of them in the same way.

Suppose incorrect data is received by your program, and the LENGERR condition is raised. What happens then? How does your program know that there is a problem? Notice the RESP option in the RECEIVE command in STUBPGM. RESP is an option that can be placed in any CICS command to set up a **response code field**. Your program can then test the value which CICS places in the response code field by comparing it to DFHRESP(NORMAL), DFHRESP(LENGERR), or other CICS-supplied response values. The CICS translator automatically substitutes the proper numeric comparison values for DFHRESP(condition-name). RESP2 is a second, optional field that can also be added, to provide further detail in some cases. Note that DFHRESP(condition-name) works only with RESP, not with RESP2.

A full-word binary data area must be supplied with RESP and RESP2. After the CICS command is executed, you can test the RESP field by coding statements such as these:

```
IF your-resp-field = DFHRESP (NORMAL)
    PERFORM NORMAL-ROUTINE
ELSE
    IF your-resp-field = DFHRESP(ENDFILE)
        PERFORM ENDFILE-ROUTINE
    ELSE
        PERFORM ERROR-ROUTINE.
```

As we will see later, using RESP means that you must test the EIBAID field directly after using a RECEIVE MAP command, for example.

Remember that RESP and RESP2 can be added to any CICS command. When this book lists the parameters available with each CICS command, RESP and RESP2 will be omitted in order to save space in the text.

4.1.4 HANDLE CONDITION Command

In versions of CICS prior to 1.7, RESP did not exist. Instead, the HANDLE CONDITION command was used. If STUBPGM had been written prior to release 1.7, the first statement in the procedure division of STUBPGM would have been a HANDLE CONDITION command, as follows:

```
EXEC CICS HANDLE CONDITION
          LENGERR (LENGTH-ERR-ROUTINE)
          END-EXEC.
```

HANDLE CONDITION tells your program that you want to branch to a specified error-handler routine if an error condition is raised later in the program. Notice that the HANDLE CONDITION does not cause anything at all to be executed *unless the error condition is actually invoked later.* The HANDLE CONDITION routines insert an implied "GO TO" statement into your program, which is undesirable because it makes it harder to write a structured CICS program. CICS now allows you to specify the RESP and RESP2 options in your CICS commands as a substitute for a separate HANDLE CONDITION command. HANDLE is obsolete; don't use it if RESP and RESP2 are available on your system. **Be aware that, under CICS OS/2 1.20, HANDLE CONDITION and similar HANDLE commands are supported only in the COBOL language, not in C.**
It is important to realize that the RESP and RESP2 options turn off both HANDLE CONDITION and HANDLE AID actions. (Coding the NOHAN-DLE parameter in a command would turn off these actions too.)

4.1.5   Terminating the Task

Notice the RETURN command in STUBPGM. The RETURN command terminates program execution, terminates the task, and returns control to CICS. That means, in this instance, that the CICS terminal control program will be waiting for the terminal user to enter another transaction request code on the terminal. To avoid compiler diagnostics, it's customary to put a GOBACK statement into CICS programs, but the GOBACK is placed after the RETURN command so that it will never be executed. We will discuss program and task termination in more detail in Chapter 5.

4.1.6   Data Structures: Which Options Should You Choose?

Many CICS commands offer us the choice of whether to define a working storage field or to use areas defined in the linkage section. Using the linkage section complicates program coding, but may cause system resources to be used slightly more efficiently, because data need not be moved into the program's working storage before it can be accessed. If a linkage section address pointer is used, then the data can be accessed without first being moved. However, it takes a little more programming effort.

Why did we choose to use a working storage field, rather than a linkage section field, in Figure 4.1? Observe that the example uses a very small amount of system resources. This leaves no significant room for improvement. Adding more lines of code would cause efficiency losses that would cancel any gains obtained by organizing the storage usage differently. **It makes sense to try to make a program more efficient only when the program consumes a large amount of system resources.** For that to be the case, the module must be executed often and each execution must produce a noticeable impact upon the system. This is true of only a minority of program modules. Perhaps 20% of your site's program code results in 80% of the total resource expenditure. If you are in a position to make decisions concerning these issues, common sense should be your guide.

4.1.7   An Optional Topic: Terminal I/O Using the Linkage Section

Sometimes we will want to increase program efficiency by using the linkage section to work with data. For example, it may make sense to use linkage section address pointers for I/O processing when the record size or device buffer size is extremely large. It also may make sense to use address pointers if the pointer values themselves will be passed to another module so that the other module can use the pointers to find the required data. (Be aware of the fact that main storage requested by your programs, and certain other system resources, are freed or deallocated at end of task.) Finally, your installation may impose standards that involve use of linkage section address pointers under certain circumstances.

How could we have set up the sample program to receive its message into a linkage section field? The exact methods we will use depend on whether or not we are using VS COBOL II. However, in either case, we use the SET option on the RECEIVE command, in place of the INTO option. For example:

```
EXEC CICS RECEIVE
        SET (address-pointer)
        LENGTH (ACTUAL-MESSAGE-LENGTH)
        END-EXEC.
```

Use of linkage section when NOT under VS COBOL II.   If you are not using VS COBOL II, then you must define a BLL cell group in the linkage section, immediately after the DFHCOMMAREA field. (The DFHCOMMAREA field is a communications field that CICS provides for you. We will use it in the next chapter.) A BLL cell group is specified as a COBOL 01-level group item, and each BLL cell within the group is a PIC S9(8) COMP elementary field. The first BLL cell is a "dummy" that is used by the system to point to the other cells. Each subsequent BLL cell in the group is used by the system to point to another COBOL 01-level group item in the linkage section. Here is what a typical linkage section would look like:

```
LINKAGE SECTION
01  DFHCOMMAREA          PIC X.
01  BLL-CELLS.
        02  DUMMY-BLL    PIC S9(8) COMP.
        02  INPUT-BLL    PIC S9(8) COMP.
        02  OUTPUT-BLL   PIC S9(8) COMP.
01  INPUT-LINKAGE-AREA.
        (etc.)
01  OUTPUT-LINKAGE-AREA.
        (etc.)
```

How does the system know which BLL cell points to which group item? Each appears in consecutive order, omitting the dummy BLL cell. The first BLL cell after the dummy cell points to the first 01-level group item; the next BLL cell points to the second 01-level group item, and so forth. (The only exception to this scheme occurs when an 01-level group item is longer than 4,096 bytes; in that instance, it will require an extra BLL cell for each multiple of 4,096 bytes.)

The optimizing feature of compilers such as the OS Full ANSI COBOL Version 4 compiler or the OS/VS COBOL compiler requires you to insert a SERVICE RELOAD statement in the program every time a BLL pointer value has been changed. This statement directs the compiler to insert code to establish addressability. Any CICS command that uses the SET (pointer-ref) option will change a BLL cell value. A SERVICE RELOAD statement is needed at every point to which the program can branch after the CICS command with the SET option has been executed. This means that if you set up a HANDLE CONDITION, you should place a SERVICE RELOAD statement at the beginning of each error handler routine. In this instance, the first part of the procedure division would look like this:

```
PROCEDURE DIVISION.
SERVICE RELOAD BLL-CELLS.
.   .   .   .   (etc.)
EXEC CICS RECEIVE
         SET (INPUT-BLL)
         LENGTH (ACTUAL-MESSAGE-LENGTH)
         END-EXEC.
SERVICE RELOAD INPUT-LINKAGE-AREA.
.  .  .  .  .  (etc.)
```

Use of linkage section under VS COBOL II. Command-level CICS when used with the VS COBOL II compiler provides some features which automatically determine the address and length of storage areas referenced in CICS commands. Earlier versions of COBOL required the programmer to set up a BLL cell in the linkage section for every 01-level storage area defined in the linkage section, except for the DFHCOMMAREA. **Under VS COBOL II, it is no longer necessary to provide BLL cells when using the linkage section; it is only necessary to code the 01 levels which will actually hold your data.** All CICS commands that contain the SET option may reference the data area directly. For example, if the 01 level is called YOUR-STORAGE-AREA, instead of using:

```
SET (bll-cell-name)
```

you may specify the following:

```
SET (ADDRESS OF YOUR-STORAGE-AREA).
```

Note that the phrase "ADDRESS OF" is a COBOL reserved word which refers to a special register. This phrase can be used in COBOL SET statements as well as in the SET option in CICS commands. This allows you to save and restore address values. For instance, you can specify:

```
SET SAVE-POINTER TO ADDRESS OF YOUR-STORAGE-AREA.
```

which will put the virtual storage address of YOUR- STORAGE-AREA into SAVE-POINTER. Note that SAVE-POINTER must be a field defined with the clause, USAGE IS POINTER. You can restore the value by specifying:

```
SET ADDRESS OF ANY-STORAGE-AREA TO SAVE-POINTER.
```

It is not necessary to code SERVICE RELOAD instructions when an address value is updated. In fact, SERVICE RELOAD statements are prohibited under VS COBOL II.

If SAVE-POINTER is a field defined with the clause, USAGE IS POINTER, then SAVE-POINTER can be used directly in the SET clause of a CICS command. These two groups of statements provide the same result:

Option 1:

```
EXEC CICS READ
      DATASET ("ddname")
      SET (ADDRESS OF YOUR-STORAGE-AREA)
      LENGTH (length-field)
      END-EXEC.
SET SAVE-POINTER TO ADDRESS OF YOUR-STORAGE-AREA.
```

Option 2:

```
EXEC CICS READ
      DATASET ("ddname")
      SET (SAVE-POINTER)
      LENGTH (length-field)
      END-EXEC.
SET ADDRESS OF YOUR-STORAGE-AREA TO SAVE-POINTER.
```

One additional advantage to VS COBOL II: when you move data between areas containing OCCURS DEPENDING ON statements, you no longer need to move the occurrence counter field to itself in order to insure correct data length and addressability.

Old programs that already contain BLL cell definitions in the linkage section can be left as is, if SERVICE RELOAD statements are removed.

Received Data Length.   Notice the RECEIVE command in Figure 4.3. The LENGTH parameter works differently in programs that use the SET (pointer-ref) option that we just discussed. Using the SET option causes CICS to set a linkage section BLL pointer to the beginning of the received data. In that case, CICS does not use the current contents of the LENGTH parameter field to restrict the length of the received data. This means that your program must examine the LENGTH parameter field to find out how much data has been received. If you want to place a limit on how much data you want the program to process at one time, then you use the MAXLENGTH parameter. If the received data is longer than the MAX-LENGTH field, then CICS will truncate the data to the appropriate length and will signal your program that the LENGERR condition has been invoked, The MAXLENGTH option was introduced with CICS 1.6.

```
IDENTIFICATION DIVISION.
PROGRAM-ID. STUBPG2.
AUTHOR. ALIDA M. JATICH AND PHIL NOWAK.
********************************************************************
* STUBPG2 RECEIVES A MESSAGE FROM THE USER'S TERMINAL. IF THE     *
* USER ENTERED TOO MUCH DATA, MAKING THE MESSAGE LONGER THAN      *
* EXPECTED, STUBPG2 WILL SEND AN ERROR MESSAGE BACK TO THE        *
* USER'S TERMINAL. OTHERWISE, STUBPG2 WILL ECHO THE USER'S        *
* ORIGINAL MESSAGE BACK TO THE TERMINAL.                          *
*                                                                 *
* STUBPG2 PERFORMS THE SAME FUNCTIONS AS DOES STUBPGM.            *
* HOWEVER, INSTEAD OF USING WORKING STORAGE I/O AREAS,            *
* STUBPG2 USES I/O AREAS IN THE LINKAGE SECTION.                  *
*                                                                 *
* THIS IS THE VS COBOL II VERSION. IT USES THE SET (POINTER)      *
* OPTION RATHER THAN THE BLL CELLS AND SERVICE RELOADS USED IN    *
* OLDER VERSIONS OF COBOL.                                        *
********************************************************************
ENVIRONMENT DIVISION.
DATA DIVISION.
WORKING-STORAGE SECTION.
77  INPUT-MESSAGE-LENGTH        PIC S9(4) COMP VALUE +0.
77  OUTPUT-MESSAGE-LENGTH       PIC S9(4) COMP VALUE +0.
77  BLANK-BYTE                  PIC X          VALUE SPACES.
77  INPUT-POINTER               USAGE IS POINTER.
77  OUTPUT-POINTER              USAGE IS POINTER.
01  OUTPUT-MESSAGE-CONSTANT.
    05  FILLER                  PIC X(34)      VALUE
    ' MESSAGE RECEIVED BY STUBPG2 WAS: '.
01  BAD-NEWS.
    05  FILLER                  PIC X(36)      VALUE
    ' STUBPG2 TERMINAL INPUT WAS TOO LONG'.
LINKAGE SECTION.
01  DFHCOMMAREA.
    05  FILLER                  PIC X.
01  INPUT-MESSAGE-FIELD.
    05  TRAN-CODE               PIC XXXX.
    05  INPUT-MESSAGE-VAR       PIC X(20).
01  OUTPUT-MESSAGE-FIELD.
    05  OUTPUT-MESSAGE-VAR1     PIC X(34).
    05  OUTPUT-MESSAGE-VAR2     PIC X(24).
PROCEDURE DIVISION.
MAIN-PROG.
********************************************************************
* THIS RECEIVE MAP INSTRUCTION SETS A POINTER CALLED INPUT-       *
* POINTER. THIS WILL POINT TO THE MEMORY LOCATION CONTAINING      *
* THE ACTUAL TERMINAL INPUT MESSAGE. THE SET ADDRESS             *
* INSTRUCTION ASSOCIATES THE FIELD DEFINITION IN THE LINKAGE      *
* SECTION WITH THE POINTER.                                       *
*                                                                 *
* NOTICE THAT THE LENGTH FIELD DOES NOT ACT AS A LIMIT ON THE     *
* INPUT MESSAGE LENGTH. INSTEAD, IT ACTS AS A MEANS FOR PASSING   *
* THE ACTUAL MESSAGE LENGTH BACK TO STUBPG2.                      *
********************************************************************
        EXEC CICS RECEIVE
                  SET (INPUT-POINTER)
                  LENGTH (INPUT-MESSAGE-LENGTH)
                  END-EXEC.
        IF INPUT-MESSAGE-LENGTH   24
            EXEC CICS SEND
                      FROM (BAD-NEWS)
                      LENGTH (36)
                      END-EXEC
            EXEC CICS RETURN
                      END-EXEC.
*
        SET ADDRESS OF INPUT-MESSAGE-FIELD TO INPUT-POINTER.
********************************************************************
* STUBPG2 OBTAINS A LINKAGE SECTION OUTPUT AREA LONG ENOUGH TO    *
* HOLD THE MAXIMUM LENGTH OUTPUT MESSAGE.                         *
```

FIGURE 4.3 STUBPG2 source code.

```
*******************************************************************
     EXEC CICS GETMAIN
               SET (OUTPUT-POINTER)
               LENGTH (58)
               INITIMG (BLANK-BYTE)
               END-EXEC.
     SET ADDRESS OF OUTPUT-MESSAGE-FIELD TO OUTPUT-POINTER.
     MOVE OUTPUT-MESSAGE-CONSTANT TO OUTPUT-MESSAGE-VAR1.
     MOVE INPUT-MESSAGE-VAR TO OUTPUT-MESSAGE-VAR2.
     COMPUTE OUTPUT-MESSAGE-LENGTH = INPUT-MESSAGE-LENGTH + 30.
     EXEC CICS SEND
               FROM (OUTPUT-MESSAGE-FIELD)
               LENGTH (OUTPUT-MESSAGE-LENGTH)
               END-EXEC
   *
     EXEC CICS RETURN
               END-EXEC.
        GOBACK.
```

FIGURE 4.3   *(Continued)*

The NOTRUNCATE option changes the way in which excessively long data input is handled. If NOTRUNCATE is specified, then the overflow portion of the data is saved by CICS so that your program can obtain it by issuing more RECEIVE commands. The NOTRUNCATE option was also introduced with CICS 1.6.

As mentioned above, VS COBOL II provides a LENGTH special register which holds the actual data lengths of storage areas referenced in CICS commands. In general, you can omit the LENGTH, FROMLENGTH, MAX-LENGTH, and other similar options from CICS commands that use them. There are some exceptions: you provide the LENGTH parameter when you want CICS to tell you what is the actual received length of a data item. You also need to use the LENGTH option when you work with data of a length different from the length of the 01-level storage area. For instance, if you want to write only a small portion of a record, or if you are adding or deleting table entries from within a variable-length record that contains an OCCURS DEPENDING ON option, you will need to specify the LENGTH option.

Obtaining More Storage in the Linkage Section.   As   STUBPGM   and STUBPG2 demonstrate, you also have the choice of whether or not to write a program so that it will send its message from a linkage section area. Obtaining storage areas in the linkage section saves resources only when the program is capable of using a large piece of storage, but when it will only need this storage occasionally or for short periods of time. If you know that your program will always need a work area or an output area, then you may as well define that area within working storage. For purposes of illustration, however, we demonstrate this technique here.

To obtain a linkage section work area in order to build output data, you must first use a GETMAIN command. Here is the syntax of this command:

```
EXEC CICS GETMAIN
        SET (pointer-ref)
        (LENGTH(data-value)|FLENGTH(data-value))
        (INITIMG(data-value)
        END-EXEC.
```

To use this command, you must have a linkage section work area specified, and a corresponding BLL cell if you are not under VS COBOL II. The LENGTH parameter should match the length of the linkage section work area that you are using. (If you are using CICS 1.6 or later on a large-scale mainframe system that supports extended addressing (XA), you may substitute the FLENGTH parameter for the LENGTH parameter if you wish to be able to allocate space from above the 16-megabyte line.) The INITIMG parameter refers to the initialization character that should be spread through the newly allocated work area. The (data-value) argument must be a one-byte COBOL field containing zero, space, low-values, or whatever else you wish to spread through the work area.

When your task terminates, all of the main storage will be freed by the CICS storage control program. If your program executes a RETURN command immediately after it is finished using the storage, you do not need to do anything else to free the storage. However, if your program does other processing, links to another program, or for any reason does not execute a RETURN command when it no longer needs the storage, you should use a FREEMAIN command to free the linkage section storage that you acquired by using the GETMAIN. Here is the command:

```
EXEC CICS FREEMAIN
        DATA(data-area)
        END-EXEC.
```

When using FREEMAIN, specify the name of the linkage section data area itself, not the name of the address variable or BLL pointer. The FREEMAIN command differs from the GETMAIN command in this regard. **Do not try to FREEMAIN a piece of data that does not belong to your program. Never FREEMAIN an area that was never successfully acquired in the first place or an area that has already been FREEMAINed. This can cause storage violations or other errors.**

4.2 USING MAP I/O COMMANDS

4.2.1 SEND MAP Command Format

Commands to send and receive BMS maps are similar to the terminal control SEND and RECEIVE commands that we just discussed. We will show some options available under minimum function basic mapping support (BMS).

Here is the syntax for the SEND MAP command:

```
EXEC CICS SEND MAP(name)
       [MAPSET(name)]
       [DATAONLY|MAPONLY]
       [FROM(data-area)
       LENGTH(data-value)]
       [CURSOR]
       [ERASE|ERASEAUP]
       [FREEKB]
       [FRSET]
       [ALARM]
       [other device control options]
       END-EXEC.
```

How the SEND MAP Command Works.   Let's look at what is happening when a program sends a map to a terminal. Remember that some of the data that will be sent is stored in the physical map, which CICS obtains from the core image or load library at execution time. The data from the physical map is *default data:* captions, headers, original cursor position, initial values of attribute bytes, and so forth. The rest of the data that will be sent comes from your program. Your program will use the symbolic map copy member as a guide for organizing its override data before the map is sent. The data contributed by your program can override some of the default data coming from the physical map, such as the cursor position, field data, and attribute values. (Your program can affect only those named fields that actually appear in the symbolic map.)

Suppose you want to send a map to the terminal with no changes at all to the data coming from the physical map. To do this, you need to tell the CICS system to send a command to clear the user's terminal screen, and then to send the map to the terminal, using the physical map information only, with no data coming from the program. **Specifying MAPONLY in the SEND MAP command indicates that only the physical map contents will be sent.** In most applications, the first map sent to the terminal user will be a menu. It often makes sense to send the menu with the MAPONLY and ERASE options, since your program typically will not need to insert any variable data into the menu. ERASE clears old data from the terminal screen. Always send a map using ERASE if the terminal screen might possibly contain some other data from an old message or map. If this is not done, part of the old data will remain visible between the new fields that you sent. Figure 4.4 shows the use of MAPONLY and ERASE.

Now suppose that you want to send a different map to the screen, such as a file inquiry screen. You want the screen to show constant information such as headers, but you also want your program to insert some file look up information into the data fields. To do this, you need to tell the CICS system to send a command to clear the user's terminal screen and to send the map to the terminal, using data both from the physical map and from

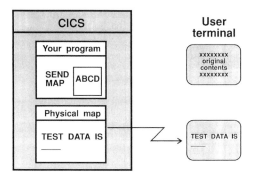

```
EXEC CICS SEND MAP (mapname)
         MAPSET (mapsetname)
         MAPONLY
         ERASE
         END-EXEC.
```

With **MAPONLY**, information sent to
user terminal consists only of default
information from physical map.

FIGURE 4.4   SEND MAP options: MAPONLY (physical map).

your program. **Omitting MAPONLY and DATAONLY in the SEND MAP command causes data to be sent from both the physical map and the symbolic map.** Another parameter is needed in the SEND MAP command: FROM(data-area). As shown in Figure 4.5, FROM(data-area) tells CICS where to find the symbolic map data from your program that should be merged with the data from the physical map.

Merging of map and program data is done on a field-by-field basis. In other words, CICS looks at your symbolic map work area one field at a time. If any of the symbolic map fields are filled with hexadecimal zeros (low-values), CICS will insert the value from the physical map, or if no default value is specified, CICS will allow the existing value to remain in the field at the user's terminal. This means that you can change the attribute byte of a field without changing the field data itself, and vice versa. Since the attribute becomes a separate field in your symbolic map work area, you can move hexadecimal zeros to it if you do not wish to change it at the same time that you are changing your field data.

Suppose all of the constant data from the physical map has been sent to the user's terminal screen already. There is no need to waste transmission time by sending it again. Suppose you want to change a few attribute bytes, or the contents of a few fields on the screen, without disturbing anything else. To do this, you must tell CICS to send some data from your symbolic map work area, without erasing the screen and without sending any data from the physical map. **Specifying FROM(data-area) and**

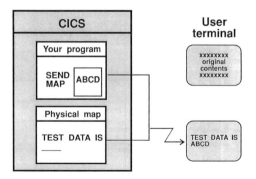

```
EXEC CICS SEND MAP (mapname)
          MAPSET (mapsetname)
          FROM (area)
          ERASE
          END-EXEC.
```

Information sent to user terminal is a
combination of physical map contents and
symbolic map contents.

FIGURE 4.5   SEND MAP options: merging map data with program data.

**DATAONLY in the SEND MAP command causes only the data from the
symbolic map to be sent to the terminal.** This is shown in Figure 4.6.

**Never use ERASE with DATAONLY. Never use DATAONLY to send a
map to a terminal unless the same map has already been sent to that
terminal by a previous command.** If you send a map using DATAONLY to
a terminal screen that is not already displaying your map, then the screen
contents will look like garbage. Why is this so? Using DATAONLY causes
BMS to assume that all necessary control information has already been
sent to the terminal device, and therefore that no more control information
need be sent. If this control information has in fact been wiped out, then
the terminal will receive some data but will not have the information it
needs to display it properly.

If you have FSET (modified) attributes on fields in your physical map,
the modified data tags will NOT be turned on when you send your map
with the DATAONLY option. Why is this? DATAONLY causes your physical map default data to be ignored. To turn these modified data tags on,
your program must place modified attribute values in each of the attribute
fields in your symbolic map before sending the map.

If you have any invalid or "garbage" data anywhere in your symbolic
map work area, then the use of the SEND MAP instruction will bring about
unpredictable results. The most unusual results come from bad data in the
first 12 bytes of the symbolic map work area. (This is the area that is

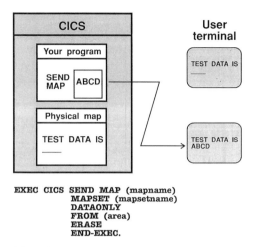

```
EXEC CICS SEND MAP (mapname)
          MAPSET (mapsetname)
          DATAONLY
          FROM (area)
          ERASE
          END-EXEC.
```

Information sent to user terminal
consists only of information placed
by your program in the symbolic map
work area.

DATAONLY should be used only if data from the
correct physical map is already present on the
user's terminal screen. DATAONLY should never
be used with ERASE.

FIGURE 4.6   SEND MAP options: DATAONLY (program data only).

generated when you specify TIOAPFX=YES in your DFHMSD macro.)
Avoid this by clearing the entire symbolic map area to hexadecimal zeros
(low-values) before placing new values into the fields.

If you have just *successfully* received data formatted by the appropriate
map into a symbolic map work area, then you can send the same map from
the same work area again after making any desired changes to field contents. You can do this because basic mapping support clears the receiving
field to hexadecimal zeros before inserting the data from the terminal.
(This means that fields whose modified data tags are turned off will be
represented by hexadecimal zeros in the symbolic map. Any good data
that was in these fields will disappear.) However, if BMS determines that
no map data is available from that terminal, then the receiving field will
not be cleared.

Determining Correct Map Length.   Since map commands use the map
length, how do you know what length to specify? The length parameter is
used only when the map is being sent using symbolic map data in your
program. In other words, if you are sending the map with the MAPONLY
option, you do not need to specify the length. You can also omit the length
if you are using the VS COBOL II compiler. If you do need to specify the
length, it should be the length of the symbolic map work area in your
program. How can you obtain this? Examine all of the named data fields

on your map, and find the total of their lengths in bytes. Then add an extra three bytes for each of the named data fields. The three extra bytes for each field come from the one-byte attribute and the two-byte field length parameter. (There will be more bytes if your site supports the extended data stream feature.) Verify your arithmetic by checking the DMAP when you compile your program.

Program Control of Cursor Position.   The SEND MAP command has a CURSOR option that can be used in two ways. If you supply an argument value with the CURSOR option, this argument will be the screen address offset at which the cursor should be positioned. These are the addresses that begin at location zero in the upper left corner of the terminal screen. The address argument should represent the beginning of a user-enterable field on the screen. *This method is not recommended, because many of the cursor addresses in each program will have to be changed whenever changes are made to any field positions.*

A better way to set the cursor position is available whenever the map is defined as INOUT, which is the commonest situation. Defining the map as INOUT causes separate fields to be generated in the symbolic map for the length and attribute settings. Simply move -1 to the field length position of the field whose first byte should be the cursor position. Include the CURSOR option, with no argument value, in the SEND MAP command. This instructs CICS to look for a field with -1 in the field length position, and to send an instruction to place the cursor there. This is known as **symbolic cursor positioning.** Obviously, this method cannot be used with the MAPONLY option, because the MAPONLY option tells CICS to ignore whatever might be in your program's symbolic map work area. See Figure 4.7.

ERASE and ERASEUP.   The ERASE option tells CICS to send a brief command to clear all data from the user's screen. This will empty the device's buffer. It is useful when changing from one map to another. The ERASEUP option erases all *unprotected fields* from the user's screen, allowing all protected and autoskip field data to remain. This can be useful when using the same map over and over to enter data. All of the constant information can remain on the screen. Any variable data can be cleared efficiently between input operations by using a SEND MAP command with the ERASEUP option. Keep in mind, however, that ERASEUP will not clear old displayed text from error message fields defined with autoskip attributes. You will have to place blanks in the error fields to do that.

Suppose you would like to send some device control information to the terminal, such as ERASEUP, but you have no need to send any map data from your program or from the physical map. In that case, you can use this command in place of the SEND MAP command:

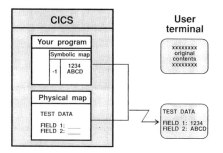

```
EXEC CICS SEND MAP (mapname)
          MAPSET (mapsetname)
          CURSOR
          ERASE
          END-EXEC.
```

The CURSOR parameter in this SEND MAP command causes CICS to use the symbolic map contents to determine cursor placement. CICS will find the first field in the symbolic map with length -1, and will place the cursor at the start of that field.

The CURSOR parameter causes the default cursor position in the physical map to be ignored.

FIGURE 4.7 Symbolic cursor positioning.

```
EXEC CICS SEND CONTROL
          [device control options]
          END-EXEC.
```

The SEND CONTROL command was introduced with CICS 1.6. (In older versions of CICS, programmers substituted a "kludge": a dummy SEND command with a field length of zero, but with various desired device control options. You may find this when maintaining old programs.)

When can you omit certain parameters?   If the map name and the map set name happen to be the same, you need to specify only the map name. Ordinarily, you will not need to specify the LENGTH option. LENGTH is used only if you are sending the map from the beginning of a data area that is longer than the map data itself. Device control parameters work in the same way when specified here as they do when specified in the DFHMSD macro. Anything specified in CICS commands overrides whatever was in the DFHMSD or DFHMDI macro. If you specified FREEKB, FRSET, or ALARM in your DFHMSD macro, supplying them again in the SEND MAP command will have no effect. If you did not specify them in the DFHMSD macro, you can supply them here. For instance, you can use the SEND MAP command with the ALARM feature if your program has discovered an error, and you can use the SEND MAP command without ALARM if all data is valid.

4.2.2   RECEIVE MAP Command

Here is what the RECEIVE MAP actually does:

- It receives raw data that has been read by the CICS terminal control program.
- It formats this data according to information in the appropriate physical map.
- It clears out the receiving area used by your program. (This is the work area that is formatted using the symbolic map copy library member.)
- It places data from each modified field into the appropriate receiving field within this work area.

When we discussed the RECEIVE command earlier, we mentioned that the RECEIVE command takes data that the CICS terminal control program has already received from the terminal and passes it to your program. In essence, this is also what the RECEIVE MAP command does.

Notice the way in which these terminal commands differ greatly from other types of I/O such as a CICS READ from a data set. The CICS READ eventually results in a request that the operating system obtain data from a data set and pass this data back to your program. The data set read operation typically begins during the execution of the CICS command. Terminal I/O is different because it is *user dependent*. When the I/O device is a terminal, it is not possible to obtain data on demand from the device as one would do if the device were a disk drive. Data comes from the terminal only when the user presses a function key. The CICS terminal control program uses teleprocessing access methods to poll or accept interrupts from each active terminal at all times in order to determine whether a function key has been pressed. This means that terminal control is constantly receiving any data that is coming in from the terminals, and is setting this data aside in order to satisfy any future RECEIVE and RECEIVE MAP commands that pertain to each device. When the RECEIVE MAP command is being serviced, it usually is not necessary to wait for any I/O to arrive from the terminal, because the desired data has already been obtained by the terminal control program.

Here are the options for the RECEIVE MAP command:

```
EXEC CICS RECEIVE MAP(name)
          [MAPSET(name)]
          [INTO(data-area)|SET(pointer-ref)]
          [FROM(data-area)LENGTH(data-value)|
```

```
TERMINAL[ASIS]]
END-EXEC.
```

When we discussed the RECEIVE command, we mentioned that there is a choice as to whether to set up your receiving field in working storage or in the linkage section. Similarly, you can set up the RECEIVE MAP command to receive the map data into a working storage area or into a linkage section area. The only difference has to do with the fact that you are provided a symbolic map copy member with which to format this working storage or linkage section area. Just as with the RECEIVE command, use the INTO(data-area) option if the area is in working storage, and use the SET(pointer-ref) option if the area is in the linkage section.

Let us look at the other command parameters. You must always specify the map name, but if the map set name happens to be the same as the map name, you may omit the map set name. There is also an ASIS option. This option overrides any upper-case translation features built into the system, but it is not set up to work for terminal I/O that has already been read by terminal control before your command-level program began to run. It works only for subsequent RECEIVE MAP command executions within that program. A properly designed program module ordinarily will execute only one RECEIVE MAP command each time it is invoked, and therefore will not be able to make use of this option.

The RECEIVE MAP command format also contains an option for FROM(data-area) LENGTH(data-value). These options are used when the map data has already been received into a storage area, but the data has not been formatted as a map. This option allows the program to format the terminal input so that it can be dealt with in the same manner as any other map. This option is seldom used.

4.3 PROGRAMMING CONSIDERATIONS FOR MAP I/O

4.3.1 Error Handling

Earlier in this chapter, we discussed use of the RESP command parameter for error checking. Each time a CICS command is executed, we need to determine whether the execution was successful. If it was not, we need to determine exactly what problem was encountered. Why does the application programmer need to worry about this? Actually, the CICS system has some default mechanism for handling each of the invalid situations that could come up for a given command. For most of them, the CICS system will terminate your application program and issue a memory dump. For unrecoverable errors that you cannot do anything about in your program, the CICS system default mechanism is satisfactory. However, you might not want to deal with every unusual situation as though it were an error.

The RESP option command places error handling under your program's control.

With each command, there are different possible error situations. Although these error situations are listed with each command in the CICS *Application Programmer's Reference Manual,* most are relatively uncommon. It is important for you to know which exceptional conditions are likeliest to concern you. We will discuss treatment of these conditions in detail here.

For a RECEIVE MAP command, the likeliest error situation that you will encounter will be MAPFAIL. MAPFAIL simply means that the RECEIVE MAP command failed to receive data from the terminal that is in a format recognizable as a map. This happens if the user's screen has been cleared, or if the data on it was put there by a SEND command and not by a SEND MAP command. It could also happen if there is a map on the user's terminal screen, but none of the modified data tags on any of the fields are turned on. (Some programmers always set one field on each BMS map to a permanent FSET attribute, in order to prevent this.) Finally, it could happen if the attention key pressed by the user was a key, such as CLEAR, that does not cause terminal data fields to be sent. Use the RESP option in your RECEIVE MAP command, and then check the response code field by comparing it with DFHRESP(MAPFAIL) immediately after the command is executed.

Even though you specify a map name in the RECEIVE MAP command, the command can be satisfied by any map. **The presence of the wrong map on the screen does not in itself raise the MAPFAIL condition.** You are responsible for determining which map is on the screen. When you prepare a map, you can embed the map name or some other identifier in a labeled field in the map, so that your program can verify that it read the correct map, and not some map that belongs to a different application.

Taming the HANDLE CONDITION Command. We have seen that the HANDLE CONDITION command looks like this:

```
EXEC CICS HANDLE CONDITION
          exceptional condition[(label)]
          [exceptional condition[(label)]]
          END-EXEC.
```

If you are using CICS 1.7 or above, or if you are using CICS OS/2, you should use RESP instead of HANDLE CONDITION. Figures 4.8 and 4.9 show the effects of HANDLE and RESP on program structure. However, if RESP is not available to you, here is how to use HANDLE CONDITION without causing too much confusion:

• In a COBOL program, the "label" is a COBOL paragraph or section. Program execution will branch to this label if the exceptional condi-

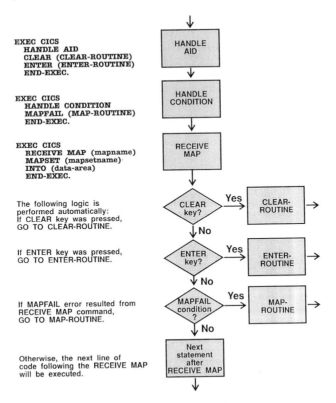

```
EXEC CICS
    HANDLE AID
    CLEAR (CLEAR-ROUTINE)
    ENTER (ENTER-ROUTINE)
    END-EXEC.


EXEC CICS
    HANDLE CONDITION
    MAPFAIL (MAP-ROUTINE)
    END-EXEC.


EXEC CICS
    RECEIVE MAP (mapname)
    MAPSET (mapsetname)
    INTO (data-area)
    END-EXEC.
```

The following logic is performed automatically: If CLEAR key was pressed, GO TO CLEAR-ROUTINE.

If ENTER key was pressed, GO TO ENTER-ROUTINE.

If MAPFAIL error resulted from RECEIVE MAP command, GO TO MAP-ROUTINE.

Otherwise, the next line of code following the RECEIVE MAP will be executed.

FIGURE 4.8 HANDLE CONDITION command.

tion is triggered. This is the equivalent of a GO TO, not a PERFORM. Program execution will GO TO the handler routine whenever the special condition occurs as the result of another statement or command. Programmers who are accustomed to writing structured code will need to be aware of this. If you use HANDLE commands, you will be forced to use other GO TO statements whenever you need to return from a handler routine, or whenever you need to "jump over" unwanted error-handler code. However, it is best to avoid any GO TO statements that branch upward in the program. Here is an example:

```
READ-NEXT-ROUTINE.
    EXEC CICS HANDLE CONDITION
    ENDFILE (SET-EOF-FLAG)
    END-EXEC.
    EXEC CICS READNEXT
        DATASET ("FILE01")
        INTO (WS-BUFFER)
        LENGTH (FILE01-LENGTH)
```

```
        RIDFLD (FILE01-KEY)
        END-EXEC.
    GO TO READ-NEXT-ROUTINE-EXIT.
SET-EOF-FLAG.
    MOVE "Y" TO FILE01-EOF-FLAG.
READ-NEXT-ROUTINE-EXIT.
    EXIT.
```

A routine of this type can be PERFORMed from wherever it is needed in the program, but it should be placed as close as possible to the statement that PERFORMs it most often.

- Up to 16 conditions can be specified in one command. If you want to specify more, just use another HANDLE CONDITION command.
- If you specify an exceptional condition without a label, then you will "turn off" any previous HANDLE CONDITION set up for that exceptional condition. This means that if that condition is triggered, then the CICS default error handling that exists for that condition will be used. This example turns off error handling for MAPFAIL:

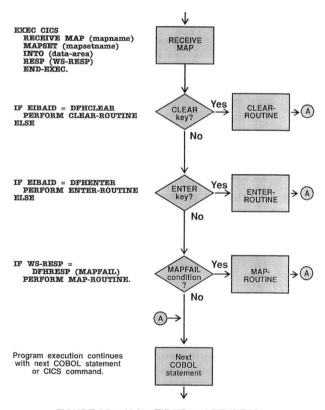

FIGURE 4.9   Using EIBAID and DFHRESP.

```
EXEC CICS HANDLE CONDITION
          MAPFAIL
          END-EXEC.
```

- Many exceptional conditions can be triggered by more than one command. For example, the MAPFAIL condition can only be triggered by the RECEIVE MAP command, but the DISABLED condition can be triggered by every CICS command that performs I/O against any data set. If you set up a HANDLE CONDITION for the DISABLED condition, then the same error handler routine can be executed for many data sets that cannot be opened when I/O is attempted. Unless you set up your own code to keep track of this, your program won't know which file is affected.

- If your program links to a subprogram, the HANDLE CONDITION in the main program will not exist in the subprogram. The subprogram will need its own HANDLE CONDITION. When control returns to the main program, the main program's HANDLE CONDITION will once again be in effect.

- If you are PERFORMing a paragraph or section within your program, you may want to use a different HANDLE CONDITION temporarily while you are within that paragraph or section. If you are using CICS 1.6 or later, you may code this at the beginning of your paragraph or section:

```
EXEC CICS PUSH HANDLE
          END-EXEC.
```

This suspends the old HANDLE CONDITION, in effect by placing it on a stack. Follow the PUSH HANDLE command with the new HANDLE CONDITION. Then, at the end of the paragraph or section, restore the old HANDLE CONDITION with the following command:

```
EXEC CICS POP HANDLE
          END-EXEC.
```

Here is an example of the use of these commands:

```
ROUTINE-1.
          EXEC CICS HANDLE CONDITION
                    NOTOPEN(ERROR-MESS-ROUTINE)
                    END-EXEC.
          (etc.)
          PERFORM ROUTINE-2.
          (etc.)
ROUTINE-1-EXIT.
     EXIT.
          (etc.)
ROUTINE-2.
```

```
            EXEC CICS PUSH HANDLE
                      END-EXEC.
            EXEC CICS HANDLE CONDITION
                      NOTOPEN(ABNORMAL-END-ROUTINE)
                      END-EXEC.
*
* ABNORMAL-END-ROUTINE is now in effect for NOTOPEN
* condition.
*
            EXEC CICS POP HANDLE
                      END-EXEC.
*
*ERROR-MESS-ROUTINE is once again in effect for NOTOPEN
*condition.
*
 ROUTINE-2-EXIT.
      EXIT.
```

- Suppose you do not want any automatic error handling at all to take place if a certain situation occurs. There are three ways to turn off HANDLE CONDITION:

If you want to turn off *all* error handling for any particular command, then specify NOHANDLE as an option within that command. For instance:

```
EXEC CICS RECEIVEMAP(name)
          MAPSET(name)
          FROM(data-area)
          LENGTH(data-value)
          NOHANDLE
          END-EXEC.
```

NOHANDLE became available with CICS Release 1.6. If you use NOHANDLE, and if you do not use RESP, your program must examine the EIBRCODE field in the EXEC interface block to determine whether the command executed successfully. EIBRCODE is a PIC X(6) field placed in your linkage section automatically by the CICS command translator. (CICS provides addressability to all EXEC interface block fields; you do not need to set up a BLL cell.) If the EIBRCODE field contains hexadecimal zeros (low-values), then the command executed successfully. Otherwise, EIBRCODE field contents will depend on the particular command and error condition that took place. Using EIBRCODE to determine exactly which error has occurred can involve a considerable amount of programming. There are many possible bit patterns within EIBRCODE that must be interpreted differently depending upon what activity was in progress when the error occurred. This is a nuisance and is not recommended for general use.

On the other hand, if you want to turn off HANDLE CONDITION for one specific type of invalid condition throughout your program, without regard for what command triggered that invalid condition, then use this command:

```
EXEC CICS IGNORE CONDITION
        condition-name
        [condition-name]
        END-EXEC.
```

The best way, of course, is to use the RESP option in the CICS command, with CICS 1.7 or greater.

- If you want to specify your own *default* error handler routine to be used for all error conditions that are not otherwise specified in a HANDLE CONDITION command, you can use ERROR as one of the condition names in the command. Here is an example:

```
EXEC CICS HANDLE CONDITION
        MAPFAIL(MAPFAIL-ROUTINE)
        IOERR
        ERROR(GENERAL-ERROR-HANDLER)
        END-EXEC.
```

This routine specifies GENERAL-ERROR-HANDLER as the error routine for all exceptional conditions other than MAPFAIL and IOERR. For MAPFAIL, MAPFAIL-ROUTINE will be used. For IOERR, the CICS default, which is abnormal task termination, will be used.

Be very careful with the HANDLE CONDITION ERROR routine that you provide. An error within this routine can force the error handler routine to invoke itself, causing a loop. The first statement within the error handler routine itself should be:

```
EXEC CICS HANDLE CONDITION
        ERROR
        END-EXEC.
```

This will turn off the logic that could cause the default error handler to reinvoke itself.

4.3.2 The Attention Identifier

In the sample sales reporting application, the terminal user presses various function keys in order to obtain access to different features of the application. PF3, for example, goes back to the previous screen. The program module that receives the menu map from the user terminal must determine which function key was selected. The function key setting is known as the **attention identifier**.

There is a choice of methods for testing the function keys: using the HAN-

DLE AID command and examining the EIBAID field directly. HANDLE AID, like HANDLE CONDITION, has the effect of introducing branches or GO TO instructions into your program. Those who want to write structured programs will test the EIBAID field instead. However, it is important to understand how HANDLE CONDITION and HANDLE AID work, because you will encounter them when maintaining existing programs.

The HANDLE AID Command.   The HANDLE AID command works in the same way as does the HANDLE CONDITION command, with the exception of the fact that it applies to the attention identifier rather than to error conditions. HANDLE AID allows you to set up a separate routine for each possible attention identifier. Suppose a HANDLE AID command setting up a routine for PF3 is in effect. Whenever any RECEIVE or RECEIVE MAP command is executed, if the user has pressed PF3, program execution will branch to the routine that was specified for PF3.

Nothing happens until a RECEIVE or RECEIVE MAP command is executed. **No matter what key the user has pressed, the HANDLE AID logic will not be triggered until a RECEIVE or a RECEIVE MAP command has been executed.**
It is possible for the same CICS command to attempt to trigger both a HANDLE AID routine and a HANDLE CONDITION routine. Suppose a HANDLE CONDITION MAPFAIL routine and a HANDLE AID routine for the CLEAR key are both active. Suppose that the terminal user has pressed the CLEAR key. When RECEIVE MAP is executed, the attention identifier (AID) for CLEAR will be received, and the MAPFAIL condition will be raised. Which routine will be executed? The HANDLE AID routine takes priority over the HANDLE CONDITION routine, which means that program execution will branch to the HANDLE AID routine for the CLEAR key. (If something were to go wrong with the terminal I/O so that the attention identifier (AID) could not be received, then the HANDLE CONDITION routine for MAPFAIL would be executed instead.) This is shown in Figure 4.9.
Here is the syntax for HANDLE AID:

```
EXEC CICS HANDLE AID
          aid-name(label)
          [aid-name[(label)]
          [ANYKEY[(label)]]
          END-EXEC.
```

The rules for its use are similar to the rules for using HANDLE CONDITION. Note the following:

- AID names are specified as ENTER, CLEAR, PA1, PA2, PA3, PF1 through PF24, DFHPEN for a light pen, DFHTRIG for a trigger field, and so forth.

- The default action for an unspecified AID is none at all: Program execution continues with the statement following the RECEIVE or RECEIVE MAP command. To "turn off" a previously active HANDLE AID routine, and to substitute the CICS system default action, use a new HANDLE AID specifying that AID with no label. Decide which attention keys are meaningful to your program. If the user presses any key other than one of those, then send back an error message telling the user that the key is invalid or undefined.

- PUSH HANDLE and POP HANDLE commands affect HANDLE AID routines in the same manner as they affect HANDLE CONDITION routines. The NOHANDLE or RESP option in a RECEIVE MAP command also suppresses the HANDLE AID routine.

- The option ANYKEY applies to CLEAR, the PA keys, and the PF keys, unless they are specified individually. ANYKEY does not apply to ENTER. If you do not want ANYKEY to apply to a particular AID in this group, then specify that AID individually, with or without a label.

```
RECEIVE-MAP-ROUTINE.
        EXEC CICS HANDLE AID
        ENTER(ENTER-ROUTINE)
        ANYKEY(PF-KEY-ROUTINE)
        PA1
        PA2
        PA3
        END-EXEC.
EXEC CICS RECEIVE MAP("EXAMPL4")
        MAPSET ("EXP4SET")
        INTO(MAPWORK)
        END-EXEC.
PA-KEY-ROUTINE.
        etc. etc.
```

In RECEIVE-MAP-ROUTINE, if the user presses ENTER, then ENTER-ROUTINE will be executed. If the user presses any PF key, then PF-KEY-ROUTINE will be executed. If the user presses any PA key, then execution will default to PA-KEY-ROUTINE, which immediately follows the RECEIVE MAP command.

Examining the Attention Identifier Directly. Instead of using HANDLE AID routines to deal with attention identifier processing requirements, it is much preferable to examine the EIBAID field in the EXEC interface block. Copying the IBM-supplied DFHAID copy library member into your program provides you the EIBAID value for each attention identifier. After executing RECEIVE or RECEIVE MAP, simply compare EIBAID to each of the expected values in DFHAID, and perform appropriate routines in each case. (Do not expect valid information to be in EIBAID until a RECEIVE or RECEIVE MAP command has been completed.) If you find that the EIBAID field contents do not match any of the expected values, then perform an error handler routine that sends a message to the user telling him or her that an invalid function key was pressed.

Warning: You should trap the MAPFAIL condition to prevent abnormal termination if the user presses CLEAR or a PA key, preferably by using the RESP option in the RECEIVE MAP command. Remember that the CLEAR and PA keys do not transmit the data that is on the user's terminal screen. They only transmit the attention key identifier signal. This causes the MAPFAIL condition to be triggered when the CLEAR or PA keys have been pressed (A HANDLE AID routine for these keys would override the MAPFAIL condition.) If you use neither HANDLE AID nor RESP nor HANDLE CONDITION MAPFAIL, the CICS default action will take place: The program will be terminated abnormally whenever the CLEAR or PA keys are pressed. Your MAPFAIL error handler routine might begin with a statement that compares the EIBAID value with DFHCLEAR, DFHPA1, and so forth, in order to determine which key has been pressed. This method is used in our sample programs.

4.3.3 Other Programming Considerations

Where Was the User's Cursor?   If you are writing an application that lets the terminal user point at something on the screen with the cursor, such as an action bar, you will want to know where the cursor was when the data was transmitted from the terminal. The cursor position may be found in the EXEC interface block, in a field called EIBCPOSN. This field is a half-word binary representation of the screen address offset that we discussed in Chapter 2. Here again, do not expect valid information to be in EIBCPOSN until a RECEIVE or RECEIVE MAP instruction has been completed.

What Did the User Actually Enter?   Remember that only those fields whose modified data tags are turned on will be included in the transmission from the terminal to the CICS system. Remember also that basic mapping support clears out the receiving area passed to your program before placing map data in it. This means there is no guarantee that any field will contain good data. **The programmer is responsible for checking each field to determine whether the data is good before using it.** Failure to do this gives rise to data exceptions. Your program will be terminated abnormally; the user's terminal will display an ABEND ASRA message. This is an ABEND code generated by the CICS system when it determines that your program contains data exceptions or other program check errors. CICS traps the error, terminating the offending application and issuing its own messages; since the error is handled in this manner, the operating system remains essentially uninvolved.

Each field length parameter in your symbolic map work area can be checked. If its length is zero, there will be no data in the field. Otherwise, if you have some need to know how much of the field was actually keyed by the terminal operator, you can use the field length parameter. If the user pressed ERASE EOF while within the field, the field length will be cleared, but the flag byte (a redefinition of the field attribute byte) will contain hexadecimal 80.

Resetting the User's Terminal.   Suppose you want to terminate an application in an orderly manner. You would like to clear the user's screen, to return the cursor to the upper left corner, and to reset the user's terminal so that data can be entered again. You can do this with SEND CONTROL ERASE, or with a SEND command which sends a dummy field. You can use any field in working storage, but you should use a field containing hexadecimal zero for the message length. ERASE should also be specified in the SEND command. If you do not reset the user's terminal, then the SYSTEM indicator will still be on, and the user will have to press RESET before entering a new transaction code.

Transmission Time versus Programming Complexity.   As we discussed earlier, it is possible to reduce transmission time between the mainframe computer and the terminals. Sending maps using the MAPONLY or the DATAONLY options causes less data to flow outward from the computer. Turning modified data tags off on fields from which input is not needed causes less data to flow inward from the terminals. In each case, however, your program must do somewhat more work.

The number of remote terminals attached to CICS installations through dial-up or leased telephone lines is growing rapidly. For reasons of reliability or economy, these telephone lines may be slow, perhaps only 1,200 or 2,400 baud. This means that it takes noticeably longer to update the user's screen display on a remote device. Many remote sites consist of one telephone line shared by a terminal control unit and several terminal devices. If one or more of these terminal devices sends or receives large volumes of data, the other devices become locked out from time to time. For these reasons, if you are programming for a system that includes remote sites accessed over telephone lines, you should emphasize techniques for reducing transmission time. Using more efficient techniques allows the update effort to be restricted to those parts of the user's screen that actually need to be changed or to be reread. This results in faster response time for the terminal user. The sample programs that begin in the next chapter display some of these techniques. An attempt was made to make them reasonably efficient in terms of transmission time, while still keeping them simple enough to use in an introductory text.

Suppose you are writing applications only for local terminals or for terminals running at high speeds. If transmission line usage is not a problem, you could simplify your programming task by setting up all map fields with FSET attributes, and by using neither DATAONLY nor MAPONLY in your SEND MAP commands. If you do this, then everything on the user's screen will be retransmitted every time the screen needs to be changed. Also, the contents of every named field in your symbolic map will be refreshed from the user terminal whenever a RECEIVE MAP takes place. CICS purists may make disparaging remarks, but the decision to program in this way is reasonable for low-volume, local applications.

Preventing Terminal "Lockup" Errors   3270-type devices can become locked out if data is sent to them which cannot be interpreted properly by that type of device. In that case, error codes such as PROG470 will appear at the bottom of the display. These codes are from the telecommunications system, not from CICS. They can appear when a display field being sent to the screen contains non-displayable characters other than spaces or nulls (low-values). Characters of that type have to be translated into something else before being sent. For example, programs which show hexadecimal dumps in character format on the screen ordinarily change all of those characters to spaces or dots before sending the data to the terminal. Packed numeric fields or hex fields must be translated to display numeric before being sent to the screen.

When your program sends a map using variable data kept in a symbolic map work area, be sure that there isn't "garbage" left in the TIOA prefix (the first 12 bytes) or in other fields you might not be using. If you are resending a map that your program has received from a previous task, this is not a problem, because the RECEIVE MAP operation clears the work area before filling it with received data. However, if you are building a new map to be sent, you need to clear the symbolic map work area to low-values before you put your own data into it.

A similar type of error occurs if the program sends an invalid cursor position in the data stream. In a program using BMS, if you plan to use SEND MAP with the CURSOR option, you must set the cursor position by moving -1 to the length field associated with the desired field in your symbolic map. If you fail to set a length field in that way, the terminal can "hang up."

TEST YOUR UNDERSTANDING

Questions and Exercises

1. What are the situations detected by HANDLE CONDITION and HANDLE AID?

2. What programming techniques can you use in place of HANDLE AID and HANDLE CONDITION?

3. What is transmitted when DATAONLY is specified? What is transmitted when MAPONLY is specified? What is transmitted when neither DATAONLY nor MAPONLY is specified?

4. How and when can you use DATAONLY and MAPONLY to reduce transmission of data from your program to the terminal?

5. What happens to your task when EXEC CICS RETURN END-EXEC is executed at the end of your main program?

6. What is one way to tell CICS what transaction to execute next?

7. What happens if your program receives a map after the terminal user has pressed the CLEAR key?

8. Describe at least one sequence of events that could cause the MAPFAIL condition to occur.

9. When would you specify ERASE in a SEND or a SEND MAP command? Under what circumstances would you avoid using ERASE?

10. Modify STUBPGM so that it will receive and send the map STUBMAP that you coded in the last set of exercises. STUBPGM should be made to do the following:

    • Receive STUBMAP.

    • Using a RESP field, test for the MAPFAIL condition.

    • Using EIBAID and the DFHAID copy library member, test for the CLEAR key.

    • If the MAPFAIL condition is detected, then we can assume that the STUB transaction has just been initiated. In other words, someone typed STUB on the screen and pressed ENTER. In this case, send a fresh copy of STUBMAP, using MAPONLY and ERASE. Then, return to CICS to terminate the task.

    • Otherwise, check the transaction identifier that appears in the upper left corner of the map. If this transaction identifier is anything other than STUB, send STUBMAP in the same manner as described in d. above.

    • If the transaction identifier on the map is STUB, we can assume that STUBMAP has been sent to the user's terminal at least once already. Move the two input fields in the STUBMAP symbolic map area to the two output fields, and send STUBMAP DATAONLY. Execute a RETURN to CICS to terminate the task.

- You may be wondering why we do not need to check for the CLEAR or PA keys. Here is the reason: It happens that STUBPGM is invoked only by a user's typing STUB on a terminal screen and then pressing ENTER or a PF key. Remember that the CLEAR and PA keys do not cause screen contents to be sent. If the user presses PA1, for example, the computer will not receive the transaction code STUB, which would ordinarily cause STUBPGM to be run. Therefore, STUBPGM will never encounter the PA1 attention key signal.

11. *Optional Problem:* Modify STUBPG2 in the same way that you were asked to modify STUBPGM.

In the next chapter, we will learn ways to invoke a transaction other than by using a transaction code embedded on a terminal screen. Once a transaction has already been invoked in some manner that does not involve the terminal screen, the transaction may still perform a RECEIVE MAP and encounter a PA or CLEAR attention key signal. The programs in the next chapter will need to check for the PA and CLEAR keys.

5

Communication Between
Program Modules

In this chapter, we will discuss some of the ways in which CICS programs can pass data from one module to another. We will explore the ways in which tasks are initiated and terminated, and the ways in which program modules can link or transfer control to other program modules. This knowledge will make it possible to allocate functions between modules in an efficient manner.

5.1 PSEUDOCONVERSATIONAL DESIGN

5.1.1 Conversational vs. Pseudoconversational Programming

Online applications written before CICS became available were often run with a dedicated terminal. This meant that the terminal was treated as an I/O device belonging only to that application. Such an application might run all day, alternately sending messages to the terminal and polling the terminal to find out whether a response was forthcoming. Since the slowest part of an online system is usually the terminal operator, the program would spend most of its time waiting in a loop for the operator to press some keys. The terminal device itself, the memory needed by the application, and any other resources dedicated to that application would also be occupied all day, but doing useful work only a small fraction of the time.

This is known as **conversational processing.** A conversational program is one that resides in memory the whole time it is carrying on a conversation with a terminal user. Such a program might send a map to the user, wait for a response, receive the response, do some other processing, and possibly repeat this cycle many times. Since the terminal user typically does not respond to the terminal instantly, the program will very likely use large amounts of time waiting in memory, doing practically nothing. Since the entire application is being performed within one program module, the whole module will have to remain loaded in memory, even though only a small portion of it is useful at any given moment. Conversational processing is shown in Figure 5.1.

We can improve on this situation. Since the CICS terminal control program, using the teleprocessing access method software, already monitors all of the terminals anyway, why not let it take care of waiting for user response? Why not let CICS bring in the correct modules to service the response when it actually arrives? This method requires application programs to be present only when they are needed to do some useful work.

This method is known as **pseudoconversational processing.** It is called

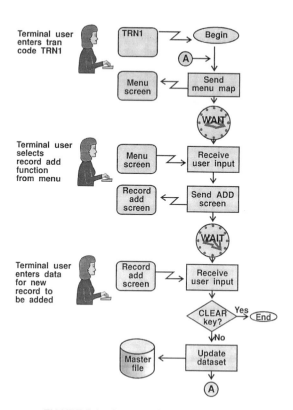

FIGURE 5.1 Conversational programming.

pseudoconversational because it is not really conversational processing, but it looks to the terminal user as though it is conversational. Although you may tell CICS to use a large variety of different modules to service the user's requests, the user will not know that more than one module was invoked. This is possible because **each program can pass information to the next program** about user input, file contents, completion of previous processing steps, and so forth.

How are pseudoconversational applications written? First of all, **the application must be built up from separate modules.** Many separate tasks within the application must each perform a part of the work. For example, the first task in an application could send the first map to the terminal user and then terminate processing by returning control to CICS. The RETURN command could contain a transaction ID, which tells the CICS system what transaction to invoke when the terminal user finally responds to the display on the terminal screen. **While the first map is visible on the screen, no CICS user-written programs for that application need to be in memory.** When the user responds to the terminal, CICS will find the next transaction ID in a work area associated with that terminal. CICS can then load the program needed to service the new transaction, and begin executing it.

A good CICS pseudoconversational application is made up, for the most part, of many separate tasks, each of which executes the following steps in the following order:

1. Initializing work areas;
2. Receiving input from a user terminal;
3. Editing the input for accuracy;
4. Reading records from data sets;
5. Updating data sets as needed;
6. Sending output to the user terminal;
7. Passing control to CICS, perhaps specifying which transaction to invoke next.

This cycle should be executed only once for each task within the application. Of course, there may be variations: If editing errors are discovered, the data set update step might be skipped. Several programs might be used to implement one task; for instance, it might be necessary to link to another program to do some other processing. **The important thing to realize, however, is that once a task has sent its output to the user terminal, it terminates. Processing the next piece of terminal input is the duty of another task.** To satisfy the next transaction request, another module will be loaded and executed. This process is shown in Figure 5.2.

The allocation of functions among the different programs and tasks

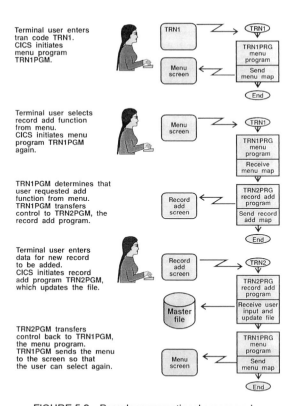

FIGURE 5.2   Pseudoconversational programming.

must be done thoughtfully. **Do not try to make one program module serve too many purposes.** Probably the most common CICS design mistake is the use of one module to do everything that needs to be done in a system. For instance, it might be reasonable to use a program to send out a menu map, and then to use the same program again to receive the user's response and to send out the next map. Unless the application is very small, it usually would *not* be reasonable to use the same program a third time to read the data on the second map, interpret it, update files, and send the menu map again.

Why should a program module perform only a few functions? If a program module is serving too many purposes, then it must contain many routines, most of which are not needed at any given time. These pieces of code sit idle in memory, and waste I/O resources as they are loaded initially and as they are paged in and out. Extra program code is needed to decide upon the correct routine to use, and to bypass execution of un-needed routines. The extra control logic tends to introduce bugs, to lengthen response times, and to make it harder for maintenance program-mers to understand the program. In addition, it takes less time to find several small pieces of storage in which to load small modules, than it does to find one large contiguous piece in which to load a big program. This affects response time. We can summarize by saying that the larger and more complex the activities, the fewer the activities that should be combined into one module.

Some people will say that a program that combines many functions may be able to reuse some parts of the same coding routines for different purposes. Be careful if your program does this. First of all, you are likely to find that the code that you do want to reuse and the code that you do not want to reuse are thoroughly intermixed. This means that you will need to add many new lines of code to avoid executing the wrong code. These added lines of code can rob you of any efficiency gains. Second, if a routine is used for too many different purposes, the module becomes hard to maintain. For example, a new feature that would be convenient when a routine is used for file inquiry might cause ABENDs or destroy files when the same routine is used for record deletions.

5.2 THE RETURN COMMAND

5.2.1 Format and Function of the RETURN Command

In the last chapter, we mentioned the RETURN command. As we observed, the RETURN command can be used to terminate a task. It also frees all memory and other resources associated with your task. (The terminal control table user area, which is associated with the user terminal, rather than with the task, is not freed. As we will discuss later, it remains allocated to that terminal.) The example showed the RETURN command being used to give control back to CICS. One of the chapter exercises required the next transaction code to be placed in the upper left corner of the user's terminal screen. In effect, this exercise used the terminal screen as means of communicating a small amount of data from one task to the next. This can be done because both the old and the new tasks are using the same terminal. However, the RETURN command itself can be used to establish the next transaction ID and to pass data from one program or task to another.

Here is the format of the RETURN command:

```
EXEC CICS RETURN
          [TRANSID(name)
          [COMMAREA(data-area)
          [LENGTH(data-value)]]]
          END-EXEC.
```

If you just want to end the task, giving control back to CICS, specify EXEC CICS RETURN END-EXEC. This is typically what is done when the user wishes to exit from an application. (Incidentally, this form of the RETURN command serves a different purpose when executed in a CICS program that was invoked by linking from another CICS program. If you specify RETURN with no transaction ID in such a case, you will exit from the present program and return to the calling program, instead of directly to CICS. We will explore this further in Section 5.4.)

Suppose you want to end the task, and suppose also that you want to use the RETURN command to specify which transaction should be executed next. To do this, you can use the TRANSID option. Specifying the TRANSID option causes CICS to start the indicated transaction as soon as someone presses an attention key on the terminal device. This gives the same result as does placing the transaction identifier in the upper left corner of the terminal screen. It is very important to realize that the RETURN TRANSID option overrides any transaction identifier that you might place in the corner of the terminal screen.

Suppose you also want to pass data to the next task. You could use the terminal as a mechanism for passing data. One task can send the information to the terminal, using a field with an FSET attribute, and the next task can receive data from this field. Unfortunately, the more data you pass in this way, the more transmission time it takes. A large amount of data will not fit on the screen at all. Also, if a particular task might possibly be receiving several different maps from different sources, it might not always be convenient to set up the maps so that the task can always find its information in the same place on every map.

The RETURN command offers a simple method for passing data between tasks. Recall that one of the things that the CICS command translator inserts into your program is a linkage section area called DFHCOMMAREA. This is a communications area intended for your use in passing data to other programs and to other tasks, as is shown in the next example. The translator provides a one-byte DFHCOMMAREA in your linkage section whether or not you intend to use it for anything. However, if you want DFHCOMMAREA to be larger than one byte, you can specify its size and format yourself, as a COBOL 01-level named DFHCOMMAREA placed immediately after the linkage section header. In the program listing, DFHCOMMAREA appears after the EXEC interface block (also inserted by the translator) and before the BLL cell group, if there is one. Even if you don't have VS COBOL II, there is no need to provide a BLL cell for DFHCOMMAREA. The CICS system makes this field available to your program automatically.

To use DFHCOMMAREA as a communications area, you need to consider both the "sending" program and the "receiving" program. A given DFHCOMMAREA may be accessed only by those programs to which it is explicitly passed. In the "sending" program, specify COMMAREA (data area) in your RETURN command. "Data-area" is the name of a field that contains the data that you want to pass to the next task. This field may be anywhere in the sending program's working storage or linkage sections. You must also specify the length of this field. For example:

```
IDENTIFICATION DIVISION.
PROGRAM-ID. PROG1.
* (etc.)
DATA DIVISION.
WORKING-STORAGE SECTION.
01  WS-COMMAREA            PIC X(80) VALUE LOW- VALUES.
01  COMM-DATA-LENGTH       PIC S9(4) COMP VALUE +80.
PROCEDURE DIVISION.
PARAGRAPH-1.
* (etc.)
END-OF-PROGRAM.
        EXEC CICS RETURN
                TRANSID (TRN2)
                COMMAREA (WS-COMMAREA)
                LENGTH (COMM-DATA-LENGTH)
                END-EXEC.
        GOBACK.

IDENTIFICATION DIVISION.
PROGRAM-ID. PROG2.
* (etc.)
DATA DIVISION.
WORKING-STORAGE SECTION.
01  EXPECTED-COMM-LGTH      PIC S9(4) COMP VALUE +80.
01  WS-COMMAREA             PIC X(80) VALUE LOW- VALUES.
* (etc.)
LINKAGE SECTION.
01  DFHCOMMAREA             PIC X(80).
* (etc.)
PROCEDURE DIVISION.
PARAGRAPH-1.
      IF EIBCALEN NOT = EXPECTED-COMM-LGTH
          PERFORM COMM-ERROR-ROUTINE
      ELSE
          MOVE DFHCOMMAREA TO WS-COMMAREA.
* (etc.)
```

The first program in the following task will be able to access this DFHCOMMAREA data without having to execute a CICS I/O command. The only requirement is that you define a DFHCOMMAREA at the beginning of the linkage section of the "receiving" program. This field must be at least as long as the DFHCOMMAREA data being passed along by the "sending" program. When the new program is loaded, the data passed by PROG1 will be placed in the DFHCOMMAREA in the new program's linkage section.

Any program using data from its DFHCOMMAREA should test the EIBCALEN field, which is the actual DFHCOMMAREA length. CICS passes EIBCALEN to your program in the EXEC interface block. It tells you whether the correct length of DFHCOMMAREA data has been received.

Program ABEND will very likely result if a program tries to use data from a DFHCOMMAREA that does not actually exist. If EIBCALEN is a length other than what your program expects, then perhaps your transaction is being called by a faulty program, or by a program that should not be invoking it at all. If no data is being passed, EIBCALEN will be zero. This will be the case, for instance, if a program is being executed because it is the first program in the transaction that a terminal operator has just requested. In that particular case, the program should probably send the first menu map in the application and then terminate.

5.3 THE XCTL COMMAND

5.3.1 Format and Function of the XCTL Command

The XCTL command looks like this:

```
EXEC CICS XCTL
          PROGRAM(name)
          [COMMAREA(data-area)
          LENGTH(data-value)]
          END-EXEC.
```

XCTL means "transfer control." *The XCTL command always contains a program name operand, not a transaction ID.* When the XCTL command is executed, the new program is loaded, it begins to run, and the old program is released from main storage. XCTL, like RETURN, lets the system rid itself of object code that it will not be using for a while.

Why do we sometimes XCTL to a new program instead of using RETURN to invoke a new transaction? The XCTL command serves a different purpose. **When the system XCTLs to another program, it does not wait for a terminal user to respond before the new program begins to execute. It starts up the new program immediately.** There are times when you will want to bring in a new program without first sending anything to the terminal and receiving a reply.

Suppose your program has just finished a file update. After the update is complete, it is necessary to send out a new menu map to the terminal user. There might be several more tasks that all finish by sending the same menu map to the user. All of these programs can terminate by issuing an XCTL to a menu handler program that places some fields on the menu map, sends out the menu map, and returns to its own transaction ID. This makes it possible to avoid repeating the same menu-building code in each program. Also, if changes need to be made to the menu-building code, these changes will only need to be made in one program. The SALEP000 program shown here is an example of this.

The XCTL command refers to a program directly, rather than through a transaction identifier. This decreases the number of transaction entries required in the PCT, because many programs do not need to be set up under a separate CICS transaction in order to be invoked.

5.4 THE LINK COMMAND

5.4.1 Format and Function of the LINK Command

The LINK command looks like this:

```
EXEC CICS LINK
          PROGRAM(name)
          [COMMAREA(data-area)
          LENGTH(data-value)]
          END-EXEC.
```

The parameters for the LINK command are the same as the parameters for the XCTL command. However, the LINK command works like a subprogram call in certain respects. The called program will ordinarily give program control back to the calling program by executing a RETURN command with no transaction identifier. In the calling program, control will return to the statement following the LINK command. Incidentally, while VS COBOL II lets you make static or dynamic subroutine calls to other CICS command-level COBOL programs, earlier versions of COBOL do not. The LINK command should be used at run time instead.

It is possible to nest program LINKs. It is also possible to LINK to a called program, then XCTL to another program, then use RETURN to get back to the original calling program. Each time LINK is executed, the task moves down one **logical nest level**. (XCTL keeps you at the same logical nest level.) To get back up to the next higher logical nest level within your task, use the RETURN command without specifying a TRANSID. This will bring you back to the next statement after the LINK command in the calling program. CICS itself is at the highest logical nest level; the last RETURN that your task specifies will be a RETURN to CICS, which terminates the task. Figure 5.3 shows this.

When LINK is used, the resources belonging to the calling program remain allocated while the called program is running. This is not true of XCTL. If several programs are expected to use a large routine on an occasional basis, it might make sense to create a separate module from that routine and to allow the other programs to LINK to it. However, do not use LINK unless there is a good reason why the called program will need to RETURN to the calling program in order to complete processing.

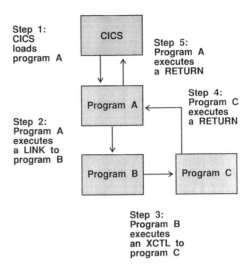

Step 1:
CICS
loads
program A

Step 5:
Program A
executes
a RETURN

Step 4:
Program C
executes
a RETURN

Step 2:
Program A
executes
a LINK to
program B

Step 3:
Program B
executes
an XCTL to
program C

FIGURE 5.3   Illustration of LINK, XCTL, and RETURN.

5.5   PROGRAMMING CONSIDERATIONS

5.5.1   Possible Error Situations

Suppose a program is trying to XCTL or to LINK to a program that cannot
be found using the CICS tables. What happens then? A PGMIDERR error
condition is raised. Although you can use RESP to check for PGMIDERR,
some programmers omit this. If a needed module does not exist, it might
make sense to allow CICS to terminate your task abnormally, because this
is an unrecoverable error requiring attention by the systems staff. When
PGMIDERR occurs, the CICS tables should be updated and the application
rerun.

If the RETURN command is being used without a TRANSID, to get back
to a calling program from a called program, the COMMAREA option is not
available for use. A COMMAREA may be specified only when you are
using RETURN to terminate a task. If the COMMAREA option is used in a
RETURN command that is being used to return control back to a calling
program rather than to CICS, then using COMMAREA with the RETURN
command will raise an INVREQ error condition. Here again, CICS ordinarily should be allowed to terminate the task if this happens.

However, if the calling program originally passed a DFHCOMMAREA
to the called program in the LINK command, any changes made to the
DFHCOMMAREA by the called program will be passed back to the calling
program automatically when it RETURNs. Nothing needs to be specified
in the RETURN command.

We already discussed the fact that you should exit from a CICS program by using RETURN, LINK, or XCTL, and not by using GOBACK or STOP RUN. In addition, you should be careful never to allow program execution to "fall out the end of the program." All logic paths within any CICS program should end at a RETURN, LINK, or XCTL command. There is only one exception to this: It is possible to use a CICS ABEND command to force a task to terminate abnormally. This will be discussed in a later chapter.

5.5.2 Maintaining Control over Your Application

You should know which programs should be allowed to SEND and RE-CEIVE each of the maps that you use. You should also know which transactions and programs should be invoked in which ways. Typically, the first task in a pseudoconversational application should be requested by direct user input such as by typing the transaction identifier on a blank terminal screen. All subsequent tasks needed in the application should be invoked only under the direct control of your programs.

Never allow the terminal user to invoke any transaction directly, other than the transaction that is used to start the application. If security constraints so indicate, the transaction code field on the maps can be made nondisplay (DRK) and modified (FSET), so that the transaction identifiers can be used to begin the next task without being seen by the terminal user. Preferably, you can use the RETURN command to specify the next transaction ID. In that case, some other naming scheme can then be used for identifying the maps to the terminal users. Also, if you want to make sure that a certain task runs only when a certain map is on the screen, you should send an error message and terminate your task if the wrong map, or no map at all, is on the screen.

You must also maintain control over the manner in which each program is accessed. For example, if program PAY2000 is loaded and executed whenever transaction PAY2 is invoked, then obviously it is possible to run PAY2000 by requesting transaction PAY2. Notice, however, that it is also possible to run PAY2000 by LINK or XCTL from another program. If you plan to allow one of your programs to be run in more than one way, this program may need to execute different routines depending on what transaction invoked the program. EIBTRNID in the EXEC interface block will tell you which transaction is currently active. For example, if EIBTRNID in the PAY2000 program contains PAY2, the module was invoked through transaction PAY2. Otherwise, the module was invoked through LINK or XCTL from a different program.

Some programmers use flags, switches, or module identifiers passed in the DFHCOMMAREA or in other CICS work areas in order to determine what execution path has been followed. These should be used only when the EXEC interface block does not provide all the information you need.

In any case, never allow your program to continue running after being invoked by other programs or transactions that do not pass them the correct input data.

5.5.3   A Warning about DFHCOMMAREA Length

Even if you read manuals to help you get to sleep at night, you probably never noticed an obscure warning about DFHCOMMAREA length on page 344 of the CICS/MVS 2.1 APRM. It says, "The receiving data area need not be of the same length as the original communication area; if access is required only to the first part of the data, the new data area can be shorter. It must not be longer than the length of the communication area being passed, because the results in this situation are unpredictable." This is important and it can cause you serious problems.

What exactly does this mean? If your program moves the received DFHCOMMAREA contents from the linkage section to a working storage area, and if your program's linkage section DFHCOMMAREA definition is longer than needed to contain the actual received data, the data might not be moved successfully from the linkage section to working storage. Your working storage definition will end up containing low-values instead of the correct data. This problem occurs under CICS 1.6 and later releases and under both OS/VS COBOL 2.4 and VS COBOL II.

For the purposes of discussion, we have three separate communications area definitions coming into play:

1.   The COMMAREA definition referenced in the RETURN or XCTL command of the previous program. This will govern the actual received data length as shown in EIBCALEN in the current program.
2.   The DFHCOMMAREA definition appearing in the linkage section of the current program.
3.   The WS-DFHCOMMAREA definition (or whatever it is called) appearing in the working storage section of the current program.

The correct data will be passed from area 1 (the previous program) to area 2 (the linkage section of the current program) but sometimes will not be moved from there to area 3 (working storage). The whole situation is not at all what one would expect. First of all, you might expect data loss or truncation if the current program's receiving DFHCOMMAREA were shorter than the sending DFHCOMMAREA, but not the other way around. Second, you might expect that the data loss would occur in the receiving program's linkage section, but instead the data loss doesn't take place until you try to move the data from there to working storage. The length of the working storage definition is NOT the cause of this problem, even though the data actually gets lost only when the data is moved to the working storage area.

According to IBM, this problem can occur when area 2 is longer than area 1, causing improper code to be generated when moving area 2 to area 3. The improper code involves an MVCL, which produces a destructive overlapping move. For example, suppose your program has a 2500-byte linkage section DFHCOMMAREA definition, but it receives a DFHCOMMAREA with an EIBCALEN of only 1000 bytes. You might have a problem later when you move your 2500-byte linkage section DFHCOMMAREA to a 2500-byte working storage area.

So how do you get around this problem? **Probably the easiest way is to set a standard requiring all programs which use DFHCOMMAREA to communicate with one another must use the same length DFHCOMMAREA, even though some of them might need to pass much less data.** This is not always a desirable solution. You might want all of your programs within an application to share some system-wide common data followed by varying amounts of program-dependent data. If most programs don't need this, you'll waste storage. There are other alternatives. You can test EIBCALEN and use only the valid portion of the data directly in the linkage section DFHCOMMAREA. However, if you change anything outside of the portion which belongs to your program, or if you attempt to pass along "trailer" data that isn't rightfully yours to another program, you'll probably get either a protection exception or a storage violation. If program #1 passes 1000 bytes to program #2, but program #2 needs to pass 2500 bytes to program #3, don't try to "cheat" by reusing the same linkage section data and setting the length parameter in the command to 2500. In that case, do a CICS GETMAIN for 2500 bytes, move the 1000 bytes to the beginning of the GETMAINed area, and pass that along to program #3.

Since this problem doesn't seem to occur with received DFHCOMMAREA less than 512 bytes, a simple work around of this type might be adequate for your purposes:

```
WORKING-STORAGE SECTION.
01   WS-DFHCOMMAREA-2500.
     05   WS-DFHCOMMAREA-500 PIC X(500) VALUE LOW-VALUES.
     05   FILLER             PIC X(2000) VALUE LOW-VALUES.
LINKAGE SECTION.
01   DFHCOMMAREA.
     05   DFHCOMMAREA-500    PIC X(500).
     05   FILLER             PIC X(2000).
PROCEDURE DIVISION.
     IF EIBCALEN = 500
         MOVE DFHCOMMAREA-500 TO WS-DFHCOMMAREA-500
     ELSE
         IF EIBCALEN = 2500
             MOVE DFHCOMMAREA TO WS-DFHCOMMAREA-2500
         ELSE
             PERFORM WRONG-LENGTH-COM.
```

Another possibility might be to define DFHCOMMAREA as variable length depending on EIBCALEN. This example shows the use of the VS COBOL II LENGTH OF statement:

```
WORKING-STORAGE SECTION.
01  WS-FULL-COMMAREA.
    05  WS-SHORT-COMMAREA  PIC X(500) VALUE LOW-VALUES.
    05  FILLER             PIC X(2000) VALUE LOW-VALUES.
LINKAGE SECTION.
01  DFHCOMMAREA.
    05  FILLER                 PIC X
                               OCCURS 1 TO 32767 TIMES
                               DEPENDING ON EIBCALEN.
PROCEDURE DIVISION.
    IF EIBCALEN = LENGTH OF WS-SHORT-COMMAREA
        MOVE DFHCOMMAREA     TO WS-SHORT-COMMAREA
    ELSE
        IF EIBCALEN = LENGTH OF WS-FULL-COMMAREA
            MOVE DFHCOMMAREA TO WS-FULL-COMMAREA
        ELSE
            PERFORM WRONG-LENGTH-COM.
```

5.6 OTHER METHODS FOR PASSING DATA BETWEEN PROGRAMS

5.6.1 Common Work Area

Some other data structures are provided for your use as work areas for communication between programs as well as for program "scratch pad" use. These work areas are set up and used in a variety of ways.

There is only one common work area (CWA) in a CICS region or partition. The size is specified by the systems programmer in the system initialization table. It is shared by all tasks running in the region or partition. When CICS is brought up at the beginning of the day, the CWA contains binary zeros. Whenever a task places some data in this area, this data will stay there until some other task changes it or the system is brought down. The CWA is useful for anything that must be accessed by many tasks within the system. One example would be sequential assignment of invoice numbers or customer numbers to prevent skipped numbers or duplicates. Whenever a new number is needed, the old number could be taken from the CWA and incremented. Once the new number has been assigned, the CWA entry could be updated.

If your installation uses the CWA, find out about the format of the data that is expected to be in this area. Ideally, this format should be available in a copy library. Also, find out which programs are responsible for placing good data in which fields, and find out what provisions are made for recovery in case the system goes down unexpectedly. Remember that your application must not interfere with use of the CWA by other applications. **An applications programmer should never place anything in the CWA without first coordinating with whoever is in charge of the CWA.**

5.6.2   Transaction Work Area

A new transaction work area (TWA) is set up each time a transaction is executed. For instance, if three people are using transaction PAY4, there will be three separate transaction work areas, one for each task. Each TWA is initialized with binary zeros. A task may access only its own TWA, and the TWA disappears after the task ends. It can be used for program "scratch pad" purposes, or for passing data to a program being accessed through LINK or XCTL. If you want your transaction to have a TWA, the TWA size must be specified in the transaction's PCT entry. Most sites use DFHCOMMAREA in preference to TCTUA or TWA.

5.6.3   Terminal Control Table User Area

A terminal control table user area (TCTUA) is set up for each terminal when CICS starts up or when the terminal control table entry is established for that terminal. (This depends on how the TCT is built and maintained.) The TCTUA is initialized at that time with binary zeros. Any data placed in the TCTUA remains there until another task changes the data or until the terminal is removed from the TCT or the CICS system is brought down. Since the TCTUA data is stored in the mainframe and not in the terminal device, shutting off the terminal has no effect on the TCTUA. It might be useful for passing data between tasks, if the volume of data is not too large. The TCTUA size is specified in the TCT entry for the terminal.

5.6.4   Accessing the CWA, TWA, and TCTUA

In order to access each of these areas, you must set up a linkage section work area and obtain the required addresses from CICS. If you are not under VS COBOL II, you will need BLL pointers. Be sure your linkage section work area is set up with the correct length and format for the data that you expect to find in these areas. **All of these areas are optional. Before trying to use any of them, make sure that they exist and that they are of the expected length.** You can do this by using the ASSIGN command:

```
EXEC CICS ASSIGN
          CWALENG(data-area)
          TWALENG(data-area)
          TCTUALENG(data-area)
          END-EXEC.
```

In each case, the data-area is a binary (COMP) field that you provide. After executing the ASSIGN command, each data- area will contain the length of the CICS system area you are inquiring about. If any data-area contains zero, then that system area does not exist.

Once you know that each desired area exists, you can use the ADDRESS command to acquire addressability to it:

```
EXEC CICS ADDRESS
          CWA(pointer-ref)
          TWA(pointer-ref)
          TCTUA(pointer-ref)
          END-EXEC.
```

The ADDRESS command works much like the SET option in the RE-CEIVE command, which we discussed in Chapter 4. In other words, executing the ADDRESS command allows you to refer directly to each of the corresponding data areas in the linkage section.

5.6.5 Which Areas to Use?

In our sample application, several types of work areas are used in order to illustrate their use. In a real application, use the terminal screen for passing small amounts of data that the user might need to modify some of the time. It is preferable to use DFHCOMMAREA for most other purposes, unless the volume of data is unusually large. If there is a large amount of data, many installations suggest the use of temporary storage, which is covered in Chapter 7. Avoid scattering small amounts of data among many different work areas, data sets, and so forth, because the effort involved in accessing them increases program complexity and overhead.

5.6.6 More about the ASSIGN Command

The ASSIGN command is useful for many things other than for finding out whether a particular system area has been defined. The same command format is always used, but different parameters cause the system to give you different types of information. Here are a few examples out of the many available:

ABCODE

If the program is ABENDing, this contains the CICS ABEND code.

FACILITY

This gives the identifier of the entity that caused your transaction to begin.

OPCLASS, OPID, OPERKEYS, OPSECURITY

These parameters are used to obtain information associated with the sign on and security privileges of the operator at the terminal associated with your task. OPERKEYS is used under Release 1.6 and greater to obtain a full-word binary security key. OPSECURITY retrieves only the first 24 bits of the operator's security key, which is all that was available under Release 1.5.

STARTCODE

This option tells you how the current task was started. Here are the possibilities:

QD: Task was begun because a transient data queue became large enough to reach its preassigned trigger level. This will be discussed later in the book.

S: Another task issued an EXEC CICS START command for this task, effective immediately or later, but without data. (See Section 5.8.)

SD: Another task issued an EXEC CICS START command for this task, with a data area passed to the new task.

TD: Task was started as a response to terminal input.

U: Task was attached by user.

TERMCODE

This option tells you the type and model number of the physical terminal device to which your task is attached.

5.7   STORING DATA IN PROGRAM FORM

5.7.1   LOAD under Mainframe CICS

Anything that can be compiled or assembled in the form of a program or map can be given an entry in the PPT. It may contain executable code, constants such as tables, working storage, or all of the above. If it contains executable code, it can be accessed through XCTL or LINK in the normal manner. If a program is used very often, the LOAD command with the HOLD option can be used to keep the program in main memory until the RELEASE command is executed. If the module contains only constants or working storage, the LOAD command with the set option can be used to set a BLL pointer to make the data available to your program in your linkage section. This is useful for tables containing such things as error messages, weeks and months, unit of measure codes, and so forth.

The LOAD command looks like this:

```
EXEC CICS LOAD PROGRAM(name)
          SET(pointer-ref)
          [LENGTH(data-area)|FLENGTH(data-area)]
          [HOLD]
          [ENTRY(pointer-ref)]
          END-EXEC.
```

The LOAD command does not necessarily load a fresh copy of the requested module. If the module you want is already in memory, the command need not do anything unless the SET option is specified. In that case, the USAGE IS POINTER data field or BLL pointer will be set to the current memory address of the module and the LENGTH or FLENGTH field will be set to the module's length. FLENGTH implies that you are using a four-byte binary field rather than a two-byte field.

If the HOLD option was used to keep a module in main memory, the RELEASE command should be used to allow it to be deleted when it is no longer needed:

```
EXEC CICS RELEASE PROGRAM(name)
          END-EXEC.
```

5.7.2 LOAD under CICS OS/2 1.20

The LOAD PROGRAM command is similar under CICS OS/2. If you are using it to load a data file (OS/2 suffix .DAT), the SET parameter is required, as is the LENGTH or FLENGTH parameter. If you are using it to load a program file (OS/2 suffix .DLL), you would use ENTRY(pointer-ref) instead of SET/LENGTH. Using the wrong parameters raises a PGMIDERR condition. An entry in the PPT is required for data modules, but not for executable modules. CICS OS/2 does not support the RELEASE PROGRAM command. If you load a program with HOLD, it remains resident, and available to all new tasks, until you bring down CICS OS/2. Be aware of how much memory you are using with resident programs.

5.8 STARTING NEW TASKS FROM AN APPLICATION PROGRAM

5.8.1 START and RETRIEVE

Suppose you want your application to begin another task, perhaps attached to some other terminal device, without terminating the existing task. RETURN TRANSID will not do this, because RETURN terminates the current task before starting the new task. The START command allows you to specify that another transaction be invoked, either immediately, or at a specific time of day, or after a specific time interval has elapsed. The START command also allows you to pass data from your application program to a program in the transaction being invoked. It even lets you specify whether or not the new task should be attached to a terminal, and, if so, to which terminal. There are several uses for this. A task that is not attached to a terminal might do something, such as backing up a file, that does not need direct user input. A task which is attached to a printer terminal can print data which has been passed to it. We will show only the more frequently used options available in the START command.

```
EXEC CICS START
          TRANSID(name)
          [INTERVAL(hhmmss)|INTERVAL (0)|TIME(hhmmss)]
          [FROM(data-area)
          LENGTH(data-value)]
          [TERMID(NAME)]
          (REQID(name)]
          END-EXEC.
```

If the INTERVAL or TIME options are not specified, the CICS system will begin the new task immediately. Otherwise, the CICS system will begin the new task at the specified time or after the specified interval has elapsed. You can identify the command by supplying a request ID parameter (REQID). Why might you need to do this? If your program has issued a START command that will activate a task in the future, and you change your mind and wish to prevent the new task from being dispatched, the REQID will allow you to cancel the START command:

```
EXEC CICS CANCEL
          REQID(name)
          END-EXEC.
```

The FROM option in the START command allows you to send data to a program in the new task. To obtain this data, this program must issue a RETRIEVE command:

```
EXEC CICS RETRIEVE
          [INTO(data-area)|SET(pointer-ref)]
          LENGTH(data-area)
          END-EXEC.
```

If the new task is not associated with a terminal, then it will have most one piece of data to be retrieved. If the new task is associated with a terminal, then there could be several pieces of data waiting to be retrieved. One piece of data could come in from each task that issued a START command for that transaction on that terminal. In that case, your program should keep executing RETRIEVE commands to fetch the data until the ENDDATA exceptional condition is encountered. Timing for the START command is provided by the interval control program or, in CICS 3.1 and later, the timer domain.

5.9 SUBPROGRAMS

5.9.1 The COBOL CALL Statement

A CICS command-level program compiled with VS COBOL II (with the
NODYNAM compiler option) can make both static and dynamic calls to
other modules. In those situations calling for *repeated* calls to the same
subprogram, the COBOL CALL is much more efficient than the CICS LINK
command for the second and later calls.

Static calls can be made to other VS COBOL II programs or to assembler
programs that have been link-edited together with the calling program. If
the called program contains CICS commands or references CICS system
areas, it must go through the CICS translator step before it is compiled. In
that case, the calling program must call it using the following statement:

```
CALL "PROGNAME' USING DFHEIBLK DFHCOMMAREA YOUR-PARM.
```

where YOUR-PARM is an optional field containing any other data that you
want to pass. You can add more of your own parameters to the CALL
statement following DFHCOMMAREA; if there is only one user parm, the
called program would contain the following statement:

```
PROCEDURE DIVISION USING YOUR-PARM.
```

Dynamic calls can be made to other VS COBOL II or assembler programs. CICS 2.1.1 or later also allows dynamic calls to programs containing CICS commands and system areas. The called module can be in the
link pack area or in a shared library. Other CICS and batch regions can use
the same module. The calling program should contain a data area that
holds the name of the desired module. If this field is called PROG-NAME-
FIELD, the CALL statement will look like this:

```
CALL PROG-NAME-FIELD.
```

The called program should end with an EXIT PROGRAM or GOBACK
statement. You might remember that GOBACK and similar statements can
cause serious problems when used with older versions of COBOL. Under
VS COBOL II, GOBACK and EXIT PROGRAM now mean "return to the
calling module," while STOP RUN now works like an EXEC CICS RE-
TURN command. If the called program is called again, it will be found in
the state in which it was left from the last call, unless the called module
contains the INITIAL clause. In contrast, a LINKed subprogram will always be found in a "refreshed" state.

Incidentally, VS COBOL II now allows the use of the INSPECT, STRING,
and UNSTRING COBOL statements.

5.10   USEFUL INFORMATION PROVIDED BY THE CICS SYSTEM

5.10.1   The EXEC Interface Block

The EXEC interface block provides much useful information that can sometimes take the place of user-defined flags and switches. Before defining any switches in your program, determine whether the EIB already contains something that can be used to provide the same information. **Remember that your program must not change anything in the EIB.** The EXEC interface block has been expanded from one release of CICS to the next. Many of the fields in the EIB concern only those programmers who are writing applications that communicate with another system or "logical unit," which we will not discuss at this point. The fields that you will be likely to use are EIBAID, EIBCALEN, EIBCPOSN, EIBDATE, EIBFN, EIBRCODE, EIBREQID, EIBRSRCE, EIBTASKN, EIBTIME, EIBTRMID, AND EIBTRNID. We will discuss these and some others.

EIBAID, PIC(X)

This field contains the attention identifier that came in with the most recent RECEIVE or RECEIVE MAP command executed in your program. If you test this field before executing a RECEIVE or RECEIVE MAP, it will contain the most recent attention identifier received by CICS from the terminal attached to your task.

EIBATT, PIC X

This field indicates that attach header data is included in data coming in from a logical unit.

EIBCALEN, PIC S9(4) COMP

This field contains the length of the DFHCOMMAREA data that has been placed in your program's linkage section. If this field contains zero, there is no DFHCOMMAREA data.

EIBCOMPL, PIC X

If this field contains hexadecimal FF, then the last time your program performed a RECEIVE, it obtained the entire message. If this field contains anything else, then your program should perform more RECEIVEs to obtain the rest of the data. This was introduced with Release 1.6. (See Chapter 4.)

EIBCONF, PIC X

This field indicates that a CONFIRM request has been received from another system (intro. Rel. 1.6).

EIBCPOSN, PIC S9(4) COMP

This field contains the location (screen address offset) at which the cursor was resting when the most recent RECEIVE or RECEIVE MAP was executed.

EIBDATE, PIC S9(7) COMP-3, format 000yyddd+

This field contains the date at which your task started. Whenever you use this command:

```
EXEC CICS ASKTIME
        END-EXEC.
```

the EIBDATE field and the EIBTIME field will be updated.

EIBDS, PIC X(8)

This field contains the file name or DDNAME of the random-access file most recently accessed with an I/O command.

EIBEOC, PIC X

This field indicates that an end-of-chain indicator has been received from another system.

EIBERR, PIC X

This field is set to hexadecimal FF only when an error has occurred in communicating with another logical unit (intro. Rel. 1.6). EIBERR and EIBERRCD are not the same as EIBRCODE, which is set for all error situations.

EIBERRCD, PIC X(4)

This field is the return code that is set along with EIBERR when there is a problem with logical unit communications (intro. Rel. 1.6).

EIBFN, PIC XX

This field contains a function code that indicates which CICS command was most recently used in your program.

EIBFREE, PIC X

This field indicates that your program should free its resources so that another task can use them.

EIBNODAT, PIC X

This field indicates that a null message (containing no data) was received from a logical unit (intro. Rel. 1.6).

EIBRCODE, PIC X(6)

This field indicates whether the most recent CICS command executed successfully. If it did, EIBRCODE will be zeros. Otherwise, EIBRCODE will contain some other value, depending on the error and on the type of CICS command that was executed. In general, it's easier to use RESP and perhaps RESP2 for this purpose.

EIBRECV, PIC X

If set to hexadecimal FF, this field indicates that there is more data for your program to receive from the logical unit.

EIBREQID, PIC X(8)

This field contains a request identifier that is used only when the current task was begun by a CICS START command.

EIBRSRCE, PIC X(8)

This field contains the name of the resource accessed in the most recent CICS command. This could be a file, a queue, or some other entity.

EIBSIG, PIC X

This field indicates that a signal has been received from a logical unit (intro. Rel. 1.6).

EIBSYNC, PIC X

If this field is set to hexadecimal FF, it indicates that your application program should free its resources, execute a SYNCPOINT command (which is a break point for recovery purposes), and terminate.

EIBSYNRB, PIC X

This field warns that the program should execute a SYNCPOINT ROLL-BACK command (intro. Rel. 1.6).

EIBTASKN, PIC S9(7) COMP-3

This field contains a sequential task number assigned by CICS to your task.

EIBTIME, PIC S9(7) COMP-3, format 0hhmmss+

This field contains the time at which the current task was started. It, too, may be updated by using the ASKTIME command.

EIBTRMID, PIC X(4)

This field contains the terminal identification number of the terminal device attached to your task.

EIBTRNID, PIC X(4)

This field contains the transaction identifier for your task, exactly as it appears in the PCT.

5.10.2　CICS 1.7 and Above: Options on ASSIGN Command

New types of system information have been made available under CICS/VS 1.7; these are listed in the *Application Programmer's Reference Manual.* Of particular usefulness are the following:

```
EXEC CICS ASSIGN
QNAME (data-area)
USERID (data-area)
PARTNS (data-area)
TERMCODE (data-area)
END-EXEC.
```

QNAME will be useful to you only if you are working with transient data queues, which we will discuss in Chapter 8. TD queues, in a nutshell, are sequential datasets. You can tell CICS to run a task whenever CICS finds a certain number of records in the TD queue. This uses a facility called automatic transaction initiation (ATI). If your task was started in this manner, the ASSIGN QNAME command can be used to find out which TD queue started your task. The QNAME(data-area) field must be four characters long. If your task was not started by a TD queue, then the INVREQ condition will be raised.

On the other hand, if your task was initiated from a terminal, then that terminal will ordinarily have an 8-character operator ID that belongs to the person who has signed on. The USERID option will return this identifier to your program. If your task was not initiated from a terminal (for instance, if it was initiated by ATI), then the INVREQ condition will be raised. If your task was initiated from a terminal, but there is no operator ID, then the USERID option will return nulls.

Various other options exist for tasks that were initiated from a terminal. These options provide your program with information about the characteristics of the terminal. For instance, you can use the PARTNS option to find out whether the terminal supports partition sets. If it does, the PARTNS option will return one byte of high-values (hex FF); if not, the PARTNS option will return one byte of nulls (hex 00). (The OUTLINE option works the same way; it indicates whether the terminal supports the field outlining option.) The TERMCODE option will return a two-byte character field which indicates the type and model number of the terminal. In either case, if the task was not initiated from a terminal, the INVREQ condition will be raised.

5.10.3 Time and Date Commands

As mentioned above, the EXEC CICS ASKTIME command updates the date and time in the EIBDATE and EIBTIME fields. Starting with CICS 1.7 and above, the ASKTIME command still does that, but now it will also place an "absolute time" value into a full-word data area that you specify.

```
EXEC CICS ASKTIME
          ABSTIME (data-area)
          END-EXEC
```

The value placed in this data area reflects both the date and the time. The FORMATTIME command will take this value and reformat the date and time as you choose.

```
EXEC CICS FORMATTIME
          ABSTIME (data-value)
          [YYDDD (data-area)]
          [DDMMYY (data-area)]
          [MMDDYY (data-area)]
          [DATE (data-area)]
          [DATEFORM (data-area)]
          [DATESEP (data-area)]
          [DAYCOUNT (data-area)]
          [DAYOFWEEK (data-area)]
          [DAYOFMONTH (data-area)]
          [MONTHOFYEAR (data-area)]
          [YEAR (DATA-AREA)]
          [TIME (data-area)]
          [TIMESEP (data-area)]
          END-EXEC
```

If the following command is executed, the results will be as follows:

```
EXEC CICS FORMATTIME
          ABSTIME (data-area)
          MMDDYY (data-area)
          DATESEP ('/')
          TIME (data-area)
          TIMESEP (':')
          END-EXEC
```

The date field could contain 12/20/91 and the time field could contain 09:33:05.

The DATESEP and TIMESEP characters, if specified, will cause the date and time to be separated by those characters for display purposes. The DATEFORM field, if specified, simply returns the date format—in this case, MMDDYY. The DAYCOUNT field, if specified, gives the number of days since January 1, 1900, in full word binary form. January 1, 1900 is day zero in this format.

In all cases, the data areas that you supply must be long enough to fit the desired data. Remember that the separator characters take up two extra positions.

5.11   SAMPLE APPLICATION PROGRAMS

5.11.1   A Menu Program

You are about to see part of a CICS application. See Figures 5.4 through 5.6. SALEP000 begins by sending the menu map SALE000 to the user's terminal. SALEP000 ends by issuing a RETURN command specifying TRANSID(SALE). SALE is the transaction that invokes SALEP000 again to process that menu.

If the user presses an attention key when the menu map is visible, SALEP000 will be executed. It does the following:

- If the user has pressed PF3, SALEP000 clears the screen and terminates the task.
- If the user has pressed PF10, SALEP000 moves the cursor up to the action bar, sends the map, and returns to its own transaction ID.
- If the user has pressed PF12, SALEP000 refreshes the screen contents, sends the map, and returns to its own transaction ID.
- If the user has pressed the enter key, SALEP000 processes user input as described in Chapter 3 and in the comments in the program. In a nutshell, it will determine which object and action were requested. It will show a small popup map, CUST000, to obtain a customer number from the user. After that, SALEP000 will XCTL to another program, which will perform the action selected by the user.
- When that other program is done, it will XCTL back to SALEP000, which in turn will send out a new menu map.

When you examine the sample programs, pay particular attention to the terminal I/O commands and to the methods used for passing data between programs and tasks. These programs also contain a few file I/O commands which we shall discuss in the next chapter.

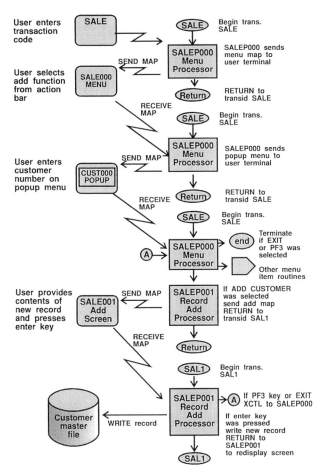

FIGURE 5.4 Logic flow diagram of record add function.

What's Next? VSAM or other random-access data sets, SQL data bases, DL/I data bases, and sequential files should be used for working with large amounts of data, for data with stringent integrity and security requirements, and for data that will be needed by batch or online programs outside the CICS region or partition. The next three chapters will cover random and queued data set access under CICS. Chapter 6 explores VSAM file handling, Chapter 7 discusses the use of temporary storage queues, and Chapter 8 covers sequential transient data queues and CICS journaling.

```
        IDENTIFICATION DIVISION.
        PROGRAM-ID. SALEP000.
        AUTHOR. ALIDA M. JATICH AND PHIL NOWAK.
       **********************************************************
       * ON THE FIRST PASS, SALEP000 SENDS THE MENU SCREEN. AFTER THAT,*
       * IT CHECKS THE USER'S INPUT TO DETERMINE WHICH OTHER PROGRAM  *
       * TO INVOKE NEXT. THIS PROGRAM ALSO PRESENTS A POPUP MENU WHICH *
       * CAN BE USED TO ENTER THE CUSTOMER NUMBER TO SELECT THE RECORD *
       * TO BE SHOWN BY THE NEXT PROGRAM.                             *
       **********************************************************
        ENVIRONMENT DIVISION.
        DATA DIVISION.
        WORKING-STORAGE SECTION.
        01  MISC-WORK.
            05  WS-CICS-RESPONSE1      PIC S9(8) COMP VALUE +0.
            05  WS-XCTL-PGM            PIC X(8)       VALUE SPACES.
            05  WS-DUMMY-FIELD         PIC X         VALUE SPACES.
            05  WS-DUMMY-LENGTH        PIC S9(4) COMP VALUE +0.
            05  WS-HOLD-MSG            PIC X(79)      VALUE SPACES.
        01  QID-NAME.
            05  QID-TRMID             PIC XXXX       VALUE SPACES.
            05  FILLER               PIC XXXX       VALUE 'SALE'.
        01  ERROR-MESSAGES.
            05  BAD-KEY-MSG           PIC X(22)      VALUE
                'Function key undefined'.
            05  BAD-OBJECT-MSG        PIC X(20)      VALUE
                'Select object 1 or 2'.
            05  BAD-COMBO-MSG         PIC X(31)      VALUE
                'Cannot change or delete history'.
            05  CUST-NUM-MSG          PIC X(27)      VALUE
                'Customer number not numeric'.
            05  NOTFND-MSG            PIC X(16)      VALUE
                'Record not found'.
            05  DISABLED-MSG          PIC X(16)      VALUE
                'File is disabled'.
            05  DSIDERR-MSG           PIC X(14)      VALUE
                'File not found'.
            05  DUPREC-MSG            PIC X(22)      VALUE
                'Record already on file'.
            05  INVREQ-MSG            PIC X(15)      VALUE
                'Invalid request'.
            05  IOERR-MSG             PIC X(9)       VALUE
                'I/O error'.
            05  ITEMERR-MSG           PIC X(16)      VALUE
                'Item not defined'.
            05  LENGERR-MSG           PIC X(19)      VALUE
                'Record length error'.
            05  NOSPACE-MSG           PIC X(17)      VALUE
                'File out of space'.
            05  PGMIDERR-MSG          PIC X(29)      VALUE
                'Program not found, PRESS PF12'.
            05  QIDERR-MSG            PIC X(17)      VALUE
                'Queue not defined'.
       *
            05  BUILD-MSG.
                10  DISPLAY-OPERATION    PIC X(12)    VALUE SPACES.
                10  FILLER               PIC X        VALUE SPACES.
                10  DISPLAY-RESOURCE     PIC X(8)     VALUE SPACES.
                10  FILLER               PIC X        VALUE SPACES.
                10  DISPLAY-DESCRIPTION  PIC X(38)    VALUE SPACES.
                10  FILLER               PIC X        VALUE SPACES.
                10  DISPLAY-CALL-WHOM    PIC X(16)    VALUE SPACES.
       *
            05  DEFAULT-DESCRIPTION.
                10  FILLER               PIC X(22)    VALUE
                'SALEP000 ERROR: RESP1='.
                10  DISPLAY-RESPONSE     PIC 9(8)     VALUE ZEROES.
       *
        COPY SALECOMM.
        COPY MSALE00.
```

FIGURE 5.5   Source code for SALEP000, the add screen processor.

```
      COPY MCUST00.
      COPY ATTRIBUT.
      COPY DFHAID.
      COPY DFHBMSCA.
      COPY CUSTMST.
      LINKAGE SECTION.
      01  DFHCOMMAREA              PIC X(68).
  *
      PROCEDURE DIVISION.
      MAIN-PROG.
  *
  ************************************************************************
  * DETERMINE WHICH POINT IN THE CYCLE APPLIES TO THE CURRENT    *
  * SITUATION. THE FIRST TIME THROUGH, NEITHER MENU IS PRESENT.  *
  * IN THAT CASE, SEND THE MAIN MENU MAP. ON SUBSEQUENT PASSES,  *
  * EITHER THE MAIN MENU OR THE CUSTOMER POPUP WILL BE ON THE    *
  * SCREEN. RECEIVE USER INPUT FROM WHICHEVER MAP IS THERE.      *
  ************************************************************************
  *
          MOVE LOW-VALUES TO SALE000I.
          MOVE LOW-VALUES TO CUST000I.
  *
          IF EIBCALEN NOT = WS-EXPECTED-EIBCALEN
                  OR EIBTRNID NOT = 'SALE'
              PERFORM FIRST-TIME-THROUGH
          ELSE
              MOVE DFHCOMMAREA TO WS-COMMAREA
              IF WS-COMM-PREV-MAP = 'SALE000'
                  PERFORM PROCESS-MAIN-MENU
              ELSE
                  IF WS-COMM-PREV-MAP = 'CUST000'
                      PERFORM PROCESS-POPUP
                  ELSE
                      PERFORM FIRST-TIME-THROUGH.
  *
          GOBACK.
  *
  ************************************************************************
  * AT THIS POINT, THE PROGRAM HAS DETERMINED THAT THE MAIN MENU  *
  * MAP WAS THE MAP MOST RECENTLY DISPLAYED TO THE USER.          *
  *                                                               *
  * DETERMINE WHAT FUNCTION KEY THE USER PRESSED. NOTE THAT       *
  * A FUNCTION KEY WHICH IS VALID WHEN THE MAIN MENU IS ON THE    *
  * SCREEN MIGHT NOT BE VALID WHEN THE POPUP IS ACTIVE. THIS IS   *
  * WHY WE SOMETIMES NEED DIFFERENT FUNCTION KEY LOGIC IN THE     *
  * ROUTINES THAT RECEIVE DIFFERENT MAPS.                         *
  ************************************************************************
  *
      PROCESS-MAIN-MENU.
  *
          IF EIBAID = DFHCLEAR OR DFHPF3
              PERFORM EXIT-ROUTINE
          ELSE
              IF EIBAID = DFHPF10
                  PERFORM CURSOR-TO-ACTION-BAR
              ELSE
                  IF EIBAID = DFHPF12
                      PERFORM FIRST-TIME-THROUGH
                  ELSE
                      IF EIBAID NOT = DFHENTER
                          MOVE BAD-KEY-MSG TO WS-HOLD-MSG
                          PERFORM SEND-MAP-WITH-ERROR.
  *
          MOVE 'MSALE00' TO DISPLAY-RESOURCE.
          MOVE 'RECEIVE MAP' TO DISPLAY-OPERATION.
  *
          EXEC CICS RECEIVE MAP ('SALE000')
                  MAPSET ('MSALE00')
                  INTO (SALE000I)
                  RESP (WS-CICS-RESPONSE1)
```

FIGURE 5.5 *(Continued)*

```
                            END-EXEC.
        *
            IF WS-CICS-RESPONSE1 = DFHRESP(MAPFAIL)
                PERFORM FIRST-TIME-THROUGH
            ELSE
                IF WS-CICS-RESPONSE1 NOT = DFHRESP(NORMAL)
                    PERFORM CHECK-CICS-RESPONSE
                    PERFORM SEND-MAP-WITH-ERROR.
        *
        *****************************************************************
        * IF YOUR TERMINALS SUPPORT COLOR, FOR EXAMPLE, 3279-TYPE      *
        * TERMINALS OR PS/2'S, CHANGE THE COLOR OF A FIELD TO INDICATE *
        * ERRORS. THE COLOR IS SET WITH AN 'EXTENDED ATTRIBUTE' BYTE.  *
        * THE EXTENDED ATTRIBUTE DOES NOT TAKE UP SPACE ON THE DISPLAY. *
        * THIS EXAMPLE IS BEING RUN ON A PS/2. IF YOUR TERMINALS ARE   *
        * MONOCHROME, CHANGE THE ATTRIBUTE BYTE TO A 'BRIGHT' SETTING  *
        * TO INDICATE ERRORS.                                          *
        *****************************************************************
            MOVE DFHTURQ TO SOSEL1C.
            MOVE SPACES TO WS-HOLD-MSG SOMSGO COMSGO.
        *
            PERFORM SALE000-CHECK-ACTION-BAR.
        *
            IF SOSEL1I = '1'
                MOVE 'CUSTMST' TO WS-COMM-OBJECT
            ELSE
                IF SOSEL1I = '2'
                    MOVE 'LINEITM' TO WS-COMM-OBJECT
                ELSE
                    IF WS-COMM-ACTION = 'EXIT' OR 'CANCEL'
                        NEXT SENTENCE
                    ELSE
                        MOVE '_' TO SOSEL1O
                        MOVE DFHRED TO SOSEL1C
                        MOVE BAD-OBJECT-MSG TO WS-HOLD-MSG
                        PERFORM SEND-MAP-WITH-ERROR.
        *
        *****************************************************************
        * SALES HISTORY TRANSACTIONS CANNOT BE CHANGED OR DELETED. IF  *
        * YOU WANT TO MAKE AN ADJUSTMENT, YOU CAN DO IT BY ADDING A NEW *
        * ADJUSTMENT ENTRY WITH THE OPPOSITE SIGN. THIS PRESERVES THE  *
        * AUDIT TRAIL OF UPDATES.                                      *
        *****************************************************************
            IF WS-COMM-OBJECT = 'LINEITM'
                IF WS-COMM-ACTION = 'CHANGE' OR 'DELETE'
                    MOVE BAD-COMBO-MSG TO WS-HOLD-MSG
                    PERFORM SEND-MAP-WITH-ERROR.
        *
            IF WS-COMM-ACTION = 'EXIT'
                PERFORM EXIT-ROUTINE
            ELSE
                IF WS-COMM-ACTION = 'CANCEL'
                    PERFORM FIRST-TIME-THROUGH
                ELSE
                    PERFORM SHOW-POPUP.
        *
        *****************************************************************
        * IF THE CURSOR WAS ANYWHERE ON THE ACTION BAR, USE THE        *
        * POSITION TO SELECT THE ACTION. IF THE CURSOR WAS SOMEWHERE   *
        * ELSE, THEN JUST GO WITH THE DEFAULT CHOICE, WHICH IS "VIEW". *
        *                                                              *
        *****************************************************************
        *
         SALE000-CHECK-ACTION-BAR.
        *
            IF EIBCPOSN  8
                MOVE 'VIEW' TO WS-COMM-ACTION
            ELSE
                IF EIBCPOSN  13
```

FIGURE 5.5   *(Continued)*

```
                 MOVE 'ADD' TO WS-COMM-ACTION
            ELSE
              IF EIBCPOSN  21
                MOVE 'CHANGE' TO WS-COMM-ACTION
              ELSE
                IF EIBCPOSN  29
                  MOVE 'DELETE' TO WS-COMM-ACTION
                ELSE
                  IF EIBCPOSN  35
                    MOVE 'CANCEL' TO WS-COMM-ACTION
                  ELSE
                    IF EIBCPOSN  43
                      MOVE 'EXIT' TO WS-COMM-ACTION
                    ELSE
                      MOVE 'VIEW' TO WS-COMM-ACTION.
 *
 ********************************************************************
 * PROCESS THE CUSTOMER NUMBER POPUP WINDOW MAP. IF THERE IS A    *
 * CUSTOMER NUMBER (NUMERIC), PLACE IT IN THE COMMAREA AND        *
 * SELECT THE NEXT PROGRAM. OTHERWISE, DISPLAY AN ERROR MESSAGE.  *
 ********************************************************************
  PROCESS-POPUP.
 *
      IF EIBAID = DFHPF12
          PERFORM FIRST-TIME-THROUGH
      ELSE
          IF EIBAID NOT = DFHENTER
              MOVE BAD-KEY-MSG TO WS-HOLD-MSG
              PERFORM SEND-MAP-WITH-ERROR.
 *
      MOVE 'MCUST00' TO DISPLAY-RESOURCE.
      MOVE 'RECEIVE MAP' TO DISPLAY-OPERATION.
 *
      EXEC CICS RECEIVE MAP ('CUST000')
              MAPSET ('MCUST00')
              INTO (CUST000I)
              RESP (WS-CICS-RESPONSE1)
              END-EXEC.
 *
      IF WS-CICS-RESPONSE1 = DFHRESP(MAPFAIL)
          PERFORM FIRST-TIME-THROUGH
      ELSE
          IF WS-CICS-RESPONSE1 NOT = DFHRESP(NORMAL)
              PERFORM CHECK-CICS-RESPONSE
              PERFORM SEND-MAP-WITH-ERROR.
 *
      IF WS-COMM-ACTION = 'ADD'
          IF WS-COMM-OBJECT = 'CUSTMST'
              MOVE 'SALEP001' TO WS-XCTL-PGM
          ELSE
              MOVE 'SALEP004' TO WS-XCTL-PGM
      ELSE
          IF WS-COMM-ACTION = 'VIEW'
              IF WS-COMM-OBJECT = 'CUSTMST'
                  MOVE 'SALEP005' TO WS-XCTL-PGM
              ELSE
                  MOVE 'SALEP006' TO WS-XCTL-PGM
          ELSE
              IF WS-COMM-ACTION = 'CHANGE'
                  MOVE 'SALEP002' TO WS-XCTL-PGM
              ELSE
                  IF WS-COMM-ACTION = 'DELETE'
                      MOVE 'SALEP003' TO WS-XCTL-PGM.
 *
      IF COCUSTI IS NUMERIC
          MOVE COCUSTI TO WS-COMM-CUST-NO
      ELSE
          IF WS-XCTL-PGM = 'SALEP005'
              MOVE LOW-VALUES TO WS-COMM-CUST-NO
          ELSE
```

FIGURE 5.5 *(Continued)*

```
                    MOVE CUST-NUM-MSG TO WS-HOLD-MSG
                    PERFORM SEND-MAP-WITH-ERROR.
*
      PERFORM XCTL-NEXT-PGM.
*
  XCTL-NEXT-PGM.
*
      MOVE WS-XCTL-PGM TO DISPLAY-RESOURCE.
      MOVE 'XCTL' TO DISPLAY-OPERATION.
*
      EXEC CICS XCTL
                PROGRAM (WS-XCTL-PGM)
                COMMAREA (WS-COMMAREA)
                RESP (WS-CICS-RESPONSE1)
                END-EXEC.
*
      IF WS-CICS-RESPONSE1 NOT = DFHRESP(NORMAL)
         PERFORM CHECK-CICS-RESPONSE
         PERFORM SEND-MAP-WITH-ERROR.
*
**********************************************************************
* THIS ROUTINE SENDS THE INITIAL MAIN MENU MAP AND/OR REFRESHES *
* IT IF 'CANCEL' WAS SELECTED.                                  *
**********************************************************************
*
  FIRST-TIME-THROUGH.
*
      MOVE LOW-VALUES TO SALE000I.
      MOVE 'SALE000' TO WS-COMM-PREV-MAP.
      MOVE SPACES TO WS-HOLD-MSG
                     WS-COMM-CUST-NO
                     WS-COMM-OBJECT
                     WS-COMM-ACTION
                     WS-COMM-NEXT-CUST-NO.
      MOVE ZEROES TO WS-COMM-COUNTER
                     WS-COMM-DATE
                     WS-COMM-NEXT-DATE
                     WS-COMM-TIME
                     WS-COMM-NEXT-TIME.
      MOVE LOW-VALUES TO WS-COMM-ITEM-CODE
                         WS-COMM-NEXT-ITEM-CODE.
*
      EXEC CICS SEND MAP ('SALE000')
                MAPSET ('MSALE00')
                MAPONLY
                ERASE
                END-EXEC.
*
      EXEC CICS RETURN
                TRANSID ('SALE')
                COMMAREA (WS-COMMAREA)
                END-EXEC.
*
*
**********************************************************************
* THIS ROUTINE SENDS THE CUSTOMER NUMBER POPUP MAP.             *
**********************************************************************
*
  SHOW-POPUP.
*
*
**********************************************************************
* WE ALSO CHANGE THE APPEARANCE OF THE ACTION BAR TO SHOW       *
* WHAT THE USER HAS CHOSEN. IF YOU DON'T HAVE A COLOR TERMINAL, *
* MOVE A 'BRIGHT' ATTRIBUTE CHARACTER TO THE ATTRIBUTE BYTE     *
* FOR THE ITEM TO BE HIGHLIGHTED; 'NORMAL' FOR THE OTHERS.      *
* THIS REQUIRES US TO SEND THE MAIN MAP ONCE AGAIN BEFORE WE    *
* SEND THE POPUP MAP.                                           *
**********************************************************************
*
```

FIGURE 5.5   *(Continued)*

```
*
      MOVE LOW-VALUES TO SALE000I.
*
      MOVE DFHNEUTR TO SOVIEWC SOADDC SOCHGC SODLTC
                      SOEXITC SOCANC.
*
      IF WS-COMM-ACTION = 'VIEW'
        MOVE DFHYELLO TO SOVIEWC
      ELSE
        IF WS-COMM-ACTION = 'ADD'
          MOVE DFHYELLO TO SOADDC
        ELSE
          IF WS-COMM-ACTION = 'CHANGE'
            MOVE DFHYELLO TO SOCHGC
          ELSE
            IF WS-COMM-ACTION = 'DELETE'
              MOVE DFHYELLO TO SODLTC
            ELSE
              IF WS-COMM-ACTION = 'CANCEL'
                MOVE DFHYELLO TO SOCANC
              ELSE
                IF WS-COMM-ACTION = 'EXIT'
                  MOVE DFHYELLO TO SOEXITC
                ELSE
                  MOVE DFHYELLO TO SOVIEWC
                  MOVE 'VIEW' TO WS-COMM-ACTION.
*
      EXEC CICS SEND MAP ('SALE000')
                MAPSET ('MSALE00')
                FROM (SALE000I)
                END-EXEC.
*
      MOVE LOW-VALUES TO CUST000I.
      MOVE 'CUST000' TO WS-COMM-PREV-MAP.
      MOVE SPACES TO WS-COMM-CUST-NO.
*
      EXEC CICS SEND MAP ('CUST000')
                MAPSET ('MCUST00')
                FROM (CUST000I)
                END-EXEC.
*
      EXEC CICS RETURN
                TRANSID ('SALE')
                COMMAREA (WS-COMMAREA)
                END-EXEC.
*
**********************************************************************
* THIS ROUTINE WILL RE-SEND WHATEVER MAP IS CURRENTLY ON THE     *
* SCREEN, WITH THE ERROR MESSAGE SET UP BY THE CALLING ROUTINE. *
**********************************************************************
*
 SEND-MAP-WITH-ERROR.
*
      IF WS-COMM-PREV-MAP = 'CUST000'
          MOVE WS-HOLD-MSG TO COMSGO
          PERFORM SEND-CUST000-BEEP
      ELSE
          MOVE WS-HOLD-MSG TO SOMSGO
          PERFORM SEND-SALE000-BEEP.
*
**********************************************************************
* THIS ROUTINE SENDS CUST000 WITH A WARNING 'BEEP', WITHOUT      *
* DISTURBING OTHER SCREEN CONTENTS.                             *
**********************************************************************
*
 SEND-CUST000-BEEP.
*
      EXEC CICS SEND MAP ('CUST000')
                MAPSET ('MCUST00')
```

FIGURE 5.5   *(Continued)*

```
                     FROM (CUST000I)
                     ALARM
                     END-EXEC.
     *
           EXEC CICS RETURN
                     TRANSID ('SALE')
                     COMMAREA (WS-COMMAREA)
                     END-EXEC.
     *
     ********************************************************************
     * THIS ROUTINE SENDS SALE000 WITH A WARNING 'BEEP'.               *
     ********************************************************************
     *
      SEND-SALE000-BEEP.
     *
           EXEC CICS SEND MAP ('SALE000')
                     MAPSET ('MSALE00')
                     FROM (SALE000I)
                     ALARM
                     END-EXEC.
     *
           EXEC CICS RETURN
                     TRANSID ('SALE')
                     COMMAREA (WS-COMMAREA)
                     END-EXEC.
     *
     ********************************************************************
     * THIS ROUTINE SENDS SALE000 WITH THE CURSOR ON THE ACTION BAR. *
     ********************************************************************
     *
      CURSOR-TO-ACTION-BAR.
     *
           MOVE LOW-VALUES TO SALE000I.
           MOVE 'SALE000' TO WS-COMM-PREV-MAP.
           EXEC CICS SEND MAP ('SALE000')
                     MAPSET ('MSALE00')
                     FROM (SALE000I)
                     CURSOR (1)
                     END-EXEC.
     *
           EXEC CICS RETURN
                     TRANSID ('SALE')
                     COMMAREA (WS-COMMAREA)
                     END-EXEC.
     *
     ********************************************************************
     * DELETE ANY REMAINING TEMP STORAGE QUEUE LEFT FROM OTHER        *
     * PROGRAMS IN THIS SYSTEM. CLEAR THE USER'S SCREEN AND RETURN    *
     * TO CICS. WE IGNORE THE RESPONSE CODE WHEN DELETING TS QUEUE.   *
     ********************************************************************
      EXIT-ROUTINE.
     *
           MOVE EIBTRMID TO QID-TRMID.
           EXEC CICS DELETEQ TS
                     QUEUE (QID-NAME)
                     RESP (WS-CICS-RESPONSE1)
                     END-EXEC.
     *
           EXEC CICS SEND
                     FROM (WS-DUMMY-FIELD)
                     LENGTH (WS-DUMMY-LENGTH)
                     ERASE
                     END-EXEC.
     *
           EXEC CICS RETURN
                     END-EXEC.
     *
     *
     ********************************************************************
```

FIGURE 5.5   *(Continued)*

```
* CHECK THE CICS RESPONSE CODE AND BUILD A MESSAGE EXPLAINING   *
* THE ERROR. IT IS THE RESPONSIBILITY OF THE CALLING ROUTINE    *
* TO INITIALIZE SOME DISPLAY FIELDS IN THE MESSAGE WORK AREA    *
* TO INDICATE THE TYPE OF COMMAND BEING PROCESSED.              *
*                                                               *
* WE DO NOTHING ABOUT CERTAIN RESPONSE CODES HERE SO THAT       *
* THOSE SITUATIONS CAN BE HANDLED WITH LOGIC ELSEWHERE IN THE   *
* PROGRAM.                                                      *
*                                                               *
*****************************************************************
*
 CHECK-CICS-RESPONSE.
*
     EVALUATE WS-CICS-RESPONSE1
     WHEN DFHRESP(NORMAL)
         CONTINUE
     WHEN DFHRESP(MAPFAIL)
         CONTINUE
     WHEN DFHRESP(ENDFILE)
         CONTINUE
     WHEN DFHRESP(DISABLED)
         MOVE 'CALL OPERATIONS' TO DISPLAY-CALL-WHOM
         MOVE DISABLED-MSG TO DISPLAY-DESCRIPTION
         MOVE BUILD-MSG TO WS-HOLD-MSG
     WHEN DFHRESP(DUPREC)
         MOVE DUPREC-MSG TO DISPLAY-DESCRIPTION
         MOVE BUILD-MSG TO WS-HOLD-MSG
     WHEN DFHRESP(DSIDERR)
         MOVE 'CALL PROGRAMMER' TO DISPLAY-CALL-WHOM
         MOVE DSIDERR-MSG TO DISPLAY-DESCRIPTION
         MOVE BUILD-MSG TO WS-HOLD-MSG
     WHEN DFHRESP(INVREQ)
         MOVE 'CALL PROGRAMMER' TO DISPLAY-CALL-WHOM
         MOVE INVREQ-MSG TO DISPLAY-DESCRIPTION
         MOVE BUILD-MSG TO WS-HOLD-MSG
     WHEN DFHRESP(IOERR)
         MOVE 'CALL PROGRAMMER' TO DISPLAY-CALL-WHOM
         MOVE IOERR-MSG TO DISPLAY-DESCRIPTION
         MOVE BUILD-MSG TO WS-HOLD-MSG
     WHEN DFHRESP(ITEMERR)
         MOVE 'CALL PROGRAMMER' TO DISPLAY-CALL-WHOM
         MOVE ITEMERR-MSG TO DISPLAY-DESCRIPTION
         MOVE BUILD-MSG TO WS-HOLD-MSG
     WHEN DFHRESP(LENGERR)
         MOVE 'CALL PROGRAMMER' TO DISPLAY-CALL-WHOM
         MOVE LENGERR-MSG TO DISPLAY-DESCRIPTION
         MOVE BUILD-MSG TO WS-HOLD-MSG
     WHEN DFHRESP(NOSPACE)
         MOVE 'CALL OPERATIONS' TO DISPLAY-CALL-WHOM
         MOVE NOSPACE-MSG TO DISPLAY-DESCRIPTION
         MOVE BUILD-MSG TO WS-HOLD-MSG
     WHEN DFHRESP(NOTFND)
         MOVE NOTFND-MSG TO DISPLAY-DESCRIPTION
         MOVE BUILD-MSG TO WS-HOLD-MSG
     WHEN DFHRESP(PGMIDERR)
         MOVE 'CALL PROGRAMMER' TO DISPLAY-CALL-WHOM
         MOVE PGMIDERR-MSG TO DISPLAY-DESCRIPTION
         MOVE BUILD-MSG TO WS-HOLD-MSG
     WHEN DFHRESP(QIDERR)
         MOVE 'CALL PROGRAMMER' TO DISPLAY-CALL-WHOM
         MOVE QIDERR-MSG TO DISPLAY-DESCRIPTION
         MOVE BUILD-MSG TO WS-HOLD-MSG
     WHEN OTHER
         MOVE 'CALL PROGRAMMER' TO DISPLAY-CALL-WHOM
         MOVE WS-CICS-RESPONSE1 TO DISPLAY-RESPONSE
         MOVE DEFAULT-DESCRIPTION TO DISPLAY-DESCRIPTION
         MOVE BUILD-MSG TO WS-HOLD-MSG
     END-EVALUATE.
*
*
```

FIGURE 5.5 *(Continued)*

```
IDENTIFICATION DIVISION.
PROGRAM-ID. SALEP001.
AUTHOR. ALIDA M. JATICH AND PHIL NOWAK.
******************************************************************
* SALEP001: ADD A NEW CUSTOMER RECORD                            *
* ON THE FIRST PASS, SALEP001 SHOWS A RECORD ADD SCREEN, WITH    *
* THE NEW CUSTOMER NUMBER TAKEN FROM THE COMMAREA. THE TERMINAL  *
* USER ENTERS DATA ON THE SCREEN. ON THE NEXT PASS, SALEP001     *
* ADDS THE NEW RECORD AND DISPLAYS THE RECORD ADD SCREEN AGAIN.  *
******************************************************************
ENVIRONMENT DIVISION.
DATA DIVISION.
WORKING-STORAGE SECTION.
01  MISC-WORK.
    05  WS-CICS-RESPONSE1       PIC S9(8) COMP VALUE +0.
    05  WS-XCTL-PGM             PIC X(8)       VALUE SPACES.
    05  WS-ERROR-FLAG           PIC X          VALUE 'N'.
01  ERROR-MESSAGES.
    05  BAD-KEY-MSG               PIC X(22)      VALUE
        'Function key undefined'.
    05  CUST-NUM-MSG              PIC X(27)      VALUE
        'Customer number not numeric'.
    05  MISSING-DATA-MSG          PIC X(26)      VALUE
        'Please supply missing data'.
    05  SUCCESSFUL-ADD-MSG        PIC X(25)      VALUE
        'Record added successfully'.
    05  DISABLED-MSG              PIC X(16)      VALUE
        'File is disabled'.
    05  DSIDERR-MSG               PIC X(14)      VALUE
        'File not found'.
    05  DUPREC-MSG                PIC X(22)      VALUE
        'Record already on file'.
    05  INVREQ-MSG                PIC X(15)      VALUE
        'Invalid request'.
    05  IOERR-MSG                 PIC X(9)       VALUE
        'I/O error'.
    05  ITEMERR-MSG               PIC X(16)      VALUE
        'Item not defined'.
    05  LENGERR-MSG               PIC X(19)      VALUE
        'Record length error'.
    05  NOSPACE-MSG               PIC X(17)      VALUE
        'File out of space'.
    05  NOTFND-MSG                PIC X(18)      VALUE
        'Record not on file'.
    05  PGMIDERR-MSG              PIC X(27)      VALUE
        'Program not defined to CICS'.
    05  QIDERR-MSG                PIC X(17)      VALUE
        'Queue not defined'.
*
    05  BUILD-MSG.
        10  DISPLAY-OPERATION   PIC X(12)      VALUE SPACES.
        10  FILLER              PIC X          VALUE SPACES.
        10  DISPLAY-RESOURCE    PIC X(8)       VALUE SPACES.
        10  FILLER              PIC X          VALUE SPACES.
        10  DISPLAY-DESCRIPTION PIC X(40)      VALUE SPACES.
        10  FILLER              PIC X          VALUE SPACES.
        10  DISPLAY-CALL-WHOM   PIC X(16)      VALUE SPACES.
*
    05  DEFAULT-DESCRIPTION.
        10  FILLER              PIC X(22)      VALUE
        'SALEP001 ERROR: RESP1='.
        10  DISPLAY-RESPONSE    PIC 9(8)       VALUE ZEROES.
*
COPY SALECOMM.
COPY MSALE01.
COPY ATTRIBUT.
COPY DFHAID.
COPY DFHBMSCA.
COPY CUSTMST.
LINKAGE SECTION.
```

FIGURE 5.6   Source code for SALEP001, the add screen processor.

```
 01  DFHCOMMAREA                   PIC X(68).
*
 PROCEDURE DIVISION.
 MAIN-PROG.
*
*****************************************************************
* DETERMINE WHICH POINT IN THE CYCLE APPLIES TO THE CURRENT    *
* SITUATION. THE FIRST TIME THROUGH, SHOW THE RECORD ADD SCREEN *
* FOR THE FIRST TIME. ON SUBSEQUENT PASSES, PROCESS USER INPUT *
* AND SHOW THE SCREEN AGAIN (OR TRANSFER CONTROL BACK TO THE   *
* MENU PROGRAM, DEPENDING ON FUNCTION KEY).                    *
*****************************************************************
*
     MOVE LOW-VALUES TO SALE001I.
*
     IF EIBCALEN NOT = WS-EXPECTED-EIBCALEN
         PERFORM FIRST-TIME-THROUGH
     ELSE
         MOVE DFHCOMMAREA TO WS-COMMAREA
         IF EIBTRNID = 'SAL1'
                 AND WS-COMM-PREV-MAP = 'SALE001'
             PERFORM PROCESS-ADD-SCREEN
         ELSE
             PERFORM FIRST-TIME-THROUGH.
*
     GOBACK.
*
*****************************************************************
* DETERMINE WHAT FUNCTION KEY THE USER PRESSED.                *
*****************************************************************
*
 PROCESS-ADD-SCREEN.
*
     IF EIBAID = DFHCLEAR OR DFHPF3
         MOVE 'SALEP000' TO WS-XCTL-PGM
         PERFORM XCTL-NEXT-PGM
     ELSE
         IF EIBAID = DFHPF10
             PERFORM CURSOR-TO-ACTION-BAR
         ELSE
             IF EIBAID = DFHPF12
                 PERFORM FIRST-TIME-THROUGH
             ELSE
                 IF EIBAID NOT = DFHENTER
                     MOVE BAD-KEY-MSG TO S1MSGO
                     MOVE -1 TO S1CUSTL
                     PERFORM SEND-SALE001-BEEP.
*
     MOVE 'MSALE01' TO DISPLAY-RESOURCE.
     MOVE 'RECEIVE MAP' TO DISPLAY-OPERATION.
*
     EXEC CICS RECEIVE MAP ('SALE001')
             MAPSET ('MSALE01')
             INTO (SALE001I)
             RESP (WS-CICS-RESPONSE1)
             END-EXEC.
*
     IF WS-CICS-RESPONSE1 = DFHRESP(MAPFAIL)
         PERFORM FIRST-TIME-THROUGH
     ELSE
         IF WS-CICS-RESPONSE1 NOT = DFHRESP(NORMAL)
             PERFORM CHECK-CICS-RESPONSE
             MOVE -1 TO S1CUSTL
             PERFORM SEND-SALE001-BEEP.
*
     MOVE SPACES TO S1MSGO.
*
*****************************************************************
* IF THE CURSOR WAS ANYWHERE ON THE ACTION BAR, USE THE        *
* POSITION TO SELECT THE ACTION. IF THE CURSOR WAS SOMEWHERE   *
```

FIGURE 5.6 *(Continued)*

```
* ELSE, THEN JUST GO WITH THE DEFAULT CHOICE, WHICH IS "ADD".    *
*********************************************************************
*
     IF EIBCPOSN  7
         MOVE 'ADD' TO WS-COMM-ACTION
     ELSE
         IF EIBCPOSN  13
             MOVE 'EXIT' TO WS-COMM-ACTION
         ELSE
             IF EIBCPOSN  21
                 MOVE 'CANCEL' TO WS-COMM-ACTION
             ELSE
                 MOVE 'ADD' TO WS-COMM-ACTION.
*
     IF WS-COMM-ACTION = 'EXIT'
         MOVE 'SALEP000' TO WS-XCTL-PGM
         PERFORM XCTL-NEXT-PGM
     ELSE
         IF WS-COMM-ACTION = 'CANCEL'
             PERFORM FIRST-TIME-THROUGH.
*
*********************************************************************
* EDIT THE DATA IN EACH OF THE USER INPUT FIELDS. YOUR METHODS   *
* MAY VARY DEPENDING ON THE TERMINAL DEVICE FEATURES YOU PLAN    *
* TO SUPPORT AND ON THE STANDARDS AT YOUR INSTALLATION.          *
*                                                                *
* UNDERLINING IS A WAY OF INDICATING HOW MUCH DATA THE USER      *
* CAN ENTER INTO EACH FIELD. IF YOUR TERMINALS OR WORKSTATIONS   *
* SUPPORT THE "UNDERLINE" EXTENDED ATTRIBUTE IN SUCH A WAY       *
* THAT THE APPEARANCE IS ACCEPTABLE TO THE TERMINAL USERS, YOU   *
* CAN OMIT THE LOGIC FOR FILLING EMPTY FIELDS WITH UNDERSCORE    *
* CHARACTERS AND FOR REMOVING TRAILING UNDERSCORES. IN THAT      *
* CASE, YOU WOULD DEFINE THE UNDERSCORES BY USING THE HIGHLIGHT  *
* ATTRIBUTE ON THE BMS MAP.                                      *
*                                                                *
* IF YOUR TERMINALS SUPPORT COLOR, FOR EXAMPLE, 3279-TYPE        *
* TERMINALS OR PS/2'S, CHANGE THE COLOR OF A FIELD TO INDICATE   *
* ERRORS. THE COLOR IS SET WITH AN 'EXTENDED ATTRIBUTE' BYTE.    *
* THE EXTENDED ATTRIBUTE DOES NOT TAKE UP SPACE ON THE DISPLAY.  *
* THIS EXAMPLE IS BEING RUN ON A PS/2. IF YOUR TERMINALS ARE     *
* MONOCHROME, DON'T TRY TO USE THE COLOR EXTENDED ATTRIBUTE.     *
* MOVE A 'BRIGHT' ATTRIBUTE CHARACTER TO THE ATTRIBUTE BYTE.     *
*********************************************************************
*
     IF S1CUSTI = LOW-VALUES OR SPACES OR '_____'
         MOVE ALL '_' TO S1CUSTO
         MOVE DFHRED TO S1CUSTC
         IF WS-ERROR-FLAG = 'N'
             MOVE -1 TO S1CUSTL
             MOVE 'Y' TO WS-ERROR-FLAG
             MOVE MISSING-DATA-MSG TO S1MSGO
         END-IF
     ELSE
         IF S1CUSTI IS NUMERIC
             MOVE S1CUSTI TO CUST-NO
             MOVE DFHTURQ TO S1CUSTC
         ELSE
             MOVE DFHRED TO S1CUSTC
             IF WS-ERROR-FLAG = 'N'
                 MOVE -1 TO S1CUSTL
                 MOVE 'Y' TO WS-ERROR-FLAG
                 MOVE CUST-NUM-MSG TO S1MSGO.
*
     INSPECT S1NAMEI REPLACING ALL '_' BY SPACES.
     IF S1NAMEI  SPACES
         MOVE S1NAMEI TO CUST-NAME
         MOVE DFHTURQ TO S1NAMEC
         MOVE ALP-REG-MOD-UNP TO S1NAMEA
     ELSE
         MOVE DFHRED TO S1NAMEC
         MOVE ALL '_' TO S1NAMEO
```

FIGURE 5.6   *(Continued)*

```
            IF WS-ERROR-FLAG = 'N'
                MOVE -1 TO S1NAMEL
                MOVE 'Y' TO WS-ERROR-FLAG
                MOVE MISSING-DATA-MSG TO S1MSGO.
*
        INSPECT S1CNTCTI REPLACING ALL '_' BY SPACES.
        IF S1CNTCTI    SPACES
            MOVE S1CNTCTI TO CUST-CONTACT
            MOVE DFHTURQ TO S1CNTCTC
            MOVE ALP-REG-MOD-UNP TO S1CNTCTA
        ELSE
            MOVE DFHRED TO S1CNTCTC
            MOVE ALL '_' TO S1CNTCTO
            IF WS-ERROR-FLAG = 'N'
                MOVE DFHRED TO S1CNTCTC
                MOVE -1 TO S1CNTCTL
                MOVE 'Y' TO WS-ERROR-FLAG
                MOVE MISSING-DATA-MSG TO S1MSGO.
*
        INSPECT S1ADDRI REPLACING ALL '_' BY SPACES.
        IF S1ADDRI    SPACES
            MOVE S1ADDRI TO CUST-STREET-ADDRESS
            MOVE DFHTURQ TO S1ADDRC
            MOVE ALP-REG-MOD-UNP TO S1ADDRA
        ELSE
            MOVE DFHRED TO S1ADDRC
            MOVE ALL '_' TO S1ADDRO
            IF WS-ERROR-FLAG = 'N'
                MOVE -1 TO S1ADDRL
                MOVE 'Y' TO WS-ERROR-FLAG
                MOVE MISSING-DATA-MSG TO S1MSGO.
*
        INSPECT S1CITYI REPLACING ALL '_' BY SPACES.
        IF S1CITYI    SPACES
            MOVE S1CITYI TO CUST-CITY
            MOVE DFHTURQ TO S1CITYC
            MOVE ALP-REG-MOD-UNP TO S1CITYA
        ELSE
            MOVE DFHRED TO S1CITYC
            MOVE ALL '_' TO S1CITYO
            IF WS-ERROR-FLAG = 'N'
                MOVE -1 TO S1CITYL
                MOVE 'Y' TO WS-ERROR-FLAG
                MOVE MISSING-DATA-MSG TO S1MSGO.
*
        IF S1STATEI    SPACES AND S1STATEI IS ALPHABETIC
            MOVE S1STATEI TO CUST-STATE
            MOVE DFHTURQ TO S1STATEC
            MOVE ALP-REG-MOD-UNP TO S1STATEA
        ELSE
            MOVE DFHRED TO S1STATEC
            MOVE ALL '_' TO S1STATEO
            IF WS-ERROR-FLAG = 'N'
                MOVE -1 TO S1STATEL
                MOVE 'Y' TO WS-ERROR-FLAG
                MOVE MISSING-DATA-MSG TO S1MSGO.
*
        INSPECT S1ZIPI REPLACING ALL '_' BY SPACES.
        IF S1ZIPI    SPACES
            MOVE S1ZIPI TO CUST-ZIP
            MOVE DFHTURQ TO S1ZIPC
            MOVE ALP-REG-MOD-UNP TO S1ZIPA
        ELSE
            MOVE DFHRED TO S1ZIPC
            MOVE ALL '_' TO S1ZIPO
            IF WS-ERROR-FLAG = 'N'
                MOVE -1 TO S1ZIPL
                MOVE 'Y' TO WS-ERROR-FLAG
                MOVE MISSING-DATA-MSG TO S1MSGO.
*
********************************************************************
```

FIGURE 5.6 *(Continued)*

```
* IF THE DATA IS GOOD, INITIALIZE THE ACCUMULATOR FIELDS IN THE *
* OUTPUT RECORD TO ZERO AND ATTEMPT TO WRITE A NEW RECORD.      *
* LET THE USER KNOW WHETHER THE WRITE WAS SUCCESSFUL.           *
****************************************************************
      IF WS-ERROR-FLAG = 'Y'
          PERFORM SEND-SALE001-BEEP
      ELSE
          MOVE ZEROES TO CUST-LAST-BILL-DATE
                         CUST-LAST-BILL-BAL-DUE
                         CUST-CURR-WK-SALES
          MOVE 'CUSTMST' TO DISPLAY-RESOURCE
          MOVE 'WRITE' TO DISPLAY-OPERATION
          EXEC CICS WRITE
                DATASET ('CUSTMST')
                FROM (CUSTMST-REC)
                RIDFLD (CUST-VSAM-KEY)
                RESP (WS-CICS-RESPONSE1)
                END-EXEC
          MOVE -1 TO S1CUSTL
          IF WS-CICS-RESPONSE1 = DFHRESP(NORMAL)
             MOVE SUCCESSFUL-ADD-MSG TO S1MSGO
             PERFORM SEND-SALE001-RETURN
          ELSE
             PERFORM CHECK-CICS-RESPONSE
             PERFORM SEND-SALE001-BEEP.
*
*
 XCTL-NEXT-PGM.
*
     MOVE WS-XCTL-PGM TO DISPLAY-RESOURCE.
     MOVE 'XCTL' TO DISPLAY-OPERATION.
     EXEC CICS XCTL
               PROGRAM (WS-XCTL-PGM)
               COMMAREA (WS-COMMAREA)
               RESP (WS-CICS-RESPONSE1)
               END-EXEC.
*
     IF WS-CICS-RESPONSE1 NOT = DFHRESP(NORMAL)
         PERFORM CHECK-CICS-RESPONSE
         MOVE -1 TO S1CUSTL
         PERFORM SEND-SALE001-BEEP.
*
*
****************************************************************
* THIS ROUTINE SENDS THE RECORD ADD MAP AND/OR REFRESHES IT    *
* IF 'CANCEL' WAS SELECTED.                                    *
****************************************************************
*
 FIRST-TIME-THROUGH.
*
     MOVE SPACES TO S1MSGO.
     IF WS-COMM-CUST-NO IS NUMERIC
         MOVE WS-COMM-CUST-NO TO S1CUSTO
         MOVE -1 TO S1NAMEL
     ELSE
         MOVE '_____' TO S1CUSTO
         MOVE -1 TO S1CUSTL.
*
     PERFORM SEND-SALE001-RETURN.
*
****************************************************************
* THIS ROUTINE SENDS SALE001 WITH A WARNING 'BEEP'. WE USE THIS *
* ONLY WHEN THE CALLING ROUTINE WANTS TO DISPLAY A WARNING ON   *
* THE MESSAGE LINE OF THIS MAP. CURSOR POSITION MUST BE SET.    *
****************************************************************
*
 SEND-SALE001-BEEP.
*
     IF WS-COMM-PREV-MAP = 'SALE001'
         EXEC CICS SEND MAP ('SALE001')
                   MAPSET ('MSALE01')
```

FIGURE 5.6   *(Continued)*

```
                        FROM (SALE001I)
                        DATAONLY
                        ALARM
                        CURSOR
                        END-EXEC
        ELSE
            MOVE 'SALE001' TO WS-COMM-PREV-MAP
            EXEC CICS SEND MAP ('SALE001')
                        MAPSET ('MSALE01')
                        FROM (SALE001I)
                        ERASE
                        ALARM
                        CURSOR
                        END-EXEC.
*
        EXEC CICS RETURN
                    TRANSID ('SAL1')
                    COMMAREA (WS-COMMAREA)
                    END-EXEC.
*
*
**********************************************************************
* THIS ROUTINE SENDS SALE001 WITH WHATEVER DATA HAS BEEN PLACED *
* ON IT. IF THE PREDEFINED PORTIONS OF THE MAP ARE ALREADY ON   *
* THE SCREEN, SALE001 WILL BE SENT 'DATAONLY'.                  *
**********************************************************************
*
 SEND-SALE001-RETURN.
*
        IF WS-COMM-PREV-MAP = 'SALE001'
            EXEC CICS SEND MAP ('SALE001')
                        MAPSET ('MSALE01')
                        FROM (SALE001I)
                        DATAONLY
                        CURSOR
                        END-EXEC
        ELSE
            MOVE 'SALE001' TO WS-COMM-PREV-MAP
            EXEC CICS SEND MAP ('SALE001')
                        MAPSET ('MSALE01')
                        FROM (SALE001I)
                        ERASE
                        CURSOR
                        END-EXEC.
*
        EXEC CICS RETURN
                    TRANSID ('SAL1')
                    COMMAREA (WS-COMMAREA)
                    END-EXEC.
*
**********************************************************************
* THIS ROUTINE SENDS SALE001 WITH CURSOR ON ACTION BAR.         *
**********************************************************************
*
 CURSOR-TO-ACTION-BAR.
*
        MOVE 'SALE001' TO WS-COMM-PREV-MAP.
        EXEC CICS SEND MAP ('SALE001')
                    MAPSET ('MSALE01')
                    FROM (SALE001I)
                    CURSOR (1)
                    DATAONLY
                    END-EXEC.
*
        EXEC CICS RETURN
                    TRANSID ('SAL1')
                    COMMAREA (WS-COMMAREA)
                    END-EXEC.
*
*
**********************************************************************
```

FIGURE 5.6 *(Continued)*

```
* CHECK THE CICS RESPONSE CODE AND BUILD A MESSAGE EXPLAINING    *
* THE ERROR. IT IS THE RESPONSIBILITY OF THE CALLING ROUTINE     *
* TO INITIALIZE SOME DISPLAY FIELDS IN THE MESSAGE WORK AREA     *
* TO INDICATE THE TYPE OF COMMAND BEING PROCESSED.               *
*                                                                *
* WE DO NOTHING ABOUT CERTAIN RESPONSE CODES HERE SO THAT        *
* THOSE SITUATIONS CAN BE HANDLED WITH LOGIC ELSEWHERE IN THE    *
* PROGRAM.                                                       *
*                                                                *
******************************************************************
*
 CHECK-CICS-RESPONSE.
*
     EVALUATE WS-CICS-RESPONSE1
     WHEN DFHRESP(NORMAL)
         CONTINUE
     WHEN DFHRESP(MAPFAIL)
         CONTINUE
     WHEN DFHRESP(ENDFILE)
         CONTINUE
     WHEN DFHRESP(DISABLED)
         MOVE 'CALL OPERATIONS' TO DISPLAY-CALL-WHOM
         MOVE DISABLED-MSG TO DISPLAY-DESCRIPTION
         MOVE BUILD-MSG TO S1MSGO
     WHEN DFHRESP(DUPREC)
         MOVE DUPREC-MSG TO DISPLAY-DESCRIPTION
         MOVE BUILD-MSG TO S1MSGO
     WHEN DFHRESP(DSIDERR)
         MOVE 'CALL PROGRAMMER' TO DISPLAY-CALL-WHOM
         MOVE DSIDERR-MSG TO DISPLAY-DESCRIPTION
         MOVE BUILD-MSG TO S1MSGO
     WHEN DFHRESP(INVREQ)
         MOVE 'CALL PROGRAMMER' TO DISPLAY-CALL-WHOM
         MOVE INVREQ-MSG TO DISPLAY-DESCRIPTION
         MOVE BUILD-MSG TO S1MSGO
     WHEN DFHRESP(IOERR)
         MOVE 'CALL PROGRAMMER' TO DISPLAY-CALL-WHOM
         MOVE IOERR-MSG TO DISPLAY-DESCRIPTION
         MOVE BUILD-MSG TO S1MSGO
     WHEN DFHRESP(ITEMERR)
         MOVE 'CALL PROGRAMMER' TO DISPLAY-CALL-WHOM
         MOVE ITEMERR-MSG TO DISPLAY-DESCRIPTION
         MOVE BUILD-MSG TO S1MSGO
     WHEN DFHRESP(LENGERR)
         MOVE 'CALL PROGRAMMER' TO DISPLAY-CALL-WHOM
         MOVE LENGERR-MSG TO DISPLAY-DESCRIPTION
         MOVE BUILD-MSG TO S1MSGO
     WHEN DFHRESP(NOSPACE)
         MOVE 'CALL OPERATIONS' TO DISPLAY-CALL-WHOM
         MOVE NOSPACE-MSG TO DISPLAY-DESCRIPTION
         MOVE BUILD-MSG TO S1MSGO
     WHEN DFHRESP(NOTFND)
         MOVE NOTFND-MSG TO DISPLAY-DESCRIPTION
         MOVE BUILD-MSG TO S1MSGO
     WHEN DFHRESP(PGMIDERR)
         MOVE 'CALL PROGRAMMER' TO DISPLAY-CALL-WHOM
         MOVE PGMIDERR-MSG TO DISPLAY-DESCRIPTION
         MOVE BUILD-MSG TO S1MSGO
     WHEN DFHRESP(QIDERR)
         MOVE 'CALL PROGRAMMER' TO DISPLAY-CALL-WHOM
         MOVE QIDERR-MSG TO DISPLAY-DESCRIPTION
         MOVE BUILD-MSG TO S1MSGO
     WHEN OTHER
         MOVE 'CALL PROGRAMMER' TO DISPLAY-CALL-WHOM
         MOVE WS-CICS-RESPONSE1 TO DISPLAY-RESPONSE
         MOVE DEFAULT-DESCRIPTION TO DISPLAY-DESCRIPTION
         MOVE BUILD-MSG TO S1MSGO
     END-EVALUATE.
*
*
```

FIGURE 5.6   *(Continued)*

TEST YOUR UNDERSTANDING

Questions and Exercises

1. Modify programs SALEP000 and SALEP001 to pass the customer number and other data in the TCTUA instead of on the terminal screen. Remember to check the TCTUA length.

2. Modify program SALEP000 so that it will ignore the customer number on the map and will use the CWA customer number whenever PF1 has been used to request addition of a new customer. SALEP000 must do the following:

   a. Check CWA length

   b. Obtain addressability to CWA

   c. Take last assigned customer number from CWA and increment it by 1, updating the value that is in the CWA

   d. Place the new customer number on the SALE001 map

3. Answer these questions regarding RETURN, XCTL, and LINK:

   a. Which of these commands can terminate both the current program and the current task, and which can terminate only the current program?

   b. Which of these commands can cause the TWA to disappear?

   c. How does a program accessed by using LINK terminate so that the calling program will resume control?

   d. If RETURN is used with a TRANSID, how soon will the new transaction begin running? What must take place first?

   e. Which module will be executing if the following sequence of events takes place?

      i.   Program A links to program B

      ii. Program B links to program C

      iii. Program C XCTLs to program D

      iv. Program D links to program E

      v.   Two RETURN commands are executed

4. Here is a problem that will get you to think about what happens to data when several users are performing updates to it:

   Program SALEP001 ordinarily adds a new customer to the file, but under certain circumstances, it may terminate without doing this. If SALEP001 finds that it will be adding a new customer to the file, then everything is correct. If SALEP001 finds that it will not be adding a new customer to the file, we may want to free the unused customer number for future reassignment. This appears simple enough; we can usually do this by decrementing the number in the CWA to return it to its original value.

However, what if some other user has also been adding new customers? In that case, the customer number in the CWA will be larger than the current number plus one. If this is the case, then it is no longer possible to free the customer number. Your assignment is to indicate the changes that could be made to SALEP001 that would free an unused customer number when this is appropriate.

6

Indexed File I/O and Related Topics

We will begin this chapter by reviewing indexed file access concepts. By far, the most frequently used file access method under CICS is VSAM. IBM encourages CICS sites to convert files used in online systems to VSAM whenever this is practical. This chapter will concentrate on the use of VSAM in CICS applications. However, we will not assume that the reader already knows about VSAM. We have found that, despite the vast number of VSAM installations, many programmers in VSAM installations say that they do not feel very comfortable with VSAM and would benefit if they had more training and if someone were available to answer VSAM questions. We will cover enough background material here to allow the reader to use VSAM files under CICS.

The discussion of VSAM internal structure and of Access Method Services (IDCAMS) applies to the mainframe environment. The implementation of VSAM under CICS OS/2 has a different internal structure and will be discussed further in the chapter on CICS OS/2.

Our next topic will be programming techniques for indexed file I/O operations. We will cover command formats and discuss techniques for error handling and for ensuring file integrity. The command formats themselves are fairly straightforward, once you understand how VSAM files work. The real challenge lies in designing an application that will provide protection against invalid or incomplete updates without tying up too many system resources. Since you are probably more interested in results than in challenges, we will suggest some programming exercises that will give you a chance to work with the design issues involved in file I/O.

6.1 INTRODUCTION TO VSAM AND ACCESS METHOD SERVICES

6.1.1 Brief Review of Indexed File Concepts

In this section, we will show you how indexed files are built and accessed, and we will introduce you to the roles they play in online applications. Our aim is to present what you need to know in order to access VSAM files under CICS. We will not take the time to cover the use of VSAM files in batch COBOL or assembler language programs. We will discuss the use of the Access Method Services (IDCAMS) utility to delete, define, print, and reproduce VSAM files, but this discussion will be quite limited in scope. To do justice to those topics would require at least one complete book.

Familiarize yourself as much as possible with all of the file access methods and data base management systems that are used in your installation. These might include SAM, VSAM, and possibly BDAM, as well as data base management systems such as DL/I, DB2, or the OS/2 EE database manager. Mainframe data base management systems, in fact, use VSAM and other file access methods to do their work. Familiarity with these access methods is essential when testing an online application or when turning it over to be put into production. You will need to know how to allocate, define, back up, restore, print, and delete each type of file that is used. You should also be able to interpret catalog entries and to determine whether resource usage is under control.

Principles of Indexing.   VSAM is an enormously powerful tool that allows several applications to do both random and sequential accesses against the same files at the same time. Random accesses may take place through the use of one or more indexes defined against each file. VSAM takes care of index management for you, so you will not see the index in your program, but you should know how an index works. Let us look at an indexed VSAM file, which is also known as a **VSAM key-sequenced data set.**

We can compare an indexed file to an ordinary telephone book. Suppose you want to find Acme Data Processing Supplies in the White Pages. To find it, you use the index at the top of each page. In other words, you start at the beginning of the book and flip through the pages until you find something like ACE—-ACT at the top of a page. Acme falls between ACE and ACT, so you know that if ACME is in the book, then it must be on this page. Therefore, you search the items (data records) on this Page, either until you find Acme or until you find that Acme is not present. You need not search data records on any other page. (See Figure 6.1.)

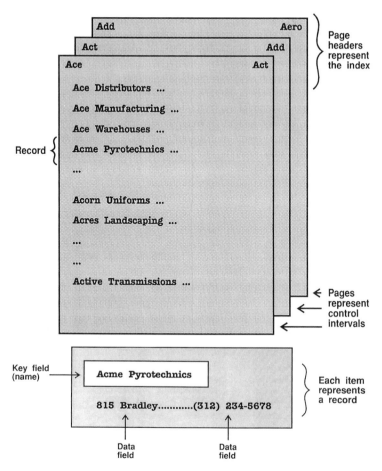

FIGURE 6.1 Indexed file structure of a telephone book.

The data records in a VSAM file may be compared to the actual entries in the telephone book. The name, address, and telephone number correspond to fields within each record. In this case, the name is the key, although special telephone books also exist in which the key is address or telephone number. The key is the identifier field for each record. When you use VSAM to do random accesses, the index tells VSAM where to look to find records with that particular key value.

Suppose the telephone book is very large, and you do not want to spend so much time looking at the indexes to find the right page. You can add another level of indexing to your telephone book by attaching plastic tabs to the pages so that you can find the A's, the B's, the C's, and so forth. In the example, you would use the upper level of the index to find the A's, and you would use the lower level of the index to find the ACE–ACT page within the A's. Similarly, VSAM adds more levels of indexing automatically if a file grows.

Now suppose you have a small-town telephone directory and you want to make up a mailing list of every business in the town. You can start at the beginning of the book and read through it to select the entries that appear to be businesses. You do not need to pay any attention to the index values at the top of each page. What you are doing is processing the telephone directory file *sequentially.* A VSAM file may also be accessed in sequential order, in similar manner.

When we read a VSAM file in **sequential order,** this means that we have requested that the VSAM software give us the records in the order that would exist if they were sorted on their key field. The VSAM records need not be physically stored in sequential order on disc, because VSAM stores records wherever it can find enough free space. However, VSAM will present the records to your program in sequential order. How does VSAM do this? The lowest level of the index is called the **sequence set.** In the sequence are pointers which tell VSAM where to find the next sequential group of records. If a group of records is added or deleted, VSAM adjusts these pointers automatically to reflect the new status. These groups of records in sequential order are contained in units called **VSAM control intervals.**

Perhaps you have worked with **direct access files** before. The direct access method software stores your record after having performed an arithmetic calculation to find out where on the disc it should go. It uses the reverse of this calculation to locate the record again later. This method works very well for random accesses only, but not for sequential accesses. The arithmetic calculation scatters the records all over the output disc extents in order to allow space for the insertion of more records throughout the file. No pointer chain is provided to get from one record to the next. This means that a direct access method file would have to be copied and sorted before it could be used to produce any reporting in sequential order. This is why direct access method files are less practical for online applications. Many online applications require a **file browse**, which presents a portion of a file to the terminal user in sequential order. The terminal user will not want to wait while an entire direct access method file is sorted so that a piece of it can be presented on the terminal screen. However, direct access method files, or BDAM files, are supported under CICS and are practical for use in applications that do not require file browses in a definite key sequence.

VSAM is a more powerful indexed file access method than ISAM. ISAM file access support was dropped from CICS starting with release 1.7. IBM encourages all installations to convert ISAM files to VSAM, because VSAM supports all of the features present under ISAM, and in addition offers certain other advantages. When a record in an ISAM file needs to be deleted, the applications program must place high-values in the delete flag at the beginning of the record. Later, another utility must be run to copy the file over and rebuild it without the flagged records. If there is a high level of file update activity, including deletions, additions, and changes to record length, then the data set can become clogged with deleted records waiting to be removed from the file. The main advantage of VSAM over ISAM is the fact that VSAM frees any space obtained by deleting or shortening existing records so that it can be used again immediately. This means that a VSAM file needs to be reorganized or rebuilt much less often than does an ISAM file.

In addition, VSAM is better equipped to deal with situations in which file additions are heavily concentrated in one portion of a file. VSAM can open up another level of indexing and can incorporate more free space if needed. It can do this because it uses a pointer chain to keep track of where the next group of records, or **control interval**, is stored on disc. If it is necessary to use some space at the end of the file to create a new **control area** (group of control intervals), VSAM again adjusts its pointer values to incorporate the new control area in the chain. These pointers are invisible to your CICS program. Only individual records are presented to your program, so you need not concern yourself with deblocking records from the control intervals.

It is still worthwhile to know about control intervals and control areas because this knowledge will help you to interpret useful information the VSAM catalog listing. Access Method Services can be used to print the contents of a VSAM catalog. The catalog listing can tell you how much activity there has been against the file. It can also warn you about problems. For instance, if the listing says that there have been many **control interval splits** and **control area splits** for a particular file, this means that it is time to redefine the VSAM file with a larger free space allocation and rebuild it.

What are control interval splits and control area splits? Remember that we just said that VSAM can expand the structure of an indexed file to incorporate more free space if necessary. Whenever VSAM needs to add a record, it finds the control area and control interval to which the record should belong, based on the key value of the record being added. If there is enough free space inside the control interval, VSAM will use this free space to add the record.

Splits occur when there is not enough free space inside the control interval. In that case, VSAM will first look for a free control interval inside the same control area. If it finds one, it will make two new control intervals out of the contents of the one that is full, and it will insert the new record in the appropriate position. This activity is called a control interval split. See Figure 6.2.

If there are no free control intervals inside the affected control area, VSAM will look for unoccupied space at the end of the file. If it finds enough, it will use this space to build a new control area, and it will move

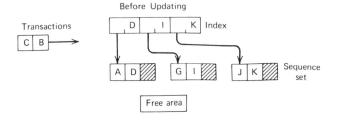

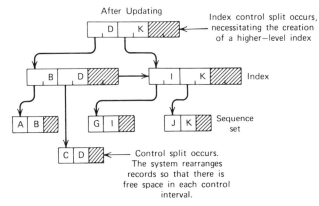

FIGURE 6.2 VSAM control area split. (Source: System/370 Job Control Language, by Gary De Ward Brown, John Wiley & Sons, Inc., 1977. Reprinted with permission.)

some of the data in the old control area into the new control area. The new record can then be added in the appropriate position. VSAM opens up another level of indexing when it does this. This activity is called a control area split.

If you list the contents of a VSAM catalog, you should also check the **highest allocated relative byte address** and the **highest used relative byte address.** Comparing these indicates how much of the extra space at the end of the file has been used. The relative byte addressing scheme numbers each byte in the file in ascending sequential order. In other words, it describes the offset of each byte from the beginning of the file. If the highest used RBA is getting close to the highest allocated RBA, this means that most of the space in the VSAM file has been used up. In that case, it is time to allocate more space to the file.

Types of VSAM files.   There are three types of files supported under VSAM. A VSAM indexed file, such as we have been discussing, is known as a **VSAM key-sequenced data set, or KSDS.** This is the type of VSAM file that is most often used in a CICS environment. It is called a key-sequenced data set because records are added to it in sequence by their principal key.

If your program reads a KSDS sequentially, it will obtain records in sequence by this key.

Another type of VSAM file is known as a **VSAM entry sequenced data set, or ESDS.** As the name implies, records are added to the end of an entry-sequenced data set in the order that they are entered. For some applications, it may make sense to keep the records in chronological order. However, an entry- sequenced data set may only be accessed sequentially, unless other software uses relative byte addresses to build its own index against it, or unless Access Method Services is used to build an alternate index against it. IMS data base software, for example, can use ESDS files for storing data, and it can perform random accesses against this data, because IMS builds its own pointer structure. A CICS program can access records in an ESDS directly by RBA if it has some means of knowing the desired RBA, although this is generally impractical.

You can use Access Method Services to build one or more alternate indexes against any mainframe KSDS or ESDS file, but you must remember that, for a KSDS file, random or sequential accesses through the prime key will be much faster and more efficient than accesses through an alternate key. Also, once an alternate key is defined against a file, there are more pointers to reorganize each time the file is updated.

There is a third type of VSAM file that is used much less often, called a **VSAM relative record data set, or RRDS.** A relative record data set works very much like a table or array. In place of an index or subscript, a relative record number is used. The data set contains a finite number of compartments or slots into which records may be placed. Each compartment or slot is numbered sequentially. If you wish to read record number 5, VSAM will look in compartment 5 to determine whether a record is there. If so, VSAM will present the record to your program. If not, VSAM will set the return code to indicate that the record is not there. You can add a new record to a relative record data set only by placing the record in one of the unoccupied compartments. If you tell VSAM to delete the record from compartment 5, then you will be able to place a new record in compartment 5 after this is done.

Types of File Access.   Experienced COBOL programmers may already know that, in a batch COBOL program, sequential, random, or dynamic access may be specified for each VSAM KSDS file. Dynamic access implies that both sequential and random access will be supported against the same file in the program. In a batch COBOL program, READ (file-name) is used to perform random accesses, and READ (file-name) NEXT is used to perform sequential accesses, if dynamic access has been specified. In a CICS program, dynamic access is assumed. The READ command is used for random accesses, and the READNEXT command is used for sequential accesses. CICS, in addition, supports backward sequential accesses, using the READPREV command. Backward sequential access is not supported under batch COBOL.

When VSAM updates a key-sequenced data set, it uses the primary key field within the record to perform a random access in order to carry out the update. However, if you know that you will be adding a large number of records in sequential order, and you know that there are no existing records in the file in that key range, then you can use the MASSINSERT option under CICS to load the records more efficiently.

6.1.2   Introduction to Access Method Services Utilities (IDCAMS)

VSAM files and catalogs should be manipulated only by programs or utilities designed for that specific purpose. Anything else either will not run at all or will destroy VSAM data sets and catalogs. Old OS/VS batch file management utilities that support ISAM do not support VSAM. VSAM files also cannot be edited interactively in the normal manner under TSO/ISPF, unless a special non-IBM online utility is purchased for that purpose. Since VSAM has its own catalog structure and pointer structure, *never* attempt to manipulate VSAM files or catalogs by using DITTO or any other utility based on physical I/O commands. **The utility most often used with VSAM files is** Access Method Services. **It is available under both MVS and DOS/VSE. It may be run as a batch job, with one or more IDCAMS commands embedded in JCL. Otherwise, individual IDCAMS commands may be run as a foreground job under TSO. Access Method Services allows you to build VSAM catalogs, allocate space, define files, copy data into files, delete files, print file contents, print catalog entries, and so forth.**

IDCAMS is NOT used to define VSAM files supported by CICS OS/2 on a microcomputer. These have a different internal structure and are defined using the CICS OS/2 file control table (FCT). VSAM under OS/2 will be discussed later in Chapter 13, which deals with CICS OS/2. However, the CICS commands used for VSAM file I/O in applications programs under CICS OS/2 are completely identical to the mainframe versions of those commands. Only the setup methods are different.

All information concerning mainframe VSAM files is stored in a **VSAM catalog.** Since DOS/VS does not have a system catalog, some installations use one or more VSAM catalogs to keep track of all files in the system, both VSAM and non-VSAM. There is always one VSAM master catalog, and there may be one or more VSAM user catalogs. In the VSAM master catalog, there is an entry for each VSAM file defined directly under the master catalog, and there is an entry for each VSAM user catalog defined directly under the master catalog. In an OS/VS1 system, the system master catalog must contain an entry that refers to a separate VSAM master catalog. In an MVS system, on the other hand, the system master catalog does double duty as the VSAM master catalog.

User catalogs may contain catalog entries for VSAM and non-VSAM data sets, and, under MVS systems, for CVOLs. User catalogs make it easier to apply password protection to groups of files, to separate test data from production data, to set up backup and recovery procedures, and to isolate any problem areas. You might not need to know about the catalog structure if you are only interested in reading an existing file in a CICS program. However, if you will need to set up a new VSAM file for test purposes, you will have to know where you will be permitted to catalog your new file. See Figure 6.3, which shows the relationship between VSAM catalogs and files.

A catalog entry for a VSAM file describes a **VSAM cluster**. A cluster is the combination of the entities that make up one particular VSAM file. In other words, for a KSDS file, a cluster is the combination of the data portion of the file and the index portion of the file. One data set name is provided for the cluster, and two other data set names are provided for the

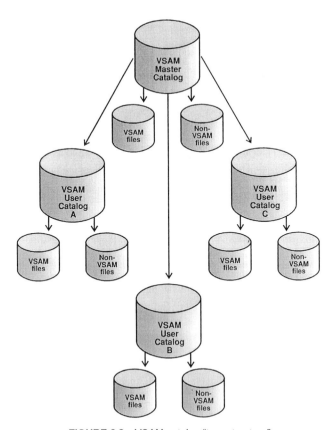

FIGURE 6.3 VSAM catalog "tree structure"

separate data and index portions of the file. For an ESDS file, a cluster is made up of only the data file. When you use Access Method Services to define a file, you should supply a data set name for all entities involved. If you fail to do so, IDCAMS software will provide rather strange-looking names containing time stamps. These will be different each time you run the file definition job.

For each VSAM file that you use, you probably will want to set up a job to delete the file, to redefine it, and to reload data into the file from a sequential backup file. Such a job may be used for building test data or for recovering a VSAM file if some mishap takes place.

Many installations have DASD management standards which apply to VSAM file definition jobs. These standards cover such things as file sharing, security, naming conventions, space allocation, and so forth. It's a good idea to talk with your manager or your systems programmer to find out what formal or informal policies exist.

Here is a job that is intended to create test data; it contains a delete command to dispose of the old file if a file with the same name is on the catalog, it defines a new VSAM KSDS cluster that is to be cataloged in a user catalog, it copies data into the file from an existing sequential data set, it prints the catalog entry for the new VSAM KSDS file, and it prints the test data that has been loaded into the file. This job uses five different IDCAMS commands to do this: DELETE, DEFINE, REPRO, LISTCAT, and PRINT. Access Method Services commands are free- format, but should begin to the right of column 1. Each command is used with one or more keyword parameters. Some keyword parameters are followed by arguments, which are placed within parentheses. For instance, the PRINT command is followed by the INDATASET parameter. The argument used with INDATASET indicates the file to be printed. Notice that each opening parenthesis must be paired with a closing parenthesis. A hyphen may be used to indicate that the command is being continued on the following line.

```
//VSAMBLD   JOB     (account),'ALIDA JATICH'
//                  EXEC    PGM=IDCAMS
//STEPCAT  DD       DSN=USERCAT.NAME,DISP=SHR
//BACKUP   DD       DSN=SEQ.BACKUP.NAME,DISP=OLD
//SYSPRINT DD       SYSOUT=A
//SYSIN    DD       *
   DELETE(YOUR.CLUSTER) -
           CLUSTER
   DEFINE CLUSTER -
           (NAME(YOUR.CLUSTER) -
           VOL(USER01) -
           KEYS(3,0) -
           RECORDSIZE(150 150) -
           SHAREOPTIONS(2) -
           FREESPACE(20 15) -
           CYLINDERS(20)) -
```

```
            INDEXED -
        DATA -
            (NAME(YOUR.DATA)) -
        INDEX -
            (NAME(YOUR.INDEX)) -
        CATALOG(USERCAT.NAME)
    REPRO -
        INFILE(BACKUP) -
        OUTDATASET(YOUR.CLUSTER)
    LISTCAT -
        ENTRIES(YOUR.CLUSTER) -
        CATALOG(USERCAT.NAME)
    PRINT
        INDATASET(YOUR.CLUSTER)
//
```

DELETE

The DELETE command removes the catalog entry for a VSAM file. To delete a VSAM cluster, specify the cluster name and the word CLUSTER so that IDCAMS will know that you want to delete an entire cluster, and will not look for some other type of entity with that name. If the cluster is not in the catalog, which will be the case the first time you run this job, an internal return code of 8 will be generated from this command, but this should not cause any difficulties. The IDCAMS return code exists only within the job step and has nothing to do with the MVS return code with which you might be familiar.

DEFINE CLUSTER

This command creates a catalog entry describing a VSAM file, but it does not place any records in the file. Notice that this command has three parts. It allows you to specify parameters for the cluster as a whole, and to override them, if you choose, for the data and index portions of the file. In this example, only the file names will be specified separately for the data and index portions of the file. Notice also that the user catalog name is specified at the end. There are an enormous number of parameters available for use in this command, so we will only touch on some of the more important ones. The others all have default values and can ordinarily be omitted.

   In this example, the new cluster will go on a volume that already contains VSAM data space, or usable space for VSAM files, allocated in the appropriate VSAM user catalog. If we wished to place the file on a volume that has no VSAM data space, we would need to specify UNIQUE and FILE(ddname), and we would need to supply a DD statement corresponding with the FILE parameter to specify the unit and volume serial number of the desired pack.

NAME

Do *not* specify the DDNAME that you will want to use later. Specify the actual file name (DSNAME).

VOL(VOLSER)

Supply the volume serial number of the pack that should contain the data set.

KEYS(LENGTH OFFSET)

KEYS is a misnomer: Only one primary KEY field per record can be specified for a given cluster. (Alternate indexes are defined and built using separate IDCAMS commands.) The key field must be one contiguous piece, but it may be concatenated from various fields within the record, regardless of data type. Key length is in bytes. Key offset is the number of bytes in the record that appear before the beginning of the key field. If the key is in the first position of the record, the offset is zero.

RECORDSIZE(AVERAGE MAXIMUM)

Average and maximum record length are given in bytes. For a file with fixed-length records, average and maximum length will be identical.

SHAREOPTIONS(OPTION OPTION)

This parameter refers to sharing of the VSAM file between all batch and online partitions or regions that need to access it. 2 is usually specified for the first option, because it allows all regions or partitions to read the file, but only one to update the file. If you want to lock out all update processing while one or more regions are reading the file, specify 1 for the first option. File sharing takes place only if the JCL used within each region or partition is set up properly. In an MVS system, the VSAM file must be specified as DISP = SHR. Avoid using 3 or 4 for the first share option. Share option 3 provides no file integrity checking whatsoever. Batch programs which access files defined with share option 3 protect themselves by issuing ENQ and DEQ macros to reserve the resource during updates. Share option 4 works much like share option 3, except for the fact that it does not allow any program to increase the high-used RBA, and because it fetches a fresh copy of the record from disc for each READ, and locks the record during each WRITE until it is completed.

The second share option is meaningful only in multiple- system environments. File sharing and data integrity in this environment is a complex issue. The systems programmer usually enforces site standards in this regard.

FREESPACE(CI CA)

This parameter allows you to specify the percentage of free space to allow within each control interval, and the percentage of free control intervals to allow within each control area. If zero is specified for both parameters, then all unused space will be at the end of the file, and any record additions will bring about a control area split. Zero should be specified only if no data is to be added to the file, which is an unlikely situation.

CYLINDERS(NUMBER)

This parameter is a substitute for the space parameter that you use in your JCL for defining other types of files.

INDEXED

This parameter indicates that the file is to be a KSDS file. An ESDS file would be specified as NONINDEXED. (For an ESDS file, you would also eliminate the INDEX specification, the KEYS, and the FREESPACE.)

REPRO

The REPRO command reproduces, or copies, data from one data set into another. The data sets may be VSAM or non-VSAM. REPRO is used most often to perform backup and recovery. If you have DD statements for the input or output files, you can specify the DDNAMEs in the INFILE or OUTFILE arguments. Otherwise, if the data sets are already listed in your VSAM catalog, you can substitute the actual file names in the INDATASET or OUTDATASET arguments.

Suppose you want to make a test file by copying only a portion of an existing file. To copy a fixed number of records, starting at the beginning of the input file, you can specify COUNT(number) in the REPRO command. If you want to skip past a fixed number of records before beginning to copy another fixed number of records, you can specify SKIP(number) followed by COUNT(number) in the REPRO command. If the input file is a KSDS VSAM file, and if you happen to know the beginning and ending keys of the desired portion of the file, there is another method: You can specify the beginning key by using FROMKEY(key) and the ending key by using TOKEY(key). File keys can be given as character literals, which should be enclosed in quotation marks if any special characters are included. They can also be given as assembler-format hexadecimal literals. The REPRO command using these options might look like this:

```
REPRO -
INFILE(indd) -
OUTFILE(outdd) -
FROMKEY(X'F1F9F0F0') -
```

```
TOKEY(X'F2F0F0F0')
LISTCAT
```

The LISTCAT command lists catalog entries for VSAM clusters, non-VSAM files, data space, alternate indexes, and user catalogs. To get a listing of just the names that are in the catalog, LISTCAT may be specified with no parameters. To get a full listing of the entire catalog, LISTCAT ALL may be specified. To get a listing of just a few entries, the ENTRIES parameter may be used to specify the ones that are needed.

PRINT

The PRINT command prints VSAM file contents. Results look somewhat like a storage dump. INDATASET or INFILE may be used to specify the file to be printed, as in the REPRO command. FROMKEY, TOKEY, SKIP, and COUNT may be used with the PRINT command to limit the printed output to those portions of the file that are most needed. These options are used the same way in the PRINT command as they are used in the REPRO command.

A suggestion: Although Access Method Services is not really part of CICS, proficiency with it is vital for anyone who wants to work successfully in a mainframe CICS installation. Since this is not primarily a VSAM textbook, we present only a small sample of what Access Method Services will do. Each command shown here contains other useful options. Use this section as a guide, but refer to appropriate manuals for materials not covered here.

6.2   CONCEPTS OF ONLINE INDEXED FILE PROCESSING

6.2.1   Relationship between Files and CICS

As we discussed in the first chapter, the random-access data sets used within the CICS region or partition are defined in the CICS file control table and sometimes also in a DD statement or DLBL and EXTENT statements in a mainframe CICS startup job. This applies to sequential and other data sets as well as to indexed data sets. The file control table entry specifies what CICS will be allowed to do with the file when it is opened. (VSAM KSDS files are ordinarily intended to support all types of reads and updates.) The FCT supplies the information that, in a batch COBOL program, would come from the SELECT statement, the FD specification, and the OPEN statement. When you use the CEMT transaction to open a file defined under CICS, you need not specify whether the file is to be opened as input, output, or I/O. The file control table entry takes care of this. The same is true if the FCT specifies that the file is to be opened automatically at system startup time.

Since the CICS system appears to the operating system as though it is an ordinary program, the operating system allows a VSAM file to be shared between batch and online regions or partitions. If the file is open under CICS, and if the CICS system is allowed to access the file for update purposes, then batch programs may still be able to open it for input, depending upon how the file was defined. Since VSAM KSDS files are ordinarily opened for all available types of access under CICS, it may be necessary to close and disable the VSAM files under CICS before running batch updates.

Under CICS releases prior to 1.7, CICS could open a VSAM file only when the VSAM file has been **loaded**. What does this mean? If a VSAM file has been defined, but it has never had any records in it, then certain formatting has not been done, and the file is considered to be **non-loaded**. A file from which all records have been deleted is considered to be **unloaded**, but could still be opened under CICS. In other words, a file must have had records in it in order to be available for opening under CICS. You may need to use a batch program or an IDCAMS job to place the first record in a VSAM file.

The CICS file control program was rewritten for CICS 1.7. Therefore, with CICS 1.7 and greater, it is no longer necessary to create a dummy record in a new VSAM file in order to put it into the loaded state so that CICS can access it. Any file that is not in the loaded state (no records have been written to it since it was created) will be opened by CICS in the load mode. The first I/O access will obviously have to be a write, since there is nothing there to read update, or delete. CICS will do the first write in the load mode, and then will close and reopen the file to do the rest of the accesses in the update mode.

6.2.2 Sharing Files among Applications in a CICS System

Data sets may also be shared among CICS tasks running within the same region or partition. The number of pending I/O requests that can be active against a file at a given time is given in the "number of strings" parameter in the FCT. Obviously, this sharing could not work if each task locked up the whole file while it performed its updates. What actually happens? The CICS READ command allows you to specify that the READ is for a subsequent update. If UPDATE is specified, the VSAM control interval for that record is locked up, or **enqueued**, until a command has been used to unlock or dequeue the record, or a successful update or deletion of that record has been executed, or the task ends. Also, the DELETE and WRITE commands keep the control interval enqueued until the I/O operation is complete, even though both commands can be executed without a prior READ for UPDATE.

What happens if task AAAA has enqueued record 1 of FILE001 and is waiting to enqueue record 1 of FILE002, and task BBBB has enqueued record 1 of FILE002 and is waiting to enqueue record 1 of FILE001? Neither task will be able to do anything; in other words, they will both "hang up." This is known as a **lockout or "deadly embrace."** Applications that access the same file resources should be designed to access all of them in the same order. No program or task should keep resources enqueued longer than necessary.

6.3 PROGRAMMING TECHNIQUES FOR INDEXED FILE I/O

6.3.1 I/O Commands for VSAM KSDS Files

The command that you will use most often is the READ command. Here is its format:

```
EXEC CICS READ
           DATASET(name)
           [UPDATE]
           RIDFLD(data-area)
           {SET(pointer-ref)|INTO(data-area)}
           [LENGTH(data-area)]
           [KEYLENGTH(data-value)[GENERIC]]
           [RBA|RRN]
           [GTEQ|EQUAL]
           END-EXEC.
```

The data set name, as we mentioned before, is the DDNAME or logical name that appears in the CICS startup job and in the CICS file control table. The SET and INTO options work in much the same way here as they do in other CICS commands. UPDATE is specified to lock a record being read so that it can be updated later without interference from other programs. For CICS releases 1.6 and greater, command-level programs are restricted from executing another READ for UPDATE against a file if the same program has already executed a READ for UPDATE against another record in the same file and if the record is still enqueued (locked).

RIDFLD stands for *record identification field.* You should specify the name of a field accessible to your program and outside of the VSAM record description. This field should contain the VSAM file key that is to be used as a search argument for finding the desired record.

KEYLENGTH and GENERIC are used to find a record in a key-sequenced data set if only the higher-order (most significant) part of the key is known. The KEYLENGTH specifies the number of bytes in the known portion of the file key. If you specify EQUAL, the I/O operation will fail if no record with those bytes in its key is on the file. If you specify GTEQ, the I/O operation will find the record with the next higher key if no record with those bytes in its key is on the file. Suppose TSTFILE contains two records beginning with A, no records beginning with B, and one record beginning with C. Suppose also that the search argument for the file is set up in this way:

If the following READ command with the EQUAL option is executed, the NOTFND condition will be raised. This tells your program that no record beginning with B is on the file.

```
EXEC CICS READ
           INTO(YOUR-WORK-AREA)
           LENGTH(YOUR-RECORD-LENGTH)
           DATASET('TSTFILE')
           RIDFLD(KEY-B)
           GENERIC
           KEYLENGTH(GEN-KEY-LENGTH)
           EQUAL
           END-EXEC
```

On the other hand, if GTEQ is substituted for EQUAL in the same command, the I/O operation will successfully return the record with the next higher key; in other words, the record beginning with C. Do not use generic keys or GTEQ when you are reading a record for UPDATE. A READ for UPDATE using a generic key will not work if the file control table entry for the data set specifies logging for dynamic transaction backout. Dynamic transaction backout is an IBM-supplied recovery tool that is used in many installations. You will not want your application to stop working suddenly if someone decides to install DTB at your site in the future.

The RBA parameter is specified if your program somehow has obtained the binary relative byte address of the desired record, and has placed this relative byte address search argument in the RIDFLD. RRN is specified if your program is using a binary relative record number to find the desired record in a relative record data set. These two options are not used very often in CICS applications.

VSAM Error Checking.   Batch COBOL programmers who use VSAM should already be accustomed to testing the VSAM return code in their programs each time a VSAM file is opened, closed, or accessed. This must be done because the COBOL compiler does not insert any routines to check for VSAM I/O failure and terminate the program if I/O failure has taken place. If a batch COBOL program does not check the VSAM return code after each I/O operation, it will continue running even if it is working with a garbage record.

The CICS system does VSAM error checking and will terminate the task if an I/O command has failed. However, if you use the RESP error-checking parameter with CICS 1.7 or greater, the CICS default of terminating abnormally on an I/O failure will be turned off. In other words, once you specify RESP, you are responsible for checking the value in your response code field and handling all unexpected situations accordingly. The CICS default of abnormal termination is generally *not* appropriate for every situation in which an I/O command has failed. For example, for a READ command, you usually will not want to "bomb" your application whenever a NOTFND (record not on file) condition occurs. Instead, you would send a message to the terminal user. Similarly, for a WRITE command, you would likely want to send a message to the user if you encountered the DUPREC condition, which is raised whenever a program tries to add a record with the same key as a record already on the file. For any file I/O command, there is always a possibility that someone may have used CEMT commands to close and disable the required data set. Ordinarily, it makes sense to terminate the task abnormally if a required file is not open under CICS. CICS will automatically put out an error message in that case. However, if you check for the NOTOPEN condition yourself, you can substitute your own error message and explain the situation to the terminal users in their own terms.

File Update Commands. Here are the parameters available for the WRITE command:

```
EXEC CICS WRITE
          DATASET(name)
          RIDFLD(data-area)
          FROM(data-area)
          [KEYLENGTH(data-value)]
          [RBA|RRN]
          [MASSINSERT]
          END-EXEC.
```

The WRITE command is used for writing a new record to a VSAM file. (The REWRITE command is used for updating a record that is *already on the file*.) Most of the parameters for the WRITE command are used in the same way as the corresponding parameters for the READ command that we just discussed. The record should be prepared in a work area of the appropriate length in working storage or in the linkage section. The name of this work area is specified in the FROM option. If the file contains variable-length records, such as with OCCURS DEPENDING ON, you will need to specify the LENGTH option.

If you are writing a record to a VSAM key-sequenced data set, or KSDS, the VSAM access method software will place the record in the correct position depending on the key in the record. **You must use the RIDFLD parameter to specify the correct file key value. The RIDFLD contents must agree with whatever is in the key field defined within the record that you are writing to the file.** For a KSDS file, you can specify the correct key field name within your FROM area in the RIDFLD parameter, or you can use a separate work area. In the latter case, it is your responsibility to see that these fields agree with one another. If they do not, the record could end up in the wrong part of the file, or worse. Where is the key field defined within the record? If you do not know, you can find the answer by looking at the Access Method Services commands in the job that was used to define the KSDS file. The KEYS parameter in the DEFINE CLUSTER command will indicate the length and offset of the key field. (Under OS/2, as we will see later, you would look at the FCT table entry.)

If you are placing a record in a VSAM relative record data set, or RRDS, use the RRN option to indicate that your search argument field (RIDFLD) contains a binary relative record number instead of a file key. The record will go into the appropriate compartment in the file.

If you are adding a new record to a VSAM entry-sequenced data set, or ESDS, the record will go at the end of the file. You need not place any data in the RIDFLD before writing the record. However, you must still specify RBA and specify a binary RIDFLD. The system will use the RIDFLD to return the relative byte address to which the new record was written.

Suppose many records are being added to a VSAM key-sequenced data set at the same time in ascending key sequence. In this case, for greater efficiency, the MASSINSERT option may be specified in the WRITE command used to write each record. Since MASSINSERT locks VSAM control intervals, your program should write all of the records to the file at once, without interspersing any other processing. After the records have been written, the UNLOCK command should be used to unlock (dequeue) the affected control intervals, so that other programs can use them.

The UNLOCK command should also be used whenever a READ for UPDATE was used, but your program decided for some reason not to complete the update or delete operation. Under most circumstances, issuing the UNLOCK allows other applications to access the affected records without waiting for your task to terminate.

Here is the format of the UNLOCK command:

```
EXEC CICS UNLOCK
          DATASET(name)
          END-EXEC.
```

In order to update an existing record on a VSAM file, your program must first have read it successfully by using a READ command with the UPDATE option. When your program updates the record, it does not need to specify the RIDFLD, because the system assumes that the record that was READ for UPDATE will be written back into the same place on the file. The LENGTH parameter is needed if the record is part of a file with variable-length records. If you are dealing with a key-sequenced data set, make sure that the key field inside the record matches the contents of the RIDFLD that was used in the READ for UPDATE. In other words, **never tamper with the contents of the key field inside a record that is being updated**. If you need to change the key of an existing record, you must DELETE the existing record and WRITE a new one with a different key.

Only one READ for UPDATE may be pending against any one data set at any given time.

```
EXEC CICS REWRITE
          DATASET(name)
          FROM(data-area)
          [LENGTH(data-value)]
          END-EXEC.
```

The method most often used for deleting a record from a VSAM key sequenced data set resembles the method used for updating a record. The record is obtained from the file by using a READ for UPDATE. It is then deleted using this command:

```
EXEC CICS DELETE
          DATASET(name)
          END-EXEC.
```

The sample record deletion program, SALEP003, uses this form of the delete command. The terminal user may request the delete function from the main menu. The main menu program requests the customer number from the terminal user and then XCTLs to the delete program, SALEP003. The delete screen shows the contents of the record that is about to be deleted. If the terminal user wishes to go ahead with the deletion, he or she may press ENTER. In that case, SALEP003 will perform a READ for UPDATE against the same record. If no updates have been made against the current week sales field, SALEP003 will perform a DELETE command, using the syntax that we have just shown. Since the record has already been locked for update, it is not necessary to identify it again by specifying the RIDFLD in the DELETE command.

It is also possible to delete a record or group of records directly, without previously doing a READ for UPDATE. This is done by specifying the record key in the DELETE command:

```
EXEC CICS DELETE
          DATASET(name)
          [RIDFLD(data-area)]
          [KEYLENGTH(data-value)]
          [GENERIC[NUMREC(data-area)]]]]
          [RBA|RRN]
          END-EXEC.
```

The record key parameters work in the same way as they do in the READ for UPDATE command, except for the NUMREC parameter. The NUMREC parameter allows you to specify a maximum number of records to delete, if you are using generic keys. Obviously, deleting records without reading them first, or deleting whole groups of records, could lead to unintentional loss of desired records. If you are not absolutely sure about what you are doing, you could obliterate good records accidentally. **Well-designed applications allow the user to see the contents of any record before it is deleted, and allow the user to end the task without deleting the record if desired.** Notice that, in the sample application, the user begins by requesting a deletion from the menu screen. The contents of the record to be deleted are shown on the delete screen. At this point, the user can either delete the record or return to the menu without deleting the record. The user should always be given an opportunity to change his or her mind about a deletion. See Figure 6.4.

```
       IDENTIFICATION DIVISION.
       PROGRAM-ID. SALEP003.
       AUTHOR. ALIDA M. JATICH AND PHIL NOWAK.
      ************************************************************
      * SALEP003: DELETE CUSTOMER RECORD CONTENTS               *
      * ON THE FIRST PASS, SALEP003 GETS THE CUSTOMER NUMBER FROM THE *
      * COMMAREA AND READS THE CUSTOMER RECORD HAVING THAT KEY. IT    *
      * SHOWS THE EXISTING CONTENTS ON THE DELETE SCREEN. THE TERMINAL*
      * USER PRESSES ENTER TO DELETE. ON THE NEXT PASS, SALEP003      *
      * DELETES THE RECORD AND DISPLAYS THE DELETE SCREEN AGAIN.      *
      ************************************************************
       ENVIRONMENT DIVISION.
       DATA DIVISION.
       WORKING-STORAGE SECTION.
       01  MISC-WORK.
           05  WS-CICS-RESPONSE1        PIC S9(8) COMP VALUE +0.
           05  WS-TSQ-ITEM1             PIC S9(4) COMP VALUE +1.
           05  WS-XCTL-PGM              PIC X(8)       VALUE SPACES.
       01  QID-NAME.
           05  QID-TRMID                PIC XXXX       VALUE SPACES.
           05  FILLER                   PIC XXXX       VALUE 'SALE'.
       01  CUSTMST-Q.
           05  CUSTNO-Q                 PIC X(6)       VALUE SPACES.
           05  FILLER                   PIC X(144)     VALUE SPACES.
       01  ERROR-MESSAGES.
           05  BAD-KEY-MSG              PIC X(22)      VALUE
               'Function key undefined'.
           05  CUST-NUM-MSG             PIC X(27)      VALUE
               'Customer number not numeric'.
           05  MISSING-DATA-MSG         PIC X(26)      VALUE
               'Please supply missing data'.
           05  SUCCESSFUL-DELETE-MSG    PIC X(27)      VALUE
               'Record deleted successfully'.
           05  ENTER-CUST-NO-MSG        PIC X(29)      VALUE
               'Please enter customer number.'.
           05  DELETE-RECORD-MSG        PIC X(44)      VALUE
               'Press enter key to delete or PF12 to cancel.'.
           05  CANNOT-DELETE-MSG        PIC X(39)      VALUE
               'Cannot delete - sales greater than zero'.
           05  RECORD-CHANGED-MSG       PIC X(39)      VALUE
               'Cannot delete - record has been changed'.
           05  DISABLED-MSG             PIC X(16)      VALUE
               'File is disabled'.
           05  DSIDERR-MSG              PIC X(14)      VALUE
               'File not found'.
           05  DUPREC-MSG               PIC X(22)      VALUE
               'Record already on file'.
           05  INVREQ-MSG               PIC X(15)      VALUE
               'Invalid request'.
           05  IOERR-MSG                PIC X(9)       VALUE
               'I/O error'.
           05  ITEMERR-MSG              PIC X(16)      VALUE
               'Item not defined'.
           05  LENGERR-MSG              PIC X(19)      VALUE
```

FIGURE 6.4   Source code for SALEP003, the record deletion screen processor.

```
                 'Record length error'.
        05   NOSPACE-MSG              PIC X(17)        VALUE
                 'File out of space'.
        05   NOTFND-MSG               PIC X(18)        VALUE
                 'Record not on file'.
        05   PGMIDERR-MSG             PIC X(27)        VALUE
                 'Program not defined to CICS'.
        05   QIDERR-MSG               PIC X(17)        VALUE
                 'Queue not defined'.
   *
        05   BUILD-MSG.
             10   DISPLAY-OPERATION   PIC X(12)        VALUE SPACES.
             10   FILLER              PIC X            VALUE SPACES.
             10   DISPLAY-RESOURCE    PIC X(8)         VALUE SPACES.
             10   FILLER              PIC X            VALUE SPACES.
             10   DISPLAY-DESCRIPTION PIC X(38)        VALUE SPACES.
             10   FILLER              PIC X            VALUE SPACES.
             10   DISPLAY-CALL-WHOM   PIC X(16)        VALUE SPACES.
   *
        05   DEFAULT-DESCRIPTION.
             10   FILLER              PIC X(22)        VALUE
                 'SALEP003 ERROR: RESP1='.
             10   DISPLAY-RESPONSE    PIC 9(8)         VALUE ZEROES.
   *
   *
    COPY SALECOMM.
    COPY MSALE03.
    COPY ATTRIBUT.
    COPY DFHAID.
    COPY DFHBMSCA.
    COPY CUSTMST.
    LINKAGE SECTION.
    01   DFHCOMMAREA                  PIC X(68).
   *
    PROCEDURE DIVISION.
    MAIN-PROG.
   *
   ***********************************************************************
   * DETERMINE WHICH POINT IN THE CYCLE APPLIES TO THE CURRENT          *
   * SITUATION. THE FIRST TIME THROUGH, SHOW THE DELETE SCREEN          *
   * FOR THE FIRST TIME. ON SUBSEQUENT PASSES, PROCESS USER INPUT       *
   * AND SHOW THE SCREEN AGAIN (OR TRANSFER CONTROL BACK TO THE         *
   * MENU PROGRAM, DEPENDING ON FUNCTION KEY).                          *
   ***********************************************************************
   *
        MOVE LOW-VALUES TO SALE003I.
   *
        IF EIBCALEN NOT = WS-EXPECTED-EIBCALEN
            PERFORM REQUEST-NEW-CUST-NO
        ELSE
            MOVE DFHCOMMAREA TO WS-COMMAREA
            IF EIBTRNID = 'SAL3' AND WS-COMM-PREV-MAP = 'SALE003'
                PERFORM PROCESS-DELETE-SCREEN
            ELSE
                PERFORM CUST-NO-FROM-COMMAREA.
   *
        GOBACK.
   *
   ***********************************************************************
   * DETERMINE WHAT FUNCTION KEY THE USER PRESSED.                      *
   ***********************************************************************
   *
    PROCESS-DELETE-SCREEN.
   *
        IF EIBAID = DFHCLEAR OR DFHPF3
            MOVE 'SALEP000' TO WS-XCTL-PGM
            PERFORM XCTL-NEXT-PGM
        ELSE
            IF EIBAID = DFHPF10
                PERFORM CURSOR-TO-ACTION-BAR
```

FIGURE 6.4   *(Continued)*

```
                ELSE
                    IF EIBAID = DFHPF12
                        PERFORM REQUEST-NEW-CUST-NO
                    ELSE
                        IF EIBAID NOT = DFHENTER
                            MOVE BAD-KEY-MSG TO S3MSGO
                            MOVE -1 TO S3CUSTL
                            PERFORM SEND-SALE003-BEEP.
*
        MOVE 'MSALE03' TO DISPLAY-RESOURCE.
        MOVE 'RECEIVE MAP' TO DISPLAY-OPERATION.
*
        EXEC CICS RECEIVE MAP ('SALE003')
                  MAPSET ('MSALE03')
                  INTO (SALE003I)
                  RESP (WS-CICS-RESPONSE1)
                  END-EXEC.
*
        IF WS-CICS-RESPONSE1 = DFHRESP(MAPFAIL)
            PERFORM CUST-NO-FROM-COMMAREA
        ELSE
            IF WS-CICS-RESPONSE1 NOT = DFHRESP(NORMAL)
                PERFORM CHECK-CICS-RESPONSE
                MOVE -1 TO S3CUSTL
                PERFORM SEND-SALE003-BEEP.
*
        MOVE SPACES TO S3MSGO.
*
**********************************************************************
* IF THE CURSOR WAS ANYWHERE ON THE ACTION BAR, USE THE             *
* POSITION TO SELECT THE ACTION. IF THE CURSOR WAS SOMEWHERE        *
* ELSE, THEN JUST GO WITH THE DEFAULT CHOICE, WHICH IS "DELETE".*
**********************************************************************
*
        IF EIBCPOSN  9
            MOVE 'DELETE' TO WS-COMM-ACTION
        ELSE
            IF EIBCPOSN  15
                MOVE 'EXIT' TO WS-COMM-ACTION
            ELSE
                IF EIBCPOSN  23
                    MOVE 'CANCEL' TO WS-COMM-ACTION
                ELSE
                    MOVE 'DELETE' TO WS-COMM-ACTION.
*
        IF WS-COMM-ACTION = 'EXIT'
            MOVE 'SALEP000' TO WS-XCTL-PGM
            PERFORM XCTL-NEXT-PGM
        ELSE
            IF WS-COMM-ACTION = 'CANCEL'
                PERFORM REQUEST-NEW-CUST-NO.
*
*
**********************************************************************
* THREE POSSIBLE SITUATIONS:                                        *
* 1. IF A RECORD IS BEING DISPLAYED ON THE SCREEN FOR POSSIBLE      *
*    DELETION, ATTEMPT TO DELETE THE RECORD. IN THAT CASE, A        *
*    VALID (NUMERIC) CUSTOMER NUMBER WILL APPEAR IN THE             *
*    COMMAREA AND WILL AGREE WITH THE CUSTOMER NUMBER ON THE        *
*    SCREEN.                                                        *
* 2. IF THE COMMAREA DOES NOT CONTAIN A VALID CUSTOMER NUMBER,      *
*    OR IF THE CUSTOMER NUMBER ON THE SCREEN HAS BEEN CLEARED,      *
*    ASK THE TERMINAL USER TO ENTER A NEW CUSTOMER NUMBER.          *
* 3. IF A NEW CUSTOMER NUMBER HAS BEEN ENTERED ON THE SCREEN,       *
*    SEND A SCREEN TO THE TERMINAL USER DISPLAYING THE             *
*    CONTENTS OF THAT RECORD.                                       *
*                                                                  *
**********************************************************************
*
        IF WS-COMM-CUST-NO IS NUMERIC
```

FIGURE 6.4   *(Continued)*

```
                    AND S3CUSTI = WS-COMM-CUST-NO
                PERFORM ATTEMPT-DELETE
        ELSE
            IF S3CUSTI IS NOT NUMERIC
                PERFORM REQUEST-NEW-CUST-NO
            ELSE
                MOVE S3CUSTO TO WS-COMM-CUST-NO
                PERFORM CUST-NO-FROM-COMMAREA.
*
**********************************************************************
* THIS ROUTINE OBTAINS ORIGINAL CUSTOMER MASTER RECORD CONTENTS *
* FROM A TEMPORARY STORAGE RECORD WRITTEN ON THE PREVIOUS PASS. *
*                                                                   *
* BEFORE ALLOWING DELETION TO TAKE PLACE, SALEP003 READS            *
* THE CUSTOMER MASTER RECORD AGAIN AND COMPARES THE CONTENTS        *
* WITH THE CONTENTS OF THE TEMPORARY STORAGE RECORD. IF THEY        *
* MATCH, PROCESSING CAN CONTINUE.                                   *
*                                                                   *
* HOWEVER, IF THE CUSTOMER MASTER RECORDS DIFFER FROM THE           *
* CONTENTS OF THE TEMPORARY STORAGE RECORD, THEN SOME OTHER         *
* USER HAS ALSO BEEN WORKING WITH THE SAME RECORD. IN THAT          *
* CASE, PROCESSING IS DISCONTINUED TO PREVENT CONFLICTS.            *
**********************************************************************
*
 ATTEMPT-DELETE.
*
     MOVE EIBTRMID TO QID-TRMID.
     MOVE QID-NAME TO DISPLAY-RESOURCE.
     MOVE 'READQ TS' TO DISPLAY-OPERATION.
     EXEC CICS READQ TS
               QUEUE (QID-NAME)
               INTO (CUSTMST-Q)
               ITEM (WS-TSQ-ITEM1)
               RESP (WS-CICS-RESPONSE1)
               END-EXEC.
*
     IF WS-CICS-RESPONSE1 NOT = DFHRESP(NORMAL)
         PERFORM CHECK-CICS-RESPONSE
         MOVE -1 TO S3CUSTL
         PERFORM SEND-SALEO03-BEEP.
*
**********************************************************************
* READ THE EXISTING RECORD FOR UPDATE.                              *
**********************************************************************
*
     MOVE 'CUSTMST' TO DISPLAY-RESOURCE.
     MOVE 'READ UPDATE' TO DISPLAY-OPERATION.
*
     EXEC CICS READ
               DATASET ('CUSTMST')
               INTO (CUSTMST-REC)
               RIDFLD (WS-COMM-CUST-NO)
               UPDATE
               RESP (WS-CICS-RESPONSE1)
               END-EXEC.
*
     IF WS-CICS-RESPONSE1 NOT = DFHRESP(NORMAL)
         PERFORM CHECK-CICS-RESPONSE
         MOVE -1 TO S3CUSTL
         PERFORM SEND-SALEO03-BEEP.
*
     IF CUSTMST-REC NOT = CUSTMST-Q
         MOVE RECORD-CHANGED-MSG TO S3MSGO
         MOVE -1 TO S3CUSTL
         PERFORM SEND-SALEO03-BEEP.
*
     IF CUST-CURR-WK-SALES NOT = ZEROES
                OR CUST-LAST-BILL-BAL-DUE NOT = ZEROES
                OR CUST-LAST-BILL-DATE NOT = ZEROES
```

FIGURE 6.4   *(Continued)*

```
                MOVE CANNOT-DELETE-MSG TO S3MSGO
                MOVE -1 TO S3CUSTL
                PERFORM SEND-SALE003-BEEP.
        *
            MOVE 'CUSTMST' TO DISPLAY-RESOURCE.
            MOVE 'DELETE' TO DISPLAY-OPERATION.
        *
            EXEC CICS DELETE
                DATASET ('CUSTMST')
                RESP (WS-CICS-RESPONSE1)
                END-EXEC.
        *
            MOVE -1 TO S3CUSTL.
        *
        ****************************************************************
        * IF THE DELETE WAS SUCCESSFUL, THE TERMINAL USER MAY OVERKEY  *
        * THE CUSTOMER NUMBER TO DELETE A DIFFERENT RECORD NEXT TIME.  *
        * IF THE DELETE WAS NOT SUCCESSFUL, DISPLAY A MESSAGE          *
        * EXPLAINING WHY NOT.                                          *
        ****************************************************************
        *
            IF WS-CICS-RESPONSE1 = DFHRESP(NORMAL)
                MOVE SUCCESSFUL-DELETE-MSG TO S3MSGO
                MOVE -1 TO S3CUSTL
                MOVE ENTER-CUST-NO-MSG TO S3INSTRO
                PERFORM SEND-SALE003-RETURN
            ELSE
                PERFORM CHECK-CICS-RESPONSE
                PERFORM SEND-SALE003-BEEP.
        *
        *
        XCTL-NEXT-PGM.
        *
            MOVE WS-XCTL-PGM TO DISPLAY-RESOURCE.
            MOVE 'XCTL' TO DISPLAY-OPERATION.
            EXEC CICS XCTL
                    PROGRAM (WS-XCTL-PGM)
                    COMMAREA (WS-COMMAREA)
                    RESP (WS-CICS-RESPONSE1)
                    END-EXEC.
        *
            IF WS-CICS-RESPONSE1 NOT = DFHRESP(NORMAL)
                PERFORM CHECK-CICS-RESPONSE
                MOVE -1 TO S3CUSTL
                PERFORM SEND-SALE003-BEEP.
        *
        *
        ****************************************************************
        * THIS ROUTINE TAKES THE CUSTOMER NUMBER FROM THE WORKING      *
        * STORAGE COPY OF THE DFHCOMMAREA AND USES IT TO READ A        *
        * CUSTOMER RECORD. IT SHOWS THE RECORD ON THE DELETE SCREEN.   *
        ****************************************************************
        *
        CUST-NO-FROM-COMMAREA.
        *
            IF WS-COMM-CUST-NO IS NOT NUMERIC
                PERFORM REQUEST-NEW-CUST-NO.
        *
            MOVE WS-COMM-CUST-NO TO S3CUSTO.
            MOVE -1 TO S3NAMEL.
            MOVE SPACES TO S3MSGO.
        *
        ****************************************************************
        * READ THE EXISTING RECORD.                                    *
        ****************************************************************
        *
            MOVE 'CUSTMST' TO DISPLAY-RESOURCE.
            MOVE 'READ' TO DISPLAY-OPERATION.
        *
            EXEC CICS READ
```

FIGURE 6.4   *(Continued)*

```
                        DATASET ('CUSTMST')
                        INTO (CUSTMST-REC)
                        RIDFLD (WS-COMM-CUST-NO)
                        RESP (WS-CICS-RESPONSE1)
                        END-EXEC.
    *
        IF WS-CICS-RESPONSE1 NOT = DFHRESP(NORMAL)
            PERFORM CHECK-CICS-RESPONSE
            PERFORM SEND-SALE003-BEEP.
    *
    ***********************************************************************
    * DELETE THE OLD TEMP STORAGE QUEUE THAT MIGHT BE LEFT FROM        *
    * PREVIOUS TASKS. THE QUEUE ID IS BUILT FROM THE TRAN CODE AND     *
    * THE TERMINAL ID.                                                 *
    ***********************************************************************
    *
        MOVE EIBTRMID TO QID-TRMID.
        MOVE QID-NAME TO DISPLAY-RESOURCE.
        MOVE 'DELETEQ TS' TO DISPLAY-OPERATION.
    *
        EXEC CICS DELETEQ TS
                QUEUE (QID-NAME)
                RESP (WS-CICS-RESPONSE1)
                END-EXEC.
    *
        IF WS-CICS-RESPONSE1 NOT = DFHRESP(NORMAL)
                AND WS-CICS-RESPONSE1 NOT = DFHRESP(QIDERR)
            PERFORM CHECK-CICS-RESPONSE
            PERFORM SEND-SALE003-BEEP.
    *
        MOVE QID-NAME TO DISPLAY-RESOURCE.
        MOVE 'WRITEQ TS' TO DISPLAY-OPERATION.
    *
        EXEC CICS WRITEQ TS
                QUEUE (QID-NAME)
                FROM (CUSTMST-REC)
                ITEM (WS-TSQ-ITEM1)
                RESP (WS-CICS-RESPONSE1)
                END-EXEC.
    *
        IF WS-CICS-RESPONSE1 NOT = DFHRESP(NORMAL)
            PERFORM CHECK-CICS-RESPONSE
            PERFORM SEND-SALE003-BEEP.
    *
    ***********************************************************************
    * PUT EXISTING RECORD CONTENTS ON THE SCREEN (DISPLAY-ONLY).       *
    ***********************************************************************
    *
        MOVE CUST-NO TO S3CUSTO.
        MOVE CUST-NAME TO S3NAMEO.
        MOVE CUST-CONTACT TO S3CNTCTO.
        MOVE CUST-STREET-ADDRESS TO S3ADDRO.
        MOVE CUST-CITY TO S3CITYO.
        MOVE CUST-STATE TO S3STATEO.
        MOVE CUST-ZIP TO S3ZIPO.
        MOVE CUST-CURR-WK-SALES TO S3SALESO.
        MOVE CUST-LAST-BILL-BAL-DUE TO S3BALO.
        MOVE CUST-LAST-BILL-DATE TO S3BDATEO.
    *
        MOVE DELETE-RECORD-MSG TO S3INSTRO.
        MOVE SPACES TO S3MSGO.
    *
        PERFORM SEND-SALE003-RETURN.
    *
    *
    ***********************************************************************
    * THIS ROUTINE CLEARS THE SCREEN AND ASKS THE USER TO ENTER THE    *
    * KEY OF THE NEXT RECORD TO BE DELETED.                            *
    ***********************************************************************
    *
```

FIGURE 6.4   *(Continued)*

```
REQUEST-NEW-CUST-NO.
*
    MOVE SPACES TO WS-COMM-CUST-NO.
    MOVE -1 TO S3CUSTL.
    MOVE ENTER-CUST-NO-MSG TO S3INSTRO.
    MOVE SPACES TO S3MSGO.
*
    MOVE ALL '_' TO S3CUSTO.
    MOVE SPACES TO S3NAMEO
                   S3CNTCTO
                   S3ADDRO
                   S3CITYO
                   S3STATEO
                   S3ZIPO
                   S3SALESO
                   S3BALO
                   S3BDATEO.
*
*********************************************************************
* DELETE THE OLD TEMP STORAGE QUEUE THAT MIGHT BE LEFT FROM        *
* PREVIOUS TASKS. THE QUEUE ID IS BUILT FROM THE TRAN CODE AND     *
* THE TERMINAL ID.                                                 *
*********************************************************************
*
    MOVE EIBTRMID TO QID-TRMID.
    MOVE QID-NAME TO DISPLAY-RESOURCE.
    MOVE 'DELETEQ TS' TO DISPLAY-OPERATION.
*
    EXEC CICS DELETEQ TS
              QUEUE (QID-NAME)
              RESP (WS-CICS-RESPONSE1)
              END-EXEC.
*
    IF WS-CICS-RESPONSE1 NOT = DFHRESP(NORMAL)
           AND WS-CICS-RESPONSE1 NOT = DFHRESP(QIDERR)
       PERFORM CHECK-CICS-RESPONSE
       PERFORM SEND-SALE003-BEEP.
*
    PERFORM SEND-SALE003-RETURN.
*
*
*********************************************************************
* THIS ROUTINE SENDS SALE003 WITH A WARNING 'BEEP'. WE USE THIS    *
* ONLY WHEN THE CALLING ROUTINE WANTS TO DISPLAY A WARNING ON      *
* THE MESSAGE LINE OF THIS MAP. CURSOR POSITION MUST BE SET.       *
*********************************************************************
*
SEND-SALE003-BEEP.
*
    IF WS-COMM-PREV-MAP = 'SALE003'
       EXEC CICS SEND MAP ('SALE003')
                 MAPSET ('MSALE03')
                 FROM (SALE003I)
                 DATAONLY
                 ALARM
                 CURSOR
                 END-EXEC
    ELSE
       MOVE 'SALE003' TO WS-COMM-PREV-MAP
       EXEC CICS SEND MAP ('SALE003')
                 MAPSET ('MSALE03')
                 FROM (SALE003I)
                 ERASE
                 ALARM
                 CURSOR
                 END-EXEC.
*
    EXEC CICS RETURN
              TRANSID ('SAL3')
              COMMAREA (WS-COMMAREA)
```

FIGURE 6.4   *(Continued)*

```
                    END-EXEC.
 *
 *
 ****************************************************************
 * THIS ROUTINE SENDS SALE003 WITH WHATEVER DATA HAS BEEN PLACED *
 * ON IT. IF THE PREDEFINED PORTIONS OF THE MAP ARE ALREADY ON   *
 * THE SCREEN, SALE003 WILL BE SENT 'DATAONLY'.                  *
 ****************************************************************
 *
  SEND-SALE003-RETURN.
 *
      IF WS-COMM-PREV-MAP = 'SALE003'
          EXEC CICS SEND MAP ('SALE003')
                    MAPSET ('MSALE03')
                    FROM (SALE003I)
                    DATAONLY
                    CURSOR
                    END-EXEC
      ELSE
          MOVE 'SALE003' TO WS-COMM-PREV-MAP
          EXEC CICS SEND MAP ('SALE003')
                    MAPSET ('MSALE03')
                    FROM (SALE003I)
                    ERASE
                    CURSOR
                    END-EXEC.
 *
      EXEC CICS RETURN
                TRANSID ('SAL3')
                COMMAREA (WS-COMMAREA)
                END-EXEC.
 *
 ****************************************************************
 * THIS ROUTINE SENDS SALE003 WITH CURSOR ON ACTION BAR.        *
 ****************************************************************
 *
  CURSOR-TO-ACTION-BAR.
 *
      MOVE 'SALE003' TO WS-COMM-PREV-MAP.
      EXEC CICS SEND MAP ('SALE003')
                MAPSET ('MSALE03')
                FROM (SALE003I)
                CURSOR (1)
                DATAONLY
                END-EXEC.
 *
      EXEC CICS RETURN
                TRANSID ('SAL3')
                COMMAREA (WS-COMMAREA)
                END-EXEC.
 *
 *
 ****************************************************************
 * CHECK THE CICS RESPONSE CODE AND BUILD A MESSAGE EXPLAINING  *
 * THE ERROR. IT IS THE RESPONSIBILITY OF THE CALLING ROUTINE   *
 * TO INITIALIZE SOME DISPLAY FIELDS IN THE MESSAGE WORK AREA   *
 * TO INDICATE THE TYPE OF COMMAND BEING PROCESSED.             *
 *                                                              *
 * WE DO NOTHING ABOUT CERTAIN RESPONSE CODES HERE SO THAT      *
 * THOSE SITUATIONS CAN BE HANDLED WITH LOGIC ELSEWHERE IN THE  *
 * PROGRAM.                                                     *
 *                                                              *
 ****************************************************************
 *
  CHECK-CICS-RESPONSE.
 *
      EVALUATE WS-CICS-RESPONSE1
      WHEN DFHRESP(NORMAL)
          CONTINUE
      WHEN DFHRESP(MAPFAIL)
```

FIGURE 6.4 *(Continued)*

```
                CONTINUE
        WHEN DFHRESP(ENDFILE)
                CONTINUE
        WHEN DFHRESP(DISABLED)
            MOVE 'CALL OPERATIONS' TO DISPLAY-CALL-WHOM
            MOVE DISABLED-MSG TO DISPLAY-DESCRIPTION
            MOVE BUILD-MSG TO S3MSGO
        WHEN DFHRESP(DUPREC)
            MOVE DUPREC-MSG TO DISPLAY-DESCRIPTION
            MOVE BUILD-MSG TO S3MSGO
        WHEN DFHRESP(DSIDERR)
            MOVE 'CALL PROGRAMMER' TO DISPLAY-CALL-WHOM
            MOVE DSIDERR-MSG TO DISPLAY-DESCRIPTION
            MOVE BUILD-MSG TO S3MSGO
        WHEN DFHRESP(INVREQ)
            MOVE 'CALL PROGRAMMER' TO DISPLAY-CALL-WHOM
            MOVE INVREQ-MSG TO DISPLAY-DESCRIPTION
            MOVE BUILD-MSG TO S3MSGO
        WHEN DFHRESP(IOERR)
            MOVE 'CALL PROGRAMMER' TO DISPLAY-CALL-WHOM
            MOVE IOERR-MSG TO DISPLAY-DESCRIPTION
            MOVE BUILD-MSG TO S3MSGO
        WHEN DFHRESP(ITEMERR)
            MOVE 'CALL PROGRAMMER' TO DISPLAY-CALL-WHOM
            MOVE ITEMERR-MSG TO DISPLAY-DESCRIPTION
            MOVE BUILD-MSG TO S3MSGO
        WHEN DFHRESP(LENGERR)
            MOVE 'CALL PROGRAMMER' TO DISPLAY-CALL-WHOM
            MOVE LENGERR-MSG TO DISPLAY-DESCRIPTION
            MOVE BUILD-MSG TO S3MSGO
        WHEN DFHRESP(NOSPACE)
            MOVE 'CALL OPERATIONS' TO DISPLAY-CALL-WHOM
            MOVE NOSPACE-MSG TO DISPLAY-DESCRIPTION
            MOVE BUILD-MSG TO S3MSGO
        WHEN DFHRESP(NOTFND)
            MOVE NOTFND-MSG TO DISPLAY-DESCRIPTION
            MOVE BUILD-MSG TO S3MSGO
        WHEN DFHRESP(PGMIDERR)
            MOVE 'CALL PROGRAMMER' TO DISPLAY-CALL-WHOM
            MOVE PGMIDERR-MSG TO DISPLAY-DESCRIPTION
            MOVE BUILD-MSG TO S3MSGO
        WHEN DFHRESP(QIDERR)
            MOVE 'CALL PROGRAMMER' TO DISPLAY-CALL-WHOM
            MOVE QIDERR-MSG TO DISPLAY-DESCRIPTION
            MOVE BUILD-MSG TO S3MSGO
        WHEN OTHER
            MOVE 'CALL PROGRAMMER' TO DISPLAY-CALL-WHOM
            MOVE WS-CICS-RESPONSE1 TO DISPLAY-RESPONSE
            MOVE DEFAULT-DESCRIPTION TO DISPLAY-DESCRIPTION
            MOVE BUILD-MSG TO S3MSGO
        END-EVALUATE.
*
*
```

FIGURE 6.4 *(Continued)*

```
IDENTIFICATION DIVISION.
PROGRAM-ID. SALEP004.
AUTHOR. ALIDA M. JATICH AND PHIL NOWAK.
******************************************************************
* SALEP004: PROCESSOR FOR ENTRY OF CURRENT WEEK SALES             *
*                                                                 *
* SALEP004 READS "ENTER CURRENT WEEK SALES" SCREEN INPUT          *
* AND PERFORMS THE FOLLOWING ACTIONS:                             *
*                                                                 *
* 1. IT UPDATES CURRENT WEEK SALES AMOUNT IN CUSTOMER MASTER      *
*    RECORD.                                                      *
*                                                                 *
* 2. IT WRITES A L'NE ITEM RECORD TO THE LINE ITEM VSAM FILE      *
*    FOR EVENTUAL USE IN A BILLING SYSTEM.                        *
*                                                                 *
* 3. IT WRITES A COPY OF THE LINE ITEM RECORD TO A TRANSIENT      *
*    DATA QUEUE FOR EVENTUAL PRINTING.                            *
*                                                                 *
* 4. IT REFRESHES THE "ENTER CURRENT WEEK SALES" SCREEN TO        *
*    ALLOW THE TERMINAL USER TO ENTER MORE DATA.                  *
*                                                                 *
* 5. UNLESS THE USER SELECTS OTHERWISE. IT RETURNS TO             *
*    TRANSACTION SAL4. CAUSING THIS PROGRAM TO BE INVOKED         *
*    AGAIN.                                                       *
*                                                                 *
******************************************************************
ENVIRONMENT DIVISION.
DATA DIVISION.
WORKING-STORAGE SECTION.
01  MISC-WORK.
    05  WS-CICS-RESPONSE1        PIC S9(8) COMP VALUE +0.
    05  WS-XCTL-PGM              PIC X(8)       VALUE SPACES.
    05  WS-ERROR-FLAG            PIC X          VALUE 'N'.
    05  WS-QTY                   PIC S9(6)      VALUE ZEROES.
    05  WS-SALES-ENTERED         PIC S9(5)V99   VALUE ZEROES.
01  ERROR-MESSAGES.
    05  BAD-KEY-MSG              PIC X(22)      VALUE
        'Function key undefined'.
    05  CUST-NUM-MSG             PIC X(27)      VALUE
        'Customer number not numeric'.
    05  MISSING-DATA-MSG         PIC X(26)      VALUE
        'Please supply missing data'.
    05  PLUS-OR-MINUS-MSG        PIC X(24)      VALUE
        'Enter plus or minus sign'.
    05  NUMERIC-MSG              PIC X(40)      VALUE
        'Field must be numeric, greater than zero'.
    05  SUCCESSFUL-ADD-MSG       PIC X(25)      VALUE
        'Record added successfully'.
    05  NOTFND-MSG               PIC X(28)      VALUE
        'Customer number not on file'.
    05  DISABLED-MSG             PIC X(16)      VALUE
        'File is disabled'.
    05  DSIDERR-MSG              PIC X(14)      VALUE
        'File not found'.
    05  DUPREC-MSG               PIC X(22)      VALUE
        'Record already on file'.
    05  INVREQ-MSG               PIC X(15)      VALUE
        'Invalid request'.
    05  IOERR-MSG                PIC X(9)       VALUE
        'I/O error'.
    05  ITEMERR-MSG              PIC X(16)      VALUE
        'Item not defined'.
    05  LENGERR-MSG              PIC X(19)      VALUE
        'Record length error'.
    05  NOSPACE-MSG              PIC X(17)      VALUE
        'File out of space'.
    05  PGMIDERR-MSG             PIC X(27)      VALUE
        'Program not defined to CICS'.
    05  QIDERR-MSG               PIC X(17)      VALUE
        'Queue not defined'.
```

FIGURE 6.5   Source code for SALEP004, the Enter Current Week Sales screen processor.

```
*
    05  BUILD-MSG.
        10  DISPLAY-OPERATION    PIC X(12)      VALUE SPACES.
        10  FILLER               PIC X          VALUE SPACES.
        10  DISPLAY-RESOURCE      PIC X(8)       VALUE SPACES.
        10  FILLER               PIC X          VALUE SPACES.
        10  DISPLAY-DESCRIPTION  PIC X(38)      VALUE SPACES.
        10  FILLER               PIC X          VALUE SPACES.
        10  DISPLAY-CALL-WHOM    PIC X(16)      VALUE SPACES.
*
    05  DEFAULT-DESCRIPTION.
        10  FILLER               PIC X(22)      VALUE
        'SALEP004 ERROR: RESP1='.
        10  DISPLAY-RESPONSE     PIC 9(8)       VALUE ZEROES.
*
  COPY SALECOMM.
  COPY MSALE04.
  COPY ATTRIBUT.
  COPY DFHAID.
  COPY DFHBMSCA.
  COPY CUSTMST.
  COPY LINEITM.
  LINKAGE SECTION.
  01  DFHCOMMAREA              PIC X(68).
*
  PROCEDURE DIVISION.
  MAIN-PROG.
*
 ****************************************************************
 * DETERMINE WHICH POINT IN THE CYCLE APPLIES TO THE CURRENT    *
 * SITUATION. THE FIRST TIME THROUGH, SHOW THE RECORD ADD SCREEN *
 * FOR THE FIRST TIME. ON SUBSEQUENT PASSES, PROCESS USER INPUT  *
 * AND SHOW THE SCREEN AGAIN (OR TRANSFER CONTROL BACK TO THE    *
 * MENU PROGRAM, DEPENDING ON FUNCTION KEY).                     *
 ****************************************************************
*
     MOVE LOW-VALUES TO SALE004I.
*
     IF EIBCALEN NOT = WS-EXPECTED-EIBCALEN
         PERFORM FIRST-TIME-THROUGH
     ELSE
         MOVE DFHCOMMAREA TO WS-COMMAREA
         IF EIBTRNID = 'SAL4'
                 AND WS-COMM-PREV-MAP = 'SALE004'
             PERFORM PROCESS-ADD-SCREEN
         ELSE
                 PERFORM FIRST-TIME-THROUGH.
*
     GOBACK.
*
 ****************************************************************
 * DETERMINE WHAT FUNCTION KEY THE USER PRESSED.                *
 ****************************************************************
*
 PROCESS-ADD-SCREEN.
*
     IF EIBAID = DFHCLEAR OR DFHPF3
         MOVE 'SALEP000' TO WS-XCTL-PGM
         PERFORM XCTL-NEXT-PGM
     ELSE
         IF EIBAID = DFHPF10
             PERFORM CURSOR-TO-ACTION-BAR
         ELSE
             IF EIBAID = DFHPF12
                 PERFORM FIRST-TIME-THROUGH
             ELSE
                 IF EIBAID NOT = DFHENTER
                     MOVE BAD-KEY-MSG TO S4MSGO
                     MOVE -1 TO S4CUSTL
                     PERFORM SEND-SALE004-BEEP.
```

FIGURE 6.5 *(Continued)*

```
       *
       MOVE 'SALE004' TO DISPLAY-RESOURCE.
       MOVE 'RECEIVE MAP' TO DISPLAY-OPERATION.
       *
       EXEC CICS RECEIVE MAP ('SALE004')
                MAPSET ('MSALE04')
                INTO (SALE004I)
                RESP (WS-CICS-RESPONSE1)
                END-EXEC.
       *
       IF WS-CICS-RESPONSE1 = DFHRESP(MAPFAIL)
           PERFORM FIRST-TIME-THROUGH
       ELSE
           IF WS-CICS-RESPONSE1 NOT = DFHRESP(NORMAL)
               PERFORM CHECK-CICS-RESPONSE
               PERFORM SEND-SALE004-BEEP.
       *
       MOVE SPACES TO S4MSGO.
       *
       **********************************************************************
       * IF THE CURSOR WAS ANYWHERE ON THE ACTION BAR, USE THE            *
       * POSITION TO SELECT THE ACTION. IF THE CURSOR WAS SOMEWHERE       *
       * ELSE, THEN JUST GO WITH THE DEFAULT CHOICE, WHICH IS "ADD".      *
       **********************************************************************
       *
       IF EIBCPOSN  7
           MOVE 'ADD' TO WS-COMM-ACTION
       ELSE
           IF EIBCPOSN  13
               MOVE 'EXIT' TO WS-COMM-ACTION
           ELSE
               IF EIBCPOSN  21
                   MOVE 'CANCEL' TO WS-COMM-ACTION
               ELSE
                   MOVE 'ADD' TO WS-COMM-ACTION.
       *
       IF WS-COMM-ACTION = 'EXIT'
           MOVE 'SALEP000' TO WS-XCTL-PGM
           PERFORM XCTL-NEXT-PGM
       ELSE
           IF WS-COMM-ACTION = 'CANCEL'
               PERFORM FIRST-TIME-THROUGH.
       *
       **********************************************************************
       * EDIT THE DATA IN EACH OF THE USER INPUT FIELDS. YOUR METHODS     *
       * MAY VARY DEPENDING ON THE TERMINAL DEVICE FEATURES YOU PLAN      *
       * TO SUPPORT AND ON THE STANDARDS AT YOUR INSTALLATION.            *
       *                                                                  *
       * UNDERLINING IS A WAY OF INDICATING HOW MUCH DATA THE USER        *
       * CAN ENTER INTO EACH FIELD. IF YOUR TERMINALS OR WORKSTATIONS     *
       * SUPPORT THE "UNDERLINE" EXTENDED ATTRIBUTE IN SUCH A WAY         *
       * THAT THE APPEARANCE IS ACCEPTABLE TO THE TERMINAL USERS, YOU     *
       * CAN OMIT THE LOGIC FOR FILLING EMPTY FIELDS WITH UNDERSCORE      *
       * CHARACTERS AND FOR REMOVING TRAILING UNDERSCORES. IN THAT        *
       * CASE, YOU WOULD DEFINE THE UNDERSCORES BY USING THE HIGHLIGHT    *
       * ATTRIBUTE ON THE BMS MAP.                                        *
       *                                                                  *
       * IF YOUR TERMINALS SUPPORT COLOR, FOR EXAMPLE, 3279-TYPE          *
       * TERMINALS OR PS/2'S, CHANGE THE COLOR OF A FIELD TO INDICATE     *
       * ERRORS. THE COLOR IS SET WITH AN 'EXTENDED ATTRIBUTE' BYTE.      *
       * THE EXTENDED ATTRIBUTE DOES NOT TAKE UP SPACE ON THE DISPLAY.    *
       * THIS EXAMPLE IS BEING RUN ON A PS/2. IF YOUR TERMINALS ARE       *
       * MONOCHROME, DON'T TRY TO USE THE COLOR EXTENDED ATTRIBUTE.       *
       * MOVE A 'BRIGHT' ATTRIBUTE CHARACTER TO THE ATTRIBUTE BYTE.       *
       **********************************************************************
       *
       IF S4CUSTI = LOW-VALUES OR SPACES OR '_____'
           MOVE ALL '_' TO S4CUSTO
           MOVE DFHRED TO S4CUSTC
           IF WS-ERROR-FLAG = 'N'
```

FIGURE 6.5   *(Continued)*

```
                MOVE -1 TO S4CUSTL
                MOVE 'Y' TO WS-ERROR-FLAG
                MOVE MISSING-DATA-MSG TO S4MSGO
            END-IF
        ELSE
            IF S4CUSTI IS NUMERIC
                MOVE S4CUSTI TO WS-COMM-CUST-NO
                MOVE DFHTURQ TO S4CUSTC
            ELSE
                MOVE DFHRED TO S4CUSTC
                IF WS-ERROR-FLAG = 'N'
                    MOVE -1 TO S4CUSTL
                    MOVE 'Y' TO WS-ERROR-FLAG
                    MOVE CUST-NUM-MSG TO S4MSGO.
*
        INSPECT S4ITEMI REPLACING ALL '_' BY SPACES.
        IF S4ITEMI   SPACES
            MOVE DFHTURQ TO S4ITEMC
            MOVE ALP-REG-MOD-UNP TO S4ITEMA
        ELSE
            MOVE DFHRED TO S4ITEMC
            MOVE ALL '_' TO S4ITEMO
            IF WS-ERROR-FLAG = 'N'
                MOVE -1 TO S4ITEML
                MOVE 'Y' TO WS-ERROR-FLAG
                MOVE MISSING-DATA-MSG TO S4MSGO.
*
        IF S4UNITPI IS NUMERIC AND S4UNITPI   ZEROES
            MOVE DFHTURQ TO S4UNITPC
            MOVE NUM-REG-MOD-UNP TO S4UNITPA
        ELSE
            MOVE DFHRED TO S4UNITPC
            MOVE ZEROES TO S4UNITPO
            IF WS-ERROR-FLAG = 'N'
                MOVE DFHRED TO S4UNITPC
                MOVE -1 TO S4UNITPL
                MOVE 'Y' TO WS-ERROR-FLAG
                MOVE NUMERIC-MSG TO S4MSGO.
*
        IF S4QTYI IS NUMERIC AND S4QTYI   ZEROES
            MOVE DFHTURQ TO S4QTYC
            MOVE NUM-REG-MOD-UNP TO S4QTYA
        ELSE
            MOVE DFHRED TO S4QTYC
            MOVE ZEROES TO S4QTYO
            IF WS-ERROR-FLAG = 'N'
                MOVE -1 TO S4QTYL
                MOVE 'Y' TO WS-ERROR-FLAG
                MOVE NUMERIC-MSG TO S4MSGO.
*
        IF S4SIGNI = '_' OR SPACES OR LOW-VALUES
            MOVE '+' TO S4SIGNI.
        IF S4SIGNI = '+' OR '-'
            MOVE DFHTURQ TO S4SIGNC
            MOVE ALP-REG-MOD-UNP TO S4SIGNA
        ELSE
            MOVE DFHRED TO S4SIGNC
            MOVE ALL '_' TO S4SIGNO
            IF WS-ERROR-FLAG = 'N'
                MOVE -1 TO S4SIGNL
                MOVE 'Y' TO WS-ERROR-FLAG
                MOVE PLUS-OR-MINUS-MSG TO S4MSGO.
*
****************************************************************
* REFRESH THE DATE AND TIME PROVIDED BY CICS IN THE EXEC      *
* INTERFACE BLOCK.                                            *
****************************************************************
*
        EXEC CICS ASKTIME
                END-EXEC.
```

FIGURE 6.5 *(Continued)*

```
*
*************************************************************
* IF THE DATA IS GOOD, MOVE DATA TO THE WORK AREA FOR THE LINE  *
* ITEM RECORD.                                                  *
*************************************************************
*
     IF WS-ERROR-FLAG = 'N'
         MOVE S4CUSTI TO LINEITM-CUST-NO
         MOVE EIBDATE TO LINEITM-DATE
         MOVE EIBTIME TO LINEITM-TIME
         MOVE S4ITEMI TO LINEITM-ITEM-CODE
         MOVE S4UNITPI TO LINEITM-UNIT-PRICE
         MOVE ZEROES TO WS-QTY
         IF S4SIGNI = '+'
             ADD S4QTYI TO WS-QTY
         ELSE
             SUBTRACT S4QTYI FROM WS-QTY
         END-IF
         MOVE WS-QTY TO LINEITM-QUANTITY.

*
*************************************************************
* IF EVERYTHING IS OK SO FAR, ATTEMPT TO READ THE CUSTOMER      *
* MASTER RECORD FOR UPDATE. IF CUSTOMER NUMBER IS NOT ON FILE,  *
* MOVE AN ERROR MESSAGE TO THE SCREEN AND DON'T UPDATE ANYTHING.*
*************************************************************
*
     IF WS-ERROR-FLAG = 'N'
         MOVE 'CUSTMST' TO DISPLAY-RESOURCE
         MOVE 'READ' TO DISPLAY-OPERATION
         EXEC CICS READ
                 DATASET ('CUSTMST')
                 INTO (CUSTMST-REC)
                 RIDFLD (WS-COMM-CUST-NO)
                 UPDATE
                 RESP (WS-CICS-RESPONSE1)
                 END-EXEC
         IF WS-CICS-RESPONSE1 NOT = DFHRESP(NORMAL)
             PERFORM CHECK-CICS-RESPONSE
             MOVE DFHRED TO S4CUSTC
             MOVE -1 TO S4CUSTL
             MOVE 'Y' TO WS-ERROR-FLAG.
*
     IF WS-ERROR-FLAG = 'Y'
         PERFORM SEND-SALE004-BEEP.
*
*************************************************************
* IF THE READ WAS SUCCESSFUL, UPDATE THE CUSTOMER RECORD. THEN  *
* WRITE A LINE ITEM VSAM RECORD.                                *
*************************************************************
*
     COMPUTE WS-SALES-ENTERED = S4UNITPI * WS-QTY.
     COMPUTE CUST-CURR-WK-SALES = WS-SALES-ENTERED +
                 CUST-CURR-WK-SALES.
     MOVE 'CUSTMST' TO DISPLAY-RESOURCE.
     MOVE 'REWRITE' TO DISPLAY-OPERATION.
     EXEC CICS REWRITE
             DATASET ('CUSTMST')
             FROM (CUSTMST-REC)
             RESP (WS-CICS-RESPONSE1)
             END-EXEC.
     IF WS-CICS-RESPONSE1 NOT = DFHRESP(NORMAL)
         PERFORM CHECK-CICS-RESPONSE
         MOVE 'Y' TO WS-ERROR-FLAG.
*
     IF WS-ERROR-FLAG = 'N'
         MOVE 'LINEITM' TO DISPLAY-RESOURCE
         MOVE 'WRITE' TO DISPLAY-OPERATION
         EXEC CICS WRITE
                 DATASET ('LINEITM')
                 FROM (LINEITM-REC)
```

FIGURE 6.5   *(Continued)*

```
                          RIDFLD (LINEITM-KEY)
                          RESP (WS-CICS-RESPONSE1)
                          END-EXEC
              IF WS-CICS-RESPONSE1 NOT = DFHRESP(NORMAL)
                  PERFORM CHECK-CICS-RESPONSE
                  MOVE 'Y' TO WS-ERROR-FLAG.
      *
      *********************************************************************
      * WRITE THE LINE ITEM RECORD TO A TRANSIENT DATA QUEUE.            *
      *********************************************************************
      *
              IF WS-ERROR-FLAG = 'N'
                  MOVE 'LMSG' TO DISPLAY-RESOURCE
                  MOVE 'WRITEQ TD' TO DISPLAY-OPERATION
                  EXEC CICS WRITEQ TD
                          QUEUE ('LMSG')
                          FROM (LINEITM-REC)
                          RESP (WS-CICS-RESPONSE1)
                          END-EXEC
                  IF WS-CICS-RESPONSE1 NOT = DFHRESP(NORMAL)
                      PERFORM CHECK-CICS-RESPONSE
                      MOVE 'Y' TO WS-ERROR-FLAG.
      *
      *********************************************************************
      * IF ALL ACTIVITY WAS SUCCESSFUL SO FAR, LET THE TERMINAL USER     *
      * KNOW THIS. OTHERWISE, ROLL BACK ANY UPDATES THAT HAVE GONE       *
      * THROUGH, SO THAT ALL FILES WILL BE PUT BACK TO THEIR             *
      * ORIGINAL STATE.                                                  *
      *********************************************************************
      *
              IF WS-ERROR-FLAG = 'N'
                  MOVE -1 TO S4CUSTL
                  MOVE SUCCESSFUL-ADD-MSG TO S4MSGO
                  PERFORM SEND-SALE004-RETURN
              ELSE
                  EXEC CICS SYNCPOINT
                          ROLLBACK
                          END-EXEC
                  MOVE -1 TO S4CUSTL
                  PERFORM CHECK-CICS-RESPONSE
                  PERFORM SEND-SALE004-BEEP.
      *
      *
       XCTL-NEXT-PGM.
      *
          MOVE WS-XCTL-PGM TO DISPLAY-RESOURCE.
          MOVE 'XCTL' TO DISPLAY-OPERATION.
          EXEC CICS XCTL
                  PROGRAM (WS-XCTL-PGM)
                  COMMAREA (WS-COMMAREA)
                  RESP (WS-CICS-RESPONSE1)
                  END-EXEC.
      *
          IF WS-CICS-RESPONSE1 NOT = DFHRESP(NORMAL)
              PERFORM CHECK-CICS-RESPONSE
              MOVE -1 TO S4CUSTL
              PERFORM SEND-SALE004-BEEP.
      *
      *
      *********************************************************************
      * THIS ROUTINE SENDS THE RECORD ADD MAP AND/OR REFRESHES IT        *
      * IF 'CANCEL' WAS SELECTED.                                        *
      *********************************************************************
      *
       FIRST-TIME-THROUGH.
      *
          MOVE SPACES TO S4MSGO.
          IF WS-COMM-CUST-NO IS NUMERIC
              MOVE WS-COMM-CUST-NO TO S4CUSTO
              MOVE -1 TO S4ITEML
```

FIGURE 6.5 *(Continued)*

```
         ELSE
             MOVE ALL '_' TO S4CUSTO
             MOVE -1 TO S4CUSTL.
*
         MOVE ALL '_' TO S4ITEMO.
         MOVE '+' TO S4SIGNO.
*
         PERFORM SEND-SALE004-RETURN.
*
*
*********************************************************************
* THIS ROUTINE SENDS SALE004 WITH A WARNING 'BEEP'. WE USE THIS    *
* ONLY WHEN THE CALLING ROUTINE WANTS TO DISPLAY A WARNING ON      *
* THE MESSAGE LINE OF THIS MAP. CURSOR POSITION MUST BE SET.       *
*********************************************************************
*
 SEND-SALE004-BEEP.
*
         IF WS-COMM-PREV-MAP = 'SALE004'
             EXEC CICS SEND MAP ('SALE004')
                            MAPSET ('MSALE04')
                            FROM (SALE004I)
                            DATAONLY
                            ALARM
                            CURSOR
                            END-EXEC
         ELSE
             MOVE 'SALE004' TO WS-COMM-PREV-MAP
             EXEC CICS SEND MAP ('SALE004')
                            MAPSET ('MSALE04')
                            FROM (SALE004I)
                            ERASE
                            ALARM
                            CURSOR
                            END-EXEC.
*
         EXEC CICS RETURN
                       TRANSID ('SAL4')
                       COMMAREA (WS-COMMAREA)
                       END-EXEC.
*
*
*********************************************************************
* THIS ROUTINE SENDS SALE004 WITH WHATEVER DATA HAS BEEN PLACED    *
* ON IT. IF THE PREDEFINED PORTIONS OF THE MAP ARE ALREADY ON      *
* THE SCREEN, SALE004 WILL BE SENT 'DATAONLY'.                     *
*********************************************************************
*
 SEND-SALE004-RETURN.
*
         IF WS-COMM-PREV-MAP = 'SALE004'
             EXEC CICS SEND MAP ('SALE004')
                            MAPSET ('MSALE04')
                            FROM (SALE004I)
                            DATAONLY
                            CURSOR
                            END-EXEC
         ELSE
             MOVE 'SALE004' TO WS-COMM-PREV-MAP
             EXEC CICS SEND MAP ('SALE004')
                            MAPSET ('MSALE04')
                            FROM (SALE004I)
                            ERASE
                            CURSOR
                            END-EXEC.
*
         EXEC CICS RETURN
                       TRANSID ('SAL4')
                       COMMAREA (WS-COMMAREA)
                       END-EXEC.
```

FIGURE 6.5   *(Continued)*

```
*
***********************************************************************
* THIS ROUTINE SENDS SALE004 WITH CURSOR ON ACTION BAR.              *
***********************************************************************
*
 CURSOR-TO-ACTION-BAR.
*
     MOVE 'SALE004' TO WS-COMM-PREV-MAP.
     EXEC CICS SEND MAP ('SALE004')
               MAPSET ('MSALE04')
               FROM (SALE004I)
               CURSOR (1)
               DATAONLY
               END-EXEC.
*
     EXEC CICS RETURN
               TRANSID ('SAL4')
               COMMAREA (WS-COMMAREA)
               END-EXEC.
*
*
***********************************************************************
* CHECK THE CICS RESPONSE CODE AND BUILD A MESSAGE EXPLAINING        *
* THE ERROR. IT IS THE RESPONSIBILITY OF THE CALLING ROUTINE         *
* TO INITIALIZE SOME DISPLAY FIELDS IN THE MESSAGE WORK AREA         *
* TO INDICATE THE TYPE OF COMMAND BEING PROCESSED.                   *
*                                                                    *
* WE DO NOTHING ABOUT CERTAIN RESPONSE CODES HERE SO THAT            *
* THOSE SITUATIONS CAN BE HANDLED WITH LOGIC ELSEWHERE IN THE        *
* PROGRAM.                                                           *
*                                                                    *
***********************************************************************
*
 CHECK-CICS-RESPONSE.
*
     EVALUATE WS-CICS-RESPONSE1
     WHEN DFHRESP(NORMAL)
         CONTINUE
     WHEN DFHRESP(MAPFAIL)
         CONTINUE
     WHEN DFHRESP(ENDFILE)
         CONTINUE
     WHEN DFHRESP(DISABLED)
         MOVE 'CALL OPERATIONS' TO DISPLAY-CALL-WHOM
         MOVE DISABLED-MSG TO DISPLAY-DESCRIPTION
         MOVE BUILD-MSG TO S4MSGO
     WHEN DFHRESP(DUPREC)
         MOVE DUPREC-MSG TO DISPLAY-DESCRIPTION
         MOVE BUILD-MSG TO S4MSGO
     WHEN DFHRESP(DSIDERR)
         MOVE 'CALL PROGRAMMER' TO DISPLAY-CALL-WHOM
         MOVE DSIDERR-MSG TO DISPLAY-DESCRIPTION
         MOVE BUILD-MSG TO S4MSGO
     WHEN DFHRESP(INVREQ)
         MOVE 'CALL PROGRAMMER' TO DISPLAY-CALL-WHOM
         MOVE INVREQ-MSG TO DISPLAY-DESCRIPTION
         MOVE BUILD-MSG TO S4MSGO
     WHEN DFHRESP(IOERR)
         MOVE 'CALL PROGRAMMER' TO DISPLAY-CALL-WHOM
         MOVE IOERR-MSG TO DISPLAY-DESCRIPTION
         MOVE BUILD-MSG TO S4MSGO
     WHEN DFHRESP(ITEMERR)
         MOVE 'CALL PROGRAMMER' TO DISPLAY-CALL-WHOM
         MOVE ITEMERR-MSG TO DISPLAY-DESCRIPTION
         MOVE BUILD-MSG TO S4MSGO
     WHEN DFHRESP(LENGERR)
         MOVE 'CALL PROGRAMMER' TO DISPLAY-CALL-WHOM
         MOVE LENGERR-MSG TO DISPLAY-DESCRIPTION
         MOVE BUILD-MSG TO S4MSGO
     WHEN DFHRESP(NOSPACE)
```

FIGURE 6.5 *(Continued)*

```
            MOVE 'CALL OPERATIONS' TO DISPLAY-CALL-WHOM
            MOVE NOSPACE-MSG TO DISPLAY-DESCRIPTION
            MOVE BUILD-MSG TO S4MSGO
     WHEN DFHRESP(NOTFND)
            MOVE NOTFND-MSG TO DISPLAY-DESCRIPTION
            MOVE BUILD-MSG TO S4MSGO
     WHEN DFHRESP(PGMIDERR)
            MOVE 'CALL PROGRAMMER' TO DISPLAY-CALL-WHOM
            MOVE PGMIDERR-MSG TO DISPLAY-DESCRIPTION
            MOVE BUILD-MSG TO S4MSGO
     WHEN DFHRESP(QIDERR)
            MOVE 'CALL PROGRAMMER' TO DISPLAY-CALL-WHOM
            MOVE QIDERR-MSG TO DISPLAY-DESCRIPTION
            MOVE BUILD-MSG TO S4MSGO
     WHEN OTHER
            MOVE 'CALL PROGRAMMER' TO DISPLAY-CALL-WHOM
            MOVE WS-CICS-RESPONSE1 TO DISPLAY-RESPONSE
            MOVE DEFAULT-DESCRIPTION TO DISPLAY-DESCRIPTION
            MOVE BUILD-MSG TO S4MSGO
     END-EVALUATE.
   *
   *
   *
```

FIGURE 6.5   *(Continued)*

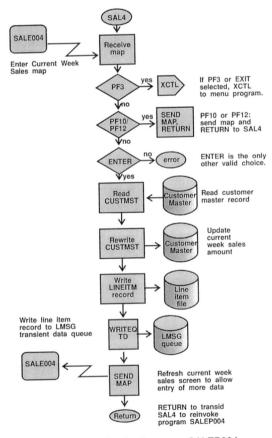

FIGURE 6.6   Logic of program SALEP004.

Sample Programs. Here is an example of a program that updates existing records on one VSAM file and adds records to another. SALEP004 is a program that allows the terminal user to enter current week sales for a customer. This function may be selected from the main menu. The main menu program will request a customer number from the terminal user and will then XCTL to the current week sales program, SALEP004. See Figures 6.5 and 6.6.

The terminal user may enter an item number, price, and quantity on map SALE004. Pressing ENTER invokes the current week sales processor, SALEP004, which does the following:

- SALEP004 updates the current week sales figure in the customer master record.
- SALEP004 writes a time-stamped line item record to the line item VSAM file.
- SALEP004 writes the line item to a sequential queue for later printing. (We will discuss this in detail in Chapter 8.)
- SALEP004 refreshes the user screen by clearing the item, quantity, and price fields, leaving the customer number on the screen. It sends the same map to the user's terminal again.
- SALEP004 executes a RETURN to its own TRANSID (SAL4). This means that SALEP004 will be executed again to process the new input on SALE004. This allows the terminal user to enter more line items for the same customer without having to go back to the menu screen.

6.3.2 Commands for File Browsing

As we mentioned earlier, a file browse is an application that reads a portion of a file sequentially and that presents an extract from these records to the terminal user. To the terminal user, a file browse looks like a table or a report on the terminal screen. Headers appear at the top of the screen, and detail fields are arranged in columns below the header fields. The user can use the ENTER key or other function keys to move up or down through the file. File browses can use a significant amount of system resources, but if they are designed correctly, resource usage will not be excessive. It is important to include file browses in many applications because terminal users tend to like them and to find them useful. A file browse can serve as a substitute for a printed report; it usually costs less and takes less time to browse the file on the terminal screen than it does to print the entire file and ship the report to the user. It also saves trees!

A file browse is started with the STARTBR command. The parameters used with it are similar to those used in the READ command. **The STARTBR command does not actually place any records in your**

program's working storage or linkage section. It only sets the current record pointer, which is invisible to your program. The current record pointer is a software indicator that points at the record that will be made available in the next sequential READNEXT or READPREV statement.

```
EXEC CICS STARTBR
           DATASET(name)
           RIDFLD(data-area)
           [KEYLENGTH(data-value)[GENERIC]]
           [RBA|RRN]
           [GTEQ|EQUAL]
           END-EXEC.
```

Ordinarily, you will want to specify GTEQ in the STARTBR command. If you specify GTEQ, and no record exists with the specified RIDFLD key, the STARTBR will point at the record with the next higher key. On the other hand, if EQUAL is specified, and no record exists with the specified RIDFLD key, then the NOTFND exceptional condition will be raised. This is why you typically should not specify EQUAL.

How do you position the pointer at the beginning or at the end of the file? If you specify GENERIC with a KEYLENGTH of zero, or if you specify a RIDFLD containing hexadecimal zeros (low-values), the STARTBR will point at the first record in the file. If you specify a RIDFLD containing hexadecimal FFs (high-values), the STARTBR will point past the last record in the file. A key of high-values can be useful when you wish to begin a backward browse. Do not use GENERIC if you are starting a backward browse. You must successfully execute STARTBR before it is possible for you to obtain a record by using READPREV.

Be sure to provide a RESP routine for NOTFND before beginning a browse. You may also wish to check for DUPKEY and possibly to ignore this condition; it results from reading records using a VSAM alternate key when this key has been defined as nonunique and when several records share this alternate key.

To obtain the next record on the file in ascending sequence, the READNEXT command is used. Whenever READNEXT is executed successfully, CICS updates the RIDFLD so that its new contents will correspond with the record that was just retrieved. If you wish to skip certain portions of the file, your program may also update the RIDFLD between READNEXT commands. You may change the RIDFLD contents to a higher value if you wish to skip all of the records between the current position in the file and the record corresponding with the new RIDFLD value. This is known as **skip-sequential processing.** It can only be done with forward browses. If the NOTFND condition occurs, the forward browse must be reset or ended.

```
EXEC CICS READNEXT
           DATASET(name)
           {SET(ptr-ref)|INTO(data-area)}
```

```
          [LENGTH(data-area)]
          RIDFLD(data-area)
          [KEYLENGTH(data-value)[GENERIC]]
          [RBA|RRN]
          END-EXEC.
```

The READPREV command is used to carry out backward browses. If you perform a READNEXT command and then a READPREV command, the first READPREV will retrieve the same record as did the last READNEXT.

```
EXEC CICS READPREV
          DATASET(name)
          {SET(ptr-ref)|INTO(data-area)}
          [LENGTH(data-area)]
          RIDFLD(data-area)
          [KEYLENGTH(data-value)[GENERIC]]
          [RBA|RRN]
          END-EXEC.
```

The ENDBR command is used to terminate a browse, freeing resources so that other processing can take place. **Always issue an ENDBR command to terminate a browse before you do a READ UPDATE.** Otherwise, lockouts or file access conflicts can occur.

```
EXEC CICS ENDBR
          DATASET(name)
          END-EXEC.
```

Suppose you wish to end a browse and start a new browse against the same file immediately. You may wish to do this in order to move further back toward the beginning of the file without executing READPREV again and again. The RESETBR command can be used to do this. Its parameters are similar to those used in the STARTBR command. In fact, RESETBR behaves much like an ENDBR followed by a STARTBR.

```
EXEC CICS RESETBR
          DATASET(name)
          RIDFLD(data-area)
          [KEYLENGTH(data-value)[GENERIC]]
          [RBA|RRN]
          [GTEQ|EQUAL]
          END-EXEC.
```

Sample Browse Program. SALEP005 is a file browse program that shows the customer list on the screen. The terminal user may request this program from the main menu. The main menu program will ask the user to enter a starting customer number. If none is given, the browse will start at the beginning of file. The menu processor, SALEP000, XCTLs to SALEP005, passing the starting browse key along to it in the DFHCOMMAREA. See Figures 6.7 and 6.8.

```
      IDENTIFICATION DIVISION.
      PROGRAM-ID. SALEP005.
      AUTHOR. ALIDA M. JATICH AND PHIL NOWAK.
     *****************************************************************
     * SALEP005: CUSTOMER RECORD BROWSE SCREEN PROCESSOR.           *
     *                                                              *
     * SALEP005 STARTS THE BROWSE OPERATION AND READS ENOUGH        *
     * OF THE CUSTOMER MASTER FILE TO FILL UP ONE SCREEN. IT        *
     * THEN ENDS THE BROWSE AND SENDS THE MAP TO THE TERMINAL       *
     * SCREEN.                                                      *
     *                                                              *
     * SALEP005 IS INITIALLY INVOKED BY XCTL FROM THE MENU          *
     * PROCESSOR PROGRAM, SALEP000. IF IT IS INVOKED IN THAT WAY,   *
     * THE STARTING BROWSE KEY IS OBTAINED FROM THE DFHCOMMAREA.    *
     * A FORWARD BROWSE SCREEN IS CREATED AND SENT TO THE USER.     *
     *                                                              *
     * THE USER MAY CHANGE THE BROWSE KEY ON THE SCREEN IF DESIRED. *
     * HE OR SHE MAY PRESS PF7 FOR A BACKWARD BROWSE OR PF8 FOR     *
     * A FORWARD BROWSE. WHEN THE KEY IS PRESSED, TRANSACTION SAL5  *
     * WILL BEGIN, INVOKING SALEP005, WHICH WILL PICK UP THE        *
     * CUSTOMER NUMBER FROM THE TERMINAL SCREEN. IT WILL CREATE A   *
     * FORWARD OR BACKWARD BROWSE SCREEN, SEND IT TO THE USER,      *
     * AND RETURN TO TRANSACTION SAL5 TO ALLOW MORE BROWSE ACTIVITY.*
     *                                                              *
     * IF WE SCROLL BACKWARD OR FORWARD, WE REPEAT ONE LINE THAT    *
     * APPEARED ON THE LAST SCREEN, PER THE RECOMMENDATION OF IBM   *
     * IN THE SYSTEMS APPLICATION ARCHITECTURE COMMON USER ACCESS   *
     * (SAA CUA) STANDARDS MANUAL.                                  *
     *****************************************************************
      ENVIRONMENT DIVISION.
      DATA DIVISION.
      WORKING-STORAGE SECTION.
      01  MISC-WORK.
          05  FILLER                  PIC X(24)       VALUE
              '>SALEP005 WS BEGINS>'.
          05  WS-CICS-RESPONSE1       PIC S9(8) COMP VALUE +0.
          05  WS-ACTIVE-ITEMS         PIC S9(8) COMP VALUE +0.
          05  WS-XCTL-PGM             PIC X(8)        VALUE SPACES.
          05  WS-EOF-FLAG             PIC X           VALUE 'N'.
          05  WS-CUSTNO-RIDFLD        PIC X(6)        VALUE LOW-VALUES.
     *
      COPY SALECOMM.
     *
      01  ERROR-MESSAGES.
          05  BAD-KEY-MSG             PIC X(22)       VALUE
              'Function key undefined'.
          05  FILE-EMPTY-MSG          PIC X(25)       VALUE
              'No customer records exist'.
          05  DISABLED-MSG            PIC X(16)       VALUE
              'File is disabled'.
          05  DSIDERR-MSG             PIC X(14)       VALUE
              'File not found'.
          05  DUPREC-MSG              PIC X(22)       VALUE
              'Record already on file'.
          05  INVREQ-MSG              PIC X(15)       VALUE
              'Invalid request'.
          05  IOERR-MSG               PIC X(9)        VALUE
              'I/O error'.
          05  ITEMERR-MSG             PIC X(16)       VALUE
              'Item not defined'.
          05  LENGERR-MSG             PIC X(19)       VALUE
              'Record length error'.
          05  NOSPACE-MSG             PIC X(17)       VALUE
              'File out of space'.
          05  NOTFND-MSG              PIC X(18)       VALUE
              'Record not on file'.
          05  PGMIDERR-MSG            PIC X(27)       VALUE
              'Program not defined to CICS'.
          05  QIDERR-MSG              PIC X(17)       VALUE
              'Queue not defined'.
```

FIGURE 6.7   Source code for SALEP005, customer file browse program, and for SALEP006.

```
*
      05  BUILD-MSG.
          10  DISPLAY-OPERATION    PIC X(12)       VALUE SPACES.
          10  FILLER               PIC X           VALUE SPACES.
          10  DISPLAY-RESOURCE      PIC X(8)        VALUE SPACES.
          10  FILLER               PIC X           VALUE SPACES.
          10  DISPLAY-DESCRIPTION  PIC X(38)       VALUE SPACES.
          10  FILLER               PIC X           VALUE SPACES.
          10  DISPLAY-CALL-WHOM    PIC X(16)       VALUE SPACES.
*
      05  DEFAULT-DESCRIPTION.
          10  FILLER               PIC X(22)       VALUE
          'SALEP005 ERROR: RESP1='.
          10  DISPLAY-RESPONSE     PIC 9(8)        VALUE ZEROES.
*
  COPY MSALE05.
*
 ********************************************************************
 * IN ORDER TO GROUP FIELDS WITHIN THE SYMBOLIC MAP AS AN ARRAY, *
 * A REDEFINITION IS NEEDED. THE NUMBER OF FILLER CHARACTERS     *
 * WILL VARY DEPENDING ON WHETHER YOU ARE USING EXTENDED         *
 * ATTRIBUTE SETTINGS.                                           *
 ********************************************************************
 *
  01  MAP-ARRAY REDEFINES SALE005I.
      02  FILLER                   PIC X(85).
      02  SCREEN-LINE OCCURS 12 TIMES INDEXED BY MAP-INDX.
          05  FILLER               PIC X(5).
          05  SCR-CUSTNO           PIC X(6).
          05  FILLER               PIC X(5).
          05  SCR-CUSTNAME         PIC X(25).
      02  FILLER                   PIC X(168).
 *
 ********************************************************************
 * THIS TABLE IS USED FOR CHANGING THE ORDER OF RECORDS FROM     *
 * DESCENDING TO ASCENDING, FOR BACKWARD BROWSE DISPLAY.         *
 ********************************************************************
 *                                                               *
  01  WORK-ARRAY.
      02  WORK-LINE OCCURS 12 TIMES INDEXED BY WORK-INDX.
          05  WORK-CUSTNO          PIC X(6).
          05  WORK-CUSTNAME        PIC X(25).
 *
  COPY ATTRIBUT.
  COPY DFHAID.
  COPY DFHBMSCA.
  COPY CUSTMST.
  LINKAGE SECTION.
  01  DFHCOMMAREA                  PIC X(68).
 *
  PROCEDURE DIVISION.
  MAIN-PROG.
 *
 ********************************************************************
 * DETERMINE WHICH POINT IN THE CYCLE APPLIES TO THE CURRENT     *
 * SITUATION. THE FIRST TIME THROUGH, SHOW THE BROWSE SCREEN     *
 * FOR THE FIRST TIME. ON SUBSEQUENT PASSES, PROCESS USER INPUT  *
 * AND SHOW THE SCREEN AGAIN (OR TRANSFER CONTROL BACK TO THE    *
 * MENU PROGRAM, DEPENDING ON FUNCTION KEY).                     *
 ********************************************************************
 *
      MOVE LOW-VALUES TO SALE005I.
 *
      IF EIBCALEN NOT = WS-EXPECTED-EIBCALEN
          PERFORM REFRESH-SCREEN
      ELSE
          MOVE DFHCOMMAREA TO WS-COMMAREA
          IF EIBTRNID = 'SAL5'
                  AND WS-COMM-PREV-MAP = 'SALE005'
              PERFORM CHECK-FOR-INPUT
```

FIGURE 6.7 *(Continued)*

```
                ELSE
                    MOVE WS-COMM-CUST-NO TO WS-COMM-NEXT-CUST-NO
                    PERFORM FORWARD-BROWSE.
        *
            GOBACK.
        *
        ********************************************************************
        * DETERMINE WHAT FUNCTION KEY THE USER PRESSED.                    *
        ********************************************************************
        *
        CHECK-FOR-INPUT.
        *
            IF EIBAID = DFHCLEAR OR DFHPF3
                MOVE 'SALEP000' TO WS-XCTL-PGM
                PERFORM XCTL-NEXT-PGM
            ELSE
                IF EIBAID = DFHPF10
                    PERFORM CURSOR-TO-ACTION-BAR
                ELSE
                    IF EIBAID = DFHPF12
                        PERFORM REFRESH-SCREEN
                    ELSE
                        IF EIBAID = DFHENTER
                                OR DFHPF7 OR DFHPF8
                            NEXT SENTENCE
                        ELSE
                            MOVE BAD-KEY-MSG TO S5MSGO
                            MOVE -1 TO S5CUSTL
                            PERFORM SEND-SALE005-BEEP.
        *
            MOVE 'SALE005' TO DISPLAY-RESOURCE.
            MOVE 'RECEIVE MAP' TO DISPLAY-OPERATION.
        *
            EXEC CICS RECEIVE MAP ('SALE005')
                    MAPSET ('MSALE05')
                    INTO (SALE005I)
                    RESP (WS-CICS-RESPONSE1)
                    END-EXEC.
        *
            IF WS-CICS-RESPONSE1 = DFHRESP(MAPFAIL)
                PERFORM REFRESH-SCREEN
            ELSE
                IF WS-CICS-RESPONSE1 NOT = DFHRESP(NORMAL)
                    PERFORM CHECK-CICS-RESPONSE
                    PERFORM SEND-SALE005-BEEP.
        *
            MOVE SPACES TO S5MSGO.
        *
        ********************************************************************
        * IF THE ENTER KEY WAS PRESSED, AND THE CURSOR WAS ANYWHERE        *
        * ON THE ACTION BAR, USE THE CURSOR POSITION TO SELECT THE         *
        * ACTION. IF THE CURSOR WAS ANYWHERE ELSE, JUST GO WITH THE        *
        * DEFAULT VALUE. IN THIS CASE, THE DEFAULT ACTION IS WHATEVER      *
        * IS IN THE COMMAREA FROM THE PREVIOUS ACTION, BECAUSE WE          *
        * ASSUME PEOPLE USUALLY KEEP SCROLLING IN THE SAME DIRECTION.      *
        *                                                                  *
        * IF THE USER ENTERED A NEW CUSTOMER NUMBER, USE THAT FOR          *
        * THE STARTING POSITION FOR THE NEXT SCREEN. OTHERWISE,            *
        * START FROM THE PREVIOUS VALUE IN THE COMMAREA.                   *
        *                                                                  *
        ********************************************************************
        *
            IF EIBAID = DFHPF7
              MOVE 'BACKWARD' TO WS-COMM-ACTION
            ELSE
              IF EIBAID = DFHPF8
                MOVE 'FORWARD' TO WS-COMM-ACTION
              ELSE
                IF EIBCPOSN  10
                  MOVE 'FORWARD' TO WS-COMM-ACTION
```

FIGURE 6.7   *(Continued)*

```
              ELSE
                IF EIBCPOSN  20
                  MOVE 'BACKWARD' TO WS-COMM-ACTION
                ELSE
                  IF EIBCPOSN  26
                    MOVE 'EXIT' TO WS-COMM-ACTION
                  ELSE
                    IF EIBCPOSN  33
                      MOVE 'CANCEL' TO WS-COMM-ACTION.
*
       IF WS-COMM-ACTION = 'EXIT'
          MOVE 'SALEP000' TO WS-XCTL-PGM
          PERFORM XCTL-NEXT-PGM
       ELSE
           IF WS-COMM-ACTION = 'CANCEL'
              PERFORM REFRESH-SCREEN
           ELSE
              IF S5CUSTO IS NUMERIC
                 MOVE S5CUSTO TO WS-COMM-CUST-NO
                                 WS-COMM-NEXT-CUST-NO
                 MOVE ALL '_' TO S5CUSTO
                 PERFORM FORWARD-BROWSE
              ELSE
                 IF WS-COMM-ACTION = 'BACKWARD'
                     PERFORM BACKWARD-BROWSE
                 ELSE
                     PERFORM FORWARD-BROWSE.
*
***********************************************************************
* 1. START A BROWSE WITH KEY FROM PRIOR SCREEN OR FROM USER.        *
* 2. READ NEXT RECORD UNTIL END OF FILE OR SCREEN IS FULL.          *
* 3. DETERMINE CORRECT SETTING FOR ON-SCREEN PAGING INDICATORS.     *
* 4. MOVE THE FIRST AND LAST CUSTOMER NUMBERS ON THE SCREEN TO      *
*    THE WORKING STORAGE COPY OF THE COMMAREA.                      *
* 5. END BROWSE.                                                    *
* 6. CHANGE THE APPEARANCE OF ACTION BAR TO SHOW THAT 'FORWARD'     *
*    IS NOW THE DEFAULT. IF YOU HAVE A COLOR DISPLAY, USE THE       *
*    COLOR EXTENDED ATTRIBUTE. OTHERWISE, CHANGE THE ATTRIBUTE      *
*    BYTE OF THE SELECTED ACTION TO A BRIGHT SETTING.               *
* 7. SEND MAP AND RETURN.                                          *
***********************************************************************
*
 FORWARD-BROWSE.
*
     MOVE ZEROES TO WS-ACTIVE-ITEMS.
     MOVE 'N' TO WS-EOF-FLAG.
     SET MAP-INDX TO 1.
     MOVE SPACES TO S5MSGO.
*
     MOVE WS-COMM-NEXT-CUST-NO TO WS-CUSTNO-RIDFLD.
*
     MOVE 'CUSTMST' TO DISPLAY-RESOURCE.
     MOVE 'START BROWSE' TO DISPLAY-OPERATION.
     EXEC CICS STARTBR GTEQ
               DATASET ('CUSTMST')
               RIDFLD (WS-CUSTNO-RIDFLD)
               RESP (WS-CICS-RESPONSE1)
               END-EXEC.
*
     IF WS-CICS-RESPONSE1 = DFHRESP(NOTFND)
        MOVE 'Y' TO WS-EOF-FLAG
        MOVE SPACES TO S5PLUSO
     ELSE
        IF WS-CICS-RESPONSE1 NOT = DFHRESP(NORMAL)
            PERFORM CHECK-CICS-RESPONSE
            MOVE -1 TO S5CUSTL
            PERFORM SEND-SALE005-BEEP
     ELSE
         PERFORM FORWARD-BROWSE-LOOP
             UNTIL MAP-INDX  +12
```

FIGURE 6.7 *(Continued)*

```
                    OR WS-EOF-FLAG = 'Y'
              IF WS-ACTIVE-ITEMS  ZEROES
                   PERFORM FWD-BROWSE-HOUSEKEEPING
              END-IF
              PERFORM END-BROWSE.
*
        MOVE 'FORWARD' TO WS-COMM-ACTION.
        MOVE DFHYELLO TO S5FWDC.
        MOVE DFHNEUTR TO S5BKWC.
*
        MOVE -1 TO S5CUSTL.
        PERFORM SEND-SALE005-RETURN.
*
  *************************************************************************
  * THE SCREEN HAS A PLUS AND MINUS SIGN TO INDICATE WHETHER             *
  * MORE RECORDS CAN BE REACHED BY SCROLLING FORWARD OR BACKWARD.        *
  * THESE SIGNS ARE REQUIRED BY IBM IN THE SAA COMMON USER ACCESS        *
  * STANDARDS.                                                           *
  *                                                                      *
  * IF WE ARE PAGING AHEAD FROM A PREVIOUS SCREEN, THE COUNTER           *
  * FIELD IN THE COMMAREA WILL INDICATE HOW MANY RECORDS WERE            *
  * SHOWN ON THE PREVIOUS PASS. THE SCREEN CONTENTS "OVERLAP"            *
  * BY ONE RECORD. IF MORE THAN ONE RECORD WAS SHOWN ON THE              *
  * PREVIOUS SCREEN, WE SET THE MINUS SIGN ON THE CURRENT                *
  * SCREEN TO INDICATE THAT THERE ARE SOME RECORDS ON FILE               *
  * WITH KEYS LOWER THAN THE ONES WE ARE NOW SHOWING.                    *
  *                                                                      *
  * WE READ ONE RECORD AHEAD OF THE LAST ITEM ON THE SCREEN              *
  * TO DETERMINE WHETHER THERE ARE MORE RECORDS TO WHICH                 *
  * THE USER MAY SCROLL FORWARD ON THE NEXT SCREEN. IF SO,               *
  * WE SET THE PLUS SIGN. WHEN WE READ THIS RECORD, WE DON'T             *
  * WANT IT TO GO ON THE SCREEN AND WE DON'T WANT TO UPDATE THE          *
  * SAVED COMMAREA KEY.                                                  *
  *                                                                      *
  * NOTE THAT THESE INDICATORS ARE NOT PERFECTLY ACCURATE BECAUSE        *
  * WE DON'T CONTROL THE WHOLE FILE. OTHER USERS COULD BE ADDING         *
  * OR DELETING RECORDS.                                                 *
  *************************************************************************
  *
   FWD-BROWSE-HOUSEKEEPING.
  *
        MOVE SCR-CUSTNO (1) TO WS-COMM-CUST-NO.
        MOVE WS-CUSTNO-RIDFLD TO WS-COMM-NEXT-CUST-NO.
  *
        PERFORM CLEAR-UNUSED-LINES
              UNTIL MAP-INDX  +12.
  *
        IF WS-COMM-COUNTER  +1
              MOVE '-' TO S5MINUSO.
  *
        MOVE WS-ACTIVE-ITEMS TO WS-COMM-COUNTER.
  *
        IF WS-EOF-FLAG = 'Y'
              MOVE SPACES TO S5PLUSO
        ELSE
              MOVE 'CUSTMST' TO DISPLAY-RESOURCE
              MOVE 'READNEXT' TO DISPLAY-OPERATION
              EXEC CICS READNEXT
                        DATASET ('CUSTMST')
                        INTO (CUSTMST-REC)
                        RIDFLD (WS-CUSTNO-RIDFLD)
                        RESP (WS-CICS-RESPONSE1)
                        END-EXEC
              IF WS-CICS-RESPONSE1 = DFHRESP(ENDFILE)
                   MOVE SPACES TO S5PLUSO
              ELSE
                   IF WS-CICS-RESPONSE1 = DFHRESP(NORMAL)
                        MOVE '+' TO S5PLUSO
                   ELSE
                        PERFORM CHECK-CICS-RESPONSE
```

FIGURE 6.7   *(Continued)*

```
                    MOVE -1 TO S5CUSTL
                    PERFORM SEND-SALE005-BEEP.
*
**********************************************************************
* ATTEMPT TO READ THE NEXT RECORD. IF FOUND, PUT IT IN THE          *
* NEXT AVAILABLE PLACE IN THE MAP ARRAY.                            *
**********************************************************************
*
 FORWARD-BROWSE-LOOP.
*
     MOVE 'CUSTMST' TO DISPLAY-RESOURCE.
     MOVE 'READNEXT' TO DISPLAY-OPERATION.
     EXEC CICS READNEXT
               DATASET ('CUSTMST')
               INTO (CUSTMST-REC)
               RIDFLD (WS-CUSTNO-RIDFLD)
               RESP (WS-CICS-RESPONSE1)
               END-EXEC.
*
     IF WS-CICS-RESPONSE1 = DFHRESP(ENDFILE)
        MOVE 'Y' TO WS-EOF-FLAG
     ELSE
         IF WS-CICS-RESPONSE1 = DFHRESP(NORMAL)
            MOVE CUST-NO TO SCR-CUSTNO (MAP-INDX)
            MOVE CUST-NAME TO SCR-CUSTNAME (MAP-INDX)
            SET MAP-INDX UP BY +1
            ADD +1 TO WS-ACTIVE-ITEMS
         ELSE
            PERFORM CHECK-CICS-RESPONSE
            MOVE -1 TO S5CUSTL
            PERFORM SEND-SALE005-BEEP.
*
 CLEAR-UNUSED-LINES.
*
     MOVE SPACES TO SCR-CUSTNO (MAP-INDX)
                    SCR-CUSTNAME (MAP-INDX).
*
     SET MAP-INDX UP BY +1.
*
**********************************************************************
* A BACKWARD BROWSE DIFFERS FROM A FORWARD BROWSE IN TWO WAYS.      *
*                                                                  *
* FIRST OF ALL, THE START BROWSE MUST BEGIN AT A VALID KEY          *
* ON THE FILE. THE ONLY EXCEPTION TO THIS IS A BACKWARD BROWSE      *
* STARTING FROM THE END OF THE FILE, WHICH IS BEGUN WITH A          *
* KEY OF HIGH-VALUES. THUS, IF THE START BROWSE INSTRUCTION         *
* FAILS, THEN WE TRY AGAIN WITH A KEY OF HIGH-VALUES TO GET A       *
* VALID STARTING POINT. NOTE THAT THE START BROWSE WILL FAIL        *
* AGAIN IF IN FACT THERE ARE NO RECORDS ON FILE.                    *
*                                                                  *
* SECOND, THE RECORDS ARE READ IN DESCENDING ORDER, BUT FOR         *
* THE SAKE OF CONSISTENT VISUAL APPEARANCE, WE WANT TO DISPLAY      *
* THEM IN ASCENDING ORDER ON THE SCREEN. NOT ONLY THAT, BUT         *
* IF THERE IS LESS THAN A SCREENFUL OF RECORDS, WE WANT TO          *
* START OVER AT THE BEGINNING OF THE FILE AND READ UP TO A          *
* FULL SCREEN OF RECORDS STARTING FROM THERE.                       *
**********************************************************************
* 1. START A BROWSE WITH KEY FROM PRIOR SCREEN OR FROM USER.        *
* 2. TRY THE START BROWSE AGAIN WITH A KEY OF HIGH-VALUES IF        *
*    THE FIRST ATTEMPT DOESN'T WORK.                                *
* 3. READ PREVIOUS RECORD UNTIL BEGINNING OF FILE OR WORK TABLE     *
*    IS FULL.                                                        *
* 4. MOVE THE FIRST AND LAST CUSTOMER NUMBERS FROM THE WORK         *
*    TABLE TO THE WORKING STORAGE COPY OF THE COMMAREA.             *
* 5. REVERSE THE ORDER OF THE SCREEN ITEMS BY COPYING FROM THE      *
*    WORK TABLE TO THE SCREEN TABLE.                                *
* 6. DETERMINE CORRECT SETTING FOR ON-SCREEN PAGING INDICATORS.     *
* 7. END BROWSE.                                                    *
* 8. CHANGE THE APPEARANCE OF ACTION BAR TO SHOW THAT 'BACKWARD'    *
*    IS NOW THE DEFAULT. IF YOU HAVE A COLOR DISPLAY, USE THE       *
```

FIGURE 6.7   *(Continued)*

```
*     COLOR EXTENDED ATTRIBUTE. OTHERWISE, CHANGE THE ATTRIBUTE  *
*     BYTE OF THE SELECTED ACTION TO A BRIGHT SETTING.            *
* 9. SEND MAP AND RETURN.                                         *
*****************************************************************
*
 BACKWARD-BROWSE.
*
     MOVE ZEROES TO WS-ACTIVE-ITEMS.
     MOVE 'N' TO WS-EOF-FLAG.
     SET MAP-INDX TO +1.
     SET WORK-INDX TO +1.
     MOVE SPACES TO WORK-ARRAY.
     MOVE SPACES TO S5MSGO.
*
     MOVE WS-COMM-CUST-NO TO WS-CUSTNO-RIDFLD.
     MOVE 'CUSTMST' TO DISPLAY-RESOURCE.
     MOVE 'START BROWSE' TO DISPLAY-OPERATION.
     EXEC CICS STARTBR GTEQ
             DATASET ('CUSTMST')
             RIDFLD (WS-CUSTNO-RIDFLD)
             RESP (WS-CICS-RESPONSE1)
             END-EXEC.
*
     IF WS-CICS-RESPONSE1 = DFHRESP(NOTFND)
        MOVE HIGH-VALUES TO WS-COMM-CUST-NO
        EXEC CICS STARTBR GTEQ
                DATASET ('CUSTMST')
                RIDFLD (WS-CUSTNO-RIDFLD)
                RESP (WS-CICS-RESPONSE1)
                END-EXEC.
*
     IF WS-CICS-RESPONSE1 = DFHRESP(NOTFND)
        MOVE FILE-EMPTY-MSG TO S5MSGO
        MOVE SPACES TO S5PLUSO S5MINUSO
        MOVE -1 TO S5CUSTL
        PERFORM SEND-SALE005-BEEP
     ELSE
        IF WS-CICS-RESPONSE1 NOT = DFHRESP(NORMAL)
           PERFORM CHECK-CICS-RESPONSE
           MOVE -1 TO S5CUSTL
           PERFORM SEND-SALE005-BEEP
        ELSE
           PERFORM BACKWARD-BROWSE-LOOP
              UNTIL WORK-INDX  +12
              OR WS-EOF-FLAG = 'Y'
           IF WS-ACTIVE-ITEMS = 12
              PERFORM BUILD-BKWD-BROWSE-SCREEN
           ELSE
              PERFORM END-BROWSE
              MOVE LOW-VALUES TO WS-COMM-CUST-NO
                                 WS-COMM-NEXT-CUST-NO
              MOVE ZEROES TO WS-COMM-COUNTER
              MOVE SPACES TO S5PLUSO S5MINUSO
              PERFORM FORWARD-BROWSE.
*
 BUILD-BKWD-BROWSE-SCREEN.
*
*****************************************************************
* IF WE HAVE OBTAINED A FULL SCREEN OF RECORDS, MOVE THOSE       *
* RECORDS TO THE SCREEN IN THE PROPER ORDER. THEN, MOVE THE      *
* KEYS FOR THE FIRST AND LAST SCREEN LINE TO THE WORKING         *
* STORAGE COPY OF THE COMMAREA.                                  *
*****************************************************************
*
     PERFORM INVERT-SCREEN-ORDER 12 TIMES.
     MOVE WORK-CUSTNO (1) TO WS-COMM-NEXT-CUST-NO.
     MOVE WORK-CUSTNO (12) TO WS-COMM-CUST-NO.
*
*****************************************************************
* THE SCREEN HAS A PLUS AND MINUS SIGN TO INDICATE WHETHER       *
```

FIGURE 6.7   *(Continued)*

```
* MORE RECORDS CAN BE REACHED BY SCROLLING FORWARD OR BACKWARD. *
* THESE SIGNS ARE REQUIRED BY IBM IN THE SAA COMMON USER ACCESS *
* STANDARDS.                                                    *
*                                                               *
* IF WE ARE PAGING BACK FROM A PREVIOUS SCREEN, THE COUNTER     *
* FIELD IN THE COMMAREA WILL INDICATE HOW MANY RECORDS WERE     *
* SHOWN ON THE PREVIOUS PASS. THE SCREEN CONTENTS "OVERLAP"     *
* BY ONE RECORD. IF MORE THAN ONE RECORD WAS SHOWN ON THE       *
* PREVIOUS SCREEN, WE SET THE PLUS SIGN ON THE CURRENT          *
* SCREEN TO INDICATE THAT THERE ARE SOME RECORDS ON FILE        *
* WITH KEYS HIGHER THAN THE ONES WE ARE NOW SHOWING.            *
*                                                               *
* WE READ ONE RECORD BEFORE THE FIRST ITEM ON THE SCREEN        *
* TO DETERMINE WHETHER THERE ARE MORE RECORDS TO WHICH          *
* THE USER MAY SCROLL BACKWARD ON THE NEXT SCREEN. IF SO,       *
* WE SET THE MINUS SIGN. WHEN WE READ THIS RECORD, WE DON'T     *
* WANT IT TO GO ON THE SCREEN AND WE DON'T WANT TO UPDATE THE   *
* SAVED COMMAREA KEY.                                           *
*                                                               *
* NOTE THAT THESE INDICATORS ARE NOT PERFECTLY ACCURATE BECAUSE *
* WE DON'T CONTROL THE WHOLE FILE. OTHER USERS COULD BE ADDING  *
* OR DELETING RECORDS.                                          *
*****************************************************************
*
      IF WS-COMM-COUNTER  +1
          MOVE '+' TO S5PLUSO.
*
      MOVE WS-ACTIVE-ITEMS TO WS-COMM-COUNTER.
*
      IF WS-EOF-FLAG = 'Y'
          MOVE SPACES TO S5MINUSO
      ELSE
          MOVE 'CUSTMST' TO DISPLAY-RESOURCE
          MOVE 'READPREV' TO DISPLAY-OPERATION
          EXEC CICS READPREV
                  DATASET ('CUSTMST')
                  INTO (CUSTMST-REC)
                  RIDFLD (WS-CUSTNO-RIDFLD)
                  RESP (WS-CICS-RESPONSE1)
                  END-EXEC
          IF WS-CICS-RESPONSE1 = DFHRESP(ENDFILE)
              MOVE SPACES TO S5MINUSO
          ELSE
              IF WS-CICS-RESPONSE1 = DFHRESP(NORMAL)
                  MOVE '-' TO S5MINUSO
              ELSE
                  PERFORM CHECK-CICS-RESPONSE
                  MOVE -1 TO S5CUSTL
                  PERFORM SEND-SALE005-BEEP.
*
      PERFORM END-BROWSE.
*
      MOVE 'BACKWARD' TO WS-COMM-ACTION.
      MOVE DFHYELLO TO S5BKWC.
      MOVE DFHNEUTR TO S5FWDC.
*
      MOVE -1 TO S5CUSTL.
      PERFORM SEND-SALE005-RETURN.
*
*****************************************************************
* ATTEMPT TO READ THE PREVIOUS RECORD. IF FOUND, PUT IT IN      *
* THE NEXT AVAILABLE PLACE IN THE WORKING STORAGE ARRAY.        *
*****************************************************************
*
 BACKWARD-BROWSE-LOOP.
*
*
      MOVE 'CUSTMST' TO DISPLAY-RESOURCE.
      MOVE 'READPREV' TO DISPLAY-OPERATION.
      EXEC CICS READPREV
```

FIGURE 6.7 (Continued)

```
                        DATASET ('CUSTMST')
                        INTO (CUSTMST-REC)
                        RIDFLD (WS-CUSTNO-RIDFLD)
                        RESP (WS-CICS-RESPONSE1)
                        END-EXEC.
    *
        IF WS-CICS-RESPONSE1 = DFHRESP(ENDFILE)
            MOVE 'Y' TO WS-EOF-FLAG
        ELSE
            IF WS-CICS-RESPONSE1 = DFHRESP(NORMAL)
                MOVE CUST-NO TO WORK-CUSTNO (WORK-INDX)
                MOVE CUST-NAME TO WORK-CUSTNAME (WORK-INDX)
                SET WORK-INDX UP BY +1
                ADD +1 TO WS-ACTIVE-ITEMS
            ELSE
                PERFORM CHECK-CICS-RESPONSE
                MOVE -1 TO S5CUSTL
                PERFORM SEND-SALE005-BEEP.
    *
    ***********************************************************************
    * THE BACKWARD BROWSE ROUTINE GETS THE RECORDS IN REVERSE ORDER *
    * AND STORES THEM IN A WORKING STORAGE ARRAY. IT THEN PUTS THE  *
    * RECORDS INTO THE SCREEN ARRAY IN ASCENDING ORDER BY CUSTOMER  *
    * NUMBER.                                                        *
    ***********************************************************************
    *
     INVERT-SCREEN-ORDER.
    *
        SET WORK-INDX DOWN BY +1.
        MOVE WORK-CUSTNO (WORK-INDX) TO SCR-CUSTNO (MAP-INDX).
        MOVE WORK-CUSTNAME (WORK-INDX) TO SCR-CUSTNAME (MAP-INDX).
        SET MAP-INDX UP BY +1.
    *
    *
     XCTL-NEXT-PGM.
    *
        MOVE ZEROES TO WS-COMM-COUNTER.
        MOVE WS-XCTL-PGM TO DISPLAY-RESOURCE.
        MOVE 'XCTL' TO DISPLAY-OPERATION.
        EXEC CICS XCTL
                PROGRAM (WS-XCTL-PGM)
                COMMAREA (WS-COMMAREA)
                RESP (WS-CICS-RESPONSE1)
                END-EXEC.
    *
        IF WS-CICS-RESPONSE1 NOT = DFHRESP(NORMAL)
            PERFORM CHECK-CICS-RESPONSE
            MOVE -1 TO S5CUSTL
            PERFORM SEND-SALE005-BEEP.
    *
    ***********************************************************************
    * ENDBR (END BROWSE) COMMAND WILL FAIL IF STARTBR (START BROWSE)*
    * COMMAND WAS UNSUCCESSFUL. THIS IS NOT A MATTER OF CONCERN, SO *
    * BYPASS ANY ERROR HANDLING FOR THAT SITUATION.                 *
    ***********************************************************************
    *
     END-BROWSE.
    *
        MOVE 'CUSTMST' TO DISPLAY-RESOURCE.
        MOVE 'END BROWSE' TO DISPLAY-OPERATION.
        EXEC CICS ENDBR
                DATASET ('CUSTMST')
                RESP (WS-CICS-RESPONSE1)
                END-EXEC.
    *
        IF WS-CICS-RESPONSE1 NOT = DFHRESP(INVREQ)
                AND WS-CICS-RESPONSE1 NOT = DFHRESP(NORMAL)
            PERFORM CHECK-CICS-RESPONSE
            MOVE -1 TO S5CUSTL
            PERFORM SEND-SALE005-BEEP.
```

FIGURE 6.7   *(Continued)*

```
*
**********************************************************************
* THIS ROUTINE SENDS THE RECORD BROWSE MAP WITH NO DATA ON IT.  *
**********************************************************************
*
 REFRESH-SCREEN.
*
     MOVE ZEROES TO WS-COMM-COUNTER.
     MOVE 'FORWARD' TO WS-COMM-ACTION.
     MOVE DFHYELLO TO S5FWDC.
     MOVE DFHNEUTR TO S5BKWC.
     MOVE 'SALE005' TO WS-COMM-PREV-MAP.
     MOVE SPACES TO S5MSGO.
     MOVE SPACES TO WS-COMM-CUST-NO
                    WS-COMM-NEXT-CUST-NO.
     MOVE '_____' TO S5CUSTO.
     MOVE -1 TO S5CUSTL.
     MOVE SPACES TO S5PLUSO S5MINUSO.
     SET MAP-INDX TO +1.
     PERFORM CLEAR-UNUSED-LINES
         UNTIL MAP-INDX  +12.
     PERFORM SEND-SALE005-RETURN.
*
*
**********************************************************************
* THIS ROUTINE SENDS SALE005 WITH A WARNING 'BEEP'. WE USE THIS *
* ONLY WHEN THE CALLING ROUTINE WANTS TO DISPLAY A WARNING ON   *
* THE MESSAGE LINE OF THIS MAP. CURSOR POSITION MUST BE SET.    *
**********************************************************************
*
 SEND-SALE005-BEEP.
*
     IF WS-COMM-PREV-MAP = 'SALE005'
         EXEC CICS SEND MAP ('SALE005')
                    MAPSET ('MSALE05')
                    FROM (SALE005I)
                    DATAONLY
                    ALARM
                    CURSOR
                    END-EXEC
     ELSE
         MOVE 'SALE005' TO WS-COMM-PREV-MAP
         EXEC CICS SEND MAP ('SALE005')
                    MAPSET ('MSALE05')
                    FROM (SALE005I)
                    ERASE
                    ALARM
                    CURSOR
                    END-EXEC.
*
     EXEC CICS RETURN
             TRANSID ('SAL5')
             COMMAREA (WS-COMMAREA)
             END-EXEC.
*
*
**********************************************************************
* THIS ROUTINE SENDS SALE005 WITH WHATEVER DATA HAS BEEN PLACED *
* ON IT. IF THE PREDEFINED PORTIONS OF THE MAP ARE ALREADY ON   *
* THE SCREEN, SALE005 WILL BE SENT 'DATAONLY'.                  *
**********************************************************************
*
 SEND-SALE005-RETURN.
*
     IF WS-COMM-PREV-MAP = 'SALE005'
         EXEC CICS SEND MAP ('SALE005')
                    MAPSET ('MSALE05')
                    FROM (SALE005I)
                    DATAONLY
                    CURSOR
```

FIGURE 6.7   *(Continued)*

```
                              END-EXEC
            ELSE
                MOVE 'SALE005' TO WS-COMM-PREV-MAP
                EXEC CICS SEND MAP ('SALE005')
                          MAPSET ('MSALE05')
                          FROM (SALE005I)
                          ERASE
                          CURSOR
                          END-EXEC.
       *
            EXEC CICS RETURN
                      TRANSID ('SAL5')
                      COMMAREA (WS-COMMAREA)
                      END-EXEC.
       *
       **********************************************************************
       * THIS ROUTINE SENDS SALE005 WITH CURSOR ON ACTION BAR.         *
       **********************************************************************
       *
        CURSOR-TO-ACTION-BAR.
       *
            MOVE 'SALE005' TO WS-COMM-PREV-MAP.
            EXEC CICS SEND MAP ('SALE005')
                      MAPSET ('MSALE05')
                      FROM (SALE005I)
                      CURSOR (1)
                      DATAONLY
                      END-EXEC.
       *
            EXEC CICS RETURN
                      TRANSID ('SAL5')
                      COMMAREA (WS-COMMAREA)
                      END-EXEC.
       *
       *
       **********************************************************************
       * CHECK THE CICS RESPONSE CODE AND BUILD A MESSAGE EXPLAINING   *
       * THE ERROR. IT IS THE RESPONSIBILITY OF THE CALLING ROUTINE    *
       * TO INITIALIZE SOME DISPLAY FIELDS IN THE MESSAGE WORK AREA    *
       * TO INDICATE THE TYPE OF COMMAND BEING PROCESSED.              *
       *                                                               *
       * WE DO NOTHING ABOUT CERTAIN RESPONSE CODES HERE SO THAT       *
       * THOSE SITUATIONS CAN BE HANDLED WITH LOGIC ELSEWHERE IN THE   *
       * PROGRAM.                                                      *
       *                                                               *
       **********************************************************************
       *
       *
        CHECK-CICS-RESPONSE.
       *
            EVALUATE WS-CICS-RESPONSE1
            WHEN DFHRESP(NORMAL)
                CONTINUE
            WHEN DFHRESP(MAPFAIL)
                CONTINUE
            WHEN DFHRESP(ENDFILE)
                CONTINUE
            WHEN DFHRESP(DISABLED)
                MOVE 'CALL OPERATIONS' TO DISPLAY-CALL-WHOM
                MOVE DISABLED-MSG TO DISPLAY-DESCRIPTION
                MOVE BUILD-MSG TO S5MSGO
            WHEN DFHRESP(DUPREC)
                MOVE DUPREC-MSG TO DISPLAY-DESCRIPTION
                MOVE BUILD-MSG TO S5MSGO
            WHEN DFHRESP(DSIDERR)
                MOVE 'CALL PROGRAMMER' TO DISPLAY-CALL-WHOM
                MOVE DSIDERR-MSG TO DISPLAY-DESCRIPTION
                MOVE BUILD-MSG TO S5MSGO
            WHEN DFHRESP(INVREQ)
                MOVE 'CALL PROGRAMMER' TO DISPLAY-CALL-WHOM
```

FIGURE 6.7   *(Continued)*

```
                MOVE INVREQ-MSG TO DISPLAY-DESCRIPTION
                MOVE BUILD-MSG TO S5MSGO
            WHEN DFHRESP(IOERR)
                MOVE 'CALL PROGRAMMER' TO DISPLAY-CALL-WHOM
                MOVE IOERR-MSG TO DISPLAY-DESCRIPTION
                MOVE BUILD-MSG TO S5MSGO
            WHEN DFHRESP(ITEMERR)
                MOVE 'CALL PROGRAMMER' TO DISPLAY-CALL-WHOM
                MOVE ITEMERR-MSG TO DISPLAY-DESCRIPTION
                MOVE BUILD-MSG TO S5MSGO
            WHEN DFHRESP(LENGERR)
                MOVE 'CALL PROGRAMMER' TO DISPLAY-CALL-WHOM
                MOVE LENGERR-MSG TO DISPLAY-DESCRIPTION
                MOVE BUILD-MSG TO S5MSGO
            WHEN DFHRESP(NOSPACE)
                MOVE 'CALL OPERATIONS' TO DISPLAY-CALL-WHOM
                MOVE NOSPACE-MSG TO DISPLAY-DESCRIPTION
                MOVE BUILD-MSG TO S5MSGO
            WHEN DFHRESP(NOTFND)
                MOVE NOTFND-MSG TO DISPLAY-DESCRIPTION
                MOVE BUILD-MSG TO S5MSGO
            WHEN DFHRESP(PGMIDERR)
                MOVE 'CALL PROGRAMMER' TO DISPLAY-CALL-WHOM
                MOVE PGMIDERR-MSG TO DISPLAY-DESCRIPTION
                MOVE BUILD-MSG TO S5MSGO
            WHEN DFHRESP(QIDERR)
                MOVE 'CALL PROGRAMMER' TO DISPLAY-CALL-WHOM
                MOVE QIDERR-MSG TO DISPLAY-DESCRIPTION
                MOVE BUILD-MSG TO S5MSGO
            WHEN OTHER
                MOVE 'CALL PROGRAMMER' TO DISPLAY-CALL-WHOM
                MOVE WS-CICS-RESPONSE1 TO DISPLAY-RESPONSE
                MOVE DEFAULT-DESCRIPTION TO DISPLAY-DESCRIPTION
                MOVE BUILD-MSG TO S5MSGO
            END-EVALUATE.
    *
    *

    IDENTIFICATION DIVISION.
    PROGRAM-ID. SALEP006.
    AUTHOR. ALIDA M. JATICH AND PHIL NOWAK.
    **********************************************************************
    * SALEP006: LINEITM RECORD BROWSE SCREEN PROCESSOR.                 *
    *                                                                    *
    * SALEP006 STARTS THE BROWSE OPERATION AND READS ENOUGH             *
    * OF THE LINE ITEM VSAM FILE TO FILL UP ONE SCREEN. IT              *
    * THEN ENDS THE BROWSE AND SENDS THE MAP TO THE TERMINAL            *
    * SCREEN.                                                            *
    *                                                                    *
    * SALEP006 IS INITIALLY INVOKED BY XCTL FROM THE MENU               *
    * PROCESSOR PROGRAM, SALEP000. IF IT IS INVOKED IN THAT WAY,        *
    * THE STARTING BROWSE KEY IS OBTAINED FROM THE DFHCOMMAREA.         *
    * A FORWARD BROWSE SCREEN IS CREATED AND SENT TO THE USER.          *
    *                                                                    *
    * THE USER MAY CHANGE THE BROWSE KEY ON THE SCREEN IF DESIRED.      *
    * HE OR SHE MAY PRESS PF7 FOR A BACKWARD BROWSE OR PF8 FOR          *
    * A FORWARD BROWSE. WHEN THE KEY IS PRESSED, TRANSACTION SAL6       *
    * WILL BEGIN, INVOKING SALEP006, WHICH WILL PICK UP THE             *
    * CUSTOMER NUMBER FROM THE TERMINAL SCREEN. IT WILL CREATE A        *
    * FORWARD OR BACKWARD BROWSE SCREEN, SEND IT TO THE USER,           *
    * AND RETURN TO TRANSACTION SAL6 TO ALLOW MORE BROWSE ACTIVITY.     *
    *                                                                    *
    * IF WE SCROLL BACKWARD OR FORWARD, WE REPEAT ONE LINE THAT         *
    * APPEARED ON THE LAST SCREEN, PER THE RECOMMENDATION OF IBM        *
    * IN THE SYSTEMS APPLICATION ARCHITECTURE COMMON USER ACCESS        *
    * (SAA CUA) STANDARDS MANUAL.                                       *
    **********************************************************************
```

FIGURE 6.7 *(Continued)*

```
ENVIRONMENT DIVISION.
DATA DIVISION.
WORKING-STORAGE SECTION.
01  MISC-WORK.
    05  FILLER                     PIC X(24)      VALUE
        '>SALEP006 WS BEGINS>'.
    05  WS-CICS-RESPONSE1          PIC S9(8) COMP VALUE +0.
    05  WS-ACTIVE-ITEMS            PIC S9(8) COMP VALUE +0.
    05  WS-XCTL-PGM                PIC X(8)       VALUE SPACES.
    05  WS-EOF-FLAG                PIC X          VALUE 'N'.
*
    05  WS-RIDFLD.
        10  WS-RIDFLD-CUST-NO  PIC X(6).
        10  WS-RIDFLD-DATE     PIC S9(7) COMP-3.
        10  WS-RIDFLD-TIME     PIC S9(7) COMP-3.
        10  WS-RIDFLD-ITEM-CODE PIC X(6).
    05  WS-1ST-RIDFLD.
        10  WS-1ST-RIDFLD-CUST-NO
                               PIC X(6).
        10  WS-1ST-RIDFLD-DATE PIC S9(7) COMP-3.
        10  WS-1ST-RIDFLD-TIME PIC S9(7) COMP-3.
        10  WS-1ST-RIDFLD-ITEM-CODE
                               PIC X(6).
    05  WS-LAST-RIDFLD.
        10  WS-LAST-RIDFLD-CUST-NO
                               PIC X(6).
        10  WS-LAST-RIDFLD-DATE PIC S9(7) COMP-3.
        10  WS-LAST-RIDFLD-TIME PIC S9(7) COMP-3.
        10  WS-LAST-RIDFLD-ITEM-CODE
                               PIC X(6).
*
*
COPY SALECOMM.
*
01  ERROR-MESSAGES.
    05  BAD-KEY-MSG                PIC X(22)      VALUE
        'Function key undefined'.
    05  NO-RECS-FOR-CUST-MSG       PIC X(26)      VALUE
        'No line item records exist'.
    05  DISABLED-MSG               PIC X(16)      VALUE
        'File is disabled'.
    05  DSIDERR-MSG                PIC X(14)      VALUE
        'File not found'.
    05  DUPREC-MSG                 PIC X(22)      VALUE
        'Record already on file'.
    05  INVREQ-MSG                 PIC X(15)      VALUE
        'Invalid request'.
    05  IOERR-MSG                  PIC X(9)       VALUE
        'I/O error'.
    05  ITEMERR-MSG                PIC X(16)      VALUE
        'Item not defined'.
    05  LENGERR-MSG                PIC X(19)      VALUE
        'Record length error'.
    05  NOSPACE-MSG                PIC X(17)      VALUE
        'File out of space'.
    05  NOTFND-MSG                 PIC X(18)      VALUE
        'Record not on file'.
    05  PGMIDERR-MSG               PIC X(27)      VALUE
        'Program not defined to CICS'.
    05  QIDERR-MSG                 PIC X(17)      VALUE
        'Queue not defined'.
*
    05  BUILD-MSG.
        10  DISPLAY-OPERATION   PIC X(12)     VALUE SPACES.
        10  FILLER              PIC X         VALUE SPACES.
        10  DISPLAY-RESOURCE    PIC X(8)      VALUE SPACES.
        10  FILLER              PIC X         VALUE SPACES.
        10  DISPLAY-DESCRIPTION PIC X(38)     VALUE SPACES.
        10  FILLER              PIC X         VALUE SPACES.
        10  DISPLAY-CALL-WHOM   PIC X(16)     VALUE SPACES.
```

FIGURE 6.7 *(Continued)*

```
*
    05  DEFAULT-DESCRIPTION.
        10  FILLER                  PIC X(22)      VALUE
            'SALEP006 ERROR: RESP1='.
        10  DISPLAY-RESPONSE   PIC 9(8)       VALUE ZEROES.
*
 COPY MSALE06.
*
******************************************************************
* IN ORDER TO GROUP FIELDS WITHIN THE SYMBOLIC MAP AS AN ARRAY, *
* A REDEFINITION IS NEEDED. THE NUMBER OF FILLER CHARACTERS     *
* WILL VARY DEPENDING ON WHETHER YOU ARE USING EXTENDED         *
* ATTRIBUTE SETTINGS.                                           *
******************************************************************
*
 01  MAP-ARRAY REDEFINES SALE006I.
     05  FILLER                     PIC X(96).
     05  SCREEN-LINE OCCURS 16 TIMES INDEXED BY MAP-INDX.
         10  FILLER                 PIC X(5).
         10  SCR-ITEM-CODE          PIC X(6).
         10  FILLER                 PIC X(5).
         10  SCR-QUANTITY-X.
             15  SCR-QUANTITY       PIC ZZZ,ZZ9-.
         10  FILLER                 PIC X(5).
         10  SCR-UNIT-PRICE-X.
             15  SCR-UNIT-PRICE  PIC $$$,$$$.99.

     05  FILLER                     PIC X(168).
*
******************************************************************
* THIS TABLE IS USED FOR CHANGING THE ORDER OF RECORDS FROM     *
* DESCENDING TO ASCENDING, FOR BACKWARD BROWSE DISPLAY.         *
******************************************************************
*                                                               *
 01  WORK-ARRAY.
     02  WORK-LINE OCCURS 16 TIMES INDEXED BY WORK-INDX.
         05  WORK-ITEM-CODE     PIC X(6).
         05  WORK-QUANTITY      PIC S9(6).
         05  WORK-UNIT-PRICE    PIC S9(5)V99.
*
 COPY ATTRIBUT.
 COPY DFHAID.
 COPY DFHBMSCA.
 COPY LINEITM.
 LINKAGE SECTION.
 01  DFHCOMMAREA                    PIC X(68).
*
 PROCEDURE DIVISION.
 MAIN-PROG.
*
******************************************************************
* DETERMINE WHICH POINT IN THE CYCLE APPLIES TO THE CURRENT     *
* SITUATION. THE FIRST TIME THROUGH, SHOW THE BROWSE SCREEN     *
* FOR THE FIRST TIME. ON SUBSEQUENT PASSES, PROCESS USER INPUT  *
* AND SHOW THE SCREEN AGAIN (OR TRANSFER CONTROL BACK TO THE    *
* MENU PROGRAM, DEPENDING ON FUNCTION KEY).                     *
******************************************************************
*
     MOVE LOW-VALUES TO SALE006I.
*
     IF EIBCALEN NOT = WS-EXPECTED-EIBCALEN
         PERFORM REFRESH-SCREEN
     ELSE
         MOVE DFHCOMMAREA TO WS-COMMAREA
         IF EIBTRNID = 'SAL6'
                 AND WS-COMM-PREV-MAP = 'SALE006'
             PERFORM CHECK-FOR-INPUT
         ELSE
             MOVE WS-COMM-KEY TO WS-COMM-NEXT-KEY
             PERFORM FORWARD-BROWSE.
```

FIGURE 6.7   (Continued)

```
*
      GOBACK.
*
***********************************************************************
* DETERMINE WHAT FUNCTION KEY THE USER PRESSED.                       *
***********************************************************************
*
 CHECK-FOR-INPUT.
*
      IF EIBAID = DFHCLEAR OR DFHPF3
          MOVE 'SALEP000' TO WS-XCTL-PGM
          PERFORM XCTL-NEXT-PGM
      ELSE
          IF EIBAID = DFHPF10
              PERFORM CURSOR-TO-ACTION-BAR
          ELSE
              IF EIBAID = DFHPF12
                  PERFORM REFRESH-SCREEN
              ELSE
                  IF EIBAID = DFHENTER
                          OR DFHPF7 OR DFHPF8
                      NEXT SENTENCE
                  ELSE
                      MOVE BAD-KEY-MSG TO S6MSGO
                      MOVE -1 TO S6CUSTL
                      PERFORM SEND-SALE006-BEEP.
*
      MOVE 'SALE006' TO DISPLAY-RESOURCE.
      MOVE 'RECEIVE MAP' TO DISPLAY-OPERATION.
*
      EXEC CICS RECEIVE MAP ('SALE006')
                MAPSET ('MSALE06')
                INTO (SALE006I)
                RESP (WS-CICS-RESPONSE1)
                END-EXEC.
*
      IF WS-CICS-RESPONSE1 = DFHRESP(MAPFAIL)
          PERFORM REFRESH-SCREEN
      ELSE
          IF WS-CICS-RESPONSE1 NOT = DFHRESP(NORMAL)
              PERFORM CHECK-CICS-RESPONSE
              PERFORM SEND-SALE006-BEEP.
*
      MOVE SPACES TO S6MSGO.
*
***********************************************************************
* IF THE ENTER KEY WAS PRESSED, AND THE CURSOR WAS ANYWHERE          *
* ON THE ACTION BAR, USE THE CURSOR POSITION TO SELECT THE           *
* ACTION. IF THE CURSOR WAS ANYWHERE ELSE, JUST GO WITH THE          *
* DEFAULT VALUE. IN THIS CASE, THE DEFAULT ACTION IS WHATEVER        *
* IS IN THE COMMAREA FROM THE PREVIOUS ACTION, BECAUSE WE            *
* ASSUME PEOPLE USUALLY KEEP SCROLLING IN THE SAME DIRECTION.        *
*                                                                    *
* IF THE USER ENTERED A NEW CUSTOMER NUMBER, USE THAT FOR            *
* THE STARTING POSITION FOR THE NEXT SCREEN. OTHERWISE,              *
* START FROM THE PREVIOUS VALUE IN THE COMMAREA.                     *
*                                                                    *
***********************************************************************
*
      IF EIBAID = DFHPF7
        MOVE 'BACKWARD' TO WS-COMM-ACTION
      ELSE
        IF EIBAID = DFHPF8
          MOVE 'FORWARD' TO WS-COMM-ACTION
        ELSE
          IF EIBCPOSN 10
            MOVE 'FORWARD' TO WS-COMM-ACTION
          ELSE
            IF EIBCPOSN 20
              MOVE 'BACKWARD' TO WS-COMM-ACTION
```

FIGURE 6.7 *(Continued)*

```
              ELSE
                IF EIBCPOSN  26
                  MOVE 'EXIT' TO WS-COMM-ACTION
                ELSE
                   IF EIBCPOSN  33
                     MOVE 'CANCEL' TO WS-COMM-ACTION.
*
      IF WS-COMM-ACTION = 'EXIT'
         MOVE 'SALEP000' TO WS-XCTL-PGM
         PERFORM XCTL-NEXT-PGM
      ELSE
          IF WS-COMM-ACTION = 'CANCEL'
             PERFORM REFRESH-SCREEN
          ELSE
             IF S6CUSTO IS NUMERIC
                SET MAP-INDX TO 1
                PERFORM CLEAR-REMAINING-ITEMS
                   UNTIL MAP-INDX  16
                MOVE S6CUSTO TO WS-COMM-CUST-NO
                                WS-COMM-NEXT-CUST-NO
                MOVE LOW-VALUES TO WS-COMM-ITEM-CODE
                                   WS-COMM-NEXT-ITEM-CODE
                MOVE ZEROES TO WS-COMM-DATE
                               WS-COMM-TIME
                               WS-COMM-NEXT-DATE
                               WS-COMM-NEXT-TIME
                               WS-COMM-COUNTER
                MOVE ALL '_' TO S6CUSTO
                PERFORM FORWARD-BROWSE
             ELSE
                IF WS-COMM-ACTION = 'BACKWARD'
                    PERFORM BACKWARD-BROWSE
                ELSE
                    PERFORM FORWARD-BROWSE.
*
*
***************************************************************************
* 1. START A BROWSE WITH KEY FROM PRIOR SCREEN OR FROM USER.       *
* 2. READ NEXT RECORD UNTIL END OF FILE OR SCREEN IS FULL.         *
* 3. DETERMINE CORRECT SETTING FOR ON-SCREEN PAGING INDICATORS.    *
* 4. MOVE THE FIRST AND LAST ITEM NUMBERS ON THE SCREEN TO         *
*    THE WORKING STORAGE COPY OF THE COMMAREA.                     *
* 5. END BROWSE.                                                   *
* 6. CHANGE THE APPEARANCE OF ACTION BAR TO SHOW THAT 'FORWARD'    *
*    IS NOW THE DEFAULT. IF YOU HAVE A COLOR DISPLAY, USE THE      *
*    COLOR EXTENDED ATTRIBUTE. OTHERWISE, CHANGE THE ATTRIBUTE     *
*    BYTE OF THE SELECTED ACTION TO A BRIGHT SETTING.              *
* 7. SEND MAP AND RETURN.                                          *
***************************************************************************
*
 FORWARD-BROWSE.
*
     MOVE ZEROES TO WS-ACTIVE-ITEMS.
     MOVE 'N' TO WS-EOF-FLAG.
     SET MAP-INDX TO 1.
     MOVE SPACES TO S6MSGO.
*
     MOVE WS-COMM-NEXT-KEY TO WS-RIDFLD
                             WS-1ST-RIDFLD.
*
     MOVE 'LINEITM' TO DISPLAY-RESOURCE.
     MOVE 'START BROWSE' TO DISPLAY-OPERATION.
     EXEC CICS STARTBR GTEQ
             DATASET ('LINEITM')
             RIDFLD (WS-RIDFLD)
             RESP (WS-CICS-RESPONSE1)
             END-EXEC.
*
     IF WS-CICS-RESPONSE1 = DFHRESP(NOTFND)
         MOVE 'Y' TO WS-EOF-FLAG
```

FIGURE 6.7   *(Continued)*

```
              MOVE SPACES TO S6PLUSO
          ELSE
              IF WS-CICS-RESPONSE1 NOT = DFHRESP(NORMAL)
                  PERFORM CHECK-CICS-RESPONSE
                  MOVE -1 TO S6CUSTL
                  PERFORM SEND-SALE006-BEEP
          ELSE
              PERFORM FORWARD-BROWSE-LOOP
                  UNTIL MAP-INDX  +16
                  OR WS-EOF-FLAG = 'Y'
              IF WS-ACTIVE-ITEMS  ZEROES
                  PERFORM FWD-BROWSE-HOUSEKEEPING
              END-IF
              PERFORM END-BROWSE.
*
          MOVE 'FORWARD' TO WS-COMM-ACTION.
          MOVE DFHYELLO TO S6FWDC.
          MOVE DFHNEUTR TO S6BKWC.
*
          MOVE -1 TO S6CUSTL.
          PERFORM SEND-SALE006-RETURN.
*
*****************************************************************
* THE SCREEN HAS A PLUS AND MINUS SIGN TO INDICATE WHETHER      *
* MORE RECORDS CAN BE REACHED BY SCROLLING FORWARD OR BACKWARD. *
* THESE SIGNS ARE REQUIRED BY IBM IN THE SAA COMMON USER ACCESS *
* STANDARDS.                                                    *
*                                                               *
* IF WE ARE PAGING AHEAD FROM A PREVIOUS SCREEN, THE COUNTER    *
* FIELD IN THE COMMAREA WILL INDICATE HOW MANY RECORDS WERE     *
* SHOWN ON THE PREVIOUS PASS. THE SCREEN CONTENTS "OVERLAP"     *
* BY ONE RECORD. IF MORE THAN ONE RECORD WAS SHOWN ON THE       *
* PREVIOUS SCREEN, WE SET THE MINUS SIGN ON THE CURRENT         *
* SCREEN TO INDICATE THAT THERE ARE SOME RECORDS ON FILE        *
* WITH KEYS LOWER THAN THE ONES WE ARE NOW SHOWING.             *
*                                                               *
* WE READ ONE RECORD AHEAD OF THE LAST ITEM ON THE SCREEN       *
* TO DETERMINE WHETHER THERE ARE MORE RECORDS TO WHICH          *
* THE USER MAY SCROLL FORWARD ON THE NEXT SCREEN. IF SO,        *
* WE SET THE PLUS SIGN. WHEN WE READ THIS RECORD, WE DON'T      *
* WANT IT TO GO ON THE SCREEN AND WE DON'T WANT TO UPDATE THE   *
* SAVED COMMAREA KEY.                                           *
*                                                               *
* NOTE THAT THESE INDICATORS ARE NOT PERFECTLY ACCURATE BECAUSE *
* WE DON'T CONTROL THE WHOLE FILE. OTHER USERS COULD BE ADDING  *
* OR DELETING RECORDS.                                          *
*****************************************************************
*
     FWD-BROWSE-HOUSEKEEPING.
*
         MOVE WS-1ST-RIDFLD TO WS-COMM-KEY.
         MOVE WS-LAST-RIDFLD TO WS-COMM-NEXT-KEY.
*
         PERFORM CLEAR-REMAINING-ITEMS
             UNTIL MAP-INDX  +16.
*
         IF WS-COMM-COUNTER  +1
             MOVE '-' TO S6MINUSO.
*
         MOVE WS-ACTIVE-ITEMS TO WS-COMM-COUNTER.
*
         IF WS-EOF-FLAG = 'Y'
             MOVE SPACES TO S6PLUSO
         ELSE
             MOVE 'LINEITM' TO DISPLAY-RESOURCE
             MOVE 'READNEXT' TO DISPLAY-OPERATION
             EXEC CICS READNEXT
                     DATASET ('LINEITM')
                     INTO (LINEITM-REC)
                     RIDFLD (WS-RIDFLD)
```

FIGURE 6.7   *(Continued)*

```
                          RESP (WS-CICS-RESPONSE1)
                          END-EXEC
              IF WS-CICS-RESPONSE1 = DFHRESP(ENDFILE)
                  OR WS-RIDFLD-CUST-NO NOT =
                      WS-1ST-RIDFLD-CUST-NO
                  MOVE SPACES TO S6PLUSO
              ELSE
                  IF WS-CICS-RESPONSE1 NOT = DFHRESP(NORMAL)
                      PERFORM CHECK-CICS-RESPONSE
                      MOVE -1 TO S6CUSTL
                      PERFORM SEND-SALE006-BEEP
                  ELSE
                      MOVE '+' TO S6PLUSO.
     *
     ****************************************************************
     * ATTEMPT TO READ THE NEXT RECORD. IF FOUND, PUT IT IN THE    *
     * NEXT AVAILABLE PLACE IN THE MAP ARRAY.                      *
     ****************************************************************
     *
      FORWARD-BROWSE-LOOP.
     *
          MOVE 'LINEITM' TO DISPLAY-RESOURCE.
          MOVE 'READNEXT' TO DISPLAY-OPERATION.
          EXEC CICS READNEXT
                    DATASET ('LINEITM')
                    INTO (LINEITM-REC)
                    RIDFLD (WS-RIDFLD)
                    RESP (WS-CICS-RESPONSE1)
                    END-EXEC.
     *
          IF WS-CICS-RESPONSE1 = DFHRESP(ENDFILE)
              MOVE 'Y' TO WS-EOF-FLAG
          ELSE
              IF WS-CICS-RESPONSE1 NOT = DFHRESP(NORMAL)
                  PERFORM CHECK-CICS-RESPONSE
                  MOVE -1 TO S6CUSTL
                  PERFORM SEND-SALE006-BEEP
              ELSE
                  IF WS-1ST-RIDFLD-CUST-NO = LOW-VALUES
                      MOVE WS-RIDFLD TO WS-1ST-RIDFLD
                  END-IF
                  IF WS-RIDFLD-CUST-NO =
                          WS-1ST-RIDFLD-CUST-NO
                      MOVE LINEITM-ITEM-CODE
                          TO SCR-ITEM-CODE (MAP-INDX)
                      MOVE LINEITM-QUANTITY
                          TO SCR-QUANTITY (MAP-INDX)
                      MOVE LINEITM-UNIT-PRICE
                          TO SCR-UNIT-PRICE (MAP-INDX)
                      IF MAP-INDX = +1
                          MOVE WS-RIDFLD TO WS-1ST-RIDFLD
                      END-IF
                      MOVE WS-RIDFLD TO WS-LAST-RIDFLD
                      SET MAP-INDX UP BY +1
                      ADD +1 TO WS-ACTIVE-ITEMS
                  ELSE
                      MOVE 'Y' TO WS-EOF-FLAG.
     *
     *
     ****************************************************************
     * A BACKWARD BROWSE DIFFERS FROM A FORWARD BROWSE IN TWO WAYS. *
     *                                                             *
     * FIRST OF ALL, THE START BROWSE MUST BEGIN AT A VALID KEY    *
     * ON THE FILE. THE ONLY EXCEPTION TO THIS IS A BACKWARD BROWSE *
     * STARTING FROM THE END OF THE FILE, WHICH IS BEGUN WITH A    *
     * KEY OF HIGH-VALUES. THUS, IF THE START BROWSE INSTRUCTION   *
     * FAILS, THEN WE TRY AGAIN WITH A KEY OF HIGH-VALUES TO GET A *
     * VALID STARTING POINT. NOTE THAT THE START BROWSE WILL FAIL  *
     * AGAIN IF IN FACT THERE ARE NO RECORDS ON FILE.             *
     *                                                             *
     ****************************************************************
```

FIGURE 6.7 *(Continued)*

```
* SECOND, THE RECORDS ARE READ IN DESCENDING ORDER, BUT FOR      *
* THE SAKE OF CONSISTENT VISUAL APPEARANCE, WE WANT TO DISPLAY    *
* THEM IN ASCENDING ORDER ON THE SCREEN. NOT ONLY THAT, BUT       *
* IF THERE IS LESS THAN A SCREENFUL OF RECORDS, WE WANT TO        *
* START OVER AT THE BEGINNING OF THE FILE AND READ UP TO A        *
* FULL SCREEN OF RECORDS STARTING FROM THERE.                     *
******************************************************************
* 1. START A BROWSE WITH KEY FROM PRIOR SCREEN OR FROM USER.      *
* 2. TRY THE START BROWSE AGAIN WITH A KEY OF HIGH-VALUES IF      *
*    THE FIRST ATTEMPT DOESN'T WORK.                              *
* 3. READ PREVIOUS RECORD UNTIL BEGINNING OF FILE OR WORK TABLE   *
*    IS FULL.                                                     *
* 4. MOVE THE FIRST AND LAST LINEITM FILE KEYS FROM THE WORK      *
*    TABLE TO THE WORKING STORAGE COPY OF THE COMMAREA.           *
* 5. REVERSE THE ORDER OF THE SCREEN ITEMS BY COPYING FROM THE    *
*    WORK TABLE TO THE SCREEN TABLE.                              *
* 6. DETERMINE CORRECT SETTING FOR ON-SCREEN PAGING INDICATORS.   *
* 7. END BROWSE.                                                  *
* 8. CHANGE THE APPEARANCE OF ACTION BAR TO SHOW THAT 'BACKWARD'* 
*    IS NOW THE DEFAULT. IF YOU HAVE A COLOR DISPLAY, USE THE     *
*    COLOR EXTENDED ATTRIBUTE. OTHERWISE, CHANGE THE ATTRIBUTE    *
*    BYTE OF THE SELECTED ACTION TO A BRIGHT SETTING.             *
* 9. SEND MAP AND RETURN.                                         *
******************************************************************
*
 BACKWARD-BROWSE.
*
     MOVE ZEROES TO WS-ACTIVE-ITEMS.
     MOVE 'N' TO WS-EOF-FLAG.
     SET MAP-INDX TO +1.
     SET WORK-INDX TO +1.
     MOVE SPACES TO WORK-ARRAY.
     MOVE SPACES TO S6MSGO.
*
     MOVE WS-COMM-KEY TO WS-RIDFLD
                         WS-LAST-RIDFLD-CUST-NO.
     MOVE 'LINEITM' TO DISPLAY-RESOURCE.
     MOVE 'START BROWSE' TO DISPLAY-OPERATION.
     EXEC CICS STARTBR GTEQ
               DATASET ('LINEITM')
               RIDFLD (WS-RIDFLD)
               RESP (WS-CICS-RESPONSE1)
               END-EXEC.
*
     IF WS-CICS-RESPONSE1 = DFHRESP(NOTFND)
         MOVE HIGH-VALUES TO WS-COMM-KEY
         EXEC CICS STARTBR GTEQ
                   DATASET ('LINEITM')
                   RIDFLD (WS-RIDFLD)
                   RESP (WS-CICS-RESPONSE1)
                   END-EXEC.
*
     IF WS-CICS-RESPONSE1 = DFHRESP(NOTFND)
         MOVE SPACES TO S6PLUSO S6MINUSO
         MOVE -1 TO S6CUSTL
         PERFORM SEND-SALE006-RETURN
     ELSE
         IF WS-CICS-RESPONSE1 NOT = DFHRESP(NORMAL)
             PERFORM CHECK-CICS-RESPONSE
             MOVE -1 TO S6CUSTL
             PERFORM SEND-SALE006-BEEP
         ELSE
             PERFORM BACKWARD-BROWSE-LOOP
                 UNTIL WORK-INDX  +16
                 OR WS-EOF-FLAG = 'Y'
             IF WS-ACTIVE-ITEMS = 16
                 PERFORM BUILD-BKWD-BROWSE-SCREEN
             ELSE
                 PERFORM END-BROWSE
                 MOVE LOW-VALUES TO WS-COMM-ITEM-CODE
```

FIGURE 6.7 *(Continued)*

```
                                          WS-COMM-NEXT-ITEM-CODE
                      MOVE ZEROES TO WS-COMM-DATE
                                     WS-COMM-TIME
                                     WS-COMM-NEXT-DATE
                                     WS-COMM-NEXT-TIME
                      MOVE ZEROES TO WS-COMM-COUNTER
                      MOVE SPACES TO S6PLUS0 S6MINUS0
                      PERFORM FORWARD-BROWSE.
     *
      BUILD-BKWD-BROWSE-SCREEN.
     *
     *****************************************************************
     * IF WE HAVE OBTAINED A FULL SCREEN OF RECORDS, MOVE THOSE      *
     * RECORDS TO THE SCREEN IN THE PROPER ORDER. THEN, MOVE THE     *
     * KEYS FOR THE FIRST AND LAST SCREEN LINE TO THE WORKING        *
     * STORAGE COPY OF THE COMMAREA.                                 *
     *****************************************************************
     *
          PERFORM INVERT-SCREEN-ORDER 16 TIMES.
          MOVE WS-1ST-RIDFLD TO WS-COMM-KEY.
          MOVE WS-LAST-RIDFLD TO WS-COMM-NEXT-KEY.
     *
     *****************************************************************
     * THE SCREEN HAS A PLUS AND MINUS SIGN TO INDICATE WHETHER      *
     * MORE RECORDS CAN BE REACHED BY SCROLLING FORWARD OR BACKWARD. *
     * THESE SIGNS ARE REQUIRED BY IBM IN THE SAA COMMON USER ACCESS *
     * STANDARDS.                                                    *
     *                                                               *
     * IF WE ARE PAGING BACK FROM A PREVIOUS SCREEN, THE COUNTER     *
     * FIELD IN THE COMMAREA WILL INDICATE HOW MANY RECORDS WERE     *
     * SHOWN ON THE PREVIOUS PASS. THE SCREEN CONTENTS "OVERLAP"     *
     * BY ONE RECORD. IF MORE THAN ONE RECORD WAS SHOWN ON THE       *
     * PREVIOUS SCREEN, WE SET THE PLUS SIGN ON THE CURRENT          *
     * SCREEN TO INDICATE THAT THERE ARE SOME RECORDS ON FILE        *
     * WITH KEYS HIGHER THAN THE ONES WE ARE NOW SHOWING.            *
     *                                                               *
     * WE READ ONE RECORD BEFORE THE FIRST ITEM ON THE SCREEN        *
     * TO DETERMINE WHETHER THERE ARE MORE RECORDS TO WHICH          *
     * THE USER MAY SCROLL BACKWARD ON THE NEXT SCREEN. IF SO,       *
     * WE SET THE MINUS SIGN. WHEN WE READ THIS RECORD, WE DON'T     *
     * WANT IT TO GO ON THE SCREEN AND WE DON'T WANT TO UPDATE THE   *
     * SAVED COMMAREA KEY.                                           *
     *                                                               *
     * NOTE THAT THESE INDICATORS ARE NOT PERFECTLY ACCURATE BECAUSE *
     * WE DON'T CONTROL THE WHOLE FILE. OTHER USERS COULD BE ADDING  *
     * OR DELETING RECORDS.                                          *
     *****************************************************************
     *
          IF WS-COMM-COUNTER  +1
              MOVE '+' TO S6PLUS0.
     *
          MOVE WS-ACTIVE-ITEMS TO WS-COMM-COUNTER.
     *
          IF WS-EOF-FLAG = 'Y'
              MOVE SPACES TO S6MINUS0
          ELSE
              MOVE 'LINEITM' TO DISPLAY-RESOURCE
              MOVE 'READPREV' TO DISPLAY-OPERATION
              EXEC CICS READPREV
                      DATASET ('LINEITM')
                      INTO (LINEITM-REC)
                      RIDFLD (WS-RIDFLD)
                      RESP (WS-CICS-RESPONSE1)
                      END-EXEC
              IF WS-CICS-RESPONSE1 = DFHRESP(ENDFILE)
                      OR WS-RIDFLD-CUST-NO NOT =
                      WS-LAST-RIDFLD-CUST-NO
                  MOVE SPACES TO S6MINUS0
              ELSE
                  IF WS-CICS-RESPONSE1 NOT = DFHRESP(NORMAL)
```

FIGURE 6.7   *(Continued)*

```
                        PERFORM CHECK-CICS-RESPONSE
                        MOVE -1 TO S6CUSTL
                        PERFORM SEND-SALE006-BEEP
                    ELSE
                        MOVE '-' TO S6MINUSO.
*
        PERFORM END-BROWSE.
*
        MOVE 'BACKWARD' TO WS-COMM-ACTION.
        MOVE DFHYELLO TO S6BKWC.
        MOVE DFHNEUTR TO S6FWDC.
*
        MOVE -1 TO S6CUSTL.
        PERFORM SEND-SALE006-RETURN.
*
***********************************************************************
* ATTEMPT TO READ THE PREVIOUS RECORD. IF FOUND, PUT IT IN          *
* THE NEXT AVAILABLE PLACE IN THE WORKING STORAGE ARRAY.            *
***********************************************************************
*
 BACKWARD-BROWSE-LOOP.
*
*
        MOVE 'LINEITM' TO DISPLAY-RESOURCE.
        MOVE 'READPREV' TO DISPLAY-OPERATION.
        EXEC CICS READPREV
                DATASET ('LINEITM')
                INTO (LINEITM-REC)
                RIDFLD (WS-RIDFLD)
                RESP (WS-CICS-RESPONSE1)
                END-EXEC.
*
        IF WS-CICS-RESPONSE1 = DFHRESP(ENDFILE)
            MOVE 'Y' TO WS-EOF-FLAG
        ELSE
            IF WS-CICS-RESPONSE1 NOT = DFHRESP(NORMAL)
                PERFORM CHECK-CICS-RESPONSE
                MOVE -1 TO S6CUSTL
                PERFORM SEND-SALE006-BEEP
            ELSE
                IF WS-RIDFLD-CUST-NO =
                        WS-LAST-RIDFLD-CUST-NO
                    MOVE LINEITM-ITEM-CODE
                        TO WORK-ITEM-CODE (WORK-INDX)
                    MOVE LINEITM-QUANTITY
                        TO WORK-QUANTITY (WORK-INDX)
                    MOVE LINEITM-UNIT-PRICE
                        TO WORK-UNIT-PRICE (WORK-INDX)
                    IF WORK-INDX = +1
                        MOVE WS-RIDFLD TO WS-LAST-RIDFLD
                    END-IF
                    MOVE WS-RIDFLD TO WS-1ST-RIDFLD
                    SET WORK-INDX UP BY +1
                    ADD +1 TO WS-ACTIVE-ITEMS
                ELSE
                    MOVE 'Y' TO WS-EOF-FLAG.
*
***********************************************************************
* THE BACKWARD BROWSE ROUTINE GETS THE RECORDS IN REVERSE ORDER *
* AND STORES THEM IN A WORKING STORAGE ARRAY. IT THEN PUTS THE  *
* RECORDS INTO THE SCREEN ARRAY IN ASCENDING ORDER BY CUSTOMER  *
* NUMBER.                                                        *
***********************************************************************
*
 INVERT-SCREEN-ORDER.
*
        SET WORK-INDX DOWN BY +1.
        MOVE WORK-ITEM-CODE (WORK-INDX) TO SCR-ITEM-CODE (MAP-INDX).
        MOVE WORK-QUANTITY (WORK-INDX) TO SCR-QUANTITY (MAP-INDX).
        MOVE WORK-UNIT-PRICE (WORK-INDX)
```

FIGURE 6.7 *(Continued)*

```
                TO SCR-UNIT-PRICE (MAP-INDX).
          SET MAP-INDX UP BY +1.
*
*
 XCTL-NEXT-PGM.
*
      MOVE ZEROES TO WS-COMM-COUNTER.
      MOVE WS-XCTL-PGM TO DISPLAY-RESOURCE.
      MOVE 'XCTL' TO DISPLAY-OPERATION.
      EXEC CICS XCTL
              PROGRAM (WS-XCTL-PGM)
              COMMAREA (WS-COMMAREA)
              RESP (WS-CICS-RESPONSE1)
              END-EXEC.
*
      IF WS-CICS-RESPONSE1 NOT = DFHRESP(NORMAL)
          PERFORM CHECK-CICS-RESPONSE
          MOVE -1 TO S6CUSTL
          PERFORM SEND-SALE006-BEEP.
*
*********************************************************************
* ENDBR (END BROWSE) COMMAND WILL FAIL IF STARTBR (START BROWSE)*
* COMMAND WAS UNSUCCESSFUL. THIS IS NOT A MATTER OF CONCERN, SO *
* BYPASS ANY ERROR HANDLING FOR THAT SITUATION.                *
*********************************************************************
*
 END-BROWSE.
*
      MOVE 'LINEITM' TO DISPLAY-RESOURCE.
      MOVE 'END BROWSE' TO DISPLAY-OPERATION.
      EXEC CICS ENDBR
              DATASET ('LINEITM')
              RESP (WS-CICS-RESPONSE1)
              END-EXEC.
*
      IF WS-CICS-RESPONSE1 NOT = DFHRESP(INVREQ)
          AND WS-CICS-RESPONSE1 NOT = DFHRESP(NORMAL)
          PERFORM CHECK-CICS-RESPONSE
          MOVE -1 TO S6CUSTL
          PERFORM SEND-SALE006-BEEP.
*
*********************************************************************
* THIS ROUTINE SENDS THE RECORD BROWSE MAP WITH NO DATA ON IT.  *
*********************************************************************
*
 REFRESH-SCREEN.
*
      MOVE ZEROES TO WS-COMM-COUNTER.
      MOVE 'FORWARD' TO WS-COMM-ACTION.
      MOVE DFHYELLO TO S6FWDC.
      MOVE DFHNEUTR TO S6BKWC.
      MOVE 'SALE006' TO WS-COMM-PREV-MAP.
      MOVE SPACES TO S6MSGO.
      MOVE SPACES TO WS-COMM-CUST-NO
                     WS-COMM-NEXT-CUST-NO.
      MOVE LOW-VALUES TO WS-COMM-ITEM-CODE
                          WS-COMM-NEXT-ITEM-CODE.
      MOVE ZEROES TO WS-COMM-DATE
                     WS-COMM-TIME
                     WS-COMM-NEXT-DATE
                     WS-COMM-NEXT-TIME.
      MOVE '_____' TO S6CUSTO.
      MOVE -1 TO S6CUSTL.
      MOVE SPACES TO S6PLUSO S6MINUSO.
      SET MAP-INDX TO +1.
      PERFORM CLEAR-REMAINING-ITEMS UNTIL MAP-INDX  16.
      PERFORM SEND-SALE006-RETURN.
*
*
 CLEAR-REMAINING-ITEMS.
```

FIGURE 6.7   *(Continued)*

```
*
      MOVE SPACES TO SCR-ITEM-CODE (MAP-INDX)
                     SCR-QUANTITY-X (MAP-INDX)
                     SCR-UNIT-PRICE-X (MAP-INDX).
*
      SET MAP-INDX UP BY 1.
*
*****************************************************************
* THIS ROUTINE SENDS SALE006 WITH A WARNING 'BEEP'. WE USE THIS *
* ONLY WHEN THE CALLING ROUTINE WANTS TO DISPLAY A WARNING ON   *
* THE MESSAGE LINE OF THIS MAP. CURSOR POSITION MUST BE SET.    *
*****************************************************************
*
 SEND-SALE006-BEEP.
*
      IF WS-COMM-PREV-MAP = 'SALE006'
         EXEC CICS SEND MAP ('SALE006')
                   MAPSET ('MSALE06')
                   FROM (SALE006I)
                   DATAONLY
                   ALARM
                   CURSOR
                   END-EXEC
      ELSE
         MOVE 'SALE006' TO WS-COMM-PREV-MAP
         EXEC CICS SEND MAP ('SALE006')
                   MAPSET ('MSALE06')
                   FROM (SALE006I)
                   ERASE
                   ALARM
                   CURSOR
                   END-EXEC.
*
      EXEC CICS RETURN
                TRANSID ('SAL6')
                COMMAREA (WS-COMMAREA)
                END-EXEC.
*
*
*****************************************************************
* THIS ROUTINE SENDS SALE006 WITH WHATEVER DATA HAS BEEN PLACED *
* ON IT. IF THE PREDEFINED PORTIONS OF THE MAP ARE ALREADY ON   *
* THE SCREEN, SALE006 WILL BE SENT 'DATAONLY'.                  *
*****************************************************************
*
 SEND-SALE006-RETURN.
*
      IF WS-COMM-PREV-MAP = 'SALE006'
         EXEC CICS SEND MAP ('SALE006')
                   MAPSET ('MSALE06')
                   FROM (SALE006I)
                   DATAONLY
                   CURSOR
                   END-EXEC
      ELSE
         MOVE 'SALE006' TO WS-COMM-PREV-MAP
         EXEC CICS SEND MAP ('SALE006')
                   MAPSET ('MSALE06')
                   FROM (SALE006I)
                   ERASE
                   CURSOR
                   END-EXEC.
*
      EXEC CICS RETURN
                TRANSID ('SAL6')
                COMMAREA (WS-COMMAREA)
                END-EXEC.
*
*****************************************************************
* THIS ROUTINE SENDS SALE006 WITH CURSOR ON ACTION BAR.        *
```

FIGURE 6.7 *(Continued)*

```
****************************************************************
*
 CURSOR-TO-ACTION-BAR.
*
     MOVE 'SALE006' TO WS-COMM-PREV-MAP.
     EXEC CICS SEND MAP ('SALE006')
               MAPSET ('MSALE06')
               FROM (SALE006I)
               CURSOR (1)
               DATAONLY
               END-EXEC.
*
     EXEC CICS RETURN
               TRANSID ('SAL6')
               COMMAREA (WS-COMMAREA)
               END-EXEC.
*
*
****************************************************************
* CHECK THE CICS RESPONSE CODE AND BUILD A MESSAGE EXPLAINING  *
* THE ERROR. IT IS THE RESPONSIBILITY OF THE CALLING ROUTINE   *
* TO INITIALIZE SOME DISPLAY FIELDS IN THE MESSAGE WORK AREA   *
* TO INDICATE THE TYPE OF COMMAND BEING PROCESSED.             *
*                                                              *
* WE DO NOTHING ABOUT CERTAIN RESPONSE CODES HERE SO THAT      *
* THOSE SITUATIONS CAN BE HANDLED WITH LOGIC ELSEWHERE IN THE  *
* PROGRAM.                                                     *
*                                                              *
****************************************************************
*
*
 CHECK-CICS-RESPONSE.
*
     EVALUATE WS-CICS-RESPONSE1
     WHEN DFHRESP(NORMAL)
          CONTINUE
     WHEN DFHRESP(MAPFAIL)
          CONTINUE
     WHEN DFHRESP(ENDFILE)
          CONTINUE
     WHEN DFHRESP(DISABLED)
          MOVE 'CALL OPERATIONS' TO DISPLAY-CALL-WHOM
          MOVE DISABLED-MSG TO DISPLAY-DESCRIPTION
          MOVE BUILD-MSG TO S6MSGO
     WHEN DFHRESP(DUPREC)
          MOVE DUPREC-MSG TO DISPLAY-DESCRIPTION
          MOVE BUILD-MSG TO S6MSGO
     WHEN DFHRESP(DSIDERR)
          MOVE 'CALL PROGRAMMER' TO DISPLAY-CALL-WHOM
          MOVE DSIDERR-MSG TO DISPLAY-DESCRIPTION
          MOVE BUILD-MSG TO S6MSGO
     WHEN DFHRESP(INVREQ)
          MOVE 'CALL PROGRAMMER' TO DISPLAY-CALL-WHOM
          MOVE INVREQ-MSG TO DISPLAY-DESCRIPTION
          MOVE BUILD-MSG TO S6MSGO
     WHEN DFHRESP(IOERR)
          MOVE 'CALL PROGRAMMER' TO DISPLAY-CALL-WHOM
          MOVE IOERR-MSG TO DISPLAY-DESCRIPTION
          MOVE BUILD-MSG TO S6MSGO
     WHEN DFHRESP(ITEMERR)
          MOVE 'CALL PROGRAMMER' TO DISPLAY-CALL-WHOM
          MOVE ITEMERR-MSG TO DISPLAY-DESCRIPTION
          MOVE BUILD-MSG TO S6MSGO
     WHEN DFHRESP(LENGERR)
          MOVE 'CALL PROGRAMMER' TO DISPLAY-CALL-WHOM
          MOVE LENGERR-MSG TO DISPLAY-DESCRIPTION
          MOVE BUILD-MSG TO S6MSGO
     WHEN DFHRESP(NOSPACE)
          MOVE 'CALL OPERATIONS' TO DISPLAY-CALL-WHOM
          MOVE NOSPACE-MSG TO DISPLAY-DESCRIPTION
```

FIGURE 6.7 (Continued)

```
         MOVE BUILD-MSG TO S6MSGO
WHEN DFHRESP(NOTFND)
         MOVE NOTFND-MSG TO DISPLAY-DESCRIPTION
         MOVE BUILD-MSG TO S6MSGO
WHEN DFHRESP(PGMIDERR)
         MOVE 'CALL PROGRAMMER' TO DISPLAY-CALL-WHOM
         MOVE PGMIDERR-MSG TO DISPLAY-DESCRIPTION
         MOVE BUILD-MSG TO S6MSGO
WHEN DFHRESP(QIDERR)
         MOVE 'CALL PROGRAMMER' TO DISPLAY-CALL-WHOM
         MOVE QIDERR-MSG TO DISPLAY-DESCRIPTION
         MOVE BUILD-MSG TO S6MSGO
WHEN OTHER
         MOVE 'CALL PROGRAMMER' TO DISPLAY-CALL-WHOM
         MOVE WS-CICS-RESPONSE1 TO DISPLAY-RESPONSE
         MOVE DEFAULT-DESCRIPTION TO DISPLAY-DESCRIPTION
         MOVE BUILD-MSG TO S6MSGO
END-EVALUATE.
*
*
```

FIGURE 6.7   *(Continued)*

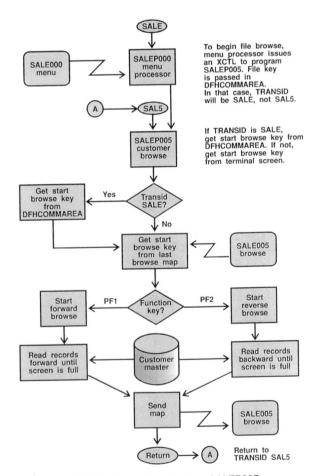

FIGURE 6.8   Logic of program SALEP005.

SALEP005 uses the starting browse key to perform a STARTBR command. It reads enough records to fill the screen. It then performs an ENDBR command and sends the browse map to the terminal user. The new starting browse key is saved in the DFHCOMMAREA. If the user presses PF8, the next browse operation will continue forward from the point at which the first browse ended. If the user presses PF7, on the other hand, the next browse operation will begin reading records in reverse. In addition to this, the user can enter a new starting browse key on the screen, in order to begin the next browse operation at any desired point in the file.

Notice that this browse affects only a small part of the VSAM file at a time, and that it is fully pseudoconversational.

What about Alternate Indexes?   If you have worked with VSAM extensively in batch applications, you are probably familiar with alternate indexes. An alternate index is a VSAM KSDS file containing a secondary set of keys for accessing data in another VSAM file. Access by the alternate keys can be done in sequential or random order. Prior to CICS 1.7, there were some file integrity problems when alternate keys are being updated under CICS. Problems sometimes occurred when there were too many occurrences of nonunique (duplicate) alternate keys. Also, when the original VSAM file, or base cluster, is updated, VSAM software provides for updating the other alternate indexes. Since these updates took place asynchronously, as soon as VSAM has finished updating the base cluster, CICS assumed that the update was complete, even if the alternate index updates have not been completed.

One way to avoid these problems was to build your own VSAM cross reference KSDS file. Depending upon design requirements, your cross reference file might contain one record for each record on the base cluster. Each cross-reference record would contain the value of the secondary key followed by the value of the primary key. (If there will be repeated occurrences of a given secondary key, then you could provide uniqueness by defining the entire cross-reference file record as a VSAM key. The secondary key can be accessed on its own if it is considered as a generic key.) However, using this method required you to update your cross-reference file whenever you add records to the base cluster, or delete records from the base cluster, or change the secondary key field within a base cluster record.

Under CICS 1.7 and above, it is now possible to do updates to recoverable files using alternate-index paths without loss of file integrity.

6.4 CHANGES TO CICS VSAM FILE PROCESSING

6.4.1 File Opening Procedures

The file control program was rewritten completely with CICS 1.7 to make it more efficient and more convenient to use. File open/close logic was changed at that time, which affects the applications programmer. In releases of CICS prior to 1.7, availability of a dataset under CICS file control depended upon whether it was OPEN or CLOSED. This setting still exists in the file control table, but with 1.7, it no longer matters to your application program. This is because CICS now automatically opens all ENABLED datasets the first time they are accessed by a CICS program. A dataset that is not being used immediately does not have to be opened at CICS initialization. There is also no need to use a CEMT command to open it manually before using it. This adds convenience and efficiency to CICS file handling. Therefore, if your program contains routines which test for NOTOPEN, and the file is in a CICS 1.7 (or greater) region, those routines will never be executed.

If you want to lock everyone out of a file, possibly so that some other non-CICS region can update it, you can still use a CEMT command to set the dataset DISABLED. In that case, it will not be opened, and the DISABLED condition will be raised.

Another way now exists to ENABLE, DISABLE, OPEN, or CLOSE a dataset under file control. This is the EXEC CICS SET DATASET command, which is also described in the CICS/VS Customization Guide. Other SET command formats exist for other system parameters. SET allows you do some of the same functions as does CEMT, but from within an application program.

```
EXEC CICS SET
        DATASET(data-value)
        ENABLED
        END-EXEC.
```

The data-value should contain the ddname.

```
EXEC CICS SET
        DATASET(data-value)
        DISABLED
        [WAIT|NOWAIT|FORCE]
        END-EXEC
```

FORCE will abend all tasks that are trying to access the dataset and will disable the dataset immediately. WAIT and NOWAIT will disable the dataset only after these accesses are complete. WAIT, however, will suspend your own application until the file is disabled, while NOWAIT will return control to your application and allow the disabling operation to take place asynchronously.

```
EXEC CICS SET
         DATA SET(data-value)
         OPEN
         [EMPTY]
         END-EXEC.
```

Specify EMPTY only if you want the dataset to be a scratch data set for use as a temporary work space. EMPTY clears out the old data when the dataset is reopened. This works only when the file has been defined as REUSE in the VSAM catalog.

```
EXEC CICS SET
         DATASET(data-value)
         CLOSED
         [EMPTY]
         [WAIT|NOWAIT|FORCE]
         END-EXEC.
```

SET commands can be used to change some of the other settings in the file control table, such as the number of concurrent accesses permitted against the file at any one time. These are not settings which you would ordinarily change in an application program, but if you are interested you will find this information in the *Customization Guide*.

Under MVS, CICS 1.7 and above will verify your VSAM files automatically as they are being opened. (Verification means making sure that the end-of-file mark is set properly.) Batch jobs being run under MVS operating systems also enjoy that feature. It is better to take out the verify step from all jobs, both CICS and batch, and to let the system take care of verifying files. The new method is not entirely compatible with the old, so all jobs on the system should be using the same method with any given file. Otherwise, some VSAM catalog problems can appear.

6.4.2   More Application Programming Changes

Since the file control program was rewritten with CICS 1.7, an error in the dynamic transaction backout processing which caused some good records to be backed out has now been corrected. This error was triggered when a program attempted to add a record when an existing record had the same key (DUPREC condition). Prior to CICS 1.7, dynamic transaction backout, which we will discuss later, mistakenly backed out the "good" existing record on the file when this happened. This has been corrected, so that special processing in the application program is no longer needed.

Also with CICS 1.7, generic-key reads for update, generic deletes, and use of key GE (greater than or equal) now work properly against data sets defined as recoverable. Whether this is a good idea is another matter. Before deleting or updating any records, your program needs to check to make sure that it is working with the right record. You don't want to delete the wrong record without knowing it.

CICS/MVS 2.1 introduced a new feature, **extended recovery facility (XRF)**. XRF allows the systems staff to set up CICS with redundant resources for greater fault tolerance (data integrity and uptime). XRF requires the switching or sharing of datasets between the active and the passive ("backup") system. This is taken care of by CICS and requires no effort on the part of the applications programmer.

Data tables were introduced with CICS/MVS 2.1.1. Data tables, in a nutshell, are VSAM files which CICS copies into virtual memory above the 16 megabyte line. They provide faster access to data, particularly for read-only files. They are defined to CICS by means of FCT entries. With CICS-maintained data tables, CICS keeps the data tables in synch with the actual files on disk. Your application programs will treat CICS-maintained data tables exactly the same as any normal VSAM file. With user-maintained data tables, applications programs or user exits installed by the systems staff are responsible for keeping the data tables in synch with the disk files, and sometimes also for building the data table at startup time. If your site has user-maintained data tables, ask your systems programming staff about which routines to use.

With mainframe CICS/ESA 3.1, and with CICS OS/2, RDO (resource definition online) is available for the file control table. RDO lets you build FCT entries through online screens without having to use FCT macros in a batch job. In fact, with CICS OS/2, all CICS tables are maintained exclusively through screens. This will eventually be true for mainframe CICS as well.

TEST YOUR UNDERSTANDING

Questions and Exercises

1. Define each of these terms:
   a. Key-sequenced data set
   b. Entry-sequenced data set
   c. Relative record data set
   d. "Loaded" file
   e. Cluster
   f. Data (file type)
   g. Index (file type)
   h. Sequential access

    i.   Random access

    j.   Sequence set

    k.   Control interval

    l.   Control area

    m. File browse

    n.   READ for UPDATE

    o.   Free space

    p.   Enqueue/dequeue

    q.   Master catalog

    r.   User catalog

    s.   VSAM data space

    t.   Relative byte address

    u.   Relative record number

    v.   Access Method Services

    w. LISTCAT

    x.   REPRO

    y.   RIDFLD

    z.   GENERIC

2. How can you find out whether a VSAM file needs to be reorganized with more free space?

3. Suppose you know that it is time to reorganize a VSAM KSDS file. You will need to use Access Method Services to build a new VSAM file with more free space. You have access to the job stream that was used to define the old file. What parameter argument values will you need to change?

4. What parameters must you supply in a WRITE command in order to add a new record to the end of an entry-sequenced data set?

5. Why should you try to avoid doing any other processing after doing a READ for UPDATE and before completing the update or delete operation?

6. What happens to the affected control interval when you terminate your task after doing a READ for UPDATE, but without completing the update or delete?

7. Suppose one task in an application does a READ without the UPDATE option, in order to show the user the contents of a record. Suppose the next task does a READ for UPDATE against the same record, updates some fields, and performs a REWRITE. What two things can happen to the record between the first READ and the second READ for UPDATE? Remember that other users can access this record before it has been READ for UPDATE. In order to tell whether anything has happened to the record, some information

will need to be passed from the first task to the second. What is this information? What should the second task do if it finds that some other user has altered the record? (For some applications, it's critically important to keep two or more users from trying to update the same record at the same time. For other applications, it is unimportant.) The next chapter will show a sample program which deals with this problem.

8. VSAM file contents should be copied to backup data sets at regular intervals. Describe the way in which you would set up a job stream to back up a VSAM file. Describe the way in which you would set up a job stream to recover the VSAM file from the backup data set. In particular, what job control language and Access Method Services parameters would be contained in each job stream?

9. The CICS system raises the ILLOGIC error condition for VSAM file processing whenever anything goes wrong that does not fit under any of the other VSAM error conditions. It tends to occur when one user is trying to read a record that another user has already enqueued. Write a RESP routine for ILLOGIC that tells the terminal user that the customer master file is busy and that he or she should try again later. Place this routine in the update program SALEP002.

10. Modify the current week sales entry program, SALEP004, to make it use the item number to look up the price in a VSAM KSDS price— file. Assume that the file's DDNAME is PRICE. It is keyed on the item number, with each record formatted as follows:

```
01  PRICE-RECORD.
      05  P-VSAM-KEY.
            10 P-ITEM PIC X(6).
      05  P-PRICE PIC S9(S)V99.
```

In a real application, other inventory-related information would probably be present in the file, but we wish to keep this application simple. Assume that the price field has been removed from the ENTER CURRENT WEFK SALES map, SALE004, since the price is now being obtained from a file rather than from user input. If the price for an item is not on the PRICE file, the item number is bad. In that case, do not update any files; instead, redisplay the ENTER CURRENT WEEK SALES map, SALE004, to the user with an appropriate error message.

7

Temporary Storage

In this chapter, you will learn about the use of *temporary storage*. Temporary storage is a CICS facility that makes it possible to pass large amounts of data between programs and tasks conveniently. Temporary storage resembles a random-access file in certain respects and resembles main storage in other respects. In fact, temporary storage may be stored physically in main storage or on a disc file, depending upon the requirements of the application. We will begin by discussing the uses to which temporary storage is put in a typical application. We will discuss the different ways in which temporary storage queues may be set up. Finally, we will discuss the CICS command formats needed in order to access temporary storage within an application program.

7.1   THE ROLE OF TEMPORARY STORAGE IN A CICS APPLICATION

7.1.1   Need for Temporary Storage

If you have written much job control language for batch systems, you are probably familiar with the use of temporary files. You may build a file at the beginning of a job and delete it yourself at the end, or you may specify a temporary file under OS/VS or under some other facility that causes it to disappear or to be scratched at the end of a job. A temporary data set is a place to put data that is not yet in its final form, but that is to be passed to a later job step. After the job is complete, the good data will be placed in a permanent data set, and there will no longer be any reason to keep the intermediate results.

Temporary storage fulfills a similar role for online applications under CICS. It is used whenever a large amount of data is to be manipulated within a program, or when a large amount of data must be passed to another program or task. Here are some examples of its use:

- Suppose it is necessary to show to a terminal user a display such as a spreadsheet or other table that is too large to fit within one display screen image. The information can be built up in temporary storage. By using function keys, the user can request to view different parts of the information.

- Temporary storage can be used to pass a copy of the original contents of a record from one task to another. This can be used to determine whether other terminal users may have updated the same record between the first task and the second. If other users have been working with the same record, then the current terminal user should find out what the other users are trying to do before he or she completes any updates to it. Temporary storage will serve this purpose in our sample program, SALEP002. Recall that we discussed this issue in question 7 at the end of Chapter 6.

- Some data sets that are built during online processing may contain a very large number of fields. These fields may not all fit conveniently on one screen; a crowded display screen may confuse the user and may cause errors. It may be necessary to present a series of screens to the terminal user, with each screen showing a subset of the record being built. In a pseudoconversational application, each such display requires the execution of another task. Temporary storage may be used to pass the new record from one task to the next. The new record can easily be deleted if the terminal user decides to discontinue building it. Only when all parts of the record have been built correctly does the application write the new record to the actual permanent data set.

- When a program receives a map, if modified data tags are being reset, only those fields that have been modified by the terminal user will be made available. For example, suppose task X sends a map to the terminal user with information in all of its fields, and then terminates. The user changes the data in some of the fields in this map. Suppose task Y is invoked next in order to process the user input. When task Y receives the same map from the terminal user, **task Y will see only those field contents that have been keyed by the terminal user.** All of the other fields contain hexadecimal nulls (low-values). If task Y will need the original contents of some or all of the fields on the map, then task X must use some mechanism for passing this information. Temporary storage provides a good way to do this.

7.1.2   How Temporary Storage is Allocated and Used

Temporary storage used in a CICS region or partition may be allocated **main storage** under control of that region or partition, or it may be allocated in a **VSAM auxiliary temporary storage file** set up exclusively for that purpose. No matter how many tasks within a CICS partition or region are using auxiliary temporary storage, only one VSAM file is used to satisfy all of their requirements. DD statements or DLBL and EXTENT statements for this VSAM file are included in the CICS startup job. Its internal structure is transparent to you; CICS software performs all needed file I/O and control logic so that your program is presented with only those temporary storage records that it requires.

Groups of one or more temporary storage records are known as **temporary storage queues.** It is not necessary to make an entry in a CICS table in order to set up a temporary storage queue. Any CICS application program can set up a temporary storage queue simply by devising a queue name of up to eight characters and by writing out one or more temporary storage records using that queue name. In the temporary storage write command, the program may specify whether the queue should be allocated in main storage or in the auxiliary file.

Once a temporary storage queue is created, the queue will remain available until the CICS system is brought down or until a program uses the queue name to delete the queue. Any CICS application program that knows the queue name can read records from within the queue either sequentially or randomly. Random access is accomplished by specifying the queue name and the item number within the queue. Records in temporary storage queues may be read as many times as desired; there is no way to delete single records from within a queue, so the records will not disappear unless the whole queue is deleted. CICS applications may also update the contents of existing queue records and add new records to the end of an existing queue. Each new record added to the queue will cause the item number to be incremented by 1.

Since a temporary storage queue can be accessed by any task that knows the queue name, a temporary storage queue is a good method for passing data from one task to another. Since the temporary storage may be stored physically on a VSAM file rather than in main storage, use of temporary storage defined as AUXILIARY makes sense for storing large amounts of data. Temporary storage offers an advantage for complex applications: an IBM-supplied temporary storage browse transaction was introduced with CICS 1.6. In other words, if something seems to be wrong, a convenient method is provided for looking at the contents of the temporary storage queue. If the queue name is available, it is also possible to define temporary storage queues as being recoverable in case of abnormal task terminations.

It is important to devise queue names that uniquely identify the queue, but that are predictable. **The customary choice of temporary** storage queue names, appropriate for most purposes, is an eight-character name made up of the four-character transaction ID followed by the four-character terminal ID obtained from EIBTRMID. Suppose transaction AAAA writes a temporary storage queue record with queue name AAAAL77C whenever it is executed from terminal L77C. Suppose transaction BBBB is designed to follow transaction AAAA. Transaction BBBB will also be attached to L77C. For that reason, it can obtain the terminal ID code from EIBTRMID and append it to AAAA to obtain AAAAL77C once again. For this naming convention to work, transaction BBBB must know that it should receive its data from transaction AAAA, so that it can supply the right prefix. Using this method allows users at several terminals to use these transactions without allowing their temporary storage queues to become mixed up. Queues generated for other users might be named AAAAL77D, AAAAL77E, and so forth. Of course, if you want a temporary storage queue to be shared by many terminals, you would not do this.

It will not work to use the EIBTASKN instead of the four-character transaction ID when devising the queue name. Why is this so? Because you won't find your queue again! Keep in mind that a task is a single execution of a transaction. The transaction ID always remains the same from execution to execution, but the task number assigned by the CICS system will differ. If a task number is used to form a queue name, the queue name will be different each time the queue is built. Subsequent tasks will not have access to this original task number, and will not be able to find the queue.

Temporary storage queues allocated in an auxiliary data set may be specified as being recoverable. To do this, you must determine which queue names should be specified in this way. For the above situation, if there are four terminals from which AAAA and BBBB can be run, the resulting queue names might be AAAAL77C, AAAAL77D, AAAAL77E, and AAAAL77F. All of these queue names can be placed in a special temporary storage recovery table. This makes it possible for incomplete transactions to be backed out under certain circumstances.

You may choose how many records you wish to place in a temporary storage queue, and how long each record should be, as long as your choices remain within system limitations at your installation. Check with your systems programmer if your requirements are unusually large. If large amounts of data are being handled, the data should be broken up into separate records within the temporary storage queue. This is easy to do: If you use more than one WRITEQ TS command to put data into the queue, you will build more than one record. The first record will be item 1, the second record will be item 2, and so forth. Once they are created, these records can be read sequentially by specifying NEXT, or randomly by specifying the item number, in much the same way records are accessed in a VSAM relative record data set.

7.2   PROGRAMMING TECHNIQUES

7.2.1   I/O Commands for Reading, Writing, and Deleting Temporary Storage

The WRITEQ TS command is used to write new records to a temporary storage queue and to update existing records. If a queue with the specified queue name does not already exist, the WRITEQ TS command that creates the first new record will also create the queue. Here is the format of the WRITEQ TS command:

```
EXEC CICS WRITEQ TS
          QUEUE(name)
          FROM(data-area)
          LENGTH(data-value)
          [ITEM(data-area)[REWRITE]]
          [MAIN|AUXILIARY]
          END-EXEC.
```

The queue name should be constructed in a work area. Specify the name of this work area in the QUEUE(name) parameter. As in other output commands, FROM(data-area) indicates the source of the data to be written, and LENGTH(data-value) indicates the length in bytes. Records written to a temporary storage queue need not all be the same length. You may specify MAIN or AUXILIARY to indicate whether the temporary storage should be allocated in main storage or on a VSAM auxiliary storage data set. For most applications, AUXILIARY storage should be specified, but check the standards at your site. (Remember that temporary storage remains in existence between tasks. You might not want temporary storage to tie up main memory for long periods of time whenever a terminal user gets up to help a customer or to find something in a manual.)

If REWRITE is not specified, then the WRITEQ TS will write a new temporary storage record sequentially at the end of the queue. If ITEM(data-area) is specified, CICS will place the item number of the new record in the specified data area. The item number of the new record will be the item number of the previous record plus one. (If ITEM(data-area) is not specified, the WRITE command will still work, but the item number will not be returned to the application program.) This is shown in Figure 7.1.

REWRITE is used to cause an existing temporary storage record to be updated, as is shown in Figure 7.2. If REWRITE is specified, ITEM(data-area) must be specified also. Place the item number of the record to be updated in ITEM (data-area). This will cause the WRITEQ TS instruction to update an existing temporary storage record whose item number equals what is specified in ITEM(data-area). It is not necessary to read this queue entry before updating it, but it is good programming practice to do so. If no queue entry with the appropriate item number exists, the ITEMERR condi-

TS queue L77ATEST contains:

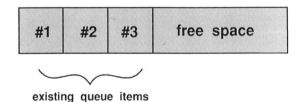

existing queue items

```
EXEC CICS WRITEQ TS
   QUEUE (L77ATEST)
   FROM (WS-BUILD-AREA)
   LENGTH (WS-ITEM-LENGTH)
   ITEM (WS-ITEM-NUMBER)
   END-EXEC.
```

After execution of this command,
TS queue L77ATEST contains:

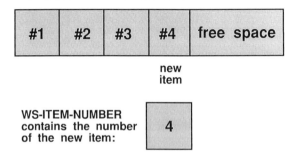

new
item

WS-ITEM-NUMBER
contains the number
of the new item:

FIGURE 7.1   Writing items to a temporary storage queue sequentially.

tion will be raised. If an attempt is made to update records in a nonexistent queue, the QIDERR condition will be triggered. (Check your queue name in that case.) RESP may be used to check for the ITEMERR and QIDERR exceptional conditions.

To read existing temporary storage queue items, the READQ TS command is used: EXEC CICS READQ TS

```
QUEUE(name)
{SET(pointer-ref)|INTO(data-area)}
LENGTH(data-area)
[ITEM(data-value)|NEXT]
[NUMITEMS(data-area)]
END-EXEC.
```

If the queue item is greater than the maximum length specified in LENGTH(data-area), the input record will be truncated and the LENGERR condition will be triggered.

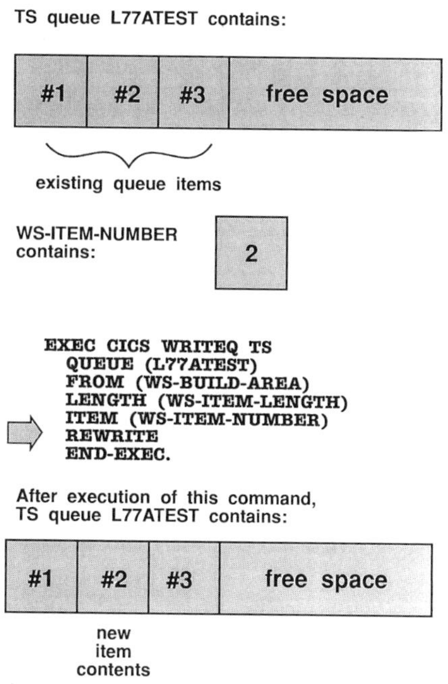

TS queue L77ATEST contains:

existing queue items

WS-ITEM-NUMBER
contains:

2

```
EXEC CICS WRITEQ TS
    QUEUE (L77ATEST)
    FROM (WS-BUILD-AREA)
    LENGTH (WS-ITEM-LENGTH)
    ITEM (WS-ITEM-NUMBER)
    REWRITE
    END-EXEC.
```

After execution of this command,
TS queue L77ATEST contains:

new
item
contents

FIGURE 7.2   Random-access update of temporary storage.

The SET(pointer-ref) or INTO(data-area) parameter is used to indicate that the input record should be placed in a linkage section or working storage data area respectively. The NUMITEMS(data-area) parameter, which first became available with CICS 1.6, provides a data area to be updated by the CICS system. This data area will contain the total number of records within the temporary storage queue.

Random accesses against specific records within the temporary storage queue are requested by using the ITEM(data-value) parameter. The same record will be read again and again as long as the same numeric value remains in the ITEM(data-value) parameter. If the requested record does not exist, the ITEMERR condition will be triggered. If the entire queue does not exist, the QIDERR condition will be triggered. (Incidentally, the READQ TS command will not read a queue that was created by a macro-level CICS program which used the DFHTS TYPE=PUT macro.) Random access to temporary storage queues is shown in Figure 7.3.

Sequential accesses against the temporary storage queue are requested by using the NEXT parameter, which is a default. For example, if there is only one record in the queue, it will be retrieved on the first READQ TS NEXT instruction. Subsequent READQ TS NEXT instructions will cause the ITEMERR condition to be raised, which in this instance means that sequential end of file has been reached. **Note that the NEXT option is**

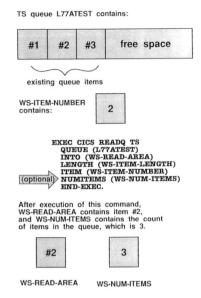

FIGURE 7.3   Random-access read of temporary storage item.

system-wide: your program gets the record immediately after the last record retrieved from that queue by any task. This is not usually a problem. Queue names that are based on terminal ID would ordinarily prevent more than one task from having access to the TS queue at the same time.

The DELETEQ TS instruction may be used to delete an entire temporary storage queue. If the queue does not exist, execution of DELETEQ TS will cause the QIDERR condition to be raised. It is important to delete any temporary storage queues that will no longer be needed, so that resources will be freed for use by other processes. If your task is creating a new temporary storage queue, it should first delete any old queues that may happen to have the same name. Such old queues might be left over from prior tasks that terminated abnormally.

```
EXEC CICS DELETEQ TS
          QUEUE(name)
          END-EXEC.
```

7.2.2   Programming Recommendations

If you are not handling fairly small amounts of data, then you may need to create only one record within your temporary storage queue. In order to update this record in place, you must still specify that the record to be updated is item number 1. Some programmers do not like to specify an item number when there is only one record in the queue. Instead of performing a normal update, they delete the entire queue and put out a new temporary storage queue containing the updated record. This is bad practice. Some programmers even delete and rebuild the queue every time they read the one record in it, so that the first record will come up again the next time the same queue is read sequentially. If there is any need to read item 1 more than once, it would be far easier to perform a random-access READQ TS against item 1 each time. Maintenance programmers should watch for and correct these programming mistakes.

Watch out for programs that create temporary storage queues but never delete them. This is wasteful of resources. Applications that create TS queues should delete their own queues when they are no longer needed. Deletion logic may be placed in the routines that allow the user to exit from those applications. When the transaction is about to begin a new TS queue, it should also take care to delete the old TS queue that might exist with that name. Old queues could remain from prior tasks that terminated abnormally without first deleting their queues.

7.2.3 Sample Program: Customer Record Change Processor

The customer record change function is selected from the main menu SALEP000. The user is asked to enter a customer number, which is passed to program SALEP002, the change program. SALEP002 will read the existing customer record and display it on the screen, using map SALE002. It also places information from the customer record in a temporary storage record. It then RETURNs to its own TRANSID, SAL2. Comments in the source code indicate each step. See Figures 7.4 and 7.5.

The user makes any desired changes on the terminal screen, and presses ENTER. This causes program SALEP002 to be run again. SALEP002 reads both the temporary storage record passed to it from its own previous execution, and the actual customer record. If there is any discrepancy between the two record images, or if the customer record is missing, this means that another user has changed or deleted the customer record during the time in which the change screen was being displayed to the first user. In that case, we inform the first user and terminate the transaction.

SALEP002 receives map SALE002, which should contain some changes entered by the terminal user. SALEP002 will transfer these changes to the customer record work area and write this record out to the VSAM file. SALEP002 will then allow the user to enter another customer number to be updated. If the user presses PF3, SALEP002 will then XCTL to the menu program, SALEP000, which will provide the user with a fresh copy of the menu.

```
              IDENTIFICATION DIVISION.
              PROGRAM-ID. SALEP002.
              AUTHOR. ALIDA M. JATICH AND PHIL NOWAK.
              ******************************************************************
              * SALEP002: CHANGE CUSTOMER RECORD CONTENTS                       *
              * ON THE FIRST PASS, SALEP002 GETS THE CUSTOMER NUMBER FROM THE    *
              * COMMAREA AND READS THE CUSTOMER RECORD HAVING THAT KEY. IT       *
              * SHOWS THE EXISTING CONTENTS ON THE CHANGE SCREEN. THE TERMINAL*
              * USER ENTERS DATA ON THE SCREEN. ON THE NEXT PASS, SALEP002      *
              * REWRITES THE RECORD AND DISPLAYS THE CHANGE SCREEN AGAIN.       *
              ******************************************************************
              ENVIRONMENT DIVISION.
              DATA DIVISION.
              WORKING-STORAGE SECTION.
              01  MISC-WORK.
                  05  WS-CICS-RESPONSE1        PIC S9(8) COMP VALUE +0.
                  05  WS-TSQ-ITEM1             PIC S9(4) COMP VALUE +1.
                  05  WS-XCTL-PGM              PIC X(8)       VALUE SPACES.
              01  QID-NAME.
                  05  QID-TRMID                PIC XXXX       VALUE SPACES.
                  05  FILLER                   PIC XXXX       VALUE 'SALE'.
              01  CUSTMST-Q.
                  05  CUSTNO-Q                 PIC X(6)       VALUE SPACES.
                  05  FILLER                   PIC X(144)     VALUE SPACES.
              01  ERROR-MESSAGES.
                  05  BAD-KEY-MSG              PIC X(22)      VALUE
                      'Function key undefined'.
                  05  CUST-NUM-MSG             PIC X(27)      VALUE
                      'Customer number not numeric'.
                  05  MISSING-DATA-MSG         PIC X(26)      VALUE
                      'Please supply missing data'.
                  05  SUCCESSFUL-CHANGE-MSG    PIC X(27)      VALUE
                      'Record changed successfully'.
                  05  ENTER-CUST-NO-MSG        PIC X(29)      VALUE
                      'Please enter customer number.'.
                  05  CHANGE-FIELDS-MSG        PIC X(47)      VALUE
                      'Make desired changes to fields and press enter.'.
                  05  CANNOT-UPDATE-MSG        PIC X(39)      VALUE
                      'Cannot update - record has been changed'.
                  05  DISABLED-MSG             PIC X(16)      VALUE
                      'File is disabled'.
                  05  DSIDERR-MSG              PIC X(14)      VALUE
                      'File not found'.
                  05  DUPREC-MSG               PIC X(22)      VALUE
                      'Record already on file'.
                  05  INVREQ-MSG               PIC X(15)      VALUE
                      'Invalid request'.
                  05  IOERR-MSG                PIC X(9)       VALUE
                      'I/O error'.
                  05  ITEMERR-MSG              PIC X(16)      VALUE
                      'Item not defined'.
                  05  LENGERR-MSG              PIC X(19)      VALUE
                      'Record length error'.
                  05  NOSPACE-MSG              PIC X(17)      VALUE
                      'File out of space'.
                  05  NOTFND-MSG               PIC X(18)      VALUE
                      'Record not on file'.
                  05  PGMIDERR-MSG             PIC X(27)      VALUE
                      'Program not defined to CICS'.
                  05  QIDERR-MSG               PIC X(17)      VALUE
                      'Queue not defined'.
              *
                  05  BUILD-MSG.
                      10  DISPLAY-OPERATION    PIC X(12)      VALUE SPACES.
                      10  FILLER               PIC X          VALUE SPACES.
                      10  DISPLAY-RESOURCE     PIC X(8)       VALUE SPACES.
                      10  FILLER               PIC X          VALUE SPACES.
                      10  DISPLAY-DESCRIPTION  PIC X(38)      VALUE SPACES.
                      10  FILLER               PIC X          VALUE SPACES.
                      10  DISPLAY-CALL-WHOM    PIC X(16)      VALUE SPACES.
```

FIGURE 7.4 Source code for SALEP002, customer record change processor.

```
*
     05  DEFAULT-DESCRIPTION.
         10  FILLER              PIC X(22)        VALUE
         'SALEP002 ERROR: RESP1='.
         10  DISPLAY-RESPONSE    PIC 9(8)         VALUE ZEROES.
*
 COPY SALECOMM.
 COPY MSALE02.
 COPY ATTRIBUT.
 COPY DFHAID.
 COPY DFHBMSCA.
 COPY CUSTMST.
 LINKAGE SECTION.
 01  DFHCOMMAREA              PIC X(68).
*
 PROCEDURE DIVISION.
 MAIN-PROG.
*
***********************************************************************
* DETERMINE WHICH POINT IN THE CYCLE APPLIES TO THE CURRENT          *
* SITUATION. THE FIRST TIME THROUGH, SHOW THE CHANGE SCREEN          *
* FOR THE FIRST TIME. ON SUBSEQUENT PASSES, PROCESS USER INPUT       *
* AND SHOW THE SCREEN AGAIN (OR TRANSFER CONTROL BACK TO THE         *
* MENU PROGRAM, DEPENDING ON FUNCTION KEY).                          *
***********************************************************************
*
     MOVE LOW-VALUES TO SALE002I.
*
     IF EIBCALEN NOT = WS-EXPECTED-EIBCALEN
         PERFORM REQUEST-NEW-CUST-NO
     ELSE
         MOVE DFHCOMMAREA TO WS-COMMAREA
         IF EIBTRNID = 'SAL2' AND WS-COMM-PREV-MAP = 'SALE002'
             PERFORM PROCESS-CHANGE-SCREEN
         ELSE
             PERFORM CUST-NO-FROM-COMMAREA.
*
     GOBACK.
*
***********************************************************************
* DETERMINE WHAT FUNCTION KEY THE USER PRESSED.                      *
***********************************************************************
*
 PROCESS-CHANGE-SCREEN.
*
     IF EIBAID = DFHCLEAR OR DFHPF3
         MOVE 'SALEP000' TO WS-XCTL-PGM
         PERFORM XCTL-NEXT-PGM
     ELSE
         IF EIBAID = DFHPF10
             PERFORM CURSOR-TO-ACTION-BAR
         ELSE
             IF EIBAID = DFHPF12
                 PERFORM REQUEST-NEW-CUST-NO
             ELSE
                 IF EIBAID NOT = DFHENTER
                     MOVE BAD-KEY-MSG TO S2MSGO
                     MOVE -1 TO S2CUSTL
                     PERFORM SEND-SALE002-BEEP.
*
     MOVE 'MSALE02' TO DISPLAY-RESOURCE.
     MOVE 'RECEIVE MAP' TO DISPLAY-OPERATION.
*
     EXEC CICS RECEIVE MAP ('SALE002')
             MAPSET ('MSALE02')
             INTO (SALE002I)
             RESP (WS-CICS-RESPONSE1)
             END-EXEC.
*
     IF WS-CICS-RESPONSE1 = DFHRESP(MAPFAIL)
```

FIGURE 7.4 *(Continued)*

```
                    PERFORM CUST-NO-FROM-COMMAREA
              ELSE
                  IF WS-CICS-RESPONSE1 NOT = DFHRESP(NORMAL)
                     PERFORM CHECK-CICS-RESPONSE
                     MOVE -1 TO S2CUSTL
                     PERFORM SEND-SALE002-BEEP.
      *
              MOVE SPACES TO S2MSGO.
      *
      *****************************************************************
      * IF THE CURSOR WAS ANYWHERE ON THE ACTION BAR, USE THE         *
      * POSITION TO SELECT THE ACTION. IF THE CURSOR WAS SOMEWHERE    *
      * ELSE, THEN JUST GO WITH THE DEFAULT CHOICE, WHICH IS "CHANGE".*
      *****************************************************************
      *
              IF EIBCPOSN  9
                  MOVE 'CHANGE' TO WS-COMM-ACTION
              ELSE
                  IF EIBCPOSN  15
                      MOVE 'EXIT' TO WS-COMM-ACTION
                  ELSE
                      IF EIBCPOSN  23
                          MOVE 'CANCEL' TO WS-COMM-ACTION
                      ELSE
                          MOVE 'CHANGE' TO WS-COMM-ACTION.
      *
              IF WS-COMM-ACTION = 'EXIT'
                  MOVE 'SALEP000' TO WS-XCTL-PGM
                  PERFORM XCTL-NEXT-PGM
              ELSE
                  IF WS-COMM-ACTION = 'CANCEL'
                      PERFORM REQUEST-NEW-CUST-NO.
      *
      *
      *****************************************************************
      * THREE POSSIBLE SITUATIONS:                                    *
      * 1. IF USER INPUT IS ON THE SCREEN, CONSISTING OF CHANGES TO   *
      *    BE APPLIED TO THE CURRENT CUSTOMER RECORD, ATTEMPT TO      *
      *    APPLY THOSE UPDATES. IN THAT CASE, A VALID (NUMERIC)       *
      *    CUSTOMER NUMBER WILL APPEAR IN THE COMMAREA AND WILL       *
      *    AGREE WITH THE CUSTOMER NUMBER ON THE SCREEN.              *
      * 2. IF THE COMMAREA DOES NOT CONTAIN A VALID CUSTOMER NUMBER,  *
      *    OR IF THE CUSTOMER NUMBER ON THE SCREEN HAS BEEN CLEARED,  *
      *    ASK THE TERMINAL USER TO ENTER A NEW CUSTOMER NUMBER.      *
      * 3. IF A NEW CUSTOMER NUMBER HAS BEEN ENTERED ON THE SCREEN,   *
      *    SEND A SCREEN TO THE TERMINAL USER DISPLAYING THOSE        *
      *    RECORD CONTENTS FOR MODIFICATION.                          *
      *                                                               *
      *****************************************************************
      *
              IF WS-COMM-CUST-NO IS NUMERIC
                      AND S2CUSTI = WS-COMM-CUST-NO
                  PERFORM ATTEMPT-UPDATE
              ELSE
                  IF S2CUSTI IS NOT NUMERIC
                      PERFORM REQUEST-NEW-CUST-NO
                  ELSE
                      MOVE S2CUSTO TO WS-COMM-CUST-NO
                      PERFORM CUST-NO-FROM-COMMAREA.
      *
      *****************************************************************
      * THIS ROUTINE OBTAINS ORIGINAL CUSTOMER MASTER RECORD CONTENTS *
      * FROM A TEMPORARY STORAGE RECORD WRITTEN ON THE PREVIOUS PASS. *
      *                                                               *
      * BEFORE ALLOWING ANY UPDATES TO TAKE PLACE, SALEP002 READS     *
      * THE CUSTOMER MASTER RECORD AGAIN AND COMPARES THE CONTENTS    *
      * WITH THE CONTENTS OF THE TEMPORARY STORAGE RECORD. IF THEY    *
      * MATCH, UPDATE PROCESSING CAN CONTINUE.                        *
      *                                                               *
      * HOWEVER, IF THE CUSTOMER MASTER RECORDS DIFFER FROM THE       *
```

FIGURE 7.4   *(Continued)*

```
* CONTENTS OF THE TEMPORARY STORAGE RECORD, THEN SOME OTHER      *
* USER HAS ALSO BEEN WORKING WITH THE SAME RECORD. IN THAT       *
* CASE, UPDATE PROCESSING IS DISCONTINUED TO PREVENT CONFLICTS.  *
******************************************************************
*
 ATTEMPT-UPDATE.
*
     MOVE EIBTRMID TO QID-TRMID.
     MOVE QID-NAME TO DISPLAY-RESOURCE.
     MOVE 'READQ TS' TO DISPLAY-OPERATION.
*
     EXEC CICS READQ TS
               QUEUE (QID-NAME)
               INTO (CUSTMST-Q)
               ITEM (WS-TSQ-ITEM1)
               RESP (WS-CICS-RESPONSE1)
               END-EXEC.
*
     IF WS-CICS-RESPONSE1 NOT = DFHRESP(NORMAL)
         PERFORM CHECK-CICS-RESPONSE
         MOVE -1 TO S2CUSTL
         PERFORM SEND-SALE002-BEEP.
*
******************************************************************
* READ THE EXISTING RECORD FOR UPDATE.                           *
******************************************************************
*
     MOVE 'CUSTMST' TO DISPLAY-RESOURCE.
     MOVE 'READ UPDATE' TO DISPLAY-OPERATION.
*
     EXEC CICS READ
               DATASET ('CUSTMST')
               INTO (CUSTMST-REC)
               RIDFLD (WS-COMM-CUST-NO)
               UPDATE
               RESP (WS-CICS-RESPONSE1)
               END-EXEC.
*
     IF WS-CICS-RESPONSE1 NOT = DFHRESP(NORMAL)
         PERFORM CHECK-CICS-RESPONSE
         MOVE -1 TO S2CUSTL
         PERFORM SEND-SALE002-BEEP.
*
     IF CUSTMST-REC NOT = CUSTMST-Q
         MOVE CANNOT-UPDATE-MSG TO S2MSGO
         MOVE -1 TO S2CUSTL
         PERFORM SEND-SALE002-BEEP.
*
     IF S2NAMEL  ZEROES AND S2NAMEI  SPACES
         MOVE S2NAMEI TO CUST-NAME.
*
     IF S2CNTCTL  ZEROES AND S2CNTCTI  SPACES
         MOVE S2CNTCTI TO CUST-CONTACT.
*
     IF S2ADDRL  ZEROES AND S2ADDRI  SPACES
         MOVE S2ADDRI TO CUST-STREET-ADDRESS.
*
     IF S2CITYL  ZEROES AND S2CITYI  SPACES
         MOVE S2CITYI TO CUST-CITY.
*
     IF S2STATEL  ZEROES AND S2STATEI IS ALPHABETIC
         MOVE S2STATEI TO CUST-STATE.
*
     IF S2ZIPL  ZEROES AND S2ZIPI  SPACES
         MOVE S2ZIPI TO CUST-ZIP.
*
     MOVE 'CUSTMST' TO DISPLAY-RESOURCE.
     MOVE 'REWRITE' TO DISPLAY-OPERATION.
*
     EXEC CICS REWRITE
```

FIGURE 7.4 *(Continued)*

```
                        DATASET ('CUSTMST')
                        FROM (CUSTMST-REC)
                        RESP (WS-CICS-RESPONSE1)
                        END-EXEC.
       *
           MOVE -1 TO S2CUSTL.
       *
       ***********************************************************************
       * IF THE UPDATE WAS SUCCESSFUL, THE TERMINAL USER MAY OVERKEY    *
       * THE CUSTOMER NUMBER TO UPDATE A DIFFERENT RECORD NEXT TIME.    *
       * IF THE UPDATE WAS NOT SUCCESSFUL, DISPLAY A MESSAGE            *
       * EXPLAINING WHY NOT.                                            *
       ***********************************************************************
       *
           IF WS-CICS-RESPONSE1 = DFHRESP(NORMAL)
               MOVE SUCCESSFUL-CHANGE-MSG TO S2MSGO
               MOVE -1 TO S2CUSTL
               MOVE ENTER-CUST-NO-MSG TO S2INSTRO
               PERFORM SEND-SALE002-RETURN
           ELSE
               PERFORM CHECK-CICS-RESPONSE
               PERFORM SEND-SALE002-BEEP.
       *
       *
        XCTL-NEXT-PGM.
       *
           MOVE WS-XCTL-PGM TO DISPLAY-RESOURCE.
           MOVE 'XCTL' TO DISPLAY-OPERATION.
           EXEC CICS XCTL
                       PROGRAM (WS-XCTL-PGM)
                       COMMAREA (WS-COMMAREA)
                       RESP (WS-CICS-RESPONSE1)
                       END-EXEC.
       *
           IF WS-CICS-RESPONSE1 NOT = DFHRESP(NORMAL)
               PERFORM CHECK-CICS-RESPONSE
               MOVE -1 TO S2CUSTL
               PERFORM SEND-SALE002-BEEP.
       *
       *
       ***********************************************************************
       * THIS ROUTINE TAKES THE CUSTOMER NUMBER FROM THE WORKING        *
       * STORAGE COPY OF THE DFHCOMMAREA AND USES IT TO READ A          *
       * CUSTOMER RECORD. IT SHOWS THE RECORD ON THE CHANGE SCREEN.     *
       ***********************************************************************
       *
        CUST-NO-FROM-COMMAREA.
       *
           IF WS-COMM-CUST-NO IS NOT NUMERIC
               PERFORM REQUEST-NEW-CUST-NO.
       *
           MOVE WS-COMM-CUST-NO TO S2CUSTO.
           MOVE -1 TO S2NAMEL.
           MOVE SPACES TO S2MSGO.
       *
       ***********************************************************************
       * READ THE EXISTING RECORD.                                      *
       ***********************************************************************
       *
           MOVE 'CUSTMST' TO DISPLAY-RESOURCE.
           MOVE 'READ' TO DISPLAY-OPERATION.
       *
           EXEC CICS READ
                       DATASET ('CUSTMST')
                       INTO (CUSTMST-REC)
                       RIDFLD (WS-COMM-CUST-NO)
                       RESP (WS-CICS-RESPONSE1)
                       END-EXEC.
       *
           IF WS-CICS-RESPONSE1 NOT = DFHRESP(NORMAL)
```

FIGURE 7.4 *(Continued)*

```
                    PERFORM CHECK-CICS-RESPONSE
                    PERFORM SEND-SALE002-BEEP.
       *
       ***********************************************************************
       * DELETE THE OLD TEMP STORAGE QUEUE THAT MIGHT BE LEFT FROM       *
       * PREVIOUS TASKS. THE QUEUE ID IS BUILT FROM THE TRAN CODE AND    *
       * THE TERMINAL ID.                                                *
       ***********************************************************************
       *
            MOVE EIBTRMID TO QID-TRMID.
            MOVE QID-NAME TO DISPLAY-RESOURCE.
            MOVE 'DELETEQ TS' TO DISPLAY-OPERATION.
       *
            EXEC CICS DELETEQ TS
                      QUEUE (QID-NAME)
                      RESP (WS-CICS-RESPONSE1)
                      END-EXEC.
       *
            IF WS-CICS-RESPONSE1 NOT = DFHRESP(NORMAL)
                   AND WS-CICS-RESPONSE1 NOT = DFHRESP(QIDERR)
               PERFORM CHECK-CICS-RESPONSE
               PERFORM SEND-SALE002-BEEP.
       *
            MOVE QID-NAME TO DISPLAY-RESOURCE.
            MOVE 'WRITEQ TS' TO DISPLAY-OPERATION.
       *
            EXEC CICS WRITEQ TS
                      QUEUE (QID-NAME)
                      FROM (CUSTMST-REC)
                      ITEM (WS-TSQ-ITEM1)
                      RESP (WS-CICS-RESPONSE1)
                      END-EXEC.
       *
            IF WS-CICS-RESPONSE1 NOT = DFHRESP(NORMAL)
               PERFORM CHECK-CICS-RESPONSE
               PERFORM SEND-SALE002-BEEP.
       *
       ***********************************************************************
       * PUT EXISTING RECORD CONTENTS ON THE SCREEN.                     *
       * THE AMOUNT FIELDS ARE DISPLAY-ONLY AND CANNOT BE CHANGED.       *
       ***********************************************************************
       *
            MOVE CUST-NO TO S2CUSTO.
            MOVE CUST-NAME TO S2NAMEO.
            MOVE CUST-CONTACT TO S2CNTCTO.
            MOVE CUST-STREET-ADDRESS TO S2ADDRO.
            MOVE CUST-CITY TO S2CITYO.
            MOVE CUST-STATE TO S2STATEO.
            MOVE CUST-ZIP TO S2ZIPO.
            MOVE CUST-CURR-WK-SALES TO S2SALESO.
            MOVE CUST-LAST-BILL-BAL-DUE TO S2BALO.
            MOVE CUST-LAST-BILL-DATE TO S2BDATEO.
       *
            MOVE CHANGE-FIELDS-MSG TO S2INSTRO.
            MOVE SPACES TO S2MSGO.
       *
            PERFORM SEND-SALE002-RETURN.
       *
       *
       ***********************************************************************
       * THIS ROUTINE CLEARS THE SCREEN AND ASKS THE USER TO ENTER THE *
       * KEY OF THE NEXT RECORD TO BE CHANGED.                           *
       ***********************************************************************
       *
        REQUEST-NEW-CUST-NO.
       *
            MOVE SPACES TO WS-COMM-CUST-NO.
            MOVE -1 TO S2CUSTL.
            MOVE ENTER-CUST-NO-MSG TO S2INSTRO.
            MOVE SPACES TO S2MSGO.
```

FIGURE 7.4 *(Continued)*

```
*
      MOVE ALL '_' TO S2CUSTO.
      MOVE SPACES TO S2NAMEO
                     S2CNTCTO
                     S2ADDRO
                     S2CITYO
                     S2STATEO
                     S2ZIPO
                     S2SALESO
                     S2BALO
                     S2BDATEO.
*
************************************************************************
* DELETE THE OLD TEMP STORAGE QUEUE THAT MIGHT BE LEFT FROM      *
* PREVIOUS TASKS. THE QUEUE ID IS BUILT FROM THE TRAN CODE AND   *
* THE TERMINAL ID.                                              *
************************************************************************
*
      MOVE EIBTRMID TO QID-TRMID.
      MOVE QID-NAME TO DISPLAY-RESOURCE.
      MOVE 'DELETEQ TS' TO DISPLAY-OPERATION.
*
      EXEC CICS DELETEQ TS
                QUEUE (QID-NAME)
                RESP (WS-CICS-RESPONSE1)
                END-EXEC.
*
      IF WS-CICS-RESPONSE1 NOT = DFHRESP(NORMAL)
             AND WS-CICS-RESPONSE1 NOT = DFHRESP(QIDERR)
         PERFORM CHECK-CICS-RESPONSE
         PERFORM SEND-SALE002-BEEP.
*
      PERFORM SEND-SALE002-RETURN.
*
*
************************************************************************
* THIS ROUTINE SENDS SALE002 WITH A WARNING 'BEEP'. WE USE THIS *
* ONLY WHEN THE CALLING ROUTINE WANTS TO DISPLAY A WARNING ON   *
* THE MESSAGE LINE OF THIS MAP. CURSOR POSITION MUST BE SET.    *
************************************************************************
*
 SEND-SALE002-BEEP.
*
      IF WS-COMM-PREV-MAP = 'SALE002'
         EXEC CICS SEND MAP ('SALE002')
                   MAPSET ('MSALE02')
                   FROM (SALE002I)
                   DATAONLY
                   ALARM
                   CURSOR
                   END-EXEC
      ELSE
         MOVE 'SALE002' TO WS-COMM-PREV-MAP
         EXEC CICS SEND MAP ('SALE002')
                   MAPSET ('MSALE02')
                   FROM (SALE002I)
                   ERASE
                   ALARM
                   CURSOR
                   END-EXEC.
*
      EXEC CICS RETURN
                TRANSID ('SAL2')
                COMMAREA (WS-COMMAREA)
                END-EXEC.
*
*
************************************************************************
* THIS ROUTINE SENDS SALE002 WITH WHATEVER DATA HAS BEEN PLACED *
* ON IT. IF THE PREDEFINED PORTIONS OF THE MAP ARE ALREADY ON   *
```

FIGURE 7.4 *(Continued)*

```
* THE SCREEN, SALE002 WILL BE SENT 'DATAONLY'.              *
*****************************************************************
*
 SEND-SALE002-RETURN.
*
     IF WS-COMM-PREV-MAP = 'SALE002'
         EXEC CICS SEND MAP ('SALE002')
                   MAPSET ('MSALE02')
                   FROM (SALE002I)
                   DATAONLY
                   CURSOR
                   END-EXEC
     ELSE
         MOVE 'SALE002' TO WS-COMM-PREV-MAP
         EXEC CICS SEND MAP ('SALE002')
                   MAPSET ('MSALE02')
                   FROM (SALE002I)
                   ERASE
                   CURSOR
                   END-EXEC.
*
     EXEC CICS RETURN
               TRANSID ('SAL2')
               COMMAREA (WS-COMMAREA)
               END-EXEC.
*
*****************************************************************
* THIS ROUTINE SENDS SALE002 WITH CURSOR ON ACTION BAR.     *
*****************************************************************
*
 CURSOR-TO-ACTION-BAR.
*
     MOVE 'SALE002' TO WS-COMM-PREV-MAP.
     EXEC CICS SEND MAP ('SALE002')
               MAPSET ('MSALE02')
               FROM (SALE002I)
               CURSOR (1)
               DATAONLY
               END-EXEC.
*
     EXEC CICS RETURN
               TRANSID ('SAL2')
               COMMAREA (WS-COMMAREA)
               END-EXEC.
*
*
*****************************************************************
* CHECK THE CICS RESPONSE CODE AND BUILD A MESSAGE EXPLAINING  *
* THE ERROR. IT IS THE RESPONSIBILITY OF THE CALLING ROUTINE   *
* TO INITIALIZE SOME DISPLAY FIELDS IN THE MESSAGE WORK AREA   *
* TO INDICATE THE TYPE OF COMMAND BEING PROCESSED.             *
*                                                             *
* WE DO NOTHING ABOUT CERTAIN RESPONSE CODES HERE SO THAT      *
* THOSE SITUATIONS CAN BE HANDLED WITH LOGIC ELSEWHERE IN THE  *
* PROGRAM.                                                     *
*                                                             *
*****************************************************************
*
 CHECK-CICS-RESPONSE.
*
     EVALUATE WS-CICS-RESPONSE1
     WHEN DFHRESP(NORMAL)
          CONTINUE
     WHEN DFHRESP(MAPFAIL)
          CONTINUE
     WHEN DFHRESP(ENDFILE)
          CONTINUE
     WHEN DFHRESP(DISABLED)
          MOVE 'CALL OPERATIONS' TO DISPLAY-CALL-WHOM
          MOVE DISABLED-MSG TO DISPLAY-DESCRIPTION
```

FIGURE 7.4 *(Continued)*

```
            MOVE BUILD-MSG TO S2MSGO
        WHEN DFHRESP(DUPREC)
            MOVE DUPREC-MSG TO DISPLAY-DESCRIPTION
            MOVE BUILD-MSG TO S2MSGO
        WHEN DFHRESP(DSIDERR)
            MOVE 'CALL PROGRAMMER' TO DISPLAY-CALL-WHOM
            MOVE DSIDERR-MSG TO DISPLAY-DESCRIPTION
            MOVE BUILD-MSG TO S2MSGO
        WHEN DFHRESP(INVREQ)
            MOVE 'CALL PROGRAMMER' TO DISPLAY-CALL-WHOM
            MOVE INVREQ-MSG TO DISPLAY-DESCRIPTION
            MOVE BUILD-MSG TO S2MSGO
        WHEN DFHRESP(IOERR)
            MOVE 'CALL PROGRAMMER' TO DISPLAY-CALL-WHOM
            MOVE IOERR-MSG TO DISPLAY-DESCRIPTION
            MOVE BUILD-MSG TO S2MSGO
        WHEN DFHRESP(ITEMERR)
            MOVE 'CALL PROGRAMMER' TO DISPLAY-CALL-WHOM
            MOVE ITEMERR-MSG TO DISPLAY-DESCRIPTION
            MOVE BUILD-MSG TO S2MSGO
        WHEN DFHRESP(LENGERR)
            MOVE 'CALL PROGRAMMER' TO DISPLAY-CALL-WHOM
            MOVE LENGERR-MSG TO DISPLAY-DESCRIPTION
            MOVE BUILD-MSG TO S2MSGO
        WHEN DFHRESP(NOSPACE)
            MOVE 'CALL OPERATIONS' TO DISPLAY-CALL-WHOM
            MOVE NOSPACE-MSG TO DISPLAY-DESCRIPTION
            MOVE BUILD-MSG TO S2MSGO
        WHEN DFHRESP(NOTFND)
            MOVE NOTFND-MSG TO DISPLAY-DESCRIPTION
            MOVE BUILD-MSG TO S2MSGO
        WHEN DFHRESP(PGMIDERR)
            MOVE 'CALL PROGRAMMER' TO DISPLAY-CALL-WHOM
            MOVE PGMIDERR-MSG TO DISPLAY-DESCRIPTION
            MOVE BUILD-MSG TO S2MSGO
        WHEN DFHRESP(QIDERR)
            MOVE 'CALL PROGRAMMER' TO DISPLAY-CALL-WHOM
            MOVE QIDERR-MSG TO DISPLAY-DESCRIPTION
            MOVE BUILD-MSG TO S2MSGO
        WHEN OTHER
            MOVE 'CALL PROGRAMMER' TO DISPLAY-CALL-WHOM
            MOVE WS-CICS-RESPONSE1 TO DISPLAY-RESPONSE
            MOVE DEFAULT-DESCRIPTION TO DISPLAY-DESCRIPTION
            MOVE BUILD-MSG TO S2MSGO
        END-EVALUATE.
    *
```

FIGURE 7.4   *(Continued)*

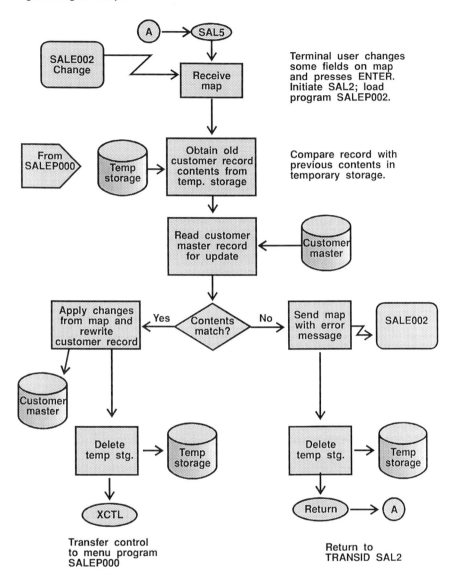

FIGURE 7.5 Logic of program SALEP002.

TEST YOUR UNDERSTANDING

Questions and Exercises

1. What should a task do when it decides that the contents of a temporary storage queue will no longer be needed? What should a task do before it builds a new queue?

2. Suppose you wish to pass data between two transactions that are being invoked in succession from the same terminal. When might it be advantageous to set up and use a temporary storage queue as opposed to passing the data in the DFHCOMMAREA or the terminal control table user area (TCTUA) for that terminal?

3. If you have already read all of the records in a temporary storage queue sequentially, and you reach end of queue, what exceptional condition will be raised? Suppose you want to start again and reread the first record in the queue. What command parameters will allow you to do this?

8

Sequential File I/O in CICS Programs

In Chapter 6, we discussed the use of VSAM files in CICS programs. We noted that the same VSAM files may be shared by CICS programs and by programs running in batch regions or partitions. In Chapter 7, we discussed temporary storage queues, which serve the purpose of temporary files for communication between CICS programs within the same region or partition. In this chapter, we will discuss two types of sequential file structures. These sequential file structures may be used for communication between CICS tasks and batch tasks, for batch processing within the CICS partition, and for providing increased file security and integrity. The file structures that we will be discussing are known as **transient data queues** and **journals.**

8.1 SEQUENTIAL I/O CONCEPTS

8.1.1 Uses for Sequential I/O under CICS

Most file I/O done in CICS programs involves random accesses against indexed files, with occasional file browses. This is because it is impractical to update existing records interactively in a sequential file. (This could be done only by presenting every record in the file to the terminal user to allow him or her to decide whether to update it, and by creating an updated copy of the file.) However, there are other ways to use sequential file processing in a CICS program. Some CICS applications write sequential records for printing, or to create an audit trail of everything that is being done. Some CICS applications may read sequential data from terminal devices that are set up for batch data collection rather than for interactive processing. Such a CICS transaction might be invoked repeatedly to gather terminal data. Each time the transaction is invoked, it will obtain another piece of data from a sequential terminal, and it will write this data to a sequential file so that a scheduled batch job running in another region or partition can use it later.

8.1.2 Transient Data Queue Concepts

What Is a Queue? **A queue might be defined as a series of persons or other entities awaiting their turn.** One example of a queue might be a line of vehicles waiting to get through a traffic signal. A "transaction" may be said to occur each time the light turns green: Several vehicles are "processed" by being allowed to go through the intersection. Sensing devices are sometimes provided so that a "transaction" occurs (the light turns green) only when at least one vehicle is waiting in the queue. It is wasteful for the light to turn green if no vehicles are waiting to go through from that direction.

Queues of this nature are very different from the temporary storage queues that we discussed in the previous chapter. **Temporary storage queues do not really behave like queues according to the strictest definition of the term.** This is because records within temporary storage queues may be accessed randomly or sequentially as many times as desired. **In a transient data queue, however, records are taken from the queue in the same order that they were placed in the queue.** They may not be updated. If one task reads a record from a transient data queue, the record becomes inaccessible. Neither that CICS task nor any other may read that record again. In addition, depending upon the type of queue, you may specify a transaction that will be invoked automatically each time a certain number of records has accumulated in the queue. This transaction can then empty the queue by processing each of its records in sequential order. This automatic feature resembles the sensing device in our traffic queue example. A transient data queue must be defined in the destination control table. (Temporary storage queues need not be defined in any CICS table.) This table entry indicates which type of transient data queue is being used. For instance, a transient data queue may be defined as an *intrapartition destination* or as an *extrapartition destination*.

Intrapartition Transient Data Destinations. **An intrapartition destination is a queue that is used for communication between programs within a CICS partition or region.** One or more CICS transactions may write records to an intrapartition destination, and one or more CICS transactions may also read records from it. The term *intrapartition* refers to the fact that the queue contents are not directly available to jobs running outside the CICS region or partition. All of the intrapartition transient data queues used by one region or partition are stored physically on the same file. A VSAM file is ordinarily allocated for storing intrapartition queues. This file is separate from the VSAM file that is set aside for auxiliary temporary storage. Each intrapartition queue stored on this VSAM file appears to your program to be a separate data set, because CICS software presents to your program only those queue elements that it requests.

In the destination control table entry for an intrapartition transient data queue, you may supply a transaction code that should be invoked when the number of records waiting to be read grows to a specified **trigger level**. For some applications, it may make sense to define the intrapartition destination as **reusable**, which means that disc space is freed every time a record is read from the queue. Whenever a record is read from a reusable transient data queue, it is removed physically from the queue. Removing all of the records from a reusable queue causes all disc space and storage allocated to the queue to be freed.

If an intrapartition transient data queue is defined as *nonreusable*, then the queue contents will continue to take up space in memory and on disc even after all of the records have been read. The resources will be freed only when a command is specifically issued to delete the queue. However, records in a nonreusable queue still cannot be read more than once by any CICS task. Since that is the case, where is the advantage in defining a queue as nonreusable?

A nonreusable intrapartition destination may be defined as **logically recoverable**. Dynan.ic transaction backout may be used to remove the effects of incomplete transactions. This means that the last record read can be made available once again if the task that previously read it ABENDed or was interrupted when the CICS system went down. It also means that records written to a logically recoverable transient data queue during a failed task will be removed. We will discuss use of dynamic transaction backout later in this chapter.

Extrapartition Transient Data Destinations. An extrapartition transient data destination is a sequential file that is available for use both inside and outside the CICS region or partition. The term **destination** is misleading in one sense; a given extrapartition destination can be set up as an input file to be read normally, as an input file to be read backward, or as an output file, but not as more than one of these. An input transient data destination and an output transient data destination may be defined against the same physical data set, as long as the device type permits both input and output. An extrapartition data set may be assigned to any device that permits sequential access, including disc, tape, line printer, and so forth. All sequential data sets used for this purpose must be included in the CICS startup JCL. Each extrapartition destination has two separate entries in the destination control table; these contain the name of the data set associated with the queue.

Extrapartition destinations are processed in the same way as are intrapartition destinations, except that they are not recoverable, they do not allow for automatic task initiation through use of a trigger level, and their storage is not freed or deallocated after their records have all been read. If you need recoverability features and if you need to pass data to a file outside of the CICS partition, use a VSAM file defined in the file control table as recoverable, instead of a transient data queue. Sequential processing of VSAM files is ordinarily quite efficient.

Suppose a CICS task is polling a sequential terminal or a remote system to collect data for a batch job. This task can use one extrapartition destination to read this data from the remote device, and another extrapartition destination to accumulate this data so that it can be used later as input to a job in a batch region or partition.

There is another use for an extrapartition destination. Let us consider something that might happen in a typical CICS file update task. The user might enter records that are correct, but that indicate that an unexpected situation is developing. Very large orders for one product might mean that special arrangements must be made to fulfill that order. A large amount due on an invoice might mean that the invoice must be approved by an officer of the company. Too small a level of output from one piece of equipment might mean that something is wrong with that equipment. The terminal user should not be restricted from entering these figures. However, any figures that look unusual in any respect should be brought to someone's attention. This may be done by writing copies of the unusual records to an extrapartition transient data destination. Whenever you are designing any application, batch or online, you should find out what combinations of data values indicate that unusual situations are developing, and you should plan to report these situations to the appropriate people.

Usage statistics may also be written to an extrapartition data set. For instance, some application programs ask for a password, and some programs should only be run from certain terminal devices. Programs that check passwords or terminal IDs can write a record to an extrapartition output queue whenever anyone tries to use an invalid password or a restricted terminal. This information can be printed later. If many security violations appear on the report, someone is probably trying to break into the system. Catching the violator is easier with knowledge of the location, date, and time of the security violations.

Indirect Destinations.   There is another type of entry in the destination control table that you may need to know about. An indirect destination is a destination that is set up as an "alias" or alternate name for another destination. Intrapartition and extrapartition destinations can both have alternate names. This feature allows the systems programmer to redirect queue output to another file without recompiling any CICS applications. When testing a CICS application, for example, an indirect transient data destination can be set up so that all output could be directed to a test file. When testing is complete, a different indirect destination can be substituted.

8.1.3 Logging and Journaling Concepts

System Log and User Journals. Mainframe CICS provides another type of sequential output data set: the journal file. Journals are used most often to hold information needed for recovering from system failures. They are also used for some of the same purposes for which output extrapartition transient data queues are used. Each journal is specified in an entry in the **journal control table**, and in JCL statements in the CICS startup job. Journals are used instead of output transient data queues for some purposes in order to take advantage of certain automatic features provided by CICS. Journals are not supported under CICS OS/2 as of current release 1.20.

Journals may be stored physically on sequential tape or disc files. Any CICS task may add records to any journal defined under its region or partition. Each journal file in a region or partition is identified by a **journal file ID number.** The system log is identified by journal file ID 1. User journals, if any, are defined with numbers 2 through 99.

Logging Recovery Information. In addition to holding records generated by user programs, the system log is used to hold data that is needed for CICS emergency restart facilities. **Restart data in the system log can be used to recover data that was affected by tasks that were interrupted by a CICS system crash.**

The CICS system also maintains another log known as the **dynamic log,** if the dynamic transaction backout facility is being used. **The dynamic log also contains data used for backing out changes to recoverable resources.** The transaction backout program is an IBM-supplied utility that is run automatically whenever a task that uses protected resources ABENDs (terminates abnormally).

Dynamic transaction backout of recoverable files is supported under CICS OS/2 1.20, with its own transaction log file. Since CICS OS/2 supports a maximum of four concurrent users, there would ordinarily be less need for multiple access to the same files. Under CICS OS/2, enqueues against recoverable datasets are held with file-level locks. This means the entire file is locked on a CICS OS/2 READ UPDATE, not just a VSAM control interval as in mainframe CICS.

In the event of a system failure, which data sets can be recovered in this way? Recoverable resources include data sets defined as recoverable in the file control table, intrapartition transient data queues defined as recoverable in the destination control table, auxiliary temporary storage queues, DB2 databases, and all DL/I data sets accessible by the CICS system.

For example, in the file control table entry for each VSAM or other random-access file, you may specify LOG=YES. This defines that data set as being recoverable, and it causes recovery and restart data to be written to the system log and to the dynamic log. When a file is defined as recoverable in the file control table, then whenever any CICS program enqueues any records on this file, these records remain enqueued until end of task or until a SYNCPOINT command has been executed. (A normal end of task is a CICS syncpoint in itself.) In other words, if the program is updating several records on different recoverable files, all other tasks will be locked out of these records until all of the file updates have completed successfully.

Why do these records on protected data sets remain locked? In many applications, several files are updated that should be related to one another in some way. In other words, whenever an update is made to one file, another update should be made to some other file. For example, an order processing task might update both an inventory file and a billing file. Suppose the task ABENDs after the inventory file has been updated, but before the billing file has been updated? The two files will become "out of sync" with one another. The easiest way to put them back into valid relationship to one another is to use dynamic transaction backout to reverse all of the effects of the failed transaction. It examines all of the recoverable resources and restores the affected portions to their original condition. This can be done successfully only if no other tasks have interfered with records involved in the incomplete transaction. To prevent this interference, records in recoverable files are automatically enqueued for a longer period of time.

When a syncpoint occurs, either at end of task or at a command issued by the program, all of the updates to recoverable files are known to be complete, and all recoverable resources are dequeued.

Automatic Journaling.   In a file control table entry, you may specify a journal file ID number to which record images should be copied automatically. This may be the system journal or a user journal. The file control table entry also indicates which file I/O operations should trigger this automatic journaling. If you specify JREC=RU in the file control table entry, then whenever any CICS program reads a record for update from that file, a copy of the original values in the record is written to the journal file. If you specify JREQ=WN, then whenever any CICS program writes a new record to that file, a copy of the new record is written to the journal file. If you specify JREQ=WU, then whenever any CICS program updates a record on that file, a copy of the updated values in the record is written to the journal file. Also, whenever any CICS program deletes a record from that file, a copy of the keys of the deleted record is written to the journal file. This is called automatic journaling; it is done without using any journal output commands in the applications programs.

User Journal Records.   Journals can be used to store other output information besides images of updated records. In your CICS command level program, you can set up a work area, formatted according to your needs from which journal records can be written. If only a small portion of a record is relevant to your application, you might want to write only that portion to a journal file. If you wish to record data taken from several files, or from user input, or from the CICS system, this data may be placed on a journal file. The application program must use CICS journal output commands to write these records to a journal file. When this is done, CICS automatically appends a prefix containing its own information to the journal output record. Some of this information may be useful to you for diagnostic or other purposes.

Journal Buffers.   Journal records are not always written to the output device immediately after a journal output command is issued, unless STARTIO is specified in the output command. Journal records accumulate in the appropriate *journal buffer* to await output activity. Ordinarily, the journal buffer is divided into two sections. The section boundary is determined by the buffer shift-up value. After enough records have been placed in the buffer, the buffer shift-up value is reached, and all of the records in the first section are written out to the journal file. While this is taking place, the second section of the journal buffer remains open for more activity. When all of the records in the first section have been written to the output device, the records in the second section are shifted up into the first section.

If journal file activity is sparse, it may take a long time for the buffer shift-up value to be reached. In that case, when there have been no new records placed in the journal buffer for one second, the journal buffer contents are written out. Also, the system journal buffer contents are written to the output file immediately whenever a SYNCPOINT command is issued by a task that has been performing I/O against recoverable data sets.

8.2   PROGRAMMING TECHNIQUES FOR SEQUENTIAL I/O OPERATIONS

8.2.1   Transient Data I/O Commands

The same read and write commands are used for intrapartition and extrapartition transient data queue I/O. Here is the output command:

```
EXEC CICS WRITEQ TD
        QUEUE(name)
        [LENGTH(data-value)]
        END-EXEC.
```

The record length must always be specified, except under one set of circumstances: If the queue is an extrapartition transient data set with fixed-length records stored on disc, and if you are building the output in a work area of the correct length, the length may be omitted. The NOSPACE exceptional condition will be raised if there is no more room in the output file extents. NOTOPEN will be raised if the destination data set is not open under CICS. LENGERR will be raised if the length specification is incorrect.

This command allows your program to read a record from a transient data queue:

```
EXEC CICS READQ TD
        QUEUE(name)
        [LENGTH(data-value)]
        END-EXEC.
```

Once again, the length must usually be specified, with the same single exception. The NOTOPEN condition will be raised if the destination data set is not open under CICS, and the LENGERR condition will be raised if the length specification is incorrect. You will need to test for the QZERO condition, which is raised when there are no more records waiting in the queue to be read.

If the queue is an intrapartition destination, it is possible to delete the contents of the entire queue with one command. All space allocated to the queue is freed. However, any CICS task may still write new records to the queue, to be read later by the same or another task. Here again, the QIDERR condition will be raised if the queue is not in the DCT.

```
EXEC CICS DELETEQ TD
        QUEUE(name)
        END-EXEC.
```

For any of the above commands, the QIDERR condition will be raised if the queue does not exist in the destination control table.

8.2.2 Commands for Writing Journal Records

The JOURNAL command is used to place user journal records in the appropriate journal output buffer, from which they will eventually be written to the journal output file. The WAIT JOURNAL command is used to suspend all other processing in the task until the user journal record has been written successfully. The specified journal must exist and must be open. For either command, if the journal file ID number has not been defined in the journal control table, the JIDERR error condition will be raised. If the journal file is not open under CICS, the NOTOPEN error condition will be raised. If some other I/O failure occurs, the IOERR error condition will be raised. HANDLE-CONDITION commands may be used to check on these conditions if necessary.

Making Certain That the Journal Records Were Written. Unless you specify otherwise, the JOURNAL output command is **asynchronous**. This means that journal output activity is not synchronized with other activities in your program. Journal output activity, once begun, continues independently of what your program is doing. Your program does not wait for it to complete successfully. If you use the JOURNAL command to place a record in the journal output buffer, you can continue with other processing and even terminate your task without waiting for the journal records in the buffer to be written out. This can help your program to run faster, but it also brings a disadvantage. Suppose you want to be absolutely sure that your application always writes its records to the journal file successfully. If something goes wrong with the journal file output, perhaps you want to write a record to a different journal, alert the user, terminate the task abnormally, or perform some other error- handling option. If your task terminates before journal I/O is complete, then it will be too late for your program to do anything about the unsuccessful I/O.

If this poses a problem, you may choose to synchronize your task with the journal output routines; in other words, to make completion of your task depend on completion of the journal output. You can do this by specifying WAIT in your JOURNAL commands. This will cause the system to suspend execution of your task until either the journal record has been written to the output device, or the output operation has failed. Using WAIT allows the task to make certain that journal output has completed successfully, but it also can slow task execution. Instead of specifying WAIT in the JOURNAL command, you can use the JOURNAL command, continue with some other processing, and then use the WAIT JOURNAL command just before the end of your task. Some time has elapsed between the JOURNAL command and the WAIT JOURNAL command; perhaps enough to allow the journal output to complete. If journal output is already complete, the WAIT JOURNAL command simply allows control to return to your program. If journal output is not yet complete, the WAIT JOURNAL command causes your task to be suspended until the journal output has either completed or failed.

Suppose your task is writing a series of records to the same journal file. This means all of the records are going to the same output buffer. In that case, it is not necessary to specify WAIT along with every JOURNAL output command. If you wish to make sure that all of the journal records have been written successfully, you need to specify WAIT only with the *last* JOURNAL output command. (Alternatively, you can specify WAIT

JOURNAL once, just before the end of your task.) Why is this sufficient? If you know that the last record in a journal buffer has been written, then you know that every other record in the buffer has been written out also.

Both the JOURNAL and the WAIT JOURNAL commands allow STARTIO to be specified. As the name implies, STARTIO causes journal I/O to be started immediately. This makes your task run faster, but it causes shorter blocks to be written to the journal file, and reduces the efficiency of the system as a whole.

STARTIO can be specified whether or not WAIT is also specified. If your program is writing records to a journal file that is not used very often, it may make sense to specify STARTIO if WAIT is specified. If the buffer seldom fills, your task will ordinarily have to wait one full second after each JOURNAL command before the journal record is actually written to the output device. STARTIO will avoid this delay.

Journal Command Formats.   Here is the format of the JOURNAL command:

```
EXEC CICS JOURNAL
          JFILEID(data-value)
          JTYPEID(data-value)
          FROM(data-area)
          LENGTH(data-value)
          [REQID(data-area)]
          [PREFIX(data-value)PFXLENG(data-value)]
          [STARTIO]
          [WAIT]
          END-EXEC.
```

JFILEID(data-value) is used to specify the journal file ID number. Since the system log is journal file 1, JFILEID(1) accesses the system log. JTYPEID(data-value) is a two-byte record-type indicator of your own choosing. You can use it to indicate the format of the record contents. You must specify the record length. The record length must be no greater than the maximum specified in the journal control table entry for that journal file. If you choose, you may specify an optional user prefix by using the PREFIX(data-value) and PFXLENG(data-value) parameters.

REQID(data-area) is used to attach an identifying label to this particular JOURNAL output command. This request identifier can be used later in a WAIT JOURNAL command to refer to a JOURNAL command for a particular record. This parameter is not used often. If REQID is omitted, the WAIT JOURNAL command will refer to the last JOURNAL output command that was issued for that journal data set.

Here is the format of the WAIT JOURNAL command. Remember that WAIT JOURNAL is used to suspend program execution until the journal records have been written from the journal buffer to the journal file.

```
EXEC CICS WAIT JOURNAL
          JFILEID(data-value)
          [REQID(data-value)]
          [STARTIO]
          END-EXEC.
```

8.2.3 Appearance of Journal File Contents

A CICS journal file may be read by a batch job if it is treated as a file with variable-length blocked records. Every block, and every record, begins with a half-word hexadecimal length field, followed by a half-word field containing hexadecimal zeros. The first record in each block is a **block label record**. It contains the record length, the system ID, the user ID, the record position within the block, the journal ID, the block number, the volume creation date, the volume sequence number, the address and the track balance field of the previous journal block (if the journal file is on disc), the run start time, the time the block was written, and the date the block was written.

Subsequent records in the block also begin with the record length, the system ID, the user ID, and the record position within the block. After this data, CICS adds a system prefix that contains the system prefix length, the task number, a time stamp, the transaction code, the terminal ID, and other information that identifies the origin of the journaled data. If you specify a user prefix in your output command, it will follow the system prefix. The actual output data follows all of these prefixes. The format of mainframe journal prefixes appears in an IBM-provided assembler language DSECT, DFHJCRDS. The format of this DSECT can change from one release to the next. If you need to access these files, you can either write an assembler program or I/O subroutine, or you can make up a COBOL version of that DSECT for use directly in a COBOL program. See Figure 8.1.

A batch utility, DFHJUP, prints journal data sets. This was introduced with CICS 1.7. Each journal record is shown in both character and hexadecimal formats. Detailed information on how to use this batch utility is in the **CICS Installation and Operations Guide**. It can be used to print or copy a complete journal file or a selected group of records on it. You can give it control statements to tell it which records to select. The control statements compare the data at a specified offset in each record with data which you supply. DFHJUP might be helpful if you want to set up a method for recovering lost file updates by applying journal records against a backup of your file. DFHJUP could be used to pick up those updates that occurred after the date and time of the backup, and to reject any updates that don't apply to that particular file.

```
*COBOL VERSION OF DFHJCRDS (CICS LOG RECORD PREFIX FORMAT)
*
01  COBOL-DFHJCRDS.
    05  J-SYSTEM-HEADER.
        10  J-LLBB-VAR-LENGTH.
            15  J-LL               PIC S9(4) COMP.
            15  J-BB               PIC S9(4) COMP.
        10  J-SYSTEM-REC-ID        PIC S9(4) COMP.
        10  J-USER-REC-ID          PIC S9(4) COMP.
        10  J-RECORD-WITHIN-BLOCK
                                   PIC S999 COMP-3.
    05  J-SYSTEM-PREFIX.
        10  J-SYS-PFX-LEN          PIC S9(4) COMP.
        10  J-RESERVED             PIC XX.
        10  J-SYS-PFX-FLAG         PIC X.
        10  J-TASK-NO              PIC S9(5) COMP-3.
        10  J-TIME-HHMMSSS         PIC S9(7) COMP-3.
        10  J-TRANS-ID             PIC XXXX.
        10  J-TERM-ID              PIC XXXX.
    05  J-SYS-PFX-OPTIONAL.
        10  J-SYS-PFX-FILE-ID      PIC X(8).
    05  J-SYS-PFX-OPTIONAL-RDF REDEFINES J-SYS-PFX-OPTIONAL.
        10  J-SYS-PFX-VTAM-SEQ-NO
                                   PIC S9(8) COMP.
        10  FILLER                 PIC XXXX.
*
*JOURNAL CONTROL LABEL RECORD FORMAT
01  COBOL-DFHJCRDS-LABEL.
    05  JC-LLBB-VAR-LENGTH.
        10  JC-LL                  PIC S9(4) COMP.
        10  JC-BB                  PIC S9(4) COMP.
    05  JC-CONSTANT-8045           PIC S9(4) COMP.
    05  JC-CONSTANT-0000           PIC S9(4) COMP.
    05  JC-CONSTANT-01             PIC S999 COMP-3.
    05  JC-EVENT-CONTROL-NO.
        10  JC-FILE-ID             PIC X.
        10  JC-BLOCK-NO            PIC S9(5) COMP-3.
        10  JC-VOL-CREATE-YYDDD    PIC S9(7) COMP-3.
        10  JC-VOL-SEQ-NO          PIC S999 COMP-3.
        10  JC-LAST-BLOCK-WRITTEN
                                   PIC S9(8) COMP.
        10  JC-TRACK-BALANCE       PIC S9(4) COMP.
        10  JC-TIME-BLOCK-WRITTEN-HHMMSSS
                                   PIC S9(7) COMP-3.
        10  JC-RUN-START-TIME-HHMMSSS
                                   PIC S9(7) COMP-3.
        10  JC-DATE-BLOCK-WRITTEN-YYDDD
                                   PIC S9(7) COMP-3.
```

FIGURE 8.1   COBOL version of DFHJCRDS.

8.2.4 Programming Techniques for Tasks Using Protected Resources

If your application accesses protected resources, you will need to organize your program differently in order to take proper advantage of the recovery facilities. This requires some systems analysis. In particular, find out which files must be updated together. If a record is added to one file, is it necessary to add, change, or delete records on any other data sets at the same time? If you find that several update actions must be performed at once, these actions should all be grouped together within one logical unit of work.

A logical unit of work is one or more update actions that should be performed together. If it is not possible to finish performing a logical unit of work, all of the incomplete update actions should be backed out using dynamic transactions backout. We have already observed that, if protected resources are being updated, the CICS system allows them to remain enqueued (locked) until the task ends or a SYNCPOINT command is executed. If the task ABENDs, dynamic transaction backout will recover all of the enqueued resources.

To make sure that the resources are all enqueued at the same time, place all of the update activity needed for one logical unit of work in one task. Complete all editing of user input, and other preliminary activity, before enqueuing any protected resources. Do not begin to do writes, deletes, or reads for update until you are reasonably sure that everything is in order. To summarize, group all related update activity together within one task. Perform the updates after all edits have been run successfully. If you still need to do some other work within your task *after all of the updates are complete,* you should use the SYNCPOINT command to terminate the logical unit of work:

```
EXEC CICS SYNCPOINT
        END-EXEC.
```

If you use DL/I in your CICS application, issuing a SYNCPOINT command will also cause a DL/I termination call to be invoked. SYNCPOINT will also terminate any basic mapping support paging commands, which we will discuss in a later chapter. Releases prior to 1.7 contained a glitch in the dynamic transaction backout processing: if the program is adding a new record to a file and the program ABENDs because a record with the same key is already present, the dynamic transaction backout processing will back out the old record that was originally on the file. To work around this problem, execute a READ command before the WRITE command. If the READ command fails to locate a record with the appropriate key, then it is safe to add a record with that key.

Many programmers think of abnormal terminations (ABENDs) as a nuisance with which they must cope. Actually, ABENDs can be used as a valuable data integrity tool. Remember that you are in control of error handling within your CICS applications. You can decide which conditions should be allowed to trigger ABEND. How does this help you maintain file integrity? Whenever something goes wrong with any of the updates within a logical unit of work, an ABEND will cause all of the updates against any of the resources to be backed out. This is because dynamic transaction backout can be invoked when an ABEND takes place.

When a file update fails, the default CICS error-handling facilities will cause the task to ABEND, unless RESP or a HANDLE CONDITION command overrides this default. Using RESP will override all default CICS error handling. So, in order to take advantage of dynamic transaction backout, you need to check for fatal error conditions yourself, and to trigger an ABEND or take other appropriate action when you find one.

Suppose a program is updating some files, and the program discovers that a file being read for update contains some invalid data. This in itself will not trigger task ABEND. However, it might make sense to back out all of the pending updates whenever a bad file is found. You can do this by using a CICS command to force task ABEND. In a typical program, you would first use the SEND command to place an appropriate message on the user's terminal. You might also write a diagnostic message to a journal file or some other device. Once this is done, you can use the CICS ABEND command to cause dynamic transaction backout to restore your recoverable data sets to their previous status. Here is the command format:

```
EXEC CICS ABEND
          [ABCODE(name)]
          [CANCEL]
          END-EXEC.
```

If you use the ABCODE(name) option, it will cause a memory dump to be placed on the dump data set, with the specified name appearing in the header. Otherwise, no dump will be produced. Dumps take considerable file space. If you have written good diagnostic messages to a journal or other data set, you may not need to see a dump.

The CANCEL parameter causes any HANDLE ABEND routine currently in effect to be suspended. Otherwise, a HANDLE ABEND routine might be invoked by the ABEND command. If you never use HANDLE ABEND in your programs, you can ignore this parameter.

Figure 8.2 shows the use of the ABEND command.

Trapping CICS Task ABEND.   Suppose you want to write diagnostic messages to a certain device before allowing a task to terminate abnormally. You can use the HANDLE ABEND command to specify your own routine to be executed, instead of the normal CICS abnormal termination routines, if task ABEND is about to take place. The HANDLE ABEND command resembles the HANDLE CONDITION and HANDLE AID commands in most respects. Note that, under CICS OS/2 1.20, HANDLE commands are supported only in the COBOL language, not in C.

```
EXEC CICS HANDLE ABEND
          [PROGRAM(name)|LABEL(label)|CANCEL|RESET]
          END-EXEC.
```

The LABEL(label) parameter allows you to specify the routine to which your program should branch if ABEND is about to take place. The PROGRAM(name) parameter causes your program to XCTL to another Program module if ABEND is about to take place. CANCEL suspends the effect of

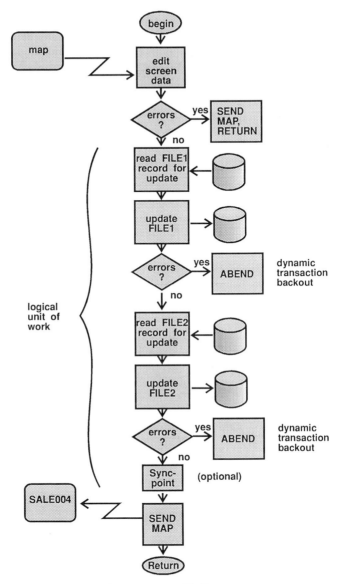

FIGURE 8.2 Updating two recoverable files.

any previous HANDLE ABEND command. RESET restores the effect of any suspended HANDLE ABEND command.

When an ABEND routine is invoked, CICS automatically cancels the HANDLE ABEND that brought the program to this point. This prevents the routine from calling itself. Your error-handler routine should write its error messages and then use an ABEND command to end the task.

Invoking Dynamic Transaction Backout without Task ABEND. We mentioned earlier that a program should not begin to perform updates until editing and validation have been completed. In other words, the program should assure itself that the updates are likely to be valid before performing them. Any further errors that are found during the updating process are likely to be serious, unrecoverable errors that could justifiably he handled by task ABEND. However, you have a choice as to whether or not you want to ABEND the task when you invoke dynamic transaction backout. This form of the SYNCPOINT command will cause dynamic transaction backout to be invoked, but without causing task ABEND:

```
EXEC CICS SYNCPOINT
           ROLLBACK
           END-EXEC.
```

TEST YOUR UNDERSTANDING

Questions and Exercises

1. Why do you suppose you should finish other program activities before enqueueing records for update?
2. Name some CICS commands that we have encountered so far that enqueue resources.
3. What is the difference between the dynamic log, the system log, and user journals?
4. Suppose task 1234 has already read the last record from transient data queue TQ1. What condition indicates that this has happened? If TQ1 were to be read again, would the same condition necessarily appear again? What could have happened between the two attempts to read TQ1?
5. Although CICS journals carry recovery data, they themselves are not recoverable resources under dynamic transaction backout. After an update has failed, but before the task terminates, what might you want to write to a CICS journal file?
6. Suppose file INVMAST is a recoverable resource, containing records AAAA through ZZZZ. Suppose task 0001 and task 0002 are running at the same time. Task 0001 has just updated record AAAA, and is about to read record BBBB for update. Task 0002 has just updated record BBBB, and is about to read record AAAA for update. What is about to happen? What rule would prevent future problems of this type?
7. Under what circumstances should you use the SYNCPOINT and SYNCPOINT ROLLBACK commands? Why?

9

Testing Methods for CICS Applications

In the previous chapters, we have covered enough commands to allow you to design and code a simple CICS application. We have shown you how to use basic mapping support macros. We have also discussed requirements for CICS table entries, and methods for creating, backing up, and printing VSAM files. In this chapter, we will discuss methods for testing a completed CICS command-level application.

Testing a CICS command level application is usually easier than testing a batch application. This is because so many good diagnostic tools are available. We will discuss the IBM-provided execution diagnostic facility (EDF) in this chapter. Other vendors offer similar interactive testing tools, some of which provide features beyond those of EDF.

There is one problem with testing in an online environment: security. If possible, testing should take place in a separate CICS test region or partition, or on your own CICS OS/2 system, with its own test files. Otherwise, it is only a matter of time before production files are damaged. Even in a test system, no one should experiment with the new transactions without first talking to the person responsible for testing. If various people play with the transactions, they will disturb the contents of files, queues, journals, and system work areas. Any testing done later will show unpredictable results.

9.1   PLANNING FOR A VALID TEST

9.1.1   Creating a Test Plan

Testing a CICS application has one thing in common with testing a batch application: In a valid test, all features of the application are exercised. To be sure that this is done, a test plan should be used. Someone other than the programmer should be involved in the testing effort, if possible. Why is this so? If you design and code an application, and then you try to test it, you may take things for granted. You may see what you think should be happening, rather than what actually is happening. For instance, every program should be able to reject various combinations of bad data. Some of these combinations of bad data might not have occurred to you when you were designing the program. They still might not occur to you when you build test data to exercise the error handlers. Your test will not discover these deficiencies in the editing routines. However, terminal users might embarrass you later by entering these combinations of data and finding out that your application does not always work.

A test plan should be developed by a person who understands the purpose of the application and the requirements of the users. This person should refer to the system and program specifications when preparing the test plan. Each application should be tested on a screen-by-screen basis. A checklist should be made up for each screen. Each item on the checklist must specify what should happen when a given action is performed. The person doing the testing writes down what actually does happen.

Certain tests should appear on every checklist. **It might be a good idea to make a standard "installation test plan" that contains certain standard items.** Here are some possible examples:

1. Function key assignments must appear in the designated area at the bottom of the screen and must conform to SAA standards.
2. Function keys should do what the labels suggest. Use of undefined function keys should result in an error message.
3. A descriptive header must appear in the header area on the screen.
4. Each data field on the screen must be correctly labeled.
5. Each user-enterable field must be followed by a skip byte, unless it is positioned immediately before another field. In other words, the terminal user must not be able to key past the end of any field.
6. Tab through all of the fields on the screen. The cursor should rest only on fields intended for user data entry or cursor selection.
7. No inappropriate or meaningless characters, numerals, or messages should appear anywhere on the screen.
8. When the screen is redisplayed after errors have been detected, all invalid fields should be highlighted and unprotected. The cursor

should be placed at the first field discovered to be in error. An error message should describe what is wrong with the first invalid field.

9. Whenever error fields are rekeyed, the system should accept the corrected data.

10. The action bar should be at the top of the screen. Test all combinations of objects and actions to make sure the selection process works.

11. If there are any pull-down menus, popup menus, or dialog boxes, make sure they appear at the correct times and accept user input. Also, make sure that the old screen contents are restored after the overlay disappears.

12. If there are any scrolling screens, they should show data in the correct sequence and should handle end-of-data and beginning-of-data conditions correctly.

13. The user should be able to exit from any screen without changing the contents of any file.

14. The PF3 key or EXIT action from the main menu should terminate the application in an orderly manner, causing a blank screen (or appropriate security menu) to be displayed.

Editing tests will depend on the application. Here are a few examples of tests that could be part of various different test plans:

1. The following 10 fields should appear on this screen. Verify that each one has the length and attributes specified on page A.

2. If file XXX is closed, message YYY should appear when the add, change, or delete functions are selected.

3. The FICA WAGES field should never show an amount greater than the FICA limit.

4. Program must display message ZZZ if AGE is either negative or greater than 120.

5. An error message should appear if this transaction is run from terminals other than L77A, L77B, and L77E.

6. After the last invoice is successfully entered, the next invoice should be assigned a higher number.

Flow of program execution should also be tested. For instance:

1. When an adjustment has been entered, menu XXXX should reappear.

2. Menu YYYY should appear in place of menu XXXX if the correct authorization code has been entered.

3. Program should display message AAAA and ABEND if file record is missing or damaged.

9.1.2   Creating Good Test Data

The person in charge of testing should decide what user input should be used to test each screen. A list of this data should accompany the test plan. Some of this test data should represent good records that are likely to be entered. The remainder should represent bad information that should be rejected. If existing data must be available on other files, this data should be built using IEBDG, FILE-AID, or some other test data generator. If none is available, use COBOL programs. It is a mistake to rely exclusively on small extracts from production files, unless someone has made sure that they contain every combination of data that is to be tested, including data which should be rejected as invalid.

After testing is done, all updated files should be printed or dumped to determine whether each field contains the data that the test plan says that they should contain. A COBOL program or a purchased utility may be used for this purpose.

9.1.3   System Capacity

It might also be a good idea to determine how efficiently the application actually runs. Consider allowing several users to work with the application at once, preferably during a time when other batch and online programs are also running. Observe whether the users interfere with one another or with other online tasks or batch jobs. How many times can the transaction be used successfully by five users in a 15-minute period? Will the application handle the work load expected of it? Do the users like the way the fields are arranged on each screen, or do they complain that something is slowing them down or making them do extra work? They may want the design to be changed from the specifications they approved originally. The process of keying data causes them to notice things that they overlooked before.

9.2   WHAT TO DO IF AN APPLICATION BEGINS LOOPING

9.2.1   Breaking Out of a Loop

Suppose you are testing a program and you reach a point at which it seems to be "stuck" or "hung up." In other words, you can neither get out of the application nor make it go on to the next step. The system may fail to recognize key input from your terminal, or it may keep redisplaying the same things over and over on your screen. Assuming that the problem is not caused by mainframe system outage or slow telecommunications response, your application may be in a loop. Do not panic; if you know what transactions you were trying to run, you or another authorized terminal user can use another terminal to disable the transactions that make up the application. On a mainframe, this can be done by using the CEMT command discussed in the appendix. (On a microcomputer, it's probably easiest to shut down and restart CICS OS/2, which takes very little time.)

Disabling the offending transactions will cause the application to terminate abnormally, without any need to shut down the CICS partition or region. Also, once any transaction is disabled, it cannot be run until it is enabled again. This keeps faulty transactions from invoking each other in a loop. If anyone else is also trying to work with the transactions, warn them about the problem and ask them not to use them until further notice. The transactions should be enabled again later by using CEMT so that they can be tested under execution diagnostic facility (EDF). This is fairly safe because you can use EDF to abort any task that is involved in a loop.

9.3 USING EXECUTION DIAGNOSTIC FACILITY

9.3.1 What Is EDF?

Execution diagnostic facility is an IBM-provided utility that allows the programmer to debug CICS command level applications interactively. It is available on mainframe and CICS OS/2 systems. If you use EDF to test an application, EDF will stop the execution before and after each CICS command in order to show you what is in the command parameter arguments, whether the command executed successfully, and what data is in working storage and in the EXEC interface block. When execution is stopped, you can change the contents of most of these items. You can also terminate the task, which is useful if you are testing an application that has a loop problem.

Important: EDF will not work with macro-level programs. If EDF is used to test a command-level program that also contains macro-level statements (a practice that IBM discourages), EDF may work improperly.

EDF will work with CICS programs that make DL/I data base calls. If requested, EDF will show you the DL/I interface block, and it will stop program execution if a DL/I error status occurs. However, EDF ordinarily does not stop program execution before and after each DL/I call. (EDF does stop program execution when the EXEC DLI option, or command-level interface, is used.)

9.3.2   How to Run Your Application under EDF

For security reasons, many sites allow the use of EDF in test CICS systems
but not in production systems. If you want to use EDF, check with your
systems programmer to make sure that it has been installed under a
security key that allows you to use it. You can run your application under
EDF in two ways: using one terminal or using two terminals. For some, it
is less confusing to run EDF using two terminals, because the application
itself runs on one terminal while the debugging information appears on
the other. (If your application uses partitioned displays, you must use two
terminals. On another occasion, I found it necessary to use two terminals
to debug an application which manipulated terminal I/O area (TIOA)
fields directly, because EDF didn't work with one terminal.)

To begin EDF on one terminal, enter CEDF on a blank terminal screen.
A message will come up saying that EDF mode is on. To run your transaction, clear the screen and enter your own transaction code. The next
screen that appears will be the EDF transaction initialization screen. **To
make EDF step through your program exactly as it is normally executed,
simply press ENTER each time an EDF screen becomes visible.**

To begin EDF on two terminals, clear both screens. On one terminal
enter CEDF (terminal-id). A message will appear stating the EDF mode is
on. Then, go to the other terminal and enter your application's transaction
code. Under CICS OS/2, you can use two terminal windows as two separate EDF terminals. If a task is already running on terminal L77A (let's say
that it is in a loop), you can go to another terminal and enter CEDF L77A
to put that task into debug mode. Once you've found the problem, you can
also terminate the task from there.

Suppose you are testing a pseudoconversational application using one
terminal. Your first task will send a map and will RETURN, specifying
another transaction ID. What will EDF show? Here are the steps:

1.   EDF will show you the SEND MAP command itself.

2.   EDF will show an image of the user screen. Do not enter data or
     press PF keys when this screen is visible; simply press ENTER.

3.   EDF will show you the response code from the SEND MAP com-
     mand.

     EDF will show you the RETURN command.

5.   EDF will show you a program termination screen.

6.   EDF will show you a task termination screen. This screen will ask
     whether you want to continue using EDF. You may enter YES or
     NO. The default is NO, which is not usually what you want.

7.   The user screen will appear. Enter your test data and press whatever
     function key is appropriate.

8. If you requested that EDF be continued, EDF will show a transaction initiation screen for the new task.

This sounds more complicated than it actually is. If you try it out, you will see that EDF works conveniently with pseudo-conversational applications.

9.3.3 Features Available under EDF

Figure 9.1 shows some examples of screen images produced by EDF. At the bottom of each EDF screen is a display showing the features that can be selected with PF keys. This display changes from screen to screen. Certain functions are not available on all screens. However, a given function does not move from one PF key assignment to another. If your terminal does not have all of the PF keys shown on the screen, you may move the cursor under the desired option and press ENTER, Here are the available functions:

CONTINUE (ENTER key):

Continue stepping through the program under EDF.

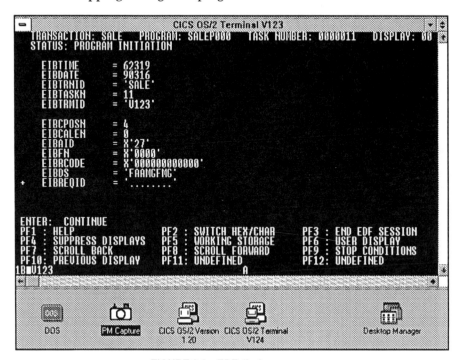

FIGURE 9.1   EDF display screens.

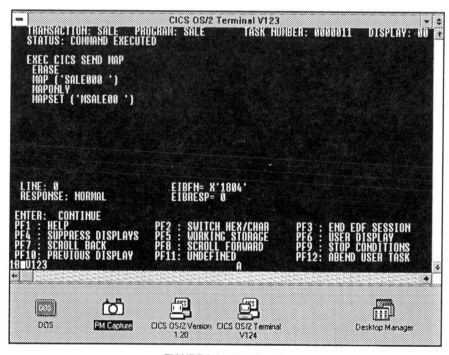

FIGURE 9.1   *(Continued)*

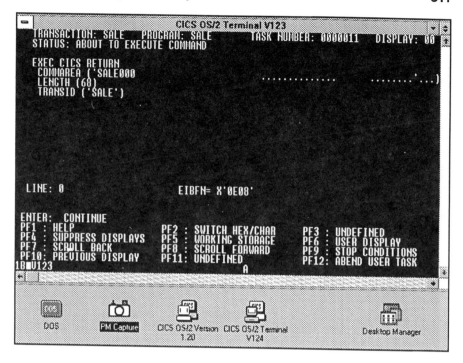

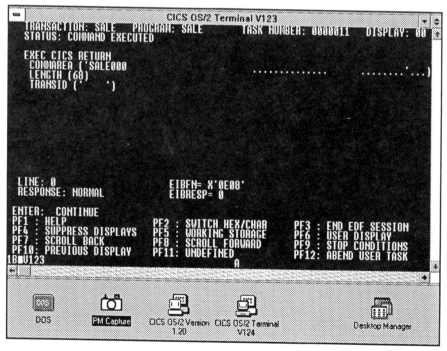

FIGURE 9.1 *(Continued)*

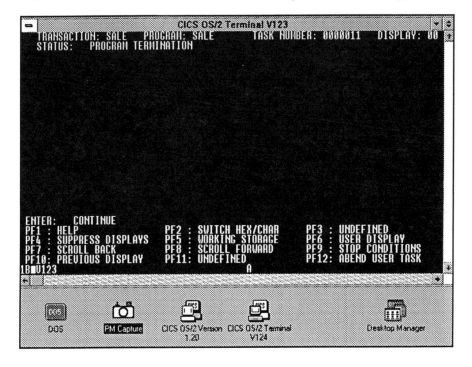

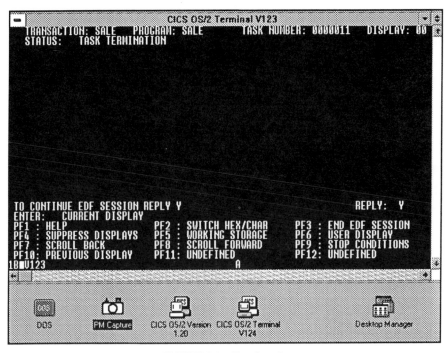

FIGURE 9.1   *(Continued)*

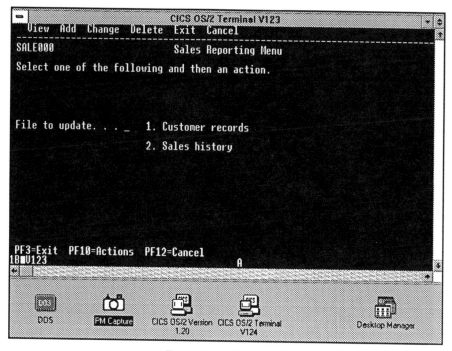

FIGURE 9.1 *(Continued)*

ABEND USER TASK:

Terminate the task abnormally. EDF will show you another screen that will allow you to request a memory dump and assign an identifier to print out with the dump.

BROWSE TEMP STORAGE:

This option allows you to use transaction CEBR, which is discussed in a later section. CEBR first became available with CICS 1.6.

CURRENT DISPLAY:

If you have used a PF key to view some other display, this key will return you to the current EDF screen. The current EDF screen is the screen from the command that was most recently executed or is about to be executed.

DIB DISPLAY:

This shows DL/I interface block, if present.

EIB DISPLAY:

This shows EXEC interface block. This is full of useful information. Review Chapter 5, Section 9 for an explanation of EIB contents.

END EDF SESSION:

This terminates EDF, but does not terminate your application. The remainder of your task will run as it would when EDF is not in use.

NEXT DISPLAY:

EDF stores up to 10 previous command displays. If you have been looking at a previous display, this option will show you the next newer command display.

PREVIOUS DISPLAY:

This option will show you the next older command display.

REGISTERS AT ABEND:

This display shows register contents if an ABEND ASRA (program check) has taken place. You can use these register contents, along with the WORKING STORAGE displays, to find the bad instruction.

REMEMBER DISPLAY:

This option adds a special display such as WORKING STORAGE or EIB to the EDF storage queue. You can look at it again if you use the PREVIOUS DISPLAY option.

SCROLL BACK, SCROLL FORWARD:

These options are for examining a command or EIB display that takes up more than one screen.

SCROLL BACK HALF, SCROLL BACK FULL, SCROLL FORWARD HALF, SCROLL FORWARD FULL:

These options are for examining different portions of the WORKING STORAGE DISPLAY.

STOP CONDITIONS, SUPPRESS DISPLAYS:

EDF takes up considerable storage and execution time. If you think that a large portion of your application is working, you may want to shut off EDF until a certain transaction is invoked or until an error has taken place. Pressing the STOP CONDITIONS key will give you a screen on which you can specify what conditions should stop program execution. For instance, if your program was translated using the DEBUG option, you can ask EDF to stop at a certain line number. After you complete the answers on this screen, you can select the SUPPRESS DISPLAYS key to suspend EDF until one of the conditions occurs.

SWITCH HEX/CHAR:

This option allows you to choose whether argument values and other screen data will be displayed in hexadecimal or in character format.

WORKING STORAGE:

In a COBOL program, this display shows your working storage contents. To see a particular field when you know the offset, you can type the offset value in the address field on the WORKING STORAGE display, and press ENTER. Otherwise, you can use PF keys to scroll up and down. If you want to see something that is in the linkage section—for instance, a record that you have read using the SET(pointer) option—you will need to use this pointer value to locate it. Find the pointer value on the EDF command screen that read the record. Type this pointer value in the address field on the WORKING STORAGE display, and press ENTER. Your record will appear.

Changing Fields on EDF Screens.   You can overtype many areas visible on EDF screens, including working storage, command parameter argument values, some EIB fields, and so forth. You can skip execution of a command by typing NOP (meaning "no operation") over it. You may not add new command arguments or delete old ones, nor may you change anything on a previous screen.

An EDF screen that appears just before a command is executed contains a copy of the original argument values. If you change the data on such a screen, only the current command is affected. The original data, which might be in a record buffer or in working storage, is affected only if you change it by using the working storage display.

On an EDF screen that appears after command execution, you may change the response code to NORMAL or to some appropriate error condition such as MAPFAIL, IOERR, and so forth. Changing the response code to NORMAL will inhibit error handling, while changing the response code to an error condition will trigger error handling.

9.3.4   Using EDF Instead of a Memory Dump

Getting a memory dump under CICS involves printing the dump file. In most installations, you cannot do this instantly. However, if you know what user input caused the ABEND, you can try to reproduce the ABEND when the application is running under EDF. This will allow you to use the REGISTERS AT ABEND display and the WORKING STORAGE displays to find data exceptions and the like. The ABEND address and register values are used with the program listing to find the bad instruction and the contents of the bad operands. This is done in exactly the same manner as debugging a batch COBOL dump, which is covered in many other texts. Debugging a printed CICS dump is not as simple; we will look at printed CICS dumps later. From your point of view, it is always easier to use EDF or another debugging tool if it is available, and to use dumps only if you do not know what input caused the problem.

9.3.5   Temporary Storage Browse

With CICS 1.6 and above, you can use your terminal to look at temporary storage queues through the IBM-supplied CEBR transaction. CEBR can be invoked through EDF by selecting PF2 when the WORKING STORAGE display screen is visible. CEBR can also be run freestanding by entering the characters CEBR on a cleared terminal screen. A browse display will appear, which looks somewhat like the EDF displays. A display of PF key options appears at the bottom. PF1 brings up a HELP screen, which describes the commands that you can use. To use a command, type it on the screen and press ENTER. Here are some CEBR commands:

QUEUE nnnnnnnn:

This command allows you to specify which queue you would like to see.

TERMINAL nnnn:

This command replaces the last four characters of the queue name. (Remember that the terminal ID is customarily used as the last four characters in a temporary storage queue name.)

PURGE:

This purges the records from the queue being browsed. It can cause problems if used by unauthorized persons.

TOP:

This command moves to the beginning of the queue.

BOTTOM:

This command moves to the end of the queue.

LINE, COLUMN, and FIND/string/:

These are used to move around in the queue display.

GET nnnn:

This copies the transient data queue named nnnn into the current tempo-rary storage queue. The transient data queue must be an intrapartition queue or an input extrapartition queue.

PUT nnnn:

This copies the temporary storage queue now being browsed into a tran-sient data queue named nnnn. The transient data queue must be an intrapartition queue or an output extrapartition queue. If the output queue represents a print file, this command will allow the temporary storage contents to be printed.

9.3.6 CECI and CECS

CICS provides another troubleshooting tool that lets you do two useful things: You can check command syntax, and you can use CICS commands in a freestanding manner to put data into test files, repair damaged files, examine data set contents online, and so forth. CECI is an IBM-provided CICS transaction that invokes the **command level interpreter** one com-mand at a time. If you have used a microcomputer that comes equipped with a BASIC interpreter, and have entered and executed BASIC state-ments one line at a time, you will be familiar with what a command interpreter does. CECI prompts you to enter each command; when you are finished, it executes that command. Obviously, CECI could give rise to some security problems. CECI is very powerful and should be made available only on test CICS systems, except under very unusual circum-stances. CECI and CECS are available under CICS OS/2 as well as under mainframe CICS.

To run CECI, enter the transaction code CECI followed by the command name, such as READ or SEND MAP. A screen will appear containing prompts that will help you to enter the correct command parameters. After you do so, the command will execute.

To route the output of one command (such as a record that was just read) for use as input to another command, you can specify a variable in both commands. The variable may be set up ahead of time if desired. Pressing PF5 will bring up the VARIABLES screen. While on this screen, you can enter the name of any new variable that you wish to define, and press ENTER. The first character of a variable name should be an amper-sand.

Substituting CECS for CECI causes the interpreter to check your command syntax without actually executing the command. It can be used as a reminder of the available command parameters.

9.4   USING THE ANIMATOR FOR DEBUGGING UNDER OS/2

9.4.1   What Animated Debugging Is All About

Animated source-level debugging provides you with a visual trace through your COBOL source code as your program is executing. Various debugging packages provide this feature in mainframe and microcomputer CICS.

If you are using a microcomputer to develop CICS COBOL command level programs under OS/2, with the Micro Focus or IBM COBOL/2 compiler, you can use the Animator for debugging under CICS. (The IBM COBOL/2 compiler is actually written by Micro Focus and distributed by IBM.) The Animator is packaged with the COBOL/2 compiler itself. It was originally developed to provide source-level interactive debugging in free-standing COBOL/2 programs, which use the screen handling built into the COBOL compiler itself. However, CICS OS/2 contains built-in interfaces, which enable you to use the Animator for debugging CICS programs.

Animated source-level debugging is different from EDF, although you can use both at once. EDF stops only at CICS commands and shows you working storage in hexadecimal format. The Animator shows you a full-screen display of your CICS COBOL source code, highlighting the line currently being executed. To see contents of working storage fields, you use Animator commands to query the desired fields by name. When the actual "user" screen is sent to the terminal, it will replace the Animator display temporarily, much as the user screen replaces the current EDF display temporarily. The source code shown to you by the Animator is the output from the translator step, with the CICS commands translated into EXEC interface calls.

An expanded version of the Animator product, the Advanced Animator, is offered as part of the Micro Focus Workbench. This product contains some extra commands for greater convenience, such as a shorthand Watch command to set up a query for the data fields on the line currently being executed. It also can produce an animated structure diagram of a program.

9.4.2   Compiling Programs to Run under Animator

To use the Animator to debug a program under CICS, you need to compile the program using the COBOL/2 compiler with the ANIM directive. You may also need to compile subprograms invoked from that program. Normally, a CICS program is part of a hierarchy of applications programs. If the faulty program is not associated with the first screen in your application, you might want to suppress debugging until you get to that module. Simply omit the ANIM directive when compiling programs that you don't want to debug.

How do you set the ANIM directive? If you want to set up all of your CICS programs for debugging, which is not the usual case, you can specify ANIM as one line in the COBOL.DIR compiler directives file and then recompile them all. You can also specify ANIM in the compiler directive line at the beginning of the source code for the modules you want to debug, if you remember to remove it after debugging is complete. The easiest way is to specify ANIM on the command line when you submit your compile or translate/compile/link job. For example:

```
CICSTCL SALEP006 ANIM
```

Ordinarily, when you compile a CICS program using the COBOL/2 compiler, you get a file suffixed with .OBJ, from which the link editor builds an executable .DLL file. CICS OS/2 will then execute your .DLL file as a subroutine. When you specify the ANIM directive, the COBOL/2 compiler will also produce an .INT file and an .IDY file. These are "intermediate" code files which the Animator will use at run time in place of the executable file. The Animator requires the .INT file, the .IDY file, and the .CBL file (COBOL source) to be present at run time. However, if a .DLL file is present in your subdirectory at run time, CICS OS/2 will use it. The CICS application program will run at machine speed, as it normally would, and the Animator debugging facilities will not be invoked. **To run a CICS application program in Animator mode, you must remove its .DLL file from the subdirectory being used as your object library.**

9.4.3 Telling CICS OS/2 to Use Animator

To make CICS OS/2 recognize the Animator, you need to provide debug parameters with the CICSRUN command. Parameters can be provided either directly on the OS/2 command line following the CICSRUN command itself, or in the Parameters option of the OS/2 Start Programs or Desktop Manager menu facility. The Animator requires a parameter of this type, where in this case V124 is the identifier of the terminal which will be used for debugging:

```
/D-V124(ANIM)
```

CICS OS/2 configuration will be discussed in more detail in a later chapter. In the default CICS OS/2 configuration as supplied by IBM, V123 and V124 are the identifiers of the two logical terminals defined under CICS. These appear as separate windows on your monitor when you bring up CICS. You can use CESN to sign on to either of them or to both. For those who are familiar with OS/2 terminology, both terminal windows will appear as Presentation Manager windows in the same screen group with whatever other icons and windows happen to be there when you start up CICS. Like other PM windows, they can be scrolled, resized, moved, or minimized to icons. To see all the text at once, you will have to maximize the active window. In that case, it will cover all but the lowest portion of the monitor. If you want one or both of those terminals to come up in full screen mode rather than in PM windows, you can change the setting in the Terminal Control Table (TCT) using the CEDA transaction.

At Last! Applications Development Software that Comes with Its Own Fly Swatter!   Yes, there really is a fly swatter. When you bring up CICS with one terminal defined as a debugging terminal, your debugging session will display in full-screen mode, occupying the entire monitor. (It will not display in an OS/2 window, even if its TCT entry indicates it will.) To switch from that session to the other CICS terminal session or to other OS/2 applications that might be running, hold the Ctrl key and press Esc. This will cause your OS/2 Task List to appear, from which you can select whatever else you want to display. Whenever the Animator session is not being displayed, it appears on the OS/2 PM screen as an icon. This icon is a fly swatter with a tag on it which reads "CICS", captioned "CICS OS/2 Animator V124" (or whatever terminal ID you are using). Clicking on the fly swatter icon will get you back into the Animator session. By contrast, when you minimize a normal CICS terminal session to an icon, the icon looks like a terminal.

If you define V123 as the Animator terminal, then CICS will come up with that terminal in full-screen mode. The V124 terminal will, in effect, be hidden in the background, though you can select it with the OS/2 Task List. If you define V124 as the Animator terminal, CICS will come up with the V123 terminal in the active PM window, and with the V124 terminal minimized to the fly swatter icon, which you can select with the mouse. My own preference is to use V124 as the Animator terminal rather than V123.

9.4.4 Running a Program with Animator

To begin debugging, sign on to the Animator terminal and enter the beginning transaction ID of the application you want to debug. When you reach the program that has been compiled with the ANIM directive, the Animator display will appear on your logical terminal in full-screen mode, in place of the usual CICS screen displays. Most of the screen will contain your COBOL source code, starting with the first line of the Procedure Division. The Animator inserts a READY TRACE at the beginning of the source. Using cursor arrow keys or the Page Up/Page Down keys, you can scroll very rapidly through your entire source file, including working storage and linkage section definitions.

If we use Animator to debug SALEP006, this is how the first screen will look:

```
1066  PROCEDURE DIVISION USING DFHEIBLK DFHCOMMAREA.
1067        READY TRACE.
1068        SET EIB-EDF-ON OF DFHEIBLK TO TRUE
1069        MOVE 0 TO EIB-EDF-LINE-NUMBER OF DFHEIBLK
1070        MOVE 0 TO EIB-KEYN OF DFHEIBLK
1071        MOVE 97 TO EIB-FCTN OF DFHEIBLK
1072        CALL '_COBTMCS' USING DFHEIBLK EIB- WSTART EIB-WEND
1073         DFHCOMMAREA.
1074        IF EIB-CC OF DFHEIBLK NOT = 0
1075              GO TO Z99-HANDLE-CONDITION
1076        END-IF.
1077  MAIN-PROG.
1078  *
1079  ********************************************************************
1080  * DETERMINE WHICH POINT IN THE CYCLE APPLIES TO THE CURRENT     *
1081  * SITUATION. THE FIRST TIME THROUGH, SHOW THE BROWSE SCREEN     *
1082  * FOR THE FIRST TIME. ON SUBSEQUENT PASSES, PROCESS USER INPUT  *
1083  * AND SHOW THE SCREEN AGAIN (OR TRANSFER CONTROL BACK TO THE    *
1084  * MENU PROGRAM, DEPENDING ON FUNCTION KEY).                     *
1085  ********************************************************************
Animate—SALEP006————————-Level=01-Speed=5—-Ins-Caps-Num-Scroll
F1=help F2=view F3=align F4=exchange F5=where F6=look- up F9/10=word=/ Escape
Step Go Zoom next-If Perform Reset Break Env Query Find Locate Text Do 0-9
Speed
```

The function key commands work as follows:

Escape

Allows you to get back to the previous Animator menu from a sub-menu, or allows you to get out of Animator entirely.

F1=help

Help information for Animator.

F2=view

Shows the screen display as the user would normally see it. Pressing any other key will clear the user display and return to the Animator display.

F3=align

Repositions the display within the source code so that the cursor line becomes the third line on the display.

F4=exchange

Swaps between split-screen displays (see "Text" option).

F5=where

Returns the cursor to the statement currently being executed.

F6=look-up

Lets you enter a line number, to which the display will scroll.

F9=WORD

Moves cursor to the previous word.

F10=WORD

Moves cursor to the next word.

The "hot key" commands work as follows:

Step

Executes the current statement and moves the cursor to the next executable statement in the source code file. This is called **Step mode**.

Go

Runs the program in **Go mode**. The program automatically steps through the source code line by line, highlighting the current line as it proceeds. Pressing keys 0 through 9 lets you adjust the speed of execution in go mode.

Zoom

Runs the program in **Zoom mode**, which means full speed without animation. To break out of Zoom mode, hold the Ctrl key and press the Break key.

Next-If

Runs the program in Zoom mode until the next IF statement is reached. The Animator display returns at that point.

Perform

Causes a Perform-level sub-menu to appear. If your cursor is on a PERFORM or CALL statement, or if it is within a PERFORMed or CALLed routine, you can press S (Step) to zoom through the routine named in the PERFORM statement. If your cursor is already within such a routine, you can press E (Exit) to zoom through all remaining statements of that routine.

Reset

Brings up a sub-menu which lets you change program execution sequence. **Here are the options on the Reset menu:**

Cursor-position

Executes the statement at the cursor position.

Next

Skips the current statement and executes the next statement.

Start

Restarts program execution sequence with the first executable statement in the program. Make sure all of your variables are set to desired initial values before doing this.

Quit-perform

Skips to the end of the current PERFORMed paragraph, omitting all remaining statements.

Break

Brings up a menu for setting temporary program breakpoints which become effective when you go into Go or Zoom mode. **Here are the options on the Break menu:**

Set

Sets a breakpoint on the current line which will cause execution to halt there.

Go

Sets a breakpoint which displays a message showing that this statement has just been executed.

If

Brings up a command line which lets you enter the activating condition for a conditional breakpoint. Only one of these is allowed per program. Enter an IF statement which is valid according to the rules of COBOL syntax.

On

Brings up a command line which lets you enter the frequency with which this breakpoint will be triggered. If you enter 5, for example, the breakpoint will occur every fifth time this line is executed.

Examine

Cycles your cursor position through each line on which you have already set a breakpoint.

Environment

Provides additional breakpoint and execution sequence features. **Here are the options on the Environment menu:**

Program-break

If you want to execute all of your programs except for one program in Zoom mode, use this option to select which program should be the exception. On this menu, press This to select the current program, or Select to enter the name of some other program. When you go into Zoom mode, the Animator screen will reappear when you get to that module.

Threshold-level

If you want to Zoom through all lower-level PERFORMs and CALLs, this will let you select the nest level for that purpose.

Until

Lets you enter a conditional breakpoint which can be triggered from anywhere in the program. Program execution will stop whenever that condition becomes true. Only one of these is allowed per program.

Backtrack

Brings up a sub-menu which lets you record and play back the program execution sequence. This does NOT re-execute the code; it only shows you what was executed in case you missed it the first time around. Set begins the recording process, Unset stops the recording process, and E lets you examine it.

Query

Brings up a Query sub-menu, which lets you examine and change working storage and linkage section items. This is probably the most important Animator command that you will use.

Cursor-name

Shows the contents of the field whose name is at the current cursor position. The cursor must be pointing at a valid data name for this to work.

Enter-name

Lets you enter the name of the field to be displayed.

Monitor-off

Turns off the facility which lets you monitor the changing contents of a field.

Dump-list

Saves a list of test data values for the current queried data item. A list of this type can be built using the Query Alt menu.

Once you have chosen a data field, the **Query Data-name menu** will appear. Function keys on this menu let you clear data contents so that you can rekey them (F2), toggle between hex and character format (F3), go up to the group item (F7), go down to the individual items contained within the current group item (F8), or move to the next data item at the same level (F9). Cursor arrow keys let you move around in the data. The Escape key gets you out of this menu.

The Alt key brings up another sub-menu which lets you produce a list of test data values for the current queried data item. Once you have produced a query list, you can scroll up or down until you have found the value you want to use for testing. Pressing the enter key will insert that value into the data field in your program.

Find

Lets you search forward for a desired text string in your source code file. The search is case-sensitive.

Locate

Locates the place where a selected name was declared in your program. The name can be a file name, data name, or procedure name.

Text

Lets you split the display into two "windows", rejoin the display, or refresh it.

Do

Provides a command line on which you can enter a COBOL statement to be executed immediately in interpretive mode. Your source code file will not be affected.

TEST YOUR UNDERSTANDING

Questions and Exercises

1. Why should you be careful about which people are allowed to use CEDF and CEBR? What problems could occur if unauthorized individuals were to use these transactions?

2. What could happen to production data sets if CEDF is enabled for use in a "live" CICS region or partition, as opposed to a "test" partition or region?

3. Suppose you have just written your first large CICS application. Your supervisor thinks that it is working and wants to make it available immediately. After all, it costs money and takes time to test something thoroughly. You, on the other hand, are not sure that all of the bugs are out, and you do not want to be embarrassed later. What arguments might persuade your supervisor to allocate more resources for testing?

4. Choose a portion of our sample sales reporting application and make up a test plan for it.

10

Troubleshooting Program ABENDs

In the previous chapter, we learned how to test new CICS applications under EDF or Animator. The easiest way to rid an application of known bugs is to test the application under EDF, Animator, or other interactive debugging software. If you know what input triggers the problem, you can reproduce the error situation yourself to see exactly what is happening. Suppose, however, that your program has terminated abnormally, and that you are unable to find out what input caused it to fail. Your only clues at this point are the contents of the CICS dump files and trace table.

Why is it sometimes so hard to tell what input caused a program to fail? For one thing, it may take some time for you to hear about the problem. By then, the terminal user may have forgotten the exact sequence of keystrokes and screen images that led to the failure. Some terminal users blame themselves if something goes wrong when they are using the computer. They may be afraid that someone will scold them or even fire them because they made the system break down by pressing the wrong key. These worries may cause them to avoid discussing the problem with you. The problem could also be something that rarely happens. A faulty application could "bomb" when two users try to get at the same records, or when a certain terminal device has been shut off. The terminal users in each case might be completely unaware of what is happening.

10.1 USING DUMPS

10.1.1 Dump Concepts

A memory dump is simply a printed listing of the contents of some portion of system memory at the time the dump was taken, usually at the time of system or application failure. CICS dumps can be somewhat more difficult to use than batch COBOL or assembler language dumps that you may be accustomed to reading. They contain vast amounts of information about CICS control blocks and so forth, most of which is irrelevant to the applications programmer. It would take another whole book to describe all of it. However, CICS dumps also contain information needed for troubleshooting program checks caused by data exceptions and other fatal errors, which applications programmers are called upon to solve.

Note to mainframe programmers: Starting with CICS/ESA 3.1, new routines exist for capturing and printing dumps, with more debugging information built in. This may make some of the effort described in this section unnecessary. As of this writing, CICS 3.1 is available only for MVS/ESA sites. The interactive problem control system (IPCS) provides various parameters for formatting a system dump which was written to an MVS SYS1.DUMPxx file; further information is available in the CICS/ESA Operations Guide.

Note to CICS OS/2 programmers: Watch your disk space! Troubleshooting information is kept in three files, none of which should grow out of control. CICS OS/2 1.20 memory dumps are written to a file called FAAUTFDM.LST. You can view the file with the OS/2 system editor or with any other ASCII text editor. Memory dumps are less helpful on microcomputers, because microcomputers typically have less disk space for storing dump files. Dumps exhaust disk space in a hurry, especially if the problem occurs repeatedly. System outages can, and do, result from running out of disk space. A CICS OS/2 system initialization table (SIT) setting lets you choose whether or not to produce dumps automatically on program ABEND. Automatic dumps of this type show all areas of CICS memory. If you produce dumps with a CICS command, try to confine the dumped data to what you will actually need. Remember to delete the file after use (or cold start CICS to get rid of the file).

CICS OS/2 1.20 substitutes a file called CICSMSG.LOG for the "system console" monitor that would exist on a mainframe. System messages concerning startup, shutdown (normal or otherwise), or task-related errors are stored there as ASCII text. CICS displays these messages in an OS/2 window as they are written. When the message log file gets too big, just delete it. CICS will open a new one the next time you bring it up.

Under CICS OS/2 1.20, the auxiliary trace file (which we will discuss in more detail later) is called FAATAFEN.TRC. Use of this file is controlled by the IBM-supplied CTRA transaction. Here again, this file increases in size very rapidly.

10.1.2   Step-by-Step Method for Reading Mainframe ABEND Dumps

If you use batch COBOL or assembler language dumps to find program checks, you may be in the habit of finding your working storage and file buffers by visually scanning the dump until you recognize the data. This technique may not work for CICS debugging. The CICS storage control program constantly obtains and releases storage areas for the other CICS control programs to use in satisfying your CICS commands. These storage areas may be used for file buffers, terminal I/O areas, and so forth. Releasing a storage area does not automatically erase its contents. Familiar-looking data may continue to occupy an area until some other module writes over it. In addition, the CICS system sometimes uses temporary storage to store images of data to be sent to your terminal screen. This repeated data can make the dump listing look confusing. The solution is to follow the directions given in the next section when looking for a program check. Visual inspection is not the best way to approach a CICS dump.

The first thing you need to do is to print the dump file and find your dump. You may be accustomed to seeing batch COBOL and assembler language dumps printed automatically after being sent to the list queue. This is not true of CICS dumps. A CICS system startup job ordinarily contains JCL for a DFHDMPA file and a DFHDMPB file. The CICS system cycles back and forth between these files. If one of them becomes filled with dumps, the system operator uses a master terminal command to switch the active dump file to the empty data set. The full data set is then printed and its contents cleared so that it can be used again later. While one data set is being printed, the other can keep accepting more dumps. The CICS system should be set up with enough dump file space to hold a reasonable number of dumps. The CICS tables should be set up so that task ABEND will cause a memory dump to be placed on the active dump file. This must be done by the systems programmer.

To get a mainframe dump, you will have to ask the operator to switch the dump files and to print the old dump file using the dump print program, DFHDUP. Details about DFHDUP may be found in the Operations Guide. (If it is not practical to switch the dump files, you will have to wait for the dump file to be printed the next time CICS is shut down.) Many dumps other than your own will probably be in the dump file. Identify yours by the transaction code at the top of the listing. Since dumps waste a large amount of paper, some environmentally conscious sites have a separate utility for viewing dumps without printing them. Otherwise, you can leave the printed output in the spool file and browse it with a spool utility.

A dump code should appear on a mainframe dump listing. If the dump came from an EXEC CICS ABEND or DUMP command, then the dump code will be the one that you supplied in the CICS command itself. If the dump came from a program check ABEND, the dump code will probably be ASRA. If the dump came from an ABEND raised by CICS internal error handling, some other dump code will be assigned. If the dump came from an EDF session in which you pressed a PF key to request task ABEND, the dump code that you supplied under EDF will appear on the listing. Incidentally, whenever a CICS program ABENDs for any reason, the dump code will appear on the screen of the terminal to which the task was attached.

If the dump resulted from a program check (ABEND ASRA), you will need to find the address of the offending instruction, and probably the contents of the bad operands, in order to correct the problem. Besides the dump itself, you will need a program compilation listing showing addresses both for data elements and for coding statements. See Figures 10.1 and 10.2.

1. Look through the dump. On a separate sheet, list all of the hexadecimal address ranges for each area labeled PROGRAM STORAGE. In Figure 10.2, the only such range is hex 164008-164FCF.

2. Look at page 1 of the dump. At the top, you should see a field labeled PSW. Copy down the last three bytes (six hexadecimal digits) of this field. This is the address of the faulty instruction, or of the instruction immediately following the faulty one. In Figure 10.2, the PSW address is hex 164512.

3. Compare the addresses. If the PSW address from part 2 is within one of the address ranges from part 1, the problem is in your program somewhere. Otherwise, it may be in some other module, and you will probably need to use the trace table to find it. Some other module may have been executing which performs I/O or other services on behalf of your program. It's also possible that a program executed a "wild" branch somewhere outside of the area it should occupy. This can happen if a pointer was reset to zero or if program code was overlaid with other data.

4. Find the linkage editor map in your program listing. There will be a list of CSECTs. One of them will have the same name as your CICS application program. Copy down the offset of this CSECT. In Figure 10.1, the offset of EXAMP001 is hex 18.

5. In the linkage editor map, you will also find the address of another CSECT, DFHECI. This is a part of CICS that is linked together with your program. Copy down this offset also. In Figure 10.1, the offset of DFHECI is hex 00.

6. Subtract the offset in part 4 from the offset in part 5. The result will be the relative location in program storage of the beginning of your own object code. In this case, the offset is hex 18.

```
CICS/VS COMMAND LANGUAGE TRANSLATOR VERSION 1.5

        CBL XOPTS(LANGLVL(2),CICS)                                      00000100

  LINE          SOURCE LISTING

 00001          IDENTIFICATION DIVISION.                                00000100
 00002          PROGRAM-ID.  EXAMP001.                                  00000200
 00003          AUTHOR.  ALIDA JATICH AND PHIL NOWAK.                   00000300
 00004          ********************************************************
 00005          *                                                      *
 00006          * EXAMP001 IS A VARIATION OF STUBPGM CONTAINING A BUG WHICH *
 00007          * SHOULD BE FOUND BY USING A MEMORY DUMP.              *
 00008          *                                                      *
 00009          ********************************************************
 00010          * STUBPGM RECEIVES A MESSAGE FROM THE USER'S TERMINAL.  IF THE *
 00011          * USER ENTERED TOO MUCH DATA, MAKING THE MESSAGE LONGER THAN *
 00012          * EXPECTED, STUBPGM WILL SEND AN ERROR MESSAGE BACK TO THE *
 00013          * USER'S TERMINAL.  OTHERWISE, STUBPGM WILL ECHO THE USER'S *
 00014          * ORIGINAL MESSAGE BACK TO THE TERMINAL.               *
 00015          ********************************************************
 00016          ENVIRONMENT DIVISION.                                   00000400
 00017          DATA DIVISION.                                          00000500
 00018          WORKING-STORAGE SECTION.                                00000600
 00019          01  EXPECTED-MESSAGE-LENGTH     PIC S9(4)  COMP  VALUE +9.   00000700
 00020          01  OUTPUT-LENGTH               PIC S9(4)  COMP  VALUE +37.  00000700
 00021          01  INPUT-MESSAGE-FIELD.                                00000800
 00022              05  TRAN-CODE               PIC XXXX         VALUE SPACES.  00000900
 00023              05  INPUT-MESSAGE-VAR       PIC 99999        VALUE ZEROES.  00001000
 00024          01  OUTPUT-MESSAGE-FIELD.                               00001100
 00025              05  FILLER                  PIC X(34)        VALUE   00001200
 00026          ' NUMERAL RECEIVED BY EXAMP001 WAS '.                   00001300
 00027              05  OUTPUT-MESSAGE-VAR      PIC S9(5) COMP   VALUE +0.   00001000
 00028          01  BAD-NEWS.                                           00001400
 00029              05  FILLER                  PIC X(28)        VALUE   00001500
 00030          ' TERMINAL INPUT WAS TOO LONG'.                         00001600
 00031          PROCEDURE DIVISION.                                     00001700
 00032          MAIN-PROG.                                              00001800
 00033              EXEC CICS HANDLE CONDITION                          00001900
 00034                  LENGERR (SEND-BAD-NEWS)                         00002000
 00035                  END-EXEC.                                       00002100
 00036              EXEC CICS RECEIVE                                   00002200
 00037                  INTO (INPUT-MESSAGE-FIELD)                      00002300
 00038                  LENGTH (EXPECTED-MESSAGE-LENGTH)                00002400
 00039                  END-EXEC.                                       00002500
 00040              MOVE INPUT-MESSAGE-VAR TO OUTPUT-MESSAGE-VAR.       00002600
 00041              EXEC CICS SEND                                      00002700
 00042                  FROM (OUTPUT-MESSAGE-FIELD)                     00002800
 00043                  LENGTH (OUTPUT-LENGTH)                          00002900
 00044                  END-EXEC.                                       00003000
 00045              EXEC CICS RETURN                                    00003100
 00046                  END-EXEC.                                       00003200
 00047              GOBACK.                                             00003300
 00048          SEND-BAD-NEWS.                                          00003400
 00049              EXEC CICS SEND                                      00003500
```

FIGURE 10.1 Listing of program EXAMP001 that produced a dump.

```
CICS/VS COMMAND LANGUAGE TRANSLATOR VERSION 1.5

LINE            SOURCE LISTING

00050                         FROM (BAD-NEWS)                           00003600
00051                         LENGTH (28)                              00003700
00052                         END-EXEC.                                00003800
00053              EXEC CICS RETURN                                     00003900
00054                         END-EXEC.                                00004000
```

```
CICS/VS COMMAND LANGUAGE TRANSLATOR VERSION 1.5

*OPTIONS IN EFFECT*      APOST, NODEBUG, FLAGW, LANGLVL(2), LIST, NONUM, OPT, SEQ, SPACE1, NOXREF, CICS

NO MESSAGES PRODUCED BY TRANSLATOR.

TRANSLATION TIME:-    0.00 MINS.
```

FIGURE 10.1   *(Continued)*

```
PP 5740-CB1 RELEASE 2.3 + PTF R - UP13477          IBM OS/VS COBOL   JULY 24, 1978

    1                        23.32.39      OCT  3,1983

00001           IDENTIFICATION DIVISION.                                    00000100
00002           PROGRAM-ID.  EXAMP001.                                      00000200
00003           AUTHOR.  ALIDA JATICH AND PHIL NOWAK.                       00000300
00004           ***********************************************************
00005           *                                                         *
00006           * EXAMP001 IS A VARIATION OF STUBPGM CONTAINING A BUG WHICH *
00007           * SHOULD BE FOUND BY USING A MEMORY DUMP.                  *
00008           *                                                         *
00009           ***********************************************************
00010           * STUBPGM RECEIVES A MESSAGE FROM THE USER'S TERMINAL.  IF THE  *
00011           * USER ENTERED TOO MUCH DATA, MAKING THE MESSAGE LONGER THAN   *
00012           * EXPECTED, STUBPGM WILL SEND AN ERROR MESSAGE BACK TO THE     *
00013           * USER'S TERMINAL.  OTHERWISE, STUBPGM WILL ECHO THE USER'S    *
00014           * ORIGINAL MESSAGE BACK TO THE TERMINAL.                       *
00015           ***********************************************************
00016           ENVIRONMENT DIVISION.                                      00000400
00017           DATA DIVISION.                                             00000530
00018           WORKING-STORAGE SECTION.                                   00000600
00019           01  EXPECTED-MESSAGE-LENGTH      PIC S9(4)  COMP  VALUE +9.  00000700
00020           01  OUTPUT-LENGTH               PIC S9(4)  COMP  VALUE +37. 00000700
00021           01  INPUT-MESSAGE-FIELD.                                   00000800
00022               05  TRAN-CODE           PIC XXXX         VALUE SPACES.  00000900
00023               05  INPUT-MESSAGE-VAR   PIC 99999        VALUE ZEROES.  00001000
00024           01  OUTPUT-MESSAGE-FIELD.                                  00001100
00025               05  FILLER              PIC X(34)        VALUE          00001200
00026               ' NUMERAL RECEIVED BY EXAMP001 WAS '.                  00001300
00027               05  OUTPUT-MESSAGE-VAR  PIC S9(5) COMP   VALUE +0.      00001400
00028           01  BAD-NEWS.                                              00001400
00029               05  FILLER              PIC X(28)        VALUE          00001500
00030               ' TERMINAL INPUT WAS TOO LONG'.                        00001600
00031           COPY DFHEIVAR.
00032 C         01  DFHEIV.                                                 04000000
00033 C             02   DFHEIV0  PICTURE X(26).                            08000000
00034 C             02   DFHEIV1  PICTURE X(8).                             12000000
00035 C             02   DFHEIV2  PICTURE X(8).                             16000000
00036 C             02   DFHEIV3  PICTURE X(8).                             20000000
00037 C             02   DFHEIV4  PICTURE X(6).                             24000000
00038 C             02   DFHEIV5  PICTURE X(4).                             28000000
00039 C             02   DFHEIV6  PICTURE X(4).                             32000000
00040 C             02   DFHEIV7  PICTURE X(2).                             36000000
00041 C             02   DFHEIV8  PICTURE X(2).                             40000000
00042 C             02   DFHEIV9  PICTURE X(1).                             44000000
00043 C             02   DFHEIV10 PICTURE S9(7) USAGE COMPUTATIONAL-3.      48000000
00044 C             02   DFHEIV11 PICTURE S9(4) USAGE COMPUTATIONAL.        52000000
00045 C             02   DFHEIV12 PICTURE S9(4) USAGE COMPUTATIONAL.        56000000
00046 C             02   DFHEIV13 PICTURE S9(4) USAGE COMPUTATIONAL.        60000000
00047 C             02   DFHEIV14 PICTURE S9(4) USAGE COMPUTATIONAL.        64000000
00048 C             02   DFHEIV15 PICTURE S9(4) USAGE COMPUTATIONAL.        68000000
00049 C             02   DFHEIV16 PICTURE S9(9) USAGE COMPUTATIONAL.        72000000
00050 C             02   DFHEIV17 PICTURE X(4).                             76000000
00051 C             02   DFHEIV18 PICTURE X(4).                             80000000
00052 C             02   DFHEIV19 PICTURE X(4).                             84000000
00053 C             02   DFHEIV97 PICTURE S9(7) USAGE COMPUTATIONAL-3 VALUE ZERO. 88000000
00054 C             02   DFHEIV98 PICTURE S9(4) USAGE COMPUTATIONAL VALUE ZERO.   92000000
```

FIGURE 10.1   *(Continued)*

```
00055 C          02  DFHEIV99 PICTURE X(1)  VALUE SPACE.              96000000
00056        LINKAGE SECTION.
00057        COPY DFHEIBLK REPLACING EIBLK BY DFHEIBLK.
00058 C    *     EIBLK EXEC INTERFACE BLOCK                            02000000
00059 C    01    DFHEIBLK.                                             04000000
00060 C    *     EIBTIME     TIME IN OHHMMSS FORMAT                    06000000
00061 C          02 EIBTIME     PICTURE S9(7) USAGE COMPUTATIONAL-3.   08000000
00062 C    *     EIBDATE     DATE IN OOYYDDD FORMAT                    10000000
00063 C          02 EIBDATE     PICTURE S9(7) USAGE COMPUTATIONAL-3.   12000000
00064 C    *     EIBTRNID    TRANSACTION IDENTIFIER                    14000000
00065 C          02 EIBTRNID    PICTURE X(4).                          16000000
00066 C    *     EIBTASKN    TASK NUMBER                               18000000
00067 C          02 EIBTASKN    PICTURE S9(7) USAGE COMPUTATIONAL-3.   20000000
00068 C    *     EIBTRMID    TERMINAL IDENTIFIER                       22000000
00069 C          02 EIBTRMID    PICTURE X(4).                          24000000
00070 C    *     DFHEIGDI    RESERVED                                  26000000
00071 C          02 DFHEIGDI    PICTURE S9(4) USAGE COMPUTATIONAL.     28000000
00072 C    *     EIBCPOSN    CURSOR POSITION                           30000000
00073 C          02 EIBCPOSN    PICTURE S9(4) USAGE COMPUTATIONAL.     32000000
00074 C    *     EIBCALEN    COMMAREA LENGTH                           34000000
00075 C          02 EIBCALEN    PICTURE S9(4) USAGE COMPUTATIONAL.     36000000
00076 C    *     EIBAID      ATTENTION IDENTIFIER                      38000000
00077 C          02 EIBAID      PICTURE X(1).                          40000000
00078 C    *     EIBFN       FUNCTION CODE                             42000000
00079 C          02 EIBFN       PICTURE X(2).                          44000000
00080 C    *     EIBRCODE    RESPONSE CODE                             46000000
00081 C          02 EIBRCODE    PICTURE X(6).                          48000000
00082 C    *     EIBDS       DATASET NAME                              50000000
00083 C          02 EIBDS       PICTURE X(8).                          52000000
00084 C    *     EIBREQID    REQUEST IDENTIFIER                        54000000
00085 C          02 EIBREQID    PICTURE X(8).                          56000000
00086 C    *     EIBRSRCE    RESOURCE NAME                             58000000
00087 C          02 EIBRSRCE    PICTURE X(8).                          60000000
00088 C    *     EIBSYNC     SYNCPOINT REQUIRED                        62000000
00089 C          02 EIBSYNC     PICTURE X.                             64000000
00090 C    *     EIBFREE     TERMINAL FREE REQUIRED                    66000000
00091 C          02 EIBFREE     PICTURE X.                             68000000
00092 C    *     EIBRECV     DATA RECEIVE REQUIRED                     70000000
00093 C          02 EIBRECV     PICTURE X.                             73000000
00094 C    *     EIBSEND     RESERVED                                  76000000
00095 C          02 EIBSEND     PICTURE X.                             79000000
00096 C    *     EIBATT      ATTACH DATA EXISTS                        82000000
00097 C          02 EIBATT      PICTURE X.                             85000000
00098 C    *     EIBEOC      GOTTEN DATA IS COMPLETE                   88000000
00099 C          02 EIBEOC      PICTURE X.                             91000000
00100 C    *     EIBFMH      GOTTEN DATA CONTAINS FMH                  94000000
00101 C          02 EIBFMH      PICTURE X.                             97000000
00102        01  DFHCOMMAREA PICTURE X(1).
00103        01  DFHBLLSLOT1 PICTURE X(1).
00104        01  DFHBLLSLOT2 PICTURE X(1).
00105        PROCEDURE DIVISION USING DFHEIBLK DFHCOMMAREA.            00001700
00106           SERVICE RELOAD DFHEIBLK.
00107        MAIN-PROG.                                                00001800
00108      *     EXEC CICS HANDLE CONDITION
00109      *          LENGERR (SEND-BAD-NEWS)
00110      *          END-EXEC.
00111          . MOVE '              ' TO DFHEIVO CALL 'DFHEI1' USING  00001900

     3                    23.32.39     OCT  3,1983


00112            DFHEIVO GO TO SEND-BAD-NEWS DEPENDING ON DFHEIGDI.
00113
00114      *     EXEC CICS RECEIVE
00115      *          INTO (INPUT-MESSAGE-FIELD)
00116      *          LENGTH (EXPECTED-MESSAGE-LENGTH)
00117      *          END-EXEC.
00118          MOVE '              ' TO DFHEIVO CALL 'DFHEI1' USING    00002200
00119            DFHEIVO INPUT-MESSAGE-FIELD EXPECTED-MESSAGE-LENGTH.
00120
00121
00122            MOVE INPUT-MESSAGE-VAR TO OUTPUT-MESSAGE-VAR.         00002600
00123      *     EXEC CICS SEND
00124      *          FROM (OUTPUT-MESSAGE-FIELD)
00125      *          LENGTH (OUTPUT-LENGTH)
00126      *          END-EXEC.
00127          MOVE '              ' TO DFHEIVO CALL 'DFHEI1' USING    00002700
00128            DFHEIVO DFHEIV99 DFHEIV98 OUTPUT-MESSAGE-FIELD
00129            OUTPUT-LENGTH.
00130
00131      *     EXEC CICS RETURN
00132      *          END-EXEC.
00133          MOVE '              ' TO DFHEIVO CALL 'DFHEI1' USING DFHEIVO.  00003100
00134                                                                 00003300
00135            GOBACK.                                               00003400
00136        SEND-BAD-NEWS.
00137      *     EXEC CICS SEND
00138      *          FROM (BAD-NEWS)
00139      *          LENGTH (28)
00140      *          END-EXEC.
00141          MOVE 28 TO DFHEIV11 MOVE '              ' TO DFHEIVO CALL '00003500
00142        -  'DFHEI1' USING DFHEIVO DFHEIV99 DFHEIV98 BAD-NEWS DFHEIV11.
00143
00144
00145      *     EXEC CICS RETURN
00146      *          END-EXEC.
00147          MOVE '              ' TO DFHEIVO CALL 'DFHEI1' USING DFHEIVO.  00003900
00148
```

FIGURE 10.1 (Continued)

EXAMP001   23.32.39   OCT 3,1983

INTRNL NAME	LVL	SOURCE NAME
DNM=1-068	01	EXPECTED-MESSAGE-LENGTH
DNM=1-101	01	OUTPUT-LENGTH
DNM=1-124	01	INPUT-MESSAGE-FIELD
DNM=1-156	02	TRAN-CODE
DNM=1-175	02	INPUT-MESSAGE-VAR
DNM=1-202	01	OUTPUT-MESSAGE-FIELD
DNM=1-235	02	FILLER
DNM=1-246	02	OUTPUT-MESSAGE-VAR
DNM=1-274	01	BAD-NEWS
DNM=1-295	02	FILLER
DNM=1-309	01	DFHEIV
DNM=1-328	02	DFHEIV0
DNM=1-345	02	DFHEIV1
DNM=1-362	02	DFHEIV2
DNM=1-379	02	DFHEIV3
DNM=1-399	02	DFHEIV4
DNM=1-416	02	DFHEIV5
DNM=1-433	02	DFHEIV6
DNM=1-450	02	DFHEIV7
DNM=1-467	02	DFHEIV8
DNM=1-484	02	DFHEIV9
DNM=2-000	02	DFHEIV10
DNM=2-021	02	DFHEIV11
DNM=2-039	02	DFHEIV12
DNM=2-057	02	DFHEIV13
DNM=2-075	02	DFHEIV14
DNM=2-093	02	DFHEIV15
DNM=2-111	02	DFHEIV16
DNM=2-129	02	DFHEIV17
DNM=2-147	02	DFHEIV18
DNM=2-165	02	DFHEIV19
DNM=2-183	02	DFHEIV97
DNM=2-201	02	DFHEIV98
DNM=2-219	02	DFHEIV99
DNM=2-237	01	DFHEIBLK
DNM=2-258	02	EIBTIME
DNM=2-275	02	EIBDATE
DNM=2-292	02	EIBTRNID
DNM=2-310	02	EIBTASKN
DNM=2-331	02	EIBTRMID
DNM=2-349	02	DFHEIGDI
DNM=2-367	02	EIBCPOSN
DNM=2-385	02	EIBCALEN
DNM=2-403	02	EIBAID
DNM=2-419	02	EIBFN
DNM=2-434	02	EIBRCODE
DNM=2-452	02	EIBDS
DNM=2-467	02	EIBREQID
DNM=2-485	02	EIBRSRCE
DNM=3-000	02	EIBSYNC
DNM=3-017	02	EIBFREE
DNM=3-037	02	EIBRECV
DNM=3-054	02	EIBSEND
DNM=3-071	02	EIBATT
DNM=3-087	02	EIBEOC

BASE	DISPL	INTRNL NAME	DEFINITION	USAGE
BL=1	000	DNM=1-068	DS 2C	COMP
BL=1	008	DNM=1-101	DS 2C	COMP
BL=1	010	DNM=1-124	DS 0CL9	GROUP
BL=1	010	DNM=1-156	DS 4C	DISP
BL=1	014	DNM=1-175	DS 5C	DISP-NM
BL=1	020	DNM=1-202	DS 0CL38	GROUP
BL=1	020	DNM=1-235	DS 34C	DISP
BL=1	042	DNM=1-246	DS 4C	COMP
BL=1	048	DNM=1-274	DS 0CL28	GROUP
BL=1	048	DNM=1-295	DS 28C	DISP
BL=1	068	DNM=1-309	DS 0CL106	GROUP
BL=1	068	DNM=1-328	DS 26C	DISP
BL=1	082	DNM=1-345	DS 8C	DISP
BL=1	08A	DNM=1-362	DS 8C	DISP
BL=1	092	DNM=1-379	DS 8C	DISP
BL=1	09A	DNM=1-399	DS 6C	DISP
BL=1	0A0	DNM=1-416	DS 4C	DISP
BL=1	0A4	DNM=1-433	DS 4C	DISP
BL=1	0A8	DNM=1-450	DS 2C	DISP
BL=1	0AA	DNM=1-467	DS 2C	DISP
BL=1	0AC	DNM=1-484	DS 1C	DISP
BL=1	0AD	DNM=2-000	DS 4P	COMP-3
BL=1	0B1	DNM=2-021	DS 2C	COMP
BL=1	0B3	DNM=2-039	DS 2C	COMP
BL=1	0B5	DNM=2-057	DS 2C	COMP
BL=1	0B7	DNM=2-075	DS 2C	COMP
BL=1	0B9	DNM=2-093	DS 2C	COMP
BL=1	0BB	DNM=2-111	DS 4C	COMP
BL=1	0BF	DNM=2-129	DS 4C	DISP
BL=1	0C3	DNM=2-147	DS 4C	DISP
BL=1	0C7	DNM=2-165	DS 4C	DISP
BL=1	0CB	DNM=2-183	DS 4P	COMP-3
BL=1	0CF	DNM=2-201	DS 2C	COMP
BL=1	0C1	DNM=2-219	DS 1C	DISP
BLL=3	000	DNM=2-237	DS 0CL66	GROUP
BLL=3	000	DNM=2-258	DS 4P	COMP-3
BLL=3	004	DNM=2-275	DS 4P	COMP-3
BLL=3	008	DNM=2-292	DS 4C	DISP
BLL=3	00C	DNM=2-310	DS 4P	COMP-3
BLL=3	010	DNM=2-331	DS 4C	DISP
BLL=3	014	DNM=2-349	DS 2C	COMP
BLL=3	016	DNM=2-367	DS 2C	COMP
BLL=3	018	DNM=2-385	DS 2C	COMP
BLL=3	01A	DNM=2-403	DS 1C	DISP
BLL=3	01B	DNM=2-419	DS 2C	DISP
BLL=3	01D	DNM=2-434	DS 6C	DISP
BLL=3	023	DNM=2-452	DS 8C	DISP
BLL=3	02B	DNM=2-467	DS 8C	DISP
BLL=3	033	DNM=2-485	DS 8C	DISP
BLL=3	03B	DNM=3-000	DS 1C	DISP
BLL=3	03C	DNM=3-017	DS 1C	DISP
BLL=3	03D	DNM=3-037	DS 1C	DISP
BLL=3	03E	DNM=3-054	DS 1C	DISP
BLL=3	03F	DNM=3-071	DS 1C	DISP
BLL=3	040	DNM=3-087	DS 1C	DISP

FIGURE 10.1 *(Continued)*

DNM=3-103	02	EIBFMH			BLL=3	041	DNM=3-103	DS 1C	DISP
DNM=3-119	01	DFHCOMMAREA			BLL=4	000	DNM=3-119	DS 1C	DISP
DNM=3-140	01	DFHBLLSLOT1			BLL=5	000	DNM=3-140	DS 1C	DISP
DNM=3-161	01	DFHBLLSLOT2			BLL=6	000	DNM=3-161	DS 1C	DISP

```
          6      EXAMP001       23.32.39       OCT  3,1983

                            MEMORY MAP

                    TGT                     00178

               SAVE AREA                    00178
               SWITCH                       001C0
               TALLY                        001C4
               SORT SAVE                    001C8
               ENTRY-SAVE                   001CC
               SORT CORE SIZE               001D0
               RET CODE                     001D4
               SORT RET                     001D6
               WORKING CELLS                001D8
               SORT FILE SIZE               00308
               SORT MODE SIZE               0030C
               PGT-VN TBL                   00310
               TGT-VN TBL                   00314
               RESERVED                     00318
               LENGTH OF VN TBL             0031C
               LABEL RET                    0031E
               RESERVED                     0031F
               DBG R14 SAVE                 00320
               COBOL INDICATOR              00324
               A(INIT1)                     00328
               DEBUG TABLE PTR              0032C
               SUBCOM PTR                   00330
               SORT-MESSAGE                 00334
               SYSOUT DDNAME                0033C
               RESERVED                     0033D
               COBOL ID                     0033E
               COMPILED POINTER             00340
               COUNT TABLE ADDRESS          00344
               RESERVED                     00348
               DBG R11 SAVE                 00350
               COUNT CHAIN ADDRESS          00354
               PRBL1 CELL PTR               00358
               RESERVED                     0035C
               TA LENGTH                    00361
               RESERVED                     00364
               PCS LIT PTR                  0036C
               DEBUGGING                    00370
               CD FOR INITIAL INPUT         00374
               OVERFLOW CELLS               0037B
               BL CELLS                     0037B
               DECBADR CELLS                0037C
               FIB CELLS                    0037C
               TEMP STORAGE                 00380
               TEMP STORAGE-2               0038B
               TEMP STORAGE-3               0038B
               TEMP STORAGE-4               0038B
               BLL CELLS                    0038B
               VLC CELLS                    003A4
               SBL CELLS                    003A4
               INDEX CELLS                  003A4
               SUBADR CELLS                 003A4
               ONCTL CELLS                  003A4
          7      EXAMP001       23.32.39       OCT  3,1983


               PFMCTL CELLS                 003A4
               PFMSAV CELLS                 003A4
               VN CELLS                     003A4
               SAVE AREA =2                 003A4
               SAVE AREA =3                 003A4
               XSASW CELLS                  003A4
               XSA CELLS                    003A4
               PARAM CELLS                  003A4
               RPTSAV AREA                  003BB
               CHECKPT CTR                  003BB

     LITERAL POOL (HEX)

     003E0 (LIT+0)      001C0204  80000416  00C00000  00000000  000CCCC0  00010402
     003F8 (LIT+24)     C0000400  00001400  00400000  00040430  00040000  00010000
     00410 (LIT+48)     40000004  0E080000  04000010  00

                    PGT                     003C0

               OVERFLOW CELLS               003C0
               VIRTUAL CELLS                003C0
               PROCEDURE NAME CELLS         003D0
               GENERATED NAME CELLS         003DB
               DCB ADDRESS CELLS            003DC
               VNI CELLS                    003DC
               LITERALS         *           003E0
               DISPLAY LITERALS             0041D

     REGISTER ASSIGNMENT

        REG 6   BL =1

     WORKING-STORAGE STARTS AT LOCATION 000A0 FOR A LENGTH OF 000D4.
```

FIGURE 10.1 *(Continued)*

8   EXAMP001   23.32.39   OCT 3,1983

CONDENSED LISTING

105	ENTRY	00041E		106	SERVICE	000436		111	MOVE	000436
111	CALL	000446		112	GO	000470		118	MOVE	00049E
118	CALL	0004AE		122	MOVE	0004E8		127	MOVE	0004F6
127	CALL	000506		133	MOVE	000550		133	CALL	000560
135	GOBACK	00058A		141	MOVE	0005B4		141	MOVE	0005BA
141	CALL	0005CA		147	MOVE	000614		147	CALL	000624

9   EXAMP001   23.32.39   OCT 3,1983

```
*STATISTICS*      SOURCE RECORDS =   148      DATA DIVISION STATEMENTS =    59      PROCEDURE DIVISION STATEMENTS =    17
*OPTIONS IN EFFECT*      SIZE =  131072  BUF =   16384  LINECNT = 57  SPACE1, FLAGW,   SEQ,   SOURCE
*OPTIONS IN EFFECT*      DMAP, NOPMAP,   CLIST,   SUPMAP, NOXREF,   SXREF,   LOAD, NODECK, APOST, NOTPUNC, NOFLOW
*OPTIONS IN EFFECT*      NOTERM, NONUM, NOBATCH, NONAME, COMPILE=01, NOSTATE, NORESIDENT, NODYNAM,  LIB, NOSYNTAX
*OPTIONS IN EFFECT*      NOOPTIMIZE, NOSYMDMP, NOTEST,   VERB,   ZWB, SYST, NOENDJOB, NCLVL
*OPTIONS IN EFFECT*      NOLST , NOFDECK,NOCDECK, LCOL2, L120,   DUMP ,   ADV , NOPRINT,
*OPTIONS IN EFFECT*      NOCOUNT, NOVBSUM, NOVBREF, LANGLVL(2)
```

FIGURE 10.1   *(Continued)*

```
 10        EXAMP001        23.32.39        OCT  3,1983


                                          CROSS-REFERENCE DICTIONARY


DATA NAMES                       DEFN     REFERENCE


BAD-NEWS                         000028   000141
DFHBLLSLOT1                      000103
DFHBLLSLOT2                      000104
DFHCOMMAREA                      000102
DFHEIBLK                         000059
DFHEIGDI                         000071   000112
DFHEIV                           000032
DFHEIVO                          000033   000111   000118   000127   000133   000141   000147
DFHEIV1                          000034
DFHEIV10                         000043
DFHEIV11                         000044   000141
DFHEIV12                         000045
DFHEIV13                         000046
DFHEIV14                         000047
DFHEIV15                         000048
DFHEIV16                         000049
DFHEIV17                         000050
DFHEIV18                         000051
DFHEIV19                         000052
DFHEIV2                          000035
DFHEIV3                          000036
DFHEIV4                          000037
DFHEIV5                          000038
DFHEIV6                          000039
DFHEIV7                          000040
DFHEIV8                          000041
DFHEIV9                          000042
DFHEIV97                         000053
DFHEIV98                         000054   000127   000141
DFHEIV99                         000055   000127   000141
EIBAID                           000077
EIBATT                           000097
EIBCALEN                         000075
EIBCPOSN                         000073
EIBDATE                          000063
EIBDS                            000083
EIBEOC                           000099
EIBFMH                           000101
EIBFN                            000079
EIBFREE                          000091
EIBRCODE                         000081
EIBRECV                          000093
EIBREQID                         000085
EIBRSRCE                         000087
EIBSEND                          000095
EIBSYNC                          000089
EIBTASKN                         000067
EIBTIME                          000061
EIBTRMID                         000069
EIBTRNID                         000065
EXPECTED-MESSAGE-LENGTH          000019   000118


 11        EXAMP001        23.32.39        OCT  3,1983


INPUT-MESSAGE-FIELD              000021   000118
INPUT-MESSAGE-VAR                000023   000122
OUTPUT-LENGTH                    000020   000127
OUTPUT-MESSAGE-FIELD             000024   000127
OUTPUT-MESSAGE-VAR               000027   000122
TRAN-CODE                        000022


 12        EXAMP001        23.32.39        OCT  3,1983


PROCEDURE NAMES                  DEFN     REFERENCE


MAIN-PROG                        000107
SEND-BAD-NEWS                    000136   000112
```

FIGURE 10.1   *(Continued)*

```
F64-LEVEL LINKAGE EDITOR OPTIONS SPECIFIED XREF,LIST,MAP
         DEFAULT OPTION(S) USED -  SIZE=(196608,65536)
IEW0000     INCLUDE SYSLIB(DFHECI)                                    50000000
```

```
                              CROSS REFERENCE TABLE

 CONTROL SECTION                    ENTRY

  NAME      ORIGIN  LENGTH            NAME    LOCATION     NAME  LOCATION     NAME   LOCATION     NAME   LOCATION
 DFHECI       00      18
                                    DFHCBLT      4       DFHEI1     A      DLZEI01     A       DLZEI02     A
                                    DLZEI03      A       DLZEI04    A      DFHAICBA   14
 EXAMP001     18      70A
 ILBOCOMO•   728      16D
                                    ILBOCOM     728
 ILBOSRV •   898      4A4
                                    ILBOSRVO    8A2      ILPOSR5    8A2     ILBOSR3     8A2     ILBOSR     8A2
                                    ILBOSRV1    8A6      ILPOSTP1   8A6     ILBOST      8AA     ILBOSTPO   8AA
 ILBOBEG •   D40      188
                                    ILBOBEGO    D42
 ILBOMSG •   EC8      100
                                    ILBOMSGO    ECA


 LOCATION  REFERS TO SYMBOL  IN CONTROL SECTION        LOCATION  REFERS TO SYMBOL  IN CONTROL SECTION
   3D8          ILBOSRVO        ILBOSRV                  3DC          ILBOSR5         ILBOSRV
   3E0          DFHEI1          DFHECI                   3E4          ILBOSRV1        ILBOSRV
   348          ILBOCOMO        ILBOCOMO                 C24          ILBOCOM         ILBOCOMO
   C38          ILBOSTTO        $UNPE SOLVED(W)          C28          ILBOCMMO        $UNRESOLVED(W)
   C2C          ILBOBEGO        ILBOBEG                  C30          ILBOMSGO        ILBOMSG
   C34          ILBOSNO2        $UNRESOLVED(W)           EE0          ILBOPRMO        $UNRESOLVED(W)

 ENTRY ADDRESS        18

 TOTAL LENGTH       FC8
 ••••EXAMP001  NOW REPLACED IN DATA SET
 AUTHORIZATION CODE IS       0.
```

FIGURE 10.1   *(Continued)*

```
CUSTOMER INFORMATION CONTROL SYSTEM STORAGE DUMP    CODE=ASRA    TASK=EX01        DATE=10/04/83    TIME=01:09:34    PAGE    1

PSW               078D0007   90164512

REGS 14-4         501CD838   C0164730   00000000   00124850          501644A2   001643F0   0012436E

REGS 5-11         FF000000   0012454C   0012482E   0012482C          001646C4   00164020   00164020

TASK CONTROL AREA (USER AREA)             ADDRESS  124100  TO  1244FF       LENGTH  000400

000000    00124000 001B36D4 011D5998 001EF7D8    C0124210 00000000 1400FF00 003100A0    *..  ....M...o..7(..................*    124100
000020    051E4CC8 00000000 00000000 00000000    00000000 00000000 00000000 00000000    *...H...............................*    124120
000040    00000000 00000000 00000000 00000000    00000000 00000000 501CD838 00124960    *.........................Q.....-*    124140
000060    401CD6C6 C1E2D9C1 00000000 00006000    001CE00C 001643F0 001A5560 001CD540    * .OFASRA.......-.........0...-..N *    124160
000080    FE000014 00004000 D7F00000 C1E2D9C1    078D0007 90164512 00000000 00000000    *....... .PO..ASFA..................*    124180
0000A0    501CD838 00164730 00000000 00124850    501644A2 001643F0 00124368 FF000000    *..Q....................s...0..........*    1241A0
0000C0    0012454C 0012482E 0012482C 001646C4    00164020 00164020 04020000 001D5998    *...................D.. ... .........q*    1241C0
0000E0    00124960 8C0000A8 24F40005 00000000    00000000 00000000 00000000 00000000    *...-...y.4..........................*    1241E0
000100    00000000 00000000 D3C9C6D6 E2E3D6D9    42000090 00000000 FF124420 051E4CC8    *..........LIFOSTOR..................H*    124200
000120    00000000 00000000 00000000 00000000    00000000 00000000 00000000 00000000    *...................................*    124220
000140    00000000 00000000 00000000 011D5998    C01D4FEC 00124100 001EF0F0 FE124420    *...................q..+.........00....*    124240
000160    F0002C3 001EE5A4 00000000 00000000    8B000028 00000000 00000000 00000000    *0.KC...u.............................*    124260
000180    00000000 00000000 00000000 00000000    00000000 00000000 8B000028 00000000    *...................................*    124280
0001A0    00000178 00000000 001243D0 00000000    00000000 00000000 00000000 00000000    *...................................*    1242A0
0001C0    40404040 001D5998 00000000 00000000    00000000 00000000 00000000 00000000    *     ...q............................*    1242C0
0001E0    00000000 00000000 00000000 00000000    00000000 00000000 00000000 00000000    *...................................*    1242E0
000200    00000000 00000000 00000000 00000000    00000000 00000000 00124368 8012436C    *...................................*    124300
000220    00124910 A01E5C14 00000000 00000000    00000000 00000000 00000000 00000000    *.......*...........................*    124320
000240    00000000 00000000 00000000 00124880    00000000 00000000 00000004 00000000    *...................................*    124340
000260    00000000 00000000 001243D0 FF000000    00124624 0012454C 00000000 001CE610    *..............................W.*    124360
000280    00124624 401ED1F2 00164020 001CE610    00124368 00164060 00124510 00164068    *.... .J2.. ...k......... -....... .*    124380
0002A0    001CE850 00124000 00164020 001ECFF4    0016443E FE1CC2BC FE1242A0 00124100    *..Y... ... ....4.......B..........*    1243A0
0002C0    82000000 00000000 4CC4C6C6 C5C9C240    0010934C 0083277F C5E7F0F1 0000098C    *b........ DFHEIF ..1..c..EX01....*    1243C0
0002E0    D9C9C3C8 00000009 00007D04 02000000    00000000 00000000 00000000 00000000    *RICH.......'.......................*    1243E0
000300    000000D9 C9C3C840 40404000 00000000    00000000 00000000 00000178 00000000    *...RICH     ......................*    124400
000320    480000B8 00124210 00000000 00000000    00000000 00000000 00000000 00000000    *...................................*    124420
000340    00000000 00000000 00000000 00000000    00000000 00000000 00000000 00000000    *...................................*    124440
000360    00000000 00000000 00000000 FE1244D8    FCC5E9E2 001E536C 01000000 00000000    *.................(..ZS...............*    124460
000380    02000000 C5E7C1D4 D7F0F0F1 011D5998    00000000 00040000 00000000 00000000    *....EXAMP001...q......................*    124480
0003A0    00000000 00000000 00000000 00000000    00000000 000C0000 00000000 001CF80C    *..............................8.*    1244A0
0003C0    00000000 00000000 00000000 011D5998    001F0FD4 00000000 00000000 00000000    *.................q...M..............*    1244C0
0003E0    00000000 00000000 00000000 00000000    00000000 00000000 8A0404F8 00124960    *...........................8...-*    1244E0

TASK CONTROL AREA (SYSTEM AREA)           ADDRESS  124000  TO  1240FF       LENGTH  000100

000000    8A0404F8 00124960 00124A10 00124A10    E000096C 001CF80C 00116180 00000000    *...8...-...............8.../......*    124000
000020    001EFB48 00000000 00000000 00000000    00000000 FE1CC2BC 00000000 00124624    *........................B.........*    124020
000040    00124500 00124270 00000000 00000000    00000000 00000000 00000000 00000000    *...................................*    124040
000060    00000000 0000000C 00000000 C1E2D9C1    00000000 00000000 00000000 7E1242A0    *.............ASFA.............=...*    124060
000080    FE1244D8 00000000 FE124200 FE1244F8    001F0E68 00124210 00000000 00000000    *...Q............8.................*    124080
0000A0    001D5998 00000000 00000000 00000000    C5E7F0F1 00000000 00000000 00000000    *...q.............EX01.............*    1240A0
0000C0    C1E2D9C1 00000000 00124960 00000000    00000000 00000000 00000000 00000000    *ASRA........-.......................*    1240C0
0000E0    00000000 00000000 00000000 00000000    00000000 00000000 00000000 00000000    *...................................*    1240E0
```

FIGURE 10.2 Program check dump produced by sample program EXAMP001.

```
CUSTOMER INFORMATION CONTROL SYSTEM STORAGE DUMP   CODE=ASRA   TASK=EX01      DATE=10/04/83   TIME=01:09:34   PAGE    2

LIFO STACK ENTRY                        ADDRESS  124210  TO  12441F      LENGTH  000210

000000   42000090 00000000 FE124420 051E4CC8   00000000 00000000 00000000 00000000   *..............F...............*   124210
000020   00000000 00000000 00000000 00000000   00000000 00000000 00000000 011D5998   *..............................q*   124230
000040   001D4EB0 00124100 001EF0F0 FE124420   FC00D2C3 001EB5A4 00000000 00000000   *..+.......00....C.KC...u.......*   124250
000060   8B000028 00000000 00000000 00000000   00000000 00000000 00000000 00000000   *..............................*   124270
000080   00000000 00000000 8B000028 00000000   00000178 00000000 001243D0 00000000   *..............................*   124290
0000A0   00000000 00000000 00000000 00000000   40404040 001D5998 00000000 00000000   *...............     ...q.......*   1242B0
0000C0   00000000 00000000 00000000 00000000   00000000 00000000 00000000 00000000   *..............................*   1242D0
0000E0   00000000 00000000 00000000 00000000   00000000 00000000 00000000 00000000   *..............................*   1242F0
000100   00000000 00000000 00124368 8012436C   00124510 A01E5C14 00000000 00000000   *...................*..........*   124310
000120   00000000 00000000 00000000 00000000   00000000 00000000 00000000 0012488C   *..............................*   124330
000140   00000000 00000000 00000004 00000000   00000000 00000000 001243D0 FF000000   *..............................*   124350
000160   00124624 0012454C 00000000 001CE610   00124624 401ED1F2 00164020 001CE610   *.............W..... .J2.. ...W.*   124370
000180   00124368 00164060 00124510 00164068   001CE850 00124000 00164020 001ECFF4   *...... -...... ...Y... ... ....4*   124390
0001A0   0016443E FE1CC2BC FE1242A0 00124100   E2000000 00000000 40C4C6C8 C5C9C240   *......B.........E....... DFHEIB *   1243B0
0001C0   0010934C 0083277F C5E7F0F1 000009FC   D9C9C3C8 00000009 00007D04 02000000   *..1..c..EX01....RICH......'.....*   1243D0
0001E0   00000000 00000000 00000000 00000000   000000D9 C9C3C840 40404000 00000000   *..................RICH     .....*   1243F0
000200   00000000 00000000 00000178 00000000                                          *...............               *   124410

      REGS  0 THRU 15                   ADDRESS  1B3604  TO  1B3643      LENGTH  000040

000000   00000000 00124850 501644A2 001643E0   001243E8 FF000000 0012454C 0012482E   *...........s...(..............*   1B3604
000020   0012482C 001646C4 00164020 00164C20   001643E0 00124624 501644F8 00164730   *.......D.. ... ...........8....*   1B3624

COMMON SYSTEM AREA                      ADDRESS  1EF0F0  TO  1EF7D7      LENGTH  0006E8

000000   00000000 000F4F78 00000000 701B2AA0   00000000 00000000 301D5664 801D5998   *..............................q*   1EF0F0
000020   001D9C48 00115009 0000078F 801DA2CA   801D7E70 801DA112 001D7600 001D8600   *..............s.............f.*   1EF110
000040   001D9600 001EFB46 0010050C 00124100   0109340F 00000000 07D00100 00000000   *..o...........................*   1EF130
000060   00065E7F 00012C00 00A1A558 00000FDF   00003C00 000F5000 001F6CF0 0083277F   *..;.......v...................c..*   1EF150
000080   001F02F0 F0FFFFFE 00000000 001F1F58   00000006 00000000 0018E030 D438C615   *...00.......................M.F.*   1EF170
0000A0   00000000 00116100 00116080 001160C0   001161F0 001F0050 001EFB48 C500FF00   *....../...-...-.../..........E...*   1EF190
0000C0   00190002 000006E8 001FF7D8 00000000   00000000 00000000 00000000 00000000   *.......Y..7(....................*   1EF1B0
0000E0   401EA458 001D2400 001CE00C 001F61E0   001F2A78 001D4FD8 001C92D8 001C4E6C   * .u.........../.........Q..kQ..+.*   1EF1D0
000100   001C6850 00000000 001AC024 001A5BA8   001F0FE8 001E8224 011E3310 001A99A0   *..............$y...Y..E.......r.*   1EF1F0
000120   001CF470 001CC080 001D4EB0 001C8370   001C4D80 0018EE90 00114000 001F0910   *..4........+...c...(....... .....*   1EF210
000140   001CF004 001E36B8 001E7318 001C6518   001C4F24 001C684C 00000000 00000000   *..............e...+............*   1EF230
000160   0F1B1EE0 7FFE0000 00000000 3DAA09F2   000DE590 00000000 00000000 00000000   *...............2..2............*   1EF250
000180   001F0AE8 001F0AEC 00000000 001F0B04   00000000 00000000 00000000 001EF0A0   *...Y.........................0.*   1EF270
0001A0   070E58F0 D19CC7FF 00131B7D 00131C51   0005DC00 000C0000 E6D6D9D2 C1D9C5C1   *...0J......'............WORKAREA*   1EF290
0001C0   0000000C 000C0000 004C007C 00098C00   01055C00 00955C00 0C000C00 0C000C00   *...................*..n*.........*   1EF2B0
0001E0   1C001C00 000C0000 0C000C00 0C00000C   00000C00 000C0000 0C00000C 0C000C00   *..............................*   1EF2D0
000200   00000000 00000000 00000000 00000000   00000000 00000000 00000000 00000000   *..............................*   1EF2F0
000220   LINES TO 0006C0 SAME AS ABOVE                                                                                   1EF310
0006E0   00000000 00000000                                                           *........                      *   1EF7D0

CSA OPTIONAL FEATURE LIST               ADDRESS  1EF7D8  TO  1EFA3B      LENGTH  000264

000000   00000000 00000000 001A5530 001BE8D0   801C181A 00000000 001D06E8 001D0718   *.............Y............Y....*   1EF7D8
000020   001B1D54 001B1720 001E16F4 00000C00   00000000 001D0420 00000000 00000000   *...........4...................*   1EF7F8
000040   00000000 00000000 00000000 00000000   001AD120 00000000 00000000 00000000   *..................J............*   1EF818
000060   801F0A2C 01F4D5D6 00000C00 000CFF04   001FE5C0 0083277F 001C8564 001EF0F0   *.....4NO...........V..c.....e...00*   1EF838
000080   001F0F68 001D1FB0 001BB020 001B5800   00000000 00000000 00000000 00000000   *..............................*   1EF858
```

FIGURE 10.2 *(Continued)*

CUSTOMER INFORMATION CONTROL SYSTEM STORAGE DUMP   CODE=ASRA   TASK=EX01   DATE=10/04/83   TIME=C3:C9:34   PAGE   3

CSA OPTIONAL FEATURE LIST   ADDRESS   1E87LE   TO 1EFA3B   LENGTH 00026C

TRACE TABLE   ADDRESS 1A8FC0   TO 1A99A0   LENGTH 000C80

TRACE HDR   001A97FC   001ARE0C   001A997C   0C1A99A0

TRACE TABLE   ID PEGID REQD TASK FIELD A FIELD I   TRACE TYPE

FC	1E4C4E	CH05	0093	04000000	0015E596	....	ZCP RETN ZISR ISC FREE DETACH
F1	1EB7L8	L404	KC	00124000	00000000	....	SCP FREEMAIN
F1	1E2806	4004	KC	00124000	EAC4C428	....	SCP RELEASED ICA STORAGE
F0	1F329C	4004	TC	44000000	EAC40728	.....Y	KCP WAIT DCI=LIST
F0	1D7E44	4004	TC	0011589C	E015758	....	SCP FREEMAIN
C9	1D28C6	C204	TC	E3C9D4C5	01C73C3F	.....TIME..	SCP FREEMAIN TERMINAL STORAGE
EL	C001C	E204	TC	00015000	84C00778	....	TIMING TRACE CI/07/38.3
F1	1D7AE0	0004	TC	00115000	84C00778	.....Y	SCP GETMAIN-CCND-INIT
C8	1D26DA	0004	TC	00115000	84C007B8	....	SCP ACQUIRED LINE STORAGE
FC	1E329C	4004	TC	44000000	00000000	.....Y	KCP WAIT DCI=LIST
FD	000C4C	0104	TC	0406319E	C0063JCA	....	... REPEAT 00004 TIMES
F0	1D0380	0704	TC	D9C9C3CF	C5E7FCF1	RICHEX01	KCP ATTACH-CONDITIONAL
F1	1EF1L4	EA04	TC	0000040C	F0105598	...0....	SCP GETMAIN-CCND-INIT
C8	1D26DA	0004	TC	00124000	EAC404B8	8	SCP ACQUIRED ICA STORAGE
F0	1E329C	4004	TC	44000000	001D72E8	.....Y	KCP WAIT DCI=LIST
FC	1E4CC8	0503	0094	00000001	0010559B	....	ZCP ZSCP START UP TASK
F2	1E4F2C	0204	0094	C5F7C1F4	L7F0F0F1	EXAMP001	PCP XCIL
F1	1CE19E	8C04	0094	00000364	011F5998	....	SCP GETMAIN
C8	1D26DA	0004	0094	00124500	2C00020C	....	SCP ACQUIRED USER STORAGE
E1	164480	0004	0094	00124540	00000264	....	EIP HANDLE-CONDITION ENTRY
F1	1EE868	CC04	0094	0000007F	011F5998	....	SCP GETMAIN-INIT
C8	1D26DA	0004	0094	00124880	8C000688	....	SCP ACQUIRED USER STORAGE
F1	1EE97E	CC04	0094	00000040	011D5998	....	SCP GETMAIN-INIT
C8	1D26DA	0004	0094	00124910	EC00004B	....	SCP ACQUIRED USER STORAGE
E1	164480	00F4	0094	00000020	00000204	....	EIP HANDLE-CONDITION RESPONSE
E1	164448	0004	0094	0C12454C	C0000402	....	EIP RECEIVE-IC ENTRY
F1	1E5630	4404	0094	00115000	0015559B	....	SCP FREEPIN
C9	1D26D6	0004	0094	00115000	85C00798	....	SCP RELEASED TERMINAL STORAGE

FIGURE 10.2 (Continued)

```
CUSTOMER INFORMATION CONTROL SYSTEM STORAGE DUMP   CODE=ESRA   TASK=EXO1   DATE=10/04/83   TIME=01:09:34   PAGE   4

1A80CC  E1  1644F8  00F4  0094  01000000  C0000002  ........          EIP  RECEIVE-IC RESPONSE
1A80D0  E1  164560  0004  0094  0124054C  C0000404  ........          EIP  SEND-TC INITY
1A80E2C F1  1E54D0  C304  0094  0000025   C5C00038  ........          SCP  GETMAIN-INIT
1A80E40 C8  1D26DA  0004  0094  00115590  C5C00038  ........          SCP  ACQUIRED TERMINAL STORAGE
1A80E60 FC  1E3594  0105  0094  00014000  C0115E90  ........          ZCP  ZARQ APPL FEQ WRITE
1A80E80 FC  164460  00F4  0094  0124054C  C0000F08  ........          ZCP  REIN ZARC APPL FEQ WRITE
1A80E8C F2  1CD3D4  1004  0094  C5E7C1D4  L7E0EF01  *EXAMP001         EIP  SEND-TC RESPONSE
1A80D90 F1  1CE27E  4004  0094  0124054C  C1105598  ........          PCP  RETURN ENTRY
1A80DA0 C9  1D2806  0004  0094  00115000  C0000378  ........          SCP  FREEMAIN
1A80DC0 F0  1CE1C4  8004  0094  00000000  C0000000  ........          SCP  RELEASED USER STORAGE
1FA0DD0 FC  1EB69E  0304  0094  00000000  00000000  ........          KCP  DETACH
1FA0DE0 FC  1E4C48  0004  0094  04000000  C0115598  ........          KCP  DEQALL
1A80E0C C9  1D2806  0004  0094  00120000  C0000000  ........          ZCP  ZISP ISC FREE DETACH
1A80E1C E1  1EE7D8  4A04  KC    00120000  C5C00000  ........          ZCP  RETN ZISI ISC FFEE DETACH
1A80E20 FC  1D2806  0004  KC    00120000  EAC04C F8  ........8         SCP  FREEMAIN ICA STORAGE
1FB0E30 E1  1E329C  4004  7C    00115690  C0115598  ........          SCP  RELEASED ICA STORAGE
1FB0E5C C9  1D2806  0004  7C    00115690  C0115598  ........Y         SCP  WAIT ECI=LIST
1FB0E60 E1  1D7844  4004  7C    00115690  C0115598  ........          SCP  FREEMAIN
1FB0E4C F1  1D7AE0  E404  7C    0000078F  E0105598  ........          SCP  GETMAIN-CCHD-INIT
1A80E50 C8  1D2E2A  0004  7C    00115000  E4C0077E  ........          SCP  ACQUIRE LINE STORAGE
1FB0E60 F0  1E329C  4004  7C    04C00000  C0117288  ........Y         SCP  WAIT DCI=LIST
1FB0E70 FC  00005C  0104  7C    006534A   C0063A4C  *FICHEXO1         ...  REPEAT OC005 TIMES
1FB0E80 F1  1DD380  0704  7C    D9C5C3CB  C5E7F6E1  ........          KCP  ATTACH-CONDITIONAL
1A80E90 E1  1D2E2A  EA04  1C    0000F0    F010559E  ....0...          SCP  GETMAIN-CCND-INIT
1A80EA0 C8  1D2EDA  0004  1C    00120000  EAC04F8   ........8         SCP  ACQUIRED ICA STORAGE
1A80EB0 F0  1F329C  4004  1C    04C00000  C0107128  ........          KCP  WAIT ECI=LIST
1A80ECC FC  1E4CC8  0503  0095  0C000001  C0115598  ........          PCP  ZSUP START OF TASK
1A80EE0 F2  1E4E2C  020A  0095  C5E7C1D4  E7E0EFC1  *EXAMP001         PCP  XCTL
1FB0EF0 F1  1CE19E  8C04  0095  0124054C  C1105598  ........          SCP  GETMAIN
1FB0EFC C8  1D26EA  0004  0095  0124500   C0000204  ........          SCP  ACQUIRED USER STORAGE
1AAFFC0 F1  164480  CC04  0095  0C000078  C1105598  ........          EIP  HANDLE-CONDITION ENTRY
1AAFEC0 E1  1EE868  CC04  0095  0000007E  E0000CCE  ........          SCP  ACQUIRED USER STORAGE
1AAEF2C C8  1D26DA  0004  0095  014FAF60  EC00CCF8  ........          SCP  GETMAIN-INIT
1FB0EF4 F1  1E3E97E CC04  0095  00CC0040  C0115598  ........          SCP  ACQUIRED USER STORAGE
1AAEF50 C8  1D2EDA  0004  0095  00124910  CC000E08  ........          EIP  ACQUIRED USER STORAGE
1AAF8C0 E1  164480  00F4  0095  00000000  C0000264  ........          EIP  HANDLE-CONDITION RESPONSE
1AAFEC0 F1  164498  4004  0095  0124054C  C0000C02  ........          EIP  RECEIVE-IC ENTRY
1AAF7C0 F1  1E5630  4404  0095  00115000  C0115598  ........          SCP  RELEASED TERMINAL STORAGE
1AAF8C0 C9  1D2806  0004  0095  00115000  C5C00378  ........          EIP  RECEIVE-IC RESPONSE
1AAF9C0 E1  124910  01F4  0095  0124054C  C0000404  ........          EIP  SEND-TC ENTRY
1AAFAC0 E1  1E54DC  C304  0095  0000001C  C0115598  ........          SCP  GETMAIN-INIT
1AAFBC0 C8  1D26DA  0004  0095  00115090  C5C00038  ........          SCP  ACQUIRED TERMINAL STORAGE
1A0FDC0 FC  1E5598  0103  0095  0124GC00  C0105590  ........          ZCP  ZARQ APPL FEQ WRITE
1AAFEE0 FC  1E3594  00F4  0095  00014000  C0115E90  ........          ZCP  PEIN ZAMC APPL FEQ WRITE
1AAFFE0 E1  164658  0004  0095  0124054C  00000F08  ........          EIP  SEND-TC RESPONSE
1AF9010 F2  1CD3D4  1004  0095  C5E7C1D4  E7F0F0F1  *EXAMP001         EIP  RETURN ENTRY
1A9020  F1  1CE27E  4004  0095  0124054C  C1105598  ........          PCP  RETURN
1A9030  C9  1D2806  0004  0095  00115000  8C00037E  ........          SCP  FREEMAIN
1A9040  F0  1CE1C4  8004  0095  00000000  C0000000  ........          SCP  RELEASED USER STORAGE
1A9050  FC  1EB69E  0304  0095  00000000  C0000000  ........          KCP  DETACH
1A9060  FC  1E4E48  0805  0095  04000000  C1105598  ........          KCP  DEQALL
1A9070  FC  1E4C48  0805  0095  04000000  C0000000  ........          ZCP  ZISP ISC FREE DETACH
1A9080  F1  1EF7D8  4A04  KC    00120000  C0000000  ........          ZCP  REIN ZISI ISC FFFE DETACH
                                                                      SCP  FREEMAIN
```

FIGURE 10.2 *(Continued)*

CUSTOMER INFORMATION CONTROL SYSTEM STORAGE DUMP   CODE=ASRA   TASK=EX01   DATE=10/04/83   TIME=01:C9:34   PAGE 5

Address								Description
1A9090	C9	1D2806	0004	KC	0U124000	8AC040F8	8	SCP RELEASED ICA STORAGE
1A90A0	F0	1E329C	0004	TC	40000090	01D72C8	.......Y	KCP WAIT DCI=LIST
1A90B0	F1	1D7E44	0004	TC	00115890	601D5C28	....	SCP FREEMAIN
1A90C0	C9	1D2806	0004	TC	000057BF	601D5C28	....	SCP RELEASED TERMINAL STORAGE
1A90D0	C8	1D2AE0	E404	TC	0000578B	601D0758	....	SCP GETMAIN-COND-INIT
1A90E0	C8	1E329C	4004	TC	40000090	80100758	.......Y	SCP ACQUIRED LINE STORAGE
1A90F0	FD	0000C8	0104	TC	0U06334A	00063718	....	KCP WAIT DCI=LIST
1A9100	FD	1DD380	0704	TC	D9C9C3C8	C5E7F0F1	HICHEX01	KCP REPEAT 00006 TIMES
1A9110	F1	1EE1D4	EA04	TC	000004F0	801D5998	....	KCP ATTACH-CONDITIONAL
1A9120	C8	1D26DA	0004	TC	00124000	FA040F8	0	SCP GETMAIN-COND-INIT
1A913C	F0	1E329C	4004	TC	40000090	01D72E8	.......Y	SCP ACQUIRED ICA STORAGE
1A9140	FC	1E4CC8	0503	0096	00000001	001D5998	....	KCP WAIT DCI=LIST
1A9160	F2	1E4F2C	0204	0096	C5E7FC1D4	D7F0F0F1	EXAMP001	PCP ZSUP START UP TASK
1A916C	F1	1CEE9E	8C04	0096	00000364	01D5998	....	PCP XCTL
1A9170	C8	1D26DA	000A	0096	00124500	CC000378	....	SCP GETMAIN
1A918C	F1	164420	000A	0096	00124540	00000204	....	SCP ACQUIRED USER STORAGE
1A9190	F1	1EE68	CC0A	0096	0000007F	01105998	....	EIP HANDLE-CONDITION ENTRY
1A91A0	C8	1D26DA	000A	0096	00124880	EC000E8	....	SCP GETMAIN-INIT
1A91B0	F1	1EE97E	CC0A	0096	00000040	01105998	....	SCP ACQUIRED USER STORAGE
1A91C0	C8	1D26DA	000A	0096	00124910	8C00008	....	EIP ACQUIRED USER STORAGE
1A91D0	E1	164460	000A	0096	00000000	C0000204	....	EIP HANDLE-CONDITION RESPONSE
1A91E0	E1	1644B8	000A	0096	00124540	C00000C2	....	EIP RECEIVE-TC ENTRY
1A91F0	F1	1E5E30	440A	0096	00115000	001D5998	....	SCP FREEMAIN
1A9200	C9	1D2806	000A	0096	00115000	85C0007B	....	SCP RELEASED TERMINAL STORAGE
1A9210	E1	1644B8	000A	0096	00000000	85C0007B	....	EIP RECEIVE-TC RESPONSE
1A9220	E1	164460	000A	0096	00124540	00000002	....	EIP SEND-TC ENTRY
1A9230	C8	1D26DA	C304	0096	00000025	C01151598	....	SCP GETMAIN-INIT
1A924C	E1	1E54D0	C304	0096	00C0C025	00115998	....	SCP ACQUIRED TERMINAL STORAGE
1A9250	C8	1D2EDA	000A	0096	00115890	85C00038	....	ZCP ZARQ APPL REQ WRITE
1A926C	FC	1E5598	0103	0096	00124000	00105998	....	ZCP RETN ZPK APPL REQ WRITE
1A9270	C8	1E354A	0105	0096	00124000	00115850	....	EIP SEND-TC RESPONSE
1A9280	E1	164560	000A	0096	00000000	00000404	....	EIP RETURN ENTRY
1A9290	E1	16459A	000A	0096	00124540	C0000FC8	....	PCP RETURN
1A92A0	F2	1CD3D4	000A	0096	C5E7FC1C4	D7F0F0F1	EXAMP001	SCP FREEMAIN
1A92B0	F0	1CE27E	000A	0096	00124540	01105998	....	SCP RELEASED USER STORAGE
1A92C0	C9	1D2806	000A	0096	00124540	8CC00378	....	KCP DETACH
1A92D0	F0	1CE1C4	800A	0096	00000000	00000000	....	KCP DEQALL
1A92E0	F0	1EB69E	0304	0096	00000000	00000C00	....	TIMING TRACE 01/07/55.3
1A9300	FD	00001C	0204	0096	E3C9D4C5	C1C7553F	TIME...	ZCP ZISF FREE DETACH
1A9310	FC	1EE6F2	0E03	0096	04000000	001D5998	....	ZCP RETN ZISF ISC FREE DETACH
1A9320	FC	1EDC48	0B05	0096	04000000	001D5998	....	SCP FREEMAIN
1A932C	F1	1EP7D8	4A04	KC	00124000	FA040F8	8	SCP RELEASED ICA STORAGE
1A933C	C9	1D2806	000A	KC	00124000	01D72E8	.......Y	KCP WAIT DCI=LIST
1A934C	F0	1E329C	4004	TC	40000090	001D72E8	.......Y	SCP FREEMAIN
1A935C	F1	1D7E44	4004	TC	00115890	801D5998	....	SCP FREEMAIN
1A9360	C9	1D2806	0004	TC	00115890	85C00038	....	SCP RELEASED TERMINAL STORAGE
1A937C	F1	1D7AE0	E404	TC	00000078F	8400079B	....	SCP GETMAIN-COND-INIT
1A938C	C8	1D26DA	0004	TC	00115000	8400079B	....	SCP ACQUIRED LINE STORAGE
1A939C	F0	1E329C	4004	TC	40000090	001D72E8	.......Y	KCP WAIT DCI=LIST
1P93A0	FD	0000BC	0104	TC	00063A53	C0065F51	....	KCP REPEAT 00068 TIMES
1F93C0	F0	1DD380	0704	TC	D9C9C3C8	C5E7F0F1	HICHEX01	KCP ATTACH-CONDITIONAL
1F93CC	C8	1EB1D4	EA04	TC	000004F0	801D5998	....	SCP GETMAIN-COND-INIT
1A93EC	C8	1D26DA	0004	TC	00124000	FA040F8	8	SCP ACQUIRED ICA STORAGE
1A93FC	F0	1E329C	4004	TC	40000090	001D72E8	.......Y	KCP WAIT DCI=LIST
1A94F00	FC	1E4CC6	0503	0097	00000001	001C5998	....	ZCP ZSUP START UP TASK
1A94F0	F2	1F4F2C	0204	0097	C5E7C1D4	D7F0F0F1	EXAMP001	PCP XCTL
1A9410	F1	1CEE9E	8C04	0097	00C00364	01105998	....	SCP GETMAIN

FIGURE 10.2 (Continued)

```
CUSTOMER INFORMATION CONTROL SYSTEM STORAGE DUMP   CODE=ASRA   TASK=EXO1                    DATE=10/04/83   TIME=01:05:34   PAGE 6

1A9420  C8  1D26DA  0004  0097  00124500  8C00027B  ......     SCP ACQUIRED USER STORAGE
1A943C  E1  164480  0004  0097  00124540  C0000034  ......     EIP HANDLE-CONDITION ENTRY
1F944C  F1  1FE868  CC04  0097  0000007E  C1105C66  ......     SCP GETMAIN-INIT
1A945C  C8  1D26DA  0004  0097  00124880  8C000C68  ......     SCP ACQUIRED USER STORAGE
1A946C  F1  1FE97E  CC04  0097  00000040  01105998  .-...      SCP GETMAIN-INIT
1A947C  C8  1D26DA  00F4  0097  00124910  EC000C68  ......     SCP ACQUIRED USER STORAGE
1A948C  E1  164480  0004  0097  001245AC  C00002C4  ......     EIP HANDLE-CONDITION RESPONSE
1F949C  E1  164448  00F4  0097  00124500  00000042  ......     EIP RECEIVE-TC ENTRY
1A94AC  C9  1D2806  0004  C097  00115000  00015998  ......     SCP FREEMAIN
1F94EC  E1  164448  00F4  0097  00115000  85005778  ......     SCP RELEASED TERMINAL STORAGE
1A94DC  E1  164560  0004  0097  0000000C  C0C00404  ......     EIP RECEIVE-TC RESPONSE
1A94F0  F1  1E54D0  C304  0097  0x0C0025  C01D5758  ......     EIP SEND-TC ENTRY
1A94FC  FC  1E5598  0105  0097  00115890  C01D5998  ......     SCP GETMAIN-INIT
1A9500  FC  1F354A  0105  0097  00C14000  00015840  ......     SCP ACQUIRED TERMINAL STORAGE
1A9510  E1  164560  00F4  0097  0000000C  C00156C0  ......     ZCP ZARQ APPL REQ WRITE
1A952C  E1  16A59A  0004  0097  00124540  C00004C4  ......     ZCP REIN ZARQ APPL REQ WRITE
1A9530  F2  1CD3D4  1004  0097  C5E7C1E4  L70F0F01  EXAMPOO1   EIP SEND-TC RESPONSE
1P9540  F1  1CE27E  4004  0097  00124500  C11D5998  ......     EIP RETURN ENTRY
1A9550  C9  1D2806  0004  0097  00124500  8C000378  ......     PCP RETURN
1A9560  F0  1CE1C4  8004  0097  00C00000  CC000000  ......     SCP FREEMAIN
1F9570  F0  1D26DA  0304  0097  00115000  CC0000C0  ......     SCP RELEASED USER STORAGE
1A958C  F1  1FE65E  0304  0097  00C00000  00000000  ......     KCP DETACH
1A9590  FD  00001C  0204  0097  E3C90AC5  C1C926.6  TIME..     KCP DEQALL
1A959C  FC  1E8EF2  0E03  0097  0x0C0000  C11D5998  ......     TIMING TRACE  C1/09/26.6
1A959C  FC  1E4C46  0E05  0097  04CC0000  C01D5998  ......     ZCP ZISE ISC FREE DETACH
1A95DC  F1  1EE7E8  4A04  KC    00124000  00C00000  ......     ZCP REIN ZISE ISC FREE DETACH
1A95DC  C9  1D329C  4004  1C    0C124000  8C01728.6  ......-8  SCP FREEMAIN
1A95EC  F1  1D7E44  4004  1C    40000000  C01728.6  ......     SCP RELEASED ICA STORAGE
1A95E0  C9  1D2806  0004  1C    00115890  E01155.98 ......-Y   KCP WAIT DCI=LIST
1A95E0  F1  1C28C6  000A  1C    00115540  E5000034  ......     SCP FREEMAIN
1A9610  F1  1D7AE0  E404  1C    000C07FF  EC1155.98 ......     SCP RELEASED TERMINAL STORAGE
1A9620  C8  1D26DA  0004  1C    00115000  E4C0079-B ......     SCP GETMAIN-CCAD-INIT
1A963C  FC  1E329C  4C04  1C    40000000  C01728.6  ......-Y   SCP ACQUIRED LINE STORAGE
1A964C  FL  00007C  0104  1C    0065C0C1  0065161   ......     KCP WAIT DCI=LIST
1A965C  F1  1DD380  0704  1C    L9C5C3C8  C5E7F0F1  *ICHEXO1   ... REPEAT 00007 TIMES
1A966C  F1  1F91D4  EA04  1C    00C004FC  F01D5998  .-..-0     KCP ATTACH-CONDITIONAL
1A9670  C8  1D2EDA  0004  1C    00124000  EA040AFB  ......     SCP GETMAIN-CCAD-INIT
1A9680  F0  1F329C  4004  1C    00124000  8C01728.6 ......-8   SCP ACQUIRED ICA STORAGE
1A969C  FC  1F4CC8  0503  0096  0000C001  C01D5998  ......     KCP WAIT DCI=LIST
1A96AC  F2  1F4F2C  0204  0096  C5E7C1E4  L710F0F1  EXAMPOO1   ZCP 2SUP START UP TASK
1A96BC  F1  1CEE9E  8C04  0098  00000364  C11D5998  ......     PCP XCTL
1A96CC  C8  1D26CA  0004  0098  00124500  CC000376  ......     SCP GETMAIN
1A96DC  E1  164480  0004  0098  00124SAC  C0000C2C  ......     SCP ACQUIRED USER STORAGE
1A96FC  F1  1FE868  CC04  0098  0000007F  C11D5998  ......     EIP HANDLE-CONDITION ENTRY
1A96F0  F1  1D26CA  0004  0098  00124880  8C00C0F8  ......     SCP GETMAIN-INIT
1A9700  F1  1EE97E  CC04  0098  00000040  01105998  ......     SCP ACQUIRED USER STORAGE
1A9710  C8  1D26CA  00F4  0006  00124910  EC000C68  ......     SCP GETMAIN-INIT
1A9720  E1  164480  0004  0098  00124510  CC000C46  ......     SCP ACQUIRED USER STORAGE
1A9730  E1  164448  00F4  0098  001245AC  C000C4C2  ......     EIP HANDLE-CONDITION RESPONSE
1A9740  E1  164448  0004  0098  00124540  00000042  ......     EIP RECEIVE-IC ENTRY
1A9750  C9  1D2806  0004  0096  00115000  CC015998  ......     SCP FREEMAIN
1A9760  C9  1D26C6  0004  0098  00115000  85C007-8  PSRA.      SCP RELEASED TERMINAL STORAGE
1A9770  F2  1E21A8  6004  0098  C1E2D9C1  0000000C  ......     EIP RECEIVE-TC RESPONSE
1A97BC  F1  1DC6C4  CC04  0098  00000098  C000CCFB  ......     PCP ABEND
1A97E0  C8  1D26DA  0004  0098  0C14960  CC00CFB6  ......     SCP GETMAIN-INIT
1A97A0  F4  1CL83E  FE04  0098  00000000  C1E2D9C1  ...ASRA    SCP ACQUIRED USER STORAGE
                                                              DCP TRANSACTION.
```

FIGURE 10.2 (Continued)

```
CUSTOMER INTEGRATION CONTROL SYSTEM STORAGE DUMP   CODE=ASRA   TASK=EX01          DATE=10/08/83   TIME=09:05:34   PAGE   7

1F97TC          PC 1B34EC 4004 0098 8CCCOOC 0013CF0  .........  KCP WAIT ECI=SINGLE

TRANSACTION STORAGE -USER      ADDRESS  124560  TO  124A0F          LENGTH  0000EC

000000  8CCCC0A8 00124910 00000000 00001840          C1C3C240 80600000 C1E2D9C1   .........  IFHTAPF ..-ASRA
000020  C5E7C1D4 D7F0F0F1 00000000 00000000          CLC00CC0 01000000 00000CC0   .FRAMTOO1.......*
000040  00000C00 00000000 D7E2E661 D9C5C7E2          07E10007 9C164512 00000000   *.........ISI/RECS.*
000060  50164412 0016443F0 00124368A FF000000        0012459C 0012482E 0016464C4   *......s....O....
000080  00164020 0016440208 0012A100 0011E0F0        00124B2C 0012482C 0016464C4   *.......h....CE..b*
0000A0  00000000 00000000 8C0000A8 00124910          00164730 00000000 00000CC0   *..............).*

TRANSACTION STORAGE -USER      ADDRESS  124910  TO  12495F          LENGTH  000050

000000  8C000048 00124880 50164460 0011E03CC          CC000000 CC124850 A0ICE91E 0016ACC8   *..........I.......Z..*
000020  0012423E FFCC0000 0012459C 00124426          0012482C 002b46CC4 00164020 0016ACC0   *...........i......*
000040  0016430 0012A6624 8C000048 00124880          ...........

TRANSACTION STORAGE -USER      ADDRESS  124960  TO  12490F          LENGTH  00009C

000000  8C000088 00124560 0012A8CF 007FU2C0          CC000000 00000000 00000000 00000CC0   *.......h......*
000020  00000000 01CCC000 00000000 00000000          00000000 00000000 49100412 00000CC0   *............*
000040  00000CC0 00000000 00000000 00000000          0000C000 00000112 49100412 00000CC0   *............*
000060  00000CC0 0000FF00 8C00006A 0012A56C          CC000000 CC000000 00000000 00000CC0   *............*

TRANSACTION STORAGE -USER      ADDRESS  124560  TO  12467F          LENGTH  C00380

000000  8C0CC278 00124000 00000000 00000000          5C16470C A0ICE91E A0ICE91E 0016ACC8   *.........Z.....*
000020  0016445A 50164466 01640FC 0016443F0          0016A830 0016A6C4 0016A6C4 0016A020   *.....O.....c..(..*
000040  0C1643F0 0016415F 0C1CE8A0 000900000        C022C000 CC225000 CC9E5C5 C4A00C2b6   *........q....EXO1*
000060  5C1CF450 0012459C ENE7FCF0 40D58DA4         40E3C5C3 40E7F0F1 C5E7F0F1 C4A00C2b6   *.......q..... NTPEFL RECEIVED HY*
000080  0012459C ENE7FCFE F1AGE6C1 6200000         40E9C5C3 04C905C1 D3400915 14C00040   *....EXAMPOOL WAS ...TFFMINAL IN*
0000A0  D7A41340 EbC1E24C 4CA0404C 4CCC000         0402C000 04000000 14C0C040   *FUT WAS TOC LONC....*
```

FIGURE 10.2 (Continued)

CUSTOMER INFORMATION CONTROL SYSTEM STORAGE DUMP   CODE=A5RA   TASK=EX01   DATE=10/04/83   TIME=01:09:34   PAGE   8

FIGURE 10.2 *(Continued)*

```
CUSTOMER INFORMATION CONTROL SYSTEM STORAGE DUMP    CODE=ASRA    TASK=EX01         DATE=10/04/83    TIME=01:09:34    PAGE     9

PROGRAM STORAGE                            ADDRESS  1640C8   TO   164FCF       LENGTH   000FC8

0005A0    F08058F0 D1E0900E FC4805F0 9110D046    47E0F00E 58F0C00C 07FF48F0 D05C58E0    *0..0J...0..0j.....0..0......0.*..*    1645A8
0005C0    D004980C D01458E0 D00C07FE D2016CE1    C020D20E 6068C045 92406077 D2096078    *..q..........K.-...K.-...k -.K.-.*    1645C8
0005E0    60774110 60685010 D22C4110 60D15010    D2304110 60CF5010 D2344110 60465010    *-...-...K...-J..K...-...K...-...*    1645E8
000600    D2384110 60B15010 D23C9660 D23C4110    D22C9640 D04958F0 C00805EF 94BFD049    *K...-...K.o.K...K.o ...0....m...*    164608
000620    40F0D05C 58F0D1B8 50D0F060 D2086068    C0549240 6071D20F 60726071 41106068    * 0.*.0J...0.K.-...k -.K.-.-...-.*    164628
000640    5010D22C 9680D22C 4110D22C 9640D049    58F0C008 05EF94BF D04940F0 D05C58F0    *..K.o.K...K.o ...0....m... 0.*.0*    164648
000660    D1B850D0 F0804110 02074100 00806900    C0181610 0A0D58F0 C01807FF 50D05008    *J...0..........i........0........*    164668
000680    5050D004 50E0D054 9120D048 47E0F02F    5820D1B8 9140D049 47E0F02E 96042000    *........j.....0...J.j ....0.o....*    164688
0006A0    58F02038 41F0E004 07FF94EF DC4858E0    C00005FF 12000789 9610D048 05F09120    *.0...00...m....0........io....0j.*    1646A8
0006C0    D04847E0 F0165800 E048982D B0505BE0    D05407FE 9620D048 41600004 4110C010    *....0.....q.........o....-......*    1646C8
0006E0    4170C01C 06700550 58401000 1E4B5040    10008716 50004180 D2004160 0004417C    *......... ..... ..g.....K..-.....*    1646E8
000700    D2070510 58008000 12004780 10101F0B    50008000 87861000 5860D200 58E0D054    *K...................gf...-K......*    164708
000720    07FE0000 00000000 80000000 00164196    C9D3C2D6 D5E3D9F0 00000000 00000000    *................oILBONTR0........*    164728
000740    00000000 00000000 00000000 00000000    00000000 00000000 00000000 00000000    *................................*    164748
000760    001648AA 00000000 00000000 00000000    00000000 00000000 00000000 00000000    *................................*    164768
000780    00000000 00000000 00000000 00000000    00000000 00000000 00000000 00000000    *................................*    164788
0007A0    00000000 00000000 00124624 00000000    00000000 00000000 00000000 00000000    *................................*    1647A8
0007C0    00000000 00000000 40404040 40404040    00000000 00000000 00000000 00000000    *........        ................*    1647C8
0007E0    00000000 00000000 00000000 00000000    00000000 F0F0F0F0 F0F0F0F0 00000000    *....................00000000....*    1647E8
000800    00000000 00000000 00000000 00000000    00000000 00000000 00000000 00000000    *................................*    164808
000820    00000000 00000000 00000000 0000C9D3    C2D6C3D6 D4400000 F5F7F4F0 60D3D4F1    *..............ILBOCOM ..5740-LM1*    164828
000840    404DC35D 40C3D6D7 E8D9C9C7 C8E340C9    C2D440C3 D6D9D740 F1F9F7F2 6B40F1F9    * (C) COPYRIGHT IBM CORP 1972, 19*    164848
000860    F7F640D3 C9C3C5D5 E2C5C440 D4C1E3C5    D9C9C1D3 406040D7 D9D6C7D9 C1D440D7    *76 LICENSED MATERIAL - PROGRAM P*    164868
000880    D9D6D7C5 D9E3E840 D6C640C9 C2D46BF2    F4F0F3F7 F7000000 0000000C 00164CE8    *ROPERTY OF IBM,240377...........*    164888
0008A0    000047F0 F00C47F0 F0C447F0 F08450F0    F3CE90E7 F3A6185F D50353CE 53AA4760    *...00..00D.00d.03..X3w..N.......*    1648A8
0008C0    503C58E0 53A6D503 E0005054 4780503C    48E0539E D503E000 505C4770 509858 2C    *.....wN..............N....*...q..*    1648C8
0008E0    53665840 538258F0 536A056F D50353CE    53AA4760 50605010 D1B847F0 506C58F0    *.f. .b.0....N.........-..J..0...0*    1648E8
000900    C0009140 D04A4780 506C9601 10005910    53624780 507C5010 53829601 53A21604    *..j ......o.......b.......bo..s..*    164908
000920    98EF53A6 9827F3B6 5810F382 07FE50F0    F3C64EF0 F39847F0 F0105810 53821211    *q..wq.3...3b...03E.03q.00....b..*    164928
000940    477050BC 410050AA 47F050B2 C9D3C2D6    C3D6D4FC 1B110A08 18105010 53829680    *.........0..ILBOCOM0.........bo.*    164948
000960    100050D0 100447F0 506C90EC F3CE184F    5820D1E8 91402002 47104148 91042000    *........0....3.....J.j ......j...*    164968
000980    47E0414C 47F04148 58F0438A 12FF4780    40F2056F 47F0411A 410040FA 47F04102    *.....0...0...... 2...0.... ..0..*    164988
0009A0    C9D3C2D6 D4E2C7F0 41100000 0A0618F0    056F4500 4118C9D3 C2D6D4E2 C7F00A09    *ILBOMSG0........0......ILBOMSG0..*    1649A8
0009C0    12554770 412698EC 43CE07FE 58E02038    4FE0439C 48EE0000 40E0D05C 12EE07E8    *.......q................... ..*....*    1649C8
0009E0    47F04142 80000127 5810413E 0A0D4580    40E29180 20024780 418258E0 20384EE0    *.0............... Sj......b.......*    1649E8
000A00    439C48EE 000040E0 D05C12EE 4740413A    58F0202C 12FF4780 4182943E 200241FF    *...... ..*... ...0.......bm.....*    164A08
000A20    001C05EF 47F041A0 58F0206C 12FF4780    41A0189D 41D0D0A8 50D90008 509D0004    *.....0...0..............y.R......*    164A28
000A40    1B1105EF 18D9D502 4396205D 476041C6    4110205C 18744580 4324D502 43963065    *.....RN..o.)...F...*.......N..o..*    164A48
000A60    478041C6 41130064 47E041B0 D5024396    20594760 41DA4110 20581874 45804324    *...F.....0..N..o..................*    164A68
000A80    D7072058 2058D502 43962055 47804236    58F0438E 12FF4780 41FA05EF 47F04220    *P.....N..o.......(..............0..*    164A88
000AA0    41004202 47F0420A C9D3C2D6 E2D5C4F2    1B110A08 18F005EF 4500421E C9D3C2D6    *.....0..ILBOSND2.....0......ILBO*    164AA8
000AC0    E2D5C4F2 0A099140 20024780 422C4580    40E24110 20541B77 45804324 D5024396    *SND2..j ........ S...........N..o*    164AC8
000AE0    20514780 428A9108 20504780 42564500    4254C9D3 C2D6D8E2 E2F00A09 D5024396    *......j............ILBOQSS0..N..o*    164AE8
000B00    20654780 426E4500 426CC9C5 C4D8C2F1    40400A09 41102050 1B774580 4324D502    *.e.........IEDQB1  .............N.*    164B08
000B20    43963075 4780428A 41130074 47F04274    D5024396 20614780 42D65850 20604135    *.o.............0..N..o./...0...-..*    164B28
000B40    00909110 30304780 42B25035 02144115    021418 74 45804324 583502D8 12334780    *..j.............................Q....*    164B48
000B60    42D64133 05A09110 30304780 42D65035    021492E0 52144115 02140A14 947F2000    *.0....j.......0.....k..........m...*    164B68
000B80    9101439E 478042EC D703437E 437E94FE    439E9101 200047E0 436458F0 439212FF    *j........P..=.=m...j.........0.k..*    164B88
000BA0    077F4500 4308C9D3 C2D6E2E3 E3F00A09    41004312 47F0431A C9D3C2D6 E2E3E3F0    *......ILBOSTT0........0..ILBOSTT0*    164BA8
000BC0    41100000 0A0818F0 07FF5831 00009110    303007E8 92801000 0A141277 07881813    *........0......j.....hk.........h..*    164BC8
000BE0    58F01014 96011017 1EEE43E0 F0054CE0    F0064100 E0089140 F00447E0 435C4100    *.0..o.........0....0.......j 0....*..*    164BE8
000C00    E0104110 F0000A0A 07F848F0 D05C58D0    200458D0 D00458E0 D00C980C D01407FE    *....0.....8.0.*.............q.......*    164C08
000C20    40400000 00164730 00000000 00164D4A    00164ED2 00000000 00000000 00000000    *   ............(...+K............*    164C28
000C40    00060008 00E0C27C 501646BC 001648AA    001CE61C 00124368 00164730 00124510    *......B.............W.............*    164C48
000C60    00164068 00124378 00124000 00164020    00164EAA A0A41813 4500C3E0 0C000C00    *.. ....... ... .......u.....C.....*    164C68
```

FIGURE 10.2 *(Continued)*

CUSTOMER INFORMATION CONTROL SYSTEM STORAGE DUMP   CODE=ASRA   TASK=EX01   DATE=10/04/83   TIME=01:05:34   PAGE   10

PROGRAM STORAGE   ADDRESS   164008   TO   164FCF   LENGTH   000FC8

```
000C80   00000268   58F10054   05FF07F7   05FF07F7   D203C3FC   ...h.1......7K.C....     164C88
000CA0   C4C6D9F1   FF020000   50310700   0A510F7F   D203C3FC   *DFM1.........7...u.     164CA8
000CC0   00000268   00000289   58F10054   9561C27D   47770470   *...h....l.l....7..Un.P. 164CC8
000CE0   47E0C458   18130700   4500C450   04000001   95C0C27C   *..D......D......B.      164CE8
000D00   00000000   00000000   00000000   00000000   00000000   *.......o.......h.1...O  164CE8
000D20   00000000   C9D3C2D6   E2E9E540   E5E2E4D5   E2E2E9C5   *....ILBOSHV VSFEL2.3UF13056 164D08
000D40   000047F0   F004167F   9102D049   47807024   70249204   *....0...j.......J.N.     164D28
000D60   D1C79A7F   D1C51834   12444770   70484110   D4F1411C   *JGm.JE..j........k.      164D48
000D80   00000A08   5000D1B6   18305050   303E5020   D4F14110   *..00...J.........O..ILHOCOMO. 164D68
000DA0   707A4100   706847F0   7C70C9D3   C2D6C3D4   91E03CC0   *....J......O..ILBOCMC.   164D88
000DC0   47107122   9E803000   414C0001   50D03CC4   70A4D5E3   *....o....ILBOCMC....j... 164DA8
000DE0   714A101C   47707118   9103D007   47707118   101F477C   *.........j...........WN. 164DC8
000E00   71184920   20004780   71189101   20034770   714247LC   *.........j......j...     164DE8
000E20   71B04920   711858F0   711858F0   713E12FF   C9D3C2D6   *......j......ILBO        1E4E08
000E40   D7E9D4F0   1B11CA08   18F005EF   45007116   713801LC   *PRM0....0.....ILBO       164E28
000E60   47F07138   12444770   713B4500   713BC903   D9C5C54C   *.0......JLFCCOMO....6.   164E48
000E80   00000000   0000C064   C1D5E2F4   E3C8C5C2   E3C2D6D3   *.0......JLFCCOMO....6.   164E68
000EA0   C6D6D940   C3D4E24C   E3D4C0C3   D6C2D6D3   C9E3C5C7   *FOR CMS TO COFOLI1FOBEG  164EA6
000EC0   E4E7F1F3   F4F7E740   0000047F0   F004117F   92400D10E *UP13477...00...j.....eK.J.K.J.e 164EC8
000EE0   D10FC224   D10E709F   5830D1B0   D207L133   D27401Ot   *.J.K.J...J.K.J..C....N.  164EE8
000F00   D0007D0B   4770704C   5830D1B0   D207114B   D6E1J54t   *.J.K.J...0..K.....Jm.    164EF08
000F20   200047F0   70709104   20024784   7070940FB  D10E2C23  *...0...j...K......J.K.   164F28
000F40   10007D0E   D203107E   70E2D201   001C9101   705FA1E5  *...0...j.J.0.....J.K.K.  164F48
000F60   943A2002   07F64040   C9D2C6F9   F9F2C940   C54C0C3C1 *m...6.IKF992]  RECURSIVE CA* 164F68
000F80   D3F34CE3   D640D4D6   C4E4D3C5   40740C6D9  D6E36CC3  *LL TO MODULE EFCM MODULE (NOT C* 164FA8
000FA0   D6C2C6D3   5D003080   007E80C0   02004020   E5D209C5  *OBOL)..=...  .ILBOMSG VSHEL2.3* 164FA8
000FC0   E4E7F1F3   F0F5F640                                   *UP13056                  164FC8
```

END OF CICS/VS STORAGE DUMP

FIGURE 10.2 (Continued)

7. Add the result from part 6 to the beginning of the first address range that you found in part 1. This tells you where your object code was actually relocated when it was loaded into the CICS region or partition. In this case, the result is hex 164020.

8. Subtract the load address in part 7 from the PSW address in part 2. This result is the offset of the instruction that ABENDed (or the one following it), which in this case is hex 0004F2.

9. Look up the instruction offset from part 8 in the condensed listing in your CICS compile listing. Find the highest instruction address that is less than or equal to the offset address from part 8. Then, look up the instruction in the source code listing. In this case, it is line 122: MOVE 0004E8. The source listing indicates MOVE INPUT-MESSAGE-VAR TO OUTPUT- MESSAGE-VAR. Looking at the instruction will often give you a clue to the problem, which in this case is conflicting data types. The input variable will contain whatever was entered by the user, if anything. Nonnumeric or wrong-length user input will crash the program when it is moved to the output variable.

10. If you are still unsure why an instruction went bad, check the names of the data areas used in the instruction. Look them up in the data division map in your compile listing and write down the base locators (BLs or BLLs) and displacements for each of them.

11. After the end of the data division map, you should find a few printed lines in which the base locators are equated to various registers. Find out which registers go with the base locators from part 10.

12. Look at the first page of your dump listing again. You should see a table of the register values at ABEND. Find the registers that were used as base locators for the operands for the offending instruction.

13. Add the displacements from part 10 to the base locator values from part 12 to get the actual locations of the operands.

14. Look up the addresses from part 13 in the address column on the right-hand side of the dump listing. Working storage operands should be in one of the blocks labeled TRANSACTION STORAGE. The field contents should tell you why the instruction failed.

10.1.3 ABEND Codes for CICS Application Programs

What if the problem causing the dump was not a program check (ABEND ASRA)? Four-character-transaction ABEND codes generated by the CICS system, as well as longer diagnostic codes, may be found in the IBM-supplied manual, CICS Messages and Codes. Be sure to get the manual that corresponds with the version of CICS that you are using.

```
[TABLES]
[DCT]
[FCT]
[PCT]
[PPT]
[SIT]
[TCT]
END-EXEC.
```

You should already be familiar with the DUMPCODE(name) option, which allows you to specify a code that uniquely identifies the dump listing. Avoid choosing dump codes beginning with A. If you are executing several DUMP commands in your task, you can use different dump codes to indicate which DUMP command produced which dump listing.

The other options allow you to choose how much information you want to dump. Specifying COMPLETE causes everything to come out: both CICS table contents and main storage related to your task. Ordinarily, you should specify a COMPLETE dump only once in a task, if at all, because CICS table contents do not change often enough to warrant dumping them repeatedly.

If you specify FROM(data-area) and LENGTH(data-value), you can get a dump of part of the contents of your program's working storage or linkage sections. LENGTH(data-value) is a half-word binary field. (Under CICS 1.6 or later, you can specify a full-word binary FLENGTH(data-value) in place of LENGTH(data- value), if you have some need to print an enormous amount of dump information.)

Whenever you specify FROM(data-area) in a DUMP command, you will also get some other areas in your dump listing: the task control area (TCA), the transaction work area (TWA), the common system area (CSA), the common work area (CWA), the trace table, and the register contents. The dump will also show either the destination control table entry associated with the task, or the terminal control table terminal entry for the terminal attached to the task (along with the TCTUA and various control blocks).

Specifying STORAGE instead of FROM(data-area) in a DUMP command will produce a dump that consists only of the auxiliary areas that were just listed. Your program storage will not be included.

On the other hand, specifying PROGRAM within a DUMP command will produce a dump including all of the auxiliary areas provided in a STORAGE dump, plus the register save area chain for your task, and all of the program storage currently associated with your task.

If you specify TASK in your DUMP command, you will get all of the areas included in a PROGRAM dump, plus other storage chains such as terminal I/O areas, areas chained from the TCA storage accounting field, and DL/I control blocks.

Specifying TERMINAL in a DUMP command produces a dump that includes all of the auxiliary areas present in a STORAGE dump, plus a storage chain of terminal I/O areas.

You can specify DCT to dump the destination control table, FCT to dump the file control table, PCT to dump the program control table, PPT to dump the processing program table, or SIT to dump the system initialization table. Specifying TABLES causes all of the above tables to be dumped.

10.2 TRACE TABLE

10.2.1 Relating Trace Table Entries to CICS Control Functions

As we have mentioned, the CICS system maintains some information in an internal trace table that is displayed in some CICS memory dumps. What is in the trace table, and how can this information be used?

The trace table contains information from every task running in the CICS region or partition. As new information is added to the table, old information is written over and obliterated. This means that the trace table will be full of entries, and that these entries come from many programs and tasks besides your own application programs. Some of these entries will be from unrelated activities, but many will be from CICS modules that fulfill your CICS commands. We discussed these modules in Chapter 1. Figure 10.3 may give you an idea of the sequence in which these modules are executed. Notice that storage control is invoked often in order to provide work areas for other CICS control programs. This explains the number of references to storage control in the trace table.

Each macro-level CICS program running in the region or partition will generate one trace table entry as each CICS macro begins executing, and another trace entry as each CICS macro finishes executing. Each command-level CICS program running will generate one trace table entry every time the EXEC interface program is invoked to execute a CICS command. It will generate another trace table entry whenever the EXEC interface program returns control upon completion of a command. In addition, each of the CICS modules that play a part in servicing each CICS command will generate its own trace table entries.

The trace table is likely to be cluttered with large numbers of entries generated by other CICS tasks that are not relevant to the problems that you are trying to solve. There may even be some system-generated entries intended for use by IBM field engineers. All of these items occupy so much space that you are likely to find only a small number of entries that apply to your task. (If any task was running under EDF or some other online debugging aid, the trace table will be even more cluttered.) If you are trying to determine the cause of a program ABEND, however, the trace table entries will identify the last few CICS commands executed by the program before ABEND.

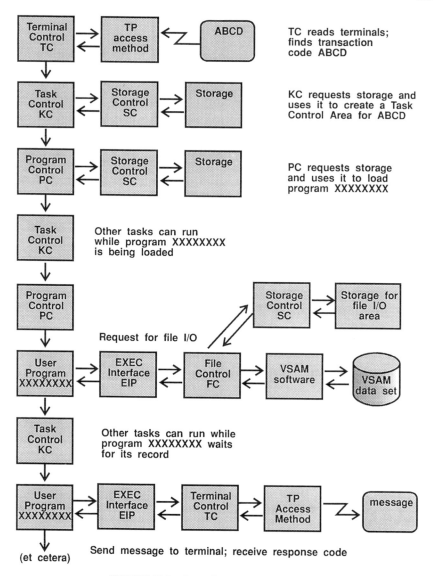

FIGURE 10.3   Control programs within CICS.

10.2.2   Finding Useful Information in Trace Table

The trace table entries that concern you the most are the entries with hexadecimal E1 in the first byte (byte 0). These are generated by the EXEC interface program before and after each CICS command. The trace entries generated at the beginning of a command have hexadecimal 0 in the first half of byte 2, while those generated at the end of a command have hexadecimal F in the first half of byte 2. Your sequential task number (not the transaction ID) will appear in packed decimal in bytes 5 through 7. In bytes 14 and 15 is the EIBFN. You may remember that this is the function identifier that appears in the EXEC interface block. It tells exactly which CICS command was executed. The EIBRCODE will appear in bytes 8 through 13 of the trace entries generated after completion of a CICS command. This is the response code that appears in the EXEC interface block. If this field contains zeros, the command was performed successfully.

A printout of the trace table appearing in a CICS dump is labeled TRACE TABLE in the left margin. Alongside the trace listing are comments that explain the EIBFN and EIBRCODE contents, making it unnecessary to look them up in Appendix A of the CICS Application Programmer's Reference Manual (Command Level). Additional comments explain some of the other trace entries.

If the trace table listing in your dump is too short to show you all of the information that you need, a master terminal operator command can be used that causes all trace table entries to be preserved on an auxiliary trace data set. Contents of this data set can be printed by the IBM-supplied CICS trace utility program, DFHTUP. This program can be used to select only those trace entries produced by the EXEC interface program, which is what a command-level programmer usually needs to see.

If you are not getting the trace entries that you expect to see, someone may be using the CICS TRACE on/off command to shut off tracing for the whole system. The command looks like this:

```
EXEC CICS TRACE (ON|OFF)
     [EI]
     [SYSTEM]
     [USER]
     [SINGLE]
     END-EXEC.
```

The word SYSTEM in this command allows the TRACE ON or OFF command to start or stop tracing for all tasks in the CICS system. The USER option affects user trace entries for all tasks in the CICS system, while the EI option affects trace entries generated by the EXEC interface program. The SINGLE option affects user entries generated by your task only. User trace entries can only be made if your systems programmer has set up event monitoring points; this is beyond the scope of this book. The TRACE on/off command is a rather dangerous command to use. Do not use it unless you are certain that you will not be working at cross-purposes with other users of the system.

TEST YOUR UNDERSTANDING

Questions and Exercises

1. Troubleshoot program EXAMP000 and dump shown in Figures 10.4 and 10.5 on the following pages.

```
CICS/VS COMMAND LANGUAGE TRANSLATOR VERSICN 1.5

          CBL XOPTS(LANGLVL(2),CICS)                                  00000100

  LINE              SOURCE LISTING

  00001             IDENTIFICATION DIVISION.                          00000200
  00002             PROGRAM-ID.  EXAMPC00.                            00000300
  00003             AUTHOR.  ALIDA JATICH AND PHIL NCWAK.             00000400
  00004             ****************************************************  *  00000500
  00005             *                                               *  00000700
  00006             *  THIS PROGRAM IS A VARIATION OF SALEP004.  IT CONTAINS  *  00000700
  00007             *  A BUG WHICH IS TO BE FOUND BY USING A MEMORY DUMP.  *  00000700
  00008             *                                               *  00000500
  00009             ****************************************************  *  00000600
  00010             *  SALEP004: PROCESSOR FOR ENTRY OF CURRENT WEEK SALES  *  00000700
  00011             *                                               *  00000800
  00012             *  SALEP004 READS "ENTER CURRENT WEEK SALES" SCREEN INPUT  *  00000900
  00013             *  AND PERFORMS THE FOLLOWING ACTIONS:          *  00001000
  00014             *                                               *  00001100
  00015             *  1.  IT UPDATES CURRENT WEEK SALES AMOUNT IN CUSTOMER  *  00001200
  00016             *      MASTER RECORD.                           *  00001300
  00017             *  2.  IT WRITES A LINE ITEM RECORD TO THE LINE ITEM VSAM  *  00001400
  00018             *      FILE FOR LATER USE IN A BILLING SYSTEM.  *  00001500
  00019             *  3.  IT CHECKS LINE ITEM TO DETERMINE IF QUANTITY FIELD  *  00001600
  00020             *      IS NEGATIVE.  IF SO, THE LINE ITEM IS AN ADJUSTMENT  *  00001700
  00021             *      TO CORRECT A PREVIOUS ERROR.  IN THAT CASE, A COPY  *  00001800
  00022             *      OF THE LINE ITEM IS WRITTEN TO THE "LIST" TRANSIENT  *  00001900
  00023             *      DATA QUEUE FOR LATER PRINTING.           *  00002000
  00024             *  4.  IT REFRESHES THE "ENTER CURRENT WEEK SALES" SCREEN  *  00002100
  00025             *      TO ALLOW THE TERMINAL USER TO ENTER MORE DATA.  *  00002200
  00026             *  5.  IT RETURNS TO TRANSACTION SAL4.  SINCE SAL4 IS  *  00002300
  00027             *      THE TRANSACTION ID ASSOCIATED WITH SALEP004, THIS  *  00002400
  00028             *      CAUSES THE SAME PROGRAM TO BE REINVOKED AGAIN LATER.  *  00002500
  00029             ****************************************************  00002600
  00030             ENVIRONMENT DIVISION.                             00002700
  00031             DATA DIVISION.                                    00002800
  00032             WORKING-STORAGE SECTION.                          00002900
  00033             01  DUMMY-FIELD          PIC X        VALUE LOW-VALUES.  00003000
  00034             01  ERROR-FLAG           PIC X        VALUE 'N'.  00003100
  00035             01  ERR-MSG.                                      00003200
  00036                 05  FILLER           PIC X(38)    VALUE       00003300
  00037             ' CUSTOMER NUMBER NOT ON FILE, RE-ENTER'.        00003400
  00038             01  MAPFAIL-MSG.                                  00003500
  00039                 05  FILLER           PIC X(20)    VALUE       00003600
  00040             'SALEP004 MAPFAIL ERR'.                           00003700
  00041             01  BAD-TRAN-MSG.                                 00003800
  00042                 05  FILLER           PIC X(17)    VALUE       00003900
  00043             'ILLEGAL TRAN CODE'.                              00004000
  00044             *                                                00004100
  00045             *  ATTRIBUTE VALUES  -  VALUES USED FOR CHANGING ATTRIBUTE  00004200
  00046             *                       BYTE SETTINGS            00004300
  00047             *                                                00004400
  00048             01  NUM-REG-MOD-PRO      PIC X        VALUE '1'.  00004500
  00049             01  NUM-REG-MOD-UNP      PIC X        VALUE 'J'.
```

FIGURE 10.4   Listing of sample program EXAMP000 to troubleshoot.

```
CICS/VS COMMAND LANGUAGE TRANSLATOR VERSION 1.5
  LINE               SOURCE LISTING
  00050        01   NUM-BRT-UNM-UNP        PIC X      VALUE  'Q'.           00004600
  00051        01   ALP-REG-MOD-UNP        PIC X      VALUE  'A'.           00004700
  00052        01   ALP-BRT-UNM-UNP        PIC X      VALUE  'I'.           00004800
  00053        01   MATH-WORK-AREAS.                                        00004900
  00054           05   SALES-ENTERED       PIC S9(5)V99.                    00004900
  00055           05   SALES-EXTENDED      PIC S9(5)V99.                    00004900
  00056        01   CUSTMST-LNGTH          PIC S9(4)   COMP VALUE +150.     00005000
  00057        01   WS-QTY                 PIC S9(6)   VALUE ZERO.          00005100
  00058        EJECT                                                        00005200
  00059        COPY MSALE04.                                                00005300
  00060        EJECT                                                        00005400
  00061        COPY CUSTMST.                                                00005500
  00062        EJECT                                                        00005600
  00063        COPY LINEVSM.                                                00005700
  00064        EJECT                                                        00005800
  00065        COPY DFHAID.                                                 00005900
  00066        EJECT                                                        00006000
  00067        PROCEDURE DIVISION.                                          00006100
  00068        INIT-ROUTINE.                                                00006200
  00069            EXEC CICS HANDLE CONDITION                               00006300
  00070                 MAPFAIL(BAD-MAP)                                    00006400
  00071                 END-EXEC.                                           00006500
  00072            EXEC CICS RECEIVE MAP('SALE004')                         00006600
  00073                 MAPSET('MSALE04')                                   00006700
  00074                 INTO (SALE004I)                                     00006800
  00075                 END-EXEC.                                           00006900
  00076            IF S4TRANI NOT EQUAL 'SAL4'                              00007000
  00077                EXEC CICS SEND                                       00007100
  00078                     FROM (BAD-TRAN-MSG)                             00007200
  00079                     ERASE                                           00007300
  00080                     LENGTH (17)                                     00007400
  00081                     END-EXEC                                        00007500
  00082                EXEC CICS RETURN                                     00007600
  00083                     END-EXEC.                                       00007700
  00084                GO TO INIT-EXIT.                                     00007800
  00085        BAD-MAP.                                                     00007900
  00086            IF EIBAID EQUAL DFHPA2                                   00008000
  00087                EXEC CICS XCTL                                       00008100
  00088                     PROGRAM ('SALEINIT')                            00008200
  00089                     END-EXEC                                        00008300
  00090            ELSE                                                     00008400
  00091                IF EIBAID EQUAL DFHCLEAR OR DFHPA1                   00008500
  00092                PERFORM CLEAR-ROUTINE                                00008600
  00093            ELSE                                                     00008700
  00094                MOVE MAPFAIL-MSG TO ERR-MSG                          00008800
  00095                EXEC CICS SEND                                       00008900
  00096                     FROM (ERR-MSG)                                  00009000
  00097                     ERASE                                           00009100
  00098                     LENGTH (20)                                     00009200
  00099                     END-EXEC                                        00009300
  00100                EXEC CICS RETURN                                     00009400
```

FIGURE 10.4   (Continued)

```
CICS/VS COMMAND LANGUAGE TRANSLATOR VERSION 1.5

    LINE            SOURCE.LISTING

    00101                              END-EXEC.                                    00009500
    00102              CLEAR-ROUTINE.                                               00009600
    00103                 EXEC CICS SEND                                            00009700
    00104                      FROM (DUMMY-FIELD)                                    00009800
    00105                      ERASE                                                 00009900
    00106                      LENGTH(0)                                             00010000
    00107                      END-EXEC.                                             00010100
    00108                 EXEC CICS RETURN                                          00010200
    00109                      END-EXEC.                                             00010300
    00110              INIT-EXIT.                                                    00010400
    00111                 EXIT.                                                      00010500
    00112              EJECT                                                         00010600
    00113              MAIN-LINE.                                                    00010700
    00114     ******************************************************************    00010800
    00115     *         VALIDATE FUNCTION KEY                               *        00010900
    00116     ******************************************************************    00011000
    00117                 IF EIBAID NOT EQUAL DFHENTER                               00011100
    00118                    MOVE NUM-REG-MOD-PRO TO S4TRANA                         00011200
    00119                    MOVE LOW-VALUES TO SALE0040                             00011300
    00120                    MOVE 'INVALID FUNCTION KEY' TO S4ERRO                   00011400
    00121                    EXEC CICS SEND                                          00011500
    00122                         MAP ('SALE004')                                    00011600
    00123                         MAPSET ('MSALE04')                                 00011700
    00124                         LENGTH (136)                                       00011800
    00125                         DATAONLY                                           00011900
    00126                         END-EXEC                                           00012000
    00127                    EXEC CICS RETURN                                        00012100
    00128                         TRANSID ('SAL4')                                   00012200
    00129                         END-EXEC.                                          00012300
    00130     ******************************************************************    00012400
    00131     *         VALIDATE MAP INPUT DATA                             *        00012500
    00132     ******************************************************************    00012600
    00133                 IF S4ITEMI IS NUMERIC                                      00012700
    00134                    MOVE NUM-REG-MOD-UNP TO S4ITEMA                         00012800
    00135                 ELSE                                                       00012900
    00136                    IF  ERROR-FLAG EQUAL 'Y'                                00013000
    00137                        MOVE NUM-BRT-UNM-UNP TO S4ITEMA                     00013100
    00138                    ELSE                                                    00013200
    00139                        MOVE 'ITEM NUMBER NOT NUMERIC - REKEY'              00013300
    00140                             TO S4ERRO                                      00013400
    00141                        MOVE NUM-BRT-UNM-UNP TO S4ITEMA                     00013500
    00142                        MOVE -1 TO S4ITEML                                  00013600
    00143                        MOVE 'Y' TO ERROR-FLAG.                             00013700
    00144                 IF S4UNITPI IS NUMERIC MOVE NUM-REG-MOD-UNP TO S4UNITPA    00013800
    00145                 ELSE                                                       00013900
    00146                    IF  ERROR-FLAG EQUAL 'Y'                                00014000
    00147                        MOVE NUM-BRT-UNM-UNP TO S4UNITPA                    00014100
    00148                    ELSE                                                    00014200
    00149                        MOVE 'UNIT PRICE NOT NUMERIC - REKEY'               00014300
    00150                             TO S4ERRO                                      00014400
    00151                        MOVE NUM-BRT-UNM-UNP TO S4UNITPA
```

FIGURE 10.4 *(Continued)*

CICS/VS COMMAND LANGUAGE TRANSLATOR VERSION 1.5

LINE   SOURCE LISTING

```
00152                        MOVE -1 TO S4UNITPL
00153                        MOVE 'Y' TO ERROR-FLAG.            00014500
00154              IF S4QTYI IS NUMERIC MOVE NUM-REG-MOD-UNP TO S4QTYA   00014600
00155              ELSE                                        00014700
00156                 IF  ERROR-FLAG EQUAL 'Y'                 00014800
00157                    MOVE NUM-BRT-UNM-UNP TO S4QTYA        00014900
00158                 ELSE                                     00015000
00159                    MOVE 'QUANTITY NOT NUMERIC - REKEY'   00015100
00160                    TO S4ERRO                            00015200
00161                    MOVE NUM-BRT-UNM-UNP TO S4QTYA        00015300
00162                    MOVE -1 TO S4QTYL                    00015400
00163                    MOVE 'Y' TO ERROR-FLAG.              00015500
00164              IF S4SIGNI = '+' OR S4SIGNI = '-'           00015600
00165                 MOVE ALP-REG-MOD-UNP TO S4SIGNA          00015700
00166              ELSE                                        00015800
00167                 IF  ERROR-FLAG EQUAL 'Y'                 00015900
00168                    MOVE ALP-BRT-UNM-UNP TO S4SIGNA       00016000
00169                 ELSE                                     00016100
00170                    MOVE 'INVALID SIGN ON QUANTITY FIELD' 00016200
00171                    TO S4ERRO                            00016300
00172                    MOVE ALP-BRT-UNM-UNP TO S4SIGNA       00016400
00173                    MOVE -1 TO S4SIGNL                   00016500
00174                    MOVE 'Y' TO ERROR-FLAG.              00016600
00175              IF ERROR-FLAG EQUAL 'Y'                     00016700
00176                 MOVE NUM-REG-MOD-PRO TO S4TRANA          00016800
00177                 EXEC CICS SEND                           00016900
00178                        MAP ('SALE004')                  00017000
00179                        MAPSET ('MSALE04')               00017100
00180                        LENGTH (136)                     00017200
00181                        DATAONLY                         00017300
00182                        END-EXEC                         00017400
00183                 EXEC CICS RETURN                         00017500
00184                        END-EXEC.                        00017600
00185              EJECT                                       00017700
00186              EXEC CICS HANDLE CONDITION                  00017800
00187                        NOTFND (BAD-SALE)                00017900
00188                        END-EXEC.                        00018000
00189              SKIP1                                       00018100
00190              MOVE S4CUSTI TO CUST-NO.                    00018200
00191              EXEC CICS READ                              00018300
00192                        DATASET('CUSTMST')               00018400
00193                        INTO (CUSTMST-REC)               00018500
00194                        RIDFLD(CUST-NO)                  00018600
00195                        LENGTH (CUSTMST-LNGTH)           00018700
00196                        UPDATE                           00018800
00197                        END-EXEC.                        00018900
00198              SKIP1                                       00019000
00199              MOVE +0 TO WS-QTY.                          00019100
00200              IF S4SIGNI = '-'                            00019200
00201                 SUBTRACT S4QTYI FROM WS-QTY              00019300
00202              ELSE                                        00019400
                                                              00019500
```

FIGURE 10.4   *(Continued)*

```
CICS/VS COMMAND LANGUAGE TRANSLATOR VERSION 1.5

  LINE                SOURCE LISTING

00203                      ADD S4QTYI TO WS-QTY.                                              00019600
00204             **************************************************************              00019700
00205             *     UPDATE CURRENT WEEK SALES FIELD IN CUSTOMER MASTER        *           00019800
00206             **************************************************************              00019900
00207                      COMPUTE SALES-ENTERED EQUAL S4UNITPI * WS-QTY.                     00020000
00208                      COMPUTE CUST-CURR-WK-SALES EQUAL SALES-EXTENDED +                  00020100
00209                              CUST-CURR-WK-SALES.                                        00020200
00210                      SKIP1                                                              00020300
00211                      EXEC CICS REWRITE                                                  00020400
00212                           DATASET('CUSTMST')                                            00020500
00213                           FROM (CUSTMST-REC)                                            00020600
00214                           LENGTH (CUSTMST-LNGTH)                                        00020700
00215                           END-EXEC.                                                     00020800
00216                      EXEC CICS ASKTIME.                                                 00020900
00217                           END-EXEC.                                                     00021000
00218                      SKIP1                                                              00021100
00219                      MOVE S4CUSTI TO LINEVSM-CUST-NO.                                   00021200
00220                      MOVE S4ITEMI TO LINEVSM-ITEM-CODE.                                 00021300
00221                      MOVE S4UNITPI TO LINEVSM-UNIT-PRICE.                               00021400
00222                      MOVE WS-QTY TO LINEVSM-QUANTITY.                                   00021500
00223                      MOVE EIBTIME TO LINEVSM-TIME.                                      00021600
00224                      MOVE EIBDATE TO LINEVSM-DATE.                                      00021700
00225                      EXEC CICS WRITE                                                    00021800
00226                           DATASET('LINEVSM')                                            00021900
00227                           FROM (LINEVSM-REC)                                            00022000
00228                           LENGTH (45)                                                   00022100
00229                           RIDFLD(LINEVSM-VSAM-KEY)                                      00022200
00230                           END-EXEC.                                                     00022300
00231                      SKIP1                                                              00022400
00232             **************************************************************              00022500
00233             *     IF QUANTITY IS NEGATIVE, THEN THE RECORD BEING ENTERED   *           00022600
00234             *     IS AN ADJUSTMENT TRANSACTION THAT IS MEANT TO REVERSE    *           00022700
00235             *     AN OLD TRANSACTION.  IN THAT CASE, WRITE A COPY OF IT    *           00022800
00236             *     TO THE 'LIST' TRANSIENT DATA OUTPUT QUEUE.               *           00022900
00237             **************************************************************              00023000
00238                      IF WS-QTY LESS THAN ZERO                                           00023100
00239                         EXEC CICS WRITEQ TD                                             00023200
00240                              FROM (LINEVSM-REC)                                         00023300
00241                              QUEUE ('LIST')                                             00023400
00242                              LENGTH (45)                                                00023500
00243                              END-EXEC.                                                  00023600
00244                      SKIP1                                                              00023700
00245             **************************************************************              00023800
00246             *     REFRESH SCREEN SO THAT IT CAN BE USED FOR MORE INPUT.    *           00023900
00247             **************************************************************              00024000
00248                      MOVE ZEROES TO S4ITEMO, S4QTYO, S4UNITPO.                          00024100
00249                      MOVE '+' TO S4SIGNO.                                               00024200
00250                      MOVE NUM-REG-MOD-UNP TO S4CUSTA.                                   00024300
00251                      MOVE NUM-REG-MOD-PRO TO S4TRANA.                                   00024400
00252                      MOVE 'ACCEPTED' TO S4EPRO.                                         00024500
00253                      EXEC CICS SEND                                                     00024600
```

FIGURE 10.4   *(Continued)*

```
CICS/VS COMMAND LANGUAGE TRANSLATOR VERSION 1.5          TIME 23.30 DATE 3 OCT 83    PAGE 6

  LINE       SOURCE LISTING

  00254            MAP ('SALE004')                                                   00024700
  00255            MAPSET ('MSALE04')                                                00024800
  00256            LENGTH (136)                                                      00024900
  00257            DATAONLY                                                          00025000
  00258            END-EXEC.                                                         00025100
  00259        EXEC CICS RETURN                                                      00025200
  00260            TRANSID ('SAL4')                                                  00025300
  00261            END-EXEC.                                                         00025400
  00262            SKIP1                                                             00025500
  00263    BAD-SALE.                                                                 00025600
  00264        MOVE ERR-MSG TO S4ERRO.                                               00025700
  00265        EXEC CICS SEND                                                        00025800
  00266            MAP ('SALE004')                                                   00025900
  00267            MAPSET ('MSALE04')                                                00026000
  00268            LENGTH (136)                                                      00026100
  00269            DATAONLY                                                          00026200
  00270            END-EXEC.                                                         00026300
  00271        EXEC CICS RETURN                                                      00026400
  00272            TRANSID ('SAL4')                                                  00026500
  00273            END-EXEC.                                                         00026600
  00274    NON-EXECUTABLE-PARAGRAPH.                                                 00026700
  00275        GOBACK.                                                               00026800


CICS/VS COMMAND LANGUAGE TRANSLATOR VERSION 1.5          TIME 23.30 DATE 3 OCT 83    PAGE 7

  *OPTIONS IN EFFECT*    APOST, NODEBUG, FLAGW, LANGLVL(2), LIST, NONUM, OPT, SEQ, SPACE1, NOXREF, CICS

  NO MESSAGES PRODUCED BY TRANSLATOR.

  TRANSLATION TIME:-   0.02 MINS.
```

FIGURE 10.4 (Continued)

```
PP 5740-CB1 RELEASE 2.3 + PTF 8 - UP13477        IBM OS/VS COBOL  JULY 24, 1978


   1                    23.30.11      OCT  3,1983


00001            IDENTIFICATION DIVISION.                                00000200
00002            PROGRAM-ID.  EXAMP000.                                  00000300
00003            AUTHOR.  ALIDA JATICH AND PHIL NOWAK.                   00000400
00004            ********************************************************00000500
00005            *                                                     *00000700
00006            *    THIS PROGRAM IS A VARIATION OF SALEP004.  IT CONTAINS*00000700
00007            *    A BUG WHICH IS TO BE FOUND BY USING A MEMORY DUMP.*00000700
00008            *                                                     *00000700
00009            ********************************************************00000500
00010            *    SALEP004: PROCESSOR FOR ENTRY OF CURRENT WEEK SALES*00000600
00011            *                                                     *00000700
00012            *    SALEP004 READS "ENTER CURRENT WEEK SALES" SCREEN INPUT*00000800
00013            *    AND PERFORMS THE FOLLOWING ACTIONS:               *00000900
00014            *                                                     *00001000
00015            *    1.  IT UPDATES CURRENT WEEK SALES AMOUNT IN CUSTOMER*00001100
00016            *        MASTER RECORD.                                *00001200
00017            *    2.  IT WRITES A LINE ITEM RECORD TO THE LINE ITEM VSAM*00001300
00018            *        FILE FOR LATER USE IN A BILLING SYSTEM.       *00001400
00019            *    3.  IT CHECKS LINE ITEM TO DETERMINE IF QUANTITY FIELD*00001500
00020            *        IS NEGATIVE.  IF SO, THE LINE ITEM IS AN ADJUSTMENT*000016C0
00021            *        TO CORRECT A PREVIOUS ERROR.  IN THAT CASE, A COPY*000017C0
00022            *        OF THE LINE ITEM IS WRITTEN TO THE "LIST" TRANSIENT*0000180C
00023            *        DATA QUEUE FOR LATER PRINTING.                *00001900
00024            *    4.  IT REFRESHES THE "ENTER CURRENT WEEK SALES" SCREEN*00002000
00025            *        TO ALLOW THE TERMINAL USER TO ENTER MORE DATA.*000021C0
00026            *    5.  IT RETURNS TO TRANSACTION SAL4.  SINCE SAL4 IS*00002200
00027            *        THE TRANSACTION ID ASSOCIATED WITH SALEP004, THIS*00002300
00028            *        CAUSES THE SAME PROGRAM TO BE REINVOKED AGAIN LATER.*000024C0
00029            ********************************************************00002500
00030            ENVIRONMENT DIVISION.                                   000026C0
00031            DATA DIVISION.                                          000027C0
00032            WORKING-STORAGE SECTION.                                0000280C
00033            01  DUMMY-FIELD              PIC X      VALUE LOW-VALUES.0000290C
00034            01  ERROR-FLAG               PIC X      VALUE 'N'.      00003000
00035            01  ERR-MSG.                                            00003100
00036                05  FILLER               PIC X(38)  VALUE          00003200
00037            ' CUSTOMER NUMBER NOT ON FILE, RE-ENTER'.              00003300
00038            01  MAPFAIL-MSG.                                        0000340C
00039                05  FILLER               PIC X(20)  VALUE          00003500
00040            'SALEP004 MAPFAIL ERR'.                                000036C0
00041            01  BAD-TRAN-MSG.                                       00003700
00042                05  FILLER               PIC X(17)  VALUE          00003800
00043            'ILLEGAL TRAN CODE'.                                   0000390C
00044            *                                                      00004000
00045            *    ATTRIBUTE VALUES  -  VALUES USED FOR CHANGING ATTRIBUTE00004100
00046            *                         BYTE SETTINGS                0000420C
00047            *                                                      0000430C
00048            01  NUM-REG-MOD-PRO          PIC X      VALUE '1'.      0000440C
00049            01  NUM-REG-MOD-UNP          PIC X      VALUE 'J'.      00004500
00050            01  NUM-BRT-UNM-UNP          PIC X      VALUE 'C'.      0000460C
00051            01  ALP-REG-MOD-UNP          PIC X      VALUE 'A'.      00004700
00052            01  ALP-BRT-UNM-UNP          PIC X      VALUE 'I'.      0000480C
00053            01  MATH-WORK-AREAS.                                    000049C0
00054                05  SALES-ENTERED        PIC S9(5)V99.             000049C0


   2                    23.30.11      OCT  3,1983


00055                05  SALES-EXTENDED       PIC S9(5)V99.             00004900
00056            01  CUSTMST-LNGTH            PIC S9(4)  COMP VALUE +150.00005000
00057            01  WS-QTY                   PIC S9(6)  VALUE ZERO.     00005100


   3                    23.30.11      OCT  3,1983


00059            COPY MSALE04.                                           00005300
00060  C         01  SALE0041.
00061  C             02  FILLER PIC X(12).
00062  C             02  S4TRANL    COMP PIC S9(4).
00063  C             02  S4TRANF    PICTURE X.
00064  C             02  S4TRANI PIC X(4).
00065  C             02  S4CUSTL    COMP PIC S9(4).
00066  C             02  S4CUSTF    PICTURE X.
00067  C             02  S4CUSTI PIC 999999.
00068  C             02  S4ITEML    COMP PIC S9(4).
00069  C             02  S4ITEMF    PICTURE X.
00070  C             02  S4ITEMI PIC 999999.
00071  C             02  S4UNITPL   COMP PIC S9(4).
00072  C             02  S4UNITPF   PICTURE X.
00073  C             02  S4UNITPI PIC 9999V99.
00074  C             02  S4QTYL     COMP PIC S9(4).
00075  C             02  S4QTYF     PICTURE X.
00076  C             02  S4QTYI PIC 999999.
00077  C             02  S4SIGNL    COMP PIC S9(4).
00078  C             02  S4SIGNF    PICTURE X.
00079  C             02  S4SIGNI PIC X(1).
00080  C             02  S4ERRL     COMP PIC S9(4).
00081  C             02  S4ERRF     PICTURE X.
00082  C             02  S4ERRI PIC X(78).
00083  C         01  SALE0040 REDEFINES SALE0041.
```

FIGURE 10.4 *(Continued)*

```
00084 C            02  FILLER PIC X(12).
00085 C            02  FILLER PICTURE X(2).
00086 C            02  S4TRANA    PICTURE X.
00087 C            02  S4TRAND    PIC X(4).
00088 C            02  FILLER PICTURE X(2).
00089 C            02  S4CUSTA    PICTURE X.
00090 C            02  S4CUSTD    PIC X(6).
00091 C            02  FILLER PICTURE X(2).
00092 C            02  S4ITEMA    PICTURE X.
00093 C            02  S4ITEMD    PIC X(6).
00094 C            02  FILLER PICTURE X(2).
00095 C            02  S4UNITPA    PICTURE X.
00096 C            02  S4UNITPD    PIC X(6).
00097 C            02  FILLER PICTURE X(2).
00098 C            02  S4QTYA    PICTURE X.
00099 C            02  S4QTYD    PIC X(6).
00100 C            02  FILLER PICTURE X(2).
00101 C            02  S4SIGNA    PICTUPE X.
00102 C            02  S4SIGND    PIC X(1).
00103 C            02  FILLER PICTURE X(2).
00104 C            02  S4ERRA    PICTURE X.
00105 C            02  S4ERRD    PIC X(78).


    4                   23.30.11      OCT  3,1983


00107              COPY CUSTMST.                                          00005500
00108 C            01  CUSTMST-REC.
00109 C               05  CUST-VSAM-KEY.
00110 C                  10  CUST-NO            PIC X(6).
00111 C               05  CUST-NAME            PIC X(25).
00112 C               05  CUST-CONTACT         PIC X(25).
00113 C               05  CUST-STREET-ADDRESS  PIC X(25).
00114 C               05  CUST-CITY            PIC X(20).
00115 C               05  CUST-STATE           PIC XX.
00116 C               05  CUST-ZIP-9.
00117 C                  10  CUST-ZIP-5        PIC X(5).
00118 C                  10  FILLER            PIC XXXX.
00119 C               05  CUST-LAST-BILL-DATE.
00120 C                  15  CUST-BILL-YY      PIC 99.
00121 C                  15  CUST-BILL-MM      PIC 99.
00122 C                  15  CUST-BILL-DD      PIC 99.
00123 C               05  CUST-LAST-BILL-BAL-DUE  PIC S9(5)V99.
00124 C               05  CUST-CURR-WK-SALES   PIC S9(5)V99.
00125 C               05  FILLER               PIC X(18).


    5                   23.30.11      OCT  3,1983


00127              COPY LINEVSM.                                          00005700
00128 C            01  LINEVSM-REC.                                       00000100
00129 C               05  LINEVSM-VSAM-KEY.                               00000200
00130 C                  10  LINEVSM-CUST-NO   PIC X(6).                  00000300
00131 C                  10  LINEVSM-DATE      PIC S9(7)    CCMP-3.       00000400
00132 C                  10  LINEVSM-TIME      PIC S9(7)    CCMP-3.       00000500
00133 C                  10  LINEVSM-ITEM-CODE PIC X(6).                  00000600
00134 C               05  LINEVSM-UNIT-PRICE   PIC S9(5)V99.              00000700
00135 C               05  LINEVSM-QUANTITY     PIC S9(6).                 00000800
00136 C               05  FILLER               PIC X(12).                 00000900


    6                   23.30.11      OCT  3,1983


00138              COPY DFHAID.                                           00005900
00139 C            01  DFHAID.                                            02000000
00140 C               02  DFHNULL    PIC  X  VALUE IS ' '.                04000000
00141 C               02  DFHENTER   PIC  X  VALUE IS QUOTE.              06000000
00142 C               02  DFHCLEAR   PIC  X  VALUE IS '_'.                08000000
00143 C               02  DFHPEN     PIC  X  VALUE IS '='.                10000000
00144 C               02  DFHOPID    PIC  X  VALUE IS 'W'.                12000000
00145 C               02  DFHMSRE    PIC  X  VALUE IS 'X'.                14000000
00146 C               02  DFHSTRF    PIC  X  VALUE IS ' '.                16000000
00147 C               02  DFHTRIG    PIC  X  VALUE IS '"'.                18000000
00148 C               02  DFHPA1     PIC  X  VALUE IS '%'.                20000000
00149 C               02  DFHPA2     PIC  X  VALUE IS '>'.                22000000
00150 C               02  DFHPA3     PIC  X  VALUE IS ','.                25000000
00151 C               02  DFHPF1     PIC  X  VALUE IS '1'.                28000000
00152 C               02  DFHPF2     PIC  X  VALUE IS '2'.                31000000
00153 C               02  DFHPF3     PIC  X  VALUE IS '3'.                34000000
00154 C               02  DFHPF4     PIC  X  VALUE IS '4'.                37000000
00155 C               02  DFHPF5     PIC  X  VALUE IS '5'.                40000000
00156 C               02  DFHPF6     PIC  X  VALUE IS '6'.                43000000
00157 C               02  DFHPF7     PIC  X  VALUE IS '7'.                46000000
00158 C               02  DFHPF8     PIC  X  VALUE IS '8'.                49000000
00159 C               02  DFHPF9     PIC  X  VALUE IS '9'.                52000000
00160 C               02  DFHPF10    PIC  X  VALUE IS ':'.                55000000
00161 C               02  DFHPF11    PIC  X  VALUE IS '#'.                58000000
00162 C               02  DFHPF12    PIC  X  VALUE IS '@'.                61000000
00163 C               02  DFHPF13    PIC  X  VALUE IS 'A'.                64000000
00164 C               02  DFHPF14    PIC  X  VALUE IS 'B'.                67000000
00165 C               02  DFHPF15    PIC  X  VALUE IS 'C'.                70000000
```

FIGURE 10.4 *(Continued)*

```
00166 C        02  DFHPF16   PIC  X  VALUE IS 'D'.              73000000
00167 C        02  DFHPF17   PIC  X  VALUE IS 'E'.              76000000
00168 C        02  DFHPF18   PIC  X  VALUE IS 'F'.              79000000
00169 C        02  DFHPF19   PIC  X  VALUE IS 'G'.              82000000
00170 C        02  DFHPF20   PIC  X  VALUE IS 'H'.              85000000
00171 C        02  DFHPF21   PIC  X  VALUE IS 'I'.              88000000
00172 C        02  DFHPF22   PIC  X  VALUE IS ' '.              91000000
00173 C        02  DFHPF23   PIC  X  VALUE IS '.'.              94000000
00174 C        02  DFHPF24   PIC  X  VALUE IS '<'.              97000000

    7                  23.30.11       OCT  3,1983

00176          COPY DFHEIVAR.                                  04000000
00177 C        01  DFHEIV.                                      08000000
00178 C            02   DFHEIVO  PICTURE X(26).                 12000000
00179 C            02   DFHEIV1  PICTURE X(8).                  16000000
00180 C            02   DFHEIV2  PICTURE X(8).                  20000000
00181 C            02   DFHEIV3  PICTURE X(8).                  24000000
00182 C            02   DFHEIV4  PICTURE X(6).                  28000000
00183 C            02   DFHEIV5  PICTURE X(4).                  32000000
00184 C            02   DFHEIV6  PICTURE X(4).                  36000000
00185 C            02   DFHEIV7  PICTURE X(2).                  40000000
00186 C            02   DFHEIV8  PICTURE X(2).                  44000000
00187 C            02   DFHEIV9  PICTURE X(1).                  48000000
00188 C            02   DFHEIV10 PICTURE S9(7) USAGE COMPUTATIONAL-3.   52000000
00189 C            02   DFHEIV11 PICTURE S9(4) USAGE COMPUTATIONAL.     56000000
00190 C            02   DFHEIV12 PICTURE S9(4) USAGE COMPUTATIONAL.     60000000
00191 C            02   DFHEIV13 PICTURE S9(4) USAGE COMPUTATIONAL.     64000000
00192 C            02   DFHEIV14 PICTURE S9(4) USAGE COMPUTATIONAL.     68000000
00193 C            02   DFHEIV15 PICTURE S9(4) USAGE COMPUTATIONAL.     72000000
00194 C            02   DFHEIV16 PICTURE S9(9) USAGE COMPUTATIONAL.     76000000
00195 C            02   DFHEIV17 PICTURE X(4).                  80000000
00196 C            02   DFHEIV18 PICTURE X(4).                  84000000
00197 C            02   DFHEIV19 PICTURE X(4).                  88000000
00198 C            02   DFHEIV97 PICTURE S9(7) USAGE COMPUTATIONAL-3 VALUE ZERC.88000000
00199 C            02   DFHEIV98 PICTURE S9(4) USAGE COMPUTATIONAL VALUE ZERO.  92000000
00200 C            02   DFHEIV99 PICTURE X(1)  VALUE SPACE.     96000000
00201          LINKAGE SECTION.
00202          COPY DFHEIBLK REPLACING EIBLK BY DFHEIBLK.
00203 C    *        EIBLK EXEC INTERFACE BLOCK                  02000000
00204 C        01  DFHEIBLK.                                    04000000
00205 C    *        EIBTIME     TIME IN OHHMMSS FORMAT          06000000
00206 C            02 EIBTIME   PICTURE S9(7) USAGE COMPUTATIONAL-3.   08000000
00207 C    *        EIBDATE     DATE IN OOYYDDD FORMAT          10000000
00208 C            02 EIBDATE   PICTURE S9(7) USAGE COMPUTATIONAL-3.   12000000
00209 C    *        EIBTRNID    TRANSACTION IDENTIFIER          14000000
00210 C            02 EIBTRNID  PICTURE X(4).                   16000000
00211 C    *        EIBTASKN    TASK NUMBER                     18000000
00212 C            02 EIBTASKN  PICTURE S9(7) USAGE COMPUTATIONAL-3.   20000000
00213 C    *        EIBTRMID    TERMINAL IDENTIFIER             22000000
00214 C            02 EIBTRMID  PICTURE X(4).                   24000000
00215 C    *        DFHEIGDI    RESERVED                        26000000
00216 C            02 DFHEIGDI  PICTURE S9(4) USAGE COMPUTATIONAL.    28000000
00217 C    *        EIBCPOSN    CURSOR POSITION                 30000000
00218 C            02 EIBCPOSN  PICTURE S9(4) USAGE COMPUTATIONAL.    32000000
00219 C    *        EIBCALEN    COMMAREA LENGTH                 34000000
00220 C            02 EIBCALEN  PICTURE S9(4) USAGE COMPUTATIONAL.    36000000
00221 C    *        EIBAID      ATTENTION IDENTIFIER            38000000
00222 C            02 EIBAID    PICTURE X(1).                   40000000
00223 C    *        EIBFN       FUNCTION CODE                   42000000
00224 C            02 EIBFN     PICTURE X(2).                   44000000
00225 C    *        EIBRCODE    RESPONSE CODE                   46000000
00226 C            02 EIBRCODE  PICTURE X(6).                   48000000
00227 C    *        EIBDS       DATASET NAME                    50000000
00228 C            02 EIBDS     PICTURE X(8).                   52000000
00229 C    *        EIBREQID    REQUEST IDENTIFIER              54000000
00230 C            02 EIBREQID  PICTURE X(8).                   56000000
00231 C    *        EIBRSRCE    RESOURCE NAME                   58000000
00232 C            02 EIBRSRCE  PICTURE X(8).                   60000000

    8                  23.30.11       OCT  3,1983

00233 C    *        EIBSYNC     SYNCPOINT REQUIRED              62000000
00234 C            02 EIBSYNC   PICTURE X.                      64000000
00235 C    *        EIBFREE     TERMINAL FREE REQUIRED          66000000
00236 C            02 EIBFREE   PICTURE X.                      68000000
00237 C    *        EIBRECV     DATA RECEIVE REQUIRED           70000000
00238 C            02 EIBRECV   PICTURE X.                      73000000
00239 C    *        EIBSEND     RESERVED                        76000000
00240 C            02 EIBSEND   PICTURE X.                      79000000
00241 C    *        EIBATT      ATTACH DATA EXISTS              82000000
00242 C            02 EIBATT    PICTURE X.                      85000000
00243 C    *        EIBEOC      GOTTEN DATA IS COMPLETE         88000000
00244 C            02 EIBEOC    PICTURE X.                      91000000
00245 C    *        EIBFMH      GOTTEN DATA CONTAINS FMH        94000000
00246 C            02 EIBFMH    PICTURE X.                      97000000
00247          01  DFHCOMMAREA PICTURE X(1).
00248          01  DFHBLLSLOT1 PICTURE X(1).
00249          01  DFHBLLSLOT2 PICTURE X(1).
00250          PROCEDURE DIVISION USING DFHEIBLK DFHCOMMAREA.          0C006100
00251              SERVICE RELOAD DFHEIBLK.
00252          INIT-ROUTINE.                                   00006200
00253      *   EXEC CICS HANDLE CONDITION
00254      *               MAPFAIL(BAD-MAP)
00255      *   END-EXEC.
00256              MOVE '                    ' TO DFHEIVO CALL 'DFHEI1' USING   00006300
00257          DFHEIVO GO TO BAD-MAP DEPENDING ON DFHEIGDI.
00258
00259      *   EXEC CICS RECEIVE MAP('SALE004')
00260      *               MAPSET('MSALE04')
00261      *               INTO (SALE004I)
00262      *   END-EXEC.
```

FIGURE 10.4 *(Continued)*

```
00263                    MOVE 'SALE004' TO DFHEIV1 MOVE 'MSALE04' TO DFHEIV2 MOVE '   00006600
00264            -        '       ' TO DFHEIVO CALL 'DFHEI1' USING DFHEIVO
00265            DFHEIV1 SALE004I DFHEIV98 DFHEIV2.
00266
00267            IF S4TRANI NOT EQUAL 'SAL4'                                          00007000
00268            *      EXEC CICS SEND
00269            *              FROM (BAD-TRAN-MSG)
00270            *              ERASE
00271            *              LENGTH (17)
00272            *              END-EXEC
00273                    MOVE 17 TO DFHEIV11 MOVE '          ' TO DFHEIVO            00007100
00274            CALL 'DFHEI1' USING DFHEIVO DFHEIV99 DFHEIV98 BAD-TRAN-MSG
00275            DFHEIV11
00276
00277
00278            *      EXEC CICS RETURN
00279            *              END-EXEC.
00280                    MOVE '         ' TO DFHEIVO CALL 'DFHEI1' USING DFHEIVO.     00007600
00281
00282               GO TO INIT-EXIT.                                                  00007800
00283            BAD-MAP.                                                             00007900
00284               IF EIBAID EQUAL DFHPA2                                            00008000
00285            *      EXEC CICS XCTL
00286            *              PROGRAM ('SALEINIT')
00287            *              END-EXEC
00288                    MOVE 'SALEINIT' TO DFHEIV3 MOVE '          ' TO DFHEIVO       00008100
00289            CALL 'DFHEI1' USING DFHEIVO DFHEIV3

        9                    23.30.11      OCT  3,1983

00290
00291            ELSE
00292               IF EIBAID EQUAL DFHCLEAR OR DFHPA1                                00008400
00293               PERFORM CLEAR-ROUTINE                                             00008500
00294            ELSE                                                                 00008600
00295               MOVE MAPFAIL-MSG TO ERR-MSG                                       00008700
00296            *      EXEC CICS SEND                                                00008800
00297            *              FROM (ERR-MSG)
00298            *              ERASE
00299            *.             LENGTH (20)
00300            *-             END-EXEC
00301                    MOVE 20 TO DFHEIV11 MOVE '          ' TO DFHEIVO 00008900
00302            CALL 'DFHEI1' USING DFHEIVO DFHEIV99 DFHEIV98 ERR-MSG
00303            DFHEIV11
00304
00305
00306            *      EXEC CICS RETURN
00307            *              END-EXEC.
00308                    MOVE '          ' TO DFHEIVO CALL 'DFHEI1' USING
00309            DFHEIVO.                                                             00009400
00310            CLEAR-ROUTINE.                                                       00009600
00311            *      EXEC CICS SEND
00312            *              FROM (DUMMY-FIELD)
00313            *              ERASE
00314            *              LENGTH(0)
00315            *              END-EXEC.
00316                    MOVE 0 TO DFHEIV11 MOVE '          ' TO DFHEIVO CALL 'D00009700
00317            -      'FHEI1' USING DFHEIVO DFHEIV99 DFHEIV98 DUMMY-FIELD DFHEIV11.
00318
00319
00320
00321            *      EXEC CICS RETURN
00322            *              END-EXEC.
00323                    MOVE '          ' TO DFHEIVO CALL 'DFHEI1' USING DFHEIVO.     00010200
00324
00325            INIT-EXIT.                                                           00010400
00326               EXIT.                                                             00010500

        10                   23.30.11      OCT  3,1983

00328            MAIN-LINE.                                                           00010700
00329            ****************************************************************     00010800
00330            *      VALIDATE FUNCTION KEY                                    *    00010900
00331            ****************************************************************     00011000
00332               IF EIBAID NOT EQUAL DFHENTER                                     00011100
00333               MOVE NUM-REG-MOD-PRO TO S4TRANA                                  00011200
00334               MOVE LOW-VALUES TO SALE004O                                      00011300
00335               MOVE 'INVALID FUNCTION KEY' TO S4ERRO                            00011400
00336            *      EXEC CICS SEND
00337            *              MAP ('SALE004')
00338            *              MAPSET ('MSALE04')
00339            *              LENGTH (136)
00340            *              DATAONLY
00341            *              END-EXEC
00342                    MOVE 'SALE004' TO DFHEIV1 MOVE 136 TO DFHEIV11 MOVE 'MSAL00011500
00343            -      'E04' TO DFHEIV2 MOVE '    0        ' TO DFHEIVO CALL 'DFHE
00344            -      'I1' USING DFHEIVO DFHEIV1 SALE004O DFHEIV11 DFHEIV2
00345
00346
00347
00348            *      EXEC CICS RETURN
00349            *              TRANSID ('SAL4')
00350            *              END-EXEC.
00351                    MOVE 'SAL4' TO DFHEIV5 MOVE '          ' TO DFHEIVO CALL '00012100
00352            -      'DFHEI1' USING DFHEIVO DFHEIV5.
00353
00354            ****************************************************************     00012300
00355            *      VALIDATE MAP INPUT DATA                                  *    00012400
00356            ****************************************************************     00012500
00357               IF S4ITEMI IS NUMERIC                                            00012600
00358               MOVE NUM-REG-MOD-UNP TO S4ITEMA                                  00012700
00359            ELSE                                                                00012800
```

FIGURE 10.4 *(Continued)*

```
00360                    IF  ERROR-FLAG EQUAL 'Y'                            00012900
00361                        MOVE NUM-BRT-UNM-UNP TO S4ITEMA                 00013000
00362                    ELSE                                               00013100
00363                        MOVE 'ITEM NUMBER NOT NUMERIC - REKEY'         00013200
00364                        TO S4ERRO                                      00013300
00365                        MOVE NUM-BRT-UNM-UNP TO S4ITEMA                00013400
00366                        MOVE -1 TO S4ITEML                             00013500
00367                        MOVE 'Y' TO ERROR-FLAG.                        00013600
00368                    IF S4UNITPI IS NUMERIC MOVE NUM-REG-MOD-UNP TO S4UNITPA  00013700
00369                    ELSE                                               00013800
00370                        IF  ERROR-FLAG EQUAL 'Y'                       00013900
00371                            MOVE NUM-BRT-UNM-UNP TO S4UNITPA           00014000
00372                        ELSE                                           00014100
00373                            MOVE 'UNIT PRICE NOT NUMERIC - REKEY'      00014200
00374                            TO S4ERRO                                  00014300
00375                            MOVE NUM-BRT-UNM-UNP TO S4UNITPA           00014400
00376                            MOVE -1 TO S4UNITPL                        00014500
00377                            MOVE 'Y' TO ERROR-FLAG.                    00014600
00378                    IF S4QTYI IS NUMERIC MOVE NUM-REG-MOD-UNP TO S4QTYA  00014700
00379                    ELSE                                               00014800
00380                        IF  ERROR-FLAG EQUAL 'Y'                       00014900
00381                            MOVE NUM-BRT-UNM-UNP TO S4QTYA             00015000
00382                        ELSE                                           00015100
00383                            MOVE 'QUANTITY NOT NUMERIC - REKEY'        00015200
00384                            TO S4ERRO                                  00015300
```

```
    11                      23.30.11        OCT  3,1983
```

```
00385                            MOVE NUM-BRT-UNM-UNP TO S4QTYA            00015400
00386                            MOVE -1 TO S4QTYL                         00015500
00387                            MOVE 'Y' TO ERROR-FLAG.                   00015600
00388                    IF S4SIGNI = '+' OR S4SIGNI = '-'                 00015700
00389                        MOVE ALP-REG-MOD-UNP TO S4SIGNA               00015800
00390                    ELSE                                              00015900
00391                        IF  ERROR-FLAG EQUAL 'Y'                      00016000
00392                            MOVE ALP-BRT-UNM-UNP TO S4SIGNA           00016100
00393                        ELSE                                          00016200
00394                            MOVE 'INVALID SIGN ON QUANTITY FIELD'     00016300
00395                            TO S4ERRO                                 00016400
00396                            MOVE ALP-BRT-UNM-UNP TO S4SIGNA           00016500
00397                            MOVE -1 TO S4SIGNL                        00016600
00398                            MOVE 'Y' TO ERROR-FLAG.                   00016700
00399                    IF ERROR-FLAG EQUAL 'Y'                           00016800
00400                        MOVE NUM-REG-MOD-PRO TO S4TRANA               00016900
00401           *         EXEC CICS SEND
00402           *             MAP ('SALE004')
00403           *             MAPSET ('MSALE04')
00404           *             LENGTH (136)
00405           *             DATAONLY
00406           *         END-EXEC
00407                     MOVE 'SALE004' TO DFHEIV1 MOVE 136 TO DFHEIV11 MOVE 'MSAL00017000
00408           -    'E04' TO DFHEIV2 MOVE ' ' 0          ' TO DFHEIV0 CALL 'DFHE
00409           -    'I1' USING DFHEIV0 DFHEIV1 SALE0040 DFHEIV11 DFHEIV2
00410
00411
00412
00413           *         EXEC CICS RETURN
00414           *             END-EXEC.
00415                     MOVE ' ' ' TO DFHEIV0 CALL 'DFHEI1' USING DFHEIV0.  00017600
00416
```

```
    12                      23.30.11        OCT  3,1983
```

```
00418           *         EXEC CICS HANDLE CONDITION
00419           *             NOTFND (BAD-SALE)
00420           *             END-EXEC.
00421                     MOVE ' '                    ' TO DFHEIV0 CALL 'DFHEI1' USING  00017900
00422                     DFHEIV0 GO TO BAD-SALE DEPENDING ON DFHEIGDI.
00423
00425                     MOVE S4CUSTI TO CUST-NO.                           00018300
00426           *         EXEC CICS READ
00427           *             DATASET('CUSTMST')
00428           *             INTO (CUSTMST-REC)
00429           *             RIDFLD(CUST-NO)
00430           *             LENGTH (CUSTMST-LNGTH)
00431           *             UPDATE
00432           *             END-EXEC.
00433                     MOVE 'CUSTMST' TO DFHEIV3 MOVE ' ' 0       ' TO DFHEIV0 CALL '0Q018400
00434           -    'DFHEI1' USING DFHEIV0 DFHEIV3 CUSTMST-REC CUSTMST-LNGTH
00435                     CUST-NO.
00436
00437
00438
00439
00441                     MOVE +0 TO WS-QTY.                                 00019200
00442                     IF S4SIGNI = '-'                                  00019300
00443                         SUBTRACT S4QTYI FROM WS-QTY                    00019400
00444                     ELSE                                              00019500
00445                         ADD S4QTYI TO WS-QTY.                         00019600
                 ************************************************************ 00019700
00446           *    UPDATE CURRENT WEEK SALES FIELD IN CUSTOMER MASTER    * 00019800
                 ************************************************************ 00019900
00449                     COMPUTE SALES-ENTERED EQUAL S4UNITPI * WS-QTY.    00020000
00450                     COMPUTE CUST-CURR-WK-SALES EQUAL SALES-EXTENDED + 00020100
00451                         CUST-CURR-WK-SALES.                           00020200
00453           *         EXEC CICS REWRITE
00454           *             DATASET('CUSTMST')
00455           *             FROM (CUSTMST-REC)
00456           *             LENGTH (CUSTMST-LNGTH)
```

FIGURE 10.4   (Continued)

```
00457        *            END-EXEC.
00458                     MOVE 'CUSTMST' TO DFHEIV3 MOVE ' \       ' TO DFHEIVO CALL '00020400
00459        -            'DFHEI1' USING DFHEIVO DFHEIV3 CUSTMST-REC CUSTMST-LNGTH.
00460
00461
00462
00463        *     EXEC CICS ASKTIME
00464        *            END-EXEC.
00465                     MOVE '       ' TO DFHEIVO CALL 'DFHEI1' USING DFHEIVO.       00020900
00466

00468              MOVE S4CUSTI TO LINEVSM-CUST-NO.                   00021200
00469              MOVE S4ITEMI TO LINEVSM-ITEM-CODE.                 00021300
00470              MOVE S4UNITPI TO LINEVSM-UNIT-PRICE.               00021400
00471              MOVE WS-QTY TO LINEVSM-QUANTITY.                   00021500
00472              MOVE EIRTIME TO LINEVSM-TIME.                      00021600
00473              MOVE EIRDATE TO LINEVSM-DATE.                      00021700
00474        *     EXEC CICS WRITE

   13                     23.30.11       OCT  3,1983

00475        *            DATASET('LINEVSM')
00476        *            FROM (LINEVSM-REC)
00477        *            LENGTH (45)
00478        *            RIDFLD(LINEVSM-VSAM-KEY)
00479        *            END-EXEC.
00480              MOVE 'LINEVSM' TO DFHEIV3 MOVE 45 TO DFHEIV11 MOVE ' 0   00021800
00481        -     ' ' TO DFHEIVO CALL 'DFHEI1' USING DFHEIVO DFHEIV3
00482              LINEVSM-REC DFHEIV11 LINEVSM-VSAM-KEY.
00483
00484
00485

00487        ***********************************************************  00022500
00488        *    IF QUANTITY IS NEGATIVE, THEN THE RECORD BEING ENTERED  *  00022600
00489        *    IS AN ADJUSTMENT TRANSACTION THAT IS MEANT TO REVERSE   *  00022700
00490        *    AN OLD TRANSACTION.  IN THAT CASE, WRITE A COPY OF IT   *  00022800
00491        *    TO THE 'LIST' TRANSIENT DATA OUTPUT QUEUE.             *  00022900
00492        ***********************************************************  00023000
00493              IF WS-QTY LESS THAN ZERO                           00023100
00494        *     EXEC CICS WRITEQ TD
00495        *            FROM (LINEVSM-REC)
00496        *            QUEUE ('LIST')
00497        *            LENGTH (45)
00498        *            END-EXEC.
00499              MOVE 'LIST' TO DFHEIV5 MOVE 45 TO DFHEIV11 MOVE ' \   00023200
00500        -     ' ' TO DFHEIVO CALL 'DFHEI1' USING DFHEIVO DFHEIV5
00501              LINEVSM-REC DFHEIV11.
00502
00503

00505        ***********************************************************  00023800
00506        *    REFRESH SCREEN SO THAT IT CAN BE USED FOR MORE INPUT.  *  00023900
00507        ***********************************************************  00024000
00508              MOVE ZEROES TO S4ITEMO, S4QTYO, S4UNITPO.          00024100
00509              MOVE '*' TO S4SIGNO.                               00024200
00510              MOVE NUM-REG-MOD-UNP TO S4CUSTA.                   00024300
00511              MOVE NUM-REG-MOD-PRD TO S4TRANA.                   00024400
00512              MOVE 'ACCEPTED' TO S4ERRO.                         00024500
00513        *     EXEC CICS SEND
00514        *            MAP ('SALE004')
00515        *            MAPSET ('MSALE04')
00516        *            LENGTH (136)
00517        *            DATAONLY
00518        *            END-EXEC.
00519              MOVE 'SALE004' TO DFHEIV1 MOVE 136 TO DFHEIV11 MOVE 'MSALE004000024600
00520        -     '' TO DFHEIV2 MOVE ' 0          ' TO DFHEIVO CALL 'DFHEI1'
00521              USING DFHEIVO DFHEIV1 SALE0040 DFHEIV11 DFHEIV2.
00522
00523
00524
00525        *     EXEC CICS RETURN
00526        *            TRANSID ('SAL4')
00527        *            END-EXEC.
00528              MOVE 'SAL4' TO DFHEIV5 MOVE '       ' TO DFHEIVO CALL 'DFH000252C0
00529        -     'EI1' USING DFHEIVO DFHEIV5.
00530

   14                     23.30.11       OCT  3,1983

00532        BAD-SALE.                                              00025600
00533              MOVE ERR-MSG TO S4ERRO.                          00025700
00534        *     EXEC CICS SEND
00535        *            MAP ('SALE004')
00536        *            MAPSET ('MSALE04')
00537        *            LENGTH (136)
00538        *            DATAONLY
00539        *            END-EXEC.
00540              MOVE 'SALE004' TO DFHEIV1 MOVE 136 TO DFHEIV11 MOVE 'MSALE004000025800
00541        -     '' TO DFHEIV2 MOVE ' 0          ' TO DFHEIVO CALL 'DFHEI1'
00542              USING DFHEIVO DFHEIV1 SALE0040 DFHEIV11 DFHEIV2.
00543
00544
00545
00546        *     EXEC CICS RETURN
00547        *            TRANSID ('SAL4')
00548        *            END-EXEC.
00549              MOVE 'SAL4' TO DFHEIV5 MOVE '       ' TO DFHEIVO CALL 'DFH000264C0
00550        -     'EI1' USING DFHEIVO DFHEIV5.
00551
00552        NON-EXECUTABLE-PARAGRAPH.                               00026700
00553              GOBACK.                                           00026800
```

FIGURE 10.4　(Continued)

```
      EXAMP000        23.30.11      OCT  3,1983


INTRNL NAME   LVL SOURCE NAME              BASE   DISPL   INTRNL NAME   DEFINITION   USAGE
DNM=1-163     01  DUMMY-FIELD              BL=1   000     DNM=1-163     DS 1C        DISP
DNM=1-184     01  ERROR-FLAG              BL=1   008     DNM=1-184     DS 1C        DISP
DNM=1-204     01  ERR-MSG                 BL=1   010     DNM=1-204     DS OCL38     GROUP
DNM=1-224     02  FILLER                  BL=1   010     DNM=1-224     DS 3AC       DISP
DNM=1-235     01  MAPFAIL-MSG             BL=1   038     DNM=1-235     DS OCL20     GROUP
DNM=1-259     02  FILLER                  BL=1   038     DNM=1-259     DS 20C       DISP
DNM=1-273     01  BAD-TRAN-MSG            BL=1   050     DNM=1-273     DS OCL17     GROUP
DNM=1-298     02  FILLER                  BL=1   050     DNM=1-298     DS 17C       DISP
DNM=1-312     01  NUM-REG-MOD-PRO         BL=1   068     DNM=1-312     DS 1C        DISP
DNM=1-337     01  NUM-REG-MOD-UNP         BL=1   070     DNM=1-337     DS 1C        DISP
DNM=1-362     01  NUM-BRT-UNM-UNP         BL=1   078     DNM=1-362     DS 1C        DISP
DNM=1-387     01  ALP-REG-MOD-UNP         BL=1   080     DNM=1-387     DS 1C        DISP
DNM=1-412     01  ALP-BRT-UNM-UNP         BL=1   088     DNM=1-412     DS 1C        DISP
DNM=1-437     01  MATH-WORK-AREAS         BL=1   090     DNM=1-437     DS OCL14     GROUP
DNM=1-465     02  SALES-ENTERED           BL=1   090     DNM=1-465     DS 7C        DISP-NM
DNM=2-000     02  SALES-EXTENDED          BL=1   097     DNM=2-000     DS 7C        DISP-NM
DNM=2-024     01  CUSTMST-LNGTH           BL=1   0A0     DNM=2-024     DS 2C        COMP
DNM=2-047     01  WS-QTY                  BL=1   0A8     DNM=2-047     DS 6C        DISP-NM
DNM=2-063     01  SALE004I                BL=1   0B0     DNM=2-063     DS OCL140    GROUP
DNM=2-084     02  FILLER                  BL=1   0B0     DNM=2-084     DS 12C       DISP
DNM=2-098     02  S4TRANL                 BL=1   0BC     DNM=2-098     DS 2C        COMP
DNM=2-115     02  S4TRANF                 BL=1   0BE     DNM=2-115     DS 1C        DISP
DNM=2-132     02  S4TRANI                 BL=1   0BF     DNM=2-132     DS 4C        DISP
DNM=2-149     02  S4CUSTL                 BL=1   0C3     DNM=2-149     DS 2C        COMP
DNM=2-166     02  S4CUSTF                 BL=1   0C5     DNM=2-166     DS 1C        DISP
DNM=2-183     02  S4CUSTI                 BL=1   0C6     DNM=2-183     DS 6C        DISP-NM
DNM=2-200     02  S4ITEML                 BL=1   0CC     DNM=2-200     DS 2C        COMP
DNM=2-217     02  S4ITEMF                 BL=1   0CE     DNM=2-217     DS 1C        DISP
DNM=2-234     02  S4ITEMI                 BL=1   0CF     DNM=2-234     DS 6C        DISP-NM
DNM=2-251     02  S4UNITPL                BL=1   0D5     DNM=2-251     DS 2C        COMP
DNM=2-269     02  S4UNITPF                BL=1   0D7     DNM=2-269     DS 1C        DISP
DNM=2-287     02  S4UNITPI                BL=1   0D8     DNM=2-287     DS 6C        DISP-NM
DNM=2-305     02  S4QTYL                  BL=1   0DE     DNM=2-305     DS 2C        COMP
DNM=2-321     02  S4QTYF                  BL=1   0E0     DNM=2-321     DS 1C        DISP
DNM=2-337     02  S4QTYI                  BL=1   0E1     DNM=2-337     DS 6C        DISP-NM
DNM=2-353     02  S4SIGNL                 BL=1   0E7     DNM=2-353     DS 2C        COMP
DNM=2-370     02  S4SIGNF                 BL=1   0E9     DNM=2-370     DS 1C        DISP
DNM=2-387     02  S4SIGNI                 BL=1   0EA     DNM=2-387     DS 1C        DISP
DNM=2-404     02  S4ERRL                  BL=1   0EB     DNM=2-404     DS 2C        COMP
DNM=2-420     02  S4ERRF                  BL=1   0ED     DNM=2-420     DS 1C        DISP
DNM=2-436     02  S4ERRI                  BL=1   0EE     DNM=2-436     DS 7AC       DISP
DNM=2-452     01  SALE0040                BL=1   0B0     DNM=2-452     DS OCL140    GROUP
DNM=2-473     02  FILLER                  BL=1   0B0     DNM=2-473     DS 12C       DISP
DNM=2-487     02  FILLER                  BL=1   0BC     DNM=2-487     DS 2C        DISP
DNM=3-000     02  S4TRANA                 BL=1   0BE     DNM=3-000     DS 1C        DISP
DNM=3-017     02  S4TRANO                 BL=1   0BF     DNM=3-017     DS 4C        DISP
DNM=3-034     02  FILLER                  BL=1   0C3     DNM=3-034     DS 2C        DISP
DNM=3-048     02  S4CUSTA                 BL=1   0C5     DNM=3-048     DS 1C        DISP
DNM=3-065     02  S4CUSTO                 BL=1   0C6     DNM=3-065     DS 6C        DISP
DNM=3-082     02  FILLER                  BL=1   0CC     DNM=3-082     DS 2C        DISP
DNM=3-096     02  S4ITEMA                 BL=1   0CE     DNM=3-096     DS 1C        DISP
DNM=3-113     02  S4ITEMO                 BL=1   0CF     DNM=3-113     DS 6C        DISP
DNM=3-133     02  FILLER                  BL=1   0D5     DNM=3-133     DS 2C        DISP
DNM=3-147     02  S4UNITPA                BL=1   0D7     DNM=3-147     DS 1C        DISP
DNM=3-165     02  S4UNITPO                BL=1   0D8     DNM=3-165     DS 6C        DISP
```

FIGURE 10.4   *(Continued)*

```
16        EXAMP000        23.30.11      OCT  3,1983
```

DNM		Name	BL	Offset	DNM	DS	Usage
DNM=3-183	02	FILLER	BL=1	0DE	DNM=3-183	DS 2C	DISP
DNM=3-197	02	S4QTYA	BL=1	0E0	DNM=3-197	DS 2C	DISP
DNM=3-213	02	S4QTYO	BL=1	0E1	DNM=3-213	DS 6C	DISP
DNM=3-229	02	FILLER	BL=1	0E7	DNM=3-229	DS 2C	DISP
DNM=3-243	02	S4SIGNA	BL=1	0E9	DNM=3-243	DS 1C	DISP
DNM=3-260	02	S4SIGNO	BL=1	0EA	DNM=3-260	DS 1C	DISP
DNM=3-277	02	FILLER	BL=1	0EB	DNM=3-277	DS 2C	DISP
DNM=3-291	02	S4ERRA	BL=1	0ED	DNM=3-291	DS 1C	DISP
DNM=3-310	02	S4ERRO	BL=1	0EE	DNM=3-310	DS 78C	DISP
DNM=3-326	01	CUSTMST-REC	BL=1	140	DNM=3-326	DS 0CL150	GROUP
DNM=3-350	02	CUST-VSAM-KEY	BL=1	14C	DNM=3-350	DS 0CL6	GROUP
DNM=3-376	03	CUST-NO	BL=1	14C	DNM=3-376	DS 6C	DISP
DNM=3-393	02	CUST-NAME	BL=1	146	DNM=3-393	DS 25C	DISP
DNM=3-412	02	CUST-CONTACT	BL=1	15F	DNM=3-412	DS 25C	DISP
DNM=3-434	02	CUST-STREET-ADDRESS	BL=1	178	DNM=3-434	DS 25C	DISP
DNM=3-463	02	CUST-CITY	BL=1	191	DNM=3-463	DS 20C	DISP
DNM=3-482	02	CUST-STATE	BL=1	1A5	DNM=3-482	DS 2C	DISP
DNM=4-000	02	CUST-ZIP-9	BL=1	1A7	DNM=4-000	DS 0CL9	GROUP
DNM=4-026	03	CUST-ZIP-5	BL=1	1A7	DNM=4-026	DS 5C	DISP
DNM=4-046	03	FILLER	BL=1	1AC	DNM=4-046	DS 4C	DISP
DNM=4-060	02	CUST-LAST-BILL-DATE	BL=1	1B0	DNM=4-060	DS 0CL6	GROUP
DNM=4-095	03	CUST-BILL-YY	BL=1	1B0	DNM=4-095	DS 2C	DISP-NM
DNM=4-117	03	CUST-BILL-MM	BL=1	1B2	DNM=4-117	DS 2C	DISP-NM
DNM=4-139	03	CUST-BILL-DD	BL=1	1B4	DNM=4-139	DS 2C	DISP-NM
DNM=4-161	02	CUST-LAST-BILL-BAL-DUE	BL=1	1B6	DNM=4-161	DS 7C	DISP-NM
DNM=4-193	02	CUST-CURR-WK-SALES	BL=1	1BD	DNM=4-193	DS 7C	DISP-NM
DNM=4-221	02	FILLER	BL=1	1C4	DNM=4-221	DS 18C	DISP
DNM=4-235	01	LINEVSM-REC	BL=1	1C8	DNM=4-235	DS 0CL45	GROUP
DNM=4-259	02	LINEVSM-VSAM-KEY	BL=1	1C8	DNM=4-259	DS 0CL20	GROUP
DNM=4-288	03	LINEVSM-CUST-NO	BL=1	1D8	DNM=4-288	DS 6C	DISP
DNM=4-313	03	LINEVSM-DATE	BL=1	1DE	DNM=4-313	DS 4P	COMP-3
DNM=4-335	03	LINEVSM-TIME	BL=1	1E2	DNM=4-335	DS 4P	COMP-3
DNM=4-360	03	LINEVSM-ITEM-CODE	BL=1	1E6	DNM=4-360	DS 6C	DISP
DNM=4-387	02	LINEVSM-UNIT-PRICE	BL=1	1EC	DNM=4-387	DS 7C	DISP-NM
DNM=4-418	02	LINEVSM-QUANTITY	BL=1	1F3	DNM=4-418	DS 6C	DISP-NM
DNM=4-444	02	FILLER	BL=1	1F9	DNM=4-444	DS 12C	DISP
DNM=4-458	01	DFHAID	BL=1	208	DNM=4-458	DS 0CL35	GROUP
DNM=4-477	02	DFHNULL	BL=1	208	DNM=4-477	DS 1C	DISP
DNM=5-000	02	DFHENTER	BL=1	2C9	DNM=5-000	DS 1C	DISP
DNM=5-018	02	DFHCLEAR	BL=1	2CA	DNM=5-018	DS 1C	DISP
DNM=5-039	02	DFHPEN	BL=1	2CB	DNM=5-039	DS 1C	DISP
DNM=5-055	02	DFHOPID	BL=1	2OC	DNM=5-055	DS 1C	DISP
DNM=5-072	02	DFHMSRE	BL=1	2CD	DNM=5-072	DS 1C	DISP
DNM=5-089	02	DFHSTRF	BL=1	2CE	DNM=5-089	DS 1C	DISP
DNM=5-106	02	DFHTRIG	BL=1	2CF	DNM=5-106	DS 1C	DISP
DNM=5-123	02	DFHPA1	BL=1	21C	DNM=5-123	DS 1C	DISP
DNM=5-139	02	DFHPA2	BL=1	211	DNM=5-139	DS 1C	DISP
DNM=5-155	02	DFHPA3	BL=1	212	DNM=5-155	DS 1C	DISP
DNM=5-171	02	DFHPF1	BL=1	213	DNM=5-171	DS 1C	DISP
DNM=5-187	02	DFHPF2	BL=1	214	DNM=5-187	DS 1C	DISP
DNM=5-203	02	DFHPF3	BL=1	215	DNM=5-203	DS 1C	DISP
DNM=5-219	02	DFHPF4	BL=1	216	DNM=5-219	DS 1C	DISP
DNM=5-235	02	DFHPF5	BL=1	217	DNM=5-235	DS 1C	DISP
DNM=5-251	02	DFHPF6	BL=1	218	DNM=5-251	DS 1C	DISP
DNM=5-267	02	DFHPF7	BL=1	219	DNM=5-267	DS 1C	DISP
DNM=5-283	02	DFHPF8	BL=1	21A	DNM=5-283	DS 1C	DISP
DNM=5-299	02	DFHPF9	BL=1	21B	DNM=5-299	DS 1C	DISP

```
17        EXAMP000        23.30.11      OCT  3,1983
```

DNM		Name	BL	Offset	DNM	DS	Usage
DNM=5-315	02	DFHPF10	BL=1	21C	DNM=5-315	DS 1C	DISP
DNM=5-335	02	DFHPF11	BL=1	21D	DNM=5-335	DS 1C	DISP
DNM=5-352	02	DFHPF12	BL=1	21E	DNM=5-352	DS 1C	DISP
DNM=5-369	02	DFHPF13	BL=1	21F	DNM=5-369	DS 1C	DISP
DNM=5-389	02	DFHPF14	BL=1	220	DNM=5-389	DS 1C	DISP
DNM=5-406	02	DFHPF15	BL=1	221	DNM=5-406	DS 1C	DISP
DNM=5-423	02	DFHPF16	BL=1	222	DNM=5-423	DS 1C	DISP
DNM=5-440	02	DFHPF17	BL=1	223	DNM=5-440	DS 1C	DISP
DNM=5-457	02	DFHPF18	BL=1	224	DNM=5-457	DS 1C	DISP
DNM=5-474	02	DFHPF19	BL=1	225	DNM=5-474	DS 1C	DISP
DNM=5-491	02	DFHPF20	BL=1	226	DNM=5-491	DS 1C	DISP
DNM=6-000	02	DFHPF21	BL=1	227	DNM=6-000	DS 1C	DISP
DNM=6-017	02	DFHPF22	BL=1	228	DNM=6-017	DS 1C	DISP
DNM=6-034	02	DFHPF23	BL=1	229	DNM=6-034	DS 1C	DISP
DNM=6-051	02	DFHPF24	BL=1	22A	DNM=6-051	DS 1C	DISP
DNM=6-068	01	DFHEIV	BL=1	230	DNM=6-068	DS 0CL106	GROUP
DNM=6-090	02	DFHEIV0	BL=1	230	DNM=6-090	DS 26C	DISP
DNM=6-107	02	DFHEIV1	BL=1	24A	DNM=6-107	DS 8C	DISP
DNM=6-127	02	DFHEIV2	BL=1	252	DNM=6-127	DS 8C	DISP
DNM=6-144	02	DFHEIV3	BL=1	25A	DNM=6-144	DS 8C	DISP
DNM=6-164	02	DFHEIV4	BL=1	262	DNM=6-164	DS 6C	DISP
DNM=6-181	02	DFHEIV5	BL=1	268	DNM=6-181	DS 4C	DISP
DNM=6-198	02	DFHEIV6	BL=1	26C	DNM=6-198	DS 4C	DISP
DNM=6-215	02	DFHEIV7	BL=1	270	DNM=6-215	DS 2C	DISP
DNM=6-232	02	DFHEIV8	BL=1	272	DNM=6-232	DS 2C	DISP
DNM=6-249	02	DFHEIV9	BL=1	274	DNM=6-249	DS 1C	DISP
DNM=6-266	02	DFHEIV10	BL=1	275	DNM=6-266	DS 4P	COMP-3
DNM=6-284	02	DFHEIV11	BL=1	279	DNM=6-284	DS 2C	COMP
DNM=6-302	02	DFHEIV12	BL=1	27B	DNM=6-302	DS 2C	COMP
DNM=6-320	02	DFHEIV13	BL=1	27D	DNM=6-320	DS 2C	COMP
DNM=6-341	02	DFHEIV14	BL=1	27F	DNM=6-341	DS 2C	COMP
DNM=6-359	02	DFHEIV15	BL=1	2E1	DNM=6-359	DS 2C	COMP
DNM=6-377	02	DFHEIV16	BL=1	2E3	DNM=6-377	DS 4C	COMP
DNM=6-395	02	DFHEIV17	BL=1	2E7	DNM=6-395	DS 4C	DISP

FIGURE 10.4 *(Continued)*

DNM=6-416	02	DFHEIV18	BL =1	28B	DNM=6-416	DS 4C	DISP
DNM=6-434	02	DFHEIV19	BL =1	28F	DNM=6-434	DS 4C	DISP
DNM=6-452	02	DFHEIV97	BL =1	293	DNM=6-452	DS 4P	COMP-3
DNM=6-470	02	DFHEIV98	BL =1	297	DNM=6-470	DS 2C	COMP
DNM=6-488	02	DFHEIV99	BL =1	299	DNM=6-488	DS 1C	DISP
DNM=7-000	01	DFHEIBLK	BLL =3	000	DNM=7-000	DS OCL66	GROUP
DNM=7-021	02	EIBTIME	BLL =3	000	DNM=7-021	DS 4P	COMP-3
DNM=7-038	02	EIBDATE	BLL =3	004	DNM=7-038	DS 4P	COMP-3
DNM=7-055	02	EIBTRNID	BLL =3	0C8	DNM=7-055	DS 4C	DISP
DNM=7-073	02	EIBTASKN	BLL =3	0CC	DNM=7-073	DS 4P	COMP-3
DNM=7-094	02	EIBTRMID	BLL =3	010	DNM=7-094	DS 4C	DISP
DNM=7-112	02	DFHEIGDI	BLL =3	014	DNM=7-112	DS 2C	COMP
DNM=7-133	02	EIBCPOSN	BLL =3	016	DNM=7-133	DS 2C	COMP
DNM=7-154	02	EIBCALEN	BLL =3	018	DNM=7-154	DS 2C	COMP
DNM=7-175	02	EIBAID	BLL =3	01A	DNM=7-175	DS 1C	DISP
DNM=7-194	02	EIBFN	BLL =3	01B	DNM=7-194	DS 2C	DISP
DNM=7-209	02	EIBRCODE	BLL =3	01D	DNM=7-209	DS 6C	DISP
DNM=7-227	02	EIBDS	BLL =3	023	DNM=7-227	DS 8C	DISP
DNM=7-242	02	EIBREQID	BLL =3	02B	DNM=7-242	DS 8C	DISP
DNM=7-260	02	EIBRSRCE	BLL =3	033	DNM=7-260	DS 8C	DISP
DNM=7-278	02	EIBSYNC	BLL =3	03B	DNM=7-278	DS 1C	DISP
DNM=7-295	02	EIBFREE	BLL =3	03C	DNM=7-295	DS 1C	DISP
DNM=7-315	02	EIBRECV	BLL =3	03D	DNM=7-315	DS 1C	DISP

18   EXAMP00C   23.30.11   OCT 3,1983

DNM=7-335	02	EIBSEND	BLL =3	03E	DNM=7-335	DS 1C	DISP
DNM=7-352	02	EIBATT	BLL =3	03F	DNM=7-352	DS 1C	DISP
DNM=7-368	02	EIBEOC	BLL =3	040	DNM=7-368	DS 1C	DISP
DNM=7-387	02	EIBFMH	BLL =3	041	DNM=7-387	DS 1C	DISP
DNM=7-403	01	DFHCOMMAREA	BLL =4	000	DNM=7-403	DS 1C	DISP
DNM=7-424	01	DFHBLLSLOT1	BLL =5	000	DNM=7-424	DS 1C	DISP
DNM=7-445	01	DFHBLLSLOT2	BLL =6	000	DNM=7-445	DS 1C	DISP

19   EXAMP000   23.30.11   OCT 3,1983

MEMORY MAP

TGT	00340
SAVE AREA	00340
SWITCH	00388
TALLY	0038C
SORT SAVE	00390
ENTRY-SAVE	00394
SORT CORE SIZE	00398
RET CODE	0039C
SORT RET	0039E
WORKING CELLS	003A0
SORT FILE SIZE	004D0
SORT MODE SIZE	004D4
PGT-VN TBL	004D8
TGT-VN TBL	004DC
RESERVED	004E0
LENGTH OF VN TBL	004E4
LABEL RET	004E6
RESERVED	004E7
DBG R14SAVE	004E8
COBOL INDICATOR	004EC
A(INIT1)	004F0
DEBUG TABLE PTR	004F4
SUBCOM PTR	004F8
SORT-MESSAGE	004FC
SYSOUT DDNAME	00504
RESERVED	00505
COBOL ID	00506
COMPILED POINTER	00508
COUNT TABLE ADDRESS	0050C
RESERVED	00510
DBG R11SAVE	00518
COUNT CHAIN ADDRESS	0051C
PRBL1 CELL PTR	00520
RESERVED	00524
TA LENGTH	00529
RESERVED	0052C
PCS LIT PTR	00534
DEBUGGING	0053B
CD FOR INITIAL INPUT	0053C
OVERFLOW CELLS	00540
BL CELLS	00540
DECBADR CELLS	00544
FIB CELLS	00544
TEMP STORAGE	00548
TEMP STORAGE-2	00558
TEMP STORAGE-3	00558
TEMP STORAGE-4	00558
BLL CELLS	00558
VLC CELLS	00574
SBL CELLS	00574
INDEX CELLS	00574
SUBADR CELLS	00574
ONCTL CELLS	00574

FIGURE 10.4   *(Continued)*

```
20          EXAMP000          23.30.11          OCT  3,1983


            PFMCTL CELLS                        00574
            PFMSAV CELLS                        00574
            VN CELLS                            0057B
            SAVE AREA =2                        00580
            SAVE AREA =3                        00580
            XSASW CELLS                         00580
            XSA CELLS                           00580
            PARAM CELLS                         0058D
            RPTSAV AREA                         00594
            CHECKPT CTR                         00594

LITERAL POOL (HEX)

00630 (LIT+0)      00110014   0000BBFF   FFF0F0F0   F0F0C000   2D0FC2C4   80000424
00648 (LIT+24)     00000000   00000000   00000000   0001E2C1   D3C5F0F0   F4D4E2C1
00660 (LIT+48)     D3C5F0F4   18320000   04000000   00050900   000020E2   C1D3F404
00678 (LIT+72)     04300004   00000081   00004000   00000E08   000C0400   001000E2
00690 (LIT+96)     C1D3C5C9   D5C9E30F   04800004   00000200   C9D5E5C1   D3C9C440
006A8 (LIT+120)    C6E4D5C3   E3C9D6D5   40D2C5E8   1804F000   04000000   00052004
006C0 (LIT+144)    0000200F   08800004   00001000   C9E3C5D4   40D5E4D4   C2C5D940
006D8 (LIT+168)    D5D6E340   D5E4D4C5   D9C9C340   6040D9C5   D2C5E8E4   D5C9E340
006F0 (LIT+192)    D7D9C9C3   C540D5D6   E340D5E4   D4C5D9C9   C3406040   D9C5D2C5
00708 (LIT+216)    EBDBE4C1   D5E3C9E3   EB40D5D6   E340D5E4   D4C5D9C9   C3406040
00720 (LIT+240)    D9C5D2C5   EBC9D5E5   C1D3C9C4   40E2C9C7   D540D6D5   40DBE4C1
00738 (LIT+264)    D5E3C9E3   EB40C6C9   C5D3C402   04B00004   0D0C0000   00000000
00750 (LIT+288)    00000000   00C3E4E2   E3D4E2E3   0602F000   040C00B4   000606E0
00768 (LIT+312)    00040000   40001002   00000400   00130003   C9D5C5F5   E2D40604
00780 (LIT+336)    F000042B   00440003   C9E2E30B   02E00004   00004000   C1C3C3C5
00798 (LIT+360)    D7E3C5C4


            PGT                                 005A0


            OVERFLOW CELLS                      005A0
            VIRTUAL CELLS                       005A0
            PROCEDURE NAME CELLS                005B4
            GENERATED NAME CELLS                005CB
            DCB ADDRESS CELLS                   0062B
            VNI CELLS                           0062B
            LITERALS                            0063D
            DISPLAY LITERALS                    0079C


     REGISTER ASSIGNMENT

     REG 6    BL =1

WORKING-STORAGE STARTS AT LOCATION 000A0 FOR A LENGTH OF 0029C.
```

FIGURE 10.4 *(Continued)*

```
21      EXAMP000        23.30.11        OCT  3,1983

                        CONDENSED LISTING

250  ENTRY     00079C    251  SERVICE  00C784    256  MOVE     00C7B4
256  CALL      0007C4    257  GO       0007EE    263  MOVE     000F1C
263  MOVE      000826    263  MOVE     000E30    264  CALL     000F40
267  IF        00088A    280  MOVE     00C896    273  CALL     00C89C
274  CALL      0008AC    294  IF       00C8F6    280  CALL     000906
282  GO        000930    289  CALL     000936    288  MOVE     000946
288  MOVE      00094C    295  MOVE     00C9D4    292  IF       000994
293  PERFORM   00098D    302  CALL     00C9FA    301  MOVE     00C9E4
301  MOVE      0009EA    316  MOVE     00CA7E    308  MOVE     000A44
308  CALL      000A54    332  IF       00CADE    316  MOVE     000AB4
316  CALL      000A94    335  MOVE     00CB1E    323  CALL     000AEE
326  EXIT      000B1E    342  MOVE     000B5E    333  MOVE     000B2F
334  MOVE      000B34    351  MOVE     00CBC2    342  MOVE     000B4E
342  MOVE      000B58    361  IF       00CC0A    343  MOVE     000B6R
343  MOVE      000B78    366  MOVE     00CC30    351  MOVE     000BCR
351  CALL      000B09    368  MOVE     000C52    358  MOVE     000C1A
360  CALL      000C26    373  MOVE     000C6C    363  MOVE     000C3C
365  IF        000C5C    377  MOVE     000CBE    367  MOVE     000C5A
368  MOVE      000C82    380  IF       000CAA    370  IF       000C7A
371  MOVE      000CA4    385  MOVE     00CCCA    375  IF       000C9E
376  MOVE      000CBE    388  IF       00CCF0    378  MOVE     000C4E
378  MOVE      000CE0    392  MOVE     000D00    381  MOVE     000CD4
383  MOVE      000CFC    397  MOVE     00002A    386  MOVE     000CF6
387  MOVE      000D20    400  MOVE     00004C    389  MOVE     000D14
391  IF        000D45    407  MOVE     00CD60    394  MOVE     000D36
396  MOVE      000D56    415  MOVE     00CD76    398  MOVE     000D52
399  IF        000D72    421  CALL     00000A    407  MOVE     000D66
407  MOVE      000D90    433  MOVE     000E24    408  MOVE     000D80
408  CALL      000E14    441  MOVE     000E82    415  CALL     000DEA
421  MOVE      000E7C    445  MOVE     000EE6    422  GO       000E4E
425  MOVE      000E9C    458  ADD      00CF14    433  MOVE     000ERC
433  CALL      000EF6    465  MOVE     000F5C    442  IF       000EEC
443  SUBTRACT  000F44    469  MOVE     00CFB8    449  COMPUTE  000F2C
450  COMPUTE   000F76    472  MOVE     00CFF8    458  MOVE     000F66
458  CALL      000FF2    480  MOVE     001016    465  CALL     000FCR
468  MOVE      001010    493  IF       001030    470  MOVF     000FFE
471  MOVE      001026    499  MOVE     001090    473  MOVE     001020
480  MOVE      001046    509  MOVE     0010AE    480  MOVE     001036
481  CALL      001048    512  MOVE     00111E    499  MOVE     0010A7
499  MOVE      001100    519  MOVE     00112E    500  CALL     0010BF
508  MOVE      001128    528  MOVE     0011B2    510  MOVE     001122
511  MOVE      001148    533  MOVE     0011FA    519  MOVE     00113E
519  MOVE      001168    540  MOVE     00121A    520  MOVE     00115B
520  CALL      0011CB    549  MOVE     00127E    528  MOVE     0011B8
528  CALL      001214    553  GOBACK   0012C6    540  MOVE     00120A
540  MOVE      001234                            541  MOVE     001274
541  CALL      001294                            549  MOVE     001284
```

FIGURE 10.4 *(Continued)*

22   EXAMP000   23.30.11   OCT 3,1983

```
*STATISTICS*     SOURCE RECORDS =     553     DATA DIVISION STATEMENTS =    176     PROCEDURE DIVISION STATEMENTS =    153
*OPTIONS IN EFFECT*     SIZE = 131072  BUF =   16384  LINECNT = 57  SPACE1,  FLAGW,   SEQ,    SOURCE
*OPTIONS IN EFFECT*     DMAP, NOPMAP,   CLIST,   SUPMAP, NOXREF,   SXREF,   LOAD, NODECK, APOST, NOTRUNC, NOFLOW
*OPTIONS IN EFFECT*     NOTERM, NONUM, NOBATCH, NONAME, COMPILE=01, NOSTATE, NORESIDENT, NODYNAM,   LIB, NOSYNTAX
*OPTIONS IN EFFECT*     NOOPTIMIZE, NOSYMDMP, NOTEST,  VERB,    ZWB, SYST, NOENDJOB, NOLVL
*OPTIONS IN EFFECT*     NOLST , NOFDECK,NOCDECK, LCOL2, L120,    DUMP ,   ADV , NOPRINT,
*OPTIONS IN EFFECT*     NOCOUNT, NOVBSUM, NOVBREF, LANGLVL(2)
```

FIGURE 10.4 (Continued)

CROSS-REFERENCE DICTIONARY

DATA NAMES	DEFN	REFERENCE
ALP-BRT-UNM-UNP	000052	000392 000396
ALP-REG-MOD-UNP	000051	000389
BAD-TRAN-MSG	000041	000274
CUST-BILL-DD	000122	
CUST-BILL-MM	000121	
CUST-BILL-YY	000120	
CUST-CITY	000114	
CUST-CONTACT	000112	
CUST-CURR-WK-SALES	000124	000450
CUST-LAST-BILL-BAL-DUE	000123	
CUST-LAST-BILL-DATE	000119	
CUST-NAME	000111	
CUST-NO	000110	000425 000433
CUST-STATE	000115	
CUST-STREET-ADDRESS	000113	
CUST-VSAM-KEY	030109	
CUST-ZIP-5	000117	
CUST-ZIP-9	000116	
CUSTMST-LNGTH	000056	000433 000458
CUSTMST-REC	000108	000433 000458
DFHAID	000139	
DFHBLLSLOT1	000248	
DFHBLLSLOT2	000249	
DFHCLEAR	000247	000292
DFHCOMMAREA	000204	
DFHEIBLK	000216	
DFHEIGD1	000177	000256 000257 000422
DFHEIVO	000178	000263 0C264 0CC273 000274 000280 000288 000289 000301 000302 000308 000316 000323 0CC343 000342 000343 000351 000407 000408 000415 000421 000433 000458 000465 000480 000481 000499 000500 000519 000520 000528 000540 000541 000549
DFHEIV1	000179	
DFHEIV10	000188	
DFHEIV11	000189	000273 000274 000301 000302 000316 000342 000343 000407 000408 000481 000499 000500 000519 000520 000540 000541
DFHEIV12	000190	
DFHEIV13	000191	
DFHEIV14	000192	
DFHEIV15	000193	
DFHEIV16	000194	
DFHEIV17	000195	
DFHEIV18	000196	000263 000264 000289 000342 000343 000408 000481 000519 000520 000540 000541
DFHEIV19	000197	000263 000288 000433 000458
DFHEIV2	000180	000264 000289 000408 000481
DFHEIV3	000181	000288 000480
DFHEIV4	000182	000351 000499 000500 000528 000549
DFHEIV5	000183	000351
DFHEIV6	000184	
DFHEIV7	000185	
DFHEIV8	000186	
DFHEIV9	000187	

FIGURE 10.4 (Continued)

```
  24        EXAMP000        23.30.11      OCT  3,1983


DFHEIV97                    000198
DFHEIV98                    000199      000264   000274   000302   0C0316
DFHEIV99                    000200      000274   000302   000316
DFHENTER                    000141      000332
DFHMSRE                     000145
DFHNULL                     000140
DFHOPID                     000144
DFHPA1                      000148      000292
DFHPA2                      000149      000284
OFHPA3                      000150
DFHPEN                      000143
DFHPF1                      000151
DFHPF10                     000160
DFHPF11                     000161
DFHPF12                     000162
DFHPF13                     000163
DFHPF14                     000164
DFHPF15                     000165
DFHPF16                     000166
DFHPF17                     000167
DFHPF18                     000168
DFHPF19                     000169
DFHPF2                      000152
DFHPF20                     000170
DFHPF21                     000171
DFHPF22                     000172
DFHPF23                     000173
DFHPF24                     000174
DFHPF3                      000153
DFHPF4                      000154
DFHPF5                      000155
DFHPF6                      000156
DFHPF7                      000157
DFHPF8                      000158
DFHPF9                      000159
DFHSTRF                     000146
DFHTRIG                     000147
DUMMY-FIELD                 000033      000316
EIBAID                      000222      000284   000292   000332
EIBATT                      000242
EIBCALEN                    000220
EIBCPOSN                    000218
EIBDATE                     000208      000473
EIBDS                       000228
EIBEOC                      000244
EIBFMH                      000246
EIBFN                       000224
EIBFREE                     000236
EIBRCODE                    000226
EIBRECV                     000238
EIBREQID                    000230
EIBRSRCE                    000232
EIBSEND                     000240
EIBSYNC                     000234
EIBTASKN                    000212
EIBTIME                     000206      000472
EIBTRMID                    000214
```

FIGURE 10.4 *(Continued)*

```
25      EXAMP000          23.30.11          OCT  3,1983                                    000377  000380  000387  000391  000398  000399

EIBTRNID             000210
ERR-MSG              000035   000295   000302   000533
ERROR-FLAG           000034   000360   000367   000370
LINEVSM-CUST-NO      000130   000468   000473
LINEVSM-DATE         000131   000469
LINEVSM-ITEM-CODE    000133   000481
LINEVSM-QUANTITY     000135   000471   000500
LINEVSM-REC          000128   000481
LINEVSM-TIME         000132   000472
LINEVSM-UNIT-PRICE   000134   000470
LINEVSM-VSAM-KEY     000129   000481
MAPFAIL-MSG          000038   000295
MATH-WORK-AREAS      000053
NUM-BRT-UNM-UNP      000050   000361   000365   000371   000533
NUM-REG-MOD-PRD      000048   000333   000400   000511
NUM-REG-MOD-UNP      000049   000358   000368   000378   000510
SALES-ENTERED        000054   000449
SALES-EXTENDED       000055   000450
SALEO04I             000041   000264
SALEO04O             000063   000334   000343   000468   0C0520   000541
S4CUSTA              000089   000510
S4CUSTF              000066
S4CUSTI              000067   000425   000468
S4CUSTL              000065
S4CUSTO              000090
S4ERRA               000104
S4ERRF               000081
S4ERRI               000082
S4ERRL               000080
S4ERRO               000105   000335   000363   000373   0CC383   000394   000512   000533
S4ITEMA              000092   000358   000361   000365
S4ITEMF              000069   000469
S4ITEMI              000070   000357
S4ITEML              000068   000366
S4ITEMO              000093   000508   000378   0C03P5   000381   000445
S4QTYA               000098   000378   000443
S4QTYF               000076
S4QTYI               000075   000386   000443   000445
S4QTYL               000074
S4QTYO               000099   000508
S4SIGNA              000101   000389   000392   000396
S4SIGNF              000078
S4SIGNI              000079   000388   000442
S4SIGNL              000077   000397
S4SIGNO              000102   000509
S4TRANA              000086   000333   000400   000511
S4TRANF              000063
S4TRANI              000064   000267
S4TRANL              000362
S4TRANO              000087
S4UNITPA             000095   000368   000371   000375
S4UNITPF             000072   000449   000470
S4UNITPI             000073   000368
S4UNITPL             000071   000376
S4UNITPO             000096   000508
WS-QTY               000357   000441   000443   000445   0CC449   000471   000493
```

FIGURE 10.4 *(Continued)*

26   EXAMP000   23.30.11   OCT   3,1983

PROCEDURE NAMES   DEFN   REFERENCE

BAD-MAP   000283   000257
BAD-SALE   000532   000422
CLEAR-ROUTINE   000310   000293
INIT-EXIT   000325   000282
INIT-ROUTINE   000252
MAIN-LINE   000328
NON-EXECUTABLE-PARAGRAPH   000552

FIGURE 10.4 (Continued)

```
F64-LEVEL LINKAGE EDITOR OPTIONS SPECIFIED XREF,LIST,MAP
         DEFAULT OPTION(S) USED -   SIZE=(196608,65536)
IEW0000  INCLUDE SYSLIB(DFHECI)

                                                        50000000

                            CROSS REFERENCE TABLE

CONTROL SECTION
  NAME      ORIGIN   LENGTH
  DFHECI    00       18

  EXAMP000  18       1300
  ILBOCOMO* 13E8     160
  ILBOSRV * 1558     4A4
  ILBOWTB * 1A00     11A
  ILBOBEG * 1B20     188
  ILBOMSG * 1CA8     10D

ENTRY
  NAME      LOCATION   NAME      LOCATION   NAME      LOCATION   NAME      LOCATION   NAME      LOCATION
  DFHCBLI   4          DFHEI1    4          DLZEI01   4          DLZEI02   A
  DLZEI03   A          DLZEI04   A          DFHAICBA  14
  ILBOCOM   13E8
  ILBOSRV0  1562       ILBOSP5   1562       ILBOSR3   1562       ILBOSR    1562
  ILBOSRV1  1566       ILBOSTP1  1566       ILBOST    156A       ILBOSTP0  156A
  ILBOWTB0  1A02
  ILBOBEG0  1B22
  ILBOMSGO  1CAA

LOCATION  REFERS TO SYMBOL  IN CONTROL SECTION     LOCATION  REFERS TO SYMBOL  IN CONTROL SECTION
  5B8       ILBOSPVO          ILBOSRV                 5BC       ILBOSP5           ILBOSRV
  5C0       DFHEI1            DFHECI                  5C4       ILBOWTBO          ILBOWTB
  5C8       ILBOSRV1          ILBOSRV                 510       ILBOCOMO          ILBOCOMO
  18E4      ILBOCMO           ILBOCOMO                18F8      ILBOSTO           $UNRESOLVED(W)
  18E8      ILBOMSGO          $UNRESOLVED(W)          18EC      ILBOBEGO          ILBOBEG
  18F0      ILBOPMO           ILBOMSG                 18F4      ILBOSND2          $UNRESOLVED(W)
  1C60                        $UNRESOLVED(W)

ENTRY ADDRESS   18

TOTAL LENGTH    10A8
****EXAMP000   NOW REPLACED IN DATA SET
AUTHORIZATION CODE IS    0.
```

FIGURE 10.4 (Continued)

```
CUSTOMER INFORMATION CONTROL SYSTEM STORAGE DUMP      CODE=ASFA    TASK=EX00              DATE=10/04/83   TIME=01:13:23   PAGE   1

PSW         078D0007   E0165F76

REGS 14-4   501CD838   001663F0   00000000   0012490C          00165F34   C01655D4   0012A0A8

REGS 5-11   FF000000   0012442C   01248D3   01248D4           00166366   0165020    00165020


TASK CONTROL AREA (USER AREA)              ADDRESS 124100 TO 1243DF      LENGTH 0002E0

000000  00124000 001B36D4 011D599A 001E47D8  00124210 00125020 001CA310 4300FF00  *.....M..q.-7U...*  124100
000020  401C95DE 00000000 00000000 00125020  501C9310 00125050 001250A4 00000000  *.n..........t..u*  124120
000040  00124FB0 001C83F0 001CAD62 00000000  00125090 00125010 501CD838 001251F0  *....c0........Q..*  124140
000060  401CD6C6 C1E2D9C1 00000000 0006C000  001CE00C 001A5560 001CD540 00124FB0  *..OFASRA........*  124160
000080  FE005090 C3E4E2E3 D4E2E340 C1E2D9C1  078D0007 E0165F76 00000000 001245BC  *....CUSTMST ASFA.*  124180
0000A0  501CD838 001663F0 00000000 0012490C  00165F34 00165504 00124A08 FF000000  *....Q........M...*  1241A0
0000C0  0012442C 00124803 24F40000 00166366  00165020 00165020 06020000 00000303  *........M.......*  1241C0
0000E0  001251F0 8C0000A8 24F40000 00000000  00125150 00000000 00000000 00000000  *...0..y.4...&....*  124200
000100  801CB8E2 00000000 0012490C 0012A65C  42000000 00000000 FF12A2A0 501CB956  *...S........LIFOST*  124220
000120  00000002 001E0920 001CB6A0 001C8370  00124666 00124100 001E0EF0 FE12A200  *.......c......0..*  124240
000140  F0000203 001E05A4 00000000 00000000  0000028  00000000 001244CC 001CC3B8  *0..R...c.......c.*  124260
000160  00000000 00000000 00000000 00000000  00000000 00000000 88000028 001CC3B8  *...............C8*  124280
000180  480000A8 00124210 00000000 401C95DE  00000000 00125020 50125050 501C9310  *...y.........-..*  1242A0
0001A0  001CA310 00125AA4 00000000 00124FE0  00000000 001CAD62 001C8370 00125050  *.t..u.....n....c.*  1242C0
0001C0  00125010 00000000 00000000 F512434A  F500C6C3 001C53B8 01000000 00000000  *.....5.FC..1....c*  1242E0
0001E0  84008370 C3E4E2E3 D4E2E340 00000303  00000000 00000000 00124566 00000000  *d.c.CUSTMST ....*  124300
000200  00000000 00000000 00000000 00000000  001F0F14 00000000 00000000 00000000  *...............*  124320
000220  00000000 00000000 00000000 00000000  00000000 00000000 00000000 00000000  *..........M.....*  124340
000240  00000000 00000000 00000000 01105998  00000000 00000000 00000000 00000000  *...............*  124360
000260  LINES TO 0002A0 SAME AS ABOVE
000280  00000000 00000000 00000000 00000000  00000000 8A0403D8 001251F0           *.........Q.0.*     1243C0


TASK CONTROL AREA (SYSTEM AREA)             ADDRESS 124000 TO 1240FF      LENGTH 000100

000000  8A0403D8 001251FC 001252A0 00125250  80001220 001CF788 00116180 00000000  *...Q.........7...*  124000
000020  001EFB48 00124FB0 00000000 00000000  00000000 FE1CC288 00000000 001246CC  *.........Bh.....*  124020
000040  001243E0 00124270 00000000 00124BA0  00000000 00000000 00000000 00000002  *...............*  124040
000060  00000000 00000000 00000000 C1E2D9C1  00000000 00000000 00000000 00124940  *..........ASRA..*  124060
000080  FE124420 00000000 FE124200 FE124308  001F0F68 00124210 00000000 00000000  *...........0....*  124080
0000A0  001D5998 00000005 001251F0 00000000  C5E7F0F0 00000000 00000000 00000000  *...q...0...EX00.*  1240A0
0000C0  C1E2D9C1 00000000 00000000 00000000  00000000 00000000 00000000 00000000  *ASRA...........*  1240C0
0000E0  00000000 00000000 00000000 00000000  00000000 00000000 00000000 00000000  *...............*  1240E0


LIFO STACK ENTRY                            ADDRESS 124210 TO 12429F      LENGTH 000090

000000  42000000 00000000 FF12A2A0 501CB956  801CBEE2 00000000 0012490C 0012A65C  *..............S*  124210
000020  00124686 00124456 00124FEF 801CB73C  00000002 001E0920 001CB6A0 001C8370  *...f........R..c.*  124230
000040  00124940 00124100 001E0EF0 FE12A2A0  F0000203 001E05A4 00000000 00000000  *......0...0..R..*  124250
000060  8B000028 00000000 00000000 001CC3F8  00000000 00000000 00000000 00000000  *..........C8....*  124270
000080  00000000 00000028 8B000028 00000000                                       *...............*  1242 90
```

FIGURE 10.5   Dump produced by sample program EXAMP000.

CUSTOMER INFORMATION CONTROL SYSTEM STORAGE DUMP   CODE=ASRA   TASK=EX00   Dflt=10/04/83   TIME=C113:23   PAGE.   2

REGS 0 THRU 15   ADDRESS 1B3604 TO 1B3643   LENGTH 000040

```
000000   00000000  0012490C  00165F34  00165654      FF000000  0012492C  0012490C  00124643                *..........P..........L*      1B3604
000020   00124BD4  00166366  CC165020  00165C20      00165660  00124600  50165EF6  0016636C      *.............................O.*      1B3624
```

COMMON SYSTEM AREA   ADDRESS 1EFFF0 TO 1EF7D7   LENGTH 0006E8

```
000000   00000000  000F4F78  00000000  701B2AA0      00000002  00125018  501C9310      *...............................1.*      1EF0F0
000020   01CA310   00125CA4  00000000  00124FE0      001C83F0  001CAD62  001C8370  001C5090      *........................C0.....C....*  1EF110
000040   00125010  00124100  001C050C  00124100      00000000  07000100  00000000  00000000      *...........................*      1EF130
000060   0006B622  00012C00  00A1A558  00000DF      CC000C66  CC0F5000  001F6CB0  008327TF      *..v.....................MF..*      1EF150
000080   001F02F0  F0FFFFEE  00000000  001F1E1F      001610F0  001F0050  001EFB48  DW36Ce15      *..00........./......E....*      1EF190
0000A0   00000000  00116100  00116080  00116CC0      00000000  C01FC050  00000000  C50uFFCO      *........................./...*      1EF180
0000C0   00190002  0016806F  001EF7D8  00000100      00000000  00000000  001C92D8  001C4F8L      *.......o..7........../.7C...*      1EF1A0
0000E0   401EA458  001D24D0  001C60CC  001E61F0      C0000000  0018FD8  001C920B  001499AC      *.u......../../......Y..b..r*      1EF1C0
000100   001C6650  00000000  001ACC24  001A51AB      C0000C60  001E6224  001E3310  001499A0      *........................{}..Y..b...*      1EF210
000120   001C1A70  001D4EE0  001E8370  001C8516      C01E8C60  001EEE90  00114000  00000000      *.......+.....C...(...{..*      1EF230
000140   001CE00A  001F36E6  001C1731P  00000C6C      001C58AC  0016CB90  00000000  00000CCC      *......V....1p...2..2.*      1EF250
000160   0F1B11E0  7FFF0000  00000060  3DAAU9F2      C0000990  00000000  00000000  00000CCC      *.Y........2.2......0.*      1EF270
000180   001F0AE8  001F0AEC  00000C00  001F0E04      CC65DCC0  0000000  E6D6D9D2  C1D9C5C1      *..Y..........WORKAREA*      1EF290
0001A0   07C6E8F0  D19CC07F  00000000  00AC007C      01429CC0  0131C000  C0C00CC0  0C000CCC      *.OJ.........................0.*      1EF2B0
0001C0   00000C0C  00C00000  00000000  0C00U000      0C0C000  C0C00000  0C000000  0C00C0C0      *............................*      1EF2D0
0001E0   2C000C00  00000000  0C000000  0C00U000      C0C00000  00000000  00000000  00000000      *............................*      1EF2F0
000200   00000000  00000000  SAME AS ABCVE              00000000  00000000  00000000  00000000      *............................*      1EF310
000220   LINES TO  0006C0  SAME AS ABCVE
00026EC   00C00000  00000000                                                                         *............*      1EF7D0
```

CSA OPTIONAL FEATURE LIST   ADDRESS 1EF718 TO 1EFA3B   LENGTH 000264

```
000000   00000000  00000000  0C1A5530  0019B800      E01C1F1A  C0000000  001D06E8  00100718      *..............Y....*      1EF7D8
000020   001B1D54  001E1720  001F16F4  00000000      00000000  00000000  00000000  00000000      *........4..............q...*      1EF7F8
000040   00000000  00000000  00000000  00000000      C01AD120  00000000  001C8564  001F0FEC      *............J..........e.*      1EF816
000060   801F0A2C  001F4D5D6  C0000C0  000C1FC4      001E1C0   00832277F  001C8564  001F0FEC      *........N0....NO....V..c..00*      1EF838
000080   001F0F68  001D1FF0  001EB020  001B5RC0      00000000  C0000000  00000C00  00000C00      *............0.......=.*      1EF858
0000A0   00000000  001CD540  001ECFF4  001E8830      001E5430  001C65R0  001C5H00  001C7E10      *....N....Y....j.*      1EF878
0000C0   001D4020  001CD140  001E7020  001EC020      001D1F90  00169130  001C2F00  001AB1LC      *.......N....Y.......*      1EF898
0000E0   001E57A0  001EF4D0  001F19E0  00000000      00000400  00000000  001E31D4  001D0F3F0      *.......M..30....*      1EF8B8
000100   00000000  001D1C50  001EFC6A  001C3398      00000CC0  001C13EA  001C4U22A  001C201CA      *....Q.....5..........0.*      1EF8D8
000120   001C139A  00000000  00000000  00000000      C0000000  C0000000  001A57F0  00C00000      *...........q..a0....*      1EF8F8
000140   0AECC000  00000000  00169170  00000000      C0000000  C01CF434  001E81F0  001F0LFC      *.............5...j.*      1EF918
000160   00000000  00000000  00000000  001A99E0      C0C00000  00000000  001E81F0  001D95.30      *.................R.*      1EF938
000180   001A7F00  001PB000  C01A6LE0  001D6E8      00000000  C0000000  00000000  00000000      *........R....*      1EF958
0001A0   001F0F00  C0C00000  C0000000  00000000      C0C00000  C0000000  0C000CC0  00000000      *....................*      1EF978
0001C0   00C00000  00000000  00000C00  030C000C      00C9000  C30C000C  0C000C00  00010300      *.........................*      1EF998
0001E0   030C0000  000F000C  0C000C30C  0C0000C      C0C0000C  C0000000  C0000000  0001C30C      *........................*      1EF9B8
000200   00000000  001EF520  030C000C  0C000C0C      C0C0000C  030C000C  0C000000  030C6C6C      *................*      1EF9D8
000220   0C000000  0C0C031C  000C000C  0C0000C      00C00300  030C000C  0C000030C  030C00C0C      *.................*      1EFA18
000240   00C00000  030C000C  0C000C30C  0C000C0      C3C30C00  0C0C00C  0C000030C  00000CC0      *............*      1EFA38
000260   00C0000C
```

FIGURE 10.5 *(Continued)*

CUSTOMER INFORMATION CONTROL SYSTEM STORAGE DUMP   COLE=ASRA   TASK=EX00   DATE=10/04/83   TIME=01:13:23   PAGE 3

TRACE TABLE

TRACE HDR   ACDRESS 1A8CC0 TO 1A997F   LENGTH 000C80

TRACE TABLE   001A9770 001A8DC0 001A997C 001A99A0

ID	REGI4	REQD	TASK	FIELD A	FIELD B	FIELD E	TRACE TYPE
1A978C	C8	1D26LA	0C04	0107	00127000	FAC4072E	....	SCP ACQUIRED ICA STORAGE
1A9790	FC	1624BA	0404	0107	00000000	00000000	....	KCP SUSPEND
1A97AC	F2	1CE0GC	0204	0121	C4C6C8C5	C4C6D74C	LFHEDFP	PCP XCTL
1A97PC	F2	16324N	0104	0121	C4C6C8C5	C4C6C4AC	LFHEDFD	PCP LINK
1A97C0	F1	1CE108	8504	0121	00000004C	011D5598	....	SCP GETMAIN
1A97DC	C8	1D26LA	0004	0121	00127730	19C000E8	....	SCP ACQUIRED ICA STORAGE
1A97E0	F1	1ED3C5	CC04	0121	00012130	C11D5598	....	SCP GETMAIN-INIT
1A97F0	C8	1D26DA	0004	0121	0012779C	7C001738	....	SCP ACQUIRED USER STORAGE
1A981C	F2	1CD8C4	2024	0121	001591 14	C0C00000	....	PCP SETXIT ROUTINE
1A9820	E1	1590CC	00F4	0121	0012777C	C0C00100	....	EIP HANDLE-ABEND EMPTY
1A983C	E1	159122	0004	0121	001277AC	C0C00000	....	PCP SETXIT ROUTINE
1A9840	E1	1590CC	00F4	0121	0000007E	C11D5598	....	EIP HANDLE-ABEND RESPONSE
1A9850	E1	1D26LA	0004	0121	001289D0	CC000C68	....	SCP ACQUIRED USER STORAGE
1A986C	E1	159122	0CF4	0121	00000000	C0C00204	....	EIP HANDLE-CONDITION RESPONSE
1A987C	E1	15913C	0C04	0121	001277AC	C0000202	....	EIP ADDRESS ENTRY
1A9680	E1	15913C	00F4	0121	00000000	C0000202	....	EIP ADDRESS RESPONSE
1A9690	E1	1591EC	0004	0121	001277F0	C0000F04	....	EIP READQ-TS ENTRY
1A98A0	F7	1C8062	8903	0121	FCC0C5C4	19C9C2C8	.EBAICH	TSP GETQ
1A98FC	F1	1C6C52	AEC4	0121	0000007F	C11C5C68	....	SCP GETMAIN-CONDITIONAL
1A9BC0	C8	1D2LLA	0CC4	0121	0012-A6C	LEU000E8	....	SCP ACQUIRED TEMPSTRC STORAGE
1A98DC	F7	1C74FC	0C15	0121	0012BA60	0EU000E8	....	TSP RETNTNCHMOL
1A98E0	F1	1C71AB	4004	0121	0012HA60	C11D5598	....	SCP FREEMAIN
1A98FC	C9	1D26C0	0004	0121	0012-A60	FEC00068	....	SCP RELEASE TEMPSTRG STORAGE
1A9900	E1	1591EC	0CF4	0121	00000000	C0C00F04	.Nh	EIP READQ-TS RESPONSE
1A9910	E1	15E3CC	0004	0121	00000079	C11L5CC8	....	EIP READQ-TS EMPTY
1A9920	F1	1D4CC0	0CF4	0121	00000079	C00000C2	....	SCP GETMAIN-INIT
1A9930	C8	1C2CEA	0CC4	0121	0012BA60	CC0007b8	....	SCP ACQUIRED USER STORAGE
1A994C	E1	15E3GC	00F4	0121	00000000	C00000C2	....	EIP GETMAIN-INIT
1A9560	E1	1595E6	0004	0121	001277AC	C00010C4	....	EIP GETMAIN RESPONSE
1A996C	FA	1C2EbE	0003	0121	000015L2	C4C0CC0	.S..	BMS SEND-MAP ENTRY
1A997C	F1	1C1672	0103	0121	00000290	C01C5598	....	SCP GETMAIN-INIT

1A8DC0	C8	1D2CUA	0004	0121	00129210	8CCC0C58	....	SCP ACQUIRED USER STORAGE
1A8D10	F1	1RFEC2	CC04	0121	00000084	011D5598	....	SCP GETMAIN-INIT
1A8D20	C8	1D26UA	0004	0121	00129AEC	8CC000C8	....	SCP ACQUIRED USER STORAGE
1A8D30	F2	1C2633	0404	0121	C4C6C8C5	C4C6D8D4	LFHEDFM	PCP LOAD-CONDITIONAL
1A8D4C	F2	1C2664	8404	0121	C4C6C8C5	C4C6D4D0	DFHEDFH	PCP LOAD
1A8D5C	F1	1C0F42	9E04	0121	0012099C	C11L5998	....	SCP GETMAIN
1A8D7C	C8	1C349C	8504	0121	00129550	9E120998	....	SCP ACQUIRED MAPCOPY STORAGE
1A8D2G	F1	1D24LR	0004	0121	00120806	011D5998	....	SCP GETMAIN.
1A8D8C	F1	1C34F6	CC04	0121	0012AC00	b5120E18	....	SCP ACQUIRED TERMINAL STORAGE
1AFDAC	C8	1D26DA	0004	0121	0000002E	011D5998	....	SCP GETMAIN-INIT
1AFDF0	F1	00001C	0C04	0121	0012957C	8C000038	.C...	SCP ACQUIRED USER STORAGE
1AFEDC	FD	1C3C3A	4C04	0121	E3C9D4C5	01111E1F	TIME..	TIMING TRACE 01/11/18.1
1A8DD0	C8	1D2806	0004	0121	00129550	011D5598	....	SCP FREEMAIN
1A8DEC	F1	1C3CCE	4004	0121	00129EF0	011L5998	.C...	SCP RELEASED MAPCOPY STORAGE
1A8DFC	C9	1D2806	0004	0121	0012AEFC	8C000038	.0...	SCP FREEMAIN
1A8E0C	FC	1C1E12	0103	0121	00810000	C01C5996	....	ZCP ZARC AIPL REQ ERASE WRITE

FIGURE 10.5 *(Continued)*

CUSTOMER INFORMATION CONTROL SYSTEM STORAGE DUMP   CODE=ASRA   TASK=EX00   DATE=10/04/83   TIME=01:13:23   PAGE   4

```
1A8E10  FC  1E354A  0105  0121  00F1000C  C012AC00  ........  ZCP  FETN ZARC APPL REQ ERASE WAIT
1A8E20  EA  1C2296  0005  0121  00000000  00001802  ........  BMS  RETN
1A8E30  E1  1595B8  00F0  0121  00000000  00001802  ........  EIP  SEND-MAP RESPONSE
1A8E40  FA  1C30E0  0003  0121  00127700  C0C001C2  ........  EIP  RECEIVE-MAP ENTRY
1A8E50  E1  1C30E0  0003  0121  00C00500  C0C001C2  ........  BMS  MAP MAPSET WAIT IN
1A8E60  FC  1F3518  4004  0121  007C0000  001D5998  ........  KCP  ZARC APPL REQ READ WAIT
1A8E70  E1  1D7AE0  4004  TC    1C0C0000  001D5998  ......Y   KCP  WAIT DCI=TERMINAL
1A8E80  C8  1E329C  E404  TC    0000078B  001F55E8  ........  SCP  GETMAIN-CCAD-INIT
1A8E90  C8  1E329C  0104  TC    00015000  001D0729  ......Y   SCP  ACQUIRED-LINE STORAGE
1A8EA0  ED  0001C   0104  TC    40060700  001D0729  ........  KCP  WAIT DCI=LIST
1A8EB0  ...  ...  ...  ...  0006B78B  C046878E  ........  :..  FREEMAIN CC001 TIMES
1A8EC0  ED  1D7E4A  4004  TC    0012A00C  601D5960  ........  SCP  RELEASED TERMINAL STORAGE
1A8ED0  C9  1D8252  0804  TC    0012A000  05120818  ........  KCP  RESUME
1A8EE0  E0  1E329C  4004  TC    00127100  C1001021  ........  KCP  WAIT DCI=LIST
1A8EF0  EA  1E354A  0105  0121  40C00C0C  C011556C  ......Y   ZCP  RETN ZARC APPL REQ
1A8F10  C9  1C3108  4004  0121  00115000  001D5998  ........  BMS  RETN CANCL MAP I/O AREA
1A8F20  C9  1D2606  0004  0121  00115C00  FSC00798  ........  SCP  FREEMAIN TERMINAL STORAGE
1A8F30  E1  1595CA  0CF4  0121  04000000  0001C2    ........  EIP  RECEIVE-MAP RESPONSE
1A8F40  E1  1595CA  0CF4  0121  00127780  00000FD4  ........  EIP  READY-TS ENTRY
1A8F50  F7  1C8062  8903  0121  FUC0CSC4  1SC4CSC8  .EDRICH   TSP  GETQ
1A8F60  F0  1C70AE  4004  0121  BC000000  C018EFFC  ........  KCP  WAIT LCI=SINGLE
1A8F70  CE  1CED52  A104  0121  0U1107BF  C11D5998  ........  SCP  GETMAIN-CONDITIONAL
1A8F80  E7  1C74FC  0004  0121  00129550  6E11D758  ........  SCP  ACQUIRED TEMPSTRG STORAGE
1A8FA0  E1  1C74FC  00F4  0121  0012955C  6E11D758  ........  ISP  RETN MONPL
1A8FB0  E1  15A0C8  0CF4  0121  00000000  00000FD4  ........  EIP  READQ-TS RESPONSE
1A8FC0  E1  15A18A  0CF4  0121  00127780  00000404  ........  EIP  SEND-TC ENTRY
1A8FD0  E1  1E540C  C304  0121  0C00074F  001D5998  ........  SCP  GETMAIT-INIT
1A8FE0  C8  1D2EDA  0004  0121  00115000  85C00758  ........  SCP  ACQUIRED TERMINAL STORAGE
1A8FF0  FC  1E5598  0103  0121  00E54000  001D5998  ........  ZCP  ZARC APPL REQ ERASE WRITE WAIT
1A9010  E1  1E361B  00F4  0121  13000000  001D5998  ......Y   KCP  WAIT LCI=TERMINAL
1A9020  F0  1E329C  4004  TC    40000000  001D72E8  ........  KCP  WAIT LCI=LIST
1A9030  E1  1E7E44  4004  TC    00115C00  E011556C  ........  SCP  FREEMAIN
1A9040  C9  1D2E06  0004  TC    00115000  001D5998  ........  SCP  RELEASED TERMINAL STORAGE
1A9050  F0  1DE252  0804  TC    00127100  C1C00121  ........  KCF  RESUME
1A9060  F0  1E329C  4004  TC    40000000  001D72E8  ........  KCP  WAIT DCI=LIST
1A9070  FC  1E354A  0105  0121  40C00C00  C00000C0  ......Y   ZCP  RETN ZARC APPL REQ
1A9080  E1  15A18A  00F4  0121  00000000  00000000  ........  EIP  SEND-TC RESPONSE
1A9090  E1  15A446  00F4  0121  00127780  00000F06  ........  EIP  DELETEQ-TS ENTRY
1A90A0  F7  1C6DFA  2103  0121  FUCCCSC4  ESC4CSC8  .EDRICH   TSP  PURGEC
1A90B0  F1  1C737E  4004  0121  00126C00  C11C5998  ........  SCP  FREEMAIN
1A90C0  C9  1D2E06  0004  0121  00126B00  S6C00C20  ........  SCP  RELEASED TSTABLE STORAGE
1A90D0  F1  1C737E  4004  0121  00126060  0011C5998  ........  SCP  FREEMAIN
1A90E0  E1  1C737E  4004  0121  00126060  0011L5558  ........  SCP  FREEMAIN
1A90F0  C9  1D2E06  0004  0121  00126B90  S8C00C20  ........  SCP  RELEASED TSTABLE STORAGE
1A9100  C9  1D2E06  0004  0121  00126B90  98C00C20  ........  SCP  RELEASED TSTABLE STORAGE
1A9110  F7  1C74FC  0005  0121  00126A00  C00000F06  ........  TSP  REIN NCPFAL
1A9120  E1  15A446  00F4  0121  00127A00  C0C00F06  ........  EIP  DELETEQ-TS RESPONSE
1A9130  E1  15A0A4  0004  0121  00127790  C0000136  ........  TSP  REIN NCPFAL
1A9140  E1  1C041E  4004  0121  00127790  011F5998  ........  SCP  FREEMAIN
1A9150  F2  1C041E  1C04  0121  00127730  0C0C440C  ........  PCP  RETURN
1A9160  E1  1C224  4004  0121  00127730  01105998  ........  SCP  FREEMAIN USER STORAGE
1A9170  C9  1D2E06  0004  0121  00127730  19C00058  ........  SCP  RELEASED USER STORAGE
1A9180  E1  1C224  4004  0121  00127330  01105998  ........  SCP  FREEMAIN
1A9190  FC  163292  0103  0121  0CC40000  001D5998  ........  ZCP  ZARC APPL REQ WAIT
```

FIGURE 10.5   *(Continued)*

CUSTOMER INFORMATION CONTROL SYSTEM STORAGE DUMP   CODE=ASRA   TASK=EX00   DATE=10/04/83   TIME=01:13:23   PAGE 5

```
1A91A0   F0  1E3618  4004  0121  13C00000  011F5998   ........   KCP WAIT DCI=TERMINAL
1A91C0   F0  1D6252  0804  1C    00127100  C1000121   ........   KCP RESUME
1A91E0   F0  1F329C  4004  1C    40000000  C01072E8   ......Y    KCP WAIT ECI=LIST
1A91E0   FC  1E354A  0105  0121  04000000  00000000   ........   ZCP RETN ZARC APPL REQ
1A91F0   F0  1633AC  0804  0121  0012410C  FF000107   ........   PCP RETURN
1A92C0   F2  1633CE  1004  0121  C4C6C8CS C4C6D740   EFHEDFF    PCP RETURN
1A920C   F0  1CE1C4  8004  0121  00000000  00000000   ........   KCP DETACH
1A9210   F1  1FB7D8  4004  KC    0110599F  00000000   ........   KCP DECALL
1A922C   F0  1D2FC6  0004  KC    00177000  00000000   ........   SCP FREEMAIN TEMPSTG STORAGE
1A9240   C9  1D2806  0004  KC    00125550  CE11078    ........   SCP RELEASED USER STORAGE
1A9250   C9  1D2806  0004  KC    00129460  BC00005E   ........   SCP RELEASED USER STORAGE
1A925C   C9  1D280C  0004  KC    00129210  CCC002C8   ........   SCP RELEASED USER STORAGE
1A9270   C9  1D2806  0004  KC    00126A60  BC0007B8   ........   SCP RELEASED USER STORAGE
1A9280   C9  1D280C  0004  KC    0012E9D0  BC000798   ........   SCP RELEASED USER STORAGE
1A929C   C9  1D280C  0004  0107  0012700C  EAC40728   ........   SCP RELEASED TCA STORAGE
1A9290   F2  1624D5  1004  0107  C4C6C8CS C4C6E740   EFHEDFX    PCP RETURN
1A92A0   F1  1CE224  4004  0107  00125460  011C5996   ........   SCP FREEMAIN
1A92C0   C9  1D280C  0004  0107  00124560  B9120046   ........   SCP RELEASED TCA STORAGE
1A92C0   F0  1CE1C4  8004  0107  00000000  00C00000   ........   KCP DETACH
1A92E0   FC  1EB6F2  0F03  0107  04000000  011C5998   ........   KCP DECALL
1A92FC   F1  1FC4B  0805  0107  04000000  001F5996   ........   ZCP ZISR ISC FREE DETACH
1A9300   F1  1E7DD8  4F04  KC    00124000  00000000   ........   ZCP RETN ZISR ISC FREE DETACH
1A9320   C9  1D2806  0004  KC    00125310  BC000076   ........   SCP FREEMAIN
1A9330   C9  1D2806  0004  KC    001252C0  BC000048   ........   SCP RELEASED USER STORAGE
1A934C   C9  1D2806  0004  KC    00125220  BC00056    ........   SCP RELEASED USER STORAGE
1A9350   C9  1D280C  0004  KC    00124E8C  FC00026    ........   SCP RELEASED USER STORAGE
1A9360   C9  1D2806  0004  KC    0012463C  1CC60048   ........   SCP RELEASED USER STORAGE
1A9370   C9  1D280C  0004  KC    00124A00  BCC000B6   ........   SCP RELEASED USER STORAGE
1A9380   C9  1D280C  0004  KC    00124000  2A040556   ........   SCP RELEASED TCA STORAGE
1A9390   F1  1D7AE0  E404  1C    0000078F  B01D5998   ........   SCP GETMAIN-CCND-INIT
1A93A0   C8  1D26A  0C04  1C    00115000  84C00798   ........   SCP ACQUIRED LINE STORAGE
1A93C0   FD  1F329C  4004  1C    40000000  C01072E8   ......Y    KCP WAIT ECI=LIST
1A93D0   FD  00033C  0104  1C    0006884P  C0069523   ........   KCP REPEAT 00033 TIMES
1A93E0   F0  00001C  0204  1C    E3C4D4C5  C111135F   TIME...    TIMING TRACE C1/11/53.9
1A93F0   F0  00007C  0104  1C    000695F3  001D72E8   ........   KCP WAIT ECI=LIST
1A9400   F0  10D380  0704  1C    D9C9C3CP  C5E7FFC0   HICHEX00   KCP REPEAT 00067 TIMES
1A9410   F1  1EB1D4  EA04  1C    00000300  E0105998   ........   SCP GETMAIN-CCAD-INIT
1A9420   F0  1E26DA  0004  7C    00124000  FAC4C308   ........   SCP ACQUIRED TCA STORAGE
1A9430   F1  1E329C  4004  7C    40000000  001D72F8   ......Y    KCP WAIT ECI=LIST
1A9440   FC  1E4CC8  0503  0122  0U0C0001  001D5996   ........   ZCP ZSUP START UP TASK
1A9450   F2  1CE19E  0204  0122  C5F7C1C4  E7F6F0F0   EXAMPO00   PCP XCTL
1A9460   C8  1D26DA  0004  0122  00000544  011D5998   ........   SCP GETMAIN
1A9470   F1  1ED03A  0004  0122  0012430  BC000558    ........   SCP ACQUIRED USER STORAGE
1A9480   F1  1D2DA   0004  0122  00124940  BC000178   ........   SCP GETMAIN-INIT
1A9490   E1  165B7E  0004  0122  0012402C  C9C00204   ........   SCP ACQUIRED USER STORAGE
1A94A0   E1  1EE868  CC04  0122  0012407B  011D5998   ........   EIP HANDLE-CONDITION ENTRY
1A94C0   C8  1D26DA  CC04  0122  0012600A  BC000088   ........   SCP GETMAIN-INIT
1A94D0   C8  1EE97E  CC04  0122  00124940  011D5998   ........   SCP GETMAIN-INIT
1A94E0   C8  1D26DA  0004  0122  0012AF50  BC000204   ........   SCP ACQUIRED USER STORAGE
1A94FC   E1  165FE1  0FF4  0122  0C000000  BC000104   ........   SCP ACQUIRED USER STORAGE
1A9500   F1  165B9A  0004  0122  0012442C  000D18C2   ........   EIP HANDLE-CONDITION RESPONSE
1A951C   FA  1C3CE0  CC04  0122  00005505  011C5998   ........   EIP RECEIVE-MAP ENTRY
1A951C   F1  1C1872  CC04  0122  00000290  011C5998   ........   BMS MAP MAPSET1 MAP IN
1A9520   C8  1D26DA  0004  0122  00124BA0  BC000298   ........   SCP ACQUIRED USER STORAGE
```

FIGURE 10.5 (Continued)

CUSTOMER INFORMATION CONTROL SYSTEM STORAGE DUMP   CODE=ASRA   TASK=EX00   DATE=10/04/83   TIME=01:13:23   PAGE 6

```
1A9530    F1 1BF8C2 CC04  0122 0000084 C11D5998  ........  SCP GETMAIN-INIT
1A9540    C8 1D26DA 0004  0122 00124E40 8C00009E  ........  SCP ACQUIRED USER STORAGE
1A95E0    F2 1C2632 8404  0122 DWE2C1E3 C5E0F440  MSALE04H  PCP LOAD-CONDITIONAL
1A95E0    F2 1C266A 0404  0122 DWF2C1E3 C5E0F440  MSALE04H  PCP LOAD
1A957C    F1 1C3DD4 C504  0122 00000087 C11D5998  ........  SCP GETMAIN-INIT
1A958C    C8 1D26DA 0004  0122 00115890 65400009E  ........  SCP ACQUIRED TERMINAL STORAGE
1A9590    F1 1C410C 4C04  0122 00115000 C11D5998  ........  SCP FREEMAIN
1A95AC    C9 1D2806 0004  0122 00115000 A5C00796  ........  SCP RELEASED TERMINAL STORAGE
1A95A0    FA 1C229E 0005  0122 6C000000 00C00000  ........  BMS RETN
1A95C0    F1 1C3108 4004  0122 00115890 C11D5998  ........  SCP FREEMAIN
1A95D0    C9 1D2806 0004  0122 00115890 A5C00796  ........  SCP RELEASED TERMINAL STORAGE
1A95E0    E1 1659A 00F4  0122 00000000 00C01EC2  ........  EIP RECEIVE-MAP RESPONSE
1A95F0    E1 1E5E5E 00F4  0122 0012442C C0000704  ........  EIP HANDLE-CONDITION ENTRY
1A9600    E1 1EE97E CC04  0122 0000004C C11D5998  ........  SCP GETMAIN-INIT
1A9610    C8 1D26DA 00F4  0142 0012AEE0 8C00048   ........  SCP ACQUIRED USER STORAGE
1A9620    E1 1E5E5E 00F4  0122 00000000 00000204  ........  EIP HANDLE-CONDITION RESPONSE
1A9630    E1 165EF6 0004  0122 0012442C C0000064  ........  EIP READ ENTRY
1A9640    E1 1C67E2 CC04  0122 0C00006F C11D5998  ........  SCP GETMAIN-INIT
1A965C    C8 1D26DA 0004  0122 00124F30 E4E2E340  ........  SCP ACQUIRED USER STORAGE
1A96F0    F5 1C6956 8403  0122 C3F4E2E3 1113235F  CLSTMST   FCP GET-UPDATE
1A9670    FD C0001C 0204  0122 E3C5D4C5 1113235F  TIME..    TIMING TRACE 01/13/23.5
1A9680    E1 1CA9C2 9D04  0122 0012004C C11D5998  ........  SCP GETMAIN
1A9690    C8 1D26DA 0004  0144 00124F50 SD12C058  ........  SCP ACQUIRED LWE STORAGE
1A96A0    E1 1CAE6C 8FC4  0122 0012006F C11D5998  ........  SCP GETMAIN
1A96A0    C8 1D2E1F 0004  0122 00125010 EF120078  ........  SCP ACQUIRED FILE STORAGE
1A96CC    C6 1CA80C 8F04  0122 0012500F C11D5998  ........  SCP GETMAIT
1A96D0    C6 1D26DA 0004  0122 00125010 EF1200E8  ........  SCP ACQUIRED FILE STORAGE
1A96EC    F0 1C95DF 4C04  0122 4J000000 00125020  ........  KCP WAIT
1A96F0    F1 1D67DC DB04  0122 00000085 C11D5998  ........  SCP GETMAIN-INIT
1A9700    C6 1D26DA 0004  0122 00125010 5EC0009E  ........  SCP ACQUIRED JCA STORAGE
1A9710    F9 1C159 0104  0122 02010001 00125150  ........  JCP WRITE
1A9720    F5 1C9974 C015  0122 00125150 9B00009E  ........  FCP RETN NORMAL
1A9730    E1 165EF6 00F4  0122 00000000 00000002  ........  EIP READ RESPONSE
1A9740    F2 1E21A6 6C04  0122 C1E2D9C1 00000000  ASRA..    PCP ABEND
1A975C    F1 1CCLC6 CC04  0122 0000005F C11D5998  ........  SCP GETMAIN-INIT
1A976C    C6 1D26DF 0004  0122 00125010 EC0C068   ........  SCP ACQUIRED USER STORAGE
1A977C    F4 1CDE3B FE04  0122 00000000 C1E2D9C1  ...ASRA   DCP TRANSACTION
```

TRANSACTION STORAGE -USER   ADDRESS 12551F0   TO 12529F   LENGTH C000EC

```
000000  1CC000A8 00125150 CC000000 C0009E40  C4C6C4E3 C1C3C240 80600000 C1E2F0C1  *....Y....... c IFHTACE -..ASRA*  1251F0
00002C  C5F7C2D4 D7F0F0F0 09750000 00000000  C0000000 C6000000 00000000 00000000  *EXAMP000...........EXAMP000.*         125210
000040  CC000000 00006006 D7E2E661 D9C5C7E2  C7E0F0007 0C5A0000 00124902 00124902  *........PSK/RECS............*         125230
000060  0015E34 00085504 0012AF08 FF000000  C012442C 0012A4B03 0016336E 0016336E  *...E34........M...(C..6..0..*         125250
00008C  0C165020 00015020 00124100 001E0E0  50165FF6 0016336F 00116336   .Y......  125270
0000AC  CC060000 00000000 00000000 00125150                                        125290
```

TRANSACTION STORAGE -JCA   ADDRESS 12515C   TO 1251EF   LENGTH 0000A0

```
000000  9FC000A8 00125090 401CB198 d01CB094  C012C578 C000001C 50lC9310 001C4310  *....q....q..E....l...t.*        125150
000020  00125078 00000009A 401C5150 001CB3E0  001CAE72 001C8370 00125090 00125010  *....q.....cC.....cC....*        125170
000040  01F00100 A111020C C6C0006 001C256C  00020000 CC9A0000 C09C0000 00C00000  *..........l.Y00RICHCUSTMST.*    125190
000060  CC000000 0000CC00 02061220 C1132355  C5F7F0F0 L9C9C3C8 C3EUE2E3 DW12E240  *.........EY00RICHCUSTMST.*     1251b0
00008C  C0000000 00000CC0 CCC00CC0 CCC00C00  C0000C00 L9C9C3C8 9B00009B 00125040  *.......q.......*                 1251D0
```

FIGURE 10.5 *(Continued)*

```
CUSTOMER INFORMATION CONTROL SYSTEM STORAGE DUMP   CODE=ASRA   TASK=EX00        DATE=10/04/83   TIME=01:13:23   PAGE    7

TRANSACTION STORAGE -FILE                       ADDRESS  125090  TO  12514F       LENGTH  0000C0

000000    8F1200B8 0012501C 0C125010 001CB370    009A0000 F0F0F0F0 F0F4E2E4 D5E2C8C9   *..............C.....000004SUNSHI*     125090
000020    D5C540E2 C8D6D7D7 C9D5C740 C3C5D5E3    C5D940C1 C2C2E840 C6C5D3C9 E7404040   *NE SHOPPING CENTER ABBY FELIX   *     1250B0
000040    40404040 40404040 40404040 F4F340D9    E4C540C4 C540C3C8 C1D9E3D9 C5E24040   *             43 RUE DE CHARTRES *     1250D0
000060    40404040 40D5C5E6 40D6D9D3 C5C1D5E2    40404040 40404040 40D3C1F4 F3F2F1F2   *     NEW ORLEANS         LA43212*     1250F0
000080    40404040 F0F0F0F0 F0F0F0F0 F0F0F0F0    C0F0F0F0 F0F0F0C0 00000000 0C000000   *    000000000000.000000.........*     125110
0000A0    00000000 0000000C 00000000 0C000000    00000000 00000000 8F1200B8 0012501C   *................................*     125130

TRANSACTION STORAGE -FILE                       ADDRESS  125010  TO  12508F       LENGTH  000080

000000    8F120078 10124FEC 0C00004C 000F9900    40000000 0C000000 00000000 0C00000C   *..............r. ...............*     125010
000020    C01C83F0 00000000 001250A4 0012416C    48E20000 C0000000 00000096 00000096   *..c0.......u.....b.........o...o*     125030
000040    C0000000 00000000 0C00012C 00000000    C0000000 801C8370 00000000 0000000C   *.....................c..........*     125050
000060    C0000000 00000000 0C000000 0200006C    C0000000 00000000 8F120078 10124FEC   *................................*     125070

TRANSACTION STORAGE -FWE                        ADDRESS  124FB0  TO  12500F       LENGTH  000060

000000    9F120058 00124F3C 00000000 001CAA40    C0F01100 00000000 00000000 0C00000C   *.............. .................*     124FB0
000020    00000000 00000000 0C000000 00000000    C0000000 C0000000 00000000 0C00000C   *................................*     124FD0
000040    00000000 00000000 00000000 00000000    C0125010 00000000 9D120058 00124F3C   *................................*     124FF0

TRANSACTION STORAGE -USER                       ADDRESS  124F30  TO  124FAF       LENGTH  000080

000000    8C000078 00124EEC C3E4E2E3 D4E2E340    C0000000 C01C8370 00000000 C3E4E2E3   *......+.CUSTMSI ......c.....CUST*     124F30
000020    D4E2E340 0000000C 40125090 0012456C    C0000000 C0000000 00000000 0C00000C   *MSI .... .......................*     124F50
000040    C0000000 00000000 0C000000 0C000000    C000000C C0000000 00000000 0C00000C   *................................*     124F70
000060    00000000 0000000C 0C000000 FF000000    C0000000 00000000 8C000078 00124EEC   *..............................+.*     124F90

TRANSACTION STORAGE -USER                       ADDRESS  124EE0  TO  124F2F       LENGTH  000050

000000    8C000048 00124F40 50165E5E 001ED3CC    C0000000 0012490C 00165E34 001655D4   *......+ ..;;..l............;....M*     124EE0
000020    00124A08 FF000000 0012442C C0124ED3    C0124FD4 00166366 00165020 0016502C   *..............L...M.............*     124F00
000040    001655C0 001246CC 8C000048 00124E40                                          *.............+                  *     124F20

TRANSACTION STORAGE -USER                       ADDRESS  124E40  TO  124EDF       LENGTH  0000A0

000000    8C000098 00124EAC D4D40000 00000000    C0010001 00010000 00000000 0000000C   *...q....MM......................*     124E40
000020    00000000 0017100E 0C000000 00000000    00000000 C0000000 00000000 D4E2C1D3   *............................MSAL*     124E60
000040    C5F0F440 00000000 00000000 00000000    18500000 40000001 01015000 0C000000   *E04 ................ ...........*     124E80
000060    07800000 0000000C C0000000 00000000    C0000000 011D5998 00404000 00000000   *.......................q.  .....*     124EA0
000080    00000000 00000000 FFFFFFFF 00000000    C0000000 00000000 8C000098 00124EAC   *...........................q....*     124EC0

TRANSACTION STORAGE -USER                       ADDRESS  124BA0  TO  124E3F       LENGTH  0002A0

000000    8C000298 00124B5C 401C1AE4 001BE5C8    701C1CE4 C01C3398 00000000 0C00000C   *...q.... ..U..*....U...q........*     124BA0
000020    00000000 00000000 0C000000 00000000    C0000000 00000000 00000000 0C00000C   *................................*     124BC0
000040    00000000 0000000C 0C000505 000000A0    E7ECF0F0 001D5998 E2C1D3C5 F0F0F4F4C  *................XC00...qSALE004 *     124BE0
000060    D4E2C1D3 C5F0F44C 0000CFF4 0000012F    C0000000 00124334 00000000 0C00000C   *MSALE04 ...4....................*     124C00
000080    00000000 00000000 C0000000 00000000    C0000000 00000000 00124E40 00124E40   *.........................+ ..+ *     124C20
0000A0    00000000 0000000C 0C000000 00000000    C0000000 001D59A4 00000000 0C00000C   *.......................u........*     124C40
```

FIGURE 10.5 (Continued)

```
CUSTOMER INFORMATION CONTROL SYSTEM STORAGE DUMP   CODE=ASRA   TASK=EX00      DATE=10/04/83   TIME=01:13:23   PAGE    8

TRANSACTION STORAGE -USER                 ADDRESS  124BA0  TO  124E3F      LENGTH  0002A0

0000C0    00000000 00000000 00000000 00000000    00000000 00000000 141CC288 00000000    *........................Bh....*    124C60
0000E0    00000001 00000000 00000000 00000000    00000000 00100000 00000000 00000000    *..............................*    124C80
000100    00000000 00000000 00000000 00000000    00000000 00000000 00000000 00000000    *..............................*    124CA0
000120    00000000 00000000 00000000 00000000    00000000 00000000 00000000 00000000    *..............................*    124CC0
000140    00000000 00000000 401C2664 001C17F8    000000FE 06115000 00000018 000000FF    *........ ......8..............*    124CE0
000160    001D59A4 00171014 901C1CC4 48000060    001ED920 00124BA0 00124E40 011E5998    *...u........D...-..R.......+ ...q*    124D00
000180    00000000 00000000 00000000 00000000    00110000 00000000 00000000 00000000    *..............................*    124D20
0001A0    00000000 00000000 00000000 00000000    00000000 00000000 00000000 00000000    *..............................*    124D40
0001C0    LINES TO 000260 SAME AS ABOVE                                                                                    124D60
000280    00000000 00000000 00000000 00000000    00000000 00000000 8C000298 00124E50    *.......................q....*    124E20

TRANSACTION STORAGE -USER                 ADDRESS  124B50  TO  124B9F      LENGTH  000050

000000    8C000048 00124AC0 501657FE 001ED3CC    00000000 0012490C A01CE91E 00165008    *.............1...........Z.....*    124B50
000020    00124A08 FF000000 0012442C 00124BD3    00124BD4 00166366 00165020 00165020    *..............L...M...........*    124B70
000040    001655C0 001246CC 8C000048 00124AC0                                           *..............                *    124B90

TRANSACTION STORAGE -USER                 ADDRESS  124AC0  TO  124B4F      LENGTH  000090

000000    8C000068 00124940 00124B0F 007F0300    00000000 00000000 00000002 00000000    *...h... ......................*    124AC0
000020    00000000 00000000 00000000 00000000    00000100 00000000 00000000 00000000    *..............................*    124AE0
000040    00000000 00000000 00000000 00000000    00000000 00000112 4B500412 46CC0112    *..............................*    124B00
000060    4FE00412 46CC0000 00000000 00000000    00000000 00000000 00000000 00000000    *+.............................*    124B20
000080    00000000 0000FF00 8C000088 00124940                                           *...........h...               *    124B40

TRANSACTION STORAGE -USER                 ADDRESS  124940  TO  124ABF      LENGTH  000180

000000    8C000178 001243E0 00124A70 00000000    00000000 00000000 00000000 00000000    *..............................*    124940
000020    40404040 001D5998 00000000 00000000    00000000 00000000 00000000 00000000    *    ...q......................*    124960
000040    00000000 00000000 00000000 00000000    00000000 00000000 00000000 001C837C    *............................c.*    124980
000060    00000000 00000000 00000000 00000000    00000000 00000000 00124A08 80124A0C    *..............................*    1249A0
000080    00124FE0 A01CBB9E 00000000 00000000    00000000 00000000 00000000 00000000    *..+....q......................*    1249C0
0000A0    00124F38 00124F4C 00000000 00124AC0    00000000 00000000 00000004 00000000    *..............................*    1249E0
0000C0    00000000 00000000 00124A70 FF000000    001246CC 0012442C 00000000 001CE610    *...........................W..*    124A00
0000E0    001246CC 401ED1F2 00165020 001CE610    00124F08 00165060 001243F0 00165068    *.... .J2......&.........-...0...*    124A20
000100    001CE850 00124000 00165020 001ECEF4    001657FC FE1CC288 00124940 0012410C    *..Y... ........4......Bh... ....*    124A40
000120    80000000 00000000 40C4C6C8 C5C9C240    0011323C 0083277F C5E7F0F0 0000122C    *........ DFHEIB .....c..EX00....*    124A60
000140    D9C9C3C8 00000304 00007D06 02000000    000000C3 E4E2E3D4 E2E34000 00000000    *RICH......'........CUSTMST .....*    124A80
000160    000000C3 E4E2E3D4 E2E34000 00000000    00000000 00000000 8C000178 001243E0    *...CUSTMST ....................*    124AA0

TRANSACTION STORAGE -USER                 ADDRESS  1243E0  TO  12493F      LENGTH  000560

000000    8C000558 00124000 00000000 00000000    00000000 501663CC A01CE91E 00165008    *...... ..................Z.....*    1243E0
000020    00165F3E 501663E0 001650C0 00165567    00165568 00166366 00165020 00165020    *..$............................*    124400
000040    001655C0 00165360 001CEB60 00000000    00000000 D5000000 00000000 40C3E4E2    *.......-...-.........N....... CUS*    124420
000060    E3D6D4C5 D940D5E4 D4C2C5D9 40D5D6E3    40D6D540 C6C9D3C5 6B40D9C5 60C5D5E3    *TOMER NUMBER NOT ON FILE, RE-ENT*    124440
000080    C5D90000 E2C1D3C5 D7F0F0F4 40D4C1D7    C6C1C9D3 40C5D9D9 00000000 C9D3D3C5    *ER..SALEP004 MAPFAIL ERR....ILLE*    124460
0000A0    C7C1D340 E3D9C1D5 40C3D6C4 C5000000    00000000 F1000000 00000000 D1000000    *GAL TRAN CODE.......1.......J...*    124480
0000C0    00000000 D8000000 00000000 C1000000    00000000 C9000000 00000000 F0F0F0F2    *....Q.......A.......I.......0002*    1244A0
0000E0    F0F0C000 00000000 00000000 00960000    00000000 F0F0F0F0 F0C20000 00000000    *00...........o......00000B......*    1244C0
000100    00000000 00000000 000400E2 C1D3F4C0    C6C0F0F0 F0F0F0F4 0006D1F0 F0F0F5F5    *...........SAL4...000004..J00055*    1244E0
```

FIGURE 10.5 (Continued)

FIGURE 10.5 *(Continued)*

```
CUSTOMER INFORMATION CONTROL SYSTEM STORAGE DUMP   CODE=ASRA   TASK=EX00        DATE=10/04/83   TIME=01:13:23   PAGE   10

PROGRAM STORAGE                              ADDRESS  165008  TO  166DAF       LENGTH  C01DA8

0000A0   F2F34BF3 F04BF1F1 D6C3E340 40F36B40   F1F9F8F3 C0000000 00000000 00000000   *23.30.11OCT  3, 1983..............*   1650A8
0000C0   D5C00000 00000000 40C3E4E2 E3D6D4C5   D940D5E4 D4C2C5D9 40D5D6E3 40D6D540   *N........ CUSTOMER NUMBER NOT ON *   1650C8
0000E0   C6C9D3C5 6B40D9C5 60C5D5E3 C5D90000   E2C1D3C5 D7F0F0F4 40D4C1D7 C6C1C9D3   *FILE, RE-ENTER..SALEP004 MAPFAIL*   1650E8
000100   40C5D9D9 00000000 C9D3D3C5 C7C1D340   E3D9C1D5 40C3D6C4 C5000000 00000000   * ERR....ILLEGAL TRAN CODE........*   165108
000120   F1000000 00000000 D1000000 00000000   D8000000 00000000 C1000000 00000000   *1.......J.......(........A........*   165128
000140   C9000000 00000000 00000000 00000000   00000000 00000000 00960000 00000000   *I.........................o......*   165148
000160   F0F0F0F0 F0C00000 00000000 00000000   00000000 00000000 00000000 00000000   *00000...........................*   165168
000180   00000000 00000000 00000000 00000000   C0000000 00000000 00000000 0000000C   *................................*   165188
0001A0   LINES TO 0002A0 SAME AS ABOVE                                                                                       1651A8
0002C0   007D6D7E E6E7887F 6C6E6BF1 F2F3F4F5   F6F7F8F9 7A7B7CC1 C2C3C4C5 C6C7C8C9   *.'.=WXh...,123456789:..ABCDEFGHI*   1652C8
0002E0   4A4B4C00 00000000 00000000 00000000   C0000000 C0000000 00000000 0000000C   *................................*   1652E8
000300   00000000 00000000 00000000 00000000   00000000 00000000 00000000 00000000   *................................*   165308
000320   00000000 00000000 00000000 00000000   00000000 00000000 00000000 0C0C0C0C   *................................*   165328
000340   00000000 0000000C 0C000000 00000C00   00400000 00000000 00300000 001CE610   *................ .............W.*   165348
000360   00000000 00000000 00000000 00000000   C0000000 00000000 00000000 00C00000   *................................*   165368
000380   00000000 0000000C 00000000 00000000   C0000000 00000000 00000000 00000000   *................................*   165388
0003A0   2002A04B 00000000 00000000 001657EC   00000000 00000000 00000000 00000000   *................................*   1653A8
0003C0   00000000 00000000 00000000 00000000   C0000000 00000000 00000000 00000000   *................................*   1653C8
0003E0   LINES TO 000420 SAME AS ABOVE                                                                                       1653E8
000440   00000000 00000000 00000000 00000000   C0000000 00000000 00000000 00000000   *................................*   165448
000460   LINES TO 0004E0 SAME AS ABOVE                                                                                       165468
000500   00000000 00000000 00165020 00000000   C01663F0 E2E8E2D6 E4E34040 E3800000   *..................OSYSOUT  T...*   165508
000520   001650A8 00000000 00000000 00000000   C0000000 00000000 00000000 0000000C   *...y............................*   165528
000540   00000000 00000000 CCC0000C 0000000C   00000000 00000000 001650C0 00000000   *................................*   165548
000560   00000000 00000000 00000000 00000000   00000000 00000000 00000000 0000000C   *................................*   165568
000580   00000000 00000000 00000000 00000000   00165E3E 00000000 00000000 00000000   *..................$.............*   165588
0005A0   00000000 0000000C 00000000 00000000   0000000C 00000000 0016656A 0016656A   *................................*   1655A8
0005C0   00165012 00166A0A 0016656E 00165C20   00165956 00165A9E 00165B3E 0016621A   *...........................$.....*   1655C8
0005E0   00165950 001659B4 001659D0 001659F4   001659E6 00165C2A 00165C46 00165C70   *..................4...W..*...*...*.*   1655E8
000600   00165C5C 00165C98 00165CCE 00165CAE   00165CFA 00165D20 00165D00 00165D34   *..**..*q..*...*...*...)...)...).*   165608
000620   00165D40 00165D76 00165D56 00165E34   00165F34 00165F4C 00166120 001662E6   *..) ..)...)...;.........../....W*   165628
000640   001658 3E 00000000 00110014 000088FF   FFF0F0F0 F0F0C000 2D0F0204 80000424   *..$............F..00000..........*   165648
000660   00000000 00000000 00000000 0001E2C1   D3C5F0F0 F4D4E2C1 D3C5F0F4 1802D000   *..................SALE004MSALE04....*   165668
000680   04000000 00050900 000020E2 C1D3F4C4   C4300004 00000081 00004000 0000E0E6   *.............SAL4........a.. .....*   165688
0006A0   00000400 001000E2 C1D3C5C9 D5C9E30E   C4800004 00000200 C9D5E5C1 D3C9C440   *........SALEINIT.........INVALID *   1656A8
0006C0   C6E4D5C3 E3C9D6D5 40D2C5E8 1804F000   C4000000 00052004 0000200E 088C0004   *FUNCTION KEY..0...................*   1656C8
0006E0   00001000 C9E3C5D4 40D5E4D4 C2C5D940   D5D6E340 D5E4D4C5 D9C9C340 6040D9C5   *....ITEM NUMBER NOT NUMERIC - RE*   1656E8
000700   D2C5E8E4 D5C9E340 D7D9C9C3 C540D5D6   E340D5E4 D4C5D9C9 C3406040 D9C5D2C5   *KEYUNIT PRICE NOT NUMERIC - REKE*   165708
000720   E8D8E4C1 D5E3C9E3 E840D5D6 E340D5E4   D4C5D9C9 C3406040 D9C5D2C5 E8C9D5E5   *YQUANTITY NOT NUMERIC - REKEYINV*   165728
000740   C1D3C9C4 40E2C9C7 D540D6D5 40D8E4C1   D5E3C9E3 E840C6C9 C5D3C402 04800004   *ALID SIGN ON QUANTITY FIELD.....*   165748
000760   0D000000 00000000 00000000 00C3E4E2   E3D4E2E3 0602F000 04000084 000606EC   *...............CUSTMST..0....d....*   165768
000780   00040000 40001002 00000400 001300D3   C9D5C5E5 E2D40604 F0000428 00440CD3   *.... ...........LINEVSM..0......L*   165788
0007A0   C9E2E308 02E00004 00004000 C1C3C3C5   D7E3C5C4 5840D004 58404018 58504000   *IST........ .ACCEPTED. ...  ... .*   1657A8
0007C0   5050D220 585C4004 5050D224 D211E230   C0A29240 6242D206 62436242 41106230   *..K...  ...K.K....sk ..K..........*   1657C8
0007E0   5010D240 9680D240 4110D240 9640D049   58F0C008 05EF94BF D04940F0 D05C58F0   *..K o.K ..K o ...0.....m... 0.*.0*   1657E8
000800   D1E850D0 F08058E0 D2204810 E0144130   C0144910 C0E40520 4720201C 8B100001   *J...0...K..........................*   165808
000820   47C0201C 48112018 89100002 58113000   07F10001 D206624A C0B69240 6251D206   *.........i..........1..K......k ..K.*   165828
000840   6252C0BD 92406259 D20E6230 C0C49240   623FD209 6240623F 41106230 5010D240   *.....k ..K.....Dk ..K.. ..........K *   165848
000860   4110624A 5010D244 411060E0 5010D248   41106297 5010D24C 41106252 5010D250   *.......K...-...K.....p..K.........K.*   165868
000880   96F0D250 4110D240 9640D049 58F0C008   C5EF94EF D04940F0 D05C58F0 D1E850D0   *o.K...K o ...C....m... 0.*.0J...*   165888
0008A0   F0F05820 C028D503 60BFC0D3 0782D201   6279C090 D20E6230 C0D79240 623FD209   *0......N.-..L.bK......K....Pk ..K.*   1658A8
0008C0   6240623F 4110623C 5010D240 41106299   5010D244 41106297 5010D248 4110605C   *. .........K ...I..K....p..K...-.*   1658C8
0008E0   5010D24C 41106279 5010D250 9680D250   4110D240 9640D049 58F0C008 05EF94EF   *..K.........K.o.K...K o ...0.....m.*   1658E8
000900   D04940F0 D05C58F0 D1E850D0 F080D208   6230C0E6 92406239 D20F623A 62394110   *.. 0.*.0J...0.K.....Wk ..K........*   165908
000920   62305010 D2409680 D2404110 D2409640   D0495FF0 C00805EF 94BFD049 40F0D05C   *....K o.K ..K c ...0....m... 0.**   165928
```

FIGURE 10.5 *(Continued)*

```
CUSTOMER INFORMATION CONTROL SYSTEM STORAGE DUMP   CODE=ASRA   TASK=EX00        DATE=10/04/83   TIME=01:13:23   PAGE   11

PROGRAM STORAGE                                  ADDRESS  165008  TO  166DAF      LENGTH  C01DA8

000940  58F0D1E8 50D0F080 5810C020 07F15E20   C02C58E0 D220D500 E01A6211 0772D207   *.0J...0.......1.......K.N.........K.*   165948
000960  625AC0EF D2086230 C0E79240 6239D20F   623A6239 41106230 5010D240 4110625A   *....K....7k ..K.............K ....*   165968
000980  5010D244 9680D244 4110D240 9640D049   58F0C008 05EF94BF D04940F0 D05C58F0   *..K.o.K...K o ...C....m... C.*.0*   165988
0009A0  D1F850D0 F08C5810 C01C07F1 5820C030   58F0D220 D500E01A 620A0782 5820C034   *J...0.......1.......K.N.......b....*   1659A8
0009C0  D500E01A 62100772 5800D238 5000D234   5800C038 5000D238 5810C01C 07F15800   *N..........K...K........K.......1..*   1659C8
0009E0  D2345000 D2385810 C01C07F1 D2136010   60389240 6024D210 60256024 D2016279   *K...K.......1K.-.-.k -.K.-.-.K...*   1659E8
000A00  C092D20E 6230C0D7 9240623F D2096240   623F4110 62305010 D2404110 6299501C   *.kK....Pk ..K.. .........K ...r..*   165A08
000A20  D2444110 62975010 D2484110 60105010   D24C4110 62795010 D2509680 D2504110   *K....p..K...-...K........K.o.K...*   165A28
000A40  D2409640 D04958F0 C00805EF 94BFD049   40F0D05C 58F0D1B8 50D0F060 D2C86230   *K o ...0....m... C.*.0J...0.K...*   165A48
000A60  C0E69240 6239D20F 623A6239 41106230   5010D240 9680D240 4110D240 9640D049   *.Wk ..K.............K o.K ..K o ..*   165A68
000A80  58F0C008 05EF94BF D04940F0 D05C58F0   D1F850D0 F060D201 6279C094 D2CF6230   *.0....m... 0.*.0J...0.K....mK...*   165A88
000AA0  C0D79240 623FD209 6240623F 41106230   5010D240 41106299 5010D244 41106297   *.Pk ..K.. .........K ...r..K....p*   165AA8
000AC0  5010D248 41106000 5010D24C 41106279   5010D250 9680D250 4110D240 9640D049   *..K...-...K........K.o.K...K o ..*   165AC8
000AE0  58F0C008 05EF94BF D04940F0 D05C58F0   D1F85CD0 F080D208 6230C0E6 92406239   *.0....m... 0.*.0J...0.K....Wk ..*   165AE8
000B00  D20F623A 6239411C 62305010 D2409680   D2404110 D2409640 D04958F0 C00805EF   *K.............K o.K ..K c ...0....*   165B08
000B20  94BFD049 40F0D05C 58F0D1B8 50D0F080   5810D238 C7E15820 C03C58F0 D220D500   *m... 0.*.0J...0...K..1.......K.N.*   165B28
000B40  E01A6209 0782D200 60EE6068 920060E0   D28A60B1 60B0D213 60EEC100 924061C2   *.....bK.-.-.k.-.K.-.-.K.-.A.k /.*   165B48
000B60  D23E6103 6102D206 624AC0B6 92406251   D2016279 C095D206 6252C0BD 92406259   *K./././K......k ..K....nK......k ..*   165B68
000B80  D2CE6230 C1149240 623FD209 6240623F   41106230 5010D240 4110624A 5010D244   *K...A.k ..K.. .........K .......K.*   165B88
000BA0  411060F0 5010D248 41106279 5010D24C   41106252 5010D250 9680D250 4110D240   *..-...K........K........K.o.K...K *   165BA8
000BC0  9640D049 58F0C008 05EF94BF D04940F0   D05C58F0 D1B850D0 F080D203 626EC0D3   *o ...0....m... 0.*.0J...0.K....L*   165BC8
000BE0  D2086230 C1239240 6239D20F 623A6239   41106230 5010D24C 41106268 5010D244   *K...A.k ..K.............K .......K.*   165BE8
000C00  9680D244 4110D240 9640D049 58F0C008   C5EF94BF D04940F0 D05C58F0 D1B850D0   *o.K...K o ...0....m... 0.*.0J...*   165C08
000C20  F0E05820 C00CDD05 60CE2000 5810C040   C771D200 60CE6070 5810C044 07F15E20   *C........-....... ..K.-.-.......1..*   165C28
000C40  C04895E8 6008C772 D2006CCE 60785810   C04407F1 D21E60EE C12C9240 6101D22D   *..nY-...K.-.-.......1K.-.A.k /.K.*   165C48
000C60  610E610D D20060CE 6078D201 60CCC097   92E86C08 5820C00C DD0560D8 20005810   */././K.-.-.K.-..pKY-.........-Q....*   165C68
000C80  C04C0771 D20060D7 60705810 C05007F1   5620C054 95E86008 0772D200 60D7607B   *....K.-P-.......1....nY-...K.-P-.*   165C88
000CA0  5810C050 07F1D21D 60EEC14E 9240610C   D22F610D 610CD200 60D76078 D20160D5   *.....1K.-.A.k /.K././.K.-P-.K.-N*   165CA8
000CC0  C09792E8 60085820 C00CDD05 60E12000   5810C058 C771D200 60E06070 5810C05C   *.pkY-........-..........K.-.-....**   165CC8
000CE0  07F15820 C06095E8 60080772 D20060E0   60785810 C05C07F1 D21B60EE C1699240   *.1...-nY-...K.-.-.....*.1K.-.A.k *   165CE8
000D00  610AD230 610E610A D20060E0 6078D201   60DFC097 92E86008 5820C064 954E60EA   */.K././.K.-.-.K.-..pkY-.....n+-.*   165D08
000D20  07825820 C068956C 60EA0772 D20060E9   60F05E10 C06C07F1 5820C070 95E86008   *.b....n--...K.-Z-.......1....nY-.*   165D28
000D40  0772D200 60E96086 5810C06C 07F1D21D   60EEC185 9240610C D22E610D 610CD200   *..K.-Z-h.....1K.-.Aek /.K././.K.*   165D48
000D60  60F96C68 D20160E7 C09792E8 60085820   C07495E8 60080772 D20060BE 6068D206   *-Z-hK.-X.pkY-.....nY-...K.-.-.K.*   165D68
000D80  624AC0B6 92406251 D2016279 C095D206   6252C0FD 92406259 D20E6230 C1149240   *....k ..K....nK.....k ..K...A.k *   165D88
000DA0  623FD209 6240623F 41106230 5010D240   4110624A 5010D244 411060B0 5010D248   *..K.. .........K .......K...-...K.*   165DA8
000DC0  41106279 5010D24C 41106252 5010D250   9680D250 4110D240 9640D049 58F0C008   *.......K.........K.o.K...K o ...0..*   165DC8
000DE0  05EF94BF D04940F0 D05C58F0 D1B850D0   F080D208 6230C0E6 92406239 D20F623A   *..m... 0.*.0J...0.K....Wk ..K...*   165DE8
000E00  62394110 62305010 D2409680 D2404110   D2409640 D04958F0 C00805EF 94BFD049   *.........K o.K ..K o ...0....m...*   165E08
000E20  40F0D05C 58F0D1B8 50D0F060 D2116230   C1A39240 6242D206 62436242 41106230   * 0.*.0J...0.K...Atk ..K..........*   165E28
000E40  5010D240 9680D240 4110D240 9640D049   58F0C008 05EF94BF D04940F0 D05C58F0   *..K o.K ..K o ...0....m... 0.*.0*   165E48
000E60  D1F850D0 F08058E0 D2204810 E0144130   C0144910 C0B40520 4720201C 8B100001   *J...0...K...........................*   165E68
000E80  47C0201C 48112018 89100002 58113000   07F10004 D2056140 60C6D206 625AC1E5   *.........i.........1..K./ -FK...A.*   165E88
000EA0  92406261 D2086230 C1BC9240 6239D20F   623A6239 41106230 5010D240 4110625A   *k ./K...A.k ..K.............K ....*   165EA8
000EC0  5010D244 41106140 5010D248 411060F0   5010D24C 41106140 5010D250 9680D250   *..K.../ ..K...-...K.../ ..K.o.K.*   165EC8
000EE0  4110D240 9640D049 58F0C008 05EF94BF   D04940F0 D05C58F0 D1B850D0 FC8CD205   *..K o ...0....m... 0.*.0J...0.K.*   165EE8
000F00  60A8C099 5820C078 956060EA 0772E275   D20860E1 F275D210 60A8FB33 D214D20C   *-y.r....n--...2.K.-.2.K.-y..K.K.*   165F08
000F20  F35360A8 D2145810 C07C07F1 F275D210   60E1F275 D20860A8 FA33D214 D20CF353   *3.-yK......12.K.-.2.K.-y..K.K.3.*   165F28
000F40  60A8D214 F275D210 60A8F275 D20860D8   FC73D21C D20CF366 6090D211 F276D210   *-yK.2.K.-y2.K.-Q..K.K.3.-.K.2.K.*   165F48
000F60  61EDF276 D2086097 FA43D213 D20CF364   61EDD213 D206625A C1B59240 6261D208   */.2.K.-p..K.K.3./.K.K...A.k ./K.*   165F68
000F80  6230C1C5 92406239 D20F623A 62394110   62305010 D2404110 625A5010 D2444110   *..AEk ..K............K .......K...*   165F88
000FA0  61405010 D2484110 60A05010 D24C9680   D24C4110 D2409640 D04958F0 C00805EF   */ ..K...-...K.o.K...K c ...0.....*   165FA8
000FC0  94BFD049 40F0D05C 58F0D1B8 50D0F080   D2086230 C1CE9240 6239D20F 623A6239   *m... 0.*.0J...0.K...A.k ..K......*   165FC8
000FE0  41106230 5010D240 9680D240 4110D240   9640D049 58F0C008 05EF94BF D04940F0   *.......K o.K ..K c ...0....m... 0*   165FE8
001000  D05C58F0 D1B850D0 F080D205 61D860C6   D20561E6 60CFD205 61ED60D8 92F061EC   *.*.0J...0.K./Q-FK./W-.K./.-QK0/.*   166008
```

FIGURE 10.5 *(Continued)*

```
CUSTOMER INFORMATION CONTROL SYSTEM STORAGE DUMP   CODE=ASRA   TASK=EX00        DATE=10/04/83   TIME=01:13:23   PAGE   12

PROGRAM STORAGE                          ADDRESS  165008  TO  166DAF       LENGTH  C01DA8

001020   94CF61F2 96C061F2 D20561F3 60A858E0   D220F633 61E2E000 F83361DE E004D206   *m./2o./2K./3-y..K.8./S..8./...K.*   166028
001040   625AC1D7 92406261 D2016279 C09FD208   6230C1DE 92406239 D20F623A 62394110   *..APk ./K.....K...A.k ..K.......*   166048
001060   62305010 D2404110 625A5010 D2444110   61D85010 D2484110 62795010 D24C4110   *....K ......K.../Ç..K.......K...*   166068
001080   61D85010 D2509680 D2504110 D2409640   D0495EF0 C00805EF 94BFD049 40F0D05C   */Q..K.o.K...K o ...0....m... 0.**   166088
0010A0   58FCD1B8 50D0F08C F275D210 60A8E930   D214C0A1 58F0C080 07AFD203 6268C1E7   *.0J...0.2.K.-y9.K....0....K...AX*   1660A8
0010C0   D2016279 C09FD208 6230C1EB 92406239   D20F623A 62394110 62305010 D2404110   *K.....K...A.k ..K...........K ..*   1660C8
0010E0   62685010 D2444110 61D85010 D2484110   62795010 D24C9680 D24C4110 D240964C   *....K.../Q..K........K.o.K...K o *   1660E8
001100   D04958F0 C00805EF 94BFD049 40F0D05C   58F0D1E8 50D0F080 92F060CF D20460D0   *...0....m... 0.*.0J...0.K0-.K.-.*   166108
001120   60CF92F0 60E1D204 60E260E1 92F060D8   D20460D9 60D8924E 60EAD200 60C56070   *-.K0-.K.-S-.K0-ÇK.-R-Qk+-.K.-E-.*   166128
001140   D20060BE 6068D207 60EEC1F4 924060F6   D24460F7 60F6D206 624AC0B6 92406251   *K.-.-.K.-.A4k -éK.-7-6K.....k ..*   166148
001160   D2016279 C095D206 6252C0BD 92406259   D20E6230 C1149240 623FD209 6240623F   *K....nK.....k ..K...A.k ..K.. ..*   166168
001180   41106230 5010D240 4110624A 5010D244   411060F0 5010D248 41106279 5010D24C   *.......K ......K...-...K.......K.*   166188
0011A0   41106252 5010D250 968CD250 4110D240   9640D049 58F0C008 05EF94BF D04940F0   *.......K.o.K...K c ...0....m... 0*   1661A8
0011C0   D05C58F0 D1B850D0 F080D203 6268C0D3   D2086230 C1239240 6239D20F 623A6239   *.*.0J...0.K....IK...A.k ..K.....*   1661C8
0011E0   41106230 5010D240 41106268 5010D244   9680D244 4110D240 9640D049 58F0C008   *.......K ......K.c.K...K o ...0..*   1661E8
001200   05EF94BF D04940F0 D05C58F0 D1B850D0   F080D225 60EE6010 92406114 D2266115   *..m... 0.*.0J...0.K.-.-.k /.K./.*   166208
001220   6114D206 624AC0B6 92406251 D2016279   C095D206 6252C0BD 92406259 D20E6230   */.K.....k ..K....nK.....k ..K...*   166228
001240   C1149240 623FD209 6240623F 41106230   5010D240 4110624A 5010D244 411060E0   *A.k ..K.. ........K ......K...-.*   166248
001260   5010D248 41106279 5010D24C 41106252   5010D250 9680D250 4110D240 9640D049   *..K........K.......K.o.K...K o ..*   166268
001280   58F0C008 05EF94BF D04940F0 D05C58F0   D1B850D0 F080D203 6268C0D3 D2086230   *.0....m... 0.*.0J...0.K....LK...*   166288
0012A0   C1239240 6239D20F 623A6239 41106230   5010D240 41106268 5010D244 9680D244   *A.k ..K............K ......K.o.K.*   1662A8
0012C0   4110D240 9640D049 58F0C008 05EF94BF   D04940F0 D05C58F0 D1B850D0 F08058F0   *..K o ...0....m... 0.*.0J...0..0*   1662C8
0012E0   D1B0900E F04805F0 9110D048 47E0F00E   58F0C010 07FF48F0 D05C58D0 D0C4960C   *J...0..0j......0..0......0.*....q.*   1662E8
001300   D01458E0 D00C07FE 41100207 410000E0   89000018 16100A0D 58F0C084 07FE50E0   *..................i.........0.d....*   166308
001320   50085050 D00450E0 D0549120 D04847E0   F02E5820 D1B89140 D04947E0 F02E96C4   *...........j......0...J.j ....0.o.*   166328
001340   200058F0 203841F0 F00407FF 94EFD048   58F0C000 05EF1200 07899610 D04605F0   *...0...00...m.....0.........io....0*   166348
001360   9120D048 47E0F016 5800B048 982DE050   58E0D054 07FE9620 D0484160 00044110   *j......0.....q...........c....-....*   166368
001380   C0144170 C0880670 05505840 10001E4B   50401000 87165000 41600008 4110C088   *.....h..... ..... ..g....-.....h*   166388
0013A0   4170C090 06700550 58401000 1E4B5040   10008716 50004180 D2004160 00044170   *.......... ..... ..o.....K..-.....*   1663A8
0013C0   D2C70510 58008000 12004780 10101E0B   50008000 87861000 D207D238 C08858C0   *K..................gf..K.K..h.-*   1663C8
0013E0   D2C058E0 D05407FE 80000000 00165360   C9D3C2D6 D5E3D9F0 00000000 00000000   *K..............-ILBONTR0.........*   1663E8
001400   00000000 00000000 00000000 00000000   00000000 00000000 00000000 00000000   *................................*   166408
001420   0016656A 00000000 00000000 00000000   00000000 00000000 00000000 00000000   *................................*   166428
001440   00000000 00000000 00000000 00000000   00000000 00000000 00000000 00000000   *................................*   166448
001460   00000000 00000000 001246CC 00000000   00000000 00000000 00000000 00000000   *................................*   166468
001480   00000000 00000000 40404040 40404040   00000000 00000000 00000000 00000000   *........         ................*   166488
0014A0   00000000 00000000 00000000 00000000   00000000 F0F0F0F0 F0F0F0F0 00000000   *....................00000000....*   1664A8
0014C0   00000000 00000000 00000000 00000000   00000000 00000000 00000000 00000000   *................................*   1664C8
0014E0   00000000 00000000 00000000 0000C9D3   C2D6C3D6 D4400000 F5F7F4F0 60D3D4F1   *..................ILBOCOM ..5740-LM1*   1664E8
001500   404DC35D 40C3D6D7 E8D9C9C7 C8E340C9   C2D440C3 D6D9D740 F1F9F7F2 6B40F1F9   * (C) COPYRIGHT IBM CORP 1972, 19*   166508
001520   F7F640D3 C9C3C5D5 E2C5C440 D4C1E3C5   D9C9C1D3 406040D7 D9D6C7D9 C1D440D7   *76 LICENSED MATERIAL - PROGRAM P*   166528
001540   D9D6D7C5 D9E3E840 D6C640C9 C2D46BF2   F4F0F3F7 F7000000 0000000C 00166978   *ROPERTY OF IBM,240377............*   166548
001560   000047F0 F00C47F0 F0C447F0 F08450F0   F3CE90E7 F3A6185F D50353CE 53AA4780   *...00..00D.00d.03..X3w..N.......*   166568
001580   503C58E0 53A6D503 E0005054 4780503C   4BE0539E D503E000 505C4770 509858E0   *.....wN...............N....*...q..*   166588
0015A0   53E65840 538258F0 536A056F D50353CE   53AA4780 50605010 D1B847F0 506C58E0   *.f. .b.0....N.........-...J..0...0*   1665A8
0015C0   C0C09140 D04A4780 506C9601 10005910   536247E0 507C5010 53829601 53A218C4   *..j ......o.......t.........bo..s..*   1665C8
0015E0   98FF53A6 9827F3B6 5810F382 07FE50F0   F3C64EF0 F39847F0 F0105810 53E21211   *q..wq.3...3b...03F.03q.00....b..*   1665E8
001600   477050BC 410050AA 47F050B2 C9D3C2D6   C3D6D4F0 1E110A08 18105010 53829680   *..........0..ILBCCOM0..........bo.*   166608
001620   100050D0 100447F0 506C90EC F3CE184F   5820D1E8 91402002 47104148 91042000   *........0....3........j .......j...*   166628
001640   47E0414C 47F04148 58F0438A 12FF4780   40F2056F 47F0411A 410040FA 47F04102   *......0...0...... 2...0.... ..0..*   166648
001660   C9D3C2D6 D4E2C7F0 41100000 0A0818E0   056F4500 4118C9D3 C2D6D4E2 C7F00AC9   *ILBOMSG0........0.......ILBOMSG0..*   166668
001680   12554770 412698EC 43CE07FE 58E02038   4EE0439C 48EE0000 40E0D05C 12EE07EE   *.......q.................. ..*.....*   166688
0016A0   47F04142 80000127 5810413E 0A0D4580   40E29180 20024780 418258E0 20364BE0   *.0................ Sj.......b.......*   1666A8
0016C0   439C485E 000040E0 D05C12EE 4740413A   58F0202C 12FF4780 4182943E 200241FF   *...... ..*... ...0.........bm......*   1666C8
0016E0   001C05EF 47F041A0 58F0208C 12FF4780   41A0189D 41D0D0A8 50D90008 509D0004   *.....0...0................y.R.......*   1666E8
```

FIGURE 10.5 *(Continued)*

```
CUSTOMER INFORMATION CONTROL SYSTEM STORAGE DUMP    CODE=ASRA    TASK=EX00        DATE=10/04/83    TIME=01:13:23    PAGE   13

PROGRAM STORAGE
                                      ADDRESS  165CC8  TO  166DAF      LENGTH  001DA6

001700  1B1105EF 18D9D502 4396205D 478041C6   411C205C 18744580 4324D502 43963065  *.....RN..o.)...F...*......N..o..*   166708
001720  478041C6 41130064 47F041E0 D502439C   20594780 41DA4110 20581874 45804324  *...F.....0..N..o..................*   166728
001740  D7072058 2058D502 43962055 47804236   58F043EE 12EF4780 41FA05EF 47F04220  *P.....N..o.........C.............0..*   166748
001760  41004202 47F0420A C9D3C2D6 E2D5C4E2   1B110A08 18F005EF 4500421E C9D3C2D6  *.....0..ILBOSND2.....0......ILBO*   166768
001780  E2D5C4F2 0A09914C 20024780 422C4580   40E24110 20541B77 45804324 D502439E  *SND2..j ........ S...........N..o*   166788
0017A0  20514780 428A9108 20504780 425645C0   4254C9D3 C2D6D8E2 E2F00A09 D502435E  *......j............ILBOQSSO..N..o*   1667A8
0017C0  20E54780 426E4500 426CC9C5 C4D8C2F1   40400A09 41102050 1B774580 4324D502  *.e.........IEDQP1  .............N.*   1667C8
0017E0  43963075 4780428A 41130074 47F04274   D5C24396 20614780 42D65850 20604135  *.o............0..N..o./...0...-..*   1667E8
001800  00909110 30304780 42B25035 02144115   02141E74 45804324 583502D8 1233478C  *..j.........................Q....*   166808
001820  42E64133 05A09110 30304780 42D65035   021492F0 52144115 02140A14 947F2000  *.0....j.......0....k...........m...*   166828
001840  9101439E 478042EC D703437E 437E94FE   439E9101 200047E0 436458F0 439212FF  *j........P..=.=m...j.........C.k..*   166848
001860  077F4500 4308C9D3 C2D6E2E3 E3F00A09   41004312 47F0431A C9D3C2D6 E2E3E3F0  *......ILBOSTTO........0..ILBOSTTO*   166868
001880  41100000 0A0818FC 07FF5831 00009110   30300788 92801000 0A141277 07E61813  *........0.......j....hk.........h..*   166888
0018A0  58F01014 96011017 1BEE43E0 F0054CF0   E0C64100 F0089140 F00447E0 435C410C  *.0..o.........0...(.....j 0....*..*   1668A8
0018C0  E0104110 F0000A0A 07F848F0 D05C58D0   20045ED0 D0C458E0 D00C980C D01407EE  *.....0....8.0.*..............q.....*   1668C8
0018E0  40400000 001663F0 00000000 00166F2A   C0166CF2 00000000 00000000 00000000  *     .....0.....,..................*   1668E8
001900  00060008 00F0C27C 5016635E 0016656A   C01CE610 00124A08 001663F0 001243F0  *.......B....;......k.........0...0*   166908
001920  00165068 00124A16 00124000 00165020   C016656A A0A41813 4500C3E0 00000000  *..........  ...........u....C.....*   166928
001940  00000288 58F10054 05EF07F7 D203C3FC   E00C4130 A0A40700 4510C404 00000000  *...h.1.....7K.C.......u....D.....*   166948
001960  C4C6D9F1 FF020000 50310000 0A5107F7   4130A0A4 18130700 4500C424 08000000  *DFR1.............7...u.......D.....*   166968
001980  0000028E 0000C289 58F10054 05EF07F7   4130A0A4 9501C27D 4770C470 9500C27C  *...h...1.1.....7...un.E'..D.n.B.*   166988
0019A0  4780C458 18130700 4500C450 04000001   00000288 58F10054 47F04456 00000000  *..D.......D.........h.1...0.......*   1669A8
0019C0  00000000 00000000 00000000 00000000   00000000 00000000 00000000 00000000  *...................................*   1669C8
0019E0  00000000 C9D3C2D6 E2D9E540 E5E2D9C5   D3F24EF3 E4D7F1F3 F0F5F640 04000002  *....ILBOSRV VSREL2.3UP13056 ....*   1669E8
001A00  00000101 01010101 01010101 01010101   01010101 01010101 01010101 01010101  *...................................*   166A08
001A20  01010101 01010101 01010101 01010101   01010101 01010101 01010101 01010101  *...................................*   166A28
001A40  LINES TO 001AC0 SAME AS ABOVE                                                                                          166A46
001AE0  01010101 01010101 01010101 01010101   01010000 00000000 00000000 01010101  *...................................*   166AE8
001B00  0101C9D3 C2D6E6E3 C240E5E2 D9C5D3F2   4BF3E4D7 F1F3F0F5 F6409550 5A10E018  *..ILBOWTB VSREL2.3UP13056 n.....*   166B08
001B20  000047F0 F004167F 9102D049 47807024   5830D1E0 D5033014 71464770 70249204  *...00...j..........J.N..........k.*   166B28
001B40  D1C7947F D1C51834 12444770 70484100   703447F0 703CC9D3 C2D6C3D6 D4F0411C  *JGm.JE...............0..ILBOCOMO..*   166B48
001B60  00000A08 5000D1E8 18305050 30385020   30AC1222 4770707A 58203010 1222478C  *......J......................:........*   166B68
001B80  707A4100 706847F0 7070C9D3 C2D6C3D4   D4F04110 00000A08 500030AC 91803000  *.:......0..ILBOCMMO...........j...*   166B88
001BA0  47107122 96803000 41400001 50D03004   5610D004 58201004 12224780 70A8D523  *....o....  ......................wN.*   166BA8
001BC0  714A101C 47707118 9103D007 47707118   5820101E 12224780 71189103 101E4770  *........j...................j.....*   166BC8
001BE0  71189180 20004780 71189101 20034770   71185E10 20004820 10004920 714247E0  *..j.......j..........................*   166BE8
001C00  71184920 71444720 711858E0 713E12FF   4770711C 410070EA 47F07102 C9D3C2D6  *...........0................0..ILBO*   166C08
001C20  D7D9D4F0 1B110A08 18F005EF 45007116   C9D3C2D6 D7D9D4F0 0A0947F0 713805EF  *PRMO.....0......ILBOPRMO...0....*   166C28
001C40  47F07138 12444770 71364500 7134C9D3   C2D6C3D6 D4F00A09 1B441813 07F60000  *.0..............ILBOCOMO.......6..*   166C48
001C60  00000000 00000064 C1D5E2F4 E3C8C9E2   40C9E240 C140E2C1 E5C540C1 D9C5C140  *.........ANS4THIS IS A SAVE AREA *   166C68
001C80  C6D6D940 C3D4E240 E3D640C3 D6C2D6D3   C9D3C2C6 C2C5C740 E5E2D9C5 D3F24EF3  *FOR CMS TO COBOLILBOBEG VSREL2.3*   166C88
001CA0  E4D7F1F3 F4F7F740 0C0047F0 F004187F   91042000 4780705C 9240D10E D276D10E  *UP13477 ...00...j.......*k J.K.J.*   166CA8
001CC0  D10ED224 D10E709E 5830D1E0 D2071133   300CD20C D13B70C3 181D58DD 0004D501  *J.K.J.....J.K.J...K.J..C.......N.*   166CC8
001CE0  D00070DB 4770704C 5830D1E0 D2071148   300C47F0 7052D20A 114870D0 18D194FE  *...........J.K.......0..K.......Jm.*   166CE8
001D00  200047F0 70709104 20024780 707094FB   20025810 D10847F0 70744110 D108D203  *...0..j........m.......J..0....J.K.*   166D08
001D20  100070DE D203107E 70E2D2C1 1004704C   0A23415C 001C9101 20024780 709A1E55  *....K..=.SK.............j..........*   166D28
001D40  943A2002 07F64040 C9D2C6F9 F9F2C940   40404040 C9C5C3E4 D9E2C9E5 C540C3C1  *m....6  IKF9921      RECURSIVE CA*   166D48
001D60  D3D340E3 D640D4D6 C4E4D3C5 4040C6D9   D6D440D4 D6C4E4D3 C5404DD5 D6E340C3  *LL TO MODULE  FROM MODULE (NOT C*   166D68
001D80  D6C2D6D3 5D003060 007E8000 02004020   C9D3C2C6 D4E2C740 E5E2D9C5 D3F24EF3  *OBOL)....=.... .ILBOMSG VSREL2.3*   166D88
001DA0  E4D7F1F3 F0F5F640                                                          *UP13056                          *   166DA8
```

FIGURE 10.5 *(Continued)*

```
CUSTOMER INFORMATION CONTROL SYSTEM STORAGE DUMP    CODE=ASRA   TASK=EX00        DATE=10/04/83   TIME=01:13:23   PAGE  14

PROGRAM STORAGE                          ADDRESS  171008  TO  1711BF        LENGTH  0001B8

000000  D4E2C1D3 C5F0F440 00404040 00000000   00000000 E2C1D3C5 F0F0F440 01A400BE   *MSALE04 .         ........SALE004 .u..*   171008
000020  00870195 C0C301BD 001850FF FE000000   00000000 00000000 000403F1 000E2C1   *.g.n.C...........1..SA*                    171028
000040  D3F40000 001802F0 001BC5D5 E3C5D940   C3E4D9D9 C5D5E340 E6C5C5D2 40E2C1D3   *L4.....0..ENTER CURRENT WEEK SAL*          171048
000060  C54E20000 001002F0 010BC3E4 E2E3D6D4   C5D940D5 E4D4C2C5 D97A0000 00060FE1   *ES.....0..CUSTOMER NUMBER:....J*           171068
000080  011CF0F0 F0F0F0F0 00000001 00F00123   0000000C 02F001AB C9E3C5D4 40D5E4D4   *..000000.....0......0..ITEM NUM*           171088
0000A0  C2C5D97A 00000006 0F5001BC F0F0F0F0   F0F00000 000100F0 01C30000 000B02F0   *BER:.....000000...0.C.....0*               1710A8
0000C0  024BE4D5 C9E340D7 D9C9C3C5 7A000000   060F5002 5CF0F0F0 F0F0F000 00000100   *..UNIT PRICE:....*000000.....*             1710C8
0000E0  F0026300 000009 02 F002EBD8 E4C1D5E3   C9E3E87A 00000006 0F5002FC F0F0F0F0   *0.....0..QUANTITY:......0000*              1710E8
000100  F0F00000 000103C1 03034E00 00000100   F0030500 00002602 F00422C3 D6D4D7L3   *00.....A..+.....0....0..COMPL*             171108
000120  C5E3C540 C1C2D6E5 C5440EC9 C5D3C4E2   40C1D5C4 40D7D9C5 E2E240C5 D5E3C5D9   *ETE ABOVE FIELDS AND PRESS ENTER*          171128
000140  4B000000 2B02F004 C2E3E6D6 40C3C5C5   E3E240D7 D3C1C3C5 E240C1D9 C540C1E2   *.....0.BTWO CENTS PLACES ARE AS*           171148
000160  E2E4D4C5 C44C6D6 D940E0E4D5 C9E34D07   D9C9C3C5 0000002A 02F006A2 D7C1F17A   *SUMED FOR UNIT PRICE....0.sPA1:*           171168
000180  40C5E7C9 E340E3D9 C1D5E2C1 C3E3C9D6   D5404007 C1F27A40 D9C5E3E4 D9D540E3   * EXIT TRANSACTION  PA2: RETURN T*          171188
0001A0  D640D4C5 D5E40000 004E01F8 0730FFFF   FFFFFFFF 00000000                     *O MENU...+.8.........*                     1711A8
```

END OF CICS/VS STORAGE DUMP

FIGURE 10.5   (Continued)

11

Advanced Topics: Screen Handling and Printing

11.1 ADVANCED BASIC MAPPING SUPPORT: PAGING AND MULTIPLE MAPS

11.1.1 How Paging Works; What Are Its Limitations

We discussed basic mapping support macros in Chapter 3, and terminal I/O commands in Chapter 4. However, we focused on one type of map: the 24 x 80-character map that fills the terminal screen. This section will show you how to build a screen image with a series of smaller maps that carry header, detail, and trailer information. We will refer to a screen image formatted in this way as a page. A CICS program may build many such pages and may send them to the user's terminal all at one time. The user may use system-defined commands to page back and forth among the collection of screen images. BMS paging is not available under CICS OS/2, as of release 1.20.

BMS paging is used when sending information to the user for examination or printing, never when receiving information from the user.
In other words, use paging when the user needs to see large amounts of data, but does not need to enter any new data. You are really sending the user a report on his or her terminal screen. Batch programmers will be familiar with this logic for a simple report program:

```
Open files.
Print headers.
Read first record.
Perform loop until end of input file:
    If report page is full,
        print trailer lines,
        print header lines.
    Print detail line.
    Read another record.
Print trailer line for last page.
Close files.
Terminate processing.
```

In a CICS file browse program in which you are supplying a certain number of pages to the user, you will not need to open and close the input file, because the file will already be open under CICS. Instead, you will need to start and end the browse. Otherwise, the logic is similar. One map is used to create the header lines at the top of the screen, another map is used repeatedly to create each detail line, and a third map is used to create the trailer lines at the bottom of the screen. The SEND MAP command, with the PAGING and ACCUM options, is used to send the maps to a special temporary storage queue. After everything is ready, the SEND PAGE command sends all of the report pages to the user's terminal. The user can enter various system-defined paging commands; these allow the user to "turn the pages" forward or backward in the simulated report. The user should also enter a command to discard the report after it is no longer needed.

In order to use some of the features of paging that we will discuss here, the CICS system must be generated to support these features. As of CICS 1.6 and later, full function BMS is required. Even so, the discussion here will only introduce you to the use of these features. We will show you one practical way in which paging can be used in an application; other methods are beyond the scope of this book.

Applications that use paging can tie up large amounts of system resources, particularly temporary storage and data transmission time. **Remember that BMS paging screen information will sit in temporary storage between tasks until the terminal user purges it.** If the terminal user has a tendency to walk away from the terminal to do other things, he or she should remember to purge the report first. Avoid using BMS paging on CICS systems that already place heavy demands on temporary storage and on data transmission. In all cases, limit the amount of information that will be sent to the user by any one task. Do no send 50 pages of file browse data. If the file has 10,000 records, decide on a subset that will be shown to the user. Let the user ask for records for one particular date, or customer, or ZIP code, or part number, or whatever. Or just send two or three pages of information starting with the key that the user requests.

11.1.2 Coding a Set of Maps to Occupy the Same Screen

It is now time to look at two of our map macros once again. The first macro that we discussed was DFHMSD, the map set definition macro. Remember that a map set is a group of maps that are loaded into memory together. **If you are using several maps to build a screen image, the maps must all be in the same map set, so that they will be loaded together.** See Figures 11.1, 11.2, and 11.3.

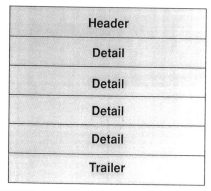

| Header |
| Detail |
| Detail |
| Detail |
| Detail |
| Trailer |

FIGURE 11.1   Using multiple maps per screen.

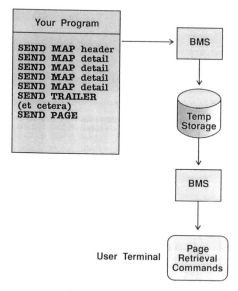

FIGURE 11.2   BMS paging.

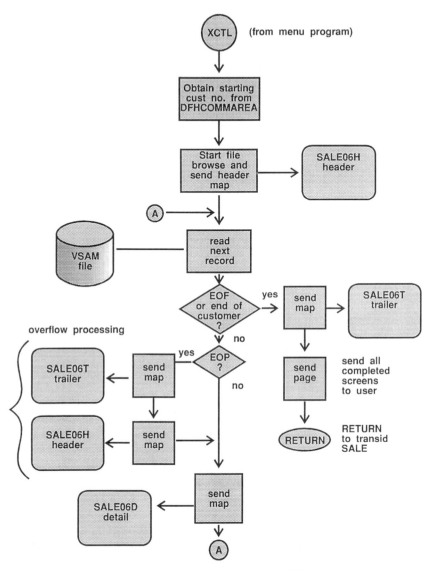

FIGURE 11.3 Browse program using BMS.

The DFHMDI macro is used to define one map. When you make up your screen image on a layout sheet, notice the way in which the maps fit together. The map at the top is the header. The map at the bottom is the trailer. Parameters in the DFHMDI macro indicate which maps are headers, which are trailers, and which are neither. Other parameters indicate how to position each map on the screen. Here is the format of the DFHMDI macro, with the options that you are likely to use for BMS paging:

```
mapname DFHMDI TIOAPFX=YES,
               [SIZE=(line,column)],
               [CTRL=(FREEKB,FRSET)],
               [HEADER=YES|TRAILER=YES],
               [COLUMN=(number)|NEXT|SAME],
               [LINE=(number)|NEXT|SAME],
               [JUSTIFY=([LEFT|RIGHT]
               [,FIRST|LAST])]
```

For the first map to appear at the top of the terminal screen, specify
HEADER and JUSTIFY=FIRST. The HEADER parameter allows the map
to be sent during page overflow processing. JUSTIFY=FIRST indicates that
the map should be placed at the beginning of a new page, and that the
previous page of data is now complete.

For the last map to appear at the bottom of the terminal screen, specify
TRAILER and JUSTIFY=LAST. The TRAILER parameter indicates that
CICS should reserve enough space for this map at the bottom of each
terminal screen page. In other words, the page overflow condition will be
invoked when the remaining space on the terminal screen is about to
become too small to hold the trailer map. The TRAILER parameter also
allows the map to be sent during page overflow processing. JUS-
TIFY=LAST indicates that the map should be placed at the bottom of the
terminal screen page, whether or not the map is sent to the terminal during
page overflow processing.

What about the "detail lines" on the terminal screen page; in other
words, the maps that appear between the header and the trailer maps?
There are many ways to specify where these maps go. Think of each map
as a "window" or "box" positioned somewhere within the terminal screen
page. Maps may touch one another, but they may not overlap. If JUS-
TIFY=LEFT is specified, which is the usual case, then the LINE and
COLUMN designations will refer to the position occupied by the upper
left corner of the map within the terminal screen page. If JUS-
TIFY=RIGHT is specified, then the LINE and COLUMN designations will
refer to the position occupied by the upper right corner of the map within
the terminal screen page.

A complex set of rules governs where the maps will go if some of the
maps on the page are specified as JUSTIFY=LEFT and others are specified as JUSTIFY=RIGHT. These results also depend on the LINE and
COLUMN specified for each map. Since there is seldom any reason to
build terminal screen pages from a patchwork of various odd-sized
maps, we will avoid this issue by making simplifying assumptions. In a
typical paging application, each "detail line" map will be left-justified,
placed with its upper left corner in column 1 of the next available line
on the terminal screen page. In other words, the map is specified as
JUSTIFY=LEFT, COLUMN=1, and LINE=NEXT. If the previous map was
also written beginning in column 1, COLUMN=SAME could be speci-

fied in place of COLUMN=1. COLUMN=SAME merely causes the current map to be positioned beginning at the same column as the previous map. LINE=NEXT indicates that this map should always be placed on a new line. SIZE=(1,80) is used if the map occupies one screen line; SIZE=(2,80) if it occupies two screen lines, and so forth. This type of map is used in our sample application.

For each page, the application program will send the header map. Then, it will repeatedly send the detail map until there is just enough space left to send the trailer map. This triggers the overflow condition. The overflow handler routine will send the trailer map for the current page, and the header map for the next page (if any). After all pages have been sent, a SEND PAGE command will be used to route all of the pages to the user's terminal.

Let's look at another way to fill the space between the header map and the trailer map. Suppose that this space is 18 lines deep, and that we want to fill this space with four maps in the form of vertical strips. If each vertical strip is 20 characters wide, four can fit on a terminal screen page. Assuming that the detail should begin on line 3, we can define the detail map as JUSTIFY=LEFT, LINE=3, COLUMN=NEXT, and SIZE=(18,20). COLUMN=NEXT means that the next available column on line 3 should be used. Page overflow occurs when there is no more room to position maps so that they begin on line 3.

When coding the macros for a map set, place the map having the largest number of labeled fields first in the map set, followed by the other maps in descending order. Also, set aside the first field on the header map as an unprotected, FSET field, so that the terminal user can enter paging commands in that field. How long should this field be? This depends upon the length of the operator paging commands that were set up in the system initialization table at your site. It is best to make these paging commands at least four characters long. Also, they should not conflict with any of the transaction codes in the PCT.

11.1.3 I/O commands for Building and Sending Pages Composed of One or More Maps per Screen

To build a series of pages, each map must be sent by a SEND MAP command that specifies PAGING and ACCUM. See Figure 11.4. ACCUM implies that the current map is only a part of a logical message that will be output later. PAGING implies that the pages should be saved on a special temporary storage queue until they are ready to be output. This temporary storage queue is created by the CICS system exclusively for this purpose;

```
CBL XOPTS (LANGLVL (2) ,CICS)                                        00000100
      IDENTIFICATION DIVISION.                                       00000200
      PROGRAM-ID.  SALEP006.                                         00000300
      AUTHOR.  ALIDA JATICH AND PHIL NOWAK.                          00000400
     ****************************************************************00000500
     *    SALEP006: VIEW CURRENT WEEK SALES FOR CUSTOMER           * 00000600
     *                                                             * 00000700
     *    SALEP006 DEMONSTRATES THE USE OF BMS PAGING IN PRODUCING* 00000800
     *    A BROWSE DISPLAY OF ONE CUSTOMER'S RECORDS ON THE VSAM   * 00000900
     *    LINE ITEM FILE.  EACH SCREEN IN THE BROWSE DISPLAY IS    * 00001000
     *    BUILT FROM A HEADER MAP, A SEQUENCE OF DETAIL LINE MAPS, * 00001100
     *    AND A TRAILER MAP.                                       * 00001200
     *                                                             * 00001300
     *    SALEP006 BEGINS THE BROWSE OPERATION BY FINDING          * 00001400
     *    THE FIRST RECORD FOR THE CUSTOMER ON THE LINE ITEM FILE. * 00001500
     *    IT CONTINUES TO READ RECORDS AND BUILD SCREENS UNTIL THERE* 00001600
     *    ARE NO MORE RECORDS FOR THAT CUSTOMER.  WHEN THIS OCCURS,* 00001700
     *    IT FINISHES BUILDING THE LAST SCREEN, AND SENDS ALL OF   * 00001800
     *    THE COMPLETED SCREEN PAGES TO THE USER TERMINAL.  IT     * 00001900
     *    TERMINATES BY ISSUING A RETURN TO TRANSID "SALE", WHICH   * 00002000
     *    WILL PUT OUT A NEW MENU MAP AS SOON AS THE TERMINAL       * 00002100
     *    USER ENTERS SOMETHING OTHER THAN A BMS PAGING COMMAND.    * 00002200
     *                                                             * 00002300
     *    THE TERMINAL USER WILL SEE A DISPLAY OF CURRENT WEEK      * 00002400
     *    SALES FOR THE CUSTOMER.  THE ONLY FIELD ON THE SCREEN     * 00002500
     *    WHICH ALLOWS USER INPUT IS THE FIELD IN THE TOP LEFT      * 00002600
     *    CORNER OF THE SCREEN.  CICS EXPECTS THE USER TO USE       * 00002700
     *    THIS FIELD TO ENTER BMS PAGING COMMANDS TO PAGE BACK      * 00002800
     *    AND FORTH THROUGH THE BROWSE DISPLAY SCREENS.  HOWEVER,   * 00002900
     *    AS SOON AS THE USER ENTERS ANYTHING OTHER THAN A VALID    * 00003000
     *    BMS PAGING COMMAND, THE BROWSE SCREENS WILL BE PURGED     * 00003100
     *    BY CICS, AND THE "SALE" TRANSACTION WILL BE INVOKED.      * 00003200
     *                                                             * 00003300
     ****************************************************************00003400
      ENVIRONMENT DIVISION.                                          00003500
      DATA DIVISION.                                                 00003600
      WORKING-STORAGE SECTION.                                       00003700
      01  BAD-DFHCOM-MSG.                                            00003800
          05  FILLER              PIC X(27)     VALUE                00003900
          'INVALID EIBCALEN - CALL D.P'.                             00004000
      01  LINEVSM-RIDFLD.                                            00003800
          05  WS-CUSTNO           PIC X(6)      VALUE SPACES.        00004100
          05  FILLER              PIC X(18)     VALUE LOW-VALUES.    00004100
      01  CUSTMST-LNGTH           PIC S9(4)     COMP VALUE +150.     00004200
      01  LINEVSM-LNGTH           PIC S9(4)     COMP VALUE +45.      00004300
          EJECT                                                      00004400
      COPY MSALE06.                                                  00004500
          EJECT                                                      00004600
      COPY LINEVSM.                                                  00004700
          EJECT                                                      00004800
      COPY DFHAID.                                                   00004900
          EJECT                                                      00005000
     *                                                               00005100
      LINKAGE SECTION.                                               00005200
      01  DFHCOMMAREA.                                               00005300
          05  CUSTOMER-NUMBER     PIC X(6).                          00005400
     *                                                               00005500
      PROCEDURE DIVISION.                                            00005600
          IF EIBCALEN NOT EQUAL 6                                    00005700
             EXEC CICS SEND                                          00005800
                     FROM (BAD-DFHCOM-MSG)                           00005900
                     ERASE                                           00006000
                     LENGTH (27)                                     00006100
                     END-EXEC                                        00006200
             EXEC CICS RETURN                                        00006300
                     END-EXEC                                        00006400
          ELSE                                                       00006500
             MOVE LOW-VALUES TO SALE06TI                             00006600
             MOVE CUSTOMER-NUMBER TO S6CUSTO.                        00006600
          SKIP1                                                      00006700
     ****************************************************************00006800
     * SEND THE HEADER MAP FOR THE FIRST SCREEN PAGE              * 00006900
     ****************************************************************00007000
```

FIGURE 11.4 Source code for SALEP006, a browse program using BMS paging.

```
        EXEC CICS SEND                                          00007100
               MAP ('SALE06H')                                  00007200
               MAPSET ('MSALE06')                               00007300
               LENGTH (28)                                      00007400
               ERASE                                            00007500
               PAGING                                           00007600
               ACCUM                                            00007700
               END-EXEC.                                        00007800
    *                                                           00007900
        EXEC CICS HANDLE CONDITION                              00008000
               ENDFILE (END-EROWSE)                             00008100
               OVERFLOW (TRAILER-HDR)                           00008200
               NOTFND (NOT-FOUND)                               00008300
               END-EXEC.                                        00008400
    ***************************************************************00008500
    * PREPARE TO READ THE FIRST VSAM FILE RECORD FOR THE CUSTOMER. *00008600
    ***************************************************************00008700
        MOVE CUSTOMER-NUMBER TO WS-CUSTNO.                      00008800
        SKIP1                                                   00008900
        EXEC CICS STARTBR GTEQ                                  00009000
               DATASET ('LINEVSM')                              00009100
               RIDFLD (LINEVSM-RIDFLD)                          00009200
               END-EXEC.                                        00009300
        SKIP1                                                   00009400
    ***************************************************************00009500
    * CONTINUE TO READ LINE ITEM RECORDS AND PRODUCE DETAIL LINE * 00009600
    * MAPS UNTIL THE DISPLAY SCREEN PAGE IS FULL (OVERFLOW), OR  * 00009700
    * END OF FILE, OR THE LAST RECORD FOR THE CURRENT CUSTOMER   * 00009800
    * HAS BEEN READ.                                             * 00009900
    ***************************************************************00010000
    READ-LINE-ITEM.                                             00010100
        EXEC CICS READNEXT                                      00010200
               DATASET ('LINEVSM')                              00010300
               INTO (LINEVSM-REC)                               00010400
               RIDFLD (LINEVSM-RIDFLD)                          00010500
               LENGTH (LINEVSM-LNGTH)                           00010600
               END-EXEC.                                        00010700
        IF LINEVSM-CUST-NO NOT = CUSTOMER-NUMBER                00010800
           GO TO END-EROWSE.                                    00010900
    ***************************************************************00012300
    * IN THE SYMBOLIC MAP WORK AREA, THE WORK AREAS FOR EACH     * 00012400
    * MAP IN THE MAP SET ARE REDEFINED OVER THE FIRST MAP IN     * 00012400
    * THE MAP SET.  BECAUSE OF THIS, THE WORK AREA MUST BE       * 00012400
    * CLEANED OUT EACH TIME IT IS USED.                          * 00012400
    ***************************************************************00012300
        MOVE LOW-VALUES TO SALE06TI.                            
        MOVE LINEVSM-ITEM-CODE TO S6ITEMO.                      00011000
        MOVE LINEVSM-QUANTITY TO S6QTYC.                        00011100
        MOVE LINEVSM-UNIT-PRICE TO S6UNITPO.                    00011200
        EXEC CICS SEND                                          00011300
               MAP ('SALE06D')                                  00011400
               MAPSET ('MSALE06')                               00011500
               FROM (SALE06DO)                                  00011600
               LENGTH (44)                                      00011700
               PAGING                                           00011800
               ACCUM                                            00011900
               END-EXEC.                                        00012000
        GO TO READ-LINE-ITEM.                                   00012100
        SKIP1                                                   00012200
    ***************************************************************00012300
    * IF THE SEND MAP COMMAND FOR THE DETAIL LINE MAP TRIGGERS THE *00012400
    * EMS PAGE OVERFLOW CONDITION, THE TRAILER-HDR ROUTINE IS    * 00012500
    * EXECUTED.  IT SENDS THE TRAILER MAP FOR THE CURRENT PAGE,  * 00012600
    * THE HEADER MAP FOR THE NEXT PAGE, AND THE DETAIL MAP THAT  * 00012700
    * TRIGGERED THE OVERFLOW CONDITION ON THE FIRST ATTEMPT TO   * 00012800
    * SEND IT.                                                   * 00012900
    ***************************************************************00013000
    TRAILER-HDR.                                                00013100
        MOVE LOW-VALUES TO SALE06TI.                            
        MOVE 'PRESS ENTER FOR MORE DATA' TO S6ERRO.             00013200
        EXEC CICS SEND                                          00013300
               MAP ('SALE06T')                                  00013400
               MAPSET ('MSALE06')                               00013500
```

FIGURE 11.4   *(Continued)*

```
                    LENGTH (93)                              00013600
                    PAGING                                   00013700
                    ACCUM                                    00013800
                    END-EXEC.                                00013900
        MOVE LOW-VALUES TO SALE06TI.
        MOVE CUSTOMER-NUMBER TO S6CUSTO.                     00006600
        EXEC CICS SEND                                       00014000
                    MAP ('SALE06H')                          00014100
                    MAPSET ('MSALE06')                       00014200
                    LENGTH (28)                              00014300
                    PAGING                                   00014400
                    ACCUM                                    00014500
                    ERASE                                    00014500
                    END-EXEC.                                00014600
        MOVE LOW-VALUES TO SALE06TI.
        MOVE LINEVSM-ITEM-CODE TO S6ITEMO.                   00011000
        MOVE LINEVSM-QUANTITY TO S6QTYO.                     00011100
        MOVE LINEVSM-UNIT-PRICE TO S6UNITPO.                 00011200
        EXEC CICS SEND                                       00014700
                    MAP ('SALE06D')                          00014800
                    MAPSET ('MSALE06')                       00014900
                    FROM (SALE06DO)                          00015000
                    LENGTH (44)                              00015100
                    PAGING                                   00015200
                    ACCUM                                    00015300
                    END-EXEC.                                00015400
        GO TO READ-LINE-ITEM.                                00015500
        SKIP1                                                00015600
*******************************************************      00015700
*  WHEN THERE IS NO MORE DATA FOR THE CUSTOMER, TERMINATE THE    *  00015800
*  FILE BROWSE.  SEND A TRAILER MAP FOR THE LAST DISPLAY SCREEN  *  00015900
*  PAGE.  SEND ALL PAGES TO THE TERMINAL USER.  RETURN TO        *  00016000
*  TRANSACTION "SALE", WHICH WILL PROVIDE THE USER WITH A NEW    *  00016100
*  MENU MAP AFTER HE OR SHE IS FINISHED WITH THE BROWSE DISPLAY.*  00016200
*******************************************************      00016300
    END-BROWSE.                                              00016400
        EXEC CICS ENDBR                                      00016500
                    DATASET ('LINEVSM')                      00016600
                    END-EXEC.                                00016700
    NOT-FOUND.                                               00016800
        MOVE LOW-VALUES TO SALE06TI.
        MOVE 'END OF DATA            ' TO S6ERRO.            00016900
        EXEC CICS SEND                                       00017000
                    MAP ('SALE06T')                          00017100
                    MAPSET ('MSALE06')                       00017200
                    LENGTH (93)                              00017300
                    PAGING                                   00017400
                    ACCUM                                    00017500
                    END-EXEC.                                00017600
        EXEC CICS SEND PAGE                                  00017700
                    END-EXEC.                                00017800
        EXEC CICS RETURN                                     00017900
                    TRANSID ('SALE')                         00018000
                    END-EXEC.                                00018100
    NEVER-EXECUTE.                                           00018200
        GOBACK.                                              00018300
```

FIGURE 11.4   (Continued)

the programmer need not write anything to it directly. Here is the format of the SEND MAP command:

```
EXEC CICS SEND MAP(name)
      MAPSET(name)
      FROM(data-area)
      LENGTH(data-value)
      PAGING
      ACCUM
      END-EXEC.
```

Suppose all of the pages have been built, and it is time to send them to the terminal user. The SEND PAGE command will send all of the pages to the terminal user:

```
EXEC CICS SEND PAGE
    [RELEASE|RETAIN]
    [OPERPURGE]
    [AUTOPAGE|NOAUTOPAGE]
    END-EXEC.
```

If the map being sent is a detail map, make certain to use the RESP field to check for the OVERFLOW condition (or use HANDLE CONDITION OVERFLOW) in case there is no more room on the current page.

If RETAIN is specified in the SEND PAGE command, page output begins immediately, while your task is still running. In effect, your task retains control while the pages are being output. On the other hand, if RELEASE is specified, the SEND PAGE command behaves as a RETURN command, ending the task immediately and sending the pages to the terminal. If neither RELEASE nor RETAIN is specified, page output occurs only after the current task ends.

AUTOPAGE is assumed when the pages are being sent to a 3287 printer. It causes pages to be written out automatically with no operator intervention. NOAUTOPAGE is assumed when the pages are being sent to a 3270-series terminal. It is not permissible to specify AUTOPAGE for a 3270-series terminal or NOAUTOPAGE for a 3287 printer.

If OPERPURGE is specified, then once the pages have been sent to the terminal, they will remain on temporary storage until the terminal operator enters a special BMS paging command to delete the pages. If OPERPURGE is not specified, then if the terminal user enters anything other than a paging command on the screen, the pages will disappear.

Suppose your program has started to build pages, but it finds that there is a problem somewhere. If so, it should delete the existing pages with the PURGE MESSAGE command in order to free system resources. Here is this command:

```
EXEC CICS PURGE MESSAGE
    END-EXEC.
```

11.1.4 Partition Sets: A Brief Discussion

Terminal devices with screens that can be partitioned are a recent development. Partitioning, in effect, divides the terminal screen into a variable number of separate I/O devices. This feature is available in mainframe CICS, beginning with version 1.6., but not under CICS OS/2. The programming required for this is somewhat complex. Since exceedingly few installations are using this feature under CICS at this time, it is not practical to show any examples of suggested uses. However, partitioning will be described here in order to familiarize you with what it does.

With the availability of higher-resolution CRT and plasma display devices, and with the availability of inexpensive memory chips, it is becoming practical to place more and more information on the face of a single display device. Readers interested in the microcomputer field may be aware of software such as Microsoft Windows or OS/2 that allows the user to run several different application programs at once from different "windows" on the display screen. Similarly, the use of partitioning on a mainframe allows more than one application to be presented to the terminal user at a given time, but with some limitations. Each application or subsystem can occupy a fixed area, or partition, on the terminal screen, and the display is text-mode only.

In contrast, BMS paging with multiple maps per screen is intended to be used with only one application at a time. The multiple maps simply make it easier to format the terminal screen as though it were a printed report.

In order to divide a terminal display screen into partitions, the terminal must be set up to support this processing. Since only one partition is the active partition at any given time, a partitionable terminal has a key that causes the cursor to "jump" into a different partition, making it the active partition. Such a terminal also has a specal clear key that clears only the active partition.

A **partition set** is defined in much the same way as a map set is defined. The DFHPSD macro is used to define the partition set, and the DFHPDI macro is used to define each partition within the set. Here is the DFHPSD macro:

```
name DFHPSD,
     [SUFFIX=(user-suffix)],
     [ALTSCRN=(lines,columns)]
```

ALTSCRN is used to specify the size of the area on the terminal device that is available for partitioning.

In the DFHPDI macro, the VIEWPOS parameter defines the position of the upper left corner of the partition's view port on the device screen. The VIEWSZE parameter defines the size of the view port in lines and columns:

```
name DFHPDI,
     VIEWPDS=(lines,columns),
     VIEWSZE=(lines,columns),
     [BUFSZE=(lines,columns)],
     [MAPSFX=mapset-suffix],
     [ATTRB=ERROR]
```

The name of a partition must be one or two characters long. ATTRB=ERROR, if specified, causes all system error messages to be routed to this partition.

These macros are assembled and stored in much the same way as are physical maps. In order to cause the terminal device to recognize the partitioning scheme, a CICS command can be used to send the partition set information to the device:

```
EXEC CICS SEND PARTNSET(name)
    END-EXEC.
```

In the SEND MAP command, the OUTPARTN(name) parameter may be used in order to specify which partition should receive the map output data. To move the user's cursor to a different partition, the ACTPARTN(name) parameter may also be placed in the SEND MAP command. ACTPARTN(name) sets the new active partition.

When using the RECEIVE MAP command, you will need to make sure that the data is being received from the correct partition. The IN-PARTN(name) parameter in the RECEIVE MAP command may be used to specify the expected input partition. If the user has entered data into the wrong partition, then CICS will send an error message and will repeat the RECEIVE MAP command.

It is also possible to receive user data from any partition, and to map the data later after it becomes clear what partition was involved. The RECEIVE PARTN command is used to determine the partition name and to obtain the unformatted terminal data. (This data should be formatted later by using a RECEIVE MAP command.)

```
EXEC CICS RECEIVE PARTN(data-area)
    {INTO(data-area)|SET(pointer-ref)}
    LENGTH(data-area)
    ASIS
    END-EXEC.
```

After command completion, the PARTN(data-area) field will contain the name of the partition from which the data was received.

11.2   PRINTING UNDER CICS

11.2.1   Using CICS Printing Terminals

As we discussed earlier, many CICS installations have printing terminals as well as CRT display terminals. The most frequently used type is the 3287, which is part of the family of 3270-compatible devices. Some terminals have a built-in hardware print key which works with the terminal controller. It causes the current screen image to be sent to a 3287 printer attached to the same printer. The hardware print key has absolutely nothing to do with CICS. In some CICS installations in which these hardware print keys do not exist, a PA key on the terminal is defined as a local copy key. When this key is pressed, the screen contents are sent to the first available 3287 printer. CICS also offers a command for printing:

```
ISSUE PRINT
```

Here again, this copies the contents of the terminal screen to the first 3270-compatible printer available. However, these alternatives allow you to print only as much data as can fit on one screen. A printed page is larger than a screen; typically, you would want to format the data somewhat differently. So how do we print larger amounts of data? To answer that question, let's take a look at the 3287 printer device.

3287 printers are output-only devices. You can use terminal control SEND commands or basic mapping support SEND MAP commands to send data to them, which will appear on the printer. Always use BMS to send your data to the printer in large amounts, if possible. It is less efficient to use the terminal control SEND command to send a series of short messages to the printer.

Handling of Blank Lines. There are certain differences between a terminal and a printer from the standpoint of programming. For example, 3287 printers ignore null lines, which means that they do not put out a line feed when a line is sent which contains only low- values. A line on a BMS map which contains no data would be a null line. This results in spacing on the printed page which would not match what you would see on a monitor. You can circumvent this by making sure each line on each map contains at least one non-null character, such as a space.

The 3287 Page Buffer. In contrast to a display terminal, output to a 3287 printer does not appear on the printed page immediately. This is because a 3287 printer contains a **page buffer**. This page buffer holds data that is being prepared for printing. If a SEND MAP or SEND CONTROL command contains the ERASE parameter, the page buffer is cleared. If a SEND MAP or SEND CONTROL command contains the PRINT parameter, all of the data that has been built in the page buffer through successive SEND MAP commands will be printed. The first SEND MAP for the printed page should contain the ERASE parameter and the last SEND MAP for the printed page should contain the PRINT parameter.

Beginning a New Printed Page. If you specify FORMFEED in the first SEND MAP command for a printed page, you will get a special form feed character (hex 0C) at the beginning of the map being sent. This causes a page eject before printing. Don't use FORMFEED in a SEND CONTROL command because that command will skip to a new page and send that page as a complete blank page. This can result either in an extra blank line or a complete blank page.

How Does CICS Access the Right Printer Terminal?   As we discussed in earlier chapters, each task is attached to one terminal. If you key a transaction code to begin running a CICS application program, that program will be attached to the display terminal on which you keyed the transaction code. All terminal control or BMS commands such as SEND or SEND MAP will access that terminal only. **To direct your printed data to a specific printer terminal, pass the data to a new task which is attached to that printer.** Note that you can't do this by an XCTL or LINK to another program or by a RETURN to another transaction. The two ways that will work are with a transient data queue with a trigger level or with the interval control START command.

We already discussed transient data queues in a previous chapter. An intrapartition transient data queue can be defined with a trigger level in the destination control table (DCT). In the DCT entry, you tell it the transaction ID which is to be initiated and the printer terminal to which the resulting task should be attached. Whenever the number of entries in the TD queue reaches the trigger level, that transaction will begin running. If the trigger level is 1, it will run every time any program writes to that queue. Associate that transaction with your own CICS print program, which will contain READQ TD commands to exhaust the TD queue and SEND MAP commands to send the contents to the printer. Using this method to begin a new transaction is known as **automatic transaction initiation (ATI)**.

Suppose many users are running the same program which puts data into a TD queue. In that case, output from the various tasks can be mixed on the TD queue, so that data could be printed in the wrong order. This isn't a problem if you make sure that all of the printed data from one task is stored in a single TD queue item, so that it all gets printed at once. (The IBM manual suggests using CICS ENQ and DEQ commands to "single-thread" access to the TD queue, but this carries the major disadvantage of making the other task wait for access.)

The CICS START and RETRIEVE Commands.   As we discussed in Chapter 5, the START command uses the timing facilities within CICS to start another task, either immediately or at some later time, which you specify in the command. If you don't specify an interval or time, the new task will start immediately. The new task can be associated with a different terminal, in this case a printer terminal. You can pass data to the new task in a data area specified in the FROM and LENGTH options within the START command. The new task issues the RETRIEVE command to get that data, and SEND MAP commands to send the data to its printer terminal.

Here is the format of the START command, showing the parameters that are relevant to this discussion:

```
EXEC CICS START
     [INTERVAL(hhmmss)|TIME(hhmmss)]
     TRANSID(name)
     [FROM(data-area) LENGTH(data-value)]
     [TERMID(name)]
     [SYSID(name)]
     END-EXEC.
```

Here is the format of the RETRIEVE command:

```
EXEC CICS RETRIEVE
     [INTO(data-area)|SET(pointer)]
     [LENGTH(data-area)]
     WAIT
     END-EXEC.
```

The START command has an optional SYSID parameter. The SYSID parameter exists in various CICS commands although we have not discussed it so far. You probably won't need it if all you want to do is to access a printer terminal next to your display terminal. However, if you want the printout to go to a printer on another connected CICS system, the SYSID command will do the job, provided that your terminal and transaction are defined in the tables on that system. The START command with the SYSID parameter will prove useful for other purposes later when we discuss intersystem communication.

The RETRIEVE command has an interesting wrinkle. The new task which issues the RETRIEVE command can pick up data not only from the transaction that STARTed the task, but also from any other tasks that have STARTed a task with the same transaction ID and terminal ID as this one. What does this mean? It means that the print task should keep issuing RETRIEVE commands until the ENDDATA exceptional condition occurs. Test for ENDDATA with the RESP clause. Alternatively, you can use the WAIT option to suspend the retrieving task until more data arrives. (The WAIT option is not supported under CICS OS/2 1.20.)

Who Gets the Printout?   Whatever method you use for printing, you should put some identifier in your data to be printed to indicate which user or terminal requested that printout. Otherwise, you'll have a problem with hardcopy printouts being lost or given to the wrong person. 3287 printers don't provide the separator pages that you get with batch JES or POWER queue output.

Printing with BMS Paging.   If you are using the ACCUM option for BMS paging, the entire set of map pages can be sent to a printer. Set up the

SEND MAP commands as shown in the previous section. In each SEND PAGE command, the parameter AUTOPAGE will be assumed, whether you code it or not. The AUTOPAGE parameter causes all of the map pages to be received in sequence on the printer without operator action. You can also specify the NLEOM option in the SEND MAP commands. NLEOM causes the print lines to be built using blanks and special new line characters, which actually saves some room in the page buffer that would otherwise be taken up with null character padding. With NLEOM, it is not necessary to place blanks in each line to be printed. However, since NLEOM posts an end-of-message character at the end of each map being sent, the ACCUM option is needed in order to cause all of the maps to come out on the printer.

For printing to work successfully, the terminals and the CICS software must be set up properly. For example, the line length of the printer terminal in the TCT must be correct. The terminal should also be defined as supporting form feeds. If you have a 3287 printer in your installation that is currently being used only for local print-key output, you will need to talk to your systems programmer before you set up an application that will send data directly to the printer from the CICS region or partition.

11.2.2   Accessing JES from CICS: Description

The JES interface is a feature introduced with CICS 1.7 that allows a CICS/VS command level application program to read from and write to mainframe JES spool files. The interface works in the same way for JES2 and for JES3. CICS commands allow the applications program to open an existing file for input or to open a new file for output, but not both operations on the same file at once. Other commands provide for reading, writing, and closing the spool file. Information on this interface is in the CICS/VS Customization Guide instead of in the command level APRM, because IBM assumes that access to the interface will be in the hands of systems programmers. However, even those programmers, who will not themselves be coding the access routines, should know what the JES interface is and what it does.

Input access (reading a spool file) is single-threaded. This means that only one CICS/VS program at a time may read any part of the JES queue. For this reason, if your program needs to read spool records, then you should open the spool file only when you are ready to use the information in it. You should read the records you need as quickly as possible and close the spool file so that other users will not be locked out. Spool access imposes much overhead on the CICS system; report processing is better handled in batch systems whenever practical. Use the JES interface only when it provides some advantage that outweighs the penalties in CICS system efficiency.

All JES interface activities must be completed within one logical unit of work. Do not end the task with a RETURN to CICS and do not execute a SYNCPOINT command when a spool file is still open. If you do, CICS will close the spool file without freeing all of the resources associated with it.

The HANDLE CONDITION command will not work with JES interface commands. Error detection must be done by testing the values returned in the RESP and RESP2 fields, which were discussed earlier. Use of RESP blocks the action of the HANDLE CONDITION command. If RESP is not used, the task will abend if spool I/O is unsuccessful. You ordinarily will not want to abend on a normal ENDFILE. Also, if you encounter a SPOLBUSY (single- thread access already in use by someone else) or SPOLERR (cannot find the desired input spool file), you might want to terminate your task, using a START command to begin it again later. RESP and RESP2 may be used in any CICS command.

To make the JES interface available, the statement DFHSIT SPOOL = YES must be included in the CICS system initialization table.

11.2.3 JES Spooling Commands

```
EXEC CICS SPOOLOPEN INPUT
    USERID(datavalue)
    TOKEN(data area)
    [CLASS(1-char. data value)]
    [RESP(full-word binary data area)]
    [RESP2(full-word binary data area)]
    END-EXEC.
```

When the SPOOLOPEN command is executed, the TOKEN is returned to your program in the specified area. It is a system identifier for the file you are using, and it must be specified on all subsequent CICS commands dealing with that spool file.

The SPOOLOPEN INPUT command is a request to retrieve a spool file from the queue. The first four characters of the USERID must match the first four characters of the CICS APPLID, for security reasons. This means that CICS programs may only open spool files intended for that use. If CLASS is specified, then the first file with the correct USERID and job class will be retrieved. Otherwise, the first file in the queue with the correct USERID will be retrieved.

```
EXEC CICS SPOOLOPEN OUTPUT
    NODE(8-character node ID)
    USERID(external writer name)
```

```
    TOKEN(8-byte data value)
    (CLASS(1-char. data value))
    NOCC|ASA|MCC)
    END-EXEC.
```

This command creates a new spool file. Output job class defaults to "A" if not specified in the command. You may specify the desired type of carriage control. The USERID and NODE can be used to send the spool file to a remote system. In that case, NODE is the remote system name, and USERID is the user on the remote system. To write your file to a local queue, specify USERID ("X") and NODE ("X").

```
EXEC CICS SPOOLREAD
    TOKEN(data area)
    INTO(data area)
    [TOFLENGTH(full word hex data area)]
    [MAXFLENGTH(full word hex data area)]
    END-EXEC.
```

This command reads one spool file record into an input data area in your program. If you want CICS to tell you how long the data area is, then specify TOFLENGTH. The actual length will be returned to you in this field. Specifying MAXFLENGTH will prevent CICS from giving you a record too long for your program to handle.

```
EXEC CICS SPOOLWRITE
    TOKEN(data area)
    FROM(data area)
    [FLENGTH(full word hex data area)]
    END-EXEC.
```

This command writes one spool file record from your data area. If you do not specify FLENGTH, then CICS will use the length of your data area.

```
EXEC CICS SPOOLCLOSE
    TOKEN(data area)
    [KEEP|DELETE]
    END-EXEC.
```

The KEEP option applies to spool files that have been opened for input. Closing an input file with DELETE will purge the file so that the next report in the queue will be retrieved on the next SPOOLOPEN INPUT command. Closing it with KEEP will retain the file so that the same file will be retrieved again on the next SPOOLOPEN INPUT command. DELETE is the default for input spool files.

The KEEP option has no meaning for a spool file that has been opened for output. Closing an output file with DELETE will purge that report, in effect backing out what has been written. The default for an output spool file is to route that file to its specified destination.

11.3 ADVANCED BASIC MAPPING SUPPORT: TEXT AND MESSAGE DATA

11.3.1 Text Processing: How It Works; When to Use It

It is possible to use CICS to write text processing applications in which application program data is fitted onto pages for display or printing without the use of maps. Text processing is an output-only operation that takes place under basic mapping support. When text data is sent, the CICS system attempts to fit the data into lines on the output device page without breaking any words in the middle. If the data overflows the page, then BMS creates a multi-page message. This is why, in mainframe CICS releases 1.6 and greater, it is preferable to do text processing under full function BMS, which supports paging operations. (CICS OS/2 does not support BMS paging as of release 1.20.)

Text processing might be useful for any application in which the output should resemble word processing output. Suppose documentation is stored on disc files, and suppose you want to allow terminal users to request a printout of this documentation from a menu. Text processing can be used to make the output look good on a variety of different-sized output devices.

11.3.2 Output Commands for Sending Text

The SEND TEXT command is used to send text data to the user's terminal. The parameters used with SEND TEXT are nearly identical to those used with SEND MAP, which we already discussed:

```
EXEC CICS SEND TEXT
      FROM(data-area)
      LENGTH(data-value)
      CURSOR(data-value)
      [FORMFEED]
      [ERASE]
      [PRINT]
      [FREEKB]
      [ALARM]
      [OUTPARTN(name)]
      [ACTPARTN(name)]
      [PAGING]
      [ACCUM]
      [HEADER(data-area)]
      [TRAILER(data-area)]
```

```
[JUSTIFY(data-value)|JUSFIRST|JUSLAST]
END-EXEC.
```

In the SEND TEXT command, JUSTIFY(data-value) specifies the line number at which to begin displaying or printing this text. JUSFIRST implies that the data should be positioned directly after the header, and JUSLAST implies that the data should be positioned directly before the trailer. HEADER(data- value) specifies the data area in which the header data is actually contained. TRAILER(data-value) performs a similar function for trailer data.

11.3.3 Message Routing

The ROUTE command can be executed before building any logical messages under BMS, in order to define the list of terminal devices that should get the message. After the route command has been issued, the pages may each be sent. When the SEND PAGE command is actually executed, the output message will go to all operators who should receive it, in accordance with the ROUTE command. ROUTE is not available under CICS OS/2 as of release 1.20.

```
EXEC CICS ROUTE
    INTERVAL(hhmmss)|INTERVAL(0)|TIME(hhmmss)]
    [ERRTERM((NAME)]
    [TITLE(data-area)]
    [LIST(data-area)]
    [OPCLASS(data-area)]
    END-EXEC.
```

INTERVAL specifies a time delay before the message is routed. ERRTERM is used to specify the terminal that is to receive CICS system messages if it is not possible to deliver the routed message. TITLE(data-area) specifies an area containing a two-byte-length field, followed by a title for the output message that will appear whenever the IBM-supplied terminal operator page query command is used to access the information. LIST specifies a list of specific terminals and/or operators who will receive the message, while OPCLASS specifies which operator class will receive the message.

Be careful when you use message routing facilities. Avoid cluttering user terminal screens with messages that appear to have no connection with the application in progress. Sending messages to a terminal that is being used to run something else may cause the other application to "bomb," if the other application was designed improperly.

TEST YOUR UNDERSTANDING

Questions and Exercises

1. Compare and contrast the browse method used in this chapter with the method shown in Chapter 6. On a system that is somewhat short on main memory and disc I/O channel availability, which method would be best to use? How would you set up an experiment to determine which method works best on your system? Observe the user response time for the browse application itself, and observe the effect on user response times for other applications running at the same time.

2. Partition sets and map sets both allow the terminal screen to be divided into sections that are used for specific purposes. Discuss possible uses for each.

3. Suppose you want to send data to different 3287 printers depending on a user's physical location. The users complain if their printout appears in a different building! Can you think of a way to prevent that? (Hint: You'll need a file or look up table which tells you which 3287 printer is nearest to any given display terminal.)

12

Advanced Topics: Interfacing

12.1 ACCESSING DL/I SEGMENTS FROM A CICS PROGRAM

12.1.1 DL/I—CICS Concepts

This section is intended for programmers who are familiar with DL/I data base concepts and CALL statements in a batch environment, and who want to use these CALL statements in CICS online programs. We will discuss what must be done in order to interface CICS with DL/I, but we will not discuss the DL/I calls themselves, or data base concepts, because these topics are beyond the scope of this book.

The same data base calls that are used for batch DL/I access are usable under CICS. This is an exception to the rule that all data set accesses in a command level program must be done by EXEC CICS commands. If CALL DL/I statements are used, the DL/I run-time software services the data base calls directly, without going through the EXEC interface program. The CICS-DL/I interface routine merely checks the parameters for correctness and passes them to the DL/I program that is running in the CICS region.

DL/I calls work in the same way under CICS in MVS and DOS/VSE systems, as long as the same CALL DL/I statements are being used. However, under DOS/VSE systems, and under MVS systems running CICS 1.6 and after, it is possible to substitute the EXEC DL/I syntax. This is described in the *CICS Command Level Application Programmer's Reference Manual*. Using EXEC DL/I will cause the commands to be passed through the EXEC interface program before being serviced by the DL/I software.

This permits online debugging through the execution diagnostic facility (EDF).

SSAs, PSB names, I/O areas, and other user-specified arguments used in DL/I calls should be defined in COBOL working storage.

Recovery data for DL/I data base files being accessed under CICS is logged in the same data sets that CICS uses for other recovery data. A CICS SYNCPOINT command will deallocate DL/I data base resources just as it deallocates other data sets. The DL/I DEQ call is not supported under CICS. DL/I and other data set resources may be freed by using a DL/I TERM call, by using a CICS SYNCPOINT command, or by terminating the task. All of these options terminate the logical unit of work, freeing all enqueued records and segments, and releasing the DL/I PSB.

Here is an example of a DL/I TERM call:

```
WORKING-STORAGE SECTION.
 01 TERM-FUNC-CODE PIC XXXX VALUE "TERM"
* (et cetera)
 PROCEDURE DIVISION.
* (et cetera)
     CALL "CBLTDLI" USING TERM-FUNC-CODE.
* (et cetera)
```

With CICS 1.7 or greater, DL/I support is no longer a part of the file control facility, so that DL/I data bases no longer require entries in the file control table. With that release was introduced a separate CEMT command for DL/I data bases. CEMT INQ or SET DLIDATABASE takes the place of CEMT INQ or SET DATASET for DL/I data bases; it allows you to allocate and deallocate data bases while CICS is running.

Reporting of statistics on DL/I was improved with CICS 1.7, so that the trace table contains the data base description (DBD).

12.1.2   DL/I Program Setup

A CICS program using DL/I data base calls must have a program specification block (PSB). The PSB contains a program communication block (PCB) for each data base needed in the program. Before using any other DL/I calls, the CICS program must use a DL/I PCB call to schedule the PSB and to get the addresses of the PCBs. What do we mean by scheduling the PSB? The system must determine that the requested PSB is correct and that the data base resources are available and are not locked up by some other process.

The scheduling call will get the address of the PCB address list, which it passes to your program in the user interface block. Assembler programmers will be familiar with the idea of passing the address of a parameter address list from one module to another. Your program obviously must use this value to locate the parameter address list, and then must use each value within this address list to find the parameters themselves. This can be done by moving values to the appropriate BLL cells, as is shown in this program excerpt:

```
WORKING STORAGE SECTION.
01  PCB-FUNC-CODE          PIC XXXX  VALUE "PCB ".
01  PSB-NAME               PIC X(8)  VALUE "TSTPSB  ".
* (ETC.)
LINKAGE SECTION.
01  BLL-CELLS.
    05  DUMMY-BLL          PIC S9(8) COMP.
    05  UIB-BLL            PIC S9(8) COMP.
    05  PCB-ADDR-LIST-BLL  PIC S9(8) COMP.
    05  FIRST-PCB-BLL      PIC S9(8) COMP.
    05  SECOND-PCB-BLL     PIC S9(8) COMP.
01  DLIUIB COPY DLIUIB.
01  PCB-ADDR-LIST.
    05  FIRST-PCB-ADDR     PIC S9(8) COMP.
    05  SECOND-PCB-ADDR    PIC S9(8) COMP.
01  FIRST-PCB.
* (ETC.)
01  SECOND-PCB.
* (ETC.)
PROCEDURE DIVISION.
*******************************************************
* SCHEDULE THE PSB                                    *
*******************************************************
    CALL "CBLTDLI" USING PCB-FUNC-CODE, PSB-NAME,
        UIB-BLL.
*******************************************************
* THE ADDRESS OF THE PCB ADDRESS LIST IS IN DLIUIB,   *
* IN A FIELD CALLED UIBPCBAL. MOVE IT TO THE BLL      *
* POINTER FOR THE PCB ADDRESS LIST, SO THAT WE CAN    *
* GET AT THE ADDRESSES IN THE LIST.                   *
*******************************************************
    MOVE UIBPCBAL TO PCB-ADDR-LIST-BLL.
*******************************************************
* NOW MOVE EACH ADDRESS IN THE PCB ADDRESS LIST TO    *
* THE CORRECT BLL POINTER FOR THAT PCB.               *
*******************************************************
    MOVE FIRST-PCB-ADDR TO FIRST-PCB-BLL.
    MOVE SECOND-PCB-ADDR TO SECOND-PCB-BLL.
*******************************************************
* YOU ARE NOW READY TO MAKE NORMAL DATABASE ACCESS    *
* CALLS.                                              *
*******************************************************
```

The INVREQ exceptional condition is likely to be triggered if it is not possible to schedule the PSB. The task should have only one PSB scheduled at a time. All DL/I resources needed by the program should be specified in the same PSB.

12.1.3 Using DL/I I/O Commands

We will not be discussing the details of DL/I call statements, because that topic is beyond the scope of this book. However, we do need to discuss the error handling that you will need to do when you use DL/I call statements under CICS. This differs somewhat from error handling used in a batch DL/I program.

After each DL/I I/O call is performed, you will need to check both the status code in the appropriate PCB and the response code in the UIB. The status code in the PCB is handled as it is in batch DL/I programs, so we will not discuss it here. The UIB response code field, UIBRCODE, is divided into two bytes. The first byte is named UIBFCTR and the second is named UIBDLTR. If the data base call was successful, UIBFCTR will contain low-values. If UIBFCTR contains hexadecimal 0C, the NOTOPEN condition was encountered for the data base that you were trying to access. If UIBFCTR contains hexadecimal 08, the INVREQ (invalid request) exceptional condition was encountered. If UIBFCTR contains hexadecimal 10, one of the PCB addresses was set up improperly. (Did you follow the example shown in the previous section?)

Suppose UIBFCTR contains hexadecimal 0C, indicating the NOTOPEN condition. In that case, the other byte, UIBDLTR, should contain either low-values, indicating that the data base is not open, or hexadecimal 02, indicating that there is an intent scheduling conflict. An intent scheduling conflict occurs when some other process has locked up the data base resources that your task needs to use.

Suppose UIBFCTR contains hexadecimal 08, indicating the INVREQ condition. Here again, the other byte, UIBDLTR, may tell you what sort of "invalid request" triggered the condition. If UIBDLTR contains low-values, then the INVREQ condition may indicate an invalid argument in your DL/I call, or it may indicate a data base that is closed or that is not listed in the FCT. If UIBDLTR contains hexadecimal 01, you tried to use a PSB name that does not exist on the system. If UIBDLTR contains hexadecimal 03, you tried to reschedule a PSB that has already been scheduled. If UIBDLTR contains hexadecimal 05, the PSB scheduling call has failed. If UIBDLTR contains high-values, the DL/I run-time software is not currently active. Other values in UIBDLTR indicate that the PSB has not been scheduled.

Under some circumstances DL/I will issue a pseudo-ABEND. This causes the CICS task to be terminated with an ABEND code of ADLA.

12.2 INTERSYSTEM COMMUNICATION AND MULTIREGION OPERATION

12.2.1 Description of ISC and MRO

It is possible to define several CICS regions or partitions on the same CPU, and to allow terminal operators to access transactions, programs, and data sets defined in regions other than those to which their terminals belong. This is known as **multiregion operation** or **MRO**. If the different CICS regions are on different CPUs, a similar feature can be used that is known as **intersystem communication** or **ISC**. ISC allows resources defined in one CICS region to be accessed by other systems of any size, including non-CICS systems, minicomputers, and microcomputers. Under either option, it is possible to access files, terminals, programs, transactions, and queues in two or more regions without the terminal user ever knowing where those resources are actually located.

Many CICS I/O commands contain an option for specifying system ID, even though we have not discussed this feature so far. The SYSID parameter can be used when an application that is running on one system needs to access a file or data base on another system. Alternatively, the entire application can run on another system, with the transactions in the PCT set up so that CICS software will allow terminals signed on to one system to run applications residing on the other. The systems programmer can set this up so that is invisible to the terminal user and to the application programmer.

ISC and MRO are not discussed in much detail in the command level APRM. See the Intercommunication Guide for more information. In this discussion, "local" will refer to the region initiating the access, and "remote" will refer to the region in which the other resource is defined.

12.2.2 LUTYPE 6.2 (APPC)

ACF/VTAM is IBM's mainframe implementation of SNA. SNA is an IBM proprietary telecommunications protocol which can be used to link a large variety of IBM and other equipment in a network. In the past, an SNA network consisted of terminals, terminal controllers, and a mainframe host. Terminals could communicate with one another only through the host. With the growing use of PC's and other computers in place of ordinary terminals, the demand arose for enhancements to SNA which would get more use out of the processing power in these devices. These devices should be able to communicate with one another directly without having to go through a host. In addition, they should be able to offload some of the actual processing burden from the mainframe host.

MRO is implemented within one CPU, and does not use SNA. ISC uses SNA; a system can be specified as LUTYPE 6.1 (Logical Unit Type 6.1) or as LUTYPE 6.2. LUTYPE 6.2 was introduced to CICS with release 1.7; it is also called APPC (Advanced Program-to-Program Communication). LUTYPE 6.2 provides new capabilities. It allows distributed transaction processing between processes under SNA, including personal computers and other non-CICS systems, **without necessarily going through a host (mainframe)**.

When you are writing CICS programs to run on a mainframe, you might be interested in offloading some of the mainframe processing burden onto another device. If the other device runs CICS, APPC provides full intercommunications capabilities; if not, APPC provides only DTP (distributed transaction processing), which will be described later. There are advantages to making the small systems appear as other CICS systems to the mainframe CICS region. Operating System/2 (OS/2) for the Personal System/2 supports APPC. CICS OS/2 will let you implement that type of processing from the microcomputer end.

12.2.3 Types of Distributed Processing

All of the connection methods, which include MRO, LUTYPE 6.1, and APPC, allow **distributed transaction processing**. The remote system need not even be a CICS system. What does distributed transaction processing let you do? If two transactions are running on two regions at the same time, each transaction can communicate synchronously with the other one. They can pass information back and forth in a conversation; the sending transaction waits for an acknowledgment from the receiving transaction before it sends anything else. Considerable applications programming effort is needed to use this feature. If more than two regions or systems are daisy-chained together, and if files are being updated on all of them, backout and recovery processing can become exceedingly complex.

Transaction routing may take place between CICS regions communicating under MRO or APPC. In a nutshell, transaction routing allows you to define your terminals under one region and your programs and transactions under another region. A terminal on one system can run a transaction on another system. Transactions on another system can also be started by CICS START commands or by a transient data queue with a trigger level. The transient data queue must be defined in the same region as is the transaction, but the terminal may be in another region or system. We discussed both of these techniques earlier in the section on CICS printing. Transaction routing can be done by setting up appropriate CICS table entries. It is not necessary to do any special applications programming. CICS uses a relay transaction to do the transaction routing; the associated CICS program is DFHCRP.

Function shipping may take place between two CICS regions communicating under APPC, LUTYPE6.1, or MRO. Function shipping lets you keep your data in a different region from your program and transaction. A transaction can request I/O from a file or queue in another region or system. A special mirror transaction on the remote system, transparent to the user, will do the I/O and will return the result to the user's transaction. CICS will create or destroy these mirror transactions without any action on the part of the applications programmer. Function shipping, like transaction routing, is done by setting up appropriate CICS table entries. It is not currently possible to access DB2 databases in this way.

Asynchronous processing can occur between CICS regions communicating under APPC, LUTYPE6.1, or MRO. It can also take place between a

CICS region and an IMS/VS region. Under asynchronous processing, the first transaction uses the START command to start a transaction in the remote region, passing along the required data in the command parameters. The first transaction terminates. The second transaction uses the RETRIEVE command to obtain the data. It processes the data, and then STARTs a transaction in the first region, passing it the results. We discussed START and RETRIEVE in an earlier section. Asynchronous processing is a cross-region or cross-system form of pseudo-conversational programming, which we have already covered in this book. It does require some applications programming effort.

You might be wondering, "Why are we bothering to do all of this? Why not define all CICS resources in one region and be done with it?" Here are some advantages of MRO or ISC use:

1. Each application area can have its own CICS region, but each can access some data for other applications or for the company as a whole. One region can be shut down to do backups, recoveries, or other batch processing, without having to shut down other CICS regions.

2. Testing activity can be "quarantined" from other CICS processing in order to avoid damage to production files or production system crashes. However, under MRO or ISC, it is possible to allow the test regions to have read-only access to production data bases. This makes it unnecessary to keep so many extra copies of these data bases.

3. Processing that requests an unusual number of CPU cycles, such as the APL interpreter, can be put into a separate region. This region can be given a lower priority, which will prevent it from slowing other processing by taking more than its rightful share of CPU cycles. MRO or ISC will still allow that region to use CICS resources defined in other regions.

4. The total processing load can be split among several multiprocessors while still allowing applications to communicate with one another. No one region will use an excessive amount of virtual memory or CPU cycles.

12.2.4 The CRTE Transaction

Suppose your terminal is defined under a region that is especially set up for support of terminal devices. A region like this would be called a **terminal-owning region**. Suppose you wanted to access a transaction in a test region. You want to test your transaction under CEDF. In order to use CEDF, your terminal must be signed on to the region in which the test transaction is defined. In effect, you can "move your sign-on" to the other region by using the CRTE transaction, as long as your terminal is defined as a remote terminal in the other region's TCT.

The CRTE transaction looks like this:

```
CRTE SYSID=xxxx
```

where xxxx is the remote system ID.

When CICS responds, you can clear the screen and proceed with your testing. To end the routing session, simply type:

```
CANCEL
```

CICS OS/2 as of Version 1.20 does not have the capability to CRTE to other systems from the OS/2 workstation. However, you can use CRTE on a host system to connect to a CICS OS/2 system.

12.2.5 Introduction to Commands for LUTYPE6.2 (APPC)

Those wishing to do synchronous communication between programs running on two different CICS systems can use LUTYPE6.2 commands. These are available only under VTAM and require a certain amount of setup in terms of CICS table entries and telecommunications software. The commands themselves are discussed in the chapter on terminal control in the command level APRM, and in more detail in the Intercommunication Guide. This is only an introduction; we will not cover all of the possible command options here.

```
EXEC CICS ALLOCATE
     SYSID(name)
     END-EXEC.
```

ALLOCATE provides your program with a telecommunications session with the other system. If this command executes successfully, a four-byte conversation ID (CONVID) will be in the EIBRSRCE field in the EXEC interface block. You will need this in all other commands that pertain to that session.

```
EXEC CICS CONNECT PROCESS
     CONVID(data-area)
     PROCNAME(data-area)
     PROCLENGTH(data-value)
     SYNCLEVEL(data-value)
     END-EXEC.
```

CONNECT PROCESS starts the back-end transaction (process) on the remote system with which the front-end program on the local system will communicate. The PROCLENGTH option is the length of the PROCNAME, which would ordinarily be four bytes for a transaction code.

The SYNCLEVEL can be 0 (no synchronization), 1 (commit only), and 2 (full synchronization with two-phase commit). Use SYNCLEVEL 0 if the application is inquiry only, if files are being updated on only one system, or if dynamic transaction backout is not being used. SYNCLEVEL 1 lets the front-end application issue a synchronization request to the back-end system and receive a reply. Once this is done, the applications themselves are responsible for committing their own updates. SYNCLEVEL 2 allows full use of the CICS SYNCPOINT and SYNCPOINT ROLLBACK commands across two or more systems. Not only that, but if you have a situation in which several remote systems are daisy-chained from one to the next, with file updates taking place across some or all of them, SYNCLEVEL 2 allows the use of an ISSUE PREPARE command to get all of the remote systems ready to take a syncpoint before the actual syncpoint is issued. This option is called "the two-phase commit". SYNCLEVEL 2 is not supported under CICS OS/2 as of release 1.20. A detailed discussion of SYNCLEVEL is beyond the scope of this book. For that, see the Intercommunication Guide.

```
EXEC CICS SEND
     [CONVID(data-area)]
     [FROM(data-area)]
     [LENGTH(data-value)]
     [INVITE|LAST]
     [CONFIRM|WAIT]
     END-EXEC.
```

This command works much like the usual terminal control SEND that you would use to send a message to a display terminal. Use the CONVID that was returned by the ALLOCATE command. The front-end program always starts the conversation by sending some data to the back-end program. The front-end program always comes up in "send" mode and the back-end program always comes up in "receive" mode. Always use IN-VITE when you expect to RECEIVE some data from the back-end program after this, because it puts your program into receive mode. On the other hand, LAST indicates that you are finished sending and are about to terminate the exchange. WAIT forces your application to wait until the command executes successfully. CONFIRM is used with SYNCLEVEL 1 or 2. It forces your application to wait until the other system replies affirmatively with an EXEC CICS ISSUE CONFIRMATION command, or negatively with an ISSUE ERROR command or an ISSUE ABEND command.

```
EXEC CICS RECEIVE
     [CONVID(data-area)]
     {INTO(data-area)|SET((pointer-ref)|
     LENGTH(data-area)
     [MAXLENGTH[(data-value)]]
     [NOTRUNCATE]
     END-EXEC.
```

In this case, most of the options are the same as those used in ordinary terminal control RECEIVE commands. NOTRUNCATE allows any extra data to be picked up on a subsequent RECEIVE command.

```
EXEC CICS CONVERSE
     [CONVID(data-area)]
     [FROM(data-area)]
     FROMLENGTH(data-value)
     {INTO(data-area)|SET((pointer-ref)}
     TOLENGTH(data-area)
     [MAXLENGTH[(data-value)]]
     [NOTRUNCATE]
     END-EXEC.
```

CONVERSE takes the place of a SEND with the INVITE option followed by a RECEIVE. Note that a similar terminal control CONVERSE command can be used to communicate with user terminals rather than with remote systems. However, you would be unwise to use CONVERSE in that environment since it implies conversational processing with a "slow" human being who stops to think while sitting at the terminal. However, a conversation between two tasks running at machine speed is what synchronous communication is all about.

```
EXEC CICS FREE
     [CONVID(data-area]
     END-EXEC.
```

This deallocates the session when you are finished conversing with the other program.

The CONVID(data-area) argument is needed when you use these commands in the front-end program, which is the one that starts the conversation. The back-end program can ignore that argument because it is always communicating with its principal facility, the front-end program. (For more typical CICS programs, the principal facility would be the user's terminal. The back-end program is attached to its session with the front-end program instead of to a user's terminal.) The entire interaction should be controlled from the front-end program as much as possible.

The commands shown here are enough for simple inquiry-only applications. If you intend to use syncpointing, you will have to check various EIB values to determine what to do next each time you issue an LUTYPE6.2 command. This is discussed in the Intercommunication Guide at great length, and will not be covered here.

CICS OS/2 supports another form of communications called **distributed program link**. It allows the OS/2 workstation to LINK to programs on a mainframe, though not vice versa at this time. This is the easiest way of getting data from a mainframe DB2 database onto the OS/2 workstation. This will be discussed in the chapter on CICS OS/2.

TEST YOUR UNDERSTANDING

Questions and Exercises

1. Explain synchronous versus asynchronous communication be-
    tween two applications programs. Is there some similarity to the
    ideas of conversational and pseudoconversational programming?

13

More About Application Design

In this chapter, we will address the issue of application design once again, in somewhat more detail. We will discuss the use of operator sign-on privileges as a method of restricting access to certain portions of the system, and we will make some suggestions about setting up and enforcing appropriate file backup procedures. We will review some of the issues connected with efficiency that we discussed earlier. Finally, we will discuss what documentation is likely to be needed.

13.1 APPLICATION SECURITY

13.1.1 Password Protection During Sign-on

The CICS system provides a method for grouping certain transactions and certain operator sign-ons under different security keys. This method allows terminal users to access only those transactions whose security keys are available under their operator sign-ons. The security key for each transaction may be specified in the PCT entry for that transaction, using the TRANSEC=(decimal-value) option. If this option is omitted, the transaction security defaults to 1, which means that any terminal user can access this transaction, even without signing on. Otherwise, under CICS 1.5, TRANSEC may be specified as any value between 1 and 24. Under CICS 1.6, TRANSEC may be specified as any value between 1 and 64. **If TRANSEC is greater than 1, then this trans-**

action may be used only by those operators whose security keys include this number.

The security keys for each terminal operator are specified in the CICS sign-on table, or SNT. Each valid operator sign-on has an entry in this table. One of the parameters is SCTYKEY = number. One or more security keys can be listed as belonging to the terminal operator. The list is enclosed in parentheses, with each security key separated by commas.

For each valid operator sign-on, the CICS sign-on table also contains an operator identifier of up to three characters, an operator name of up to twenty characters, and a password of four characters. The password and name may be specified as follows when the terminal user signs on to the CICS system:

```
CESN PS=pswd,NAME=name
```

The user can also key the tran code CESN, press the enter key, and fill in the blanks on the screen. Old releases of CICS used CSSN rather than CESN as the signon transaction; parms had to be entered on the command line.

Passwords "leak out" to unauthorized persons and become useless unless they are changed often. A sign-on password can be changed by altering the contents of the CICS sign-on table, or by entering the following:

```
CESN PS=pswd,NAME=name,NEWPS=npsw
```

Alternatively, the terminal user can simply enter CSSN at a 3270-series terminal. A screen will appear upon which password, name, and new password may be entered. The CICS system determines that the password and name entered by the operator match the password and name in a valid entry in the CICS sign-on table.

Password security is effective only when reasonable physical security measures are enforced. Employees should not write down passwords and leave them posted on walls or lying in unlocked desk drawers. Any printed listings that might show contents of the sign-on table should be shredded. System backup tapes should be stored in a secure place. Design any sensitive applications so that they can be run only from certain physical terminal devices. Arrange to install these terminals in a secure area to which access can be restricted.

Unattended CICS terminals can cause serious security problems. When leaving the terminal unattended, the terminal operator should always sign off under CICS so that unauthorized persons cannot use the terminal under a sign-on that they are not intended to have. This may be done by typing the transaction code CSSF. CSSF is an IBM-supplied transaction that disconnects whichever sign-on is in effect at that terminal.

CICS built-in security will be phased out in CICS releases after 3.1. In the words of an IBM spokesperson, "CICS is not in the security business." In other words, IBM and other vendors already offer security packages that handle both online and batch processing, and it doesn't make sense to duplicate some of those features from within CICS. Packages such as RACF will substitute for CICS internal security.

13.1.2   File Backup Procedures

You probably have plenty of experience with batch systems that update files. If the update is sequential, these systems usually merge data from the old file with data from a transactions file to create a new file. The old file is preserved as a backup for a specified period of time. If the update is random access, a backup copy of the file will usually be made before any of the changes are applied. In either case, if the update should fail or be interrupted for any reason, the system operator can recover by purging the new version of the file and by reapplying the updates against a copy of the backup file.

Backup copies should also be made from files being updated under CICS. In a typical application, CICS updates may be performed at any time during the day, and sometimes at night or on weekends as well. Backups should be taken when the CICS system has been brought down, or when online file update activity has been suspected in some other way. Otherwise, the backups might represent incomplete update activity.

How often should backups be scheduled? This depends upon the number of update transactions the system handles. If the transaction load is very light, once a week might be enough. If the transaction load is very heavy, several times a day might not be too much. Remember, if a file is destroyed, it must be replaced by its backup. The older the backup, the more transactions will have to be reentered against the backup to bring it up to date. This takes time. If only a few transactions are involved, they can be reentered manually. If many transactions are involved, a program or utility can be run, which will take the changes from the system log or from a user journal and which will reapply them against the backup file. Your responsibility as an applications programmer will be to set up any necessary journaling commands, and to provide backup job streams for each file or data base that does not already have them.

Critical data such as master files should also be backed up regularly on tapes or discs stored in a different building from the main data processing site. The backup copies can go into vault space rented from a good service bureau, or into other secure storage. Program source code, object code, JCL, and documentation should be handled in this manner as well, including CICS table information, sysgen parameters, and JCL. This may be useful in case of fire, flood, vandalism, and so forth.

13.2   SUGGESTIONS FOR EFFICIENT DESIGN

13.2.1   Working Set

The **working set** consists of the pages of object code and data that must be available in real storage at any given time. For example, if routine A repeatedly performs routines B and C, then routines A, B, and C must all be present at the same time. The storage needed for routines A, B, and C may be said to represent a working set. It is best to try to keep the working set as small as possible, in order to minimize **page faults**. A page fault takes place when a program is referencing something that is not currently in real storage. The program, and the terminal user, must wait while the item is read from virtual storage into real storage.

The working set may be kept small by writing each program so that pieces of code that are used together are adjacent to one another. Program logic should not "jump around" unnecessarily from one part of the program to another. In fact, it is best if program logic moves from the beginning of the program to the exit point in a smooth manner. Only file browses and a few other specialized CICS applications should contain loop logic.

If you are accustomed to writing structured COBOL batch programs, you often PERFORM paragraphs or sections as subroutines. In a CICS program, you might want to consider repeating small chunks of code wherever they are needed instead of performing them as subroutines. This should be done whenever the code is part of the normal processing flow. Paragraphs that are ordinarily used in sequence should be placed close to one another in the source code. On the other hand, paragraphs that are seldom used, such as some error handlers, should be grouped together at the end of the program. (The optimization in VS COBOL II will do some of these things automatically.)

If you are using more than a small amount of working storage in your program, it is worth your while to place those items next to one another that are likely to be used at the same time. Also, literals in the procedure division may be used to substitute for certain working storage areas.

Structured programming aficionados will also be aware of the tenet that each module should have only one entry point and one exit point. In the interest of efficiency, this rule is often relaxed in CICS programs. Paragraphs and sections within a CICS program should always begin execution with the statement following the label, but it does not always make sense to exit at the last statement. The same applies to the CICS program as a whole. It is usually impossible to supply only one RETURN or XCTL command at the end of the program, and to try to make this command into a universal exit from the program. For one thing, depending upon program logic, you might want to RETURN to CICS in one instance, and RETURN to a transaction ID in another instance, and XCTL to a program in another instance, and ABEND in still another instance. In addition, it is more efficient to place each RETURN, XCTL, or ABEND command where it is needed instead of at the end of the program. The object of this is to avoid having to read another page back into main memory in order to terminate the program.

If you are designing a CICS system "from scratch," so that you have some control over the types of data structures that will be used, try to avoid anything that will cause useless data to be read into memory. Avoid fancy indirect addressing schemes. Avoid long searches through chained file or data base structures, unless you actually plan to use most of the chained entries. VSAM files are better for random access. If you are using any file or data base primarily for random access under CICS, the blocks should be kept fairly small. The reverse is usually true for files or data bases used primarily for sequential access under CICS.

13.2.2 Quasi-Reentrance

CICS expects program modules to be **quasi-reentrant**. This means that many different tasks should be able to reuse the executable module without having to reload anything. One copy of the object code can be shared among many tasks. Each time a CICS command level COBOL program is executed, a new working storage section is set up for the current task that is using it. You can change anything in working storage without causing problems. There are two things that you cannot do, however. One of them is using the COBOL ALTER statement that is being removed from the newest ANSI COBOL specifications. (You wouldn't do that any more, would you?) The other is using a data set record or a CICS system area such as the CWA as a "scratch pad" work area, and forgetting to clear it before terminating your program.

13.2.3 Simulated versus Real BMS Paging

This was discussed somewhat in Chapter 11. BMS paging requires screen images to be stored by the system on a temporary storage data set. This takes channel I/O time to store and retrieve the screen images. It also takes main memory for VSAM buffers. This, however, is not usually prohibitive, as long as you limit the number of browse screens or records the program can build at a time. Experiment to find out what works best on your system. However, note that it is not possible to enter data on most screens created using BMS paging. This restricts BMS paging to inquiry-only activities.

13.2.4 Minimizing Data Transmission

This topic was discussed in Chapter 4. For applications that are carried out over long distances, special efforts should be made to reduce the number of characters being sent to the terminal by using DATAONLY and MAPONLY in the SEND MAP command. By allowing modified data tags to be turned off at the appropriate times, it is also possible to reduce transmission of unneeded characters from the terminal to the computer.

13.2.5   When to Use Linkage Section I/O Areas

If there is heavy file I/O activity, because of very large records or frequent access, the record descriptions should be placed in the linkage section and a BLL cell should be supplied. This allows the use of the SET option in I/O commands, which in turn makes it unnecessary to copy the record into working storage before using it. Linkage section work areas can be used for I/O to or from any type of file or terminal, whenever the usage level is expected to be high. An example of this type of I/O is shown in Chapter 4 [see "STUBPG2"].

13.3   DOCUMENTING YOUR APPLICATION

13.3.1   Writing Skills

This discussion will describe the types of documentation that the author believes are most likely to be useful. Some people do not think that any documentation is useful, because they have been exposed to so much bad documentation. Good documentation does not merely repeat the most obvious features of the application. It explains why the decisions were made to do things in a particular way. It tells how to fix the problem if an error occurs. It teaches the user what the application will do and how to use the application for routine purposes. A good documenter will have some writing skills: grammar, spelling, correct choice of vocabulary, and understanding of sentence structure. These can be acquired through study of grammar and usage texts and through reading well-written books, both technical and literary.

13.3.2   Technical Documentation for Programmers

Many data processing installations set their own standards for the type of technical documentation that should be provided with a finished CICS program. Some of them prefer charts generated through use of a certain systems design methodology. One possibility is Warnier-Orr charts. While these have many advantages over other methods, they must be used with care when used to document CICS programs. CICS contains many implied GO TO instructions that arise as a result of HANDLE CONDITION, HAN-DLE AID, and HANDLE ABEND commands. It takes some effort to represent these situations neatly within a Warnier-Orr chart, but it could be done. It is preferable to eliminate these things as much as possible and to use RESP and EIBAID routines instead.

I strongly discourage the preparation of detailed flowcharts of every CICS program, with one flowchart symbol for each line of source code. These charts are so detailed that they convey no impression of the purpose of each part of the program, partly because not much will fit on one page. In other words, the reader may not be able to see the forest for the trees, since he or she can only see a few trees at a time. These charts are expensive to maintain by hand. Purchased utilities that simply draw boxes around lines of source code tend to show even fewer flowchart symbols on each page.

This is not to say that flowcharts are useless. They are useful for showing the flow of control between program modules and I/O devices, and for introducing people to new concepts.

System Flowcharts. Let's step into the shoes of a new maintenance programmer who is looking for a bug in an existing CICS application. Suppose the programmer knows only that screen XXXXXXX is visible when the application hangs up. What programs build screen XXXXXXX? What programs read data from it? A chart showing which modules are executed under what circumstances might prove very useful in finding the bug. See Figure 13.1.

You can flowchart an overview of a CICS application by providing a rectangular box for each program, a CRT terminal symbol for each screen image, and an arrow for each path to be taken. Since decision paths between programs are usually governed by the choice of function keys, each arrow can be labeled with the appropriate function key.

If desired, flowchart symbols for data sets, data bases, and queues can be added to the chart. However, this may make the chart too complicated and cluttered. If a program on the chart is labeled "SALEP005 Customer File Browse," obviously the program will be reading the customer file. The presence of another symbol for the customer file will add no useful information.

Comments in the Programs. Program narratives can often be helpful to maintenance programmers, but only if they are correct and up to date. The best place to put a program narrative is in a comment block at the beginning of the program listing. Keeping the documentation in the program listing makes it impossible to misplace. If program narratives are stored separately, it is more difficult to motivate the programmer to update them when the program is updated. When the program is being updated, the maintenance programmer should add a new comment to the end of this narrative. The comment should describe what changes were made, when, and by whom.

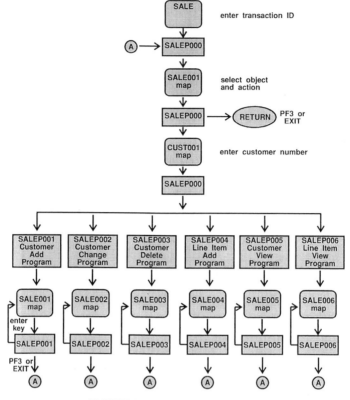

FIGURE 13.1 Module flow diagram.

What should the program narrative contain?

- Purpose. Supply one or two sentences describing what activity the program performs; for instance, "SALEP001 adds a new record to the customer master file."
- Input. Provide the name of each data set, CICS work area, or terminal device being read by the program. Describe the format of the data. If the data comes from a map, list the pertinent fields and explain their contents if their meaning is not obvious. Mention which user department is expected to supply the data. If the data comes from a file or work area, name the copy library member that describes its layout. For a file, specify the file structure being used. What other application is passing this data to the program?
- Output. Describe in same manner as program input. What other applications will be using data written by this program?
- Function. Describe the general logic flow of the program. Explain the

purposes of any unusual programming methods that are used. You may need to relate routines in the program to the business reasons for each routine.

If the program is more than a few pages long, some of the sections and paragraphs within the program should have their own brief narratives. Where necessary, insert a comment block at the head of the paragraph or section that explains what the module is expected to do. These comments should be used only where they will add something to the reader's understanding. For instance, a SEND command for map SALE000 does not need a comment that says, "**THIS COMMAND SENDS MAP SALE000 TO THE TERMINAL**."

13.3.3 User Documentation

User Manuals. You may think that it is a waste of time to write manuals for users because "they never read them anyway." If this is true, it is because so many bad manuals are written, and because so many applications are written without user participation. By the time the application is ready to install, at least some of the users should already have had some contact with it. Those who have not had contact with it should be given a demonstration of the parts of the application that they will need to use most often. The manual should remind the users of what they already have seen in the demonstration, in that it should show each step they must follow to perform a given job activity on the system.

The user manual should also list all of the error messages produced by the program. For each message, the user will need to know both the cause and the proper action to take next. Here again, the manual should do more than just repeat the error message that shows on the user terminal screen.

Help Screens. Help screens are tutorial or reference screens that terminal users can access by pressing a certain function key. Some CICS installations require help screens to be provided as part of each online application. Other installations forbid their use, for reasons of cost. **SAA CUA standards strongly recommend help screens.**

Help screen information may be hard-coded on a series of maps, assembled, and stored on the CICS system. Alternatively, the help screen information may be stored on a VSAM file. When help information is needed, the contents of the appropriate record are read and sent to the terminal using a map that contains an array of blank lines. In either case, the help information must be updated whenever the application itself is updated. Incorrect help text is worse than none at all. Some software vendors offer free-standing help packages that can be used to add help screens to existing applications and maintain the contents of the help text.

Whenever the appropriate function key has been pressed, the application program can build and send the help screen, or it can invoke another program module to produce the help screen. There is obviously some cost in terms of program overhead and terminal I/O. It may be more convenient for the user to request a help screen than to look up something in a manual, but there is more work involved in setting up and maintaining help screens than in setting up and maintaining manuals.

13.4 SYSTEM INTEGRITY IN MULTI-CPU CICS INSTALLATIONS

13.4.1 Precautions for Multi-CPU Processing

In its operating software, IBM provides less data integrity across multiple CPUs than it does within one CPU. A certain amount of care is necessary to protect programs and data under these circumstances. Here are certain things that might need to be considered in multi-CPU MVS/XA and MVS/ESA shops:

1. **Program assemblies or compilations intended for a CICS EXECLIB on one CPU should be run only on that CPU.** Suppose a CICS region is running on CPU #1, with its EXECLIB on that system also. If program compilations running on CPU #1 and CPU #2 are each trying to write an object program to the EXECLIB on CPU #1, damage can result which will make it impossible for CPU #1 to locate the programs when a NEWCOPY is done.

2. **In general, no file should be updated from two different CPUs at the same time unless special precautions are taken.** This applies whether the file is a VSAM file, a PDS, or anything else. The only exception is a file being accessed with the aid of DL/I or another data base management system which provides full support for cross-system file sharing.

    In practice, this means that only one CPU should open a file for update at any given time. The IDCAMS SHAREOPTION can be used to prevent other batch jobs or CICS regions on the same CPU from simultaneously opening the file for update, but it does not lock out update access from another CPU. This has to be prevented by manual scheduling procedures.

3. **In a multi-CPU environment, IBM recommends that the IDCAMS VERIFY step be removed from both batch and CICS jobs.** (The other alternative would be to make sure that all batch and online jobs use the IDCAMS VERIFY, but this would add extra overhead. The problem occurs when some jobs use IDCAMS VERIFY and

other jobs rely on the implicit verify which occurs during VSAM file open processing.)

Suppose a VSAM file is being updated under CICS on CPU #1. The open for output indicator in the VSAM control blocks is "ON". Suppose a batch job on CPU #2 needs to read this file. The batch job contains an IDCAMS VERIFY step, but the CICS job does not. The IDCAMS VERIFY will open this file for output even though it is already open for output on CPU #1. It will issue a verify macro and then close the file. This will cause the catalog information to be updated and the open for output indicator to be turned "OFF". However, the file actually is still open from the point of view of the CICS region on CPU #1. The CICS region is continuing to update records in the file. If CICS crashes, then the file will look as though it was not open for update at the time of the crash, because the open for output indicator will be "OFF".

Suppose the job is submitted to bring the CICS region up again. Recall that the CICS job does not contain an IDCAMS VERIFY. Since the file does not look as though it is open, the implicit verify will not be triggered either. The control blocks available to CICS describe the file at the time of its last successful close, when in fact some updates have taken place since then. Pandemonium will break loose when the CICS region attempts to access the file again while using this erroneous information.

In a nutshell, the IDCAMS VERIFY command always forces the open for output indicator to "OFF", regardless of its original setting, and regardless of whether the job will need to access the file for update. On the other hand, the implicit verify processing routine is invoked only when the open for output indicator is already "ON" and no other job on the same CPU is accessing the file. If the VSAM OPEN is read-only, the implicit verify routine will leave the open for output indicator unchanged. Since the two methods of verification are incompatible, every job on the system should use the same method.

4. **A CICS EXECLIB should not be compressed while any CICS region using it is running.** Here again, pointer damage could result. This applies to both foreground (TSO) and batch compression jobs. A PDS compression job should be scheduled to be run when all CICS regions using the library are down. Compressions are usually needed after numerous updates have taken place. This often applies to CICS EXECLIBs used for program development and testing.

5. **A CICS EXECLIB must be defined with enough space so that assemblies or compilations taking place while CICS is running will not cause an additional extent to be allocated at that time.** CICS seems to be unable to address the programs in the newly-created extent.

Here again, this issue mainly applies to CICS EXECLIBs used by programming staff. If an unusually large number of assemblies or compilations is expected, such as during conversion activity, make sure there is adequate room in the libraries.

TEST YOUR UNDERSTANDING

Questions and Exercises

1. What should a CICS command level program do after it sends a help screen to the terminal user? Think about it this way: When a terminal user has finished reading a help screen, what should he or she be able to do next? What screen will the user want to see next?

2. Why would you ordinarily not want to set up a CICS application so that it can be run from only one physical device?

3. What methods might you use to familiarize user personnel with the 3270-type keyboard and display?

14

CICS OS/2

14.1 CICS IN THE OS/2 ENVIRONMENT

14.1.1 What is OS/2?

OS/2 is IBM's current microcomputer operating environment, which replaces PC-DOS or MS-DOS. MS-DOS was written when a typical PC came with 64K of RAM on the motherboard, one or two 5 1/4" diskette drives, and a monochrome or CGA monitor. Since MS-DOS allowed only one program to run at a time, you had to end one program to load another one. MS-DOS also was limited in its handling of disk allocation and of memory addressing. MS-DOS has no support for virtual memory. Virtual memory is the swapping of unused portions of program object code and/or data out to a work file on disk so that you can run programs larger than available memory. MS-DOS is a real mode operating system, which means that if you run out of memory, you are out of luck.

To get around these limitations, some software developers wrote "terminate and stay resident" or "swap" programs, but these were failure-prone and fraught with limitations. MS-DOS provides no standardized graphics support, so programs that use anything other than plain ASCII text have to handle that themselves. OS/2 Standard Edition makes up for these MS-DOS shortcomings. OS/2 Extended Edition does all of those things and more: it provides for mainframe and network connectivity and for SQL-based database support.

OS/2 is a true protect mode **multitasking operating system**. Multitasking simply means that the operating system can run several applications at the same time. Since a workstation has only one CPU, OS/2 switches between the activities so that each gets its share of CPU time slices. Not only that, OS/2 allows more than one path of execution, or **thread**, within a single application. A program can use one thread to write to a file, for example, and another thread to check for more user input. OS/2 isolates applications from one another to prevent them from damaging each other's storage or interfering in other ways. Microsoft Windows, by contrast, is a session manager which runs under MS-DOS, providing a consistent graphics interface and bypassing some other limitations. At this time, Windows does not provide multithreading. It also does not provide networking or mainframe connectivity, although Microsoft plans to provide more capabilities in the future. It provides limited multitasking, especially in 80386 mode, but not preemptive multitasking, which means that one application can tie up the system. Windows has been positioned as a convenient end-user environment for running stand-alone applications that don't require database services or connectivity. OS/2 has been positioned as the environment for developing and running mainframe and high-end workstation applications.

Getting Used to the Environment.   Mainframe programmers who know CICS, COBOL, VSAM, and/or SQL can be productive with CICS OS/2 with little need for retraining. What areas of additional knowledge are needed? CICS OS/2 1.20 requires a minimal familiarity with OS/2 from the user's point of view. You don't need to know about the internals of OS/2 or Presentation Manager. It's easy to acquire the needed familiarity with the microcomputer environment from the user's point of view. Programmers who have used MS-DOS, Microsoft Windows, or OS/2 to run spreadsheets, word processing, or communications programs will already have most of these skills. The OS/2 windowed or full-screen command prompt takes essentially the same commands as does the MS-DOS command prompt. OS/2 command files (.CMD) replace MS-DOS batch files (.BAT), but they work much the same way. The Presentation Manager windowed environment resembles Microsoft Windows from the user's point of view. The mouse is used to resize and move windows and to make selections. Using the mouse efficiently is a manual skill which improves with practice.

Those mainframe application programmers who rely on systems programmers to do their CICS table updates will probably be expected to do their own table updates in the OS/2 environment. Allowing them to make their own updates speeds the development cycle considerably. Of course, programmers should be informed of naming conventions and other site standards before they begin updating tables. If security is handled properly on the mainframe end, so as to isolate the development environment on the workstation from the production environment on the mainframe, there is no reason why this should present any dangers.

What You'll Need. CICS OS/2 1.20 needs OS/2 Extended Edition 1.1 or later, on an 80286 machine or better. CICS needs at least 1.3 megabytes of usable memory beyond that required by OS/2 EE; more for extra terminals. Plan on at least eight megabytes and preferably more, especially if you are using OS/2 EE Database Manager for SQL support. If you run OS/2 EE without enough memory, you'll get unpredictable, intermittent errors, possibly including trashed files or databases. While in theory you can install CICS OS/2 in text mode under PC-DOS 3.3 or 4.0, the PC- DOS environment doesn't provide CICS with enough memory to do anything worthwhile. You'll also need a compiler. CICS OS/2 1.20 supports Micro Focus COBOL/2 (with the Workbench debugging tools if desired), the IBM COBOL/2 compiler, or the IBM C/2 compiler. The Microsoft C and COBOL compilers will also work. The COBOL compilers sold by IBM and Microsoft are actually Micro Focus COBOL/2. The differences have to do with which version is being shipped by whom, and which utilities are packaged with the COBOL/2 compiler.

If You also Plan to Use SQL. Examples in this book were prepared with version 2.4.31 of the Micro Focus COBOL/2 compiler. It comes with an integrated SQL preprocessor. Older versions of the COBOL/2 compiler might not. The integrated SQL preprocessor lets you debug with your original source code rather than with the expanded output of the SQL preprocessor. To use SQL with older versions of COBOL/2, you need to run the IBM SQL preprocessor for COBOL provided with CICS OS/2 1.20 before running the COBOL/2 compiler. The IBM SQL preprocessor works like a mainframe preprocessor. It scans COBOL programs containing EXEC SQL commands, commenting them out and substituting CALL statements which invoke the appropriate interface routines.

14.1.2 Installing CICS OS/2

If CICS OS/2 Was Purchased Directly from IBM. As of version 1.20, if you buy CICS OS/2 directly from IBM, it is not available on diskette for direct loading onto the microcomputer. (This may change in the future.) It has to be ordered in the form of a mainframe tape, loaded onto a mainframe under MVS or DOS/VSE, and downloaded to a microcomputer using the OS/2 EE Communications Manager or terminal emulator software, and appropriate software on the mainframe side. This process is described in the CICS OS/2 System and Application Guide. A separate license is required for each microcomputer workstation, but once you've purchased the license for a second workstation, you can copy the downloaded CICS from the first workstation to the second, and make diskette backups. You do NOT have to own or lease a mainframe to be allowed to purchase CICS OS/2. Once you have the tape and the license, you can take it to a service bureau to have it downloaded to your micro.

Once you've downloaded CICS OS/2, you will have a subdirectory called CICS120\INSTALL on whichever hard disk drive you are using. However, CICS isn't ready to run. To make up the contents of the CICS120\OS2DSD and CICS120\OS2DSD\DATA subdirectories required for running CICS, you will first need to run the CICSINST program from the INSTALL directory. The INSTALL directory will not be needed at run time, so you can back it up to diskette or tape and remove it from your hard disk. Keep the backups in case something goes wrong with your hard disk or you want to reinstall the software.

If the CICS OS/2 Option Was Purchased from Micro Focus: Micro Focus has been authorized by IBM to resell CICS OS/2 on diskette for development purposes as part of an integrated package including the COBOL/2 compiler and other utilities. This is definitely the easiest way to go for the applications programmer. Micro Focus provides a SETUP program for the diskette version which simplifies the install procedure to under 30 minutes and reduces the complexity of the install. Also, the CICS translator (preprocessor) as well as the SQL preprocessor are both integrated into this version of the COBOL/2 compiler. This integration means that the user will not have to debug the expanded code from the IBM CICS OS/2 translator. Instead, the user (using Animator) can debug his or her original source code (the .CCP version). The Animator will position on and execute the EXEC CICS...END-EXEC commands as if they were COBOL statements, simplifying the debugging task.

The CICS Working Directory.   CICS OS/2 1.20 is set up to be run from the CICS120\OS2DSD subdirectory. This means that your application programs can be kept there, along with the IBM-supplied modules. The CICS OS/2 System and Application Guide indicates that you can set up a different subdirectory to isolate your own applications from the others, using parameters in CONFIG.SYS to point at that subdirectory. When CICS OS/2 1.20 first came out, this did not work, but a "bug fix" was supplied in late 1990.

The CICS OS/2 installation process requires certain environment variables to be placed in your OS/2 CONFIG.SYS file [see Figure 14.1]. These are described in more detail in the CICS OS/2 System and Application Guide. These variables tell CICS OS/2, the translator, and the compiler where to find resources. The CONFIG.SYS file can be edited with the Micro Focus COBOL editor, the OS/2 system editor, or another ASCII text editor. You can use a word processor to update CONFIG.SYS if it can produce files in ASCII text format.

```
PROTSHELL=C:\OS2\PMSHELL.EXE C:\OS2\OS2.INI C:\OS2\OS2SYS.INI C:\OS2\CMD.EXE
FILES=128
SET COMSPEC=C:\OS2\CMD.EXE
SET PATH=C:\OS2;C:\MUGLIB;C:\SQLLIB;C:\OS2\SYSTEM;C:\OS2\IN-
STALL;C:\;K:\COBOL;K:\CICS120\OS2DSD;K:\SIDEKICK\NOTEPAD;
SET DPATH=C:\OS2;C:\MUGLIB\DLL;C:\OS2\SYSTEM;C:\OS2\IN-
STALL;C:\;K:\COBOL;K:\CICS120\OS2DSD;C:\SQLLIB;K:\CICS120\OS2DSD\DATA;
LIBPATH=.;C:\OS2\DLL;C:\MUGLIB\DLL;C:\SQLLIB\DLL;C:\;C:\OS2;C:\OS2\IN-
STALL;K:\COBOL;F:\DW5-2;K:\CICS120\OS2DSD;K:\SIDEKICK;
SET PROMPT=$e[1m$e[31m[OS2] $e[33m$p$e[36m$t$h$h$h;$e[32m$_
SET HELP=C:\OS2\HELP;
SET BOOKSHELF=C:\OS2\BOOK;
BUFFERS=60
IOPL=YES
DISKCACHE=64
MAXWAIT=3
MEMMAN=SWAP,MOVE
PROTECTONLY=NO
SWAPPATH=J:\
THREADS=255
SHELL=C:\OS2\COMMAND.COM /P
BREAK=OFF
FCBS=16,8
RMSIZE=640
DEVICE=C:\OS2\DOS.SYS
COUNTRY=001,C:\OS2\SYSTEM\COUNTRY.SYS
DEVINFO=KBD,US,C:\OS2\KEYBOARD.DCP
CODEPAGE=437,850
DEVINFO=SCR,VGA,C:\OS2\VIOTBL.DCP
SET VIDEO_DEVICES=VIO_IBMVGA
SET VIO_IBMVGA=DEVICE(BVHVGA)
DEVICE=C:\OS2\POINTDD.SYS
DEVICE=C:\OS2\IBMMOU02.SYS
DEVICE=C:\OS2\MOUSE.SYS TYPE=IBMMOU$
DEVICE=C:\OS2\PMDD.SYS
DEVICE=C:\OS2\EGA.SYS
SET KEYS=ON
DEVICE=C:\OS2\COM02.SYS
SET COBDIR=K:\COBOL;K:\CICS120\OS2DSD
SET LIB=C:\OS2;K:\CICS120\OS2DSD;K:\COBOL;C:\SQLLIB;
SET DSDIR=K:\COBOL
SET SQLUSER=USERID
SET BMSMAP=K:\CICS120\OS2DSD\DATA
SET CICSTEXT=K:\CICS120\OS2DSD\DATA
SET COBCPY=K:\CICS120\OS2DSD
SET COBWRK=K:\CICS120\OS2DSD
SET CICSRD=K:\CICS120\OS2DSD\DATA\FAACTFTB.BTR
SET CICSWRK=K:\CICS120\OS2DSD
LOG=ON
SET QRWDR=C:
SET QRWINST=C:\SQLLIB
```

FIGURE 14.1 OS/2 CONFIG.SYS.

BMSMAP   Location of map set master file (FAAMSFSC)

CICSRD   Location of CICS resource definition file where CICS tables are kept (FAACTFTB)

CICSTEXT   Location of message text file (FAAMGFMG) and help files

CICSWRK   Location of executable modules for your application programs

COBCPY   Location of "copy library" members, including BMS translation output

COBDIR   Location of files needed for COBOL compilation

COBWRK   Location of translator output files

DPATH   Data files used by your application programs

LIB   Location of run-time system library files (.LIB files)

PATH   Command files and program files outside your current directory

14.1.3 CICS OS/2 in the OS/2 Environment

CICS OS/2 1.20 is a program that runs under OS/2 Extended Edition
using Presentation Manager, much as mainframe CICS would run under a
mainframe operating system. The internal architecture of CICS OS/2 bears
no resemblance to any version of mainframe CICS, because the hardware
platform and operating system is entirely different. However, the user
interface and the application programming interface have been kept consistent with mainframe CICS as much as is practical.
CICS OS/2 is more than a program development tool which allows a
programmer to write and syntax-check command level programs to be run
on a mainframe. In fact, it is a real version of CICS that can be used for both
test and production purposes. Its capabilities are being enhanced with the
passage of time. The prior version, CICS OS/2 1.10, was introduced early
in 1988. It supported a level of functionality comparable with mainframe
CICS 1.5. Version 1.20 supports a level of functionality comparable to
CICS 3.x, with a few exceptions.

14.1.4 Advantages and Disadvantages

Let's start with the disadvantages of running CICS under OS/2. Obviously,
it costs more to get an OS/2 machine than to plug another dumb terminal
into a mainframe. A mainframe shop with plenty of excess capacity might
not be able to justify another processor. Also, there are still a few features
not supported by CICS OS/2 1.20, which will be discussed below.
  Now for the advantages. If CICS OS/2 is used as a development environment, programmers don't have to wait for CICS compiles and listings, for
test CICS to be brought up, for VTAM communication links to be restored,
or for changes to be made to test CICS. Applications programmers can take
responsibility for maintaining the CICS RDO and program libraries on their
own test machines. CICS OS/2 1.20 has the usual testing tools available

with mainframe CICS, plus some extras, such as the Micro Focus animated debug. The OS/2 environment even has a feature which CICS mainframers have been demanding for years without getting: task protected storage. As mentioned in an earlier chapter, OS/2 will display an error message if any application tries to tamper with storage which doesn't belong to it. If the programmer crashes or locks up an OS/2 workstation, he or she can reboot the workstation and recover local databases without affecting anyone else's testing. This means fewer calls to the help desk or to systems programming.

If CICS OS/2 is used for production, you have some flexibility in distributed application design. You can set it up so that users can enter data even when the link to the mainframe is down. Confidential data which is not meant to be shared with the mainframe can be isolated on an OS/2 machine. Other systems cannot get at the data if you don't set up links for them to do so. Complex user interface processing can be done without using mainframe resources.

14.2 WHAT IS SUPPORTED UNDER CICS OS/2 AND WHAT IS NOT

14.2.1 Mainframe EXEC CICS Command Set

CICS OS/2 1.20 is sufficiently compatible with mainframe CICS that it doesn't have its own application programmer's reference manual. You just use the mainframe *CICS/MVS 2.1 CICS Application Programmer's Reference Manual (Command Level)* because the EXEC CICS application program interface is virtually identical. You can download a copy of your existing mainframe command level programs, recompile them, set up test files and databases, and run them on the OS/2 machine. The transaction's displays will look much as they do on a mainframe 3270 under BMS, except that the CICS displays will be in a window.

Appendices A and B of the *CICS OS/2 System and Application Guide* contain a list of every option within every command, showing what is and what is not supported under CICS OS/2. In a nutshell, you can use everything in the CICS/MVS 2.1 or CICS/ESA 3.1 APRM except for certain specified exceptions. On the other hand, there are a few commands that are peculiar to CICS OS/2, which we will discuss below. The most notable differences from mainframe CICS are the following:

- CICS OS/2 doesn't support DL/I databases directly on your microcomputer workstation's hard disk drive, although it can access DL/I databases on a mainframe through data communications.
- Basic mapping support in CICS OS/2 is minimum-function, which means it handles neither BMS built-in paging nor unusual terminal devices such as bank teller machines. It will handle the SEND TEXT command, however.

- CICS OS/2 doesn't yet handle a two-phase commit under APPC. Usually, this would be needed only for complex recovery situations.
- It doesn't support the JOURNAL command.
- It doesn't support macro-level calls. If you have old mainframe programs with macro-level calls, you can't download them to the workstation to maintain them.

14.3.2 Access to Presentation Manager: Icing on the Cake

OS/2 "heavies" can choose to write a front end program using OS/2 Presentation Manager calls in place of BMS commands to take advantage of the graphics capabilities of the OS/2 workstation. CICS OS/2 1.20 will support the C language as well as COBOL; Presentation Manager programming is usually done in C but can also be done in COBOL. (Either way, you'll need the Developer's Toolkit.) Alternatively, the CASE/PM product can be used to generate the PM interface. In either case, you can have a mouse-ready interface to your datasets which uses windows, buttons, scroll bars, and all of the other little goodies. But if you want to port the same CICS application back to the mainframe, you will have to provide an alternative front end program using BMS commands. This may change if and when mainframes become equipped for Presentation Manager graphics.

OS/2 programmers can also use the Dialog Manager CUA interface package from IBM or the Micro Focus Dialog System in conjunction with CICS. A new version of Dialog System II (scheduled availability second quarter of 1991) will allow the application developer to paint PM graphical CUA-type applications that will also run under DOS in character graphics mode with no changes. In addition, many CASE facilities are available in the OS/2 environment. CICS OS/2 provides an excellent back end CASE tool for testing of these generated applications.

14.3 OS/2 FILE HANDLING AS IT APPLIES TO CICS

14.3.1 OS/2 vs. Mainframe Design Philosophy

Programs running under CICS OS/2 1.20 can access data on the OS/2 machine's hard disk drive, and data on other systems as well. Microcomputers don't have separate "online" and "batch" regions as do mainframes. You can reach the same resources from within a CICS OS/2 program that you would be able to reach from a non-CICS application program running under OS/2. However, if you access resources that would be unavailable to a mainframe CICS application, you will not be able to port that program back to a mainframe.

14.3.2 Program Libraries

Under OS/2, as in MS-DOS, program source code as well as executable modules are stored in subdirectories along with other files. Filename extensions are used to distinguish the various file types. For example, your own CICS COBOL source code files intended for input to the CICS translator step have an extension of .CCP. Translator output files ready for compilation have an extension of .CBL. (You can give copy library modules that extension also.) Compiler output files ready for link editing have an extension of .OBJ. Executable CICS application programs have an extension of .DLL, which is the OS/2 designation for executable subroutines. This is because your application programs are run as subroutines under CICS, not as separate programs from the OS/2 prompt.

Basic mapping support source files which you create have a filename extension of .BMS. The COBOL-format copy library modules, or symbolic maps, produced by the BMS translator have an extension of .CBL. However, all of the physical maps are stored together in a CICS-supplied map master file called FAAMSFSC.BTR, in the CICS120\OS2DSD\DATA subdirectory. You can view or delete these map sets using the IBM-supplied transaction CSCA.

14.3.3 VSAM Files

CICS OS/2 contains its own VSAM file access method. The command level interface is identical to the mainframe implementation, so that you can migrate your CICS OS/2 programs to the mainframe once they are tested. Files are defined with RDO, using the FCT screen in the CEDA transaction. The RDO definition takes care of the FCT entry and the file definition, so that there is no need for a separate IDCAMS utility on the OS/2 workstation. CICS OS/2 VSAM file support is part of CICS. It is not part of OS/2 (as is SQL), nor is it part of the COBOL compiler. OS/2 COBOL programs can get at these local CICS VSAM files only through CICS commands. The VSAM support supplied with the Micro Focus COBOL compiler for batch programming is not compatible with CICS OS/2 VSAM at this time. VSAM files created using CICS OS/2 will have a filename extension of .VSM.

14.3.4 The OS/2 Printer

Printing under CICS OS/2 works in several ways. First of all, the "print screen" key sends screen image data to a printer port on the OS/2 workstation. You indicate which printer port to use for screen printing when you define your display terminal in the TCT. On a mainframe, screen print images would go to a 3287-type printer. Second, you can define printer terminals, which are in effect mapped onto the OS/2 printer attached to your printer port, and use them the same way as you would mainframe 3287 terminals. In fact, two of these definitions are provided in the TCT in the default CICS OS/2 configuration.

Suppose you want to write a batch (non-interactive) print program which needs the OS/2 VSAM files. Since the print program won't need to interact with the user, you want it to run while the user is doing other work. Using printer terminals defined in the TCT, you can write print applications using one of the methods described above for printing under CICS. You can even provide a selection menu from which the user can select various printed reports. The print driver application can use the EXEC CICS START command to launch the desired print transaction, attaching it to the printer terminal. Once the print task is launched, the user's display terminal is free for other purposes so that the user can go back to doing something more worthwhile than waiting for the printer.

14.3.5 Sequential Files

CICS OS/2, like mainframe CICS, can use extrapartition transient data queues to read and write sequential DOS files. These files are defined in the DCT and are created with filename extensions of .TDQ. In addition, CICS OS/2 applications can access workstation files directly by using COBOL I/O statements or C library routines. This method does not take advantage of the CICS OS/2 transaction backout facilities. Applications written in this way cannot be ported back to a mainframe.

14.3.6 SQL-Based Databases

SQL-based databases can be defined in an application program using DDL (data definition language) SQL commands. They can also be defined with the OS/2 EE Query Manager, which is similar to mainframe QMF. These databases are defined under the OS/2 EE catalog structure. See next chapter for more details.

14.4 TRANSLATING PROGRAMS AND MAPS

14.4.1 Command Files

CICS COBOL source programs and BMS maps are ASCII text files. You can create them with the Micro Focus COBOL editor, the OS/2 system editor, or any other ASCII text editor. You can also use a word processor that creates ASCII files with no embedded control codes. However, a text editor specifically designed for writing programs will permit you to work more quickly. The examples shown in this book were created with the Micro Focus COBOL editor which comes with the COBOL Toolset and Workbench products.

The procedures for translating, compiling, and linking programs under OS/2 are provided with CICS OS/2. These are provided in the form of **command files** with a filename extension of .CMD. Command files are the OS/2 counterpart of MS-DOS .BAT files. If you use the compiler purchased from Micro Focus, you might need to modify the program name in the compilation step in the .CMD file so that it will access the right version of the compiler. You can edit .CMD files using any ASCII text editor.

As you would do on a mainframe, make sure all of your copy library members are ready to use before you do anything else. This means that you need to set up and translate your maps before you attempt to compile programs that use those maps. **Translate your BMS maps by entering the following command at the OS/2 prompt:**

CICSMAP filename

where "filename" is the DOS filename of your map source code file, without the .BMS extension.

The following command will translate, compile, and link edit your CICS COBOL programs:

CICSTCL filename COBOL2

Here, filename is the DOS filename of the translator input source file, without the .CCP extension. The COBOL2 parm tells the translator step that your source code is written in VS COBOL II. As described in an earlier chapter, CICS commands are coded somewhat differently under VS COBOL II; for example, the LENGTH parameter is often omitted. The translator needs to know whether VS COBOL II is being used in order to check the syntax properly. CICS OS/2 and the COBOL/2 compiler allow you to use either VS COBOL II (release 3) or old OS/VS COBOL. Omit the COBOL2 parameter for the translation step if you are using old COBOL.

As on a mainframe, the COBOL compiler needs to be given **directives** to tell it what type of code to produce. The Micro Focus compiler supports many dialects of COBOL for use on various equipment. The directives can be supplied in several ways: in the source file itself, in which case they will affect that program only; in the COBOL.DIR file, in which case they will affect all programs compiled while that file exists; and on the command line itself, following the program name, in which case they will affect that compilation only. If you are coding in VS COBOL II, be sure to use the ANS85 directive. The OSVS directive indicates which reserved word list to use. ANIM creates files for animated debugging if desired. The other directives shown here are required for SQL and will be discussed later. See the manual accompanying your compiler for the most current details concerning directives. This COBOL.DIR file was used to compile the programs used in this book:

```
ANS85
OSVS
SQL
SQLACCESS""
SQLBIND""
SQLDB(CICSBOOK)
NOSQLPASS
```

How do You Get an OS/2 Command Prompt?   There are several ways to get a command prompt in the OS/2 environment. The OS/2 operating system provides you with a **windowed command prompt** and a **full-screen command prompt**. These appear by default in the Main Group pick list in the OS/2 Desktop Manager. The windowed command prompt appears in an OS/2 window, while the full-screen command prompt uses the entire workstation screen. You can switch among these processes in the same way as you would switch among CICS terminal sessions (described below). Also, certain applications, such as the Micro Focus Workbench, provide a facility which lets you "shell" to the OS/2 command prompt and then to return to the application. For the purpose of running command files, the full-screen command prompt works better than the windowed prompt. This is because the COBOL/2 compiler switches to full-screen mode; error messages are lost when the compiler terminates and windowed mode is resumed.

14.4.2   Compilation with Micro Focus Workbench

The Micro Focus Workbench provides a menu from which you can use various editing, compilation, debugging, and integration tools for creating online and batch COBOL applications. It would take an entire book to introduce you to all of the things you can do with the Workbench, many of which have little to do with CICS.

Users of CICS OS/2 should run the Micro Focus Workbench from the directory in which the programs will be run, in this case CICS120\OS2DSD. If you install it in a "pick list" group within the OS/2 Desktop Manager, when you define the program's properties, enter your CICS directory as the working directory. This will let the Workbench find all of the files it needs without your having to type a directory path each time. It's a matter of personal preference whether you install the Workbench to run in windowed or full-screen mode. Full-screen is somewhat faster but doesn't let you keep other things visible at the same time.

You can reach the built-in editor by pressing F2 on the Workbench main menu. The editor lets you enter and update COBOL source code as well as

OS/2 command files. When the editor first comes up, it provides you with a blank screen on which you can begin entering code to create a new file. To update an existing file, hold the Alt key and press F3. At the bottom of the screen, you'll see a command line which lets you specify the name of the file you want to load into the editor. This command line is part of the Micro Focus directory system. If you enter a file name containing a "wild card", you'll get a directory pick list rather than the file itself. Comments at the bottom of the display tell you what features are available when you press the function keys [see Figure 14.2a]. If you hold the Alt or Ctrl keys, the menu changes. When you are finished editing, you can save the file by holding the Alt key and pressing F4. The Escape key gets you back to the main menu and then out of the Workbench. Details about using the editor are provided in the Micro Focus documentation.

If you have the CICS OS/2 version of the COBOL/2 compiler, which already contains the CICS translator, you can compile directly from the Workbench menu without having to translate first. It's more convenient because you won't need to set up .CMD files or run anything from the OS/2 command prompt. Otherwise, run the CICSTRAN command file from the OS/2 command prompt to take care of the translation step, as follows:

```
CICSTRAN (progname] COBOL2
```

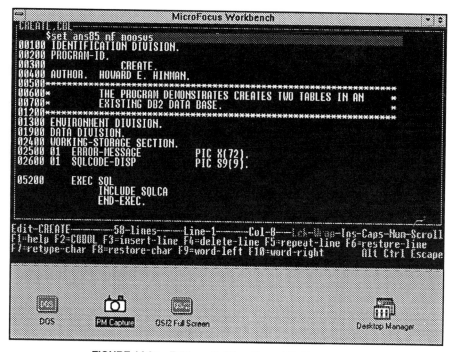

FIGURE 14.2a Editing with Micro Focus Workbench (F2).

Here, progname is the DOS filename of the translator input source file, without the .CCP extension. The COBOL2 parm tells the translator step that your source code is written in VS COBOL II.

Access the compiler from the Workbench menu by pressing F3 to reach the Check option [see Figure 14.2b and 14.2c]. As with the editor, enter the file name on the command line. Press the F6 key repeatedly to turn off the language dialect option that shows up just below the work area. This lets the compiler default to your COBOL.DIR file. The Check option will show you a syntax check of your program as it compiles. Once you've compiled with the Check option of the Workbench, you won't need to link edit, because the Workbench environment already takes care of subroutine linkages for CICS COBOL programs. Micro Focus recommends that Workbench users compile all of their CICS OS/2 programs from the Workbench, not with the COBOL compiler accessed from the command line. The compiler built into the Workbench contains features which the command line compiler doesn't have.

We discussed animation under CICS OS/2 in Chapter 9; CICS program animation is invoked from a CICS terminal session. However, if you have a batch (non-CICS) program that you want to animate, you can run it in animation mode from the Workbench menu by pressing the F4 key. You might need some batch programs for such things as setting up or rebuilding databases.

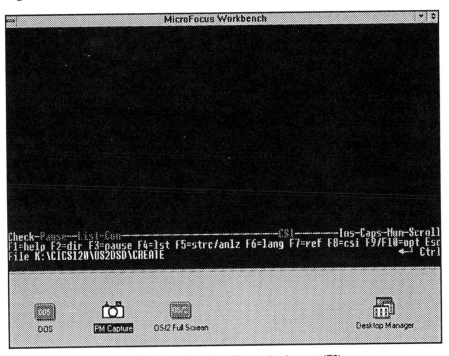

FIGURE 14.2b   The Micro Focus check menu (F3).

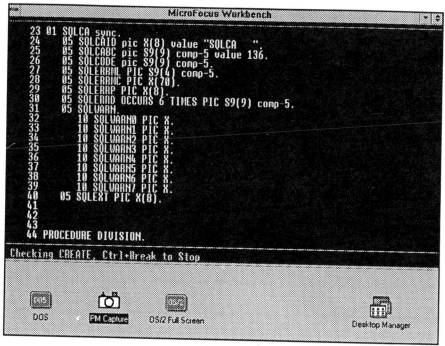

```
23 01 SQLCA sync.
24     05 SQLCAID pic X(8) value "SQLCA    ".
25     05 SQLCABC pic S9(9) comp-5 value 136.
26     05 SQLCODE pic S9(9) comp-5.
27     05 SQLERRML PIC S9(4) comp-5.
28     05 SQLERRMC PIC X(70).
29     05 SQLERRP PIC X(8).
30     05 SQLERRD OCCURS 6 TIMES PIC S9(9) comp-5.
31     05 SQLWARN.
32        10 SQLWARN0 PIC X.
33        10 SQLWARN1 PIC X.
34        10 SQLWARN2 PIC X.
35        10 SQLWARN3 PIC X.
36        10 SQLWARN4 PIC X.
37        10 SQLWARN5 PIC X.
38        10 SQLWARN6 PIC X.
39        10 SQLWARN7 PIC X.
40     05 SQLEXT PIC X(8).
41
42
43
44 PROCEDURE DIVISION.
```

Checking CREATE, Ctrl+Break to Stop

DOS   PM Capture   OS/2 Full Screen   Desktop Manager

FIGURE 14.2c Syntax check and compile.

You can also get an OS/2 command prompt from within the Micro Focus Workbench display by holding the Shift and Ctrl keys and then pressing the Break key. An OS/2 command prompt will appear at the bottom of the Workbench display [see Figure 14.2d]. Results will scroll upward within the display. To return to the Workbench, type EXIT at the OS/2 prompt and press the Enter key.

14.4.3 An Installation Glitch

If you install the Micro Focus Workbench, you'll find a COBLIB.DLL file in your \COBOL directory. So far, so good. However, when you install CICS OS/2, you may also find another COBLIB.DLL file in the CICS120\OS2DSD directory, very likely an obsolete version. Delete the older version so that it will not be run accidentally in place of the more recent version. The extra COBLIB.DLL is present because the Micro Focus Workbench with the shared run-time module was used to write CICS OS/2 itself. Let it use the more recent version from the \COBOL directory instead.

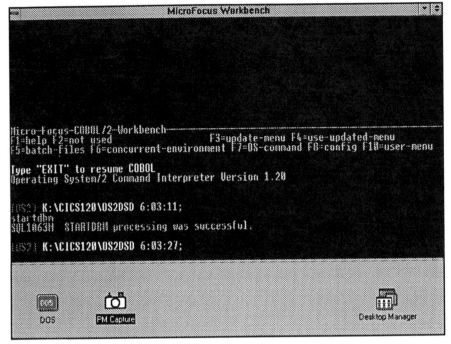

FIGURE 14.2d   OS/2 prompt from Workbench: Shift/Ctrl/Break.

14.5   CICS STARTUP AND SHUTDOWN

14.5.1   CICS Startup

You can start up CICS OS/2 by getting into the CICS120\OS2DSD sub-directory and typing CICSRUN in the OS/2 command window to invoke the CICSRUN.CMD file. (As mentioned earlier, .CMD files under OS/2 are the counterpart of .BAT files under MS-DOS.) You can also enter the startup command in the CICS "start programs" or "desktop manager" pick list. As shown in Figure 14.3a, 14.3b, 14.3c, selecting **Program** on the menu bar, and then selecting **Properties...**, displays a dialog box which allows you to examine the parms associated with the menu item. The parm windows scroll sideways to accommodate longer character strings.

To display its information to you, CICS OS/2 uses Presentation Manager windows. These can be moved, resized, scrolled, minimized to icons, or maximized to cover nearly the full screen. They will appear in the same screen group with whatever else was on your screen when you invoked the command file. When you start up CICS, the first thing you will see will be a black window labeled "CICS OS/2 1.20", or whatever you have called it on the OS/2 pick list. It will contain the text, "CICSRUN - Start up CICS OS/2". After CICS comes up, the label at the top of the window will say

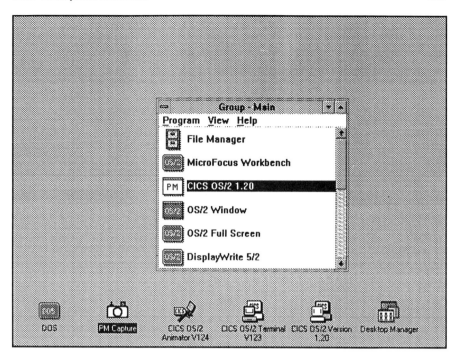

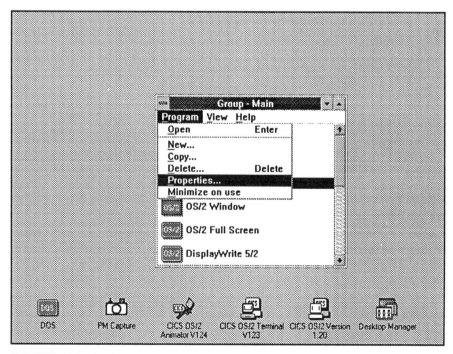

FIGURES 14.3a (top) and 14.3b (bottom) Setup to start CICS OS/2 from OS/2 Desktop Manager.

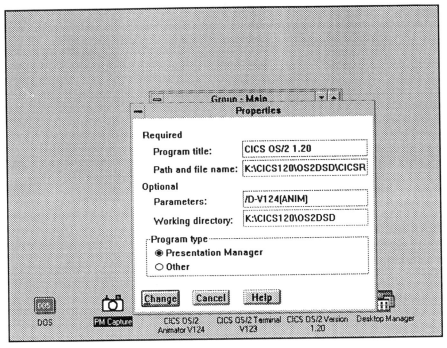

FIGURE 14.3c *(Continued)*

"Completed:", in which case you can use the mouse to close (i.e. delete) the startup window. (You can do this by keying the mouse on the system button in the upper left corner of the window frame and then selecting "Close".)

The next thing you will see is an IBM logo popup which asks you to press the enter key [Figure 14.4a]. When you do this, the logo popup will disappear, to be replaced by a white window labeled "CICS OS/2 1.20". This window is the counterpart of the system console and contains CICS messages [Figure 14.4b]. Here again, you can use the mouse to minimize the message window to an icon at the bottom of the screen; if you want to see the messages later, you can click on the icon to expand it again. Do not try to close this window unless you want to bring down CICS.

The next windows you see will be logical display terminals. CICS OS/2 comes with some prebuilt table entries. Otherwise, you'd never be able to get into CICS to do anything at all. In the default CICS OS/2 configuration as supplied by IBM, V123 and V124 are the identifiers of the two logical terminals defined under CICS. In other words, you get two separate terminal sessions that run at the same time on your OS/2 workstation screen. These appear as separate windows on your monitor when you bring up CICS. V123 is the primary terminal and will appear in front of the other windows [Figure 14.4c]. When V123 first appears, it contains another logo

FIGURE 14.4a   CICS OS2 startup; logo panel.

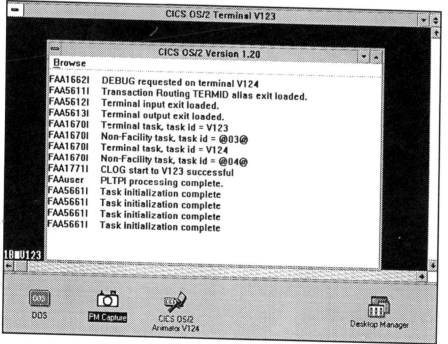

FIGURE 14.4b   CICS OS/2 startup: CICS OS/2 system console window.

FIGURE 14.4c   CICS OS/2 startup: V123 logical terminal window.

display. To see the whole screen, however, you need to use the mouse on the window frame buttons to maximize the V123 window. It will tell you to press the Enter key, but this can fool you. If you press the key labeled Enter, however, nothing will happen. This logo screen is under CICS and uses a different set of key definitions, as you will see later on. **Under CICS OS/2, the right-hand Ctrl key becomes the Enter key!**

As soon as you press the CICS Enter key, a CESN signon display appears [Figure 14.4d]. For "Sign-on Name" and for "Password", enter **SYSAD** in each case and press the CICS Enter key (right-hand Ctrl). You can change these later on in accordance with your security needs, but you have to use these values to get into CICS the first time with the ability to access system table entries. (The DEFAULT signon, with no password, will not let you work with table entries.) You can use the CESN transaction to sign on under a different identifier or to sign on to the other logical terminal if desired. Once you have signed on, you can press the CICS clear key (Esc key) to clear the screen so that you can enter another transaction ID, as in mainframe CICS.

Your display terminals will come up in windowed mode unless you specify full screen mode in the TCT, or unless you are using the Animator for debugging as described in Chapter 9. To switch among windows or full screen displays, you can bring up the OS/2 Task List by holding the Ctrl

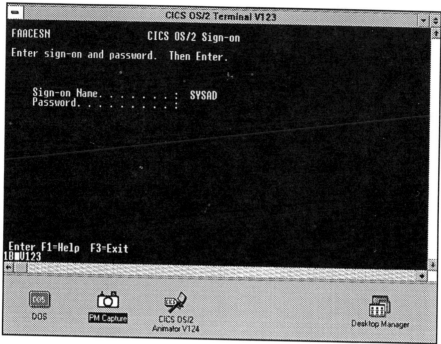

FIGURE 14.4d   CICS OS/2 startup: CESN signon.

key and pressing Esc. Alternatively, you can select among overlapping windows with the mouse. The window currently selected will have a different color on the top border. Your keystrokes will be applied to the currently selected window. This means that your CICS terminal window must be selected for you to be able to use it.

Cold vs. Warm Start: If you want to clear the message, log, and dump files associated with previous runs of CICS, you can do a **cold start**. This will also discard transient data and temporary storage records. Place the parameter /C in the parameters field when setting up your OS/2 Desktop Manager pick list entry, or specify that same parameter following the CICSRUN command at the OS/2 prompt. Without this parameter, CICS will be initialized with a **warm start**. You can set up more than one pick list entry so that you have a choice.

14.5.2   CICS Shutdown

To shut down CICS OS/2, enter the transaction CQIT on one of the terminal displays. Both terminal windows, as well as the CICS "system console" window, should disappear within a minute or less. **Always shut**

down CICS using CQIT before rebooting or turning off power to your workstation, particularly if you use SQL-based databases. Otherwise, you can leave files or SQL catalogs in an invalid state, causing difficulties in restarting CICS or accessing databases.

That's Not All, Folks...What if CICS Won't Come Down? Occasionally there are glitches at shutdown time. Here are a few things to try before you throw the big power switch:

- If your original CICS startup window remains visible after CICS is down (i.e. the window that says "Completed:"), use the mouse to close that window. Click on the button in the upper left corner of the window frame and then select Close.
- If CICS OS/2 does not come all of the way down with CQIT, you may need to re-issue CQIT in the other terminal session if it remains active. If the other terminal session contains a signon screen, enter your user ID and password on that screen.
- If you see a CICS system error message browse window during shutdown, use the action bar to EXIT from that window in order to complete the shutdown.
- If the CICS system window shows a message indicating that CICS is waiting for other processes to terminate, allow CICS a few more minutes to clean itself up. CICS will eventually "time out" the other processes if they fail to respond.

14.6   CICS SYSTEM DEFINITION TABLES

14.6.1   The CEDA Transaction

Once CICS is running, you can set up your tables with RDO (resource definition online), much as you would on mainframe CICS. Unlike on a mainframe, you cannot use macro-based CICS table definitions. Since the architecture of CICS OS/2 differs from that of mainframe CICS, all of the CICS system definition information is kept in one file on your OS/2 machine's hard disk, FAACTFTB.BTR in the CICS120\OS2DSD\DATA subdirectory. **Remember to back up FAACTFTB.BTR before you update any CICS tables!** The CEDA transaction screens in CICS OS/2 differ in appearance and structure from their mainframe counterparts, but the basic principles are the same. **Under CICS OS/2 1.20, it is necessary to bring CICS down and back up to make table entries take effect.**

The first CEDA screen contains a **pick list** which lets you choose the system table you want to update [Figure 14.5a]. Key a slash character "/" over the underscore next to the item you want to choose, and press the

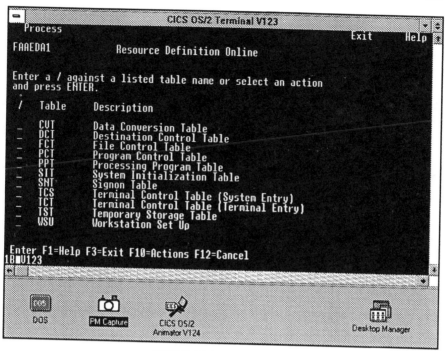

FIGURE 14.5a CEDA menu.

CICS enter key. You will see another pick list showing all table entries which currently exist for that table. Figure 14.5b is one example of this. To view an entry, key a slash character next to the desired item and press the CICS enter key. To add a new entry, move the cursor up to the word **Add** on the action bar and press the enter key. This will give you a screen with a "blank form" in which you can create a new table entry.

All of the CEDA displays contain a SAA CUA action bar which lets you view, add, change, or delete the displayed item by moving the cursor to the desired word on the action bar. The F3 key gets you back to the previous menu. The F1 key provides you with complete, detailed help information concerning all of the fields on each screen. This section will not describe all the alternatives for every field on each CEDA screen, because you can find that information on the help screens or in the *CICS OS/2 System and Application Design Guide*. Instead, we will show some examples so that you will know which table entries you will need to make for your own applications.

14.6.2 Table Contents

Data Conversion Table (CVT). The CVT lets you set up templates indicating which parts of a record need to be translated from EBCDIC to ASCII

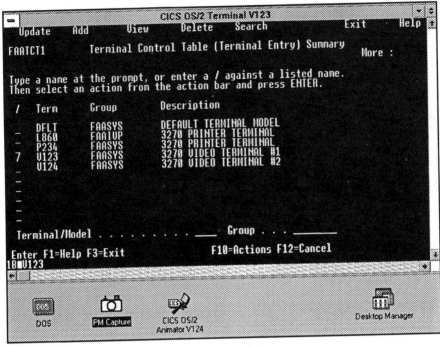

FIGURE 14.5b CEDA menu.

when transmitted from a mainframe to your OS/2 workstation [Figure 14.6]. You will need to make entries here only if your CICS OS/2 application will be downloading data from a mainframe. The CVT can be used for interval control retrieved data, file control VSAM records, temporary storage queue items, or transient data queue items. If you will need to translate data from ASCII to EBCDIC to be uploaded from your workstation to a mainframe, you will need to set up macros in the DFHCNV table on the mainframe. This is described in Chapter 19 of the CICS OS/2 System and Application Guide.

Destination Control Table (DCT). The DCT allows you to define both intrapartition and extrapartition transient data queues [Figure 14.7]. The DCT allows you to associate extrapartition TD queues with the appropriate file names.

File Control Table (FCT). All VSAM key-sequenced, entry-sequenced, relative-record, or alternative index data sets are defined in the FCT [Figure 14.8]. Notice the table at the bottom of the screen which lets you define the position and length of the keys within the record description. Unlike mainframe VSAM, you can define keys which consist of non-con-

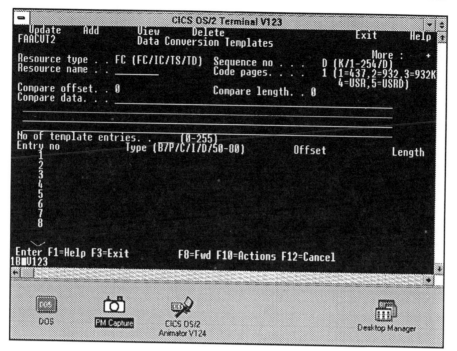

FIGURE 14.6 Data Conversion Table (CVT).

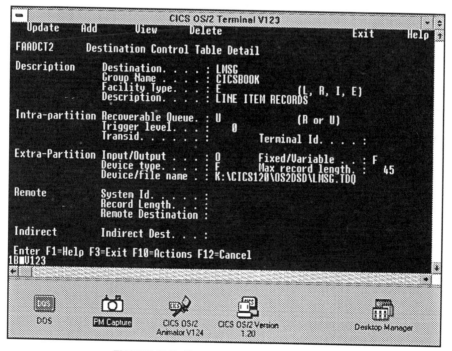

FIGURE 14.7 Destination Control Table (DCT).

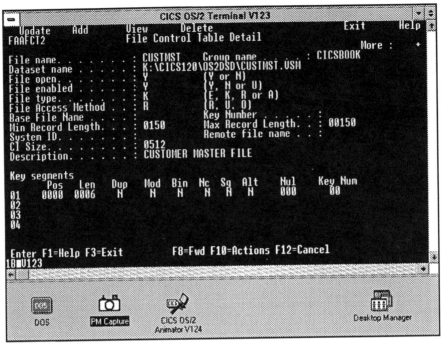

FIGURE 14.8   File Control Table (FCT).

tiguous fields, but if you do that, you won't be able to port the application back to the mainframe.

Defining the file in the FCT will not, in itself, create the OS/2 directory entry for the file. To do that, you will need to restart CICS OS/2, and then run one of the two following CICS commands to open the file:

SET FILE OPEN RESET END-EXEC

SET FILE OPENSTATUS END-EXEC

This can be done in an application program or interactively through the CECI command level interpreter transaction provided with CICS. The directory entry needs to be created only once, when the file is created for the first time. **Do not use the letters .PRE as a filename extension. Do not name two files in the same OS/2 directory with the same filename but with different extensions.** Breaking these rules can prevent CICS from recovering data in the event of a failure.

Program Control Table (PCT).   Just as in mainframe CICS, the PCT has an entry for each transaction that can be invoked on your CICS system. Each transaction is identified by a four-character transaction code [Figure

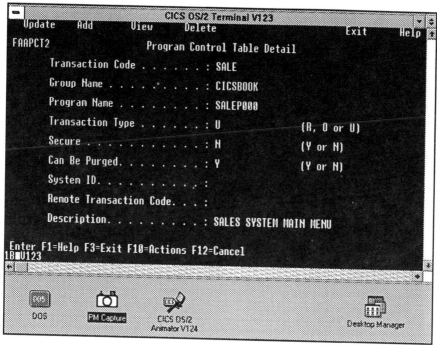

FIGURE 14.9 Program Control Table (PCT).

14.9]. You will need to make an entry for every transaction you define on your CICS OS/2 system, and for every transaction that you want to be able to run on another system through ISC. If your transaction is being run locally, provide the program name in the PCT. Otherwise, provide the system ID in the PCT and define the program on the remote system.

Processing Program Table (PPT). The mainframe CICS environment requires you to make a PPT entry for each program and map that can be used in the CICS system. **Under CICS OS/2, PPT entries for programs and maps are optional.** Make PPT entries if you want to define a group of programs to export to another system, or if you want to specify whether programs should remain resident in memory [Figure 14.10].

System Initialization Table (SIT). The SIT indicates which system-wide features should be activated in CICS the next time you start up CICS [Figure 14.11]. The scope of the SIT entry has to do with the **application group**, which can involve some or all transactions, datasets, and terminals. If you want to use the CWA or TWA, or do some system tuning, or communicate with a mainframe, you will need to add or change SIT entries.

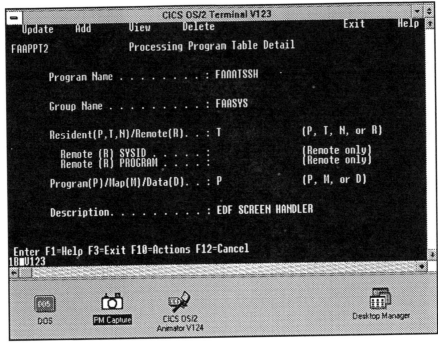

FIGURE 14.10   Processing Program Table (PPT).

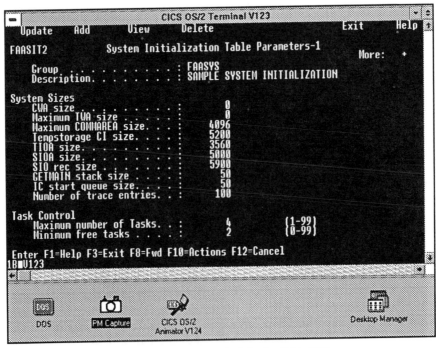

FIGURE 14.11   System Initialization Table (SIT)

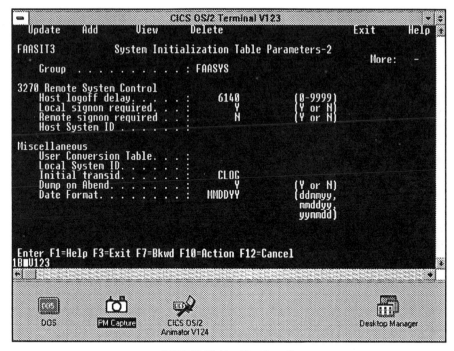

FIGURE 14.11 *(Continued)*

Signon Table (SNT).   This table contains user IDs, passwords, and security keys [Figure 14.12]. The security keys are not currently supported by CICS OS/2 for actual verification; they are supplied only for mainframe compatibility. However, the signon table does determine whether you have permission to update the CICS system tables. You also can set up signons for remote systems connected with CICS OS/2.

Terminal Control Table System Entries (TCS).   This table contains an entry for every other system to which you want to connect your CICS OS/2 system [Figure 14.13]. On a mainframe, both TCS and TCT entries would be in the TCT.

Terminal Control Table Terminal Entries (TCT).   The TCT contains an entry for each terminal connected with your CICS OS/2 system [Figure 14.14]. The entry indicates whether the terminal is a logical display terminal in an OS/2 window, a logical printer terminal, or a 3151 ASCII physical device. For a logical display terminal, the TCT entry indicates whether it will come up in full-screen mode or in a window, what special features it should support, and what printer should be associated with it for screen images. For a logical printer, the TCT entry indicates the printer port. For a 3151 ASCII device, the TCT entry indicates the terminal port.

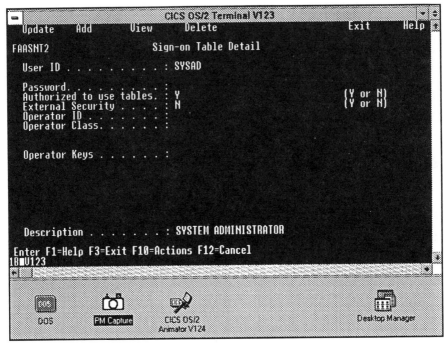

FIGURE 14.12 Signon Table (SNT).

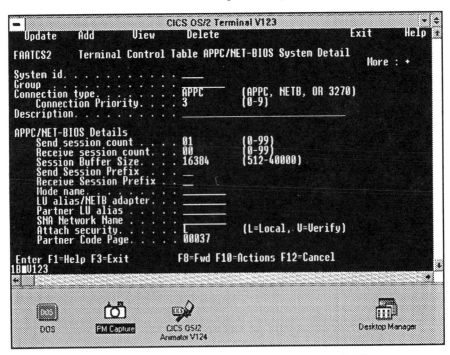

FIGURE 14.13 Terminal Control Table System Entries (TCS).

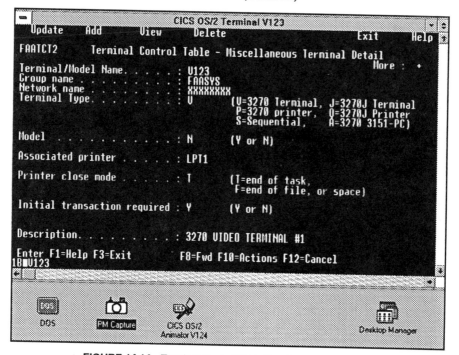

FIGURE 14.13   *(Continued)*

FIGURE 14.14   Terminal Control Table Terminal Entries (TCT).

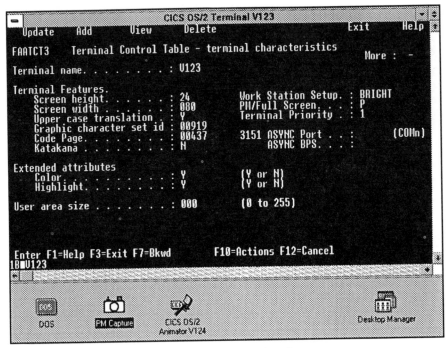

FIGURE 14.14 *(Continued)*

You'll get two logical display terminals when you install CICS; you can modify those definitions to suit your needs.

Some features in the TCT entry seem to let you customize terminal definitions to make them work like various mainframe 3270-type devices. For example, it allows you to turn off upper-case translation and to specify up to 132 character columns. However, as of CICS OS/2 1.20, some of these features do not seem to be working yet.

Temporary Storage Table (TST). Temporary storage queues, which are a type of CICS internal work file, can be defined in this table prior to use if they are on a different CICS system or if there is a need to make the queues recoverable [Figure 14.15]. If neither applies to your TS queue, you do not need to make an entry for it here.

Workstation Set Up (WSU). Like the CVT, the WSU exists only on OS/2 systems, not on mainframes. You can use it to set up your key assignments and screen colors [Figure 14.16], or to look up the default settings for these. In other words, the WSU indicates how you will simulate the 3270-series keyboard and screen on an OS/2 workstation. Once you have made a WSU entry, you can put the name of that entry in one or more TCT entries. This will make the WSU entry apply whenever you use the terminal(s) you have

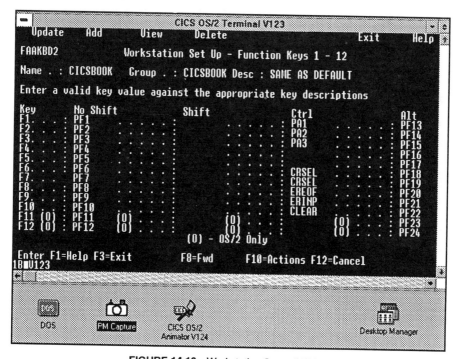

FIGURE 14.15   Temporary Storage Table (TST).

FIGURE 14.16   Workstation Setup (WSU).

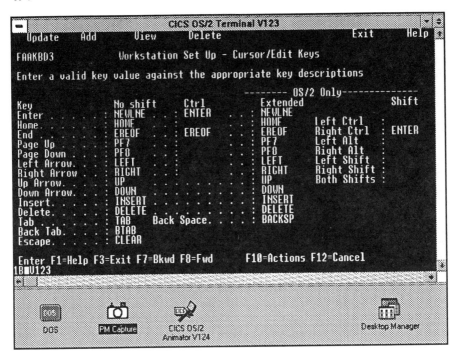

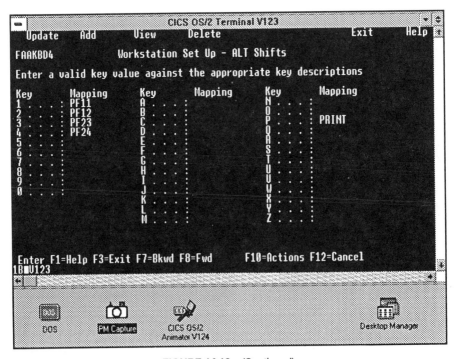

FIGURE 14.16   (Continued)

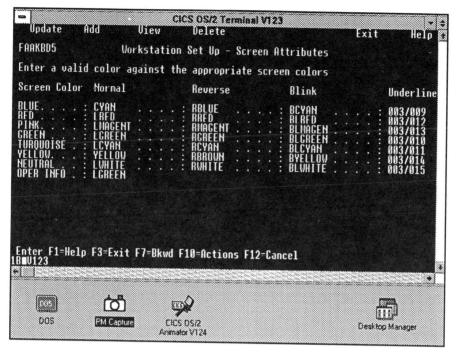

FIGURE 14.16 *(Continued)*

associated with it. A special WSU entry, in which all text was set to white, was used to brighten some of the captured screen images in this book. Ordinarily, the default settings would probably be adequate.

14.7 CICS SYSTEM UTILITY COMMANDS

14.7.1 Determining System Status

CICS OS/2 1.20 comes with the normal diagnostic tools such as CEDF, CECI, CEBR, dump, and trace table. As described earlier, its help functions take the place of a messages and codes manual. However, it does not have a CEMT or "master terminal" transaction. Persons responsible for mainframe system maintenance find CEMT useful for identifying and fixing problems. Instead, CICS OS/2 provides EXEC CICS commands which do not exist in mainframe CICS. These commands can be run from within a program or interactively through the command interpreter transaction (CECI). Either way, you will have to define appropriate variables. When you use these commands within a program, check the RESP and RESP2 fields to make sure the response was normal. These commands are listed in Appendix G of the CICS OS/2 System and Application Design Guide.

```
EXEC CICS INQUIRE {NETNAME(name)|TERMINAL(name)}
     ACQSTATUS(1-byte data-area)
     SERVSTATUS(1-byte data-area)
     TRANSACTION(4-char. data-area)
     END-EXEC.
```

ACQSTATUS and SERVSTATUS are one-byte data areas which will contain a hex value. ACQSTATUS tells you whether or not the terminal is associated with a task. If so, ACQSTATUS will equal hex 45 (decimal 69); if not, ACQSTATUS will equal hex 46 (decimal 70). SERVSTATUS tells you whether or not the terminal is in service; that is, whether it is available to be acquired. If so, SERVSTATUS will equal decimal 73; otherwise, 74. TRANSACTION will contain the four-character ID of the transaction currently attached to that terminal, if any.

```
EXEC CICS SET TERMINAL(4-char. data value)
     ACQSTATUS(1-byte data-area)
     SERVSTATUS(1-byte data-area)
     PURGETYPE(1-byte data-area)
     END-EXEC.
```

This command lets you toggle the SERVSTATUS and ACQSTATUS values to take a terminal out of service, put it back in service, and so forth. You can also purge transactions attached to the terminal. If you set PURGE-TYPE to 236, then a transaction can be purged only if CICS can maintain system and data integrity. If the transaction's PCT entry specifies **Can be purged=N**, the transaction cannot be purged. If you set PURGETYPE to 237, these safeguards are removed from tasks attached to this terminal and the transaction will be purged immediately.

```
EXEC CICS INQUIRE TASK(4-byte packed decimal task number)
     FACILITY(4-char. data-area)
     FACILITYTYPE(1-byte data-area)
     TRANSACTION(4-char. data-area)
     END-EXEC.
```

Here, the FACILITYTYPE indicates the type of **facility** to which the task is attached. This is usually a terminal ID (FACILITYTYPE=234), but it can also be a TD queue (235) or another task (233). The FACILITY data area returns the identifier of the task's **facility**. This is usually a terminal ID, but it can also be a TD queue name or blanks, if the facility is another task. The TRANSACTION data area returns the transaction ID associated with the task.

```
EXEC CICS INQUIRE TASK LIST
     LISTSIZE(full word binary data area)
     [SET(pointer)]
     END-EXEC.
```

In this case, LISTSIZE returns the total number of tasks running at the time the command was executed. SET(pointer) provides you with a pointer to a list of 4-byte packed decimal task numbers, each of which represents an active task. These commands are good for checking up on tasks that seem to be "hung up".

```
EXEC CICS SET TASK(4-byte packed value)
     PURGETYPE(1-byte data area)
     END-EXEC.
```

This command lets you purge a task. PURGETYPE works as it does in the SET TERMINAL command.

14.7.2 Signon and Signoff

```
EXEC CICS SIGNON
     USERID(data-value)
     PASSWORD(8-char. data-value)
     NATLANG(1-char. data-value)
     NATLANGINUSE(1-char. data-value)
END-EXEC.
```

This command signs on your terminal (or other principal facility) using CICS signon procedures. If you are already signed on, sign off first before using this command. NATLANG specifies the national language you want to be supported; NATLANGINUSE will be set to the NATLANG value if specified or to the system default.

```
EXEC CICS SIGNOFF
     END-EXEC.
```

This command does exactly what you would expect: it signs off from the current user ID and sets the terminal back to the default user ID.

14.8 Multiuser CICS OS/2

14.8.1 3151 ASCII Terminals

You might have heard people say that OS/2 is a multitasking system but not a multiuser system. In other words, only one user at a time can work at the OS/2 workstation, but he or she can run several programs at the same time. CICS OS/2 provides an exception to this. It will actually allow you to connect up to three 3151 ASCII terminals to the OS/2 machine. 3151 ASCII terminals are fairly inexpensive but support text only, not graphics. They work like 3270 terminals under BMS on a mainframe. A total of four people can work from the same OS/2 machine and run the CICS transactions they need: one at the workstation's keyboard and screen, the other three at the 3151 terminals. The 3151 terminal users can only access CICS; they won't be able to get to the OS/2 menus or command line prompt.

As mentioned above, one CICS OS/2 license is required for each OS/2 workstation. Just as on a mainframe, there is no license charge for adding terminals. You install the additional communication ports and cabling and enter the terminal identifiers in the CICS OS/2 TCT.

14.9   INTERSYSTEM COMMUNICATIONS WITH CICS OS/2

14.9.1   Available Communications Features

CICS OS/2 1.20 supports LU 2 (3270-type) or LU 6.2 (APPC), at the EXEC CICS level. Communications on the workstation side are handled by the OS/2 EE Communications Manager. As far as your applications are concerned, connecting an OS/2 machine with a mainframe or with another OS/2 machine under VTAM is much like connecting two mainframes. EBCDIC/ASCII translation routines are provided, as described above in the discussion of the CVT. You can use function shipping, transaction routing, asynchronous processing, and APPC, as discussed in a previous chapter. CICS OS/2 presents the programmer with a high level interface for developing APPC applications. You can reach mainframe DL/I databases on remote CICS or IMS DC systems. You can use CRTE to get from a mainframe to a CICS OS/2 system, but not vice versa. You can connect with other CICS OS/2 machines through LU 6.2 or NetBios.

14.9.2   Distributed Program Link (DPL)

CICS OS/2 provides a capability called **distributed program link (DPL)**, which mainframe CICS does not yet have. DPL simply lets you execute a program on a mainframe by EXEC CICS LINK from within an application on the OS/2 machine, as long as table entries exist and CICS security lets you sign on. To use DPL, make a PPT entry for the program and give it a SYSID which indicates the remote system on which the data should be run. The program running on the remote system should not do any terminal I/O, but should access mainframe data and communicate with the local program via the DFHCOMMAREA. Terminal I/O should be done by the local program running on your workstation.

DPL is particularly useful for communications tasks such as extracting data from mainframe DB2 databases. As of CICS 3.1, CICS does not support function shipping for access to DB2 databases on a different machine. The program which accesses the database has to run on the same machine with the database. To bring the information to another machine, you have to communicate with that program somehow. APPC lets you do this, but with considerable programming effort. It's easier to use DPL for this purpose. The front-end program on the OS/2 workstation can LINK to the mainframe program, passing parameters in the DFHCOMMAREA so that the mainframe program will know what data to extract. The mainframe program can obtain the data from the DB2 database using SQL commands, and return it to the workstation program in the DFHCOMMAREA. If security permits this, you can also update mainframe data from the workstation in similar fashion.

14.9.3 More about ASCII vs. EBCDIC

As we discussed earlier, CICS OS/2 provides EBCDIC to ASCII conversion in the CVT, though this requires some effort. CICS also provides macros on the mainframe side for converting the other way. Even with this conversion, applications might not function identically because ASCII and EBCDIC provide different **collating sequences**. On the mainframe, "1" is a hex F1 and "A" is a hex C1, so "1" is greater than "A". On the workstation, "1" is a hex 31 and "A" is a hex 41, so "1" is less than "A". The Micro Focus COBOL/2 compiler supports the directive NATIVE"EBCDIC", which ensures that COBOL internal SORTs and comparison statements (e.g. IF "1" IS LESS THAN "A") come out with the same results as on a mainframe. Since this directive does not change the sequence in which CICS VSAM files or SQL-based databases are indexed on the workstation, you can still expect EXEC CICS READNEXT and EXEC SQL SELECT...ORDER BY to return records in ASCII sequence.

14.10 SUMMARY

14.10.1 CICS OS/2 Application Development Steps

Here are the steps a typical mainframe programmer would go through to get a CICS application up and running on a CICS OS/2 workstation:

1. Transfer down from mainframe or create CICS COBOL source programs and any associated copy files.
2. Transfer down from the mainframe or create BMS map definition macros for each map set.
3. Transfer down or create test data files and/or SQL-based databases. Template definitions may be needed for EBCDIC to ASCII conversion if files are coming from a mainframe.
4. Assemble BMS maps through CICSMAP facility, being sure to create symbolic maps to copy into your program(s).

5. Check/Compile/Link your program(s), depending on whether the standalone COBOL/2 compiler or the Workbench is being used for a development facility. If the CICS OS/2 option from Micro Focus is being used, this will appear as a single step on the Workbench menu. If not, the IBM-supplied CICSTRAN translator step must be run before compilation.

6. Start up CICS OS/2.

7. Add the appropriate table entries to the PCT, FCT, and other CICS tables.

8. Bounce CICS OS/2 down and back up to get these table updates to take effect.

9. Run your transaction under CICS, using either a regular terminal session or one defined with the Animator debugging option.

TEST YOUR UNDERSTANDING

Questions and Exercises

1. List the steps involved in making the logical terminal display window V123 come up with different colors in the text. (Hint: look at both WSU and TCT.)

2. If you have access to a CICS OS/2 system on which you can run sample programs, define the CUSTMST file as it is defined here in the FCT, and then define an alternate index by customer name against the CUSTMST file. (In this case, the base file name would be the name of the CUSTMST file.) The alternate index is a separate entry in the FCT. You can get at the **Add** function by moving your cursor to the action bar. Try out the **F1** key to see the help screens that accompany the FCT.

3. Change the definition of LMSG to "local and intrapartition [L]" in its DCT entry. Provide a trigger level, transaction code, and terminal ID. For the terminal ID, use a 3287-type printer terminal which is already defined in the TCT, such as P234. Define the new transaction code and program name in a PCT entry. Then, write a program that sends the contents of each LMSG queue item to the printer terminal as a printed line. If you aren't sure what to do, look back at the discussion of printing under CICS in a previous chapter. Be sure to check for end of data.

15

SQL-Based Databases

This chapter will discuss the use of databases based on SQL (Structured Query Language) within CICS applications. It will present the basic elements of SQL syntax, along with some background on relational database concepts and database design. An exhaustive treatment of the theory and practice of relational database management using SQL-based databases would require many books. This chapter will concentrate on what a CICS application programmer will need in order to get started. Since so many vendors offer SQL-based database management systems, it is beyond the scope of this book to explore the differences between them. Examples in this chapter use the IBM OS/2 EE Database Manager. See vendor literature for specific information about other implementations of SQL-based database management systems. If you are specifically interested in DB2, which is the IBM mainframe implementation, you can find more information in *A Guide to DB2*, by Christopher Date (Addison-Wesley).

15.1 SQL CONCEPTS

15.1.1 Relational Database

What Is a Database? **A database is an organized collection of data which can be accessed and updated in a variety of ways.** A database can be small or large. Even the customer file and line item file in our sample programs can be regarded as a simple database. If you use a bookkeeping system, the set of entries you make in that system can be considered a database. Your telephone directory which you receive from the telephone company was printed out from a database which they maintain. The census forms which you fill out every ten years go into a database.

What Is the Relationship between the Database and the Database Management System? The database management system is not the same as the database itself. People sometimes use the terms interchangeably, but that is incorrect. **A database management system, or DBMS, is an automated system which makes it easier for you to manage your database.** In other words, it helps you to retrieve and update information and to reorganize the database. If you don't have a database management system, you will manage your database with routines in your own applications programs or with manual procedures.

You can think of a DBMS as being like a filing cabinet with various drawers and folders. The database itself is your own information which you store in that filing cabinet. In this chapter, the DBMS used for the sample programs will be the OS/2 Extended Edition Database Manager. The actual information will go into a database which is set up under the control of OS/2 EE Database Manager. Let's look at what a DBMS lets you do:

- A DBMS lets you define what data you will keep in your databases.
- It lets you add, change, and delete data in each database.
- It lets you retrieve selected data to show on screens or reports.
- It lets you link your data together. For example, if you have a customer file and an invoice file, you can associate each customer with the invoices belonging to him or her.
- It provides security and data integrity.
- On a multiuser system, it provides for concurrent access to data without interference between users.

What is a Relational Database Management System? A relational database management system is a DBMS which lets you see all of your data in the form of **tables** or **relations**. A table consists of **columns**, which you can think of as field definitions, and **rows**, which you can think of as data records containing those fields. Each row may be uniquely identified by a **primary key**, which is defined as a column or combination of columns that must be different for each row in the table. No two rows can have the same primary key. **Relational operators** are used to select rows from one or more tables based on their primary keys or on any other combination of selection criteria. (Within SQL, relational operators are implemented as various forms of the SELECT statement.) The **database** is a collection of tables that can be related to one another in a flexible manner. If the physical implementation of the DBMS uses any pointers or navigation links, these are hidden from the user. In fact, the relational model does not specify anything about how the data is stored on disk, which in fact is machine-dependent. It only specifies how the data will look when the DBMS returns it to the applications program or to the end user. The relational model is independent of the hardware platforms used to implement it.

Older forms of DBMS on many hardware platforms were built on the hierarchical model (such as IBM's IMS/DB or DL/I), or on the network model (such as Hewlett-Packard's TurboImage). These database models worked well in providing for data integrity and fast, efficient access, but lacked the flexibility needed for ad hoc queries. Application program logic was dependent on the physical layout of the database. This led to the development of the relational model. Its developers, Edgar F. Codd and Christopher Date, have written many books and articles covering the theoretical underpinnings of the relational model and the SQL-based implementations of that model.

What Is SQL?   SQL is a language for defining and manipulating relational databases. ANSI standards exist for SQL as they do for COBOL. SQL is not a complete programming language in itself, in that it handles only the database portion of the task. SQL commands are embedded within programs written in other languages such as COBOL, because SQL does not handle program logic, data communications, reports, or screens. EXEC SQL commands are similar to EXEC CICS commands in that regard.

SQL-based DBMSs are available from many vendors on many hardware platforms. For example, IBM provides DB2 and SQL/DS on mainframe systems and the OS/2 Extended Edition Database Manager on microcomputers. According to Codd and Date, no commercially available DBMS satisfies all of the rules of the relational model. However, SQL-based DBMSs provide many of the desired features.

Advantages Of SQL   Howard E. Hinman of Micro Focus, Inc. describes the advantages of SQL over traditional methods in this way:

"Traditionally, applications designed using a nonrelational DBMS or flat data files, are heavily constrained by the fact that relatively few data fields within a "record" (e.g. NAME, SSN, EMPLOYEE-NUMBER) may be designated as "keyed" fields. That is, data may be retrieved conditionally depending on specific values within these keyed fields, or even by combinations of values in different keyed fields. This constraint leads to the infamous problem in which customers call in who do not have their account numbers (the primary key, for example), but the operator is not given the ability to select a record by NAME instead of ACCOUNT-NUMBER because NAME is not a keyed field. Although most indexed file

systems and DBMSs offer the capability to designate ALTERNATE or SECONDARY key fields, the overhead penalty in performance and in disk space utilization is significant enough to limit this severely.

"In a relational data base using an SQL front end, ANY field may be treated as a key, so an application can offer the capability to make queries such as:

"SELECT all customers who are within the 415 area code, whose last name is SMITH, and who purchased CASSETTE TAPES during 1985.

"The power offered by this capability is sometimes very difficult for users to grasp when designing applications. In my opinion, it is the single most important feature of relational technology."

15.1.2 Data Definition and Data Manipulation

The relational model provides for two categories of commands. The first category makes up the **data definition language (DDL)**. DDL is used to define all of the objects that exist in the database environment. In other words, DDL deals exclusively with the form of the databases and not with their contents. DDL lets you create, alter, or drop databases, tables, indexes, and views. It lets you grant or revoke access privileges. A relational DBMS keeps all of its definitions for databases, tables, keys, indexes, views, and other objects in separate tables set aside for that purpose. Even though these tables are much like any other relational tables in the system, only the DDL commands are allowed to update their contents. A subcategory within DDL is the **data control language (DCL)**. The DCL is the security or authorization scheme which allows the administrator to restrict access to database resources.

In SQL, DDL is implemented as EXEC SQL commands that are embedded within applications programs or used interactively in the same manner as other SQL commands. Data definition in older, nonrelational database management or file handling systems such as IMS/DB or VSAM, by contrast, is done with separate batch utility programs.

The second category of commands makes up the **data manipulation language (DML)**. DML deals exclusively with database contents. It is used to select (retrieve), insert, update, or delete rows in existing tables. Under CICS, DML commands are embedded within programs in somewhat the same way as are CICS file control commands. You can use DML commands to display or report on the contents of the system definition tables set up by DDL commands.

15.1.3 Definition of SQL Terminology

In the first two sections of this chapter, we defined some terminology that applies to relational database systems in general. However, some terminology applies specifically to SQL- based implementations of the relational model.

The **SQL preprocessor** is somewhat like the CICS command translator, in that it comments out EXEC SQL commands and replaces them with calls to the appropriate interface routines. Depending on the implementation, the SQL preprocessor can be called from within the COBOL compiler step (if you use Micro Focus COBOL) or run as a separate step between the CICS command translator and COBOL compiler steps (if you use the preprocessor included with IBM's OS/2 EE).

An SQL preprocessor step is needed whenever hard-coded SQL commands are embedded in compiled programs. This is known as **static SQL**. On the other hand, interactive entry of SQL commands through a system such as OS/2 EE Query Manager or mainframe QMF is called **dynamic SQL**. These SQL commands are handled by the DBMS at run time. Applications programs can submit dynamic SQL commands also, for situations in which the desired processing is not known ahead of time. Using dynamic SQL from within a program offers greater flexibility at the cost of significantly slower performance.

Host variables are names of working storage or linkage section data areas within your program that you can reference in SQL statements. For instance, if you select rows from a table, you will move them into host variables in order to work with them in your COBOL program.

An **access plan** forms the relationship between a compiled application program and the database. Given a source file containing static SQL commands, and given a database containing certain tables, keys, and indexes, the access plan indicates the most efficient way to navigate through the database. The access plan is created by a **bind utility** which is provided as part of the DBMS. The design philosophy here is to isolate the applications programs from the database definition, so that the database definition can be changed without having to rewrite applications logic. The applications programmer will not need to know how to navigate through the database. The bind utility chooses the best navigation path, using its knowledge about keys, indexes, and database statistics.

On a mainframe, the plan is created by a bind procedure which is run after the compilation step. With OS/2 EE, a plan is created by the BIND function of the database manager, invoked by the precompiler services facility. The plan is stored in the database. However, you also have the option of creating a separate bind file which can be used to run the bind operation as a separate process later on. Suppose you have a test database and a production database, which are separate databases defined the same way. During testing, binding would take place against the test database. When you are finished testing, you can run the bind operation against the production database.

If you change the SQL commands within a program, it's obvious that you would need a new access plan. However, an access plan will also become invalidated if you change the definition of the database, for instance if you add or drop an index. In either case, the access plan no longer reflects the correct way to access the database on behalf of that program. At run time, the DBMS will force a rebinding of an invalidated access plan.

In the OS/2 EE database manager, access plans are stored in the database itself. If you happen to delete your test database and create it anew, you will have to put all of your access plans back into the new database, either by accessing the BIND function from the SQL precompiler or by rerunning a separate bind utility for each application program.

A **view** is, in effect, a "logical table" which provides a filter through which a user or application will see only the data it needs. A **base table** is the actual table over which the view is defined. When you create a view, the view definition is stored in the database, but no copying of the data contents takes place.

An **index** allows random access into a table by whatever key you choose to define, in ascending or descending order. SQL indexes are different from the alternate indexes that can be defined against a VSAM file, because SQL indexes are transparent to the application programmer. A program containing SQL commands will retrieve the same records without regard to the presence or absence of an index along the desired selection path. The program may run faster if the index is present, but application program logic will be the same either way. If no index is available, a sequential search will be used instead. The bind process will take into account any indexes that would be helpful in carrying out any SQL statements in the program.

The index key can consist of one or more columns, and can be defined as a unique key. In that case, the DBMS will prevent duplicate key values from being entered. The DBMS automatically creates a unique index for the primary key. Once created, an index is updated automatically by the DBMS. Indexes can make inquiry functions work faster, at the expense of some overhead at update time.

System catalogs are tables maintained by the DBMS which contain information describing each database. A separate set of system catalogs is built for each database when that database is defined with the OS/2 EE Query Manager or in a program which contains the OS/2 EE SQLGCRED (CREATE DATABASE) call. If you drop, or erase, a database using Query Manager or the SQLGDRPD (DROP DATABASE) call, the Database Manager will also delete the system catalogs associated with it. System catalog contents are modified by SQL data definition language commands. No attempt should be made to modify those or any other tables other than through commands and utilities provided by the DBMS.

Objects within a database can be grouped by prefixes known as **qualifiers.** System catalogs in the OS/2 EE database manager are given a qualifier of SYSIBM. SQL SELECT commands using that qualifier can be used to retrieve and display the contents of the system catalogs. Details about system catalog contents, and examples of the use of SELECT commands for this purpose, are presented in the *IBM OS/2 Extended Edition Database Manager Administrator's Guide.*

The *recovery log* is maintained automatically by the DBMS. It is somewhat like the CICS dynamic log in that it is used for backing out incomplete transactions in the event of a failure.

15.1.4 Database Design Principles

This section will introduce you to some basic concepts that will help you to organize and understand your data. You'll learn useful ways of looking at your data. Instead of seeing a confused mass of detail, you will see the relationships and patterns that exist. Database design is hardware and software independent. Once it's done, you can use a relational DBMS such as DB2 or the OS/2 EE Database Manager to implement those relationships on your machine. But the same database design principles apply even if you are using VSAM files and application code to manage your data.

You might ask, "Why can't I just jump in and write programs?" The more thoroughly you understand your data, the easier it will be to design good applications. If you try to design your databases by trial and error as you go along, you may find that your programs may need to be redesigned because they rely on a poor understanding of your data. Your user interface design, and the flow of logic from one program to another, should reflect an understanding of the meaning and structure of your organization's data.

Sometimes an experienced programmer chooses to bend the rules for one reason or another. I'm not enough of a purist to say that this is always wrong. However, it's important to know and understand the rules before making the decision to bend them.

Determine Your Data Requirements by Working Backward from the Output Requirements. Your database should contain whatever data is needed to produce the output which your system requires. Think of your new application as a miniature factory. Look at the products and services you want it to produce, which will be reports and screens. Then, look at the "raw materials" (in this case, data) and processing steps required to produce those results. For a billing system, for example, the output may include such things as inquiry screens, invoices, and journal entries for the general ledger. List the data that makes up those reports and screens. Obviously, the input data coming into the system will look different from the data on the reports, because calculations such as price extensions take place.

Don't Gather or Retain Data Unless You Have a Definite Use in Mind For It. If you accumulate data no one actually uses, that data will become misleading and inaccurate. It will waste processing time and disk space, and it will weaken the credibility of your application. In other words, people won't trust your system if they find bad data in part of it.

Decide How Long You Need to Keep Detailed Data on Your Computer.

If you are afraid to delete anything, remember that it costs money to keep old data around. You will need a bigger disk drive, a faster processor, and more time. How often will anyone need to look at that detailed data? At the end of the year, you may want to copy last year's historical data to an archive file which you can lock in a safe place. Then, you can delete the old rows from your active database. Even most archive files can be thrown away after seven years.

Archiving old data isn't quite the same as backing up current data. You make backup copies of current data that you still want to keep available on your disk, in case the original is damaged. You archive old data that you no longer want to keep on disk, in order to free some space. The archive contains only the old data. If you need this feature, design your application to make it convenient to identify the inactive data that should be archived. Some old data should be archived, some can be kept in summary form only, and some old data should be discarded.

How Many Times Does Each Piece of Data Occur?   Ask yourself this question for each type of data. The answers provide valuable information for database design and for projecting disk capacity needs. For example, for a billing system, you will have only one customer table row for each customer, although its contents can change with time. However, you will have an invoice line item each time a customer purchases one or more units of a particular item. This means that you will have a one-to-many relationship between customers and line item rows. The two types of information definitely need to be in separate tables. For those who diagram these relationships, a double-headed arrow indicates the side of the relationship having many occurrences:

```
CUSTOMER <-->> LINE ITEM
```

On the other hand, if you keep a comment for each customer in a comment row, so that you have only one comment row for each customer table row, those two tables will have a one-to-one relationship. In this case, you could keep both in the same table, but you might want to keep them separate for performance reasons if you seldom use the comment information.

```
CUSTOMER <--> COMMENT
```

Two tables can also have a many-to-many relationship. For instance, a customer can purchase many products, and a product can be purchased by many customers.

```
PGMCODE LAST = CUSTOMER <<-->> PRODUCT
```

No Shortcuts!   It sometimes seems easier to take shortcuts when defining your databases, but you pay for it later. Some people are tempted to crowd too much information into one table because they plan to show all of it on the same report. (People who work with big spreadsheets may acquire this habit because they don't realize that a database system gives them better alternatives.) But it's not easier in the long run. If other types of reports are needed later, using one big table does not provide the flexibility you need to get those other reports easily.

Never Crowd Several Pieces of Data under One Column Name.   Give each piece of data its own column name. Programmers who have worked with old systems such as dBASE II, which limits the number of data names for each file, sometimes acquire the untidy habit of squeezing several different pieces of information into one column in order to save the use of a data name. This is a bad idea in modern database management systems. It just makes it awkward to get at the data. For instance, don't crowd city, state, and ZIP into one column. What if sometimes you'll want to report by state, and sometimes by ZIP code? Stringing the data together means you'll have to break it apart for searching and reporting.

Each Table Should Have a Primary Key.   Each row should have a column or group of columns whose contents distinguishes that row from all others. Each table should describe a single entity, and the primary key should uniquely identify that entity. An entity can be something like a customer, an employee, a department, a product, or a check. For a primary key column, assign an identifier that won't change once entered, such as a customer number, an employee number, a department number, a product code, or a check number. People's names are bad choices for primary keys, because names can change and because two people can have the same name.

Foreign Keys Relate One Table to Another.   A row in one table can contain a key which points to another table, so that you can relate your tables to one another. For instance, you can place the customer number in the line item table so that you can refer back to the data for that customer. The customer number is called a **foreign key**. Foreign keys are an exception to the general warning not to keep the same column in more than one table, because it's necessary to have a means to relate tables to one another.

Normalizing Your Database.   When you set up your tables, how do you know which columns belong in which tables? Making the right decisions saves disk space and gives you more flexibility. The process of organizing tables to meet certain principles of relational database design is called **normalizing a database.**

Avoid Repeating Buckets Within a Row.

When you design a table, you might be tempted to put repeating buckets in each row for recurring data. Suppose you set up twelve buckets in a general ledger row for monthly totals, using the account code as the key. "After all," you say, "we never have more than twelve months in a year, right?" Right. But what if the company begins using thirteen four-week accounting periods, or what if the company wants to maintain last year's data too? Not only that, if some accounts have activity only one month out of the year, you waste disk space. And the program logic isn't THAT much easier this way.

In most instances, it's advisable to eliminate the buckets by creating separate rows. In the general ledger example, each total would occupy a separate row in a table keyed on account code/year/accounting period. If no repeating data exists in a table, the table is considered to be in **first normal form.**

Check Dependencies Among Columns.

Examine each non-key column in each table. Does it depend on the primary key value for that table? If not, that column belongs in some other table. For example, in a payroll system, it would be a bad idea to keep the pay rate in the department table. This would force the pay rate to depend on the department number key, which is illogical. You might say, "Right now, every employee in a department is paid the same rate." Don't rely on a coincidence. That situation is bound to change, leaving you with the need to change your database and application logic. In this example, if the pay rate is negotiated separately for each employee, it belongs in the employee table. If it depends on a job class code, then the job class code should be in the employee table, and a separate table should be used to maintain job class codes and their associated pay rates and descriptions.

Each Non-key Column in a Table Should Depend on the *Entire* Primary Key for that Table.

Going back to the general ledger example, if account totals are kept in a table whose primary key is account code/year/accounting period, the account description should not be in that table because the account description depends only on the account code, not on the entire key. Instead, the account description should be in another table keyed only on the account code, so that you can look up the descriptions by account code whenever you need them. If every non-key column in a table depends on the entire primary key, then the table is considered to be in **second normal form.**

Non-key Columns Should Not Depend on Other Non-Key Columns in the Same Table.   What does this mean? In the payroll example we discussed earlier, the employee table is keyed on employee number. Suppose the employee table also contains a job class code, which is a non-key column. The employee table should not also contain the job class description, because the job class description depends on a non-key field—the job class code. In this case, the job class description belongs in a table keyed on job class code. If each non-key column in a table depends only on the primary key, then the table is considered to be in **third normal form.**

In our sample programs, you might wonder why the unit price is kept in the line item record. After all, doesn't the unit price depend solely on the product number? Not in a historical record, which is what a line item record actually is. The unit price could have changed since the purchase was made. We don't want the current unit price, we want the unit price that we actually charged that customer at the time the purchase was made.

Choose Column Names That Make Sense.   Some   common-sounding names, such as DATE, are reserved words in COBOL, SQL, or both. This means that they could make COBOL or SQL work improperly if used for anything other than their intended purposes. A list of SQL reserved words appears in an appendix to the *IBM OS/2 Extended Edition Database Manager Administrator's Guide*. In any case, to name a column something like DATE would not be descriptive enough. For example, in an employee table row, you will need to specify birth-date, hire-date, term-date, and so forth.

You can use the same name for columns in two different tables, but only if the column has the same meaning in both places. Otherwise, you will mislead people. The fact that the names match should mean that the columns can be used for matching the two database files. For example, the customer number in the customer table should refer to the same entity as the customer number in the line item table, so that you can match the two tables.

Keeping Tables in Synch.   Your key columns should all contain valid information which you can use to retrieve and match rows. **Don't let rows get into your tables without valid data in all required identifier columns.** For example, in a payroll system, each paycheck history row should contain a valid check number, a valid employee ID, and a valid pay date. Why? Because you might need all of those columns later on to retrieve rows. If a row contains a blank employee ID, you won't know for whom that check was written. If the check number or check date is blank, did that mean a bad paycheck was written? SQL-based database management systems provide some features which you can use to enforce data integrity in this regard.

Since your tables relate to one another (I hope), you will want to make sure that good data exists on both sides of the relationship. Making sure that table contents refer to one another properly is known as **enforcing referential integrity.** For example, when an employee quits, you will want to prevent anyone from deleting the employee master row as long as any paycheck history rows are still on file for that employee ID. Otherwise, you will have paycheck rows floating around and you won't know whose they are. The OS/2 EE Database Manager allows you to set up **constraints** when you define your tables, which indicate what should happen when rows in a table that refers to another table are deleted.

15.2   OS/2 EXTENDED EDITION DATABASE MANAGER

15.2.1   Where Database Manager Keeps Its Data

The OS/2 Extended Edition Database Manager keeps all of its objects as files in directories within the OS/2 file system. Those files and directories should never be manipulated by anything other than the Database Manager itself. Even backups should be taken with Database Manager commands.

The Database Manager creates one **system database directory** for each workstation, on the disk drive where Database Services is installed. A database is not available to Database Manager unless it is catalogued in the system directory. When you create a database on your workstation, it is catalogued there automatically. (Databases on remote workstations must be catalogued with a CATALOG DATABASE command.)

The Database Manager also creates a **volume database directory** on each volume which contains a database. For example, suppose you have a large hard disk with various partitions set up as logical drives. If you install Database Services on the C: drive, the system database catalog will be on the C: drive also. Then, if you create one or more databases on the D: drive, Database Manager will create a volume database directory on the D: drive.

The Database Services utilities and run-time modules are kept in an OS/2 directory called \SQLLIB on the disk drive on which it was installed. Other Database Manager objects, including your actual data, are kept in OS/2 directories called \SQL00001, \SQL00002, and so forth. Each time you create a database, a consecutively-named OS/2 directory will be created under the root directory of the appropriate drive. When you use Database Manager to drop a database, it can reuse the same directory name later. Within those directories, Database Manager creates files labeled SQL00001, SQL00002, and so forth, with various different file name extensions depending on the contents. Never use OS/2 commands or any other utilities to delete, rename, copy, or move those directories or their contents. Never create any of your own OS/2 directories or file names using the letters "SQL" followed by numerals.

At installation time, Database Manager provides a **Database Manager configuration file** containing performance and tuning parameters that affect all databases on that workstation. When a database is created, it provides a **Database Configuration File** containing paramaters that affect that database only. These are initialized with default values, but can be changed by a user having system administrator capabilities.

15.2.2 Installation and Setup

The same programs which you use to install or reconfigure OS/2 Extended Edition are used to install the Database Manager. The installation program comes up the first time you boot your system from the installation diskette. If you have already installed the base system, type REINST at the OS/2 command prompt and let it prompt you for diskettes. In either case, you select features you want to install from a menu. The installation process is described in the *IBM Operating System/2 Extended Edition, Getting Started* manual packaged with OS/2 EE. For a standalone workstation, you'll need the OS/2 Base Operating System and Database Services (Standalone). For a workstation on a network, you'll need the OS/2 Base Operating System, Communications Manager, and Database Services (Server, Requestor, or Server/Requestor modules, depending on where you are keeping the actual databases). In all cases, if you have the disk space and memory, you will probably also want to install the Query Manager. The installation procedure will automatically create an entry for Query Manager in your OS/2 Desktop Manager, for convenience in starting it up.

You will need to set your swap path in CONFIG.SYS to point to a drive and directory with plenty of free space, preferably 10 mb or more. OS/2 creates a file called SWAPPER.DAT to hold whatever won't fit in actual memory. The format of the CONFIG.SYS parm is as follows:

```
SWAPPATH=D:\
```

where D: is the drive. You can define the swap file under the root directory or elsewhere. Database Manager and particularly Query Manager are big users of memory and disk space. Both will run slowly or not at all if provided with too little elbow room. If Query Manager will not come up, check available disk space on your SWAPPATH drive. Also, you should have at least 8 megabytes of system memory to run CICS OS/2 with Database Manager. OS/2 can trash files if you try to run it without enough memory.

15.2.3 What Query Manager Can Do

Query Manager is an environment running under OS/2 that lets you perform SQL functions interactively against any databases that can be accessed on your machine. You can enter SQL commands in a window in a format similar to what would be used in program source code, run those commands, and see the results. Alternatively, you can use the mouse to navigate through various selection menus in order to build query and update commands without knowing SQL. Query Manager will even convert your stored menu selections into SQL commands if you choose. Tutorials for learning to use Query Manager, including a sample database, are included with the books and software supplied with OS/2 EE, so we will not repeat that introduction here. You can use Query Manager interactively to process SQL commands that would ordinarily be embedded in an application program. Query Manager provides screen and report formatting to display your results in an attractive, readable format. You can also use it to perform system housekeeping functions such as importing and exporting data, making backups, running database statistics, and so forth.

15.2.4 Precompiler and Bind

In a previous section, we discussed the use of the SQL precompiler. Newer versions of the Micro Focus COBOL compiler invoke the SQL precompiler from within the COBOL compilation process. The SQL precompiler examines the database to verify that all data manipulation commands in your program refer correctly to objects in the database. If it does, compilation can proceed; otherwise, the SQL precompiler will produce syntax error diagnostics. If you are running the SQL precompiler as a preliminary step, the SQL precompiler will create a version of your source code in which the SQL commands have been translated into CALL statements. If you are running Micro Focus COBOL with built-in SQL support, you will not get a translated source file. This is because Micro Focus has, in effect, extended the COBOL language to include SQL, so that object code is produced directly from the untranslated source in one step. (Micro Focus chose the OS/2 EE Database Manager as the first implementation of SQL to be supported in this way.)

In either case, the SQL precompiler services facility will access the BIND function of the OS/2 EE database manager to create an access plan, which will be stored in your database. Depending on directives, it may also create a bind file which can be used for creating a new access plan if the database is changed.

Since the SQL precompiler needs to be able to access your database, Database Manager must be running. Starting the Query Manager utility will automatically start up Database Manager. You can also start up Database Manager by running the following command at the OS/2 prompt:

STARTDBM

Database Manager will keep running even after you shut down CICS or the Query Manager or terminate any programs that are using the databases.

cases, an OS/2 program development workstation will be used primarily by only one person, and that person will have authorization to be system administrator for that workstation. If sensitive data is being kept on the machine, you can set up one or more user IDs with passwords under OS/2 User Profile Management. This is provided with OS/2 and is available on the **User Profile Management Services** menu on the OS/2 Desktop Manager. Chapter 5 in the *IBM OS/2 EE Database Manager Administrator's Guide* provides details on how to go about setting up various IDs.

A user who has local administrator or administrator capabilities within User Profile Management will have system administrator capabilities within the Database Manager. At least one user must have these capabilities, so that databases can be set up. If you do not specify otherwise, one user ID with those capabilities will exist on the workstation as a default. Its user ID will be USERID and its password will be PASSWORD. This is the first thing anyone would type when attempting to guess a password. If you have sensitive data on your system, you had better replace this with something less obvious!

Once you have defined one or more user IDs, they become available within the Database Manager. Various levels of privileges exist. A user having system administrator (SYSADM) privileges can use EXEC SQL GRANT or EXEC SQL REVOKE commands to define privileges for other users. The system administrator can define databases and can affect the configuration of the system. A database administrator (DBADM), by contrast, has authority only over one specific database. Other users can be granted specific privileges which allow them to create tables and indexes, bind access plans, or access the data itself for update or read-only purposes. Here again, the *Administrator's Guide* provides details on access privileges. The Query Manager can also be used to grant and revoke privileges for a specific user and database.

The first time you bring up Query Manager or do anything else which accesses a database (such as using the SQL preprocessor), OS/2 will bring up a dialog box to prompt you for a user ID and password [Figure 15.1].

15.3 DATABASE DEFINITION

15.3.1 Defining a Database

In this context, we can think of a database as a collection of tables. There may be one or more such collections on a given workstation. Important differences exist between mainframes and OS/2 workstations in this regard.

Those familiar with DB2 on mainframes will be aware that table space has to be allocated on disk before any databases can be defined. Mainframes have large numbers of users and extensive needs for security, so it

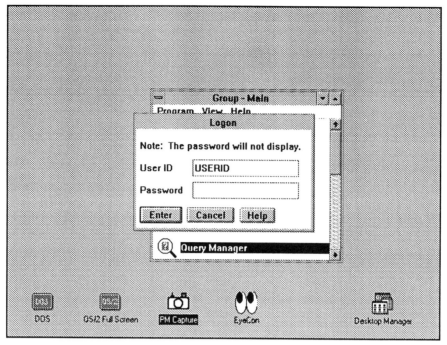

FIGURE 15.1   OS/2 dialog box for user ID and password.

makes sense to define separate databases to which different groups of users are allowed access. Under DB2, applications can use more than one database at a time, so that no real problems are created by splitting them up.

Under OS/2, on the other hand, file allocation is dynamic. You don't have to preallocate disk space with job control language before your program can write to an output file. There is no need to reserve a piece of unused disk space in case your program will need it later. OS/2 workstations have less disk space than mainframes, so OS/2 attempts to conserve that space. OS/2 dynamic file allocation eliminates the need to use SQL commands to create table space on your OS/2 workstation before defining a database, as you must do under mainframe DB2. The negative side is that an OS/2 program can attach itself to only one SQL database at a time. This means that you will need to keep all tables together that will be needed by any one application. On an OS/2 workstation, with few users, local database security is not the major concern it is on a mainframe. OS/2 programmers typically define only one database and keep all tables in it, for all applications being run on that workstation.

There is no EXEC SQL command to create a new database. There is a CALL to "__SQLGCRED" which can be used to create a database from within an application. This is described in the *OS/2 EE Database Manager Programming Reference.* However, since this is not something you need to

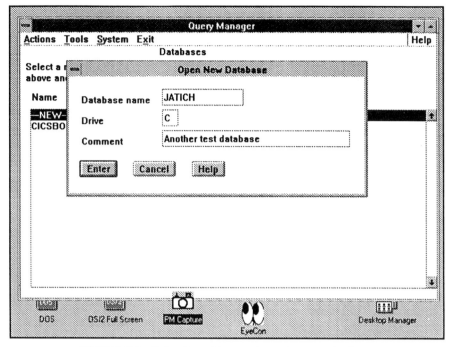

FIGURE 15.2   Using Query Manager to create a new database.

do very often, it is usually easiest to create the database interactively through Query Manager. Here's how it's done.

Using Query Manager to Create or Drop Databases.   On   the   Query Manager main menu, select the **- NEW- Open a new database** object, and select **Actions** from the action bar. From the pulldown menu, select **Open... F6**. You will be prompted for an eight-character database name, a disk drive letter, and a descriptive comment [Figure 15.2]. Supply that information and press the enter key. Query Manager will set up directory entries for your new database on the drive that you specify. It will then give you a selection menu which lets you create tables within that database. If you aren't ready to create tables immediately, or if you prefer to create your tables from within a program, you can keep selecting **Exit** from the action bar to get out of Query Manager. You can also erase a database from within Query Manager by selecting that database from the main menu and selecting **Erase... Shift+F8** from the **Actions** pulldown menu.

15.3.2   Defining Tables

This is the most important part of the data definition language. The EXEC SQL CREATE TABLE command lets you define a table with its column names and their associated data types. The available data types are the following:

OS/2 EE SQL Data Types

Column Type	Description	COBOL Data Definition
CHAR(n)	Fixed-length character string of up to 254 characters	01 dataname PIC X(n).
DATE	10-byte character string containing a date	01 dataname PIC X(10).
DECIMAL(m, n)	Packed decimal	01 dataname PIC S9(m)V9(n) COMP- 3.
INTEGER	Integer (32-bit signed)	01 dataname PIC S9(9) COMP-5.
LONG VARCHAR	Long variable-length character string of from 4001 to 32700 characters	01 dataname 05 fieldlength PIC S9(4) COMP-5. 05 fieldname PIC X(n).
SMALLINT	Small integer (16-bit signed)	01 dataname PIC S9(4) COMP-5.
TIME	8-byte character string containing a time	01 dataname PIC X(8).
TIMESTAMP	26-byte character string containing a system date and time stamp	01 dataname PIC X(26).
VARCHAR(n)	Variable-length character string of up to 4000 characters	01 dataname 05 fieldlength PIC S9(4) COMP-5. 05 fieldname PIC X(n).
Null indicator	Indicator accompanying nullable columns (anything other than NOT NULL)	01 dataname PIC S9(4) COMP-5.

The following CREATE TABLE command creates a table with five columns. The CUSTNO and ITEMCODE columns are fixed-length character format, the UNITPRICE and ORDERQTY columns are packed decimal, and the DATETIME column is a system date and time stamp. The primary key consists of CUSTNO, DATETIME, and ITEMCODE, which means that combination must be unique for each row in the table. CUSTNO is defined as a foreign key which associates this table with the CUSTOMER table. In other words, the customer numbers in the LINEITEM table will match those in the CUSTOMER table, so that one cannot delete the corresponding row from the CUSTOMER table while rows with that same customer number still exist here. This is what is meant by ON DELETE RESTRICT. I could have chosen instead to cascade deletes (which means to delete all associated LINEITEM rows if that CUSTOMER row is deleted) or to set the customer number to null.

```
EXEC SQL
      CREATE TABLE LINEITEM
           ( CUSTNO CHAR (6) NOT NULL,
             DATETIME TIMESTAMP NOT NULL,
             ITEMCODE CHAR (6) NOT NULL,
             UNITPRICE DECIMAL (7,2) NOT NULL,
             ORDERQTY DECIMAL (7,0) NOT NULL,
             PRIMARY KEY (CUSTNO, DATETIME, ITEMCODE),
             FOREIGN KEY FKEY1 (CUSTNO)
```

```
                    REFERENCES CUSTOMER ON DELETE RESTRICT
                )
    END-EXEC.
```

The COBOL data description for one of these rows is shown in the last section of this chapter.

Tables can be removed from the database with the EXEC SQL DROP TABLE command, as shown later in the sample program.

15.3.3 Defining Indexes

Additional indexes can be created against an existing table with the CREATE INDEX command. It looks like this:

```
EXEC SQL CREATE [UNIQUE] INDEX indexname
    ON tablename
    (columnname, columnname,...,columnname, ASC|DESC)
    END-EXEC.
```

ASC (ascending) is the default order. UNIQUE is optional, depending upon whether you want the DBMS to enforce no duplicate keys. Indexes can be used to make database access more efficient. If you frequently select rows from a table using that set of columns as a key, your retrievals will execute more rapidly with an index than without. However, updates against that table will take a bit longer, because indexes have to be updated too. The *OS/2 EE Database Manager Administrator's Guide* provides more information about performance monitoring and tuning.

15.3.4 Defining Views

The CREATE VIEW command lets you define views against existing tables. A view is, in effect, a subset of a **base table** which allows the user or application program to access only certain rows or columns of that table. Views are useful for enforcing security.

```
EXEC SQL CREATE VIEW viewname
    (columnname, columnname,....,columnname)
    AS selectclause
    [WITH CHECK OPTION]
    END-EXEC.
```

The select clause is a hard-coded select statement; in other words, one that contains no references to host variables or other parameters. For example, you can create a view named DEPT120 with a select clause WHERE DEPTNO = 120. WITH CHECK OPTION causes the DBMS to check all update attempts against the definition for that view. This would let the user of DEPT120 update rows for DEPTNO=120, but not other rows.

You can use a view name in an SQL command much as you would use a table name.

15.3.5 Sample "One-Time" Program to Create a Database

Sample program CREATE is shown in Figure 15.3. It is a batch SQL program compiled with the Micro Focus compiler, which puts two tables into our sample database. Since it is a batch program with no CICS commands, it does not need the CICS translator step before compilation. Note how the program checks the SQL response code in the SQLCA (SQL communications area) to determine whether the command succeeded. Batch programs of this type can be run from within the Micro Focus Workbench or from the OS/2 command prompt. (Under mainframe DB2, batch SQL programs are run under TSO.) You can use batch programs to handle housekeeping chores that don't require user interaction.

15.4 DATABASE MANIPULATION

15.4.1 SELECT Command (with a Unique Key)

The SELECT command is used to fetch rows from an SQL table. This command is extremely powerful, with many variations. Space permits only a few to be discussed in this chapter. In this section, we will look at the use of a SELECT statement to get one row from a table by means of a unique key. This is not exactly the same as the CICS commands that read a single record from a VSAM file, because the SELECT command lets you choose which columns you want to see, and because the WHERE clause allows you to search on any column or any combination of columns.

Host variables (your program's storage areas) are always preceded with a colon when used within an EXEC SQL command. Names *not* preceded with a colon are assumed to be column names or reserved words known to the Database Manager. Host variables used for retrieving column contents must be specified in the same order as the column names you use within the SQL command. For those columns that permit null values, the SELECT statement permits you to use an additional host variable to retrieve the null indicator, indicated in this example by the -NI suffix. If the null indicator contains a negative value, the column itself contains a null value and you should ignore its contents.

```
EXEC SQL SELECT
         columnname, columnname,....,columnname
         INTO hostvariable, hostvariable,....,hostvariable
         FROM tablename
         [WHERE selectclause]
```

```
$set ans85 mf noosvs
 IDENTIFICATION DIVISION.
 PROGRAM-ID.  CREATE.
 AUTHOR.  HOWARD E. HINMAN.
 ****************************************************
 * THE PROGRAM CREATES TWO NEW TABLES IN AN EXISTING *
 * OS/2 DATABASE MANAGER DATABASE.                   *
 ****************************************************
 ENVIRONMENT DIVISION.
 DATA DIVISION.
 WORKING-STORAGE SECTION.
 01   ERROR-MESSAGE          PIC X(72).
 01   SQLCODE-DISP           PIC S9(9).

      EXEC SQL
           INCLUDE SQLCA
           END-EXEC.

 PROCEDURE DIVISION.
 CREATE-TABLE-ROUTINE.
      EXEC SQL
           DROP TABLE CUSTOMER
      END-EXEC

      EXEC SQL
           DROP TABLE LINEITEM
      END-EXEC

      EXEC SQL
           CREATE TABLE CUSTOMER
                  ( CUSTNO CHAR (6) NOT NULL,
                    CUSTNAME CHAR(25) NOT NULL,
                    CONTACT CHAR (25) NOT NULL,
                    STREETADDR CHAR (25) NOT NULL,
                    CITY CHAR (20) NOT NULL,
                    STATE CHAR (2) NOT NULL,
                    ZIP CHAR (10) NOT NULL,
                    LASTBILLDATE DATE,
                    LASTBALDUE DECIMAL (7,2),
                    CURRWKSALES DECIMAL (7,2),
                    PRIMARY KEY (CUSTNO)
                  )
      END-EXEC

      IF SQLCODE NOT = ZEROES
          DISPLAY 'SQL ERROR CODE:'SQLCODE
      ELSE
          DISPLAY 'TABLE /CUSTOMER/ CREATED'.

      EXEC SQL
           CREATE TABLE LINEITEM
                  ( CUSTNO CHAR (6) NOT NULL,
                    DATETIME TIMESTAMP NOT NULL,
                    ITEMCODE CHAR (6) NOT NULL,
                    UNITPRICE DECIMAL (7,2) NOT NULL,
                    ORDERQTY DECIMAL (7,0) NOT NULL,
                    PRIMARY KEY (CUSTNO, DATETIME, ITEMCODE),
                    FOREIGN KEY FKEY1 (CUSTNO)
                    REFERENCES CUSTOMER ON DELETE RESTRICT
                  )
      END-EXEC

      IF SQLCODE NOT = ZEROES
          DISPLAY 'SQL ERROR CODE:'SQLCODE
      ELSE
          DISPLAY 'TABLE /LINEITEM/ CREATED'.
      STOP RUN.

 PROGRAM-TERMINATOR.
```

FIGURE 15.3   Sample program to create tables within a database.

```
            END-EXEC.
*
* A specific example of this would be:
*
    EXEC SQL SELECT
            CUSTNAME, CONTACT, STREETADDR,
            CITY, STATE, ZIP,
            LASTBILLDATE, LASTBALDUE, CURRWKSALES
            INTO :CUST-NAME, :CUST-CONTACT,
            :CUST-STREET-ADDRESS, :CUST-CITY,
            :CUST-STATE, :CUST-ZIP,
            :CUST-LAST-BILL-DATE:CUST-LAST-BILL-DATE-NI,
            :CUST-LAST-BILL-BAL-DUE:CUST-LAST-BILL-BAL- DUE-NI,
            :CUST-CURR-WK-SALES:CUST-CURR-WK-SALES-NI
            FROM CUSTOMER
            WHERE CUSTNO = :CUST-NO
            END-EXEC.
```

SQL provides a different way of looking at data than does COBOL. COBOL is designed to process one record at a time, while SQL can process any number of rows with one command, even an entire table or combination of tables. In fact, if you omit the WHERE clause, you get data from all of the rows in the table. This is no problem when you are entering SQL statements interactively through Query Manager. Under Query Manager, you would omit the INTO host variables, and send the entire result table to a screen or report, using as many pages as are needed. However, this is too much data for a COBOL program to handle at once, much like trying to drink water from a fire hose. In a COBOL program, you use a SELECT INTO statement with a WHERE clause or other techniques to force it to return no more than one row to your program at a time. In this particular case, we are using a WHERE clause that provides a selection on a unique key.

Substituting * (an asterisk) for the list of column names will cause all columns in the table to be selected. This comes in handy if you are entering SQL commands interactively through Query Manager, and you just want a quick look at the contents of your table.

15.4.2 INSERT Command

The INSERT command lets you put a new row into your table. Here again, you must match up the column names with the appropriate host variables for each column. You need to supply values for all columns that are NOT NULL, but not for nullable columns. If you omit a nullable column from the INSERT command, then the null indicator will be set to -1 to indicate that the value of the field is null.

Database Manager will not let you insert a row when the column values would violate its restrictions on unique keys. In other words, if CUSTNO is a unique key, you can't insert another row with the same value in CUSTNO as that of an existing row.

```
      EXEC SQL INSERT INTO tablename
             (columnname, columnname,...,columnname)
             VALUES (hostvariable, hostvariable,...,hostvariable)
             END-EXEC.
*
* A specific example of this would be:
*
      EXEC SQL INSERT INTO CUSTOMER
             (CUSTNO, CUSTNAME, CONTACT, STREETADDR,
             CITY, STATE, ZIP)
             VALUES (:CUST-NO, :CUST-NAME, :CUST- CONTACT,
             :CUST-STREET-ADDRESS, :CUST-CITY, :CUST- STATE,
             :CUST-ZIP)
             END-EXEC.
```

15.4.3 UPDATE Command

The UPDATE command lets you change values in an existing row or rows in your table. You can update whichever columns you want, without having to concern yourself with columns your program isn't using. Here again, Database Manager won't let you change values to something which would violate restrictions on unique keys. If the select clause is omitted, every row in the database will be updated.

```
      EXEC SQL UPDATE tablename
             SET columnname = hostvariable,
                 columnname = hostvariable,
                 ...,
                 columnname = hostvariable
             [WHERE selectclause]
             END-EXEC.
*
* A specific example of this would be:
*
      EXEC SQL UPDATE CUSTOMER
             SET CUSTNAME = :CUST-NAME,
                 CONTACT = :CUST-CONTACT,
                 STREETADDR = :CUST-STREET-ADDRESS,
                 CITY = :CUST-CITY,
                 STATE = :CUST-STATE,
                 ZIP = :CUST-ZIP
             WHERE CUSTNO = :CUST-NO
             END-EXEC.
```

15.4.4 DELETE Command

The DELETE command lets you delete any or all rows from a table, subject to foreign key deletion constraints as discussed above. In other words, you can't delete a row if there is a row in some other table that depends on it, and that other table carries a foreign key with a deletion constraint that refers to your table. If you omit the select clause, you will delete all rows from your table. This is useful if you want to clear out a table's contents but leave the table definition in the database. Before doing a delete with a WHERE clause, you may want to use that same WHERE clause in a SELECT statement to see which rows satisfy that condition before you delete them.

```
      EXEC SQL DELETE
          FROM tablename
          [WHERE selectclause]
          END-EXEC.
*
* A specific example of this would be:
*
      EXEC SQL DELETE
          FROM CUSTOMER
          WHERE CUSTNO = :CUST-NO
          END-EXEC.
```

15.4.5   SELECTing for More than One Record: CURSOR

A SELECT statement with a CURSOR is used when you wish to extract many rows at once, put them into the desired order, and return them to your program one by one. The initial SELECT is embedded within a DECLARE CURSOR statement, which in effect creates a work table from which you will be retrieving later. Then, you open that cursor, FETCH the records one by one into host variables, and close the cursor when you are finished. The FOR UPDATE OF clause is used if you plan to update retrieved column values later.

```
*
      EXEC SQL DECLARE cursorname CURSOR FOR
          SELECT selectclause
          [FOR UPDATE OF columnname,...,columnname]
          [ORDER BY key(s) ASC|DESC]
          END-EXEC.
*
      EXEC SQL OPEN cursorname END-EXEC.
*
* Put the FETCH statement in a loop and execute it
* repeatedly, processing records until SQLCODE is
* no longer zero:
*
      EXEC SQL FETCH cursorname
          INTO hostvariable,....,hostvariable
          END-EXEC.
*
      EXEC SQL CLOSE cursorname END-EXEC.
```

```
*
* A specific example of DECLARE CURSOR and FETCH:
*
    EXEC SQL DECLARE FWBROWSE CURSOR FOR
        SELECT
        CUSTNO, CUSTNAME
        FROM CUSTOMER
        WHERE NOT CUSTNO   :WS-CUSTNO-KEY
        ORDER BY CUSTNO ASC
        END-EXEC.
*
    EXEC SQL FETCH FWBROWSE
        INTO :CUST-NO, :CUST-NAME
        END-EXEC
```

Note that the ORDER BY clause governs the order in which the se-lected rows will be returned to your program. The OS/2 EE Database Manager will use indexes or sort operations as needed to get the se-lected rows into the desired sequence. OS/2 EE Database Manager will not necessarily provide the same retrieval sequence as would mainframe DB2, because of the difference between ASCII and EBCDIC collating se-quences.

15.4.6 More Complex SELECTs

We have only scratched the surface of SELECT statements in this chapter. There are many other things you can do with them. For example, you can nest another selection clause inside the WHERE clause of a SELECT statement, so that you can look for rows in one table that match a key built from the results of a retrieval from another table. This is called a **subquery**. You can also **join** two or more tables in a SELECT statement, so that your result table rows will contain data from both. In that case, you **qualify** the column names by prefixing them with the table names:

```
* EXAMPLE OF A JOIN:
    EXEC SQL SELECT TABLE1.COLUMN1, TABLE2.COLUMN2
        FROM TABLE1, TABLE2
        WHERE TABLE1.COLUMN3 = TABLE2.COLUMN3
        END-EXEC.
```

Another powerful feature of SQL are the aggregate operations or built-in functions. COUNT, SUM, AVG, MAX, and MIN create row counts, sums, averages, minimums, and maximums for column values across an entire table or a selected subset of that table. SQL provides a GROUP BY clause to designate control breaks based on a column or group of columns. The optional HAVING clause may be used with GROUP BY in order to select information only for those groups of rows for which a certain condition is true. HAVING is analogous to a WHERE clause for groups.

This SQL command sums up the total item count ordered by each customer:

```
EXEC SQL SELECT CUSTNO, SUM(ORDERQTY)
        FROM LINEITEM
        GROUP BY CUSTNO
END-EXEC.
```

15.4.7 Sample Programs

The following programs [Figures 15.4-15.10] are similar to those presented earlier in the book, except for the fact that they get their data from Database Manager tables rather than from VSAM files. Slightly different program logic is used in the two browse programs, because SQL contains no specific implementation of "read previous/read next" as does VSAM. See program comments for more information.

To use these programs, you will need to create the test database as described above. You will also need to change the definition of the LMSG TD queue to use variable length records with maximum length 64, as described in section 14.6 in the previous chapter (CICS tables).

The following copy library members are used in the sample programs:

```
* CUSTOMER.CBL
*******************************************************
* HOST VARIABLES FOR SQL-BASED CUSTOMER TABLE.       *
*******************************************************
  01   CUSTMST-REC.
       05   CUST-NO                   PIC X(6).
       05   CUST-NAME                 PIC X(25).
       05   CUST-CONTACT              PIC X(25).
       05   CUST-STREET-ADDRESS       PIC X(25).
       05   CUST-CITY                 PIC X(20).
       05   CUST-STATE                PIC XX.
       05   CUST-ZIP                  PIC X(10).
       05   CUST-LAST-BILL-DATE       PIC X(10).
       05   CUST-LAST-BILL-DATE-NI    PIC S9(4) COMP.
       05   CUST-LAST-BILL-BAL-DUE    PIC S9(7)V99 COMP-3.
       05   CUST-LAST-BILL-BAL-DUE-NI
                                      PIC S9(4) COMP.
       05   CUST-CURR-WK-SALES        PIC S9(7)V99 COMP-3.
       05   CUST-CURR-WK-SALES-NI     PIC S9(4) COMP.
*
* LINEITEM.CBL
*******************************************************
* HOST VARIABLES FOR SQL-BASED LINE ITEM TABLE.      *
*******************************************************
  01   LINEITM-REC.
       05   ITEM-UNIQUE-KEY.
            10   ITEM-CUST-NO         PIC X(6).
            10   ITEM-DATE-TIME       PIC X(26).
            10   ITEM-CODE            PIC X(6).
```

```
       05  ITEM-UNIT-PRICE          PIC S9(7)V99 COMP-3.
       05  ITEM-QUANTITY            PIC S9(6) COMP-3.
*
* CUSTCOMM.CBL
************************************************************
* CICS COMMAREA FOR SQL-BASED SAMPLE PROGRAMS          *
************************************************************
  01  WS-COMMAREA.
       05  WS-COMM-PREV-MAP         PIC X(8) VALUE SPACES.
       05  WS-COMM-OBJECT           PIC X(8) VALUE SPACES.
       05  WS-COMM-ACTION           PIC X(8) VALUE SPACES.
       05  WS-COMM-KEY.
           10  WS-COMM-CUST-NO      PIC X(6).
           10  WS-COMM-DATETIME     PIC X(26).
           10  WS-COMM-ITEM-CODE    PIC X(6).
       05  WS-COMM-NEXT-KEY.
           10  WS-COMM-NEXT-CUST-NO
                                    PIC X(6).
           10  WS-COMM-NEXT-DATETIME
                                    PIC X(26).
           10  WS-COMM-NEXT-ITEM-CODE
                                    PIC X(6).
       05  WS-COMM-COUNTER          PIC S9(8) COMP VALUE +0.
       *
  01  WS-EXPECTED-EIBCALEN          PIC S9(4) COMP VALUE +104.
*
* SQLCA
  01  sqlca.
       03  sqlcaid         pic x(8).
       03  sqlcabc         pic s9(9) comp-5.
       03  sqlcode         pic s9(9) comp-5.
       03  sqlerrml        pic s9(4) comp-5.
       03  sqlerrmc        pic x(70).
       03  sqlerrp         pic x(8).
       03  sqlerrd         pic s9(9) comp-5 occurs 6.
       03  sqlwarn         pic x(8).
       03  sqlext          pic x(8).
```

```
       IDENTIFICATION DIVISION.
       PROGRAM-ID. CUSTP000.
       AUTHOR. ALIDA M. JATICH AND PHIL NOWAK.
      ****************************************************************
      * SQL-BASED VERSION OF MAIN MENU PROGRAM - NO ACTUAL SQL       *
      * COMMANDS ARE EXECUTED HERE. THIS PROGRAM TRANSFERS CONTROL   *
      * TO OTHER MODULES WHICH PERFORM THE I/O.                      *
      * ON THE FIRST PASS, CUSTP000 SENDS THE MENU SCREEN. AFTER THAT,*
      * IT CHECKS THE USER'S INPUT TO DETERMINE WHICH OTHER PROGRAM  *
      * TO INVOKE NEXT. THIS PROGRAM ALSO PRESENTS A POPUP MENU WHICH *
      * CAN BE USED TO ENTER THE CUSTOMER NUMBER TO SELECT THE RECORD *
      * TO BE SHOWN BY THE NEXT PROGRAM.                             *
      ****************************************************************
       ENVIRONMENT DIVISION.
```

FIGURE 15.4 Sample CICS programs using SQL commands.

```
          DATA DIVISION.
          WORKING-STORAGE SECTION.
          01  MISC-WORK.
              05  WS-CICS-RESPONSE1        PIC S9(8) COMP VALUE +0.
              05  WS-XCTL-PGM              PIC X(8)       VALUE SPACES.
              05  WS-DUMMY-FIELD           PIC X          VALUE SPACES.
              05  WS-DUMMY-LENGTH          PIC S9(4) COMP VALUE +0.
              05  WS-HOLD-MSG              PIC X(79)      VALUE SPACES.
          01  QID-NAME.
              05  QID-TRMID                PIC XXXX       VALUE SPACES.
              05  FILLER                   PIC XXXX       VALUE 'CUST'.
          01  ERROR-MESSAGES.
              05  BAD-KEY-MSG              PIC X(22)      VALUE
                  'Function key undefined'.
              05  BAD-OBJECT-MSG           PIC X(20)      VALUE
                  'Select object 1 or 2'.
              05  BAD-COMBO-MSG            PIC X(31)      VALUE
                  'Cannot change or delete history'.
              05  CUST-NUM-MSG             PIC X(27)      VALUE
                  'Customer number not numeric'.
              05  NOTFND-MSG               PIC X(16)      VALUE
                  'Record not found'.
              05  DISABLED-MSG             PIC X(16)      VALUE
                  'File is disabled'.
              05  DSIDERR-MSG              PIC X(14)      VALUE
                  'File not found'.
              05  DUPREC-MSG               PIC X(22)      VALUE
                  'Record already on file'.
              05  INVREQ-MSG               PIC X(15)      VALUE
                  'Invalid request'.
              05  IOERR-MSG                PIC X(9)       VALUE
                  'I/O error'.
              05  ITEMERR-MSG              PIC X(16)      VALUE
                  'Item not defined'.
              05  LENGERR-MSG              PIC X(19)      VALUE
                  'Record length error'.
              05  NOSPACE-MSG              PIC X(17)      VALUE
                  'File out of space'.
              05  PGMIDERR-MSG             PIC X(29)      VALUE
                  'Program not found, PRESS PF12'.
              05  QIDERR-MSG               PIC X(17)      VALUE
                  'Queue not defined'.
          *
              05  BUILD-MSG.
                  10  DISPLAY-OPERATION    PIC X(12)      VALUE SPACES.
                  10  FILLER               PIC X          VALUE SPACES.
                  10  DISPLAY-RESOURCE     PIC X(8)       VALUE SPACES.
                  10  FILLER               PIC X          VALUE SPACES.
                  10  DISPLAY-DESCRIPTION  PIC X(38)      VALUE SPACES.
                  10  FILLER               PIC X          VALUE SPACES.
                  10  DISPLAY-CALL-WHOM    PIC X(16)      VALUE SPACES.
          *
              05  DEFAULT-DESCRIPTION.
                  10  FILLER               PIC X(22)      VALUE
                  'CUSTP000 ERROR: RESP1='.
                  10  DISPLAY-RESPONSE     PIC 9(8)       VALUE ZEROES.
          *
          COPY CUSTCOMM.
          COPY MSALE00.
          COPY MCUST00.
          COPY ATTRIBUT.
          COPY DFHAID.
          COPY DFHBMSCA.
          *
          LINKAGE SECTION.
          01  DFHCOMMAREA                  PIC X(104).
          *
          PROCEDURE DIVISION.
          MAIN-PROG.
          *
          *******************************************************************
```

FIGURE 15.4 (Continued)

```
* DETERMINE WHICH POINT IN THE CYCLE APPLIES TO THE CURRENT    *
* SITUATION. THE FIRST TIME THROUGH, NEITHER MENU IS PRESENT.   *
* IN THAT CASE, SEND THE MAIN MENU MAP. ON SUBSEQUENT PASSES,   *
* EITHER THE MAIN MENU OR THE CUSTOMER POPUP WILL BE ON THE     *
* SCREEN. RECEIVE USER INPUT FROM WHICHEVER MAP IS THERE.       *
*****************************************************************
*
      MOVE LOW-VALUES TO SALE000I.
      MOVE LOW-VALUES TO CUST000I.
*
      IF EIBCALEN NOT = WS-EXPECTED-EIBCALEN
            OR EIBTRNID NOT = 'CUST'
         PERFORM FIRST-TIME-THROUGH
      ELSE
         MOVE DFHCOMMAREA TO WS-COMMAREA
         IF WS-COMM-PREV-MAP = 'SALE000'
            PERFORM PROCESS-MAIN-MENU
         ELSE
            IF WS-COMM-PREV-MAP = 'CUST000'
               PERFORM PROCESS-POPUP
            ELSE
               PERFORM FIRST-TIME-THROUGH.
*
      GOBACK.
*
*****************************************************************
* AT THIS POINT, THE PROGRAM HAS DETERMINED THAT THE MAIN MENU  *
* MAP WAS THE MAP MOST RECENTLY DISPLAYED TO THE USER.          *
*                                                               *
* DETERMINE WHAT FUNCTION KEY THE USER PRESSED. NOTE THAT       *
* A FUNCTION KEY WHICH IS VALID WHEN THE MAIN MENU IS ON THE    *
* SCREEN MIGHT NOT BE VALID WHEN THE POPUP IS ACTIVE. THIS IS   *
* WHY WE SOMETIMES NEED DIFFERENT FUNCTION KEY LOGIC IN THE     *
* ROUTINES THAT RECEIVE DIFFERENT MAPS.                         *
*****************************************************************
*
 PROCESS-MAIN-MENU.
*
      IF EIBAID = DFHCLEAR OR DFHPF3
         PERFORM EXIT-ROUTINE
      ELSE
         IF EIBAID = DFHPF10
            PERFORM CURSOR-TO-ACTION-BAR
         ELSE
            IF EIBAID = DFHPF12
               PERFORM FIRST-TIME-THROUGH
            ELSE
               IF EIBAID NOT = DFHENTER
                  MOVE BAD-KEY-MSG TO WS-HOLD-MSG
                  PERFORM SEND-MAP-WITH-ERROR.
*
      MOVE 'MSALE00' TO DISPLAY-RESOURCE.
      MOVE 'RECEIVE MAP' TO DISPLAY-OPERATION.
*
      EXEC CICS RECEIVE MAP ('SALE000')
                MAPSET ('MSALE00')
                INTO (SALE000I)
                RESP (WS-CICS-RESPONSE1)
                END-EXEC.
*
      IF WS-CICS-RESPONSE1 = DFHRESP(MAPFAIL)
         PERFORM FIRST-TIME-THROUGH
      ELSE
         IF WS-CICS-RESPONSE1 NOT = DFHRESP(NORMAL)
            PERFORM CHECK-CICS-RESPONSE
            PERFORM SEND-MAP-WITH-ERROR.
*
*****************************************************************
* IF YOUR TERMINALS SUPPORT COLOR, FOR EXAMPLE, 3279-TYPE       *
* TERMINALS OR PS/2'S, CHANGE THE COLOR OF A FIELD TO INDICATE  *
* ERRORS. THE COLOR IS SET WITH AN 'EXTENDED ATTRIBUTE' BYTE.   *
```

FIGURE 15.4 *(Continued)*

```
* THE EXTENDED ATTRIBUTE DOES NOT TAKE UP SPACE ON THE DISPLAY. *
* THIS EXAMPLE IS BEING RUN ON A PS/2. IF YOUR TERMINALS ARE    *
* MONOCHROME, CHANGE THE ATTRIBUTE BYTE TO A 'BRIGHT' SETTING   *
* TO INDICATE ERRORS.                                          *
****************************************************************
     MOVE DFHTURQ TO SOSEL1C.
     MOVE SPACES TO WS-HOLD-MSG SOMSGO COMSGO.
*
     PERFORM SALE000-CHECK-ACTION-BAR.
*
     IF SOSEL1I = '1'
         MOVE 'CUSTMAST' TO WS-COMM-OBJECT
     ELSE
         IF SOSEL1I = '2'
             MOVE 'LINEITEM' TO WS-COMM-OBJECT
         ELSE
             IF WS-COMM-ACTION = 'EXIT' OR 'CANCEL'
                 NEXT SENTENCE
             ELSE
                 MOVE '_' TO SOSEL1O
                 MOVE DFHRED TO SOSEL1C
                 MOVE BAD-OBJECT-MSG TO WS-HOLD-MSG
                 PERFORM SEND-MAP-WITH-ERROR.
*
****************************************************************
* SALES HISTORY TRANSACTIONS CANNOT BE CHANGED OR DELETED. IF   *
* YOU WANT TO MAKE AN ADJUSTMENT, YOU CAN DO IT BY ADDING A NEW *
* ADJUSTMENT ENTRY WITH THE OPPOSITE SIGN. THIS PRESERVES THE   *
* AUDIT TRAIL OF UPDATES.                                      *
****************************************************************
     IF WS-COMM-OBJECT = 'LINEITEM'
         IF WS-COMM-ACTION = 'CHANGE' OR 'DELETE'
             MOVE BAD-COMBO-MSG TO WS-HOLD-MSG
             PERFORM SEND-MAP-WITH-ERROR.
*
     IF WS-COMM-ACTION = 'EXIT'
         PERFORM EXIT-ROUTINE
     ELSE
         IF WS-COMM-ACTION = 'CANCEL'
             PERFORM FIRST-TIME-THROUGH
         ELSE
             PERFORM SHOW-POPUP.
*
****************************************************************
* IF THE CURSOR WAS ANYWHERE ON THE ACTION BAR, USE THE         *
* POSITION TO SELECT THE ACTION. IF THE CURSOR WAS SOMEWHERE    *
* ELSE, THEN JUST GO WITH THE DEFAULT CHOICE, WHICH IS "VIEW".  *
*                                                              *
****************************************************************
*
 SALE000-CHECK-ACTION-BAR.
*
     IF EIBCPOSN  8
       MOVE 'VIEW' TO WS-COMM-ACTION
     ELSE
       IF EIBCPOSN  13
         MOVE 'ADD' TO WS-COMM-ACTION
       ELSE
         IF EIBCPOSN  21
           MOVE 'CHANGE' TO WS-COMM-ACTION
         ELSE
           IF EIBCPOSN  29
             MOVE 'DELETE' TO WS-COMM-ACTION
           ELSE
             IF EIBCPOSN  35
               MOVE 'CANCEL' TO WS-COMM-ACTION
             ELSE
               IF EIBCPOSN  43
                 MOVE 'EXIT' TO WS-COMM-ACTION
               ELSE
```

FIGURE 15.4 *(Continued)*

```
                         MOVE 'VIEW' TO WS-COMM-ACTION.
     *
     *******************************************************************
     * PROCESS THE CUSTOMER NUMBER POPUP WINDOW MAP. IF THERE IS A     *
     * CUSTOMER NUMBER (NUMERIC), PLACE IT IN THE COMMAREA AND         *
     * SELECT THE NEXT PROGRAM. OTHERWISE, DISPLAY AN ERROR MESSAGE.   *
     *******************************************************************
      PROCESS-POPUP.
     *
         IF EIBAID = DFHPF12
             PERFORM FIRST-TIME-THROUGH
         ELSE
             IF EIBAID NOT = DFHENTER
                 MOVE BAD-KEY-MSG TO WS-HOLD-MSG
                 PERFORM SEND-MAP-WITH-ERROR.
     *
         MOVE 'MCUST00' TO DISPLAY-RESOURCE.
         MOVE 'RECEIVE MAP' TO DISPLAY-OPERATION.
     *
         EXEC CICS RECEIVE MAP ('CUST000')
                   MAPSET ('MCUST00')
                   INTO (CUST000I)
                   RESP (WS-CICS-RESPONSE1)
                   END-EXEC.
     *
         IF WS-CICS-RESPONSE1 = DFHRESP(MAPFAIL)
             PERFORM FIRST-TIME-THROUGH
         ELSE
             IF WS-CICS-RESPONSE1 NOT = DFHRESP(NORMAL)
                 PERFORM CHECK-CICS-RESPONSE
                 PERFORM SEND-MAP-WITH-ERROR.
     *
         IF WS-COMM-ACTION = 'ADD'
             IF WS-COMM-OBJECT = 'CUSTMAST'
                 MOVE 'CUSTP001' TO WS-XCTL-PGM
             ELSE
                 MOVE 'CUSTP004' TO WS-XCTL-PGM
         ELSE
             IF WS-COMM-ACTION = 'VIEW'
                 IF WS-COMM-OBJECT = 'CUSTMAST'
                     MOVE 'CUSTP005' TO WS-XCTL-PGM
                 ELSE
                     MOVE 'CUSTP006' TO WS-XCTL-PGM
             ELSE
                 IF WS-COMM-ACTION = 'CHANGE'
                     MOVE 'CUSTP002' TO WS-XCTL-PGM
                 ELSE
                     IF WS-COMM-ACTION = 'DELETE'
                         MOVE 'CUSTP003' TO WS-XCTL-PGM.
     *
         IF COCUSTI IS NUMERIC
             MOVE COCUSTI TO WS-COMM-CUST-NO
         ELSE
             IF WS-XCTL-PGM = 'CUSTP005'
                 MOVE LOW-VALUES TO WS-COMM-CUST-NO
             ELSE
                 MOVE CUST-NUM-MSG TO WS-HOLD-MSG
                 PERFORM SEND-MAP-WITH-ERROR.
     *
         PERFORM XCTL-NEXT-PGM.
     *
      XCTL-NEXT-PGM.
     *
         MOVE WS-XCTL-PGM TO DISPLAY-RESOURCE.
         MOVE 'XCTL' TO DISPLAY-OPERATION.
     *
         EXEC CICS XCTL
                   PROGRAM (WS-XCTL-PGM)
                   COMMAREA (WS-COMMAREA)
                   RESP (WS-CICS-RESPONSE1)
                   END-EXEC.
```

FIGURE 15.4 *(Continued)*

```
*
      IF WS-CICS-RESPONSE1 NOT = DFHRESP(NORMAL)
          PERFORM CHECK-CICS-RESPONSE
          PERFORM SEND-MAP-WITH-ERROR.
*
**********************************************************************
* THIS ROUTINE SENDS THE INITIAL MAIN MENU MAP AND/OR REFRESHES *
* IT IF 'CANCEL' WAS SELECTED.                                  *
**********************************************************************
*
 FIRST-TIME-THROUGH.
*
      MOVE LOW-VALUES TO SALE000I.
      MOVE 'SALE000' TO WS-COMM-PREV-MAP.
      MOVE SPACES TO WS-HOLD-MSG
                     WS-COMM-OBJECT
                     WS-COMM-ACTION
                     WS-COMM-CUST-NO
                     WS-COMM-NEXT-CUST-NO
                     WS-COMM-ITEM-CODE
                     WS-COMM-NEXT-ITEM-CODE.
      MOVE ZEROES TO WS-COMM-COUNTER.
      MOVE LOW-VALUES TO WS-COMM-DATETIME
                         WS-COMM-NEXT-DATETIME.
*
      EXEC CICS SEND MAP ('SALE000')
               MAPSET ('MSALE00')
               MAPONLY
               ERASE
               END-EXEC.
*
      EXEC CICS RETURN
               TRANSID ('CUST')
               COMMAREA (WS-COMMAREA)
               END-EXEC.
*
*
**********************************************************************
* THIS ROUTINE SENDS THE CUSTOMER NUMBER POPUP MAP.            *
**********************************************************************
*
 SHOW-POPUP.
*
*
**********************************************************************
* WE ALSO CHANGE THE APPEARANCE OF THE ACTION BAR TO SHOW          *
* WHAT THE USER HAS CHOSEN. IF YOU DON'T HAVE A COLOR TERMINAL,    *
* MOVE A 'BRIGHT' ATTRIBUTE CHARACTER TO THE ATTRIBUTE BYTE        *
* FOR THE ITEM TO BE HIGHLIGHTED; 'NORMAL' FOR THE OTHERS.         *
* THIS REQUIRES US TO SEND THE MAIN MAP ONCE AGAIN BEFORE WE       *
* SEND THE POPUP MAP.                                             *
**********************************************************************
*
*
      MOVE LOW-VALUES TO SALE000I.
*
      MOVE DFHNEUTR TO SOVIEWC SOADDC SOCHGC SODLTC
                       SOEXITC SOCANC.
*
      IF WS-COMM-ACTION = 'VIEW'
        MOVE DFHYELLO TO SOVIEWC
      ELSE
        IF WS-COMM-ACTION = 'ADD'
          MOVE DFHYELLO TO SOADDC
        ELSE
          IF WS-COMM-ACTION = 'CHANGE'
            MOVE DFHYELLO TO SOCHGC
          ELSE
            IF WS-COMM-ACTION = 'DELETE'
              MOVE DFHYELLO TO SODLTC
            ELSE
```

FIGURE 15.4 *(Continued)*

```
                IF WS-COMM-ACTION = 'CANCEL'
                   MOVE DFHYELLO TO SOCANC
                ELSE
                   IF WS-COMM-ACTION = 'EXIT'
                      MOVE DFHYELLO TO SOEXITC
                   ELSE
                      MOVE DFHYELLO TO SOVIEWC
                      MOVE 'VIEW' TO WS-COMM-ACTION.
 *
       EXEC CICS SEND MAP ('SALE000')
                 MAPSET ('MSALE00')
                 FROM (SALE000I)
                 END-EXEC.
 *
       MOVE LOW-VALUES TO CUST000I.
       MOVE 'CUST000' TO WS-COMM-PREV-MAP.
       MOVE SPACES TO WS-COMM-CUST-NO.
 *
       EXEC CICS SEND MAP ('CUST000')
                 MAPSET ('MCUST00')
                 FROM (CUST000I)
                 END-EXEC.
 *
       EXEC CICS RETURN
                 TRANSID ('CUST')
                 COMMAREA (WS-COMMAREA)
                 END-EXEC.
 *
 ****************************************************************
 * THIS ROUTINE WILL RE-SEND WHATEVER MAP IS CURRENTLY ON THE   *
 * SCREEN, WITH THE ERROR MESSAGE SET UP BY THE CALLING ROUTINE. *
 ****************************************************************
 *
 SEND-MAP-WITH-ERROR.
 *
       IF WS-COMM-PREV-MAP = 'CUST000'
          MOVE WS-HOLD-MSG TO COMSGO
          PERFORM SEND-CUST000-BEEP
       ELSE
          MOVE WS-HOLD-MSG TO SOMSGO
          PERFORM SEND-SALE000-BEEP.
 *
 ****************************************************************
 * THIS ROUTINE SENDS CUST000 WITH A WARNING 'BEEP', WITHOUT    *
 * DISTURBING OTHER SCREEN CONTENTS.                           *
 ****************************************************************
 *
 SEND-CUST000-BEEP.
 *
       EXEC CICS SEND MAP ('CUST000')
                 MAPSET ('MCUST00')
                 FROM (CUST000I)
                 ALARM
                 END-EXEC.
 *
       EXEC CICS RETURN
                 TRANSID ('CUST')
                 COMMAREA (WS-COMMAREA)
                 END-EXEC.
 *
 ****************************************************************
 * THIS ROUTINE SENDS SALE000 WITH A WARNING 'BEEP'.           *
 ****************************************************************
 *
 SEND-SALE000-BEEP.
 *
       EXEC CICS SEND MAP ('SALE000')
                 MAPSET ('MSALE00')
                 FROM (SALE000I)
                 ALARM
                 END-EXEC.
```

FIGURE 15.4 *(Continued)*

```
*
      EXEC CICS RETURN
               TRANSID ('CUST')
               COMMAREA (WS-COMMAREA)
               END-EXEC.
*
*******************************************************************
* THIS ROUTINE SENDS SALE000 WITH THE CURSOR ON THE ACTION BAR. *
*******************************************************************
*
 CURSOR-TO-ACTION-BAR.
*
      MOVE LOW-VALUES TO SALE000I.
      MOVE 'SALE000' TO WS-COMM-PREV-MAP.
      EXEC CICS SEND MAP ('SALE000')
               MAPSET ('MSALE00')
               FROM (SALE000I)
               CURSOR (1)
               END-EXEC.
*
      EXEC CICS RETURN
               TRANSID ('CUST')
               COMMAREA (WS-COMMAREA)
               END-EXEC.
*
*******************************************************************
* DELETE ANY REMAINING TEMP STORAGE QUEUE LEFT FROM OTHER        *
* PROGRAMS IN THIS SYSTEM. CLEAR THE USER'S SCREEN AND RETURN    *
* TO CICS. WE IGNORE THE RESPONSE CODE WHEN DELETING TS QUEUE.   *
*******************************************************************
 EXIT-ROUTINE.
*
      MOVE EIBTRMID TO QID-TRMID.
      EXEC CICS DELETEQ TS
               QUEUE (QID-NAME)
               RESP (WS-CICS-RESPONSE1)
               END-EXEC.
*
      EXEC CICS SEND
               FROM (WS-DUMMY-FIELD)
               LENGTH (WS-DUMMY-LENGTH)
               ERASE
               END-EXEC.
*
      EXEC CICS RETURN
               END-EXEC.
*
*
*******************************************************************
* CHECK THE CICS RESPONSE CODE AND BUILD A MESSAGE EXPLAINING    *
* THE ERROR. IT IS THE RESPONSIBILITY OF THE CALLING ROUTINE     *
* TO INITIALIZE SOME DISPLAY FIELDS IN THE MESSAGE WORK AREA     *
* TO INDICATE THE TYPE OF COMMAND BEING PROCESSED.               *
*                                                                *
* WE DO NOTHING ABOUT CERTAIN RESPONSE CODES HERE SO THAT        *
* THOSE SITUATIONS CAN BE HANDLED WITH LOGIC ELSEWHERE IN THE    *
* PROGRAM.                                                       *
*                                                                *
*******************************************************************
*
 CHECK-CICS-RESPONSE.
*
      EVALUATE WS-CICS-RESPONSE1
      WHEN DFHRESP(NORMAL)
           CONTINUE
      WHEN DFHRESP(MAPFAIL)
           CONTINUE
      WHEN DFHRESP(ENDFILE)
           CONTINUE
      WHEN DFHRESP(DISABLED)
           MOVE 'CALL OPERATIONS' TO DISPLAY-CALL-WHOM
```

FIGURE 15.4   *(Continued)*

```
                  MOVE DISABLED-MSG TO DISPLAY-DESCRIPTION
                  MOVE BUILD-MSG TO WS-HOLD-MSG
              WHEN DFHRESP(DUPREC)
                  MOVE DUPREC-MSG TO DISPLAY-DESCRIPTION
                  MOVE BUILD-MSG TO WS-HOLD-MSG
              WHEN DFHRESP(DSIDERR)
                  MOVE 'CALL PROGRAMMER' TO DISPLAY-CALL-WHOM
                  MOVE DSIDERR-MSG TO DISPLAY-DESCRIPTION
                  MOVE BUILD-MSG TO WS-HOLD-MSG
              WHEN DFHRESP(INVREQ)
                  MOVE 'CALL PROGRAMMER' TO DISPLAY-CALL-WHOM
                  MOVE INVREQ-MSG TO DISPLAY-DESCRIPTION
                  MOVE BUILD-MSG TO WS-HOLD-MSG
              WHEN DFHRESP(IOERR)
                  MOVE 'CALL PROGRAMMER' TO DISPLAY-CALL-WHOM
                  MOVE IOERR-MSG TO DISPLAY-DESCRIPTION
                  MOVE BUILD-MSG TO WS-HOLD-MSG
              WHEN DFHRESP(ITEMERR)
                  MOVE 'CALL PROGRAMMER' TO DISPLAY-CALL-WHOM
                  MOVE ITEMERR-MSG TO DISPLAY-DESCRIPTION
                  MOVE BUILD-MSG TO WS-HOLD-MSG
              WHEN DFHRESP(LENGERR)
                  MOVE 'CALL PROGRAMMER' TO DISPLAY-CALL-WHOM
                  MOVE LENGERR-MSG TO DISPLAY-DESCRIPTION
                  MOVE BUILD-MSG TO WS-HOLD-MSG
              WHEN DFHRESP(NOSPACE)
                  MOVE 'CALL OPERATIONS' TO DISPLAY-CALL-WHOM
                  MOVE NOSPACE-MSG TO DISPLAY-DESCRIPTION
                  MOVE BUILD-MSG TO WS-HOLD-MSG
              WHEN DFHRESP(NOTFND)
                  MOVE NOTFND-MSG TO DISPLAY-DESCRIPTION
                  MOVE BUILD-MSG TO WS-HOLD-MSG
              WHEN DFHRESP(PGMIDERR)
                  MOVE 'CALL PROGRAMMER' TO DISPLAY-CALL-WHOM
                  MOVE PGMIDERR-MSG TO DISPLAY-DESCRIPTION
                  MOVE BUILD-MSG TO WS-HOLD-MSG
              WHEN DFHRESP(QIDERR)
                  MOVE 'CALL PROGRAMMER' TO DISPLAY-CALL-WHOM
                  MOVE QIDERR-MSG TO DISPLAY-DESCRIPTION
                  MOVE BUILD-MSG TO WS-HOLD-MSG
              WHEN OTHER
                  MOVE 'CALL PROGRAMMER' TO DISPLAY-CALL-WHOM
                  MOVE WS-CICS-RESPONSE1 TO DISPLAY-RESPONSE
                  MOVE DEFAULT-DESCRIPTION TO DISPLAY-DESCRIPTION
                  MOVE BUILD-MSG TO WS-HOLD-MSG
              END-EVALUATE.
      *
      *
```

FIGURE 15.4 *(Continued)*

```
$set ans85 sql osvs sqlaccess"" sqlbind"" sqldb(cicsbook)
 IDENTIFICATION DIVISION.
 PROGRAM-ID. CUSTP001.
 AUTHOR. ALIDA M. JATICH AND PHIL NOWAK.
 ******************************************************************
 * CUSTP001: ADD A NEW CUSTOMER RECORD (SQL VERSION OF SALEP001)  *
 * ON THE FIRST PASS, CUSTP001 SHOWS A RECORD ADD SCREEN, WITH    *
 * THE NEW CUSTOMER NUMBER TAKEN FROM THE COMMAREA. THE TERMINAL  *
 * USER ENTERS DATA ON THE SCREEN. ON THE NEXT PASS, CUSTP001     *
 * ADDS AN SQL TABLE ROW AND DISPLAYS THE ADD SCREEN AGAIN.       *
 * THIS PROGRAM USES THE SAME MAP AND USER INTERFACE LOGIC AS     *
 * SALEP001; ONLY THE DATABASE I/O IS DIFFERENT.                  *
 ******************************************************************
 ENVIRONMENT DIVISION.
 DATA DIVISION.
 WORKING-STORAGE SECTION.
```

FIGURE 15.5 Sample CICS programs using SQL commands.

```
      *
      EXEC SQL BEGIN DECLARE SECTION END-EXEC.
      COPY CUSTOMER.
      EXEC SQL END DECLARE SECTION END-EXEC.
      *
      EXEC SQL INCLUDE SQLCA END-EXEC.
      *
      01  MISC-WORK.
          05  WS-CICS-RESPONSE1       PIC S9(8) COMP VALUE +0.
          05  WS-XCTL-PGM             PIC X(8)       VALUE SPACES.
          05  WS-ERROR-FLAG           PIC X          VALUE 'N'.
      *
      01  ERROR-MESSAGES.
          05  BAD-KEY-MSG             PIC X(22)      VALUE
              'Function key undefined'.
          05  CUST-NUM-MSG            PIC X(27)      VALUE
              'Customer number not numeric'.
          05  MISSING-DATA-MSG        PIC X(26)      VALUE
              'Please supply missing data'.
          05  SUCCESSFUL-ADD-MSG      PIC X(25)      VALUE
              'Record added successfully'.
          05  DISABLED-MSG            PIC X(16)      VALUE
              'File is disabled'.
          05  DSIDERR-MSG             PIC X(14)      VALUE
              'File not found'.
          05  DUPREC-MSG              PIC X(26)      VALUE
              'Record key already on file'.
          05  INVREQ-MSG             PIC X(15)      VALUE
              'Invalid request'.
          05  IOERR-MSG               PIC X(9)       VALUE
              'I/O error'.
          05  ITEMERR-MSG             PIC X(16)      VALUE
              'Item not defined'.
          05  LENGERR-MSG             PIC X(19)      VALUE
              'Record length error'.
          05  NOSPACE-MSG             PIC X(17)      VALUE
              'File out of space'.
          05  NOTFND-MSG              PIC X(18)      VALUE
              'Record not on file'.
          05  PGMIDERR-MSG            PIC X(27)      VALUE
              'Program not defined to CICS'.
          05  QIDERR-MSG              PIC X(17)      VALUE
              'Queue not defined'.
      *
          05  BUILD-MSG.
              10  DISPLAY-OPERATION   PIC X(12)      VALUE SPACES.
              10  FILLER              PIC X          VALUE SPACES.
              10  DISPLAY-RESOURCE    PIC X(8)       VALUE SPACES.
              10  FILLER              PIC X          VALUE SPACES.
              10  DISPLAY-DESCRIPTION PIC X(40)      VALUE SPACES.
              10  FILLER              PIC X          VALUE SPACES.
              10  DISPLAY-CALL-WHOM   PIC X(16)      VALUE SPACES.
      *
          05  DEFAULT-DESCRIPTION.
              10  FILLER              PIC X(22)      VALUE
              'CUSTP001 ERROR: RESP1='.
              10  DISPLAY-RESPONSE    PIC 9(8)       VALUE ZEROES.
      *
          05  SQL-DESCRIPTION.
              10  FILLER              PIC X(24)      VALUE
              'CUSTP001 ERROR: SQLCODE='.
              10  DISPLAY-SQLCODE     PIC 9(9)-      VALUE ZEROES.
      *
      COPY CUSTCOMM.
      COPY MSALE01.
      COPY ATTRIBUT.
      COPY DFHAID.
      COPY DFHBMSCA.
      LINKAGE SECTION.
      01  DFHCOMMAREA                 PIC X(104).
```

FIGURE 15.5 *(Continued)*

```
*
 PROCEDURE DIVISION.
 MAIN-PROG.
*
***********************************************************************
* DETERMINE WHICH POINT IN THE CYCLE APPLIES TO THE CURRENT          *
* SITUATION. THE FIRST TIME THROUGH, SHOW THE RECORD ADD SCREEN      *
* FOR THE FIRST TIME. ON SUBSEQUENT PASSES, PROCESS USER INPUT       *
* AND SHOW THE SCREEN AGAIN (OR TRANSFER CONTROL BACK TO THE         *
* MENU PROGRAM, DEPENDING ON FUNCTION KEY).                          *
***********************************************************************
*
     MOVE LOW-VALUES TO SALE001I.
*
     IF EIBCALEN NOT = WS-EXPECTED-EIBCALEN
        PERFORM FIRST-TIME-THROUGH
     ELSE
        MOVE DFHCOMMAREA TO WS-COMMAREA
        IF EIBTRNID = 'CUS1'
                  AND WS-COMM-PREV-MAP = 'SALE001'
             PERFORM PROCESS-ADD-SCREEN
        ELSE
             PERFORM FIRST-TIME-THROUGH.
*
     GOBACK.
*
***********************************************************************
* DETERMINE WHAT FUNCTION KEY THE USER PRESSED.                      *
***********************************************************************
*
 PROCESS-ADD-SCREEN.
*
     IF EIBAID = DFHCLEAR OR DFHPF3
        MOVE 'CUSTP000' TO WS-XCTL-PGM
        PERFORM XCTL-NEXT-PGM
     ELSE
        IF EIBAID = DFHPF10
             PERFORM CURSOR-TO-ACTION-BAR
        ELSE
             IF EIBAID = DFHPF12
                  PERFORM FIRST-TIME-THROUGH
             ELSE
                  IF EIBAID NOT = DFHENTER
                       MOVE BAD-KEY-MSG TO S1MSGO
                       MOVE -1 TO S1CUSTL
                       PERFORM SEND-SALE001-BEEP.
*
     MOVE 'MSALE01' TO DISPLAY-RESOURCE.
     MOVE 'RECEIVE MAP' TO DISPLAY-OPERATION.
*
     EXEC CICS RECEIVE MAP ('SALE001')
               MAPSET ('MSALE01')
               INTO (SALE001I)
               RESP (WS-CICS-RESPONSE1)
               END-EXEC.
*
     IF WS-CICS-RESPONSE1 = DFHRESP(MAPFAIL)
        PERFORM FIRST-TIME-THROUGH
     ELSE
        IF WS-CICS-RESPONSE1 NOT = DFHRESP(NORMAL)
             PERFORM CHECK-CICS-RESPONSE
             MOVE -1 TO S1CUSTL
             PERFORM SEND-SALE001-BEEP.
*
     MOVE SPACES TO S1MSGO.
*
***********************************************************************
* IF THE CURSOR WAS ANYWHERE ON THE ACTION BAR, USE THE             *
* POSITION TO SELECT THE ACTION. IF THE CURSOR WAS SOMEWHERE        *
* ELSE, THEN JUST GO WITH THE DEFAULT CHOICE, WHICH IS "ADD".       *
```

FIGURE 15.5 *(Continued)*

```
*******************************************************************
*
     IF EIBCPOSN  7
         MOVE 'ADD' TO WS-COMM-ACTION
     ELSE
         IF EIBCPOSN  13
             MOVE 'EXIT' TO WS-COMM-ACTION
         ELSE
             IF EIBCPOSN  21
                 MOVE 'CANCEL' TO WS-COMM-ACTION
             ELSE
                 MOVE 'ADD' TO WS-COMM-ACTION.
*
     IF WS-COMM-ACTION = 'EXIT'
         MOVE 'CUSTP000' TO WS-XCTL-PGM
         PERFORM XCTL-NEXT-PGM
     ELSE
         IF WS-COMM-ACTION = 'CANCEL'
             PERFORM FIRST-TIME-THROUGH.
*
*******************************************************************
* EDIT THE DATA IN EACH OF THE USER INPUT FIELDS. YOUR METHODS    *
* MAY VARY DEPENDING ON THE TERMINAL DEVICE FEATURES YOU PLAN     *
* TO SUPPORT AND ON THE STANDARDS AT YOUR INSTALLATION. THIS      *
* EXAMPLE WAS RUN ON A PS/2, SO WE ARE USING COLOR CHANGES        *
* IN PLACE OF HIGHLIGHTING TO INDICATE ERRORS. WE ARE ALSO        *
* USING ACTUAL UNDERSCORE CHARACTERS IN PLACE OF THE UNDERSCORE   *
* EXTENDED ATTRIBUTE SETTING.                                     *
*                                                                 *
* THE CHARACTER FIELDS IN THIS PARTICULAR SQL TABLE ARE FIXED     *
* LENGTH. VARIABLE CHARACTER FIELDS COULD HAVE BEEN USED,         *
* BUT IN THAT CASE EACH PROGRAM WOULD HAVE TO TAKE INTO ACCOUNT   *
* HOW MUCH OF EACH FIELD IS ACTUALLY BEING USED.                  *
*******************************************************************
*
     IF S1CUSTI = LOW-VALUES OR SPACES OR '_____'
         MOVE ALL '_' TO S1CUSTO
         MOVE DFHRED TO S1CUSTC
         IF WS-ERROR-FLAG = 'N'
             MOVE -1 TO S1CUSTL
             MOVE 'Y' TO WS-ERROR-FLAG
             MOVE MISSING-DATA-MSG TO S1MSGO
         END-IF
     ELSE
         IF S1CUSTI IS NUMERIC
             MOVE S1CUSTI TO CUST-NO
             MOVE DFHTURQ TO S1CUSTC
         ELSE
             MOVE DFHRED TO S1CUSTC
             IF WS-ERROR-FLAG = 'N'
                 MOVE -1 TO S1CUSTL
                 MOVE 'Y' TO WS-ERROR-FLAG
                 MOVE CUST-NUM-MSG TO S1MSGO.
*
     INSPECT S1NAMEI REPLACING ALL '_' BY SPACES.
     IF S1NAMEI  SPACES
         MOVE S1NAMEI TO CUST-NAME
         MOVE DFHTURQ TO S1NAMEC
         MOVE ALP-REG-MOD-UNP TO S1NAMEA
     ELSE
         MOVE DFHRED TO S1NAMEC
         MOVE ALL '_' TO S1NAMEO
         IF WS-ERROR-FLAG = 'N'
             MOVE -1 TO S1NAMEL
             MOVE 'Y' TO WS-ERROR-FLAG
             MOVE MISSING-DATA-MSG TO S1MSGO.
*
     INSPECT S1CNTCTI REPLACING ALL '_' BY SPACES.
     IF S1CNTCTI  SPACES
         MOVE S1CNTCTI TO CUST-CONTACT
```

FIGURE 15.5 *(Continued)*

```
                    MOVE DFHTURQ TO S1CNTCTC
                    MOVE ALP-REG-MOD-UNP TO S1CNTCTA
               ELSE
                    MOVE DFHRED TO S1CNTCTC
                    MOVE ALL '_' TO S1CNTCTO
                    IF WS-ERROR-FLAG = 'N'
                         MOVE -1 TO S1CNTCTL
                         MOVE 'Y' TO WS-ERROR-FLAG
                         MOVE MISSING-DATA-MSG TO S1MSGO.
     *
               INSPECT S1ADDRI REPLACING ALL '_' BY SPACES.
               IF S1ADDRI  SPACES
                    MOVE S1ADDRI TO CUST-STREET-ADDRESS
                    MOVE DFHTURQ TO S1ADDRC
                    MOVE ALP-REG-MOD-UNP TO S1ADDRA
               ELSE
                    MOVE DFHRED TO S1ADDRC
                    MOVE ALL '_' TO S1ADDRO
                    IF WS-ERROR-FLAG = 'N'
                         MOVE -1 TO S1ADDRL
                         MOVE 'Y' TO WS-ERROR-FLAG
                         MOVE MISSING-DATA-MSG TO S1MSGO.
     *
               INSPECT S1CITYI REPLACING ALL '_' BY SPACES.
               IF S1CITYI  SPACES
                    MOVE S1CITYI TO CUST-CITY
                    MOVE DFHTURQ TO S1CITYC
                    MOVE ALP-REG-MOD-UNP TO S1CITYA
               ELSE
                    MOVE DFHRED TO S1CITYC
                    MOVE ALL '_' TO S1CITYO
                    IF WS-ERROR-FLAG = 'N'
                         MOVE -1 TO S1CITYL
                         MOVE 'Y' TO WS-ERROR-FLAG
                         MOVE MISSING-DATA-MSG TO S1MSGO.
     *
               IF S1STATEI  SPACES AND S1STATEI IS ALPHABETIC
                    MOVE S1STATEI TO CUST-STATE
                    MOVE DFHTURQ TO S1STATEC
                    MOVE ALP-REG-MOD-UNP TO S1STATEA
               ELSE
                    MOVE DFHRED TO S1STATEC
                    MOVE ALL '_' TO S1STATEO
                    IF WS-ERROR-FLAG = 'N'
                         MOVE -1 TO S1STATEL
                         MOVE 'Y' TO WS-ERROR-FLAG
                         MOVE MISSING-DATA-MSG TO S1MSGO.
     *
               INSPECT S1ZIPI REPLACING ALL '_' BY SPACES.
               IF S1ZIPI  SPACES
                    MOVE S1ZIPI TO CUST-ZIP
                    MOVE DFHTURQ TO S1ZIPC
                    MOVE ALP-REG-MOD-UNP TO S1ZIPA
               ELSE
                    MOVE DFHRED TO S1ZIPC
                    MOVE ALL '_' TO S1ZIPO
                    IF WS-ERROR-FLAG = 'N'
                         MOVE -1 TO S1ZIPL
                         MOVE 'Y' TO WS-ERROR-FLAG
                         MOVE MISSING-DATA-MSG TO S1MSGO.
     *
               IF WS-ERROR-FLAG = 'Y'
                    PERFORM SEND-SALE001-BEEP
               ELSE
     ***************************************************************
     * IF THE DATA IS GOOD, ADD A NEW ROW USING EXEC SQL INSERT.   *
     * THE BILLING FIELDS ARE NOT REQUIRED DATA AT THIS STAGE AND  *
     * WILL BE SET TO NULL.                                        *
     ***************************************************************
                    MOVE 'CUSTOMER' TO DISPLAY-RESOURCE
```

FIGURE 15.5 *(Continued)*

```
          MOVE 'INSERT' TO DISPLAY-OPERATION
          EXEC SQL INSERT INTO CUSTOMER
                  (CUSTNO, CUSTNAME, CONTACT, STREETADDR,
                  CITY, STATE, ZIP)
                  VALUES (:CUST-NO, :CUST-NAME, :CUST-CONTACT,
                  :CUST-STREET-ADDRESS, :CUST-CITY, :CUST-STATE,
                  :CUST-ZIP)
                  END-EXEC
**********************************************************************
* LET THE USER KNOW WHETHER THE INSERT WAS SUCCESSFUL.         *
**********************************************************************
          MOVE -1 TO S1CUSTL
          IF SQLCODE = 0
              MOVE SUCCESSFUL-ADD-MSG TO S1MSGO
              PERFORM SEND-SALE001-RETURN
          ELSE
              PERFORM CHECK-SQL-RESPONSE
              PERFORM SEND-SALE001-BEEP.
*
*
 XCTL-NEXT-PGM.
*
     MOVE WS-XCTL-PGM TO DISPLAY-RESOURCE.
     MOVE 'XCTL' TO DISPLAY-OPERATION.
     EXEC CICS XCTL
              PROGRAM (WS-XCTL-PGM)
              COMMAREA (WS-COMMAREA)
              RESP (WS-CICS-RESPONSE1)
              END-EXEC.
*
     IF WS-CICS-RESPONSE1 NOT = DFHRESP(NORMAL)
         PERFORM CHECK-CICS-RESPONSE
         MOVE -1 TO S1CUSTL
         PERFORM SEND-SALE001-BEEP.
*
*
**********************************************************************
* THIS ROUTINE SENDS THE RECORD ADD MAP AND/OR REFRESHES IT    *
* IF 'CANCEL' WAS SELECTED.                                    *
**********************************************************************
*
 FIRST-TIME-THROUGH.
*
     MOVE SPACES TO S1MSGO.
     IF WS-COMM-CUST-NO IS NUMERIC
         MOVE WS-COMM-CUST-NO TO S1CUSTO
         MOVE -1 TO S1NAMEL
     ELSE
         MOVE '_____' TO S1CUSTO
         MOVE -1 TO S1CUSTL.
*
     PERFORM SEND-SALE001-RETURN.
*
**********************************************************************
* THIS ROUTINE SENDS SALE001 WITH A WARNING 'BEEP'. WE USE THIS *
* ONLY WHEN THE CALLING ROUTINE WANTS TO DISPLAY A WARNING ON   *
* THE MESSAGE LINE OF THIS MAP. CURSOR POSITION MUST BE SET.    *
**********************************************************************
*
 SEND-SALE001-BEEP.
*
     IF WS-COMM-PREV-MAP = 'SALE001'
         EXEC CICS SEND MAP ('SALE001')
                  MAPSET ('MSALE01')
                  FROM (SALE001I)
                  DATAONLY
                  ALARM
                  CURSOR
                  END-EXEC
     ELSE
```

FIGURE 15.5 *(Continued)*

```
              MOVE 'SALE001' TO WS-COMM-PREV-MAP
              EXEC CICS SEND MAP ('SALE001')
                      MAPSET ('MSALE01')
                      FROM (SALE001I)
                      ERASE
                      ALARM
                      CURSOR
                      END-EXEC.
*
      EXEC CICS RETURN
              TRANSID ('CUS1')
              COMMAREA (WS-COMMAREA)
              END-EXEC.
*
*
******************************************************************
* THIS ROUTINE SENDS SALE001 WITH WHATEVER DATA HAS BEEN PLACED *
* ON IT. IF THE PREDEFINED PORTIONS OF THE MAP ARE ALREADY ON   *
* THE SCREEN, SALE001 WILL BE SENT 'DATAONLY'.                  *
******************************************************************
*
 SEND-SALE001-RETURN.
*
      IF WS-COMM-PREV-MAP = 'SALE001'
          EXEC CICS SEND MAP ('SALE001')
                  MAPSET ('MSALE01')
                  FROM (SALE001I)
                  DATAONLY
                  CURSOR
                  END-EXEC
      ELSE
          MOVE 'SALE001' TO WS-COMM-PREV-MAP
          EXEC CICS SEND MAP ('SALE001')
                  MAPSET ('MSALE01')
                  FROM (SALE001I)
                  ERASE
                  CURSOR
                  END-EXEC.
*
      EXEC CICS RETURN
              TRANSID ('CUS1')
              COMMAREA (WS-COMMAREA)
              END-EXEC.
*
******************************************************************
* THIS ROUTINE SENDS SALE001 WITH CURSOR ON ACTION BAR.        *
******************************************************************
*
 CURSOR-TO-ACTION-BAR.
*
      MOVE 'SALE001' TO WS-COMM-PREV-MAP.
      EXEC CICS SEND MAP ('SALE001')
              MAPSET ('MSALE01')
              FROM (SALE001I)
              CURSOR (1)
              DATAONLY
              END-EXEC.
*
      EXEC CICS RETURN
              TRANSID ('CUS1')
              COMMAREA (WS-COMMAREA)
              END-EXEC.
*
*
******************************************************************
* CHECK THE CICS RESPONSE CODE AND BUILD A MESSAGE EXPLAINING   *
* THE ERROR. IT IS THE RESPONSIBILITY OF THE CALLING ROUTINE    *
* TO INITIALIZE SOME DISPLAY FIELDS IN THE MESSAGE WORK AREA    *
* TO INDICATE THE TYPE OF COMMAND BEING PROCESSED.              *
*                                                              *
```

FIGURE 15.5 *(Continued)*

```
* WE DO NOTHING ABOUT CERTAIN RESPONSE CODES HERE SO THAT        *
* THOSE SITUATIONS CAN BE HANDLED WITH LOGIC ELSEWHERE IN THE    *
* PROGRAM.                                                       *
*                                                               *
*****************************************************************
*
 CHECK-CICS-RESPONSE.
*
     EVALUATE WS-CICS-RESPONSE1
     WHEN DFHRESP(NORMAL)
         CONTINUE
     WHEN DFHRESP(MAPFAIL)
         CONTINUE
     WHEN DFHRESP(ENDFILE)
         CONTINUE
     WHEN DFHRESP(DISABLED)
         MOVE 'CALL OPERATIONS' TO DISPLAY-CALL-WHOM
         MOVE DISABLED-MSG TO DISPLAY-DESCRIPTION
         MOVE BUILD-MSG TO S1MSGO
     WHEN DFHRESP(DUPREC)
         MOVE DUPREC-MSG TO DISPLAY-DESCRIPTION
         MOVE BUILD-MSG TO S1MSGO
     WHEN DFHRESP(DSIDERR)
         MOVE 'CALL PROGRAMMER' TO DISPLAY-CALL-WHOM
         MOVE DSIDERR-MSG TO DISPLAY-DESCRIPTION
         MOVE BUILD-MSG TO S1MSGO
     WHEN DFHRESP(INVREQ)
         MOVE 'CALL PROGRAMMER' TO DISPLAY-CALL-WHOM
         MOVE INVREQ-MSG TO DISPLAY-DESCRIPTION
         MOVE BUILD-MSG TO S1MSGO
     WHEN DFHRESP(IOERR)
         MOVE 'CALL PROGRAMMER' TO DISPLAY-CALL-WHOM
         MOVE IOERR-MSG TO DISPLAY-DESCRIPTION
         MOVE BUILD-MSG TO S1MSGO
     WHEN DFHRESP(ITEMERR)
         MOVE 'CALL PROGRAMMER' TO DISPLAY-CALL-WHOM
         MOVE ITEMERR-MSG TO DISPLAY-DESCRIPTION
         MOVE BUILD-MSG TO S1MSGO
     WHEN DFHRESP(LENGERR)
         MOVE 'CALL PROGRAMMER' TO DISPLAY-CALL-WHOM
         MOVE LENGERR-MSG TO DISPLAY-DESCRIPTION
         MOVE BUILD-MSG TO S1MSGO
     WHEN DFHRESP(NOSPACE)
         MOVE 'CALL OPERATIONS' TO DISPLAY-CALL-WHOM
         MOVE NOSPACE-MSG TO DISPLAY-DESCRIPTION
         MOVE BUILD-MSG TO S1MSGO
     WHEN DFHRESP(NOTFND)
         MOVE NOTFND-MSG TO DISPLAY-DESCRIPTION
         MOVE BUILD-MSG TO S1MSGO
     WHEN DFHRESP(PGMIDERR)
         MOVE 'CALL PROGRAMMER' TO DISPLAY-CALL-WHOM
         MOVE PGMIDERR-MSG TO DISPLAY-DESCRIPTION
         MOVE BUILD-MSG TO S1MSGO
     WHEN DFHRESP(QIDERR)
         MOVE 'CALL PROGRAMMER' TO DISPLAY-CALL-WHOM
         MOVE QIDERR-MSG TO DISPLAY-DESCRIPTION
         MOVE BUILD-MSG TO S1MSGO
     WHEN OTHER
         MOVE 'CALL PROGRAMMER' TO DISPLAY-CALL-WHOM
         MOVE WS-CICS-RESPONSE1 TO DISPLAY-RESPONSE
         MOVE DEFAULT-DESCRIPTION TO DISPLAY-DESCRIPTION
         MOVE BUILD-MSG TO S1MSGO
     END-EVALUATE.
*
 CHECK-SQL-RESPONSE.
     EVALUATE TRUE
     WHEN SQLCODE = +100
         MOVE NOTFND-MSG TO DISPLAY-DESCRIPTION
         MOVE BUILD-MSG TO S1MSGO
     WHEN SQLCODE = 0
```

FIGURE 15.5 *(Continued)*

```
        CONTINUE
   WHEN SQLCODE = -803 or +65535
        MOVE DUPREC-MSG TO DISPLAY-DESCRIPTION
        MOVE BUILD-MSG TO S1MSGO
   WHEN SQLCODE  0
        CONTINUE
   WHEN OTHER
        MOVE 'CALL PROGRAMMER' TO DISPLAY-CALL-WHOM
        MOVE SQLCODE TO DISPLAY-SQLCODE
        MOVE SQL-DESCRIPTION TO DISPLAY-DESCRIPTION
        MOVE BUILD-MSG TO S1MSGO
   END-EVALUATE.
*
*
```

FIGURE 15.5   *(Continued)*

```
$set ans85 sql osvs sqlaccess"" sqlbind"" sqldb(cicsbook)
 IDENTIFICATION DIVISION.
 PROGRAM-ID. CUSTP002.
 AUTHOR. ALIDA M. JATICH AND PHIL NOWAK.
 ***************************************************************
 * CUSTP002: CHANGE CUSTOMER RECORD CONTENTS (SQL version)     *
 * ON THE FIRST PASS, CUSTP002 GETS THE CUSTOMER NUMBER FROM THE *
 * COMMAREA AND READS THE CUSTOMER ROW HAVING THAT KEY. IT     *
 * SHOWS THE EXISTING CONTENTS ON THE CHANGE SCREEN. THE TERMINAL*
 * USER ENTERS DATA ON THE SCREEN. ON THE NEXT PASS, CUSTP002   *
 * REWRITES THE ROW AND DISPLAYS THE CHANGE SCREEN AGAIN.       *
 ***************************************************************
 ENVIRONMENT DIVISION.
 DATA DIVISION.
 WORKING-STORAGE SECTION.
 *
 EXEC SQL BEGIN DECLARE SECTION END-EXEC.
     COPY CUSTOMER.
 EXEC SQL END DECLARE SECTION END-EXEC.
 *
 EXEC SQL INCLUDE SQLCA END-EXEC.
 *
 01  MISC-WORK.
     05  WS-CICS-RESPONSE1      PIC S9(8) COMP VALUE +0.
     05  WS-TSQ-ITEM1           PIC S9(4) COMP VALUE +1.
     05  WS-XCTL-PGM            PIC X(8)       VALUE SPACES.
 01  QID-NAME.
     05  QID-TRMID              PIC XXXX       VALUE SPACES.
     05  FILLER                 PIC XXXX       VALUE 'CUST'.
 01  CUSTMST-Q.
     05  CUSTNO-Q               PIC X(6)       VALUE SPACES.
     05  FILLER                 PIC X(144)     VALUE SPACES.
 01  ERROR-MESSAGES.
     05  BAD-KEY-MSG            PIC X(22)      VALUE
         'Function key undefined'.
     05  CUST-NUM-MSG           PIC X(27)      VALUE
         'Customer number not numeric'.
     05  MISSING-DATA-MSG       PIC X(26)      VALUE
         'Please supply missing data'.
     05  SUCCESSFUL-CHANGE-MSG  PIC X(27)      VALUE
         'Record changed successfully'.
     05  ENTER-CUST-NO-MSG      PIC X(29)      VALUE
         'Please enter customer number.'.
     05  CHANGE-FIELDS-MSG      PIC X(47)      VALUE
         'Make desired changes to fields and press enter.'.
     05  CANNOT-UPDATE-MSG      PIC X(39)      VALUE
         'Cannot update - record has been changed'.
     05  DISABLED-MSG           PIC X(16)      VALUE
         'File is disabled'.
     05  DSIDERR-MSG            PIC X(14)      VALUE
         'File not found'.
```

FIGURE 15.6   Sample CICS programs using SQL commands.

```
    05  DUPREC-MSG              PIC X(26)      VALUE
        'Record key already on file'.
    05  INVREQ-MSG              PIC X(15)      VALUE
        'Invalid request'.
    05  IOERR-MSG               PIC X(9)       VALUE
        'I/O error'.
    05  ITEMERR-MSG             PIC X(16)      VALUE
        'Item not defined'.
    05  LENGERR-MSG             PIC X(19)      VALUE
        'Record length error'.
    05  NOSPACE-MSG             PIC X(17)      VALUE
        'File out of space'.
    05  NOTFND-MSG              PIC X(22)      VALUE
        'Record key not on file'.
    05  PGMIDERR-MSG            PIC X(27)      VALUE
        'Program not defined to CICS'.
    05  QIDERR-MSG              PIC X(17)      VALUE
        'Queue not defined'.
*
    05  BUILD-MSG.
        10  DISPLAY-OPERATION   PIC X(12)      VALUE SPACES.
        10  FILLER              PIC X          VALUE SPACES.
        10  DISPLAY-RESOURCE    PIC X(8)       VALUE SPACES.
        10  FILLER              PIC X          VALUE SPACES.
        10  DISPLAY-DESCRIPTION PIC X(38)      VALUE SPACES.
        10  FILLER              PIC X          VALUE SPACES.
        10  DISPLAY-CALL-WHOM   PIC X(16)      VALUE SPACES.
*
    05  DEFAULT-DESCRIPTION.
        10  FILLER              PIC X(22)      VALUE
        'CUSTP002 ERROR: RESP1='.
        10  DISPLAY-RESPONSE    PIC 9(8)       VALUE ZEROES.
*
    05  SQL-DESCRIPTION.
        10  FILLER              PIC X(24)      VALUE
        'CUSTP002 ERROR: SQLCODE='.
        10  DISPLAY-SQLCODE     PIC 9(9)-      VALUE ZEROES.
*
COPY CUSTCOMM.
COPY MSALE02.
COPY ATTRIBUT.
COPY DFHAID.
COPY DFHBMSCA.
LINKAGE SECTION.
01  DFHCOMMAREA                 PIC X(104).
*
PROCEDURE DIVISION.
MAIN-PROG.
*
******************************************************************
* DETERMINE WHICH POINT IN THE CYCLE APPLIES TO THE CURRENT      *
* SITUATION. THE FIRST TIME THROUGH, SHOW THE CHANGE SCREEN      *
* FOR THE FIRST TIME. ON SUBSEQUENT PASSES, PROCESS USER INPUT   *
* AND SHOW THE SCREEN AGAIN (OR TRANSFER CONTROL BACK TO THE     *
* MENU PROGRAM, DEPENDING ON FUNCTION KEY).                      *
******************************************************************
*
    MOVE LOW-VALUES TO SALE002I.
*
    IF EIBCALEN NOT = WS-EXPECTED-EIBCALEN
        PERFORM REQUEST-NEW-CUST-NO
    ELSE
        MOVE DFHCOMMAREA TO WS-COMMAREA
        IF EIBTRNID = 'CUS2' AND WS-COMM-PREV-MAP = 'SALE002'
            PERFORM PROCESS-CHANGE-SCREEN
        ELSE
            PERFORM CUST-NO-FROM-COMMAREA.
*
    GOBACK.
*
```

FIGURE 15.6 *(Continued)*

```
***********************************************************************
* DETERMINE WHAT FUNCTION KEY THE USER PRESSED.                       *
***********************************************************************
*
 PROCESS-CHANGE-SCREEN.
*
     IF EIBAID = DFHCLEAR OR DFHPF3
         MOVE 'CUSTP000' TO WS-XCTL-PGM
         PERFORM XCTL-NEXT-PGM
     ELSE
         IF EIBAID = DFHPF10
             PERFORM CURSOR-TO-ACTION-BAR
         ELSE
             IF EIBAID = DFHPF12
                 PERFORM REQUEST-NEW-CUST-NO
             ELSE
                 IF EIBAID NOT = DFHENTER
                     MOVE BAD-KEY-MSG TO S2MSGO
                     MOVE -1 TO S2CUSTL
                     PERFORM SEND-SALE002-BEEP.
*
     MOVE 'MSALE02' TO DISPLAY-RESOURCE.
     MOVE 'RECEIVE MAP' TO DISPLAY-OPERATION.
*
     EXEC CICS RECEIVE MAP ('SALE002')
             MAPSET ('MSALE02')
             INTO (SALE002I)
             RESP (WS-CICS-RESPONSE1)
             END-EXEC.
*
     IF WS-CICS-RESPONSE1 = DFHRESP(MAPFAIL)
         PERFORM CUST-NO-FROM-COMMAREA
     ELSE
         IF WS-CICS-RESPONSE1 NOT = DFHRESP(NORMAL)
             PERFORM CHECK-CICS-RESPONSE
             MOVE -1 TO S2CUSTL
             PERFORM SEND-SALE002-BEEP.
*
     MOVE SPACES TO S2MSGO.
*
***********************************************************************
* IF THE CURSOR WAS ANYWHERE ON THE ACTION BAR, USE THE               *
* POSITION TO SELECT THE ACTION. IF THE CURSOR WAS SOMEWHERE          *
* ELSE, THEN JUST GO WITH THE DEFAULT CHOICE, WHICH IS "CHANGE".*
***********************************************************************
*
     IF EIBCPOSN  9
         MOVE 'CHANGE' TO WS-COMM-ACTION
     ELSE
         IF EIBCPOSN  15
             MOVE 'EXIT' TO WS-COMM-ACTION
         ELSE
             IF EIBCPOSN  23
                 MOVE 'CANCEL' TO WS-COMM-ACTION
             ELSE
                 MOVE 'CHANGE' TO WS-COMM-ACTION.
*
     IF WS-COMM-ACTION = 'EXIT'
         MOVE 'CUSTP000' TO WS-XCTL-PGM
         PERFORM XCTL-NEXT-PGM
     ELSE
         IF WS-COMM-ACTION = 'CANCEL'
             PERFORM REQUEST-NEW-CUST-NO.
*
*
***********************************************************************
* THREE POSSIBLE SITUATIONS:                                          *
* 1. IF USER INPUT IS ON THE SCREEN, CONSISTING OF CHANGES TO         *
*    BE APPLIED TO THE CURRENT CUSTOMER RECORD, ATTEMPT TO            *
*    APPLY THOSE UPDATES. IN THAT CASE, A VALID (NUMERIC)             *
```

FIGURE 15.6 *(Continued)*

```
*     CUSTOMER NUMBER WILL APPEAR IN THE COMMAREA AND WILL          *
*     AGREE WITH THE CUSTOMER NUMBER ON THE SCREEN.                 *
* 2.  IF THE COMMAREA DOES NOT CONTAIN A VALID CUSTOMER NUMBER,     *
*     OR IF THE CUSTOMER NUMBER ON THE SCREEN HAS BEEN CLEARED,     *
*     ASK THE TERMINAL USER TO ENTER A NEW CUSTOMER NUMBER.         *
* 3.  IF A NEW CUSTOMER NUMBER HAS BEEN ENTERED ON THE SCREEN,      *
*     SEND A SCREEN TO THE TERMINAL USER DISPLAYING THOSE           *
*     RECORD CONTENTS FOR MODIFICATION.                             *
*                                                                   *
*********************************************************************
*
      IF WS-COMM-CUST-NO IS NUMERIC
            AND S2CUSTI = WS-COMM-CUST-NO
         PERFORM ATTEMPT-UPDATE
      ELSE
         IF S2CUSTI IS NOT NUMERIC
            PERFORM REQUEST-NEW-CUST-NO
         ELSE
            MOVE S2CUSTO TO WS-COMM-CUST-NO
            PERFORM CUST-NO-FROM-COMMAREA.
*
*********************************************************************
* THIS ROUTINE OBTAINS ORIGINAL CUSTOMER MASTER RECORD CONTENTS *
* FROM A TEMPORARY STORAGE RECORD WRITTEN ON THE PREVIOUS PASS. *
*                                                              *
* BEFORE ALLOWING ANY UPDATES TO TAKE PLACE, CUSTP002 READS    *
* THE CUSTOMER MASTER RECORD AGAIN AND COMPARES THE CONTENTS   *
* WITH THE CONTENTS OF THE TEMPORARY STORAGE RECORD. IF THEY   *
* MATCH, UPDATE PROCESSING CAN CONTINUE.                       *
*                                                              *
* HOWEVER, IF THE CUSTOMER MASTER RECORDS DIFFER FROM THE      *
* CONTENTS OF THE TEMPORARY STORAGE RECORD, THEN SOME OTHER    *
* USER HAS ALSO BEEN WORKING WITH THE SAME RECORD. IN THAT     *
* CASE, UPDATE PROCESSING IS DISCONTINUED TO PREVENT CONFLICTS. *
*********************************************************************
*
 ATTEMPT-UPDATE.
*
      MOVE EIBTRMID TO QID-TRMID.
      MOVE QID-NAME TO DISPLAY-RESOURCE.
      MOVE 'READQ TS' TO DISPLAY-OPERATION.
*
      EXEC CICS READQ TS
            QUEUE (QID-NAME)
            INTO (CUSTMST-Q)
            ITEM (WS-TSQ-ITEM1)
            RESP (WS-CICS-RESPONSE1)
            END-EXEC.
*
      IF WS-CICS-RESPONSE1 NOT = DFHRESP(NORMAL)
         PERFORM CHECK-CICS-RESPONSE
         MOVE -1 TO S2CUSTL
         PERFORM SEND-SALE002-BEEP.
*
*********************************************************************
* SELECT THE EXISTING ROW TO BE UPDATED.                         *
* OBTAIN NULL INDICATORS (-NI SUFFIX) FOR NULLABLE FIELDS.       *
*********************************************************************
      MOVE WS-COMM-CUST-NO TO CUST-NO.
      MOVE 'CUSTOMER' TO DISPLAY-RESOURCE.
      MOVE 'SELECT' TO DISPLAY-OPERATION.
      EXEC SQL SELECT
            CUSTNAME, CONTACT, STREETADDR,
            CITY, STATE, ZIP,
            LASTBILLDATE, LASTBALDUE, CURRWKSALES
            INTO :CUST-NAME, :CUST-CONTACT,
            :CUST-STREET-ADDRESS, :CUST-CITY,
            :CUST-STATE, :CUST-ZIP,
            :CUST-LAST-BILL-DATE:CUST-LAST-BILL-DATE-NI,
            :CUST-LAST-BILL-BAL-DUE:CUST-LAST-BILL-BAL-DUE-NI,
```

FIGURE 15.6   *(Continued)*

```
                    :CUST-CURR-WK-SALES:CUST-CURR-WK-SALES-NI
                    FROM CUSTOMER
                    WHERE CUSTNO = :CUST-NO
                    END-EXEC.
     *
           MOVE -1 TO S2CUSTL.
           IF SQLCODE NOT = 0
               PERFORM CHECK-SQL-RESPONSE
               PERFORM SEND-SALE002-BEEP.
     *
           IF CUST-NAME NOT  SPACES
               MOVE NOTFND-MSG TO DISPLAY-DESCRIPTION
               MOVE BUILD-MSG TO S2MSGO
               PERFORM SEND-SALE002-BEEP.
     *
           IF CUSTMST-REC NOT = CUSTMST-Q
               MOVE CANNOT-UPDATE-MSG TO S2MSGO
               MOVE -1 TO S2CUSTL
               PERFORM SEND-SALE002-BEEP.
     *
           IF S2NAMEL  ZEROES AND S2NAMEI  SPACES
               MOVE S2NAMEI TO CUST-NAME.
     *
           IF S2CNTCTL  ZEROES AND S2CNTCTI  SPACES
               MOVE S2CNTCTI TO CUST-CONTACT.
     *
           IF S2ADDRL  ZEROES AND S2ADDRI  SPACES
               MOVE S2ADDRI TO CUST-STREET-ADDRESS.
     *
           IF S2CITYL  ZEROES AND S2CITYI  SPACES
               MOVE S2CITYI TO CUST-CITY.
     *
           IF S2STATEL  ZEROES AND S2STATEI IS ALPHABETIC
               MOVE S2STATEI TO CUST-STATE.
     *
           IF S2ZIPL  ZEROES AND S2ZIPI  SPACES
               MOVE S2ZIPI TO CUST-ZIP.
     *
     *
     ********************************************************************
     * UPDATE THE CUSTOMER ROW.                                        *
     ********************************************************************
           MOVE 'CUSTOMER' TO DISPLAY-RESOURCE.
           MOVE 'UPDATE' TO DISPLAY-OPERATION.
           EXEC SQL UPDATE CUSTOMER
               SET CUSTNAME = :CUST-NAME,
                   CONTACT = :CUST-CONTACT,
                   STREETADDR = :CUST-STREET-ADDRESS,
                   CITY = :CUST-CITY,
                   STATE = :CUST-STATE,
                   ZIP = :CUST-ZIP
               WHERE CUSTNO = :CUST-NO
               END-EXEC.
     *
     *
           MOVE -1 TO S2CUSTL.
     *
     ********************************************************************
     * IF THE UPDATE WAS SUCCESSFUL, THE TERMINAL USER MAY OVERKEY     *
     * THE CUSTOMER NUMBER TO UPDATE A DIFFERENT RECORD NEXT TIME.     *
     * IF THE UPDATE WAS NOT SUCCESSFUL, DISPLAY A MESSAGE             *
     * EXPLAINING WHY NOT.                                             *
     ********************************************************************
     *
           IF SQLCODE = 0
               MOVE SUCCESSFUL-CHANGE-MSG TO S2MSGO
               MOVE -1 TO S2CUSTL
               MOVE ENTER-CUST-NO-MSG TO S2INSTRO
               PERFORM SEND-SALE002-RETURN
           ELSE
```

FIGURE 15.6 *(Continued)*

```
                PERFORM CHECK-SQL-RESPONSE
                PERFORM SEND-SALE002-BEEP.
    *
    *
     XCTL-NEXT-PGM.
    *
         MOVE WS-XCTL-PGM TO DISPLAY-RESOURCE.
         MOVE 'XCTL' TO DISPLAY-OPERATION.
         EXEC CICS XCTL
                 PROGRAM (WS-XCTL-PGM)
                 COMMAREA (WS-COMMAREA)
                 RESP (WS-CICS-RESPONSE1)
                 END-EXEC.
    *
         IF WS-CICS-RESPONSE1 NOT = DFHRESP(NORMAL)
             PERFORM CHECK-CICS-RESPONSE
             MOVE -1 TO S2CUSTL
             PERFORM SEND-SALE002-BEEP.
    *
    *
    *********************************************************************
    * THIS ROUTINE TAKES THE CUSTOMER NUMBER FROM THE WORKING          *
    * STORAGE COPY OF THE DFHCOMMAREA AND USES IT TO READ A            *
    * CUSTOMER RECORD. IT SHOWS THE RECORD ON THE CHANGE SCREEN.       *
    *********************************************************************
    *
     CUST-NO-FROM-COMMAREA.
    *
         IF WS-COMM-CUST-NO IS NOT NUMERIC
             PERFORM REQUEST-NEW-CUST-NO.
    *
         MOVE WS-COMM-CUST-NO TO S2CUSTO.
         MOVE -1 TO S2NAMEL.
         MOVE SPACES TO S2MSGO.
    *
    *
    *********************************************************************
    * SELECT THE EXISTING ROW TO BE DISPLAYED.                         *
    * OBTAIN NULL INDICATORS (-NI SUFFIX) FOR NULLABLE FIELDS.         *
    *********************************************************************
         MOVE WS-COMM-CUST-NO TO CUST-NO.
         MOVE 'CUSTOMER' TO DISPLAY-RESOURCE.
         MOVE 'SELECT' TO DISPLAY-OPERATION.
         EXEC SQL SELECT
                 CUSTNAME, CONTACT, STREETADDR,
                 CITY, STATE, ZIP,
                 LASTBILLDATE, LASTBALDUE, CURRWKSALES
                 INTO :CUST-NAME, :CUST-CONTACT,
                 :CUST-STREET-ADDRESS, :CUST-CITY,
                 :CUST-STATE, :CUST-ZIP,
                 :CUST-LAST-BILL-DATE:CUST-LAST-BILL-DATE-NI,
                 :CUST-LAST-BILL-BAL-DUE:CUST-LAST-BILL-BAL-DUE-NI,
                 :CUST-CURR-WK-SALES:CUST-CURR-WK-SALES-NI
                 FROM CUSTOMER
                 WHERE CUSTNO = :CUST-NO
                 END-EXEC.
    *
         MOVE -1 TO S2CUSTL.
         IF SQLCODE NOT = 0
             PERFORM CHECK-SQL-RESPONSE
             PERFORM SEND-SALE002-BEEP.
    *
         IF CUST-NAME NOT  SPACES
             MOVE NOTFND-MSG TO DISPLAY-DESCRIPTION
             MOVE BUILD-MSG TO S2MSGO
             PERFORM SEND-SALE002-BEEP.
    *
    *********************************************************************
    * DELETE THE OLD TEMP STORAGE QUEUE THAT MIGHT BE LEFT FROM        *
    * PREVIOUS TASKS. THE QUEUE ID IS BUILT FROM THE TRAN CODE AND     *
```

FIGURE 15.6 *(Continued)*

```
* THE TERMINAL ID.                                                     *
**********************************************************************
*
     MOVE EIBTRMID TO QID-TRMID.
     MOVE QID-NAME TO DISPLAY-RESOURCE.
     MOVE 'DELETEQ TS' TO DISPLAY-OPERATION.
*
     EXEC CICS DELETEQ TS
               QUEUE (QID-NAME)
               RESP (WS-CICS-RESPONSE1)
               END-EXEC.
*
     IF WS-CICS-RESPONSE1 NOT = DFHRESP(NORMAL)
          AND WS-CICS-RESPONSE1 NOT = DFHRESP(QIDERR)
         PERFORM CHECK-CICS-RESPONSE
         PERFORM SEND-SALE002-BEEP.
*
     MOVE QID-NAME TO DISPLAY-RESOURCE.
     MOVE 'WRITEQ TS' TO DISPLAY-OPERATION.
*
     EXEC CICS WRITEQ TS
               QUEUE (QID-NAME)
               FROM (CUSTMST-REC)
               ITEM (WS-TSQ-ITEM1)
               RESP (WS-CICS-RESPONSE1)
               END-EXEC.
*
     IF WS-CICS-RESPONSE1 NOT = DFHRESP(NORMAL)
         PERFORM CHECK-CICS-RESPONSE
         PERFORM SEND-SALE002-BEEP.
*
**********************************************************************
* PUT EXISTING RECORD CONTENTS ON THE SCREEN.                        *
* THE AMOUNT FIELDS ARE DISPLAY-ONLY AND CANNOT BE CHANGED.          *
* THREE FIELDS ARE NULLABLE...THEY HAVE A FLAG WHICH INDICATES       *
* WHETHER OR NOT VALID DATA IS IN THE FIELDS.                        *
**********************************************************************
*
     MOVE CUST-NO TO S2CUSTO.
     MOVE CUST-NAME TO S2NAMEO.
     MOVE CUST-CONTACT TO S2CNTCTO.
     MOVE CUST-STREET-ADDRESS TO S2ADDRO.
     MOVE CUST-CITY TO S2CITYO.
     MOVE CUST-STATE TO S2STATEO.
     MOVE CUST-ZIP TO S2ZIPO.
     IF CUST-CURR-WK-SALES-NI  0
         MOVE SPACES TO S2SALESI
     ELSE
         MOVE CUST-CURR-WK-SALES TO S2SALESO.
     IF CUST-LAST-BILL-BAL-DUE-NI  0
         MOVE SPACES TO S2BALI
     ELSE
         MOVE CUST-LAST-BILL-BAL-DUE TO S2BALO.
     IF CUST-LAST-BILL-DATE-NI  0
         MOVE SPACES TO S2BDATEI
     ELSE
         MOVE CUST-LAST-BILL-DATE TO S2BDATEO.
*
     MOVE CHANGE-FIELDS-MSG TO S2INSTRO.
     MOVE SPACES TO S2MSGO.
*
     PERFORM SEND-SALE002-RETURN.
*
*
**********************************************************************
* THIS ROUTINE CLEARS THE SCREEN AND ASKS THE USER TO ENTER THE *
* KEY OF THE NEXT RECORD TO BE CHANGED.                         *
**********************************************************************
*
 REQUEST-NEW-CUST-NO.
```

FIGURE 15.6 *(Continued)*

```
*
    MOVE SPACES TO WS-COMM-CUST-NO.
    MOVE -1 TO S2CUSTL.
    MOVE ENTER-CUST-NO-MSG TO S2INSTRO.
    MOVE SPACES TO S2MSGO.
*
    MOVE ALL '_' TO S2CUSTO.
    MOVE SPACES TO S2NAMEO
                  S2CNTCTO
                  S2ADDRO
                  S2CITYO
                  S2STATEO
                  S2ZIPO
                  S2SALESO
                  S2BALO
                  S2BDATEO.
*
*********************************************************************
* DELETE THE OLD TEMP STORAGE QUEUE THAT MIGHT BE LEFT FROM       *
* PREVIOUS TASKS. THE QUEUE ID IS BUILT FROM THE TRAN CODE AND    *
* THE TERMINAL ID.                                               *
*********************************************************************
*
    MOVE EIBTRMID TO QID-TRMID.
    MOVE QID-NAME TO DISPLAY-RESOURCE.
    MOVE 'DELETEQ TS' TO DISPLAY-OPERATION.
*
    EXEC CICS DELETEQ TS
            QUEUE (QID-NAME)
            RESP (WS-CICS-RESPONSE1)
            END-EXEC.
*
    IF WS-CICS-RESPONSE1 NOT = DFHRESP(NORMAL)
            AND WS-CICS-RESPONSE1 NOT = DFHRESP(QIDERR)
        PERFORM CHECK-CICS-RESPONSE
        PERFORM SEND-SALE002-BEEP.
*
    PERFORM SEND-SALE002-RETURN.
*
*
*********************************************************************
* THIS ROUTINE SENDS SALE002 WITH A WARNING 'BEEP'. WE USE THIS   *
* ONLY WHEN THE CALLING ROUTINE WANTS TO DISPLAY A WARNING ON     *
* THE MESSAGE LINE OF THIS MAP. CURSOR POSITION MUST BE SET.      *
*********************************************************************
*
 SEND-SALE002-BEEP.
*
    IF WS-COMM-PREV-MAP = 'SALE002'
        EXEC CICS SEND MAP ('SALE002')
                MAPSET ('MSALE02')
                FROM (SALE002I)
                DATAONLY
                ALARM
                CURSOR
                END-EXEC
    ELSE
        MOVE 'SALE002' TO WS-COMM-PREV-MAP
        EXEC CICS SEND MAP ('SALE002')
                MAPSET ('MSALE02')
                FROM (SALE002I)
                ERASE
                ALARM
                CURSOR
                END-EXEC.
*
    EXEC CICS RETURN
            TRANSID ('CUS2')
            COMMAREA (WS-COMMAREA)
            END-EXEC.
```

FIGURE 15.6   *(Continued)*

```
*
*
*********************************************************************
* THIS ROUTINE SENDS SALE002 WITH WHATEVER DATA HAS BEEN PLACED *
* ON IT. IF THE PREDEFINED PORTIONS OF THE MAP ARE ALREADY ON   *
* THE SCREEN, SALE002 WILL BE SENT 'DATAONLY'.                  *
*********************************************************************
*
 SEND-SALE002-RETURN.
*
     IF WS-COMM-PREV-MAP = 'SALE002'
         EXEC CICS SEND MAP ('SALE002')
                   MAPSET ('MSALE02')
                   FROM (SALE002I)
                   DATAONLY
                   CURSOR
                   END-EXEC
     ELSE
         MOVE 'SALE002' TO WS-COMM-PREV-MAP
         EXEC CICS SEND MAP ('SALE002')
                   MAPSET ('MSALE02')
                   FROM (SALE002I)
                   ERASE
                   CURSOR
                   END-EXEC.
*
     EXEC CICS RETURN
               TRANSID ('CUS2')
               COMMAREA (WS-COMMAREA)
               END-EXEC.
*
*********************************************************************
* THIS ROUTINE SENDS SALE002 WITH CURSOR ON ACTION BAR.         *
*********************************************************************
*
 CURSOR-TO-ACTION-BAR.
*
     MOVE 'SALE002' TO WS-COMM-PREV-MAP.
     EXEC CICS SEND MAP ('SALE002')
               MAPSET ('MSALE02')
               FROM (SALE002I)
               CURSOR (1)
               DATAONLY
               END-EXEC.
*
     EXEC CICS RETURN
               TRANSID ('CUS2')
               COMMAREA (WS-COMMAREA)
               END-EXEC.
*
*
*********************************************************************
* CHECK THE CICS RESPONSE CODE AND BUILD A MESSAGE EXPLAINING    *
* THE ERROR. IT IS THE RESPONSIBILITY OF THE CALLING ROUTINE    *
* TO INITIALIZE SOME DISPLAY FIELDS IN THE MESSAGE WORK AREA    *
* TO INDICATE THE TYPE OF COMMAND BEING PROCESSED.              *
*                                                               *
* WE DO NOTHING ABOUT CERTAIN RESPONSE CODES HERE SO THAT       *
* THOSE SITUATIONS CAN BE HANDLED WITH LOGIC ELSEWHERE IN THE   *
* PROGRAM.                                                      *
*                                                               *
*********************************************************************
*
 CHECK-CICS-RESPONSE.
*
     EVALUATE WS-CICS-RESPONSE1
     WHEN DFHRESP(NORMAL)
         CONTINUE
     WHEN DFHRESP(MAPFAIL)
         CONTINUE
```

FIGURE 15.6   *(Continued)*

```
          WHEN DFHRESP(ENDFILE)
              CONTINUE
          WHEN DFHRESP(DISABLED)
              MOVE 'CALL OPERATIONS' TO DISPLAY-CALL-WHOM
              MOVE DISABLED-MSG TO DISPLAY-DESCRIPTION
              MOVE BUILD-MSG TO S2MSGO
          WHEN DFHRESP(DUPREC)
              MOVE DUPREC-MSG TO DISPLAY-DESCRIPTION
              MOVE BUILD-MSG TO S2MSGO
          WHEN DFHRESP(DSIDERR)
              MOVE 'CALL PROGRAMMER' TO DISPLAY-CALL-WHOM
              MOVE DSIDERR-MSG TO DISPLAY-DESCRIPTION
              MOVE BUILD-MSG TO S2MSGO
          WHEN DFHRESP(INVREQ)
              MOVE 'CALL PROGRAMMER' TO DISPLAY-CALL-WHOM
              MOVE INVREQ-MSG TO DISPLAY-DESCRIPTION
              MOVE BUILD-MSG TO S2MSGO
          WHEN DFHRESP(IOERR)
              MOVE 'CALL PROGRAMMER' TO DISPLAY-CALL-WHOM
              MOVE IOERR-MSG TO DISPLAY-DESCRIPTION
              MOVE BUILD-MSG TO S2MSGO
          WHEN DFHRESP(ITEMERR)
              MOVE 'CALL PROGRAMMER' TO DISPLAY-CALL-WHOM
              MOVE ITEMERR-MSG TO DISPLAY-DESCRIPTION
              MOVE BUILD-MSG TO S2MSGO
          WHEN DFHRESP(LENGERR)
              MOVE 'CALL PROGRAMMER' TO DISPLAY-CALL-WHOM
              MOVE LENGERR-MSG TO DISPLAY-DESCRIPTION
              MOVE BUILD-MSG TO S2MSGO
          WHEN DFHRESP(NOSPACE)
              MOVE 'CALL OPERATIONS' TO DISPLAY-CALL-WHOM
              MOVE NOSPACE-MSG TO DISPLAY-DESCRIPTION
              MOVE BUILD-MSG TO S2MSGO
          WHEN DFHRESP(NOTFND)
              MOVE NOTFND-MSG TO DISPLAY-DESCRIPTION
              MOVE BUILD-MSG TO S2MSGO
          WHEN DFHRESP(PGMIDERR)
              MOVE 'CALL PROGRAMMER' TO DISPLAY-CALL-WHOM
              MOVE PGMIDERR-MSG TO DISPLAY-DESCRIPTION
              MOVE BUILD-MSG TO S2MSGO
          WHEN DFHRESP(QIDERR)
              MOVE 'CALL PROGRAMMER' TO DISPLAY-CALL-WHOM
              MOVE QIDERR-MSG TO DISPLAY-DESCRIPTION
              MOVE BUILD-MSG TO S2MSGO
          WHEN OTHER
              MOVE 'CALL PROGRAMMER' TO DISPLAY-CALL-WHOM
              MOVE WS-CICS-RESPONSE1 TO DISPLAY-RESPONSE
              MOVE DEFAULT-DESCRIPTION TO DISPLAY-DESCRIPTION
              MOVE BUILD-MSG TO S2MSGO
          END-EVALUATE.
      *
      *
      *
      *
       CHECK-SQL-RESPONSE.
          EVALUATE TRUE
          WHEN SQLCODE = +100
              MOVE NOTFND-MSG TO DISPLAY-DESCRIPTION
              MOVE BUILD-MSG TO S2MSGO
          WHEN SQLCODE = 0
              CONTINUE
          WHEN SQLCODE = -803 OR +65535
              MOVE DUPREC-MSG TO DISPLAY-DESCRIPTION
              MOVE BUILD-MSG TO S2MSGO
          WHEN SQLCODE   0
              CONTINUE
          WHEN OTHER
              MOVE 'CALL PROGRAMMER' TO DISPLAY-CALL-WHOM
              MOVE SQLCODE TO DISPLAY-SQLCODE
              MOVE SQL-DESCRIPTION TO DISPLAY-DESCRIPTION
              MOVE BUILD-MSG TO S2MSGO
          END-EVALUATE.
      *
```

FIGURE 15.6 *(Continued)*

```
$set ans85 sql osvs sqlaccess"" sqlbind"" sqldb(cicsbook)
IDENTIFICATION DIVISION.
PROGRAM-ID. CUSTP003.
AUTHOR. ALIDA M. JATICH AND PHIL NOWAK.
*************************************************************
* CUSTP003: DELETE CUSTOMER RECORD - SQL VERSION           *
* ON THE FIRST PASS, CUSTP003 GETS THE CUSTOMER NUMBER FROM THE *
* COMMAREA AND READS THE CUSTOMER ROW HAVING THAT KEY. IT  *
* SHOWS THE EXISTING CONTENTS ON THE DELETE SCREEN. THE TERMINAL*
* USER PRESSES ENTER TO DELETE. ON THE NEXT PASS, CUSTP003 *
* DELETES THE ROW AND DISPLAYS THE DELETE SCREEN AGAIN.    *
*************************************************************
ENVIRONMENT DIVISION.
DATA DIVISION.
WORKING-STORAGE SECTION.
*
EXEC SQL BEGIN DECLARE SECTION END-EXEC.
    COPY CUSTOMER.
EXEC SQL END DECLARE SECTION END-EXEC.
*
EXEC SQL INCLUDE SQLCA END-EXEC.
*
01  MISC-WORK.
    05  WS-CICS-RESPONSE1      PIC S9(8) COMP VALUE +0.
    05  WS-TSQ-ITEM1           PIC S9(4) COMP VALUE +1.
    05  WS-XCTL-PGM            PIC X(8)       VALUE SPACES.
01  QID-NAME.
    05  QID-TRMID              PIC XXXX       VALUE SPACES.
    05  FILLER                 PIC XXXX       VALUE 'CUST'.
01  CUSTMST-Q.
    05  CUSTNO-Q               PIC X(6)       VALUE SPACES.
    05  FILLER                 PIC X(144)     VALUE SPACES.
01  ERROR-MESSAGES.
    05  BAD-KEY-MSG            PIC X(22)      VALUE
        'Function key undefined'.
    05  CUST-NUM-MSG           PIC X(27)      VALUE
        'Customer number not numeric'.
    05  MISSING-DATA-MSG       PIC X(26)      VALUE
        'Please supply missing data'.
    05  SUCCESSFUL-DELETE-MSG  PIC X(27)      VALUE
        'Record deleted successfully'.
    05  ENTER-CUST-NO-MSG      PIC X(29)      VALUE
        'Please enter customer number.'.
    05  DELETE-RECORD-MSG      PIC X(44)      VALUE
        'Press enter key to delete or PF12 to cancel.'.
    05  CANNOT-DELETE-MSG      PIC X(39)      VALUE
        'Cannot delete - sales greater than zero'.
    05  RECORD-CHANGED-MSG     PIC X(39)      VALUE
        'Cannot delete - record has been changed'.
    05  DISABLED-MSG           PIC X(16)      VALUE
        'File is disabled'.
    05  DSIDERR-MSG            PIC X(14)      VALUE
        'File not found'.
    05  DUPREC-MSG             PIC X(22)      VALUE
        'Record already on file'.
    05  INVREQ-MSG             PIC X(15)      VALUE
        'Invalid request'.
    05  IOERR-MSG              PIC X(9)       VALUE
        'I/O error'.
    05  ITEMERR-MSG            PIC X(16)      VALUE
        'Item not defined'.
    05  LENGERR-MSG            PIC X(19)      VALUE
        'Record length error'.
    05  NOSPACE-MSG            PIC X(17)      VALUE
        'File out of space'.
    05  NOTFND-MSG             PIC X(18)      VALUE
        'Record not on file'.
    05  PGMIDERR-MSG           PIC X(27)      VALUE
        'Program not defined to CICS'.
    05  QIDERR-MSG             PIC X(17)      VALUE
```

FIGURE 15.7 Sample CICS programs using SQL commands.

```
                'Queue not defined'.
      *
          05  BUILD-MSG.
              10  DISPLAY-OPERATION   PIC X(12)       VALUE SPACES.
              10  FILLER              PIC X           VALUE SPACES.
              10  DISPLAY-RESOURCE    PIC X(8)        VALUE SPACES.
              10  FILLER              PIC X           VALUE SPACES.
              10  DISPLAY-DESCRIPTION PIC X(38)       VALUE SPACES.
              10  FILLER              PIC X           VALUE SPACES.
              10  DISPLAY-CALL-WHOM   PIC X(16)       VALUE SPACES.
      *
          05  DEFAULT-DESCRIPTION.
              10  FILLER              PIC X(22)       VALUE
              'CUSTP003 ERROR: RESP1='.
              10  DISPLAY-RESPONSE    PIC 9(8)        VALUE ZEROES.
      *
          05  SQL-DESCRIPTION.
              10  FILLER              PIC X(24)       VALUE
              'CUSTP003 ERROR: SQLCODE='.
              10  DISPLAY-SQLCODE     PIC 9(9)-       VALUE ZEROES.

      *
       COPY CUSTCOMM.
       COPY MSALE03.
       COPY ATTRIBUT.
       COPY DFHAID.
       COPY DFHBMSCA.
       LINKAGE SECTION.
       01  DFHCOMMAREA                 PIC X(104).
      *
       PROCEDURE DIVISION.
       MAIN-PROG.
      *
      **********************************************************************
      * DETERMINE WHICH POINT IN THE CYCLE APPLIES TO THE CURRENT         *
      * SITUATION. THE FIRST TIME THROUGH, SHOW THE DELETE SCREEN         *
      * FOR THE FIRST TIME. ON SUBSEQUENT PASSES, PROCESS USER INPUT      *
      * AND SHOW THE SCREEN AGAIN (OR TRANSFER CONTROL BACK TO THE        *
      * MENU PROGRAM, DEPENDING ON FUNCTION KEY).                         *
      **********************************************************************
      *
          MOVE LOW-VALUES TO SALE003I.
      *
          IF EIBCALEN NOT = WS-EXPECTED-EIBCALEN
              PERFORM REQUEST-NEW-CUST-NO
          ELSE
              MOVE DFHCOMMAREA TO WS-COMMAREA
              IF EIBTRNID = 'CUS3' AND WS-COMM-PREV-MAP = 'SALE003'
                  PERFORM PROCESS-DELETE-SCREEN
              ELSE
                  PERFORM CUST-NO-FROM-COMMAREA.
      *
          GOBACK.
      *
      **********************************************************************
      * DETERMINE WHAT FUNCTION KEY THE USER PRESSED.                     *
      **********************************************************************
      *
       PROCESS-DELETE-SCREEN.
      *
          IF EIBAID = DFHCLEAR OR DFHPF3
              MOVE 'CUSTP000' TO WS-XCTL-PGM
              PERFORM XCTL-NEXT-PGM
          ELSE
              IF EIBAID = DFHPF10
                  PERFORM CURSOR-TO-ACTION-BAR
              ELSE
                  IF EIBAID = DFHPF12
                      PERFORM REQUEST-NEW-CUST-NO
                  ELSE
```

                        FIGURE 15.7   *(Continued)*

```
                      IF EIBAID NOT = DFHENTER
                          MOVE BAD-KEY-MSG TO S3MSGO
                          MOVE -1 TO S3CUSTL
                          PERFORM SEND-SALE003-BEEP.
    *
        MOVE 'MSALE03' TO DISPLAY-RESOURCE.
        MOVE 'RECEIVE MAP' TO DISPLAY-OPERATION.
    *
        EXEC CICS RECEIVE MAP ('SALE003')
                  MAPSET ('MSALE03')
                  INTO (SALE003I)
                  RESP (WS-CICS-RESPONSE1)
                  END-EXEC.
    *
        IF WS-CICS-RESPONSE1 = DFHRESP(MAPFAIL)
            PERFORM CUST-NO-FROM-COMMAREA
        ELSE
            IF WS-CICS-RESPONSE1 NOT = DFHRESP(NORMAL)
                PERFORM CHECK-CICS-RESPONSE
                MOVE -1 TO S3CUSTL
                PERFORM SEND-SALE003-BEEP.
    *
        MOVE SPACES TO S3MSGO.
    *
    *********************************************************************
    * IF THE CURSOR WAS ANYWHERE ON THE ACTION BAR, USE THE            *
    * POSITION TO SELECT THE ACTION. IF THE CURSOR WAS SOMEWHERE       *
    * ELSE, THEN JUST GO WITH THE DEFAULT CHOICE, WHICH IS "DELETE".*
    *********************************************************************
    *
        IF EIBCPOSN  9
            MOVE 'DELETE' TO WS-COMM-ACTION
        ELSE
            IF EIBCPOSN  15
                MOVE 'EXIT' TO WS-COMM-ACTION
            ELSE
                IF EIBCPOSN  23
                    MOVE 'CANCEL' TO WS-COMM-ACTION
                ELSE
                    MOVE 'DELETE' TO WS-COMM-ACTION.
    *
        IF WS-COMM-ACTION = 'EXIT'
            MOVE 'CUSTP000' TO WS-XCTL-PGM
            PERFORM XCTL-NEXT-PGM
        ELSE
            IF WS-COMM-ACTION = 'CANCEL'
                PERFORM REQUEST-NEW-CUST-NO.
    *
    *
    *********************************************************************
    * THREE POSSIBLE SITUATIONS:                                       *
    * 1. IF A RECORD IS BEING DISPLAYED ON THE SCREEN FOR POSSIBLE     *
    *    DELETION, ATTEMPT TO DELETE THE RECORD. IN THAT CASE, A       *
    *    VALID (NUMERIC) CUSTOMER NUMBER WILL APPEAR IN THE            *
    *    COMMAREA AND WILL AGREE WITH THE CUSTOMER NUMBER ON THE       *
    *    SCREEN.                                                       *
    * 2. IF THE COMMAREA DOES NOT CONTAIN A VALID CUSTOMER NUMBER,     *
    *    OR IF THE CUSTOMER NUMBER ON THE SCREEN HAS BEEN CLEARED,     *
    *    ASK THE TERMINAL USER TO ENTER A NEW CUSTOMER NUMBER.         *
    * 3. IF A NEW CUSTOMER NUMBER HAS BEEN ENTERED ON THE SCREEN,      *
    *    SEND A SCREEN TO THE TERMINAL USER DISPLAYING THE             *
    *    CONTENTS OF THAT RECORD.                                      *
    *                                                                 *
    *********************************************************************
    *
        IF WS-COMM-CUST-NO IS NUMERIC
                AND S3CUSTI = WS-COMM-CUST-NO
            PERFORM ATTEMPT-DELETE
        ELSE
            IF S3CUSTI IS NOT NUMERIC
```

FIGURE 15.7 *(Continued)*

```
                    PERFORM REQUEST-NEW-CUST-NO
              ELSE
                    MOVE S3CUSTO TO WS-COMM-CUST-NO
                    PERFORM CUST-NO-FROM-COMMAREA.
 *
 *******************************************************************
 * THIS ROUTINE OBTAINS ORIGINAL CUSTOMER MASTER RECORD CONTENTS *
 * FROM A TEMPORARY STORAGE RECORD WRITTEN ON THE PREVIOUS PASS. *
 *                                                               *
 * BEFORE ALLOWING DELETION TO TAKE PLACE, CUSTP003 READS        *
 * THE CUSTOMER MASTER RECORD AGAIN AND COMPARES THE CONTENTS    *
 * WITH THE CONTENTS OF THE TEMPORARY STORAGE RECORD. IF THEY    *
 * MATCH, PROCESSING CAN CONTINUE.                               *
 *                                                               *
 * HOWEVER, IF THE CUSTOMER MASTER RECORDS DIFFER FROM THE       *
 * CONTENTS OF THE TEMPORARY STORAGE RECORD, THEN SOME OTHER     *
 * USER HAS ALSO BEEN WORKING WITH THE SAME RECORD. IN THAT      *
 * CASE, PROCESSING IS DISCONTINUED TO PREVENT CONFLICTS.        *
 *******************************************************************
 *
 ATTEMPT-DELETE.
 *
      MOVE EIBTRMID TO QID-TRMID.
      MOVE QID-NAME TO DISPLAY-RESOURCE.
      MOVE 'READQ TS' TO DISPLAY-OPERATION.
      EXEC CICS READQ TS
              QUEUE (QID-NAME)
              INTO (CUSTMST-Q)
              ITEM (WS-TSQ-ITEM1)
              RESP (WS-CICS-RESPONSE1)
              END-EXEC.
 *
      IF WS-CICS-RESPONSE1 NOT = DFHRESP(NORMAL)
          PERFORM CHECK-CICS-RESPONSE
          MOVE -1 TO S3CUSTL
          PERFORM SEND-SALE003-BEEP.
 *
 *******************************************************************
 * READ THE EXISTING ROW TO FIND OUT WHETHER IT CAN BE DELETED.  *
 * OBTAIN NULL INDICATORS (-NI SUFFIX) FOR NULLABLE FIELDS.      *
 *******************************************************************
      MOVE WS-COMM-CUST-NO TO CUST-NO.
      MOVE 'CUSTOMER' TO DISPLAY-RESOURCE.
      MOVE 'SELECT' TO DISPLAY-OPERATION.
      EXEC SQL SELECT
              CUSTNAME, CONTACT, STREETADDR,
              CITY, STATE, ZIP,
              LASTBILLDATE, LASTBALDUE, CURRWKSALES
              INTO :CUST-NAME, :CUST-CONTACT,
              :CUST-STREET-ADDRESS, :CUST-CITY,
              :CUST-STATE, :CUST-ZIP,
              :CUST-LAST-BILL-DATE:CUST-LAST-BILL-DATE-NI,
              :CUST-LAST-BILL-BAL-DUE:CUST-LAST-BILL-BAL-DUE-NI,
              :CUST-CURR-WK-SALES:CUST-CURR-WK-SALES-NI
              FROM CUSTOMER
              WHERE CUSTNO = :CUST-NO
              END-EXEC.
 *
      MOVE -1 TO S3CUSTL.
      IF SQLCODE NOT = 0
          PERFORM CHECK-SQL-RESPONSE
          PERFORM SEND-SALE003-BEEP.
 *
      IF CUST-NAME NOT  SPACES
          MOVE NOTFND-MSG TO DISPLAY-DESCRIPTION
          MOVE BUILD-MSG TO S3MSGO
          PERFORM SEND-SALE003-BEEP.
 *
      IF CUSTMST-REC NOT = CUSTMST-Q
          MOVE RECORD-CHANGED-MSG TO S3MSGO
```

FIGURE 15.7   *(Continued)*

```
                     MOVE -1 TO S3CUSTL
                     PERFORM SEND-SALE003-BEEP.
      *
           IF (CUST-CURR-WK-SALES-NI NOT  0
                        AND CUST-CURR-WK-SALES NOT = 0)
                        OR (CUST-LAST-BILL-BAL-DUE-NI NOT  0
                        AND CUST-LAST-BILL-BAL-DUE NOT = 0)
              MOVE CANNOT-DELETE-MSG TO S3MSGO
              MOVE -1 TO S3CUSTL
              PERFORM SEND-SALE003-BEEP.
      *
      ****************************************************************
      * DELETE THE ROW.                                             *
      ****************************************************************
           MOVE 'CUSTOMER' TO DISPLAY-RESOURCE.
           MOVE 'DELETE' TO DISPLAY-OPERATION.
           EXEC SQL DELETE
                FROM CUSTOMER
                WHERE CUSTNO = :CUST-NO
                END-EXEC.
           MOVE -1 TO S3CUSTL.
      *
      *
      ****************************************************************
      * IF THE DELETE WAS SUCCESSFUL, THE TERMINAL USER MAY OVERKEY *
      * THE CUSTOMER NUMBER TO DELETE A DIFFERENT RECORD NEXT TIME. *
      * IF THE DELETE WAS NOT SUCCESSFUL, DISPLAY A MESSAGE         *
      * EXPLAINING WHY NOT.                                         *
      ****************************************************************
      *
           IF SQLCODE = 0
              MOVE SUCCESSFUL-DELETE-MSG TO S3MSGO
              MOVE -1 TO S3CUSTL
              MOVE ENTER-CUST-NO-MSG TO S3INSTRO
              PERFORM SEND-SALE003-RETURN
           ELSE
              PERFORM CHECK-SQL-RESPONSE
              PERFORM SEND-SALE003-BEEP.
      *
      *
       XCTL-NEXT-PGM.
      *
           MOVE WS-XCTL-PGM TO DISPLAY-RESOURCE.
           MOVE 'XCTL' TO DISPLAY-OPERATION.
           EXEC CICS XCTL
                    PROGRAM (WS-XCTL-PGM)
                    COMMAREA (WS-COMMAREA)
                    RESP (WS-CICS-RESPONSE1)
                    END-EXEC.
      *
           IF WS-CICS-RESPONSE1 NOT = DFHRESP(NORMAL)
              PERFORM CHECK-CICS-RESPONSE
              MOVE -1 TO S3CUSTL
              PERFORM SEND-SALE003-BEEP.
      *
      *
      ****************************************************************
      * THIS ROUTINE TAKES THE CUSTOMER NUMBER FROM THE WORKING     *
      * STORAGE COPY OF THE DFHCOMMAREA AND USES IT TO READ A       *
      * CUSTOMER RECORD. IT SHOWS THE RECORD ON THE DELETE SCREEN.  *
      ****************************************************************
      *
       CUST-NO-FROM-COMMAREA.
      *
           IF WS-COMM-CUST-NO IS NOT NUMERIC
              PERFORM REQUEST-NEW-CUST-NO.
      *
           MOVE WS-COMM-CUST-NO TO S3CUSTO.
           MOVE -1 TO S3NAMEL.
           MOVE SPACES TO S3MSGO.
```

FIGURE 15.7 *(Continued)*

```
*
**********************************************************************
* SELECT THE EXISTING ROW TO BE DISPLAYED.                          *
* OBTAIN NULL INDICATORS (-NI SUFFIX) FOR NULLABLE FIELDS.          *
**********************************************************************
        MOVE WS-COMM-CUST-NO TO CUST-NO.
        MOVE 'CUSTOMER' TO DISPLAY-RESOURCE.
        MOVE 'SELECT' TO DISPLAY-OPERATION.
        EXEC SQL SELECT
                CUSTNAME, CONTACT, STREETADDR,
                CITY, STATE, ZIP,
                LASTBILLDATE, LASTBALDUE, CURRWKSALES
                INTO :CUST-NAME, :CUST-CONTACT,
                :CUST-STREET-ADDRESS, :CUST-CITY,
                :CUST-STATE, :CUST-ZIP,
                :CUST-LAST-BILL-DATE:CUST-LAST-BILL-DATE-NI,
                :CUST-LAST-BILL-BAL-DUE:CUST-LAST-BAL-DUE-NI,
                :CUST-CURR-WK-SALES:CUST-CURR-WK-SALES-NI
                FROM CUSTOMER
                WHERE CUSTNO = :CUST-NO
                END-EXEC.
*
        MOVE -1 TO S3CUSTL.
        IF SQLCODE NOT = 0
            PERFORM CHECK-SQL-RESPONSE
            PERFORM SEND-SALE003-BEEP.
*
        IF CUST-NAME NOT  SPACES
            MOVE NOTFND-MSG TO DISPLAY-DESCRIPTION
            MOVE BUILD-MSG TO S3MSGO
            PERFORM SEND-SALE003-BEEP.
*
*
**********************************************************************
* DELETE THE OLD TEMP STORAGE QUEUE THAT MIGHT BE LEFT FROM         *
* PREVIOUS TASKS. THE QUEUE ID IS BUILT FROM THE TRAN CODE AND      *
* THE TERMINAL ID.                                                  *
**********************************************************************
*
        MOVE EIBTRMID TO QID-TRMID.
        MOVE QID-NAME TO DISPLAY-RESOURCE.
        MOVE 'DELETEQ TS' TO DISPLAY-OPERATION.
*
        EXEC CICS DELETEQ TS
                QUEUE (QID-NAME)
                RESP (WS-CICS-RESPONSE1)
                END-EXEC.
*
        IF WS-CICS-RESPONSE1 NOT = DFHRESP(NORMAL)
                AND WS-CICS-RESPONSE1 NOT = DFHRESP(QIDERR)
            PERFORM CHECK-CICS-RESPONSE
            PERFORM SEND-SALE003-BEEP.
*
        MOVE QID-NAME TO DISPLAY-RESOURCE.
        MOVE 'WRITEQ TS' TO DISPLAY-OPERATION.
*
        EXEC CICS WRITEQ TS
                QUEUE (QID-NAME)
                FROM (CUSTMST-REC)
                ITEM (WS-TSQ-ITEM1)
                RESP (WS-CICS-RESPONSE1)
                END-EXEC.
*
        IF WS-CICS-RESPONSE1 NOT = DFHRESP(NORMAL)
            PERFORM CHECK-CICS-RESPONSE
            PERFORM SEND-SALE003-BEEP.
*
**********************************************************************
* PUT EXISTING RECORD CONTENTS ON THE SCREEN (DISPLAY-ONLY).        *
* THE AMOUNT FIELDS ARE DISPLAY-ONLY AND CANNOT BE CHANGED.         *
```

FIGURE 15.7 *(Continued)*

```
* THREE FIELDS ARE NULLABLE...THEY HAVE A FLAG WHICH INDICATES  *
* WHETHER OR NOT VALID DATA IS IN THE FIELDS.                   *
*****************************************************************
*
     MOVE CUST-NO TO S3CUSTO.
     MOVE CUST-NAME TO S3NAMEO.
     MOVE CUST-CONTACT TO S3CNTCTO.
     MOVE CUST-STREET-ADDRESS TO S3ADDRO.
     MOVE CUST-CITY TO S3CITYO.
     MOVE CUST-STATE TO S3STATEO.
     MOVE CUST-ZIP TO S3ZIPO.
     IF CUST-CURR-WK-SALES-NI  0
         MOVE SPACES TO S3SALESI
     ELSE
         MOVE CUST-CURR-WK-SALES TO S3SALESO.
     IF CUST-LAST-BILL-BAL-DUE-NI  0
         MOVE SPACES TO S3BALI
     ELSE
         MOVE CUST-LAST-BILL-BAL-DUE TO S3BALO.
     IF CUST-LAST-BILL-DATE-NI  0
         MOVE SPACES TO S3BDATEI
     ELSE
         MOVE CUST-LAST-BILL-DATE TO S3BDATEO.
*
*
     MOVE DELETE-RECORD-MSG TO S3INSTRO.
     MOVE SPACES TO S3MSGO.
*
     PERFORM SEND-SALE003-RETURN.
*
*
*****************************************************************
* THIS ROUTINE CLEARS THE SCREEN AND ASKS THE USER TO ENTER THE *
* KEY OF THE NEXT RECORD TO BE DELETED.                         *
*****************************************************************
*
 REQUEST-NEW-CUST-NO.
*
     MOVE SPACES TO WS-COMM-CUST-NO.
     MOVE -1 TO S3CUSTL.
     MOVE ENTER-CUST-NO-MSG TO S3INSTRO.
     MOVE SPACES TO S3MSGO.
*
     MOVE ALL '_' TO S3CUSTO.
     MOVE SPACES TO S3NAMEO
                    S3CNTCTO
                    S3ADDRO
                    S3CITYO
                    S3STATEO
                    S3ZIPO
                    S3SALESO
                    S3BALO
                    S3BDATEO.
*
*****************************************************************
* DELETE THE OLD TEMP STORAGE QUEUE THAT MIGHT BE LEFT FROM     *
* PREVIOUS TASKS. THE QUEUE ID IS BUILT FROM THE TRAN CODE AND  *
* THE TERMINAL ID.                                              *
*****************************************************************
*
     MOVE EIBTRMID TO QID-TRMID.
     MOVE QID-NAME TO DISPLAY-RESOURCE.
     MOVE 'DELETEQ TS' TO DISPLAY-OPERATION.
*
     EXEC CICS DELETEQ TS
               QUEUE (QID-NAME)
               RESP (WS-CICS-RESPONSE1)
               END-EXEC.
*
     IF WS-CICS-RESPONSE1 NOT = DFHRESP(NORMAL)
```

FIGURE 15.7 *(Continued)*

```
                  AND WS-CICS-RESPONSE1 NOT = DFHRESP(QIDERR)
              PERFORM CHECK-CICS-RESPONSE
              PERFORM SEND-SALE003-BEEP.
  *
       PERFORM SEND-SALE003-RETURN.
  *
  *
  *******************************************************************
  * THIS ROUTINE SENDS SALE003 WITH A WARNING 'BEEP'. WE USE THIS *
  * ONLY WHEN THE CALLING ROUTINE WANTS TO DISPLAY A WARNING ON   *
  * THE MESSAGE LINE OF THIS MAP. CURSOR POSITION MUST BE SET.    *
  *******************************************************************
  *
   SEND-SALE003-BEEP.
  *
       IF WS-COMM-PREV-MAP = 'SALE003'
           EXEC CICS SEND MAP ('SALE003')
                          MAPSET ('MSALE03')
                          FROM (SALE003I)
                          DATAONLY
                          ALARM
                          CURSOR
                          END-EXEC
       ELSE
           MOVE 'SALE003' TO WS-COMM-PREV-MAP
           EXEC CICS SEND MAP ('SALE003')
                          MAPSET ('MSALE03')
                          FROM (SALE003I)
                          ERASE
                          ALARM
                          CURSOR
                          END-EXEC.
  *
       EXEC CICS RETURN
                  TRANSID ('CUS3')
                  COMMAREA (WS-COMMAREA)
                  END-EXEC.
  *
  *
  *******************************************************************
  * THIS ROUTINE SENDS SALE003 WITH WHATEVER DATA HAS BEEN PLACED *
  * ON IT. IF THE PREDEFINED PORTIONS OF THE MAP ARE ALREADY ON   *
  * THE SCREEN, SALE003 WILL BE SENT 'DATAONLY'.                  *
  *******************************************************************
  *
   SEND-SALE003-RETURN.
  *
       IF WS-COMM-PREV-MAP = 'SALE003'
           EXEC CICS SEND MAP ('SALE003')
                          MAPSET ('MSALE03')
                          FROM (SALE003I)
                          DATAONLY
                          CURSOR
                          END-EXEC
       ELSE
           MOVE 'SALE003' TO WS-COMM-PREV-MAP
           EXEC CICS SEND MAP ('SALE003')
                          MAPSET ('MSALE03')
                          FROM (SALE003I)
                          ERASE
                          CURSOR
                          END-EXEC.
  *
       EXEC CICS RETURN
                  TRANSID ('CUS3')
                  COMMAREA (WS-COMMAREA)
                  END-EXEC.
  *
  *******************************************************************
  * THIS ROUTINE SENDS SALE003 WITH CURSOR ON ACTION BAR.        *
```

FIGURE 15.7 *(Continued)*

```
*******************************************************************
*
 CURSOR-TO-ACTION-BAR.
*
     MOVE 'SALE003' TO WS-COMM-PREV-MAP.
     EXEC CICS SEND MAP ('SALE003')
               MAPSET ('MSALE03')
               FROM (SALE003I)
               CURSOR (1)
               DATAONLY
               END-EXEC.
*
     EXEC CICS RETURN
               TRANSID ('CUS3')
               COMMAREA (WS-COMMAREA)
               END-EXEC.
*
*
*******************************************************************
* CHECK THE CICS RESPONSE CODE AND BUILD A MESSAGE EXPLAINING     *
* THE ERROR. IT IS THE RESPONSIBILITY OF THE CALLING ROUTINE      *
* TO INITIALIZE SOME DISPLAY FIELDS IN THE MESSAGE WORK AREA      *
* TO INDICATE THE TYPE OF COMMAND BEING PROCESSED.                *
*                                                                 *
* WE DO NOTHING ABOUT CERTAIN RESPONSE CODES HERE SO THAT         *
* THOSE SITUATIONS CAN BE HANDLED WITH LOGIC ELSEWHERE IN THE     *
* PROGRAM.                                                        *
*                                                                 *
*******************************************************************
*
 CHECK-CICS-RESPONSE.
*
     EVALUATE WS-CICS-RESPONSE1
     WHEN DFHRESP(NORMAL)
         CONTINUE
     WHEN DFHRESP(MAPFAIL)
         CONTINUE
     WHEN DFHRESP(ENDFILE)
         CONTINUE
     WHEN DFHRESP(DISABLED)
         MOVE 'CALL OPERATIONS' TO DISPLAY-CALL-WHOM
         MOVE DISABLED-MSG TO DISPLAY-DESCRIPTION
         MOVE BUILD-MSG TO S3MSGO
     WHEN DFHRESP(DUPREC)
         MOVE DUPREC-MSG TO DISPLAY-DESCRIPTION
         MOVE BUILD-MSG TO S3MSGO
     WHEN DFHRESP(DSIDERR)
         MOVE 'CALL PROGRAMMER' TO DISPLAY-CALL-WHOM
         MOVE DSIDERR-MSG TO DISPLAY-DESCRIPTION
         MOVE BUILD-MSG TO S3MSGO
     WHEN DFHRESP(INVREQ)
         MOVE 'CALL PROGRAMMER' TO DISPLAY-CALL-WHOM
         MOVE INVREQ-MSG TO DISPLAY-DESCRIPTION
         MOVE BUILD-MSG TO S3MSGO
     WHEN DFHRESP(IOERR)
         MOVE 'CALL PROGRAMMER' TO DISPLAY-CALL-WHOM
         MOVE IOERR-MSG TO DISPLAY-DESCRIPTION
         MOVE BUILD-MSG TO S3MSGO
     WHEN DFHRESP(ITEMERR)
         MOVE 'CALL PROGRAMMER' TO DISPLAY-CALL-WHOM
         MOVE ITEMERR-MSG TO DISPLAY-DESCRIPTION
         MOVE BUILD-MSG TO S3MSGO
     WHEN DFHRESP(LENGERR)
         MOVE 'CALL PROGRAMMER' TO DISPLAY-CALL-WHOM
         MOVE LENGERR-MSG TO DISPLAY-DESCRIPTION
         MOVE BUILD-MSG TO S3MSGO
     WHEN DFHRESP(NOSPACE)
         MOVE 'CALL OPERATIONS' TO DISPLAY-CALL-WHOM
         MOVE NOSPACE-MSG TO DISPLAY-DESCRIPTION
```

FIGURE 15.7 *(Continued)*

```
              MOVE BUILD-MSG TO S3MSGO
          WHEN DFHRESP(NOTFND)
              MOVE NOTFND-MSG TO DISPLAY-DESCRIPTION
              MOVE BUILD-MSG TO S3MSGO
          WHEN DFHRESP(PGMIDERR)
              MOVE 'CALL PROGRAMMER' TO DISPLAY-CALL-WHOM
              MOVE PGMIDERR-MSG TO DISPLAY-DESCRIPTION
              MOVE BUILD-MSG TO S3MSGO
          WHEN DFHRESP(QIDERR)
              MOVE 'CALL PROGRAMMER' TO DISPLAY-CALL-WHOM
              MOVE QIDERR-MSG TO DISPLAY-DESCRIPTION
              MOVE BUILD-MSG TO S3MSGO
          WHEN OTHER
              MOVE 'CALL PROGRAMMER' TO DISPLAY-CALL-WHOM
              MOVE WS-CICS-RESPONSE1 TO DISPLAY-RESPONSE
              MOVE DEFAULT-DESCRIPTION TO DISPLAY-DESCRIPTION
              MOVE BUILD-MSG TO S3MSGO
          END-EVALUATE.
*
*
*
  CHECK-SQL-RESPONSE.
      EVALUATE TRUE
          WHEN SQLCODE = +100
              MOVE NOTFND-MSG TO DISPLAY-DESCRIPTION
              MOVE BUILD-MSG TO S3MSGO
          WHEN SQLCODE = 0
              CONTINUE
          WHEN SQLCODE = -803 OR +65535
              MOVE DUPREC-MSG TO DISPLAY-DESCRIPTION
              MOVE BUILD-MSG TO S3MSGO
          WHEN SQLCODE   0
              CONTINUE
          WHEN OTHER
              MOVE 'CALL PROGRAMMER' TO DISPLAY-CALL-WHOM
              MOVE SQLCODE TO DISPLAY-SQLCODE
              MOVE SQL-DESCRIPTION TO DISPLAY-DESCRIPTION
              MOVE BUILD-MSG TO S3MSGO
          END-EVALUATE.
*
```

FIGURE 15.7   *(Continued)*

```
$set ans85 sql osvs sqlaccess"" sqlbind"" sqldb(cicsbook)
 IDENTIFICATION DIVISION.
 PROGRAM-ID. CUSTP004.
 AUTHOR. ALIDA M. JATICH AND PHIL NOWAK.
 *****************************************************************
 * CUSTP004: PROCESSOR FOR ENTRY OF CURRENT WEEK SALES          *
 *           (SQL VERSION)        .                             *
 *                                                              *
 * CUSTP004 READS "ENTER CURRENT WEEK SALES" SCREEN INPUT       *
 * AND PERFORMS THE FOLLOWING ACTIONS:                          *
 *                                                              *
 * 1. IT UPDATES CURRENT WEEK SALES AMOUNT IN CUSTOMER MASTER   *
 *    ROW.                                                      *
 *                                                              *
 * 2. IT WRITES A LINE ITEM ROW TO THE LINE ITEM TABLE          *
 *    FOR EVENTUAL USE IN A BILLING SYSTEM.                     *
 *                                                              *
 * 3. IT WRITES A COPY OF THE LINE ITEM ROW TO A TRANSIENT      *
 *    DATA QUEUE FOR EVENTUAL PRINTING.                         *
 *                                                              *
 * 4. IT REFRESHES THE "ENTER CURRENT WEEK SALES" SCREEN TO     *
 *    ALLOW THE TERMINAL USER TO ENTER MORE DATA.               *
 *                                                              *
 * 5. UNLESS THE USER SELECTS OTHERWISE, IT RETURNS TO          *
```

FIGURE 15.8   Sample CICS programs using SQL commands.

```
*     TRANSACTION CUS4, CAUSING THIS PROGRAM TO BE INVOKED       *
*     AGAIN.                                                      *
*                                                                *
******************************************************************
 ENVIRONMENT DIVISION.
 DATA DIVISION.
 WORKING-STORAGE SECTION.
*
 EXEC SQL BEGIN DECLARE SECTION END-EXEC.
     COPY CUSTOMER.
     COPY LINEITEM.
 EXEC SQL END DECLARE SECTION END-EXEC.
*
 EXEC SQL INCLUDE SQLCA END-EXEC.
*
 01  MISC-WORK.
     05  WS-CICS-RESPONSE1       PIC S9(8) COMP VALUE +0.
     05  WS-XCTL-PGM             PIC X(8)       VALUE SPACES.
     05  WS-ERROR-FLAG           PIC X          VALUE 'N'.
     05  WS-QTY                  PIC S9(6)      VALUE ZEROES.
     05  WS-SALES-ENTERED        PIC S9(5)V99   VALUE ZEROES.
 01  ERROR-MESSAGES.
     05  BAD-KEY-MSG             PIC X(22)      VALUE
         'Function key undefined'.
     05  CUST-NUM-MSG            PIC X(27)      VALUE
         'Customer number not numeric'.
     05  MISSING-DATA-MSG        PIC X(26)      VALUE
         'Please supply missing data'.
     05  PLUS-OR-MINUS-MSG       PIC X(24)      VALUE
         'Enter plus or minus sign'.
     05  NUMERIC-MSG             PIC X(40)      VALUE
         'Field must be numeric, greater than zero'.
     05  SUCCESSFUL-ADD-MSG      PIC X(25)      VALUE
         'Record added successfully'.
     05  NOTFND-MSG              PIC X(28)      VALUE
         'Customer number not on file'.
     05  DISABLED-MSG            PIC X(16)      VALUE
         'File is disabled'.
     05  DSIDERR-MSG             PIC X(14)      VALUE
         'File not found'.
     05  DUPREC-MSG              PIC X(22)      VALUE
         'Record already on file'.
     05  INVREQ-MSG              PIC X(15)      VALUE
         'Invalid request'.
     05  IOERR-MSG               PIC X(9)       VALUE
         'I/O error'.
     05  ITEMERR-MSG             PIC X(16)      VALUE
         'Item not defined'.
     05  LENGERR-MSG             PIC X(19)      VALUE
         'Record length error'.
     05  NOSPACE-MSG             PIC X(17)      VALUE
         'File out of space'.
     05  PGMIDERR-MSG            PIC X(27)      VALUE
         'Program not defined to CICS'.
     05  QIDERR-MSG              PIC X(17)      VALUE
         'Queue not defined'.
*
     05  BUILD-MSG.
         10  DISPLAY-OPERATION   PIC X(12)      VALUE SPACES.
         10  FILLER              PIC X          VALUE SPACES.
         10  DISPLAY-RESOURCE    PIC X(8)       VALUE SPACES.
         10  FILLER              PIC X          VALUE SPACES.
         10  DISPLAY-DESCRIPTION PIC X(38)      VALUE SPACES.
         10  FILLER              PIC X          VALUE SPACES.
         10  DISPLAY-CALL-WHOM   PIC X(16)      VALUE SPACES.
*
     05  DEFAULT-DESCRIPTION.
         10  FILLER              PIC X(22)      VALUE
         'CUSTP004 ERROR: RESP1='.
         10  DISPLAY-RESPONSE    PIC 9(8)       VALUE ZEROES.
```

FIGURE 15.8 *(Continued)*

```
*
    05  SQL-DESCRIPTION.
        10  FILLER                 PIC X(24)        VALUE
        'CUSTP004 ERROR: SQLCODE='.
        10  DISPLAY-SQLCODE        PIC 9(9)-        VALUE ZEROES.
*
 COPY CUSTCOMM.
 COPY MSALE04.
 COPY ATTRIBUT.
 COPY DFHAID.
 COPY DFHBMSCA.
 LINKAGE SECTION.
 01  DFHCOMMAREA                   PIC X(104).
*
 PROCEDURE DIVISION.
 MAIN-PROG.
*
*********************************************************************
* DETERMINE WHICH POINT IN THE CYCLE APPLIES TO THE CURRENT        *
* SITUATION. THE FIRST TIME THROUGH, SHOW THE RECORD ADD SCREEN    *
* FOR THE FIRST TIME. ON SUBSEQUENT PASSES, PROCESS USER INPUT     *
* AND SHOW THE SCREEN AGAIN (OR TRANSFER CONTROL BACK TO THE       *
* MENU PROGRAM, DEPENDING ON FUNCTION KEY).                        *
*********************************************************************
*
    MOVE LOW-VALUES TO SALE004I.
*
    EXEC CICS ASKTIME
        END-EXEC.
*
    IF EIBCALEN NOT = WS-EXPECTED-EIBCALEN
        PERFORM FIRST-TIME-THROUGH
    ELSE
        MOVE DFHCOMMAREA TO WS-COMMAREA
        IF EIBTRNID = 'CUS4'
                AND WS-COMM-PREV-MAP = 'SALE004'
            PERFORM PROCESS-ADD-SCREEN
        ELSE
            PERFORM FIRST-TIME-THROUGH.
*
    GOBACK.
*
*********************************************************************
* DETERMINE WHAT FUNCTION KEY THE USER PRESSED.                    *
*********************************************************************
*
 PROCESS-ADD-SCREEN.
*
    IF EIBAID = DFHCLEAR OR DFHPF3
        MOVE 'CUSTP000' TO WS-XCTL-PGM
        PERFORM XCTL-NEXT-PGM
    ELSE
        IF EIBAID = DFHPF10
            PERFORM CURSOR-TO-ACTION-BAR
        ELSE
            IF EIBAID = DFHPF12
                PERFORM FIRST-TIME-THROUGH
            ELSE
                IF EIBAID NOT = DFHENTER
                    MOVE BAD-KEY-MSG TO S4MSGO
                    MOVE -1 TO S4CUSTL
                    PERFORM SEND-SALE004-BEEP.
*
    MOVE 'SALE004' TO DISPLAY-RESOURCE.
    MOVE 'RECEIVE MAP' TO DISPLAY-OPERATION.
*
    EXEC CICS RECEIVE MAP ('SALE004')
            MAPSET ('MSALE04')
            INTO (SALE004I)
```

FIGURE 15.8 *(Continued)*

```
                              RESP (WS-CICS-RESPONSE1)
                              END-EXEC.
       *
           IF WS-CICS-RESPONSE1 = DFHRESP(MAPFAIL)
              PERFORM FIRST-TIME-THROUGH
           ELSE
               IF WS-CICS-RESPONSE1 NOT = DFHRESP(NORMAL)
                   PERFORM CHECK-CICS-RESPONSE
                   PERFORM SEND-SALE004-BEEP.
       *
           MOVE SPACES TO S4MSGO.
       *
       ****************************************************************
       * IF THE CURSOR WAS ANYWHERE ON THE ACTION BAR, USE THE        *
       * POSITION TO SELECT THE ACTION. IF THE CURSOR WAS SOMEWHERE   *
       * ELSE, THEN JUST GO WITH THE DEFAULT CHOICE, WHICH IS "ADD".  *
       ****************************************************************
       *
           IF EIBCPOSN  7
              MOVE 'ADD' TO WS-COMM-ACTION
           ELSE
               IF EIBCPOSN  13
                   MOVE 'EXIT' TO WS-COMM-ACTION
               ELSE
                   IF EIBCPOSN  21
                       MOVE 'CANCEL' TO WS-COMM-ACTION
                   ELSE
                       MOVE 'ADD' TO WS-COMM-ACTION.
       *
           IF WS-COMM-ACTION = 'EXIT'
              MOVE 'CUSTP000' TO WS-XCTL-PGM
              PERFORM XCTL-NEXT-PGM
           ELSE
               IF WS-COMM-ACTION = 'CANCEL'
                   PERFORM FIRST-TIME-THROUGH.
       *
       ****************************************************************
       * EDIT THE DATA IN EACH OF THE USER INPUT FIELDS. YOUR METHODS *
       * MAY VARY DEPENDING ON THE TERMINAL DEVICE FEATURES YOU PLAN  *
       * TO SUPPORT AND ON THE STANDARDS AT YOUR INSTALLATION.        *
       *                                                              *
       * UNDERLINING IS A WAY OF INDICATING HOW MUCH DATA THE USER    *
       * CAN ENTER INTO EACH FIELD. IF YOUR TERMINALS OR WORKSTATIONS *
       * SUPPORT THE "UNDERLINE" EXTENDED ATTRIBUTE IN SUCH A WAY     *
       * THAT THE APPEARANCE IS ACCEPTABLE TO THE TERMINAL USERS, YOU *
       * CAN OMIT THE LOGIC FOR FILLING EMPTY FIELDS WITH UNDERSCORE  *
       * CHARACTERS AND FOR REMOVING TRAILING UNDERSCORES. IN THAT    *
       * CASE, YOU WOULD DEFINE THE UNDERSCORES BY USING THE HIGHLIGHT*
       * ATTRIBUTE ON THE BMS MAP.                                    *
       *                                                              *
       * IF YOUR TERMINALS SUPPORT COLOR, FOR EXAMPLE, 3279-TYPE      *
       * TERMINALS OR PS/2'S, CHANGE THE COLOR OF A FIELD TO INDICATE *
       * ERRORS. THE COLOR IS SET WITH AN 'EXTENDED ATTRIBUTE' BYTE.  *
       * THE EXTENDED ATTRIBUTE DOES NOT TAKE UP SPACE ON THE DISPLAY.*
       * THIS EXAMPLE IS BEING RUN ON A PS/2. IF YOUR TERMINALS ARE   *
       * MONOCHROME, DON'T TRY TO USE THE COLOR EXTENDED ATTRIBUTE.   *
       * MOVE A 'BRIGHT' ATTRIBUTE CHARACTER TO THE ATTRIBUTE BYTE.   *
       ****************************************************************
       *
            IF S4CUSTI = LOW-VALUES OR SPACES OR '_____'
               MOVE ALL '_' TO S4CUSTO
               MOVE DFHRED TO S4CUSTC
               IF WS-ERROR-FLAG = 'N'
                   MOVE -1 TO S4CUSTL
                   MOVE 'Y' TO WS-ERROR-FLAG
                   MOVE MISSING-DATA-MSG TO S4MSGO
               END-IF
            ELSE
                IF S4CUSTI IS NUMERIC
                    MOVE S4CUSTI TO WS-COMM-CUST-NO
```

FIGURE 15.8 *(Continued)*

```
            MOVE DFHTURQ TO S4CUSTC
        ELSE
            MOVE DFHRED TO S4CUSTC
            IF WS-ERROR-FLAG = 'N'
                MOVE -1 TO S4CUSTL
                MOVE 'Y' TO WS-ERROR-FLAG
                MOVE CUST-NUM-MSG TO S4MSGO.
*
    INSPECT S4ITEMI REPLACING ALL '_' BY SPACES.
    IF S4ITEMI  SPACES
        MOVE DFHTURQ TO S4ITEMC
        MOVE ALP-REG-MOD-UNP TO S4ITEMA
    ELSE
        MOVE DFHRED TO S4ITEMC
        MOVE ALL '_' TO S4ITEMO
        IF WS-ERROR-FLAG = 'N'
            MOVE -1 TO S4ITEML
            MOVE 'Y' TO WS-ERROR-FLAG
            MOVE MISSING-DATA-MSG TO S4MSGO.
*
    IF S4UNITPI IS NUMERIC AND S4UNITPI  ZEROES
        MOVE DFHTURQ TO S4UNITPC
        MOVE NUM-REG-MOD-UNP TO S4UNITPA
    ELSE
        MOVE DFHRED TO S4UNITPC
        MOVE ZEROES TO S4UNITPO
        IF WS-ERROR-FLAG = 'N'
            MOVE DFHRED TO S4UNITPC
            MOVE -1 TO S4UNITPL
            MOVE 'Y' TO WS-ERROR-FLAG
            MOVE NUMERIC-MSG TO S4MSGO.
*
    IF S4QTYI IS NUMERIC AND S4QTYI  ZEROES
        MOVE DFHTURQ TO S4QTYC
        MOVE NUM-REG-MOD-UNP TO S4QTYA
    ELSE
        MOVE DFHRED TO S4QTYC
        MOVE ZEROES TO S4QTYO
        IF WS-ERROR-FLAG = 'N'
            MOVE -1 TO S4QTYL
            MOVE 'Y' TO WS-ERROR-FLAG
            MOVE NUMERIC-MSG TO S4MSGO.
*
    IF S4SIGNI = '_' OR SPACES OR LOW-VALUES
        MOVE '+' TO S4SIGNI.
    IF S4SIGNI = '+' OR '-'
        MOVE DFHTURQ TO S4SIGNC
        MOVE ALP-REG-MOD-UNP TO S4SIGNA
    ELSE
        MOVE DFHRED TO S4SIGNC
        MOVE ALL '_' TO S4SIGNO
        IF WS-ERROR-FLAG = 'N'
            MOVE -1 TO S4SIGNL
            MOVE 'Y' TO WS-ERROR-FLAG
            MOVE PLUS-OR-MINUS-MSG TO S4MSGO.
*
*
****************************************************************
* IF THE DATA IS GOOD, MOVE DATA TO THE WORK AREA FOR THE LINE  *
* ITEM HOST VARIABLES. WE SET THE SYSTEM DATE/TIME STAMP LATER  *
* WITHIN THE SQL INSERT COMMAND ITSELF.                        *
****************************************************************
*
    IF WS-ERROR-FLAG = 'N'
        MOVE S4CUSTI TO ITEM-CUST-NO
        MOVE S4ITEMI TO ITEM-CODE
        MOVE S4UNITPI TO ITEM-UNIT-PRICE
        MOVE ZEROES TO WS-QTY
        IF S4SIGNI = '+'
            ADD S4QTYI TO WS-QTY
```

FIGURE 15.8 *(Continued)*

```
            ELSE
                SUBTRACT S4QTYI FROM WS-QTY
            END-IF
            MOVE WS-QTY TO ITEM-QUANTITY.
 *
 ***********************************************************************
 * IF EVERYTHING IS OK SO FAR, ATTEMPT TO READ THE CUSTOMER           *
 * MASTER ROW. IF CUSTOMER NUMBER DOES NOT EXIST ON THE DATABASE,*
 * MOVE AN ERROR MESSAGE TO THE SCREEN AND DON'T UPDATE ANYTHING.*
 ***********************************************************************
 *
        IF WS-ERROR-FLAG = 'N'
            MOVE WS-COMM-CUST-NO TO CUST-NO
            MOVE 'CUSTOMER' TO DISPLAY-RESOURCE
            MOVE 'SELECT' TO DISPLAY-OPERATION
            EXEC SQL SELECT
                    CUSTNAME, CONTACT, STREETADDR,
                    CITY, STATE, ZIP, CURRWKSALES
                    INTO :CUST-NAME, :CUST-CONTACT,
                    :CUST-STREET-ADDRESS, :CUST-CITY,
                    :CUST-STATE, :CUST-ZIP,
                    :CUST-CURR-WK-SALES:CUST-CURR-WK-SALES-NI
                    FROM CUSTOMER
                    WHERE CUSTNO = :CUST-NO
                    END-EXEC
 *
        IF SQLCODE NOT = 0
            PERFORM CHECK-SQL-RESPONSE
            MOVE -1 TO S4CUSTL
            MOVE DFHRED TO S4CUSTC
            MOVE 'Y' TO WS-ERROR-FLAG.
 *
        IF CUST-NAME NOT  SPACES
            MOVE NOTFND-MSG TO DISPLAY-DESCRIPTION
            MOVE BUILD-MSG TO S4MSGO
            MOVE -1 TO S4CUSTL
            MOVE DFHRED TO S4CUSTC
            MOVE 'Y' TO WS-ERROR-FLAG.
 *
        IF WS-ERROR-FLAG = 'Y'
            PERFORM SEND-SALE004-BEEP.
 *
 ***********************************************************************
 * IF THE READ WAS SUCCESSFUL, UPDATE THE CUSTOMER ROW.               *
 * IF CURRENT WEEK SALES ACCUMULATOR CONTAINS A NULL VALUE,           *
 * INITIALIZE IT TO ZERO BEFORE ADDING TO IT.                         *
 ***********************************************************************
 *
        IF CUST-CURR-WK-SALES-NI  ZEROES
            MOVE ZEROES TO CUST-CURR-WK-SALES.
 *
        COMPUTE WS-SALES-ENTERED = S4UNITPI * WS-QTY.
        COMPUTE CUST-CURR-WK-SALES = WS-SALES-ENTERED +
                    CUST-CURR-WK-SALES.
        MOVE 'CUSTMAST' TO DISPLAY-RESOURCE.
        MOVE 'UPDATE' TO DISPLAY-OPERATION.
 *
        EXEC SQL UPDATE
            CUSTOMER
            SET CURRWKSALES = :CUST-CURR-WK-SALES
            WHERE CUSTNO = :CUST-NO
            END-EXEC.
 *
        IF SQLCODE NOT = 0
            PERFORM CHECK-SQL-RESPONSE
            MOVE -1 TO S4CUSTL
            MOVE DFHRED TO S4CUSTC
            MOVE 'Y' TO WS-ERROR-FLAG.
 *
        IF WS-ERROR-FLAG = 'Y'
```

FIGURE 15.8 *(Continued)*

```
            PERFORM SEND-SALE004-BEEP.
    *
    **********************************************************************
    * WRITE A LINE ITEM ROW. USE THE CURRENT TIMESTAMP SQL SPECIAL    *
    * REGISTER TO GET THE SYSTEM DATE AND TIME STAMP.                 *
    **********************************************************************
    *
        MOVE CUST-NO TO ITEM-CUST-NO.
        MOVE 'LINEITEM' TO DISPLAY-RESOURCE.
        MOVE 'INSERT' TO DISPLAY-OPERATION.
        EXEC SQL INSERT INTO LINEITEM
               (CUSTNO, DATETIME, ITEMCODE,
               UNITPRICE, ORDERQTY)
               VALUES (:ITEM-CUST-NO, CURRENT TIMESTAMP,
               :ITEM-CODE, :ITEM-UNIT-PRICE, :ITEM-QUANTITY)
               END-EXEC.
        IF SQLCODE NOT = 0
           PERFORM CHECK-SQL-RESPONSE
           MOVE 'Y' TO WS-ERROR-FLAG.
    *
    *
    **********************************************************************
    * WRITE THE LINE ITEM RECORD TO A TRANSIENT DATA QUEUE.          *
    **********************************************************************
    *
        IF WS-ERROR-FLAG = 'N'
           MOVE 'LMSG' TO DISPLAY-RESOURCE
           MOVE 'WRITEQ TD' TO DISPLAY-OPERATION
           EXEC CICS WRITEQ TD
                   QUEUE ('LMSG')
                   FROM (LINEITM-REC)
                   RESP (WS-CICS-RESPONSE1)
                   END-EXEC
           IF WS-CICS-RESPONSE1 NOT = DFHRESP(NORMAL)
              PERFORM CHECK-CICS-RESPONSE
              MOVE 'Y' TO WS-ERROR-FLAG.
    *
    **********************************************************************
    * IF ALL ACTIVITY WAS SUCCESSFUL SO FAR, LET THE TERMINAL USER   *
    * KNOW THIS. OTHERWISE, ROLL BACK ANY UPDATES THAT HAVE GONE     *
    * THROUGH, SO THAT ALL FILES WILL BE PUT BACK TO THEIR           *
    * ORIGINAL STATE. (SQL FILE INTEGRITY NOT SUPPORTED UNDER        *
    * CICS OS/2 1.20.)                                               *
    **********************************************************************
    *
        IF WS-ERROR-FLAG = 'N'
           MOVE -1 TO S4CUSTL
           MOVE SUCCESSFUL-ADD-MSG TO S4MSGO
           PERFORM SEND-SALE004-RETURN
        ELSE
           EXEC CICS SYNCPOINT
                   ROLLBACK
                   END-EXEC
           MOVE -1 TO S4CUSTL
           PERFORM CHECK-CICS-RESPONSE
           PERFORM SEND-SALE004-BEEP.
    *
    *
    XCTL-NEXT-PGM.
    *
        MOVE WS-XCTL-PGM TO DISPLAY-RESOURCE.
        MOVE 'XCTL' TO DISPLAY-OPERATION.
        EXEC CICS XCTL
                PROGRAM (WS-XCTL-PGM)
                COMMAREA (WS-COMMAREA)
                RESP (WS-CICS-RESPONSE1)
                END-EXEC.
    *
        IF WS-CICS-RESPONSE1 NOT = DFHRESP(NORMAL)
           PERFORM CHECK-CICS-RESPONSE
```

FIGURE 15.8 *(Continued)*

```
              MOVE -1 TO S4CUSTL
              PERFORM SEND-SALE004-BEEP.
*
*
*********************************************************************
* THIS ROUTINE SENDS THE RECORD ADD MAP AND/OR REFRESHES IT        *
* IF 'CANCEL' WAS SELECTED.                                        *
*********************************************************************
*
 FIRST-TIME-THROUGH.
*
      MOVE SPACES TO S4MSGO.
      IF WS-COMM-CUST-NO IS NUMERIC
          MOVE WS-COMM-CUST-NO TO S4CUSTO
          MOVE -1 TO S4ITEML
      ELSE
          MOVE ALL '_' TO S4CUSTO
          MOVE -1 TO S4CUSTL.
*
      MOVE ALL '_' TO S4ITEMO.
      MOVE '+' TO S4SIGNO.
*
      PERFORM SEND-SALE004-RETURN.
*
*
*********************************************************************
* THIS ROUTINE SENDS SALE004 WITH A WARNING 'BEEP'. WE USE THIS    *
* ONLY WHEN THE CALLING ROUTINE WANTS TO DISPLAY A WARNING ON      *
* THE MESSAGE LINE OF THIS MAP. CURSOR POSITION MUST BE SET.       *
*********************************************************************
*
 SEND-SALE004-BEEP.
*
      IF WS-COMM-PREV-MAP = 'SALE004'
          EXEC CICS SEND MAP ('SALE004')
                    MAPSET ('MSALE04')
                    FROM (SALE004I)
                    DATAONLY
                    ALARM
                    CURSOR
                    END-EXEC
      ELSE
          MOVE 'SALE004' TO WS-COMM-PREV-MAP
          EXEC CICS SEND MAP ('SALE004')
                    MAPSET ('MSALE04')
                    FROM (SALE004I)
                    ERASE
                    ALARM
                    CURSOR
                    END-EXEC.
*
      EXEC CICS RETURN
                TRANSID ('CUS4')
                COMMAREA (WS-COMMAREA)
                END-EXEC.
*
*
*********************************************************************
* THIS ROUTINE SENDS SALE004 WITH WHATEVER DATA HAS BEEN PLACED    *
* ON IT. IF THE PREDEFINED PORTIONS OF THE MAP ARE ALREADY ON      *
* THE SCREEN, SALE004 WILL BE SENT 'DATAONLY'.                     *
*********************************************************************
*
 SEND-SALE004-RETURN.
*
      IF WS-COMM-PREV-MAP = 'SALE004'
          EXEC CICS SEND MAP ('SALE004')
                    MAPSET ('MSALE04')
                    FROM (SALE004I)
                    DATAONLY
```

FIGURE 15.8 *(Continued)*

```
                          CURSOR
                          END-EXEC
             ELSE
                 MOVE 'SALE004' TO WS-COMM-PREV-MAP
                 EXEC CICS SEND MAP ('SALE004')
                          MAPSET ('MSALE04')
                          FROM (SALE004I)
                          ERASE
                          CURSOR
                          END-EXEC.
 *
         EXEC CICS RETURN
                 TRANSID ('CUS4')
                 COMMAREA (WS-COMMAREA)
                 END-EXEC.
 *
 **********************************************************************
 * THIS ROUTINE SENDS SALE004 WITH CURSOR ON ACTION BAR.            *
 **********************************************************************
 *
 CURSOR-TO-ACTION-BAR.
 *
         MOVE 'SALE004' TO WS-COMM-PREV-MAP.
         EXEC CICS SEND MAP ('SALE004')
                 MAPSET ('MSALE04')
                 FROM (SALE004I)
                 CURSOR (1)
                 DATAONLY
                 END-EXEC.
 *
         EXEC CICS RETURN
                 TRANSID ('CUS4')
                 COMMAREA (WS-COMMAREA)
                 END-EXEC.
 *
 *
 **********************************************************************
 * CHECK THE CICS RESPONSE CODE AND BUILD A MESSAGE EXPLAINING      *
 * THE ERROR. IT IS THE RESPONSIBILITY OF THE CALLING ROUTINE      *
 * TO INITIALIZE SOME DISPLAY FIELDS IN THE MESSAGE WORK AREA      *
 * TO INDICATE THE TYPE OF COMMAND BEING PROCESSED.               *
 *                                                                *
 * WE DO NOTHING ABOUT CERTAIN RESPONSE CODES HERE SO THAT        *
 * THOSE SITUATIONS CAN BE HANDLED WITH LOGIC ELSEWHERE IN THE    *
 * PROGRAM.                                                       *
 *                                                                *
 **********************************************************************
 *
 CHECK-CICS-RESPONSE.
 *
         EVALUATE WS-CICS-RESPONSE1
         WHEN DFHRESP(NORMAL)
             CONTINUE
         WHEN DFHRESP(MAPFAIL)
             CONTINUE
         WHEN DFHRESP(ENDFILE)
             CONTINUE
         WHEN DFHRESP(DISABLED)
             MOVE 'CALL OPERATIONS' TO DISPLAY-CALL-WHOM
             MOVE DISABLED-MSG TO DISPLAY-DESCRIPTION
             MOVE BUILD-MSG TO S4MSGO
         WHEN DFHRESP(DUPREC)
             MOVE DUPREC-MSG TO DISPLAY-DESCRIPTION
             MOVE BUILD-MSG TO S4MSGO
         WHEN DFHRESP(DSIDERR)
             MOVE 'CALL PROGRAMMER' TO DISPLAY-CALL-WHOM
             MOVE DSIDERR-MSG TO DISPLAY-DESCRIPTION
             MOVE BUILD-MSG TO S4MSGO
         WHEN DFHRESP(INVREQ)
             MOVE 'CALL PROGRAMMER' TO DISPLAY-CALL-WHOM
```

FIGURE 15.8 *(Continued)*

```
                    MOVE INVREQ-MSG TO DISPLAY-DESCRIPTION
                    MOVE BUILD-MSG TO S4MSGO
              WHEN DFHRESP(IOERR)
                    MOVE 'CALL PROGRAMMER' TO DISPLAY-CALL-WHOM
                    MOVE IOERR-MSG TO DISPLAY-DESCRIPTION
                    MOVE BUILD-MSG TO S4MSGO
              WHEN DFHRESP(ITEMERR)
                    MOVE 'CALL PROGRAMMER' TO DISPLAY-CALL-WHOM
                    MOVE ITEMERR-MSG TO DISPLAY-DESCRIPTION
                    MOVE BUILD-MSG TO S4MSGO
              WHEN DFHRESP(LENGERR)
                    MOVE 'CALL PROGRAMMER' TO DISPLAY-CALL-WHOM
                    MOVE LENGERR-MSG TO DISPLAY-DESCRIPTION
                    MOVE BUILD-MSG TO S4MSGO
              WHEN DFHRESP(NOSPACE)
                    MOVE 'CALL OPERATIONS' TO DISPLAY-CALL-WHOM
                    MOVE NOSPACE-MSG TO DISPLAY-DESCRIPTION
                    MOVE BUILD-MSG TO S4MSGO
              WHEN DFHRESP(NOTFND)
                    MOVE NOTFND-MSG TO DISPLAY-DESCRIPTION
                    MOVE BUILD-MSG TO S4MSGO
              WHEN DFHRESP(PGMIDERR)
                    MOVE 'CALL PROGRAMMER' TO DISPLAY-CALL-WHOM
                    MOVE PGMIDERR-MSG TO DISPLAY-DESCRIPTION
                    MOVE BUILD-MSG TO S4MSGO
              WHEN DFHRESP(QIDERR)
                    MOVE 'CALL PROGRAMMER' TO DISPLAY-CALL-WHOM
                    MOVE QIDERR-MSG TO DISPLAY-DESCRIPTION
                    MOVE BUILD-MSG TO S4MSGO
              WHEN OTHER
                    MOVE 'CALL PROGRAMMER' TO DISPLAY-CALL-WHOM
                    MOVE WS-CICS-RESPONSE1 TO DISPLAY-RESPONSE
                    MOVE DEFAULT-DESCRIPTION TO DISPLAY-DESCRIPTION
                    MOVE BUILD-MSG TO S4MSGO
              END-EVALUATE.
  *
  *
  *
  CHECK-SQL-RESPONSE.
        EVALUATE TRUE
        WHEN SQLCODE = +100
              MOVE NOTFND-MSG TO DISPLAY-DESCRIPTION
              MOVE BUILD-MSG TO S4MSGO
        WHEN SQLCODE = 0
              CONTINUE
        WHEN SQLCODE = -803 OR +65535
              MOVE DUPREC-MSG TO DISPLAY-DESCRIPTION
              MOVE BUILD-MSG TO S4MSGO
        WHEN SQLCODE   0
              CONTINUE
        WHEN OTHER
              MOVE 'CALL PROGRAMMER' TO DISPLAY-CALL-WHOM
              MOVE SQLCODE TO DISPLAY-SQLCODE
              MOVE SQL-DESCRIPTION TO DISPLAY-DESCRIPTION
              MOVE BUILD-MSG TO S4MSGO
        END-EVALUATE.
  *
```

FIGURE 15.8 *(Continued)*

```
$set ans85 sql osvs sqlaccess"" sqlbind"" sqldb(cicsbook)
 IDENTIFICATION DIVISION.
 PROGRAM-ID. CUSTP005.
 AUTHOR. ALIDA M. JATICH AND PHIL NOWAK.
 ****************************************************************
 * CUSTP005: CUSTOMER RECORD BROWSE SCREEN PROCESSOR           *
 *           (SQL VERSION).                                    *
 *                                                             *
 * CUSTP005 STARTS THE SELECT OPERATION AND FETCHES ENOUGH     *
 * OF THE CUSTOMER MASTER TABLE TO FILL ONE SCREEN. IT         *
```

FIGURE 15.9 **Sample CICS programs using SQL commands.**

```
* THEN CLOSES THE CURSOR FROM THE SELECT STATEMENT AND SENDS    *
* THE MAP TO THE TERMINAL SCREEN.                               *
*                                                               *
* CUSTP005 IS INITIALLY INVOKED BY XCTL FROM THE MENU           *
* PROCESSOR PROGRAM, CUSTP000. IF IT IS INVOKED IN THAT WAY,    *
* THE STARTING BROWSE KEY IS OBTAINED FROM THE DFHCOMMAREA.     *
* A FORWARD BROWSE SCREEN IS CREATED AND SENT TO THE USER.      *
*                                                               *
* THE USER MAY CHANGE THE BROWSE KEY ON THE SCREEN IF DESIRED.  *
* HE OR SHE MAY PRESS PF7 FOR A BACKWARD BROWSE OR PF8 FOR      *

* A FORWARD BROWSE. WHEN THE KEY IS PRESSED, TRANSACTION CUS5   *
* WILL BEGIN, INVOKING CUSTP005, WHICH WILL PICK UP THE         *
* CUSTOMER NUMBER FROM THE TERMINAL SCREEN. IT WILL CREATE A    *
* FORWARD OR BACKWARD BROWSE SCREEN, SEND IT TO THE USER,       *
* AND RETURN TO TRANSACTION CUS5 TO ALLOW MORE BROWSE ACTIVITY. *
*                                                               *
* IF WE SCROLL BACKWARD OR FORWARD, WE REPEAT ONE LINE THAT     *
* APPEARED ON THE LAST SCREEN, PER THE RECOMMENDATION OF IBM    *
* IN THE SYSTEMS APPLICATION ARCHITECTURE COMMON USER ACCESS    *
* (SAA CUA) STANDARDS MANUAL.                                   *
*****************************************************************
 ENVIRONMENT DIVISION.
 DATA DIVISION.
 WORKING-STORAGE SECTION.
 01  WS-LABEL                    PIC X(24)       VALUE
          '>CUSTP005 WS BEGINS>'.
*
 EXEC SQL BEGIN DECLARE SECTION END-EXEC.
     COPY CUSTOMER.
*
 01  WS-CUSTNO-KEY               PIC X(6).
 EXEC SQL END DECLARE SECTION END-EXEC.
*
 EXEC SQL INCLUDE SQLCA END-EXEC.
*
 01  WS-MISC-WORK.
     05   WS-CICS-RESPONSE1      PIC S9(8) COMP VALUE +0.
     05   WS-ACTIVE-ITEMS        PIC S9(8) COMP VALUE +0.
     05   WS-XCTL-PGM            PIC X(8)       VALUE SPACES.
     05   WS-END-OF-DATA         PIC X          VALUE 'N'.
*
 COPY CUSTCOMM.
*
 01  ERROR-MESSAGES.
     05   BAD-KEY-MSG            PIC X(22)       VALUE
          'Function key undefined'.
     05   FILE-EMPTY-MSG         PIC X(25)       VALUE
          'No customer records exist'.
     05   DISABLED-MSG           PIC X(16)       VALUE
          'File is disabled'.
     05   DSIDERR-MSG            PIC X(14)       VALUE
          'File not found'.
     05   DUPREC-MSG             PIC X(22)       VALUE
          'Record already on file'.
     05   INVREQ-MSG             PIC X(15)       VALUE
          'Invalid request'.
     05   IOERR-MSG              PIC X(9)        VALUE
          'I/O error'.
     05   ITEMERR-MSG            PIC X(16)       VALUE
          'Item not defined'.
     05   LENGERR-MSG            PIC X(19)       VALUE
          'Record length error'.
     05   NOSPACE-MSG            PIC X(17)       VALUE
          'File out of space'.
     05   NOTFND-MSG             PIC X(18)       VALUE
          'Record not on file'.
     05   PGMIDERR-MSG           PIC X(27)       VALUE
          'Program not defined to CICS'.
     05   QIDERR-MSG             PIC X(17)       VALUE
```

FIGURE 15.9 *(Continued)*

```
                  'Queue not defined'.
        *
            05  BUILD-MSG.
                10  DISPLAY-OPERATION    PIC X(12)      VALUE SPACES.
                10  FILLER               PIC X          VALUE SPACES.
                10  DISPLAY-RESOURCE     PIC X(8)       VALUE SPACES.
                10  FILLER               PIC X          VALUE SPACES.
                10  DISPLAY-DESCRIPTION  PIC X(38)      VALUE SPACES.
                10  FILLER               PIC X          VALUE SPACES.
                10  DISPLAY-CALL-WHOM    PIC X(16)      VALUE SPACES.
        *
            05  DEFAULT-DESCRIPTION.
                10  FILLER               PIC X(22)      VALUE
                'CUSTP005 ERROR: RESP1='.
                10  DISPLAY-RESPONSE     PIC 9(8)       VALUE ZEROES.
        *
            05  SQL-DESCRIPTION.
                10  FILLER               PIC X(24)      VALUE
                'CUSTP005 ERROR: SQLCODE='.
                10  DISPLAY-SQLCODE      PIC 9(9)-      VALUE ZEROES.
        *
         COPY MSALE05.
        *
        *****************************************************************
        * IN ORDER TO GROUP FIELDS WITHIN THE SYMBOLIC MAP AS AN ARRAY, *
        * A REDEFINITION IS NEEDED. THE NUMBER OF FILLER CHARACTERS     *
        * WILL VARY DEPENDING ON WHETHER YOU ARE USING EXTENDED         *
        * ATTRIBUTE SETTINGS.                                           *
        *****************************************************************
        *
         01  MAP-ARRAY REDEFINES SALE005I.
             02  FILLER                   PIC X(85).
             02  SCREEN-LINE OCCURS 12 TIMES INDEXED BY MAP-INDX.
                 05  FILLER               PIC X(5).
                 05  SCR-CUSTNO           PIC X(6).
                 05  FILLER               PIC X(5).
                 05  SCR-CUSTNAME         PIC X(25).
             02  FILLER                   PIC X(168).
        *
        *****************************************************************
        * THIS TABLE IS USED FOR CHANGING THE ORDER OF RECORDS FROM     *
        * DESCENDING TO ASCENDING, FOR BACKWARD BROWSE DISPLAY.         *
        *****************************************************************
        *                                                              *
         01  WORK-ARRAY.
             02  WORK-LINE OCCURS 12 TIMES INDEXED BY WORK-INDX.
                 05  WORK-CUSTNO          PIC X(6).
                 05  WORK-CUSTNAME        PIC X(25).
        *
         COPY ATTRIBUT.
         COPY DFHAID.
         COPY DFHBMSCA.
         LINKAGE SECTION.
         01  DFHCOMMAREA                  PIC X(104).
        *
         PROCEDURE DIVISION.
         MAIN-PROG.
        *
        *****************************************************************
        * DETERMINE WHICH POINT IN THE CYCLE APPLIES TO THE CURRENT     *
        * SITUATION. THE FIRST TIME THROUGH, SHOW THE BROWSE SCREEN     *
        * FOR THE FIRST TIME. ON SUBSEQUENT PASSES, PROCESS USER INPUT  *
        * AND SHOW THE SCREEN AGAIN (OR TRANSFER CONTROL BACK TO THE    *
        * MENU PROGRAM, DEPENDING ON FUNCTION KEY).                     *
        *****************************************************************
        *
             MOVE LOW-VALUES TO SALE005I.
        *
             IF EIBCALEN NOT = WS-EXPECTED-EIBCALEN
                 PERFORM REFRESH-SCREEN
```

FIGURE 15.9 *(Continued)*

```
        ELSE
            MOVE DFHCOMMAREA TO WS-COMMAREA
            IF EIBTRNID = 'CUS5'
                    AND WS-COMM-PREV-MAP = 'SALE005'
                PERFORM CHECK-FOR-INPUT
            ELSE
                MOVE WS-COMM-CUST-NO TO WS-COMM-NEXT-CUST-NO
                PERFORM FORWARD-BROWSE.
*
        GOBACK.
*
*********************************************************************
* DETERMINE WHAT FUNCTION KEY THE USER PRESSED.                     *
*********************************************************************
*
    CHECK-FOR-INPUT.
*
        IF EIBAID = DFHCLEAR OR DFHPF3
            MOVE 'CUSTP000' TO WS-XCTL-PGM
            PERFORM XCTL-NEXT-PGM
        ELSE
            IF EIBAID = DFHPF10
                PERFORM CURSOR-TO-ACTION-BAR
            ELSE
                IF EIBAID = DFHPF12
                    PERFORM REFRESH-SCREEN
                ELSE
                    IF EIBAID = DFHENTER
                            OR DFHPF7 OR DFHPF8
                        NEXT SENTENCE
                    ELSE
                        MOVE BAD-KEY-MSG TO S5MSGO
                        MOVE -1 TO S5CUSTL
                        PERFORM SEND-SALE005-BEEP.
*
        MOVE 'SALE005' TO DISPLAY-RESOURCE.
        MOVE 'RECEIVE MAP' TO DISPLAY-OPERATION.
*
        EXEC CICS RECEIVE MAP ('SALE005')
                MAPSET ('MSALE05')
                INTO (SALE005I)
                RESP (WS-CICS-RESPONSE1)
                END-EXEC.
*
        IF WS-CICS-RESPONSE1 = DFHRESP(MAPFAIL)
            PERFORM REFRESH-SCREEN
        ELSE
            IF WS-CICS-RESPONSE1 NOT = DFHRESP(NORMAL)
                PERFORM CHECK-CICS-RESPONSE
                PERFORM SEND-SALE005-BEEP.
*
        MOVE SPACES TO S5MSGO.
*
*********************************************************************
* IF THE ENTER KEY WAS PRESSED, AND THE CURSOR WAS ANYWHERE         *
* ON THE ACTION BAR, USE THE CURSOR POSITION TO SELECT THE          *
* ACTION. IF THE CURSOR WAS ANYWHERE ELSE, JUST GO WITH THE         *
* DEFAULT VALUE. IN THIS CASE, THE DEFAULT ACTION IS WHATEVER       *
* IS IN THE COMMAREA FROM THE PREVIOUS ACTION, BECAUSE WE           *
* ASSUME PEOPLE USUALLY KEEP SCROLLING IN THE SAME DIRECTION.       *
*                                                                   *
* IF THE USER ENTERED A NEW CUSTOMER NUMBER, USE THAT FOR           *
* THE STARTING POSITION FOR THE NEXT SCREEN. OTHERWISE,             *
* START FROM THE PREVIOUS VALUE IN THE COMMAREA.                    *
*                                                                   *
*********************************************************************
*
        IF EIBAID = DFHPF7
          MOVE 'BACKWARD' TO WS-COMM-ACTION
        ELSE
```

FIGURE 15.9 *(Continued)*

```
             IF EIBAID = DFHPF8
               MOVE 'FORWARD' TO WS-COMM-ACTION
             ELSE
               IF EIBCPOSN  10
                 MOVE 'FORWARD' TO WS-COMM-ACTION
               ELSE
                 IF EIBCPOSN  20
                   MOVE 'BACKWARD' TO WS-COMM-ACTION
                 ELSE
                   IF EIBCPOSN  26
                     MOVE 'EXIT' TO WS-COMM-ACTION
                   ELSE
                     IF EIBCPOSN  33
                       MOVE 'CANCEL' TO WS-COMM-ACTION.
  *
         IF WS-COMM-ACTION = 'EXIT'
             MOVE 'CUSTP000' TO WS-XCTL-PGM
             PERFORM XCTL-NEXT-PGM
         ELSE
             IF WS-COMM-ACTION = 'CANCEL'
                 PERFORM REFRESH-SCREEN
             ELSE
                 IF S5CUSTO IS NUMERIC
                     MOVE S5CUSTO TO WS-COMM-CUST-NO
                                     WS-COMM-NEXT-CUST-NO
                     MOVE ALL '_' TO S5CUSTO
                     PERFORM FORWARD-BROWSE
                 ELSE
                     IF WS-COMM-ACTION = 'BACKWARD'
                         PERFORM BACKWARD-BROWSE
                     ELSE
                         PERFORM FORWARD-BROWSE.
  *
  *****************************************************************
  * 1. BEGIN A SELECT WITH KEY FROM PRIOR SCREEN OR FROM USER.   *
  * 2. OPEN CURSOR.                                              *
  * 3. FETCH ROWS UNTIL END OF DATA OR SCREEN HAS BEEN FILLED.   *
  * 4. DETERMINE CORRECT SETTING FOR ON-SCREEN PAGING INDICATORS.*
  * 5. MOVE THE FIRST AND LAST CUSTOMER NUMBERS ON THE SCREEN TO *
  *    THE WORKING STORAGE COPY OF THE COMMAREA.                 *
  * 6. CLOSE CURSOR.                                             *
  * 7. CHANGE THE APPEARANCE OF ACTION BAR TO SHOW THAT 'FORWARD'*
  *    IS NOW THE DEFAULT. IF YOU HAVE A COLOR DISPLAY, USE THE  *
  *    COLOR EXTENDED ATTRIBUTE. OTHERWISE, CHANGE THE ATTRIBUTE *
  *    BYTE OF THE SELECTED ACTION TO A BRIGHT SETTING.          *
  * 8. SEND MAP AND RETURN.                                      *
  *****************************************************************
  *
  FORWARD-BROWSE.
  *
      MOVE ZEROES TO WS-ACTIVE-ITEMS.
      MOVE 'N' TO WS-END-OF-DATA.
      SET MAP-INDX TO 1.
      MOVE SPACES TO S5MSGO.
  *
      MOVE WS-COMM-NEXT-CUST-NO TO WS-CUSTNO-KEY.
  *
  *****************************************************************
  * SELECT STATEMENT WITH DECLARATION OF CURSOR                  *
  * FOR FETCHING MULTIPLE ROWS                                   *
  *****************************************************************
      MOVE WS-CUSTNO-KEY TO CUST-NO.
      MOVE 'CUSTOMER' TO DISPLAY-RESOURCE.
      MOVE 'SELECT' TO DISPLAY-OPERATION.
  *
      EXEC SQL DECLARE FWBROWSE CURSOR FOR
              SELECT
              CUSTNO, CUSTNAME
              FROM CUSTOMER
              WHERE NOT CUSTNO  :WS-CUSTNO-KEY
```

FIGURE 15.9 *(Continued)*

```
                ORDER BY CUSTNO ASC
                END-EXEC.
*
        IF SQLCODE = +100
            MOVE 'Y' TO WS-END-OF-DATA
            MOVE SPACES TO S5PLUSO
        ELSE
            IF SQLCODE NOT = ZERO
                PERFORM CHECK-SQL-RESPONSE
                MOVE -1 TO S5CUSTL
                PERFORM SEND-SALE005-BEEP
        ELSE
            MOVE 'FWBROWSE' TO DISPLAY-RESOURCE
            MOVE 'OPEN CURSOR' TO DISPLAY-OPERATION
            EXEC SQL OPEN FWBROWSE
                END-EXEC
            IF SQLCODE NOT = ZERO
                PERFORM CHECK-SQL-RESPONSE
                MOVE -1 TO S5CUSTL
                PERFORM SEND-SALE005-BEEP
            END-IF
            PERFORM FORWARD-BROWSE-LOOP
                UNTIL MAP-INDX  +12
                OR WS-END-OF-DATA = 'Y'
            IF WS-ACTIVE-ITEMS  ZEROES
                PERFORM FWD-BROWSE-HOUSEKEEPING
            END-IF
            MOVE 'FWBROWSE' TO DISPLAY-RESOURCE
            MOVE 'CLOSE CURSOR' TO DISPLAY-OPERATION
            EXEC SQL CLOSE FWBROWSE
                END-EXEC
            IF SQLCODE NOT = ZERO
                PERFORM CHECK-SQL-RESPONSE
                MOVE -1 TO S5CUSTL
                PERFORM SEND-SALE005-BEEP
            END-IF.
*
        MOVE 'FORWARD' TO WS-COMM-ACTION.
        MOVE DFHYELLO TO S5FWDC.
        MOVE DFHNEUTR TO S5BKWC.
*
        MOVE -1 TO S5CUSTL.
        PERFORM SEND-SALE005-RETURN.
*
****************************************************************
* THE SCREEN HAS A PLUS AND MINUS SIGN TO INDICATE WHETHER     *
* MORE RECORDS CAN BE REACHED BY SCROLLING FORWARD OR BACKWARD. *
* THESE SIGNS ARE REQUIRED BY IBM IN THE SAA COMMON USER ACCESS *
* STANDARDS.                                                   *
*                                                             *
* IF WE ARE PAGING AHEAD FROM A PREVIOUS SCREEN, THE COUNTER   *
* FIELD IN THE COMMAREA WILL INDICATE HOW MANY RECORDS WERE    *
* SHOWN ON THE PREVIOUS PASS. THE SCREEN CONTENTS "OVERLAP"    *
* BY ONE RECORD. IF MORE THAN ONE RECORD WAS SHOWN ON THE      *
* PREVIOUS SCREEN, WE SET THE MINUS SIGN ON THE CURRENT        *
* SCREEN TO INDICATE THAT THERE ARE SOME RECORDS ON FILE       *
* WITH KEYS LOWER THAN THE ONES WE ARE NOW SHOWING.            *
*                                                             *
* WE FETCH ONE ROW AHEAD OF THE LAST ITEM ON THE SCREEN        *
* TO DETERMINE WHETHER THERE ARE MORE RECORDS TO WHICH         *
* THE USER MAY SCROLL FORWARD ON THE NEXT SCREEN. IF SO,       *
* WE SET THE PLUS SIGN. WHEN WE FETCH THIS ROW, WE DON'T       *
* WANT IT TO GO ON THE SCREEN AND WE DON'T WANT TO UPDATE THE  *
* SAVED COMMAREA KEY.                                          *
*                                                             *
* NOTE THAT THESE INDICATORS MAY NOT BE PERFECTLY ACCURATE.    *
* IF SECURITY PERMITS, OTHER USERS COULD BE INSERTING OR       *
* DELETING ROWS WHILE WE VIEW THE TABLE.                       *
****************************************************************
*
```

FIGURE 15.9   *(Continued)*

```
 FWD-BROWSE-HOUSEKEEPING.
*
     MOVE SCR-CUSTNO (1) TO WS-COMM-CUST-NO.
     MOVE CUST-NO TO WS-CUSTNO-KEY.
     MOVE WS-CUSTNO-KEY TO WS-COMM-NEXT-CUST-NO.
*
     PERFORM CLEAR-UNUSED-LINES
         UNTIL MAP-INDX  +12.
*
     IF WS-COMM-COUNTER  +1
         MOVE '-' TO S5MINUSO.
*
     MOVE WS-ACTIVE-ITEMS TO WS-COMM-COUNTER.
*
     IF WS-END-OF-DATA = 'Y'
         MOVE SPACES TO S5PLUSO
     ELSE
         MOVE 'CUSTMAST' TO DISPLAY-RESOURCE
         MOVE 'FETCH' TO DISPLAY-OPERATION
         EXEC SQL FETCH FWBROWSE
                   INTO :CUST-NO, :CUST-NAME
                   END-EXEC
         IF SQLCODE = +100
             MOVE SPACES TO S5PLUSO
         ELSE
             IF SQLCODE = ZERO
                 MOVE '+' TO S5PLUSO
             ELSE
                 PERFORM CHECK-SQL-RESPONSE
                 MOVE -1 TO S5CUSTL
                 PERFORM SEND-SALE005-BEEP.
*
****************************************************************
* ATTEMPT TO READ THE NEXT RECORD. IF FOUND, PUT IT IN THE     *
* NEXT AVAILABLE PLACE IN THE MAP ARRAY.                       *
****************************************************************
*
 FORWARD-BROWSE-LOOP.
*
     MOVE 'CUSTMAST' TO DISPLAY-RESOURCE.
     MOVE 'FETCH' TO DISPLAY-OPERATION.
*
     EXEC SQL FETCH FWBROWSE
               INTO :CUST-NO, :CUST-NAME
               END-EXEC.
*
     IF SQLCODE = +100
         MOVE 'Y' TO WS-END-OF-DATA
     ELSE
         IF SQLCODE = ZERO
             MOVE CUST-NO TO SCR-CUSTNO (MAP-INDX)
             MOVE CUST-NAME TO SCR-CUSTNAME (MAP-INDX)
             SET MAP-INDX UP BY +1
             ADD +1 TO WS-ACTIVE-ITEMS
         ELSE
             PERFORM CHECK-SQL-RESPONSE
             MOVE -1 TO S5CUSTL
             PERFORM SEND-SALE005-BEEP.
*
 CLEAR-UNUSED-LINES.
*
     MOVE SPACES TO SCR-CUSTNO (MAP-INDX)
                    SCR-CUSTNAME (MAP-INDX).
*
     SET MAP-INDX UP BY +1.
*
****************************************************************
* SQL HAS NO COMMAND FOR READING BACKWARD PER SE.             *
* THIS IS BECAUSE ANY TABLE CAN BE INDEXED VARIOUS DIFFERENT  *
* WAYS. YOU CAN CHOOSE AMONG SEQUENCES BY USING THE "ORDER BY" *
```

FIGURE 15.9 *(Continued)*

```
* CLAUSE IN THE SELECT STATEMENT. THE DEFAULT IS "ASC"          *
* (ASCENDING) BUT YOU CAN USE "DESC" TO READ IN DESCENDING      *
* ORDER BY THE SAME SORT OR INDEX FIELD.                        *
*                                                               *
* WHILE THE ROWS ARE FETCHED IN DESCENDING ORDER, FOR THE       *
* SAKE OF CONSISTENT VISUAL APPEARANCE, WE WANT TO DISPLAY      *
* THEM IN ASCENDING ORDER ON THE SCREEN. NOT ONLY THAT, BUT     *
* IF THERE IS LESS THAN A SCREENFUL OF RECORDS, WE WANT TO      *
* START OVER AT THE BEGINNING OF THE FILE AND READ UP TO A      *
* FULL SCREEN OF RECORDS STARTING FROM THERE.                   *
*****************************************************************
* 1. BEGIN A SELECT WITH KEY FROM PRIOR SCREEN OR FROM USER.    *
* 2. OPEN CURSOR.                                               *
* 3. READ ROWS UNTIL END OF DATA OR WORK TABLE IS FULL.         *
* 4. MOVE THE FIRST AND LAST CUSTOMER NUMBERS FROM THE WORK     *
*    TABLE TO THE WORKING STORAGE COPY OF THE COMMAREA.         *
* 5. REVERSE THE ORDER OF THE SCREEN ITEMS BY COPYING FROM THE  *
*    WORK TABLE TO THE SCREEN TABLE.                            *
* 6. DETERMINE CORRECT SETTING FOR ON-SCREEN PAGING INDICATORS. *
* 7. CLOSE CURSOR.                                              *
* 8. CHANGE THE APPEARANCE OF ACTION BAR TO SHOW THAT 'BACKWARD'*
*    IS NOW THE DEFAULT. IF YOU HAVE A COLOR DISPLAY, USE THE   *
*    COLOR EXTENDED ATTRIBUTE. OTHERWISE, CHANGE THE ATTRIBUTE  *
*    BYTE OF THE SELECTED ACTION TO A BRIGHT SETTING.           *
* 9. SEND MAP AND RETURN.                                       *
*****************************************************************
*
 BACKWARD-BROWSE.
*
     MOVE ZEROES TO WS-ACTIVE-ITEMS.
     MOVE 'N' TO WS-END-OF-DATA.
     SET MAP-INDX TO +1.
     SET WORK-INDX TO +1.
     MOVE SPACES TO WORK-ARRAY.
     MOVE SPACES TO S5MSGO.
*
*
*****************************************************************
* SELECT STATEMENT WITH DECLARATION OF CURSOR                   *
* FOR FETCHING MULTIPLE ROWS                                    *
*****************************************************************
     MOVE WS-CUSTNO-KEY TO CUST-NO.
     MOVE 'CUSTOMER' TO DISPLAY-RESOURCE.
     MOVE 'SELECT' TO DISPLAY-OPERATION.
*
     EXEC SQL DECLARE BKBROWSE CURSOR FOR
          SELECT
          CUSTNO, CUSTNAME
          FROM CUSTOMER
          WHERE NOT CUSTNO   :WS-CUSTNO-KEY
          ORDER BY CUSTNO DESC
          END-EXEC.
*
     IF SQLCODE = +100
        MOVE 'Y' TO WS-END-OF-DATA
        MOVE SPACES TO S5MINUSO
     ELSE
        IF SQLCODE NOT = ZERO
           PERFORM CHECK-SQL-RESPONSE
           MOVE -1 TO S5CUSTL
           PERFORM SEND-SALE005-BEEP
        ELSE
           MOVE 'BKBROWSE' TO DISPLAY-RESOURCE
           MOVE 'OPEN CURSOR' TO DISPLAY-OPERATION
           EXEC SQL OPEN BKBROWSE
               END-EXEC
           IF SQLCODE NOT = ZERO
              PERFORM CHECK-SQL-RESPONSE
              MOVE -1 TO S5CUSTL
              PERFORM SEND-SALE005-BEEP
```

FIGURE 15.9 *(Continued)*

```
                    END-IF
                    PERFORM BACKWARD-BROWSE-LOOP
                        UNTIL WORK-INDX  +12
                        OR WS-END-OF-DATA = 'Y'
                    IF WS-ACTIVE-ITEMS = 12
                        PERFORM BUILD-BKWD-BROWSE-SCREEN
                    ELSE
                        MOVE 'BKBROWSE' TO DISPLAY-RESOURCE
                        MOVE 'CLOSE CURSOR' TO DISPLAY-OPERATION
                        EXEC SQL CLOSE BKBROWSE
                            END-EXEC
                        IF SQLCODE NOT = ZERO
                            PERFORM CHECK-SQL-RESPONSE
                            MOVE -1 TO S5CUSTL
                            PERFORM SEND-SALE005-BEEP
                        END-IF
                        MOVE LOW-VALUES TO WS-COMM-CUST-NO
                                          WS-COMM-NEXT-CUST-NO
                        MOVE ZEROES TO WS-COMM-COUNTER
                        MOVE SPACES TO S5PLUSO S5MINUSO
                        PERFORM FORWARD-BROWSE.
 *
  BUILD-BKWD-BROWSE-SCREEN.
 *
 ****************************************************************
 * IF WE HAVE OBTAINED A FULL SCREEN OF RECORDS, MOVE THOSE     *
 * RECORDS TO THE SCREEN IN THE PROPER ORDER. THEN, MOVE THE    *
 * KEYS FOR THE FIRST AND LAST SCREEN LINE TO THE WORKING       *
 * STORAGE COPY OF THE COMMAREA.                                *
 ****************************************************************
 *
        PERFORM INVERT-SCREEN-ORDER 12 TIMES.
        MOVE WORK-CUSTNO (1) TO WS-COMM-NEXT-CUST-NO.
        MOVE WORK-CUSTNO (12) TO WS-COMM-CUST-NO.
 *
 ****************************************************************
 * THE SCREEN HAS A PLUS AND MINUS SIGN TO INDICATE WHETHER     *
 * MORE RECORDS CAN BE REACHED BY SCROLLING FORWARD OR BACKWARD.*
 * THESE SIGNS ARE REQUIRED BY IBM IN THE SAA COMMON USER ACCESS*
 * STANDARDS.                                                   *
 *                                                             *
 * IF WE ARE PAGING BACK FROM A PREVIOUS SCREEN, THE COUNTER    *
 * FIELD IN THE COMMAREA WILL INDICATE HOW MANY RECORDS WERE    *
 * SHOWN ON THE PREVIOUS PASS. THE SCREEN CONTENTS "OVERLAP"    *
 * BY ONE RECORD. IF MORE THAN ONE RECORD WAS SHOWN ON THE      *
 * PREVIOUS SCREEN, WE SET THE PLUS SIGN ON THE CURRENT         *
 * SCREEN TO INDICATE THAT THERE ARE SOME RECORDS ON FILE       *
 * WITH KEYS HIGHER THAN THE ONES WE ARE NOW SHOWING.           *
 *                                                             *
 * WE READ ONE RECORD BEFORE THE FIRST ITEM ON THE SCREEN       *
 * TO DETERMINE WHETHER THERE ARE MORE RECORDS TO WHICH         *
 * THE USER MAY SCROLL BACKWARD ON THE NEXT SCREEN. IF SO,      *
 * WE SET THE MINUS SIGN. WHEN WE READ THIS RECORD, WE DON'T    *
 * WANT IT TO GO ON THE SCREEN AND WE DON'T WANT TO UPDATE THE  *
 * SAVED COMMAREA KEY.                                          *
 *                                                             *
 * NOTE THAT THESE INDICATORS ARE NOT PERFECTLY ACCURATE BECAUSE*
 * WE DON'T CONTROL THE WHOLE FILE. OTHER USERS COULD BE ADDING *
 * OR DELETING RECORDS.                                         *
 ****************************************************************
 *
        IF WS-COMM-COUNTER  +1
            MOVE '+' TO S5PLUSO.
 *
        MOVE WS-ACTIVE-ITEMS TO WS-COMM-COUNTER.
 *
        IF WS-END-OF-DATA = 'Y'
            MOVE SPACES TO S5MINUSO
        ELSE
            MOVE 'CUSTMAST' TO DISPLAY-RESOURCE
```

FIGURE 15.9   *(Continued)*

```
            MOVE 'FETCH' TO DISPLAY-OPERATION
            EXEC SQL FETCH BKBROWSE
                     INTO :CUST-NO, :CUST-NAME
                     END-EXEC
            IF SQLCODE = +100
                MOVE SPACES TO S5MINUSO
            ELSE
                IF SQLCODE = ZERO
                    MOVE '-' TO S5MINUSO
                ELSE
                    PERFORM CHECK-SQL-RESPONSE
                    MOVE -1 TO S5CUSTL
                    PERFORM SEND-SALE005-BEEP.
      *
          EXEC SQL CLOSE BKBROWSE
              END-EXEC.
      *
          MOVE 'BACKWARD' TO WS-COMM-ACTION.
          MOVE DFHYELLO TO S5BKWC.
          MOVE DFHNEUTR TO S5FWDC.
      *
          MOVE -1 TO S5CUSTL.
          PERFORM SEND-SALE005-RETURN.
      *
      ************************************************************************
      * ATTEMPT TO READ THE PREVIOUS RECORD. IF FOUND, PUT IT IN      *
      * THE NEXT AVAILABLE PLACE IN THE WORKING STORAGE ARRAY.        *
      ************************************************************************
      *
       BACKWARD-BROWSE-LOOP.
      *
      *
          MOVE 'CUSTMAST' TO DISPLAY-RESOURCE.
          MOVE 'FETCH' TO DISPLAY-OPERATION.
          EXEC SQL FETCH BKBROWSE
                   INTO :CUST-NO, :CUST-NAME
                   END-EXEC.
      *
          IF SQLCODE = +100
              MOVE 'Y' TO WS-END-OF-DATA
          ELSE
              IF SQLCODE = ZERO
                  MOVE CUST-NO TO WORK-CUSTNO (WORK-INDX)
                  MOVE CUST-NAME TO WORK-CUSTNAME (WORK-INDX)
                  SET WORK-INDX UP BY +1
                  ADD +1 TO WS-ACTIVE-ITEMS
              ELSE
                  PERFORM CHECK-SQL-RESPONSE
                  MOVE -1 TO S5CUSTL
                  PERFORM SEND-SALE005-BEEP.
      *
      ************************************************************************
      * THE BACKWARD BROWSE ROUTINE GETS THE RECORDS IN REVERSE ORDER *
      * AND STORES THEM IN A WORKING STORAGE ARRAY. IT THEN PUTS THE  *
      * RECORDS INTO THE SCREEN ARRAY IN ASCENDING ORDER BY CUSTOMER  *
      * NUMBER.                                                       *
      ************************************************************************
      *
       INVERT-SCREEN-ORDER.
      *
          SET WORK-INDX DOWN BY +1.
          MOVE WORK-CUSTNO (WORK-INDX) TO SCR-CUSTNO (MAP-INDX).
          MOVE WORK-CUSTNAME (WORK-INDX) TO SCR-CUSTNAME (MAP-INDX).
          SET MAP-INDX UP BY +1.
      *
      *
       XCTL-NEXT-PGM.
      *
          MOVE ZEROES TO WS-COMM-COUNTER.
          MOVE WS-XCTL-PGM TO DISPLAY-RESOURCE.
```

FIGURE 15.9   *(Continued)*

```
        MOVE 'XCTL' TO DISPLAY-OPERATION.
        EXEC CICS XCTL
                PROGRAM (WS-XCTL-PGM)
                COMMAREA (WS-COMMAREA)
                RESP (WS-CICS-RESPONSE1)
                END-EXEC.
*
        IF WS-CICS-RESPONSE1 NOT = DFHRESP(NORMAL)
            PERFORM CHECK-CICS-RESPONSE
            MOVE -1 TO S5CUSTL
            PERFORM SEND-SALE005-BEEP.
*
*
*********************************************************************
* THIS ROUTINE SENDS THE RECORD BROWSE MAP WITH NO DATA ON IT.  *
*********************************************************************
*
 REFRESH-SCREEN.
*
        MOVE ZEROES TO WS-COMM-COUNTER.
        MOVE 'FORWARD' TO WS-COMM-ACTION.
        MOVE DFHYELLO TO S5FWDC.
        MOVE DFHNEUTR TO S5BKWC.
        MOVE 'SALE005' TO WS-COMM-PREV-MAP.
        MOVE SPACES TO S5MSGO.
        MOVE SPACES TO WS-COMM-CUST-NO
                       WS-COMM-NEXT-CUST-NO.
        MOVE '_____' TO S5CUSTO.
        MOVE -1 TO S5CUSTL.
        MOVE SPACES TO S5PLUSO S5MINUSO.
        SET MAP-INDX TO +1.
        PERFORM CLEAR-UNUSED-LINES
            UNTIL MAP-INDX  +12.
        PERFORM SEND-SALE005-RETURN.
*
*
*********************************************************************
* THIS ROUTINE SENDS SALE005 WITH A WARNING 'BEEP'. WE USE THIS  *
* ONLY WHEN THE CALLING ROUTINE WANTS TO DISPLAY A WARNING ON    *
* THE MESSAGE LINE OF THIS MAP. CURSOR POSITION MUST BE SET.     *
*********************************************************************
*
 SEND-SALE005-BEEP.
*
        IF WS-COMM-PREV-MAP = 'SALE005'
            EXEC CICS SEND MAP ('SALE005')
                    MAPSET ('MSALE05')
                    FROM (SALE005I)
                    DATAONLY
                    ALARM
                    CURSOR
                    END-EXEC
        ELSE
            MOVE 'SALE005' TO WS-COMM-PREV-MAP
            EXEC CICS SEND MAP ('SALE005')
                    MAPSET ('MSALE05')
                    FROM (SALE005I)
                    ERASE
                    ALARM
                    CURSOR
                    END-EXEC.
*
        EXEC CICS RETURN
                TRANSID ('CUS5')
                COMMAREA (WS-COMMAREA)
                END-EXEC.
*
*
*********************************************************************
* THIS ROUTINE SENDS SALE005 WITH WHATEVER DATA HAS BEEN PLACED *
```

FIGURE 15.9 *(Continued)*

```
* ON IT. IF THE PREDEFINED PORTIONS OF THE MAP ARE ALREADY ON   *
* THE SCREEN, SALE005 WILL BE SENT 'DATAONLY'.                  *
****************************************************************
*
 SEND-SALE005-RETURN.
*
     IF WS-COMM-PREV-MAP = 'SALE005'
         EXEC CICS SEND MAP ('SALE005')
                   MAPSET ('MSALE05')
                   FROM (SALE005I)
                   DATAONLY
                   CURSOR
                   END-EXEC
     ELSE
         MOVE 'SALE005' TO WS-COMM-PREV-MAP
         EXEC CICS SEND MAP ('SALE005')
                   MAPSET ('MSALE05')
                   FROM (SALE005I)
                   ERASE
                   CURSOR
                   END-EXEC.
*
     EXEC CICS RETURN
               TRANSID ('CUS5')
               COMMAREA (WS-COMMAREA)
               END-EXEC.
*
****************************************************************
* THIS ROUTINE SENDS SALE005 WITH CURSOR ON ACTION BAR.        *
****************************************************************
*
 CURSOR-TO-ACTION-BAR.
*
     MOVE 'SALE005' TO WS-COMM-PREV-MAP.
     EXEC CICS SEND MAP ('SALE005')
               MAPSET ('MSALE05')
               FROM (SALE005I)
               CURSOR (1)
               DATAONLY
               END-EXEC.
*
     EXEC CICS RETURN
               TRANSID ('CUS5')
               COMMAREA (WS-COMMAREA)
               END-EXEC.
*
*
****************************************************************
* CHECK THE CICS RESPONSE CODE AND BUILD A MESSAGE EXPLAINING  *
* THE ERROR. IT IS THE RESPONSIBILITY OF THE CALLING ROUTINE   *
* TO INITIALIZE SOME DISPLAY FIELDS IN THE MESSAGE WORK AREA   *
* TO INDICATE THE TYPE OF COMMAND BEING PROCESSED.             *
*                                                              *
* WE DO NOTHING ABOUT CERTAIN RESPONSE CODES HERE SO THAT      *
* THOSE SITUATIONS CAN BE HANDLED WITH LOGIC ELSEWHERE IN THE  *
* PROGRAM.                                                     *
*                                                              *
****************************************************************
*
*
 CHECK-CICS-RESPONSE.
*
     EVALUATE WS-CICS-RESPONSE1
     WHEN DFHRESP(NORMAL)
         CONTINUE
     WHEN DFHRESP(MAPFAIL)
         CONTINUE
     WHEN DFHRESP(ENDFILE)
         CONTINUE
     WHEN DFHRESP(DISABLED)
```

FIGURE 15.9   *(Continued)*

```
                    MOVE 'CALL OPERATIONS' TO DISPLAY-CALL-WHOM
                    MOVE DISABLED-MSG TO DISPLAY-DESCRIPTION
                    MOVE BUILD-MSG TO S5MSGO
              WHEN DFHRESP(DUPREC)
                    MOVE DUPREC-MSG TO DISPLAY-DESCRIPTION
                    MOVE BUILD-MSG TO S5MSGO
              WHEN DFHRESP(DSIDERR)
                    MOVE 'CALL PROGRAMMER' TO DISPLAY-CALL-WHOM
                    MOVE DSIDERR-MSG TO DISPLAY-DESCRIPTION
                    MOVE BUILD-MSG TO S5MSGO
              WHEN DFHRESP(INVREQ)
                    MOVE 'CALL PROGRAMMER' TO DISPLAY-CALL-WHOM
                    MOVE INVREQ-MSG TO DISPLAY-DESCRIPTION
                    MOVE BUILD-MSG TO S5MSGO
              WHEN DFHRESP(IOERR)
                    MOVE 'CALL PROGRAMMER' TO DISPLAY-CALL-WHOM
                    MOVE IOERR-MSG TO DISPLAY-DESCRIPTION
                    MOVE BUILD-MSG TO S5MSGO
              WHEN DFHRESP(ITEMERR)
                    MOVE 'CALL PROGRAMMER' TO DISPLAY-CALL-WHOM
                    MOVE ITEMERR-MSG TO DISPLAY-DESCRIPTION
                    MOVE BUILD-MSG TO S5MSGO
              WHEN DFHRESP(LENGERR)
                    MOVE 'CALL PROGRAMMER' TO DISPLAY-CALL-WHOM
                    MOVE LENGERR-MSG TO DISPLAY-DESCRIPTION
                    MOVE BUILD-MSG TO S5MSGO
              WHEN DFHRESP(NOSPACE)
                    MOVE 'CALL OPERATIONS' TO DISPLAY-CALL-WHOM
                    MOVE NOSPACE-MSG TO DISPLAY-DESCRIPTION
                    MOVE BUILD-MSG TO S5MSGO
              WHEN DFHRESP(NOTFND)
                    MOVE NOTFND-MSG TO DISPLAY-DESCRIPTION
                    MOVE BUILD-MSG TO S5MSGO
              WHEN DFHRESP(PGMIDERR)
                    MOVE 'CALL PROGRAMMER' TO DISPLAY-CALL-WHOM
                    MOVE PGMIDERR-MSG TO DISPLAY-DESCRIPTION
                    MOVE BUILD-MSG TO S5MSGO
              WHEN DFHRESP(QIDERR)
                    MOVE 'CALL PROGRAMMER' TO DISPLAY-CALL-WHOM
                    MOVE QIDERR-MSG TO DISPLAY-DESCRIPTION
                    MOVE BUILD-MSG TO S5MSGO
              WHEN OTHER
                    MOVE 'CALL PROGRAMMER' TO DISPLAY-CALL-WHOM
                    MOVE WS-CICS-RESPONSE1 TO DISPLAY-RESPONSE
                    MOVE DEFAULT-DESCRIPTION TO DISPLAY-DESCRIPTION
                    MOVE BUILD-MSG TO S5MSGO
              END-EVALUATE.
*
*
*
  CHECK-SQL-RESPONSE.
        EVALUATE TRUE
        WHEN SQLCODE = +100
              MOVE NOTFND-MSG TO DISPLAY-DESCRIPTION
              MOVE BUILD-MSG TO S5MSGO
        WHEN SQLCODE = 0
              CONTINUE
        WHEN SQLCODE = -803 OR +65535
              MOVE DUPREC-MSG TO DISPLAY-DESCRIPTION
              MOVE BUILD-MSG TO S5MSGO
        WHEN SQLCODE   0
              CONTINUE
        WHEN OTHER
              MOVE 'CALL PROGRAMMER' TO DISPLAY-CALL-WHOM
              MOVE SQLCODE TO DISPLAY-SQLCODE
              MOVE SQL-DESCRIPTION TO DISPLAY-DESCRIPTION
              MOVE BUILD-MSG TO S5MSGO
        END-EVALUATE.
*
```

FIGURE 15.9 *(Continued)*

```
$set ans85 sql osvs sqlaccess"" sqlbind"" sqldb(cicsbook)
 IDENTIFICATION DIVISION.
 PROGRAM-ID. CUSTP006.
 AUTHOR. ALIDA M. JATICH AND PHIL NOWAK.
*******************************************************************
* CUSTP006: LINEITEM BROWSE SCREEN PROCESSOR (SQL VERSION).      *
*                                                                *
* CUSTP006 STARTS THE SELECT OPERATION AND FETCHES ENOUGH        *
* OF THE LINE ITEM TABLE TO FILL ONE SCREEN. IT THEN CLOSES      *
* THE CURSOR FROM THE SELECT AND SENDS THE MAP TO THE            *
* TERMINAL SCREEN.                                               *
*                                                                *
* CUSTP006 IS INITIALLY INVOKED BY XCTL FROM THE MENU            *
* PROCESSOR PROGRAM, CUSTP000. IF IT IS INVOKED IN THAT WAY,     *
* THE STARTING BROWSE KEY IS OBTAINED FROM THE DFHCOMMAREA.      *
* A FORWARD BROWSE SCREEN IS CREATED AND SENT TO THE USER.       *
*                                                                *
* THE USER MAY CHANGE THE BROWSE KEY ON THE SCREEN IF DESIRED.   *
* HE OR SHE MAY PRESS PF7 FOR A BACKWARD BROWSE OR PF8 FOR       *
* A FORWARD BROWSE. WHEN THE KEY IS PRESSED, TRANSACTION CUS6    *
* WILL BEGIN, INVOKING CUSTP006, WHICH WILL PICK UP THE          *
* CUSTOMER NUMBER FROM THE TERMINAL SCREEN. IT WILL CREATE A     *
* FORWARD OR BACKWARD BROWSE SCREEN, SEND IT TO THE USER,        *
* AND RETURN TO TRANSACTION CUS6 TO ALLOW MORE BROWSE ACTIVITY.  *
*                                                                *
* IF WE SCROLL BACKWARD OR FORWARD, WE REPEAT ONE LINE THAT      *
* APPEARED ON THE LAST SCREEN, PER THE RECOMMENDATION OF IBM     *
* IN THE SYSTEMS APPLICATION ARCHITECTURE COMMON USER ACCESS     *
* (SAA CUA) STANDARDS MANUAL.                                    *
*******************************************************************
 ENVIRONMENT DIVISION.
 DATA DIVISION.
 WORKING-STORAGE SECTION.
 01  WS-LABEL                        PIC X(24)       VALUE
         '>CUSTP006 WS BEGINS>'.
*
 EXEC SQL BEGIN DECLARE SECTION END-EXEC.
*
     COPY LINEITEM.

 01  WS-KEY-CUST-NO                  PIC X(6).
 01  WS-KEY-DATE-TIME                PIC X(26).
 01  WS-KEY-ITEM-CODE                PIC X(6).
*
 EXEC SQL END DECLARE SECTION END-EXEC.
*
 EXEC SQL INCLUDE SQLCA END-EXEC.
*
 01  MISC-WORK.
     05  WS-CICS-RESPONSE1           PIC S9(8) COMP VALUE +0.
     05  WS-ACTIVE-ITEMS             PIC S9(8) COMP VALUE +0.
     05  WS-XCTL-PGM                 PIC X(8)       VALUE SPACES.
     05  WS-END-OF-DATA              PIC X          VALUE 'N'.
     05  WS-STARTING-DATE-TIME.
         10  FILLER                  PIC X(26) VALUE
             '0001-01-01-00.00.00.000000'.

     05  WS-1ST-KEY.
         10  WS-1ST-KEY-CUST-NO  PIC X(6).
         10  WS-1ST-KEY-DATE-TIME
                                 PIC X(26).
         10  WS-1ST-KEY-ITEM-CODE
                                 PIC X(6).
     05  WS-LAST-KEY.
         10  WS-LAST-KEY-CUST-NO PIC X(6).
         10  WS-LAST-KEY-DATE-TIME
                                 PIC X(26).
         10  WS-LAST-KEY-ITEM-CODE
                                 PIC X(6).
```

FIGURE 15.10   **Sample CICS programs using SQL commands.**

```
*
*
 COPY CUSTCOMM.
*
 01  ERROR-MESSAGES.
     05  BAD-KEY-MSG              PIC X(22)       VALUE
         'Function key undefined'.
     05  NO-RECS-FOR-CUST-MSG     PIC X(26)       VALUE
         'No line item records exist'.
     05  DISABLED-MSG             PIC X(16)       VALUE
         'File is disabled'.
     05  DSIDERR-MSG              PIC X(14)       VALUE
         'File not found'.
     05  DUPREC-MSG               PIC X(22)       VALUE
         'Record already on file'.
     05  INVREQ-MSG               PIC X(15)       VALUE
         'Invalid request'.
     05  IOERR-MSG                PIC X(9)        VALUE
         'I/O error'.
     05  ITEMERR-MSG              PIC X(16)       VALUE
         'Item not defined'.
     05  LENGERR-MSG              PIC X(19)       VALUE
         'Record length error'.
     05  NOSPACE-MSG              PIC X(17)       VALUE
         'File out of space'.
     05  NOTFND-MSG               PIC X(18)       VALUE
         'Record not on file'.
     05  PGMIDERR-MSG             PIC X(27)       VALUE
         'Program not defined to CICS'.
     05  QIDERR-MSG               PIC X(17)       VALUE
         'Queue not defined'.
*
     05  BUILD-MSG.
         10  DISPLAY-OPERATION    PIC X(12)       VALUE SPACES.
         10  FILLER               PIC X           VALUE SPACES.
         10  DISPLAY-RESOURCE     PIC X(8)        VALUE SPACES.
         10  FILLER               PIC X           VALUE SPACES.
         10  DISPLAY-DESCRIPTION  PIC X(38)       VALUE SPACES.
         10  FILLER               PIC X           VALUE SPACES.
         10  DISPLAY-CALL-WHOM    PIC X(16)       VALUE SPACES.
*
     05  DEFAULT-DESCRIPTION.
         10  FILLER               PIC X(22)       VALUE
         'CUSTP006 ERROR: RESP1='.
         10  DISPLAY-RESPONSE     PIC 9(8)        VALUE ZEROES.
*
     05  SQL-DESCRIPTION.
         10  FILLER               PIC X(24)       VALUE
         'CUSTP006 ERROR: SQLCODE='.
         10  DISPLAY-SQLCODE      PIC 9(9)-       VALUE ZEROES.
*
 COPY MSALE06.
*
 *****************************************************************
 * IN ORDER TO GROUP FIELDS WITHIN THE SYMBOLIC MAP AS AN ARRAY, *
 * A REDEFINITION IS NEEDED. THE NUMBER OF FILLER CHARACTERS     *
 * WILL VARY DEPENDING ON WHETHER YOU ARE USING EXTENDED         *
 * ATTRIBUTE SETTINGS.                                           *
 *****************************************************************
*
 01  MAP-ARRAY REDEFINES SALE006I.
     05  FILLER                   PIC X(96).
     05  SCREEN-LINE OCCURS 16 TIMES INDEXED BY MAP-INDX.
         10  FILLER               PIC X(5).
         10  SCR-ITEM-CODE        PIC X(6).
         10  FILLER               PIC X(5).
         10  SCR-QUANTITY-X.
             15  SCR-QUANTITY     PIC ZZZ,ZZ9-.
         10  FILLER               PIC X(5).
         10  SCR-UNIT-PRICE-X.
```

FIGURE 15.10 *(Continued)*

```
           15  SCR-UNIT-PRICE  PIC $$$,$$$.99.

    05  FILLER              PIC X(168).
*
******************************************************************
* THIS TABLE IS USED FOR CHANGING THE ORDER OF RECORDS FROM      *
* DESCENDING TO ASCENDING, FOR BACKWARD BROWSE DISPLAY.          *
******************************************************************
*                                                                *
 01  WORK-ARRAY.
     02  WORK-LINE OCCURS 16 TIMES INDEXED BY WORK-INDX.
         05  WORK-ITEM-CODE     PIC X(6).
         05  WORK-QUANTITY      PIC S9(6).
         05  WORK-UNIT-PRICE    PIC S9(5)V99.
*
 COPY ATTRIBUT.
 COPY DFHAID.
 COPY DFHBMSCA.
 LINKAGE SECTION.
 01  DFHCOMMAREA             PIC X(104).
*
 PROCEDURE DIVISION.
 MAIN-PROG.
*
******************************************************************
* DETERMINE WHICH POINT IN THE CYCLE APPLIES TO THE CURRENT      *
* SITUATION. THE FIRST TIME THROUGH, SHOW THE BROWSE SCREEN      *
* FOR THE FIRST TIME. ON SUBSEQUENT PASSES, PROCESS USER INPUT   *
* AND SHOW THE SCREEN AGAIN (OR TRANSFER CONTROL BACK TO THE     *
* MENU PROGRAM, DEPENDING ON FUNCTION KEY).                      *
******************************************************************
*
     MOVE LOW-VALUES TO SALE006I.
*
     IF EIBCALEN NOT = WS-EXPECTED-EIBCALEN
         PERFORM REFRESH-SCREEN
     ELSE
         MOVE DFHCOMMAREA TO WS-COMMAREA
         IF EIBTRNID = 'CUS6'
                 AND WS-COMM-PREV-MAP = 'SALE006'
             PERFORM CHECK-FOR-INPUT
         ELSE
             MOVE WS-STARTING-DATE-TIME
                 TO WS-COMM-DATETIME
             MOVE WS-COMM-KEY TO WS-COMM-NEXT-KEY
             PERFORM FORWARD-BROWSE.
*
     GOBACK.
*
******************************************************************
* DETERMINE WHAT FUNCTION KEY THE USER PRESSED.                  *
******************************************************************
*
 CHECK-FOR-INPUT.
*
     IF EIBAID = DFHCLEAR OR DFHPF3
         MOVE 'CUSTP000' TO WS-XCTL-PGM
         PERFORM XCTL-NEXT-PGM
     ELSE
         IF EIBAID = DFHPF10
             PERFORM CURSOR-TO-ACTION-BAR
         ELSE
             IF EIBAID = DFHPF12
                 PERFORM REFRESH-SCREEN
             ELSE
                 IF EIBAID = DFHENTER
                         OR DFHPF7 OR DFHPF8
                     NEXT SENTENCE
                 ELSE
                     MOVE BAD-KEY-MSG TO S6MSGO
```

FIGURE 15.10   *(Continued)*

```
                         MOVE -1 TO S6CUSTL
                         PERFORM SEND-SALE006-BEEP.
    *
        MOVE 'SALE006' TO DISPLAY-RESOURCE.
        MOVE 'RECEIVE MAP' TO DISPLAY-OPERATION.
    *
        EXEC CICS RECEIVE MAP ('SALE006')
                  MAPSET ('MSALE06')
                  INTO (SALE006I)
                  RESP (WS-CICS-RESPONSE1)
                  END-EXEC.
    *
        IF WS-CICS-RESPONSE1 = DFHRESP(MAPFAIL)
           PERFORM REFRESH-SCREEN
        ELSE
            IF WS-CICS-RESPONSE1 NOT = DFHRESP(NORMAL)
               PERFORM CHECK-CICS-RESPONSE
               PERFORM SEND-SALE006-BEEP.
    *
        MOVE SPACES TO S6MSGO.
    *
    ***********************************************************************
    * IF THE ENTER KEY WAS PRESSED, AND THE CURSOR WAS ANYWHERE          *
    * ON THE ACTION BAR, USE THE CURSOR POSITION TO SELECT THE           *
    * ACTION. IF THE CURSOR WAS ANYWHERE ELSE, JUST GO WITH THE          *
    * DEFAULT VALUE. IN THIS CASE, THE DEFAULT ACTION IS WHATEVER        *
    * IS IN THE COMMAREA FROM THE PREVIOUS ACTION, BECAUSE WE            *
    * ASSUME PEOPLE USUALLY KEEP SCROLLING IN THE SAME DIRECTION.        *
    *                                                                    *
    * IF THE USER ENTERED A NEW CUSTOMER NUMBER, USE THAT FOR            *
    * THE STARTING POSITION FOR THE NEXT SCREEN. OTHERWISE,              *
    * START FROM THE PREVIOUS VALUE IN THE COMMAREA.                     *
    *                                                                    *
    ***********************************************************************
    *
        IF EIBAID = DFHPF7
          MOVE 'BACKWARD' TO WS-COMM-ACTION
        ELSE
          IF EIBAID = DFHPF8
            MOVE 'FORWARD' TO WS-COMM-ACTION
          ELSE
            IF EIBCPOSN  10
              MOVE 'FORWARD' TO WS-COMM-ACTION
            ELSE
              IF EIBCPOSN  20
                MOVE 'BACKWARD' TO WS-COMM-ACTION
              ELSE
                IF EIBCPOSN  26
                  MOVE 'EXIT' TO WS-COMM-ACTION
                ELSE
                  IF EIBCPOSN  33
                    MOVE 'CANCEL' TO WS-COMM-ACTION.
    *
        IF WS-COMM-ACTION = 'EXIT'
           MOVE 'CUSTP000' TO WS-XCTL-PGM
           PERFORM XCTL-NEXT-PGM
        ELSE
            IF WS-COMM-ACTION = 'CANCEL'
               PERFORM REFRESH-SCREEN
            ELSE
                IF S6CUSTO IS NUMERIC
                   SET MAP-INDX TO 1
                   PERFORM CLEAR-REMAINING-ITEMS
                       UNTIL MAP-INDX  16
                   MOVE S6CUSTO    TO WS-COMM-CUST-NO
                                      WS-COMM-NEXT-CUST-NO
                   MOVE LOW-VALUES TO WS-COMM-ITEM-CODE
                                      WS-COMM-NEXT-ITEM-CODE
                   MOVE WS-STARTING-DATE-TIME
                                   TO WS-COMM-DATETIME
```

FIGURE 15.10 *(Continued)*

```
                              WS-COMM-NEXT-DATETIME
            MOVE ZEROES    TO WS-COMM-COUNTER
            MOVE ALL '_'   TO S6CUSTO
            PERFORM FORWARD-BROWSE
        ELSE
            IF WS-COMM-ACTION = 'BACKWARD'
                PERFORM BACKWARD-BROWSE
            ELSE
                PERFORM FORWARD-BROWSE.
*
*
***********************************************************************
* 1. BEGIN A SELECT WITH KEY FROM PRIOR SCREEN OR FROM USER.        *
* 2. OPEN THE CURSOR.                                               *
* 3. FETCH NEXT RECORD UNTIL END OF FILE OR SCREEN IS FULL.         *
* 4. DETERMINE CORRECT SETTING FOR ON-SCREEN PAGING INDICATORS.     *
* 5. MOVE THE FIRST AND LAST ITEM NUMBERS ON THE SCREEN TO          *
*    THE WORKING STORAGE COPY OF THE COMMAREA.                      *
* 6. CLOSE THE CURSOR.                                              *
* 7. CHANGE THE APPEARANCE OF ACTION BAR TO SHOW THAT 'FORWARD'     *
*    IS NOW THE DEFAULT. IF YOU HAVE A COLOR DISPLAY, USE THE       *
*    COLOR EXTENDED ATTRIBUTE. OTHERWISE, CHANGE THE ATTRIBUTE      *
*    BYTE OF THE SELECTED ACTION TO A BRIGHT SETTING.               *
* 8. SEND MAP AND RETURN.                                          *
***********************************************************************
*
 FORWARD-BROWSE.
*
    MOVE ZEROES TO WS-ACTIVE-ITEMS.
    MOVE 'N' TO WS-END-OF-DATA.
    SET MAP-INDX TO 1.
    MOVE SPACES TO S6MSGO.
*
    MOVE WS-COMM-NEXT-KEY TO WS-1ST-KEY.
*
    MOVE WS-1ST-KEY-CUST-NO TO WS-KEY-CUST-NO.
    MOVE WS-1ST-KEY-DATE-TIME TO WS-KEY-DATE-TIME.
    MOVE WS-1ST-KEY-ITEM-CODE TO WS-KEY-ITEM-CODE.
*
***********************************************************************
* SELECT STATEMENT WITH DECLARATION OF CURSOR                       *
* FOR FETCHING MULTIPLE ROWS                                        *
***********************************************************************
    MOVE 'LINEITEM' TO DISPLAY-RESOURCE.
    MOVE 'SELECT' TO DISPLAY-OPERATION.
*
    EXEC SQL DECLARE FWBROWSE CURSOR FOR
        SELECT
        CUSTNO, DATETIME, ITEMCODE, UNITPRICE, ORDERQTY
        FROM LINEITEM
        WHERE CUSTNO = :WS-KEY-CUST-NO
        AND (DATETIME   :WS-KEY-DATE-TIME
        OR (DATETIME = :WS-KEY-DATE-TIME
        AND ITEMCODE   :WS-KEY-ITEM-CODE)
        OR (DATETIME = :WS-KEY-DATE-TIME
        AND ITEMCODE = :WS-KEY-ITEM-CODE))
        ORDER BY DATETIME, ITEMCODE ASC
        END-EXEC.
*
    IF SQLCODE = +100
        MOVE 'Y' TO WS-END-OF-DATA
        MOVE SPACES TO S6PLUSO
    ELSE
        IF SQLCODE NOT = ZERO
            PERFORM CHECK-SQL-RESPONSE
            MOVE -1 TO S6CUSTL
            PERFORM SEND-SALE006-BEEP
        ELSE
            MOVE 'FWBROWSE' TO DISPLAY-RESOURCE
```

FIGURE 15.10 *(Continued)*

```
                MOVE 'OPEN CURSOR' TO DISPLAY-OPERATION
                EXEC SQL OPEN FWBROWSE
                    END-EXEC
                IF SQLCODE NOT = ZERO
                    PERFORM CHECK-SQL-RESPONSE
                    MOVE -1 TO S6CUSTL
                    PERFORM SEND-SALE006-BEEP
                END-IF
                PERFORM FORWARD-BROWSE-LOOP
                    UNTIL MAP-INDX  +16
                    OR WS-END-OF-DATA = 'Y'
                IF WS-ACTIVE-ITEMS  ZEROES
                    PERFORM FWD-BROWSE-HOUSEKEEPING
                END-IF
                MOVE 'FWBROWSE' TO DISPLAY-RESOURCE
                MOVE 'CLOSE CURSOR' TO DISPLAY-OPERATION
                EXEC SQL CLOSE FWBROWSE
                    END-EXEC
                IF SQLCODE NOT = ZERO
                    PERFORM CHECK-SQL-RESPONSE
                    MOVE -1 TO S6CUSTL
                    PERFORM SEND-SALE006-BEEP
                END-IF.
  *
        MOVE 'FORWARD' TO WS-COMM-ACTION.
        MOVE DFHYELLO TO S6FWDC.
        MOVE DFHNEUTR TO S6BKWC.
  *
        MOVE -1 TO S6CUSTL.
        PERFORM SEND-SALE006-RETURN.
  *
  ******************************************************************
  * THE SCREEN HAS A PLUS AND MINUS SIGN TO INDICATE WHETHER       *
  * MORE RECORDS CAN BE REACHED BY SCROLLING FORWARD OR BACKWARD.  *
  * THESE SIGNS ARE REQUIRED BY IBM IN THE SAA COMMON USER ACCESS  *
  * STANDARDS.                                                     *
  *                                                                *
  * IF WE ARE PAGING AHEAD FROM A PREVIOUS SCREEN, THE COUNTER     *
  * FIELD IN THE COMMAREA WILL INDICATE HOW MANY ROWS WERE         *
  * SHOWN ON THE PREVIOUS PASS. THE SCREEN CONTENTS "OVERLAP"      *
  * BY ONE ROW. IF MORE THAN ONE ROW WAS SHOWN ON THE             *
  * PREVIOUS SCREEN, WE SET THE MINUS SIGN ON THE CURRENT          *
  * SCREEN TO INDICATE THAT THERE ARE SOME ROWS ON FILE            *
  * WITH KEYS LOWER THAN THE ONES WE ARE NOW SHOWING.              *
  *                                                                *
  * WE READ ONE ROW AHEAD OF THE LAST ITEM ON THE SCREEN          *
  * TO DETERMINE WHETHER THERE ARE MORE ROWS TO WHICH             *
  * THE USER MAY SCROLL FORWARD ON THE NEXT SCREEN. IF SO,         *
  * WE SET THE PLUS SIGN. WHEN WE READ THIS ROW, WE DON'T          *
  * WANT IT TO GO ON THE SCREEN AND WE DON'T WANT TO UPDATE THE    *
  * SAVED COMMAREA KEY.                                            *
  *                                                                *
  * NOTE THAT THESE INDICATORS ARE NOT PERFECTLY ACCURATE          *
  * DEPENDING ON DATABASE SECURITY. OTHER USERS COULD BE           *
  * INSERTING OR DELETING ROWS.                                   *
  ******************************************************************
  *
  FWD-BROWSE-HOUSEKEEPING.
  *
        MOVE WS-1ST-KEY TO WS-COMM-KEY.
        MOVE WS-LAST-KEY TO WS-COMM-NEXT-KEY.
  *
        PERFORM CLEAR-REMAINING-ITEMS
            UNTIL MAP-INDX  +16.
  *
        IF WS-COMM-COUNTER  +1
            MOVE '-' TO S6MINUSO.
  *
        MOVE WS-ACTIVE-ITEMS TO WS-COMM-COUNTER.
  *
```

FIGURE 15.10 *(Continued)*

```
          IF WS-END-OF-DATA = 'Y'
              MOVE SPACES TO S6PLUSO
          ELSE
              MOVE 'LINEITEM' TO DISPLAY-RESOURCE
              MOVE 'FETCH'    TO DISPLAY-OPERATION
              EXEC SQL FETCH FWBROWSE
                  INTO
                  :ITEM-CUST-NO,
                  :ITEM-DATE-TIME,
                  :ITEM-CODE,
                  :ITEM-UNIT-PRICE,
                  :ITEM-QUANTITY
                  END-EXEC
*
              IF SQLCODE = +100
                  MOVE 'Y' TO WS-END-OF-DATA
                  MOVE SPACES TO S6PLUSO
              ELSE
                  IF SQLCODE NOT = ZERO
                      PERFORM CHECK-SQL-RESPONSE
                      MOVE -1 TO S6CUSTL
                      PERFORM SEND-SALE006-BEEP
                  ELSE
                      MOVE '+' TO S6PLUSO.
*
***********************************************************************
* ATTEMPT TO READ THE NEXT RECORD. IF FOUND, PUT IT IN THE          *
* NEXT AVAILABLE PLACE IN THE MAP ARRAY.                            *
***********************************************************************
*
 FORWARD-BROWSE-LOOP.
*
      MOVE 'LINEITEM' TO DISPLAY-RESOURCE.
      MOVE 'FETCH'    TO DISPLAY-OPERATION.
*
      EXEC SQL FETCH FWBROWSE
              INTO
              :ITEM-CUST-NO,
              :ITEM-DATE-TIME,
              :ITEM-CODE,
              :ITEM-UNIT-PRICE,
              :ITEM-QUANTITY
              END-EXEC
*
      IF SQLCODE = +100
          MOVE 'Y' TO WS-END-OF-DATA
      ELSE
          IF SQLCODE NOT = ZERO
              PERFORM CHECK-SQL-RESPONSE
              MOVE -1 TO S6CUSTL
              PERFORM SEND-SALE006-BEEP
          ELSE
              MOVE ITEM-CODE
                  TO SCR-ITEM-CODE (MAP-INDX)
              MOVE ITEM-QUANTITY
                  TO SCR-QUANTITY (MAP-INDX)
              MOVE ITEM-UNIT-PRICE
                  TO SCR-UNIT-PRICE (MAP-INDX)
              IF MAP-INDX = +1
                MOVE WS-KEY-CUST-NO TO WS-1ST-KEY-CUST-NO
                MOVE WS-KEY-DATE-TIME TO WS-1ST-KEY-DATE-TIME
                MOVE WS-KEY-ITEM-CODE TO WS-1ST-KEY-ITEM-CODE
              END-IF
              MOVE WS-KEY-CUST-NO TO WS-LAST-KEY-CUST-NO
              MOVE WS-KEY-DATE-TIME TO WS-LAST-KEY-DATE-TIME
              MOVE WS-KEY-ITEM-CODE TO WS-LAST-KEY-ITEM-CODE
              SET MAP-INDX UP BY +1
              ADD +1 TO WS-ACTIVE-ITEMS.
*
*
```

FIGURE 15.10   *(Continued)*

```
*********************************************************************
* SQL HAS NO COMMAND FOR READING BACKWARD PER SE.                   *
* THIS IS BECAUSE ANY TABLE CAN BE INDEXED VARIOUS DIFFERENT        *
* WAYS. YOU CAN CHOOSE AMONG SEQUENCES BY USING THE "ORDER BY"      *
* CLAUSE IN THE SELECT STATEMENT. THE DEFAULT IS "ASC"              *
* (ASCENDING) BUT YOU CAN USE "DESC" TO READ IN DESCENDING          *
* ORDER BY THE SAME SORT OR INDEX FIELD.                            *
*                                                                   *
* WHILE THE ROWS ARE FETCHED IN DESCENDING ORDER, FOR THE           *
* SAKE OF CONSISTENT VISUAL APPEARANCE, WE WANT TO DISPLAY          *
* THEM IN ASCENDING ORDER ON THE SCREEN. NOT ONLY THAT, BUT         *
* IF THERE IS LESS THAN A SCREENFUL OF ROWS, WE WANT TO             *
* START OVER AT THE BEGINNING OF THE FILE AND READ UP TO A          *
* FULL SCREEN OF ROWS STARTING FROM THERE.                          *
*********************************************************************
* 1. BEGIN A SELECT WITH KEY FROM PRIOR SCREEN OR FROM USER.        *
* 2. OPEN THE CURSOR.                                               *
* 3. READ PREVIOUS RECORD UNTIL BEGINNING OF FILE OR WORK TABLE     *
*    IS FULL.                                                       *
* 4. MOVE THE FIRST AND LAST LINEITEM FILE KEYS FROM THE WORK       *
*    TABLE TO THE WORKING STORAGE COPY OF THE COMMAREA.             *
* 5. REVERSE THE ORDER OF THE SCREEN ITEMS BY COPYING FROM THE      *
*    WORK TABLE TO THE SCREEN TABLE.                                *
* 6. DETERMINE CORRECT SETTING FOR ON-SCREEN PAGING INDICATORS.     *
* 7. CLOSE THE CURSOR.                                              *
* 8. CHANGE THE APPEARANCE OF ACTION BAR TO SHOW THAT 'BACKWARD'*
*    IS NOW THE DEFAULT. IF YOU HAVE A COLOR DISPLAY, USE THE       *
*    COLOR EXTENDED ATTRIBUTE. OTHERWISE, CHANGE THE ATTRIBUTE      *
*    BYTE OF THE SELECTED ACTION TO A BRIGHT SETTING.               *
* 9. SEND MAP AND RETURN.                                           *
*********************************************************************
*
 BACKWARD-BROWSE.
*
     MOVE ZEROES TO WS-ACTIVE-ITEMS.
     MOVE 'N' TO WS-END-OF-DATA.
     SET MAP-INDX TO +1.
     SET WORK-INDX TO +1.
     MOVE SPACES TO WORK-ARRAY.
     MOVE SPACES TO S6MSGO.
*
     MOVE WS-COMM-KEY TO WS-LAST-KEY.
*
     MOVE WS-LAST-KEY-CUST-NO TO WS-KEY-CUST-NO.
     MOVE WS-LAST-KEY-DATE-TIME TO WS-KEY-DATE-TIME.
     MOVE WS-LAST-KEY-ITEM-CODE TO WS-KEY-ITEM-CODE.
*
     MOVE 'LINEITEM' TO DISPLAY-RESOURCE.
     MOVE 'SELECT'   TO DISPLAY-OPERATION.
*
     EXEC SQL DECLARE BKBROWSE CURSOR FOR
          SELECT
          CUSTNO, DATETIME, ITEMCODE, UNITPRICE, ORDERQTY
          FROM LINEITEM
          WHERE CUSTNO = :WS-KEY-CUST-NO
          AND NOT DATETIME   :WS-KEY-DATE-TIME
          AND (NOT DATETIME = :WS-KEY-DATE-TIME
               AND ITEMCODE  :WS-KEY-ITEM-CODE)
          ORDER BY DATETIME, ITEMCODE DESC
          END-EXEC.
*
     IF SQLCODE = +100
         MOVE 'Y' TO WS-END-OF-DATA
         MOVE SPACES TO S6PLUSO S6MINUSO
         MOVE -1 TO S6CUSTL
         PERFORM SEND-SALE006-RETURN
     ELSE
         IF SQLCODE NOT = ZERO
             PERFORM CHECK-SQL-RESPONSE
             MOVE -1 TO S6CUSTL
```

FIGURE 15.10 *(Continued)*

```
                    PERFORM SEND-SALE006-BEEP
              ELSE
                  MOVE 'BKBROWSE' TO DISPLAY-RESOURCE
                  MOVE 'OPEN CURSOR' TO DISPLAY-OPERATION
                  EXEC SQL OPEN BKBROWSE
                      END-EXEC
                  IF SQLCODE NOT = ZERO
                      PERFORM CHECK-SQL-RESPONSE
                      MOVE -1 TO S6CUSTL
                      PERFORM SEND-SALE006-BEEP
                  END-IF
                  PERFORM BACKWARD-BROWSE-LOOP
                      UNTIL WORK-INDX  +16
                      OR WS-END-OF-DATA = 'Y'
                  IF WS-ACTIVE-ITEMS = 16
                      PERFORM BUILD-BKWD-BROWSE-SCREEN
                  ELSE
                      MOVE 'BKBROWSE' TO DISPLAY-RESOURCE
                      MOVE 'CLOSE CURSOR' TO DISPLAY-OPERATION
                      EXEC SQL CLOSE BKBROWSE
                          END-EXEC
                      IF SQLCODE NOT = ZERO
                          PERFORM CHECK-SQL-RESPONSE
                          MOVE -1 TO S6CUSTL
                          PERFORM SEND-SALE006-BEEP
                      END-IF
                      MOVE LOW-VALUES TO WS-COMM-ITEM-CODE
                                         WS-COMM-NEXT-ITEM-CODE
                      MOVE WS-STARTING-DATE-TIME
                                      TO WS-COMM-DATETIME
                                         WS-COMM-NEXT-DATETIME
                      MOVE ZEROES     TO WS-COMM-COUNTER
                      MOVE SPACES     TO S6PLUSO S6MINUSO
                      PERFORM FORWARD-BROWSE.
 *
 BUILD-BKWD-BROWSE-SCREEN.
 *
 *********************************************************************
 * IF WE HAVE OBTAINED A FULL SCREEN OF RECORDS, MOVE THOSE         *
 * RECORDS TO THE SCREEN IN THE PROPER ORDER. THEN, MOVE THE        *
 * KEYS FOR THE FIRST AND LAST SCREEN LINE TO THE WORKING           *
 * STORAGE COPY OF THE COMMAREA.                                    *
 *********************************************************************
 *
     PERFORM INVERT-SCREEN-ORDER 16 TIMES.
     MOVE WS-1ST-KEY TO WS-COMM-KEY.
     MOVE WS-LAST-KEY TO WS-COMM-NEXT-KEY.
 *
 *********************************************************************
 * THE SCREEN HAS A PLUS AND MINUS SIGN TO INDICATE WHETHER         *
 * MORE RECORDS CAN BE REACHED BY SCROLLING FORWARD OR BACKWARD.    *
 * THESE SIGNS ARE REQUIRED BY IBM IN THE SAA COMMON USER ACCESS    *
 * STANDARDS.                                                       *
 *                                                                  *
 * IF WE ARE PAGING BACK FROM A PREVIOUS SCREEN, THE COUNTER        *
 * FIELD IN THE COMMAREA WILL INDICATE HOW MANY RECORDS WERE        *
 * SHOWN ON THE PREVIOUS PASS. THE SCREEN CONTENTS "OVERLAP"        *
 * BY ONE RECORD. IF MORE THAN ONE RECORD WAS SHOWN ON THE          *
 * PREVIOUS SCREEN, WE SET THE PLUS SIGN ON THE CURRENT             *
 * SCREEN TO INDICATE THAT THERE ARE SOME RECORDS ON FILE           *
 * WITH KEYS HIGHER THAN THE ONES WE ARE NOW SHOWING.               *
 *                                                                  *
 * WE READ ONE RECORD BEFORE THE FIRST ITEM ON THE SCREEN           *
 * TO DETERMINE WHETHER THERE ARE MORE RECORDS TO WHICH             *
 * THE USER MAY SCROLL BACKWARD ON THE NEXT SCREEN. IF SO,          *
 * WE SET THE MINUS SIGN. WHEN WE READ THIS RECORD, WE DON'T        *
 * WANT IT TO GO ON THE SCREEN AND WE DON'T WANT TO UPDATE THE      *
 * SAVED COMMAREA KEY.                                              *
 *                                                                  *
 * NOTE THAT THESE INDICATORS ARE NOT PERFECTLY ACCURATE BECAUSE    *
```

FIGURE 15.10 *(Continued)*

```
      * WE DON'T CONTROL THE WHOLE FILE. OTHER USERS COULD BE ADDING  *
      * OR DELETING RECORDS.                                          *
      ****************************************************************
      *
          IF WS-COMM-COUNTER  +1
              MOVE '+' TO S6PLUSO.
      *
          MOVE WS-ACTIVE-ITEMS TO WS-COMM-COUNTER.
      *
          IF WS-END-OF-DATA = 'Y'
              MOVE SPACES TO S6MINUSO
          ELSE
              MOVE 'LINEITEM' TO DISPLAY-RESOURCE
              MOVE 'FETCH'    TO DISPLAY-OPERATION
              EXEC SQL FETCH BKBROWSE
                  INTO
                  :ITEM-CUST-NO,
                  :ITEM-DATE-TIME,
                  :ITEM-CODE,
                  :ITEM-UNIT-PRICE,
                  :ITEM-QUANTITY
                  END-EXEC
      *
              IF SQLCODE = +100
                  MOVE SPACES TO S6MINUSO
              ELSE
                  IF SQLCODE NOT = ZERO
                      PERFORM CHECK-SQL-RESPONSE
                      MOVE -1 TO S6CUSTL
                      PERFORM SEND-SALE006-BEEP
                  ELSE
                      MOVE '-' TO S6MINUSO.
      *
          MOVE 'LINEITEM' TO DISPLAY-RESOURCE.
          MOVE 'CLOSE CURSOR' TO DISPLAY-OPERATION.
          EXEC SQL CLOSE BKBROWSE
              END-EXEC.
      *
          MOVE 'BACKWARD' TO WS-COMM-ACTION.
          MOVE DFHYELLO TO S6BKWC.
          MOVE DFHNEUTR TO S6FWDC.
      *
          MOVE -1 TO S6CUSTL.
          PERFORM SEND-SALE006-RETURN.
      *
      ****************************************************************
      * ATTEMPT TO READ THE PREVIOUS RECORD. IF FOUND, PUT IT IN     *
      * THE NEXT AVAILABLE PLACE IN THE WORKING STORAGE ARRAY.       *
      ****************************************************************
      *
       BACKWARD-BROWSE-LOOP.
      *
      *
          MOVE 'LINEITEM' TO DISPLAY-RESOURCE.
          MOVE 'FETCH'    TO DISPLAY-OPERATION.
          EXEC SQL FETCH BKBROWSE
                  INTO
                  :ITEM-CUST-NO,
                  :ITEM-DATE-TIME,
                  :ITEM-CODE,
                  :ITEM-UNIT-PRICE,
                  :ITEM-QUANTITY
                  END-EXEC
      *
          IF SQLCODE = +100
              MOVE 'Y' TO WS-END-OF-DATA
          ELSE
              IF SQLCODE NOT = ZERO
                  PERFORM CHECK-SQL-RESPONSE
                  MOVE -1 TO S6CUSTL
```

FIGURE 15.10 *(Continued)*

```
                    PERFORM SEND-SALE006-BEEP
              ELSE
                    MOVE ITEM-CODE
                        TO WORK-ITEM-CODE (WORK-INDX)
                    MOVE ITEM-QUANTITY
                        TO WORK-QUANTITY (WORK-INDX)
                    MOVE ITEM-UNIT-PRICE
                        TO WORK-UNIT-PRICE (WORK-INDX)
                    IF WORK-INDX = +1
                      MOVE WS-KEY-CUST-NO TO WS-LAST-KEY-CUST-NO
                      MOVE WS-KEY-DATE-TIME TO WS-LAST-KEY-DATE-TIME
                      MOVE WS-KEY-ITEM-CODE TO WS-LAST-KEY-ITEM-CODE
                    END-IF
                    MOVE WS-KEY-CUST-NO TO WS-1ST-KEY-CUST-NO
                    MOVE WS-KEY-DATE-TIME TO WS-1ST-KEY-DATE-TIME
                    MOVE WS-KEY-ITEM-CODE TO WS-1ST-KEY-ITEM-CODE
                    SET WORK-INDX UP BY +1
                    ADD +1 TO WS-ACTIVE-ITEMS.
     *
     *********************************************************************
     * THE BACKWARD BROWSE ROUTINE GETS THE RECORDS IN REVERSE ORDER *
     * AND STORES THEM IN A WORKING STORAGE ARRAY. IT THEN PUTS THE  *
     * RECORDS INTO THE SCREEN ARRAY IN ASCENDING ORDER BY CUSTOMER  *
     * NUMBER.                                                       *
     *********************************************************************
     *
      INVERT-SCREEN-ORDER.
     *
          SET WORK-INDX DOWN BY +1.
          MOVE WORK-ITEM-CODE (WORK-INDX) TO SCR-ITEM-CODE (MAP-INDX).
          MOVE WORK-QUANTITY (WORK-INDX) TO SCR-QUANTITY (MAP-INDX).
          MOVE WORK-UNIT-PRICE (WORK-INDX)
              TO SCR-UNIT-PRICE (MAP-INDX).
          SET MAP-INDX UP BY +1.
     *
     *
      XCTL-NEXT-PGM.
     *
          MOVE ZEROES TO WS-COMM-COUNTER.
          MOVE WS-XCTL-PGM TO DISPLAY-RESOURCE.
          MOVE 'XCTL' TO DISPLAY-OPERATION.
          EXEC CICS XCTL
                  PROGRAM (WS-XCTL-PGM)
                  COMMAREA (WS-COMMAREA)
                  RESP (WS-CICS-RESPONSE1)
                  END-EXEC.
     *
          IF WS-CICS-RESPONSE1 NOT = DFHRESP(NORMAL)
              PERFORM CHECK-CICS-RESPONSE
              MOVE -1 TO S6CUSTL
              PERFORM SEND-SALE006-BEEP.
     *
     *********************************************************************
     * THIS ROUTINE SENDS THE RECORD BROWSE MAP WITH NO DATA ON IT.  *
     *********************************************************************
     *
      REFRESH-SCREEN.
     *
          MOVE ZEROES     TO WS-COMM-COUNTER.
          MOVE 'FORWARD'  TO WS-COMM-ACTION.
          MOVE DFHYELLO   TO S6FWDC.
          MOVE DFHNEUTR   TO S6BKWC.
          MOVE 'SALE006'  TO WS-COMM-PREV-MAP.
          MOVE SPACES     TO S6MSGO.
          MOVE SPACES     TO WS-COMM-CUST-NO
                             WS-COMM-NEXT-CUST-NO.
          MOVE LOW-VALUES TO WS-COMM-ITEM-CODE
                             WS-COMM-NEXT-ITEM-CODE.
          MOVE WS-STARTING-DATE-TIME
                          TO WS-COMM-DATETIME
```

FIGURE 15.10   *(Continued)*

```
                        WS-COMM-NEXT-DATETIME.
    MOVE '_____'   TO S6CUSTO.
    MOVE -1          TO S6CUSTL.
    MOVE SPACES      TO S6PLUSO S6MINUSO.
    SET MAP-INDX     TO +1.
    PERFORM CLEAR-REMAINING-ITEMS UNTIL MAP-INDX  16.
    PERFORM SEND-SALE006-RETURN.
*
*
 CLEAR-REMAINING-ITEMS.
*
    MOVE SPACES TO SCR-ITEM-CODE (MAP-INDX)
                   SCR-QUANTITY-X (MAP-INDX)
                   SCR-UNIT-PRICE-X (MAP-INDX).
*
    SET MAP-INDX UP BY 1.
*
******************************************************************
* THIS ROUTINE SENDS SALE006 WITH A WARNING 'BEEP'. WE USE THIS *
* ONLY WHEN THE CALLING ROUTINE WANTS TO DISPLAY A WARNING ON   *
* THE MESSAGE LINE OF THIS MAP. CURSOR POSITION MUST BE SET.    *
******************************************************************
*
 SEND-SALE006-BEEP.
*
    IF WS-COMM-PREV-MAP = 'SALE006'
        EXEC CICS SEND MAP ('SALE006')
                  MAPSET ('MSALE06')
                  FROM (SALE006I)
                  DATAONLY
                  ALARM
                  CURSOR
                  END-EXEC
    ELSE
        MOVE 'SALE006' TO WS-COMM-PREV-MAP
        EXEC CICS SEND MAP ('SALE006')
                  MAPSET ('MSALE06')
                  FROM (SALE006I)
                  ERASE
                  ALARM
                  CURSOR
                  END-EXEC.
*
    EXEC CICS RETURN
              TRANSID ('CUS6')
              COMMAREA (WS-COMMAREA)
              END-EXEC.
*
*
******************************************************************
* THIS ROUTINE SENDS SALE006 WITH WHATEVER DATA HAS BEEN PLACED *
* ON IT. IF THE PREDEFINED PORTIONS OF THE MAP ARE ALREADY ON   *
* THE SCREEN, SALE006 WILL BE SENT 'DATAONLY'.                  *
******************************************************************
*
 SEND-SALE006-RETURN.
*
    IF WS-COMM-PREV-MAP = 'SALE006'
        EXEC CICS SEND MAP ('SALE006')
                  MAPSET ('MSALE06')
                  FROM (SALE006I)
                  DATAONLY
                  CURSOR
                  END-EXEC
    ELSE
        MOVE 'SALE006' TO WS-COMM-PREV-MAP
        EXEC CICS SEND MAP ('SALE006')
                  MAPSET ('MSALE06')
                  FROM (SALE006I)
                  ERASE
```

FIGURE 15.10 *(Continued)*

```
                              CURSOR
                              END-EXEC.
      *
           EXEC CICS RETURN
                      TRANSID ('CUS6')
                      COMMAREA (WS-COMMAREA)
                      END-EXEC.
      *
      ********************************************************************
      * THIS ROUTINE SENDS SALE006 WITH CURSOR ON ACTION BAR.           *
      ********************************************************************
      *
       CURSOR-TO-ACTION-BAR.
      *
           MOVE 'SALE006' TO WS-COMM-PREV-MAP.
           EXEC CICS SEND MAP ('SALE006')
                      MAPSET ('MSALE06')
                      FROM (SALE006I)
                      CURSOR (1)
                      DATAONLY
                      END-EXEC.
      *
           EXEC CICS RETURN
                      TRANSID ('CUS6')
                      COMMAREA (WS-COMMAREA)
                      END-EXEC.
      *
      *
      ********************************************************************
      * CHECK THE CICS RESPONSE CODE AND BUILD A MESSAGE EXPLAINING     *
      * THE ERROR. IT IS THE RESPONSIBILITY OF THE CALLING ROUTINE      *
      * TO INITIALIZE SOME DISPLAY FIELDS IN THE MESSAGE WORK AREA      *
      * TO INDICATE THE TYPE OF COMMAND BEING PROCESSED.                *
      *                                                                 *
      * WE DO NOTHING ABOUT CERTAIN RESPONSE CODES HERE SO THAT         *
      * THOSE SITUATIONS CAN BE HANDLED WITH LOGIC ELSEWHERE IN THE     *
      * PROGRAM.                                                        *
      *                                                                 *
      ********************************************************************
      *
      *
       CHECK-CICS-RESPONSE.
      *
           EVALUATE WS-CICS-RESPONSE1
           WHEN DFHRESP(NORMAL)
                CONTINUE
           WHEN DFHRESP(MAPFAIL)
                CONTINUE
           WHEN DFHRESP(ENDFILE)
                CONTINUE
           WHEN DFHRESP(DISABLED)
                MOVE 'CALL OPERATIONS' TO DISPLAY-CALL-WHOM
                MOVE DISABLED-MSG TO DISPLAY-DESCRIPTION
                MOVE BUILD-MSG TO S6MSGO
           WHEN DFHRESP(DUPREC)
                MOVE DUPREC-MSG TO DISPLAY-DESCRIPTION
                MOVE BUILD-MSG TO S6MSGO
           WHEN DFHRESP(DSIDERR)
                MOVE 'CALL PROGRAMMER' TO DISPLAY-CALL-WHOM
                MOVE DSIDERR-MSG TO DISPLAY-DESCRIPTION
                MOVE BUILD-MSG TO S6MSGO
           WHEN DFHRESP(INVREQ)
                MOVE 'CALL PROGRAMMER' TO DISPLAY-CALL-WHOM
                MOVE INVREQ-MSG TO DISPLAY-DESCRIPTION
                MOVE BUILD-MSG TO S6MSGO
           WHEN DFHRESP(IOERR)
                MOVE 'CALL PROGRAMMER' TO DISPLAY-CALL-WHOM
                MOVE IOERR-MSG TO DISPLAY-DESCRIPTION
                MOVE BUILD-MSG TO S6MSGO
           WHEN DFHRESP(ITEMERR)
                MOVE 'CALL PROGRAMMER' TO DISPLAY-CALL-WHOM
```

FIGURE 15.10 *(Continued)*

```
              MOVE ITEMERR-MSG TO DISPLAY-DESCRIPTION
              MOVE BUILD-MSG TO S6MSGO
          WHEN DFHRESP(LENGERR)
              MOVE 'CALL PROGRAMMER' TO DISPLAY-CALL-WHOM
              MOVE LENGERR-MSG TO DISPLAY-DESCRIPTION
              MOVE BUILD-MSG TO S6MSGO
          WHEN DFHRESP(NOSPACE)
              MOVE 'CALL OPERATIONS' TO DISPLAY-CALL-WHOM
              MOVE NOSPACE-MSG TO DISPLAY-DESCRIPTION
              MOVE BUILD-MSG TO S6MSGO
          WHEN DFHRESP(NOTFND)
              MOVE NOTFND-MSG TO DISPLAY-DESCRIPTION
              MOVE BUILD-MSG TO S6MSGO
          WHEN DFHRESP(PGMIDERR)
              MOVE 'CALL PROGRAMMER' TO DISPLAY-CALL-WHOM
              MOVE PGMIDERR-MSG TO DISPLAY-DESCRIPTION
              MOVE BUILD-MSG TO S6MSGO
          WHEN DFHRESP(QIDERR)
              MOVE 'CALL PROGRAMMER' TO DISPLAY-CALL-WHOM
              MOVE QIDERR-MSG TO DISPLAY-DESCRIPTION
              MOVE BUILD-MSG TO S6MSGO
          WHEN OTHER
              MOVE 'CALL PROGRAMMER' TO DISPLAY-CALL-WHOM
              MOVE WS-CICS-RESPONSE1 TO DISPLAY-RESPONSE
              MOVE DEFAULT-DESCRIPTION TO DISPLAY-DESCRIPTION
              MOVE BUILD-MSG TO S6MSGO
          END-EVALUATE.
 *
 *
 *
  CHECK-SQL-RESPONSE.
      EVALUATE TRUE
      WHEN SQLCODE = +100
          MOVE NOTFND-MSG TO DISPLAY-DESCRIPTION
          MOVE BUILD-MSG TO S6MSGO
      WHEN SQLCODE = 0
          CONTINUE
      WHEN SQLCODE = -803 OR +65535
          MOVE DUPREC-MSG TO DISPLAY-DESCRIPTION
          MOVE BUILD-MSG TO S6MSGO
      WHEN SQLCODE  0
          CONTINUE
      WHEN OTHER
          MOVE 'CALL PROGRAMMER' TO DISPLAY-CALL-WHOM
          MOVE SQLCODE TO DISPLAY-SQLCODE
          MOVE SQL-DESCRIPTION TO DISPLAY-DESCRIPTION
          MOVE BUILD-MSG TO S6MSGO
      END-EVALUATE.
```

FIGURE 15.10 *(Continued)*

TEST YOUR UNDERSTANDING

Questions and Exercises

1. Suppose you have to keep a membership system for a computer user group. Output requirements are the following:
   - Membership roster, including address, phone, type of computer, and areas of interest.
   - Mailing labels for newsletters and annual dues notice
   - Report of which members are currently paid-up.
   - Search screen to find members having any desired interest (e.g. CICS, SQL, OS/2, C programming, etc.).
   - Screens to allow the above information to be entered and updated.

   Your exercise is to set up the tables using SQL commands. You'll need at least two tables to organize this data in a logical manner. You could use more, depending on how much detail you want to keep in this system. In any case, decide what the tables should be called and what columns belong in each one. Decide on the primary key for each.

2. Familiarize yourself with Query Manager screens by going through the tutorial material packaged with OS/2 Extended Edition. Then, use Query Manager instead of the COBOL program to delete and redefine the test database containing the CUSTOMER and LINEITEM tables. What are the advantages and disadvantages of using Query Manager instead of a COBOL program for this purpose?

3. The browse operations in the sample system are not particularly efficient. The selection is repeated each time the user invokes the function. Change CUSTP000 so that the SELECT with CURSOR is done when the user selects the starting customer number from the main menu. Open the cursor, FETCH each row, write each row into a temporary storage queue for later retrieval, then close the cursor. Change CUSTP005 and CUSTP006 to retrieve the browsed records from the temporary storage queue, deleting the queue before returning to the main menu.

Appendix

MAINFRAME PROGRAM COMPILATION AND MAP ASSEMBLY

Parameters and JCL

If you are accustomed to placing a CBL card at the beginning of your COBOL source programs (or if you use *ASM with assembler language or *PROCESS with PL/I programs), you may continue doing this when you translate CICS programs. The preliminary translator step will only recognize the CICS(option1,option2,....) parameter within the CBL, *ASM, or *PROCESS statement. All other parameters will be passed along to the language compiler stage, in which they will behave exactly as they normally do. For example, suppose you submitted a job with this CBL statement:

```
CBL CICS(LANGLVL(2),DEBUG),LANGLVL(2)
```

The command level translator would recognize the CICS keyword parameter list, which contains LANGLVL(2) and DEBUG. It would interpret LANGLVL(2) to mean that the program is in ANS COBOL 1974 for an OSVS system. It would interpret DEBUG to mean that the object code should contain routines that pass translator line numbers back to CICS at run time for debugging purposes. The default options in each instance are LANGLVL(1) and NODEBUG.

Your COBOL compiler, in this example, will, in effect, receive a CBL statement containing only the parameter intended for the second job step:

```
CBL LANGLVL(2)
```

It would interpret this, in like manner, to mean that the program is in ANS COBOL 1974 for an MVS system. This parameter must be specified separately for both the translator and the compiler job steps.

Most translator options are concerned with translator listing format and resemble options that you may be accustomed to supplying for the language compiler. Defaults exist for translator options; these defaults are adequate for most purposes, so that you ordinarily will not need to concern yourself with them. However, NOTRUNC should be specified, which allows you to pass arguments to CICS commands that consist of numeric values larger than 9,999.

Figures A.1 through A.10 show some sample program translation/compilation/link and map assembly JCL for DOS/VSE and MVS systems.

```
Sample map assembly JCL for MVS systems

//MAPASMB   JOB account,'name',MSGLEVEL=1
//* ASSEMBLE A SYMBOLIC MAP FROM THE SOURCE CODE
//* CONTAINED IN YOUR.PDS(pdsmembr)
//SYMBOLIC EXEC PGM=IFOX00,REGION=320K,PARM='SYSPARM(DSECT)'
//SYSLIB    DD  DSN=SYS1.MACLIB,DISP=SHR
            DD  DSN=CICS.MACLIB,DISP=SHR
            DD  DSN=CICS.SOURCE,DISP=SHR
//SYSPRINT DD  SYSOUT=A
//SYSPUNCH DD  DSN=USER.MAPLIB.ASM(mapsetnm)
//SYSUT1    DD  UNIT=SYSDA,SPACE=(CYL,(5,5))
//SYSUT2    DD  UNIT=SYSDA,SPACE=(CYL,(5,5))
//SYSUT3    DD  UNIT=SYSDA,SPACE=(CYL,(5,5))
//SYSIN     DD  DSN=YOUR.PDS(pdsmembr),DISP=(OLD,PASS)
/*
//* ASSEMBLE AND LINK-EDIT A PHYSICAL MAP FROM THE SAME
//*   SOURCE CODE
//PHYSICAL EXEC PGM=IFOX00,REGION=320K,PARM='SYSPARM(MAP)'
//SYSLIB    DD  DSN=SYS1.MACLIB,DISP=SHR
            DD  DSN=CICS.MACLIB,DISP=SHR
            DD  DSN=CICS.SOURCE,DISP=SHR
//SYSPRINT DD  SYSOUT=A
//SYSPUNCH DD  DSN=&&TEMPNCH,SPACE=(CYL,(5,5)),UNIT=SYSDA,
//         DD  DCB=(RECFM=FB,BLKSIZE=400),DISP=(NEW,PASS)
//SYSUT1    DD  UNIT=SYSDA,SPACE=(CYL,(5,5))
//SYSUT2    DD  UNIT=SYSDA,SPACE=(CYL,(5,5))
//SYSUT3    DD  UNIT=SYSDA,SPACE=(CYL,(5,5))
//SYSIN     DD  DSN=YOUR.PDS(pdsmembr),DISP=(OLD,DELETE)
/*
//LINKEDIT EXEC PGM=IEWL,PARM='LIST,LET,XREF'
//SYSPRINT DD  SYSOUT=A
//SYSLIN    DD  DSN=&&TEMPNCH,DISP=(OLD,DELETE)
//SYSUT1    DD  UNIT=SYSDA,SPACE=(1024,(100,10))
//SYSLMOD   DD  DSN=CICS.LOADLIB,DISP=SHR
            NAME mapsetnm(R)
/*
//
```

FIGURE A.1　Sample map assembly JCL for MVS systems.

Example of MVS COBOL CICS command level compile JCL.

```
//CICSCOMP JOB account,'name',MSGLEVEL=1
          EXEC PROC=DFHEICTL,PARM.COB='LIB,BUF=4K'
//TRN.SYSIN DD *
 (insert COBOL source statements here)
/*
//LKED.SYSIN DD *
          NAME pgmname(R)
/*
//
```

This JCL invokes a PROC for COBOL, which is DFHEICTL. The PROC for Assembler is DFHEITAL; the PROC for PL/I is DFHEIPTL. These PROCs are provided along with the mainframe CICS translator.

FIGURE A.2   Example of MVS COBOL CICS command level compile JCL.

```
//NOW461CL JOB (RCCS),'COMPILE SALEP005      ',CLASS=A
//MEMBER    EXEC COMMAND,
//              NAME=SALEP005,
//              SOURCE='SSG.CICSNW.SOURCE',
//              COPY='SSG.CICSNW.COPYLIB',
//              LOAD='SSG.CICSNW.LOAD'
//LKED.SYSLIB  DD
//             DD
//             DD DSN=SSG.CICSNW.LOAD,DISP=SHR
//
```

FIGURE A.3   Another example of MVS COBOL CICS command level compile JCL.

```
//XXXXXXXX  JOB  (RCCS),NOWAK,CLASS=A
//IPO$C  PROC SUFFIX=1$,           DEFAULT COBOL TRANSLATOR
//       INDEX=CICS15,
//       OUTC='A',                 SYSOUT CLASS
//       REG=512K,                 REGION CLASS
//       NAME=XXXXXXXX,            SOURCE AND LOAD PGM NAME
//       WORK=DISK,                UNIT NAME OF WORK SPACE
//       LIB='SSG.CICSNW.SOURCE',  COBOL SOURCE LIBRARY
//       LOAD='SSG.CICSNW.LOAD'    LOAD LIBRARY NAME
//* TRANSLATOR STEP
//TRN    EXEC PGM=DFHECP&SUFFIX,
//            REGION=&REG
//STEPLIB    DD DSN=&INDEX..LOADLIB,DISP=SHR
//SYSPRINT   DD SYSOUT=&OUTC
//SYSPUNCH   DD DSN=&&SYSCIN,
//              DISP=(,PASS),UNIT=&WORK,
//              DCB=BLKSIZE=400,
//              SPACE=(400,(400,100))
//SYSIN      DD DSN=&LIB(&NAME),DISP=SHR
//* COBOL COMPILER STEP
//COB    EXEC PGM=IKFCBL00,REGION=&REG,
//  PARM=(NOTRUNC,LIB,'LANGLVL(1)',APOST,NODYNAM,NORES)
//STEPLIB    DD DSN=SYS1.VS.COBLINK,DISP=SHR
//SYSLIB     DD DSN=&INDEX..COBLIB,DISP=SHR
//           DD DSN=&LIB,DISP=SHR
//SYSPRINT   DD SYSOUT=&OUTC
//SYSIN      DD DSN=&&SYSCIN,DISP=(OLD,DELETE)
//SYSLIN     DD DSN=&&LOADSET,DISP=(MOD,PASS),
//              UNIT=&WORK,SPACE=(80,(250,100))
//SYSUT1     DD UNIT=&WORK,SPACE=(460,(350,10))
```

FIGURE A.4   Procedure showing translator step, COBOL compiler step, and linkage editor step for Figure A.3.

```
//SYSUT2    DD UNIT=&WORK,SPACE=(460,(350,10))
//SYSUT3    DD UNIT=&WORK,SPACE=(460,(350,10))
//SYSUT4    DD UNIT=&WORK,SPACE=(460,(350,10))
//* LINK EDIT STEP
//LKED      EXEC PGM=IEWL,REGION=&REG,
//               PARM=(XREF,LIST,MAP),COND=(5,LT,COB)
//SYSLIB    DD DSN=&INDEX..LOADLIB,DISP=SHR
//          DD DSN=SYS1.VS.COBLIB,DISP=SHR
//SYSLMOD   DD DSN=&LOAD(&NAME),DISP=SHR
//SYSUT1    DD UNIT=&WORK,DCB=BLKSIZE=1024,
//               SPACE=(1024,(200,20))
//SYSPRINT  DD SYSOUT=&OUTC
//SYSLIN    DD DSN=&INDEX..COBLIB(DFHEILIC),DISP=SHR
//          DD DSN=&&LOADSET,DISP=(OLD,DELETE)
//          DD DDNAME=SYSIN
//PEND
//COMMAND   EXEC IPO$C
```

FIGURE A.4   *(Continued)*

```
//NOW00006  JOB (RCCS),MSALE06,CLASS=A,TIME=1,REGION=600K
//ASMMAP06  EXEC CICSMAP4,LOADLIB='SSG.CICSNW.LOAD',
//               MEMBER=MSALE06,COND.LKED=(8,LT,ASMMAP),
//               COND.ASMDSECT=(8,LE)
//UPDT.SYSUT1 DD DSN=SSG.CICSNW.SOURCE(MSALE06),DISP=(SHR,PASS)
//ASMDSECT.SYSPUNCH DD DSN=SSG.CICSNW.COPYLIB(MSALE06),DISP=SHR
//
```

FIGURE A.5   Another example of CICS map assembly JCL for MVS systems.

```
//*        M. D. C.            SYS1.UPROCS(CICSMAP4)
//CICSMPDS PROC MEMBER=TEMPNAME,LOADLIB=DUMMY
//UPDT     EXEC PGM=IEBGENER
//SYSPRINT DD  SYSOUT=(U,,BLNK)
//SYSIN    DD  DUMMY
//SYSUT2   DD  DSN=&&TEMPPDS,UNIT=DISK,SPACE=(TRK,(5,5)),
//             DCB=(RECFM=FB,LRECL=80,BLKSIZE=6240,BUFNO=1),
//             DISP=(NEW,PASS,DELETE)
//ASMMAP   EXEC PGM=IFOX00,PARM='SYSPARM(MAP)'
//SYSLIB   DD  DSN=SYS1.MACLIB,DISP=SHR
//         DD  CICS14.MACLIB,DISP=SHR
//SYSUT1   DD  UNIT=DISK,SPACE=(CYL,(5,5)),DISP=(NEW,DELETE)
//SYSUT2   DD  UNIT=DISK,SPACE=(CYL,(5,5)),DISP=(NEW,DELETE)
//SYSUT3   DD  UNIT=DISK,SPACE=(CYL,(5,5)),DISP=(NEW,DELETE)
//SYSPUNCH DD  UNIT=DISK,DSN=&&TEMP,SPACE=(TRK,(5,5)),
//             DCB=(RECFM=FB,LRECL=80,BLKSIZE=3200),DISP=(NEW,PASS)
//SYSPRINT DD  SYSOUT=(U,,BLNK)
//SYSIN    DD  DSN=&&TEMPPDS,DISP=(OLD,PASS)
//LKED     EXEC PGM=IEWL,PARM='LIST,XREF,LET',COND=(8,LT)
//SYSUT1   DD  UNIT=DISK,SPACE=(1024,(100,100)),DISP=(NEW,DELETE)
//SYSPRINT DD  SYSOUT=(U,,BLNK)
//SYSLIN   DD  DSN=&&TEMP,DISP=(OLD,DELETE)
//         DD  DDNAME=SYSIN
//SYSLMOD  DD  DSN=&LOADLIB(&MEMBER.),DISP=SHR
//ASMDSECT EXEC PGM=IFOX00,PARM='SYSPARM(DSECT)'
//SYSLIB   DD  DSN=SYS1.MACLIB,DISP=SHR
//         DD  CICS14.MACLIB,DISP=SHR
//SYSUT1   DD  UNIT=DISK,SPACE=(CYL,(5,5)),DISP=(NEW,DELETE)
//SYSUT2   DD  UNIT=DISK,SPACE=(CYL,(5,5)),DISP=(NEW,DELETE)
//SYSUT3   DD  UNIT=DISK,SPACE=(CYL,(5,5)),DISP=(NEW,DELETE)
//SYSPRINT DD  SYSOUT=(U,,BLNK)
//SYSIN    DD  DSN=&&TEMPPDS,DISP=(OLD,DELETE)
//
```

FIGURE A.6   Procedure showing physical and symbolic map assembly for Figure A.5.

Sample map assembly JCL for DOS/VSE systems

```
// JOB MAPASM acctdata ASSEMBLE AND LINK-EDIT BMS PHYSICAL MAP
// DLBL TSTCLB,'CICS TEST CLB'
// EXTENT ,TSTLIB
// DLBL TSTRLB,'CICS TEST RLB'
// EXTENT ,TSTLIB
// DLBL TSTSLB,'CICS TEST SLB'
// EXTENT ,TSTLIB
LIBDEF SL,SEARCH=TSTSLB,FROM=TSTSLB,TO=TSTSLB
LIBDEF RL,SEARCH=TSTRLB,FROM=TSTRLB,TO=TSTRLB
LIBDEF CL,SEARCH=TSTCLB,FROM=TSTCLB,TO=TSTCLB
// OPTION CATAL,NODECK,NOXREF,SYSPARM='MAP'
 PHASE mapname,*
// EXEC ASSEMBLY,SIZE=200K
// EXEC LNKEDT

//JOB MAPSYM acctdata CREATE BMS SYMBOLIC MAP
ASSGN SYSPCH,SYSLNK
// OPTION DECK,LIST,SYSPARM='DSECT'
// EXEC ASSEMBLY,SIZE=200K
CLOSE SYSPCH,OOD
ASSGN SYSIPT,SYSLNK
// DLBL TSTCLB,'CICS TEST CLB'
// EXTENT ,TSTLIB
// DLBL TSTRLB,'CICS TEST RLB'
// EXTENT ,TSTLIB
// DLBL TSTSLB,'CICS TEST SLB'
// EXTENT ,TSTLIB
LIBDEF SL,SEARCH=TSTSLB,FROM=TSTSLB,TO=TSTSLB
LIBDEF RL,SEARCH=TSTRLB,FROM=TSTRLB,TO=TSTRLB
LIBDEF CL,SEARCH=TSTCLB,FROM=TSTCLB,TO=TSTCLB
// EXEC MAINT,SIZE=100K
```

FIGURE A.7   Sample map assembly JCL for DOS/VSE systems.

```
* $$ JOB JNM=MBONLCMP,CLASS=T,DISP=D,USER='MIKE BOUROS'
* $$ LST CLASS=L,DISP=D
// JOB MBONLCMP 17NOWSYSTCMB COMMAND LEVEL TRANSLATE/COMPILE/LINK
* $$ SLI P.CICSTEST
ASSGN SYSPCH,SYSLNK
// EXEC DFHECP1$,SIZE=150K
 CBL CICS(XREF NOLIST FLAGI),LIB,NOSXREF,NOSYM,NOSEQ,OPT,CLIST
+INC NO11SER
/*
CLOSE SYSPCH,OOD
ASSGN SYSIPT,SYSLNK
// OPTION CATAL,NOSYM,NOXREF,NOLISTX
 PHASE NO11SER,*
 INCLUDE DFHECI
// EXEC FCOBOL,SIZE=120K
// EXEC LNKEDT,SIZE=100K
/*
/&
// JOB RESETIPT 17NOWSYSTP RESET SYSIPT TO STANDARD ASSGN
CLOSE SYSIPT,OOC
/&
* $$ EOJ
```

FIGURE A.8   Sample COBOL command level compile JCL for DOS/VSE systems.

```
* $$ JOB JNM=MBMAP,CLASS=T,DISP=D,USER='MIKE BOUROS'
* $$ LST CLASS=L,DISP=D
// JOB MBMAP 17NOWSYSTCMB ASSEMBLE & LINKEDIT BMS MAP
* $$ SLI P.CICSTEST
// OPTION CATAL,NODECK,NOXREF,SYSPARM='MAP'
 PHASE NO11MAP,*
// EXEC ASSEMBLY,SIZE=200K
+INC NO11MAP
// EXEC LNKEDT
/*
/&
* $$ EOJ
```

FIGURE A.9   Sample map assembly JCL for DOS/VSE systems (physical map).

```
* $$ JOB JNM=MBMAP,CLASS=T,DISP=D,USER='MIKE BOUROS'
* $$ LST CLASS=L,DISP=D
// JOB MBMAP 17NOWSYSTCMB GENERATE COBOL MAP DSECT
ASSGN SYSPCH,SYSLNK
//OPTION DECK,LIST,SYSPARM='DSECT'
// EXEC ASSEMBLY,SIZE=200K
 PUNCH ' CATALS C.CPNO11M'
+INC NO11MAP
/*
CLOSE SYSPCH,OOD
ASSGN SYSIPT,SYSLNK
* $$ SLI P.CICSTEST
// OPTION CATAL,NOSYM,NOXREF,NOLISTX
// EXEC MAINT,SIZE=100K
/&
// JOB RESETIPT 17NOWSYSTP RESET SYSIPT TO STANDARD ASSGN
CLOSE SYSIPT,OOC
/&
* $$ EOJ
```

FIGURE A.10   Sample map assembly JCL for DOS/VSE systems (symbolic map).

Command Files for OS/2 Systems

Preparation of programs for CICS OS/2 systems was discussed in earlier chapters. Figures A.11 and A.12 show sample command files for assembling BMS maps and compiling COBOL command level programs.

THE SYSTEM PROGRAMMER'S EYE VIEW

CEMT Commands

We are about to discuss several system features that may or may not be the responsibility of the applications programmer, depending on the situation. For example, the applications programmer typically does use the CEMT command to "new copy" a program in a test region, but very often someone else will be responsible for shutting the region down. However, the applications programmer should know that these features exist even if someone else is responsible for working with them.

```
@echo off
@echo -------------------------------------------------------------------
@echo    CICSMAP  -  Translate %1.bms
@echo -------------------------------------------------------------------
if %1.==. goto msg
if not exist %1.bms goto msg1
if %2.==. goto simple
if %3.==. goto simple
faamsptr %1 SYSPARM=DSECT %2,%3
if errorlevel 12 goto aserv
if errorlevel 8 goto aerror
faamsptr %1 SYSPARM=MAP %2,%3
goto join
:simple
faamsptr %1 SYSPARM=DSECT %2
if errorlevel 12 goto aserv
if errorlevel 8 goto aerror
faamsptr %1 SYSPARM=MAP %2
:join
if errorlevel 12 goto aserv
if errorlevel 8 goto aerror
if errorlevel 4 goto awarn
goto aend
:aserv
@echo    Severe map translator errors detected
goto aend
:awarn
@echo    Map translator warning errors issued, compile can continue
goto aend
:aerror
@echo    Map translator errors issued, program may be unusable
goto aend
:msg1
@echo    %1.bms does not exist
goto aend
:msg
@echo This command will translate a BMS map. The program must be
@echo written using BMS assembler macros and have an extension of BMS
@echo To run this command enter:
@echo        CICSMAP mapname code-option
@echo mapname can be fully qualified and is required
@echo code-option refers to the treatment of the operand of XINIT,
@echo and takes one of the following forms:
@echo ASCII (the default)   - meaning that the operand is unchanged
@echo EBCDIC(ppp,qqq)       - meaning that the operand is translated
@echo                from EBCDIC page number ppp to ASCII page number qqq
@echo EBCDIC                - meaning the same as EBCDIC(037,437)
:aend
```

FIGURE A.11   CICSMAP: map assembly command file for OS/2 systems.

```
STARTDBM
@echo off
@echo ------------------------------------------------------------------------
@echo    CICSTCL  -  Translate, compile and Link %1.ccp
@echo ------------------------------------------------------------------------
if %1.==. goto msg
if not exist %1.ccp goto msg1
faaprpml %1 %2 %3 %4 COBOL2
if errorlevel 12 goto aserv
if errorlevel 8 goto aerror
if errorlevel 4 goto awarn
goto acomp
:aserv
@echo      Severe translator errors detected
goto aend
:awarn
@echo      Translator warning errors issued, compile continuing
goto acomp
:aerror
@echo      Translator errors issued, program may be unusable
goto aend
:acomp
COBOL %1,%1,%1;
if errorlevel 1 goto acerr
goto alink
:acerr
@echo      Compiler errors discovered
goto aend
:alink
if exist %1.def goto dlink
@echo ;Module definition file for %1 program    %1.def
@echo LIBRARY INITINSTANCE  >     %1.def
@echo PROTMODE              >     %1.def
@echo DATA NONSHARED        >     %1.def
@echo CODE LOADONCALL       >     %1.def
@echo EXPORTS %1 @1         >     %1.def
:dlink
link /NOD /NOP /MAP %1,%1.dll,,COBLIB+DOSCALLS+FAACLIB+SQL_STAT+SQL_DYN,%1.DEF;
if errorlevel 1 goto alerr
goto aend
:alerr
@echo      Link errors discovered
goto aend
:msg1
@echo      %1.ccp does not exist
:msg
@echo      This command will translate, compile and link a CICS program.
@echo      The source module is expected to have an extension of CCP.
@echo      -Input File-       -------Contents-------        -----Source-----
@echo      progname.CCP       CICS Source module            user defined
@echo      progname.DEF       Module definition file        user defined
@echo      PCOBOL.LIB         COBOL compiler library        Supplied with COBOL/2
@echo      DOSCALLS.LIB       OS/2 call library             Supplied with OS/2
@echo      FAACLIB.LIB        CICS OS/2 library             Supplied with CICS OS/2
@echo      The Output is:     progname.TRL    Translator listing
@echo                         progname.CBL    Translated source
@echo                         progname.LST    Compiler listing
@echo                         progname.OBJ    Object module
@echo                         progname.DLL    Executable program
@echo                         progname.MAP    Map listing
pause
@echo      To run this command enter:
@echo          CICSTCL progname  directive1 directive2 directive3
@echo      progname can be fully qualified and is required
@echo      directive1,2,3 can be COBOL2, LINECOUNT(n), QUOTE, APOST or /B
@echo      all are optional. Place directives in source file or in COBOL.DIR.
@echo      The definitions file progname.DEF is created if it does not exist
:aend
```

FIGURE A.12   CICSTCL: COBOL command level compile command file for OS/2 systems.

Master terminal commands are instructions that tell a mainframe CICS system about its current configuration. In other words, they tell the CICS system what devices are in service, what files are open, what transactions and programs are enabled, and whether a new copy of a program object module has been prepared. Master terminal commands also can be used to inquire about the current status of the configuration, and about the current usage levels of programs. Incidentally, if you hear or read about "CSMT commands", these are the old versions of CEMT commands that were used before CICS Version 1 Release 5 became available. CSMT uses a command-line format rather than a screen format; support for it is withdrawn in newer releases of CICS.

When you compile a command level program or assemble a map while mainframe CICS is running, CICS must be told that a new copy of the program or physical map object code is available. CICS will then take the address of this module and place it in the PPT entry. When you want to run a program that uses a file that is also used by batch programs, you may want to check whether the file is enabled under CICS. You may want to enable it if it is not. When a transaction is not working properly, and you do not want users to get into it before it is fixed, you will want to disable it. At the end of the day, you may want to shut down CICS to free resources to do batch processing. The effect of some of these CEMT commands is shown in Figure A.13.

There are several ways to use CEMT to do these things. More information may be found in the *Operator's Guide* or *CICS-Supplied Transactions* for your version of mainframe CICS. Only an introduction will be presented here. The easiest way to begin using CEMT is to type CEMT on a terminal screen and press ENTER. This will give you the CEMT prompting screens. The first one will ask you to enter one of the following:

INQUIRE
SET
PERFORM

INQUIRE tells you the current status of system resources; for instance, whether a file is enabled. SET allows you to change the status of system resources; it allows you to enable the file if it is disabled. PERFORM allows you to shut the system down, to create a dump, or to reset the CICS date and time to match the system date and time. These are not things that everyone should be doing; only properly authorized personnel should be able to sign onto CICS with a security key that allows access to CEMT.

If you enter INQUIRE, you will see a list of resources about which you may inquire. Type the desired option, followed by the name of the specific resource in parentheses, for example:

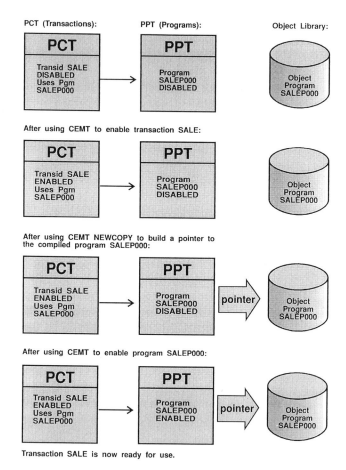

FIGURE A.13   Effect of CEMT commands on CICS tables.

DATASET (LINEITM)

A screen will appear with information about the data set status. Similar inquiries can be made concerning programs, transactions, and so forth. If you want to enable the data set, enter:

SET DATASET (LINEITM) ENABLED

To establish a new copy of a program, enter

SET PROGRAM (SALEP000) NEWCOPY

The same format is used whether the program is a command-level application or a map. CICS programs other than IBM's (i.e., those programs not beginning with DFH) may be enabled or disabled by substituting EN-

ABLED or DISABLED for NEWCOPY in the above command. Transaction codes not beginning with C may be enabled by entering the following:

SET TRANSACTION (SALE) ENABLED

Finally, to shut down CICS, the following command may be entered:

PERFORM SHUTDOWN

Extended Recovery Facility (XRF)

XRF first became available with CICS/MVS 2.1. It provides a degree of fault-tolerant processing in that it allows a partially initialized alternate CICS system to take over for an active mainframe CICS system that is down. Such an event is called an **XRF takeover**. Depending on the degree of redundancy provided, the takeover can handle a central electronic complex (CEC) outage (a mainframe hardware failure or shutdown), an operating system outage, a VTAM outage, or a CICS region outage. XRF does not affect the applications programmer except insofar as it provides increased system availability at the cost of a certain amount of overhead. Details about XRF are in the *XRF Guide.*

System Programming Interface

Sites using older versions of CICS often customized CICS by writing programs that updated CICS system control blocks, or by installing modified versions of IBM-supplied programs. IBM's stated policy is to move in the direction of providing substitute methods which allow customer sites to customize CICS without directly modifying control blocks or IBM-supplied code. This is done through **user exits** and through **system programming EXEC CICS commands**.

CICS/ESA 3.1 introduced a new exit programming interface (XPI) language which allows certain types of calls to CICS to be made from user exits. This language is described in the *Customization Guide.* The user exit language works only in user exits and differs greatly from the language used in CICS application programs.

CICS/OS/VS 1.7 introduced the concept of system programming EXEC CICS commands. These commands were intended to take the place of old macro-level calls for accessing certain CICS system functions. These commands were not listed in the command level APRM, but were instead listed in the *CICS 1.7 Customization Guide.* More commands became available with later releases; see the *CICS/ESA System Programming Reference* manual for details. Some of these system programming commands let a program do certain things which previously would have been done with the CEMT command. Other commands affect tracing, journalling, and dumping. With CICS/ESA 3.1, those commands which are defined as system programming commands are protected by a CICS translator option and can also be protected by run-time security checking through RACF. In other words, only a few programmers might be authorized to use those commands.

SOURCES OF ADDITIONAL INFORMATION

IBM Manuals for Mainframe CICS Programmers

- All programmers should have a copy of IBM's *Application Programmer's Reference Manual (Command Level)* for the relevant version of CICS. This is the reference manual most used by programmers in writing CICS applications. Mainframe CICS programmers should also have access to *Messages and Codes*, which lists the error messages. Also needed are manuals for the COBOL compiler and for Access Method Services (IDCAMS). Anyone can order these manuals directly from IBM. A bibliography of the titles and publication numbers of other CICS manuals appears at the front of each CICS manual, including the APRM.

- If you will be responsible for making entries in mainframe CICS tables with the CEDA transaction, you will need *Resource Definition (Online)*. Batch update of CICS tables is described in *Resource Definition (Batch)*. Other utility screens supplied by IBM are described in *CICS-Supplied Transactions* and *Operator's Guide*.

- For more information about debugging with dumps and trace tables, see *Problem Determination Guide* and *CICS User's Handbook*.

- For more information about programming in the MRO and ISC environment, see *Intercommunication Guide*.

- If you will be using EXEC SQL commands, see *IBM DATABASE2 Application Programming Guide for CICS Users*, SC26-4080, and *IBM DATABASE2 Reference*, SC26-4078.

- If you will be using EXEC DLI commands, see the following, depending on your version: *IMS/ESA Application Programming: EXEC DLI Commands*, SC26-4280; *IMS/VS Version 2 Application Programming for CICS/OS/VS Users*, SC26-4177; or *IMS/VS Version 1 Application Programming for CICS/VS Users*, SH20-9210.

- If you will need to be able to read macro-level programs to convert them to command level, see *CICS/VS Application Programmer's Reference Manual (Macro Level)*, SC33-0079, and the tutorial *CICS/VS Macro Level Coding Student Text*, ISP, first edition, July 1980, available through SRA under order number SR20-4687-0.

- To learn more about 3270-series terminal devices, see *An Introduction*

List of Figures

Figure:	Page:	Chapter and Section:	Caption:
Figure 1.1	2	1.1.1	Screen displays of maps used in sample programs.
Figure 1.2	8	1.1.3	Relationship of CICS to system environment (chart).
Figure 1.3	12	1.2.3	CICS COBOL command level program translation (chart).
Figure 1.4	14	1.2.3	Sample CICS COBOL command level program compilation.
Figure 1.5	22	1.2.5	Map assembly (chart).
Figure 1.6	23	1.2.5	Sample CICS map assembly.
Figure 1.7	38	1.3.1	Sample CICS table definition: PPT (processing program table).
Figure 1.8	39	1.3.1	Sample CICS table definition: SIT (system initialization table).
Figure 1.9	40	1.3.1	Sample CICS table definition: PCT (program control table).
Figure 1.10	42	1.3.1	Sample CICS table definition: FCT (file control table).
Figure 1.11	43	1.3.2	Sample CICS table definition: DCT (destination control table).
Figure 1.12	44	1.3.2	Sample CICS table definition: JCT (journal control table).
Figure 2.1	50	2.3.2	Screen addresses on a typical 3270 device.
Figure 2.2	51	2.3.2	Sample screen display.
Figure 2.3	52	2.3.2	Relationship of terminal to computer (chart).
Figure 2.4	54	2.3.4	Add screen from sample applications.
Figure 2.5	56	2.3.4	Add screen with attributes and stopper/skip bytes visible.
Figure 2.6	58	2.3.5	How the modified data tag affects the data that a program receives.

Figure:	Page:	Chapter and Section:	Caption:
Figure 3.1	65	3.1.2	Source code for map SALE000.
Figure 3.2	66	3.1.2	Source code for map CUST000.
Figure 3.3	66	3.1.2	Source code for map SALE001.
Figure 3.4	67	3.1.2	Source code for map SALE002.
Figure 3.5	69	3.1.2	Source code for map SALE003.
Figure 3.6	70	3.1.2	Source code for map SALE004.
Figure 3.7	71	3.1.2	Source code for map SALE005.
Figure 3.8	72	3.1.2	Source code for map SALE006.
Figure 3.9	87	3.5.1	Copy library members used in the sample system (record formats).
Figure 3.10	88	3.5.1	Symbolic map SALE000, as it appears in the copy library.
Figure 3.11	90	3.5.1	Symbolic map CUST000.
Figure 3.12	90	3.5.1	Symbolic map SALE001.
Figure 3.13	92	3.5.1	Symbolic map SALE002.
Figure 3.14	95	3.5.1	Symbolic map SALE003.
Figure 3.15	97	3.5.1	Symbolic map SALE004.
Figure 3.16	100	3.5.1	Symbolic map SALE005.
Figure 3.17	105	3.5.1	Symbolic map SALE006.
Figure 3.18	113	3.5.1	IBM-supplied partial table of attribute byte values and table of attention identifier values.
Figure 3.19	114	3.5.1	Table of attribute byte values.
Figure 4.1	118	4.1.1	STUBPGM source code.
Figure 4.2	120	4.1.1	How STUBPGM works (chart).
Figure 4.3	127	4.1.7	STUBPG2 source code.
Figure 4.4	131	4.2.1	SEND MAP options: MAPONLY (physical map) (chart).
Figure 4.5	132	4.2.1	SEND MAP options: merging map data with program data (chart).
Figure 4.6	133	4.2.1	SEND MAP options: DATAONLY (program data only) (chart).
Figure 4.7	135	4.2.1	Symbolic cursor positioning (chart).
Figure 4.8	139	4.3.1	HANDLE CONDITION command (chart).
Figure 4.9	140	4.3.2	Using EIBAID and DFHRESP (chart).
Figure 5.1	152	5.1.1	Conversational programming (chart).
Figure 5.2	154	5.1.1	Pseudoconversational programming (chart).
Figure 5.3	160	5.4.1	Illustration of LINK, XCTL, and RETURN (chart).
Figure 5.4	177	5.11.1	Logic flow diagram of record add function (chart).
Figure 5.5	178	5.11.1	Source code for SALEP000, the add screen processor.
Figure 5.6	186	5.11.1	Source code for SALEP001, the add screen processor.
Figure 6.1	197	6.1.1	Indexed file structure of a telephone book (chart).
Figure 6.2	200	6.1.1	VSAM control area split (chart).
Figure 6.3	203	6.1.2	VSAM catalog "tree structure" (chart).
Figure 6.4	215	6.3.1	Source code for SALEP003, the record deletion screen processor.
Figure 6.5	224	6.3.1	Source code for SALEP004, the Enter Current Week Sales screen processor.
Figure 6.6	232	6.3.1	Logic of program SALEP004 (chart).
Figure 6.7	236	6.3.2	Source code for SALEP005, customer file browse program, and for SALEP006.

Figure:	Page:	Chapter and Section:	Caption:
Figure 6.8	260	6.3.2	Logic of program SALEP005 (chart).
Figure 7.1	272	7.2.1	Writing items to a temporary storage queue sequentially (chart).
Figure 7.2	273	7.2.1	Random-access update of temporary storage (chart).
Figure 7.3	274	7.2.1	Random-access read of temporary storage item (chart).
Figure 7.4	276	7.2.3	Source code for SALEP002, customer record change processor.
Figure 7.5	285	7.2.3	Logic of program SALEP002 (chart).
Figure 8.1	298	8.2.3	COBOL version of DFHJCRDS.
Figure 8.2	301	8.2.4	Updating two recoverable files (chart).
Figure 9.1	309	9.3.3	EDF display screens.
Figure 10.1	331	10.1.2	Listing of program EXAMP001 that produced a dump.
Figure 10.2	340	10.1.2	Program check dump produced by sample program EXAMP001.
Figure 10.3	357	10.2.1	Control programs within CICS (chart).
Figure 10.4	360	Test Your Understanding	Listing of sample program EXAMP000 to troubleshoot.
Figure 10.5	383	Test Your Understanding	Dump produced by sample program EXAMP000.
Figure 11.1	399	11.1.2	Using multiple maps per screen (chart).
Figure 11.2	399	11.1.2	BMS paging (chart).
Figure 11.3	400	11.1.2	Browse program using BMS (chart).
Figure 11.4	403	11.1.3	Source code for SALEP006, a browse program using BMS paging (alternate version).
Figure 13.1	436	13.3.2	Module flow diagram (chart).
Figure 14.1	445	14.1.2	OS/2 CONFIG.SYS.
Figure 14.2a	453	14.4.2	Editing with Micro Focus Workbench (F2).
Figure 14.2b	454	14.4.2	The Micro Focus check menu (F3).
Figure 14.2c	455	14.4.2	Syntax check and compile.
Figure 14.2d	456	14.4.2	OS/2 prompt from Workbench: Shift/Ctrl/Break.
Figure 14.3	457	14.5.1	Setup to start CICS OS/2 from OS/2 Desktop Manager.
Figure 14.4a	459	14.5.1	CICS OS/2 startup: logo panel.
Figure 14.4b	459	14.5.1	CICS OS/2 startup: V123 logical terminal window.
Figure 14.4c	460	14.5.1	CICS OS/2 startup: CESN signon.
Figure 14.4d	461	14.5.1	CICS OS/2 startup: CICS OS/2 system console window.
Figure 14.5	463	14.6.1	CEDA menus.
Figure 14.6	465	14.6.2	Data Conversion Table (CVT).
Figure 14.7	465	14.6.2	Destination Control Table (DCT).
Figure 14.8	466	14.6.2	File Control Table (FCT).
Figure 14.9	467	14.6.2	Program Control Table (PCT).
Figure 14.10	468	14.6.2	Processing Program Table (PPT).
Figure 14.11	468	14.6.2	System Initialization Table (SIT).
Figure 14.12	470	14.6.2	Signon Table (SNT).
Figure 14.13	470	14.6.2	Terminal Control Table System Entries (TCS).
Figure 14.14	471	14.6.2	Terminal Control Table Terminal Entries (TCT).
Figure 14.15	473	14.6.2	Temporary Storage Table (TCT).
Figure 14.16	473	14.6.2	Workstation Setup (WSU).

Figure:	Page:	Chapter and Section:	Caption:
Figure 15.1	498	15.2.5	OS/2 dialog box for user ID and password.
Figure 15.2	499	15.3.1	Using Query Manager to create a new database.
Figure 15.3	503	15.3.5	Sample program to create tables within a database.
Figure 15.4-15.10	509	15.4.7	Sample CICS programs using SQL commands.
Figure A.1	582	Appendix	Sample map assembly JCL for MVS systems.
Figure A.2	583	Appendix	Example of MVS COBOL CICS command level compile JCL.
Figure A.3	583	Appendix	Another example of MVS COBOL CICS command level compile JCL.
Figure A.4	583	Appendix	Procedure showing translator step, COBOL compiler step, and linkage editor step for Figure A.3.
Figure A.5	584	Appendix	Another example of CICS map assembly JCL for MVS systems.
Figure A.6	584	Appendix	Procedure showing physical and symbolic map assembly for Figure A.5.
Figure A.7	585	Appendix	Sample map assembly JCL for DOS/VSE systems.
Figure A.8	585	Appendix	Sample COBOL command level compile JCL for DOS/VSE systems.
Figure A.9	586	Appendix	Sample map assembly JCL for DOS/VSE systems (physical map).
Figure A.10	586	Appendix	Sample map assembly JCL for DOS/VSE systems (symbolic map).
Figure A.11	587	Appendix	CICSMAP: map assembly command file for OS/2 systems.
Figure A.12	588	Appendix	CICSTCL: COBOL command level compile command file for OS/2 systems.
Figure A.13	590	Appendix	Effect of CEMT commands on CICS tables (chart).
(Example within text)	139	4.3.1	Coding example for use of HANDLE CONDITION within a structured program.
(Example within text)	157	5.2.1	Program sending DFHCOMMAREA data, program receiving DFHCOMMAREA data.
(Example within text)	163	5.5.3	Variable length DFHCOMMAREA.
(Example within text	204	6.1.2	IDCAMS job using DELETE, DEFINE, REPRO, LISTCAT, and PRINT.
(Example within text)	321	9.4.4	Animator display.
(Example within text)	420	12.1.2	Program setup for CICS program accessing DL/I data base.
(Example within text)	500	15.3.2	OS/2 EE SQL data types.
(Example within text)	508	15.4.7	Copy library members for SQL examples.

Index

3270-series terminals, 48–60, 592–593
  3270 data stream, 51–52, 80, 120
3287 printer terminal, 79, 406, 408–409,
    411–412, 417, 450, 480
ABEND command, 300, 330
ADDRESS command, 125–126, 166, 353,
    420, 504–505, 508
ALLOCATE command, 425
Animator, debugging with, 318–325, 327,
    353, 444, 461, 480
ASCII vs. EBCDIC considerations, 479, 507
  See also CICS OS/2, conversion table
      (CVT)
ASKTIME command, 172, 174–175
ASSIGN command, 165–166, 174
Asynchronous processing, 423–424, 478
Attention identifier (AID), 49
  attention keys, 49
  testing value of EIBAID, 145, 149
Attribute bytes
  default, 82
  defined over flag byte in symbolic map,
      87, 147
  extended attribute, 56, 76, 80–81
  See also Basic mapping support (BMS),
      DFHMDF
Automatic transaction initiation (ATI), 174

Basic mapping support (BMS)
  assembly, 23–33, 86
  BMS paging, 397–398, 401–402, 405,
      411–412, 415–416
  field definition (DFHMDF), 77, 81, 86,
      89, 116
  full function, 80, 398, 415
  map definition (DFHMDI), 77–78, 80–81,
      116, 135, 400–401

map set definition (DFHMSD), 77–78, 80,
    86, 116, 133, 135, 399
message routing, 416
minimum function, 76, 80, 130
partition sets, definition of, 174, 407–408
standard function, 76
text processing, 415–416, 448
  See also Physical map, Symbolic map
Batch data collection under CICS, 288
Batch processing
  definition, 1, 54, 64, 304
  tends to use fewer resources than CICS,
      45
BLL cells, 125, 353, 419
Browse application
  SQL examples, 553
  VSAM examples, 236, 247

CANCEL command, 169
CECI command interpreter transaction,
    317, 466
CEDA online resource definition
    transaction, 37, 45–46, 264, 320, 447,
    449, 462–475, 592
CEDF execution diagnostic facility, 303,
    307–309, 313–316, 318, 326–327, 330,
    351, 356, 424, 475
CEMT master terminal transaction, 34–35,
    46, 208, 212, 262, 307, 419, 586, 589,
    591
  not present in CICS OS/2, 475
CICS
  as subordinate operating system, 7
  command syntax, 10, 317
  command translator, 12–13, 581–582, 592
  considerations for multi-CPU
      installations, 438

CICS *(cont'd)*
  control programs (prior to 3.1), 37
  macro level (obsolete), 13–22
  startup job, 8, 208, 210, 269, 291
  system ABEND codes, 351
  tables, purpose of, 34
CICS OS/2
  3151 ASCII terminals, 478
  BMS map file (FAAMSFSC), 445, 449
  BMS map translation, 86, 451, 480
  COBOL/2 compiler, 318–319, 443–444,
    451–452, 454, 479–480
  CONFIG.SYS, 444–445, 493
  conversion table (CVT), 34–35, 37, 464,
    475, 478–479
  INQUIRE command, 476–477
  resource definition file (FAACTFTB),
    445, 463
  sequential file support (TD), 450
  SIGNOFF command, 477
  SIGNON command, 477
  terminating with CQIT, 462
  translate/compile/link, 12, 319, 451
  VSAM support, 449
  workstation setup table (WSU), 37, 475,
    480
CICS/ESA, 8, 43–44, 264, 328, 353, 447,
    591–592
  domains, 43–44, 169, 352
  gateways, 44
  kernel, 43
CICS/MVS
  data tables, 264, 593
  extended recovery facility (XRF), 264
COBOL CALL statement, 170
Common system area (CSA), 354–355
Common user access (CUA)
  action bar, 65–75, 146, 176, 305,
    462–463, 480, 499
  popup, 73–74, 176, 305, 458
  pull-down menu, 73, 305
Common work area (CWA), 164–166,
    193–194, 355, 433, 469
CONNECT PROCESS command, 425
Conversational processing, 152–153,
    427–428
CRTE routing transaction, 351, 424–425,
    478
Cursor on terminal screen
  default cursor position on BMS map, 84
  reading user's cursor position, 146,
    171–172
  setting cursor position, 53, 134
  skip bytes, 55–56, 74, 83, 116, 304
  stopper bytes, 55

Database design
  foreign key, 489, 500, 505–506
  normalization, 489–490
  primary key, 202, 261, 482–483, 486,
    489–491, 500, 580
Database management system (DBMS), 36,
    481–487, 489, 491, 501
  data control language (DCL), 484
  data definition language (DDL), 450, 484,
    486, 499
  data manipulation language (DML), 484

DELETE command, 214, 274, 294
DELETEQ TD command, 294
DELETEQ TS command, 274
Dequeue, automatic, 209, 213, 265, 292
Destination control table (DCT), 35, 294,
    355–356, 410, 450, 464, 466, 480
DFHCOMMAREA
  use of, 75, 156–158, 165–166, 479
  verifying length (EIBCALEN), 157–158,
    162–164, 171, 353
DFHMDF, DFHMDI, DFHMSD
  See Basic mapping support (BMS)
Direct access method, 198
Distributed program link (DPL), 427, 478
Distributed transaction processing (DTP),
    351, 422–423
DL/I
  debugging with EDF, 307
  programming techniques, 418–421
  termination call with SYNCPOINT, 299
Documentation, 75, 415, 429, 431,
    434–435, 453
DUMP command, 328, 330, 354–355
Dump control program, 37
Dynamic log, 291–292, 302, 487
Dynamic transaction backout (DTB), 211,
    263, 299–300, 302, 426
  dynamic transaction backout program,
    37, 291–292
  recoverable intrapartition TD queue, 289

ENDBR command, 235, 261
Enqueue, automatic, 209–210, 266,
    291–292, 299, 302, 419
EXEC interface block (EIB), 314–315, 427
  task number (EIBTASKN), 171, 173, 270
  terminal ID (EIBTRMID), 171, 174, 270
  transaction ID (EIBTRNID), 161, 171,
    174
EXEC interface program, 44–45, 351,
    356–358, 418
Execution diagnostic facility (EDF)
  See CEDF execution diagnostic facility
Extended attributes, 76, 80–81
Extrapartition destination (TD), 288–291,
    293–294, 317, 450, 465–466

Field length indicator (BMS), 59
  to determine what user entered, 86, 147
  use in setting cursor position, 59, 134
File control table (FCT), 9, 35, 208, 213,
    264, 356, 449, 466
FORMATTIME command, 175
FREE command, 427
FREEMAIN command, 129, 353
Function shipping, 478–479

GETMAIN command, 129, 163, 352–353

HANDLE ABEND command, 300–301, 434
HANDLE AID command, 122, 143–146,
    149, 300, 434
HANDLE CONDITION command, 13, 122,
    125, 138–146, 149, 299–300, 351, 406,
    413, 434

Indirect destination (TD), 290–291

Intersystem communication (ISC),
421–422, 424, 467, 592
Interval control program, 37, 169
Intrapartition destination (TD), 288–290,
294
use of trigger level to launch new task,
167, 289–290, 410, 423, 480
ISAM (obsolete), 198–199, 202
ISSUE PRINT command, 409

JES interface (spooler), 329, 411–415
JOURNAL command, 294–297, 448
Journal control table (JCT), 291, 295–296
Journals
automatic journaling, 292–293
DFHJCRDS (record layout), 297
journal buffers, 293, 296
journal file ID, 291–292, 294, 296
system log (file id 1), 291–292, 296, 302,
431
user, 293

Light pen (selector pen), 83–84
LINK command, 159, 478
Linkage editor, 13, 319, 330, 449, 451,
454
Linkage section, using data areas in,
123–129
LOAD command, 168
Lockout (deadly embrace), 210, 235
LUTYPE 6.2 (APPC), 422–423, 448,
478–479

MAPFAIL condition, 13, 75, 138, 140–141,
143–144, 146, 149, 315
avoiding ABEND with CLEAR or PA key,
146
Maps, mapsets
See Basic mapping support (BMS)
MASSINSERT (VSAM), 202, 212–213
Micro Focus Workbench, 318, 443,
451–456, 480, 502
Modified data tag
premodified (FSET), 57–58, 75, 84, 116,
132, 138, 148, 156, 161, 206, 402
turning it off, 57–58
with DATAONLY, 132
MS/DOS .BAT files, 442, 451, 456
Multiregion option (MRO), 421–424, 592

Naming conventions, 204, 442
nondisplay fields, 55, 83

Online processing
definition, 6
OS/2 .CMD files, 12, 86, 442, 451, 454,
456
OS/2 EE, 594
OS/2 EE Database Manager
CREATE DATABASE call, 486, 498
DROP DATABASE call, 486
SQLBIND utility, 452, 495–496
STARTDBM, 494
STOPDBM, 495
system database directory, 492
volume database directory, 492
OS/2, overview of, 441

Physical map, 33–34, 55, 77, 80–82, 84, 86,
116, 130–132, 135–136, 408, 449, 589
See also Basic mapping support (BMS)
Presentation Manager (OS/2), 63, 320, 442,
446, 448, 458
Processing program table (PPT), 35, 46, 80,
118, 167–168, 351, 356, 467, 478, 589
Program control program, 37
Program control table (PCT), 35, 37, 46, 75,
80, 118, 159, 165, 174, 356, 402, 422,
429, 467, 476, 480
Pseudoconversational processing, 152–153,
161, 261, 268, 308, 428
PURGE MESSAGE command, 406

QIDERR condition, 272–274, 294
Queue, defined, 288

READ command, 10, 126, 139, 210–211,
234–235, 272, 294, 479
cannot change key in existing record,
213
read for update, 209–211, 213–214, 265
READPREV command, 202, 234–235
READQ TD command, 294, 410
READQ TS command, 272–273, 275
random (ITEM), 273
sequential (NEXT), 273
RECEIVE MAP command, 122, 136–138,
141, 144–146, 148, 150, 171–172, 408
RECEIVE PARTN command, 408
Relational database, 481–484, 490
RELEASE command, 168
RESETBR command, 235
Resource definition online (RDO)
See CEDA online resource definition
RESP, use for error-checking, 121–122, 173,
413, 476
RETRIEVE command, 169, 411
RETURN command, 149, 155, 157, 170
REWRITE command, 214
ROUTE command, 416

SEND CONTROL command, 135
SEND MAP command, 130, 405
DATAONLY, 130–132, 147–150, 434
ERASEAUP, 130, 134
MAPONLY, 81, 130–131, 133–134,
147–149, 434
merged data, 131
multiple pages, 398, 402
with partitions, 408, 415
with printer, 412
SEND PAGE command, 398, 402, 406, 412,
416
SEND PARTNSET command, 408
SEND TEXT, 415–416, 448
SERVICE RELOAD, 124–126, 353
SET command, 262–263, 476–477
Signon table (SNT), 430, 469
Skip-sequential processing, 234
SQL
access plan, 485–486, 494, 496–497
bind, 485–486, 494–497
CREATE INDEX, 501
CREATE TABLE, 499–500
CREATE VIEW, 501

SQL *(cont'd)*
  DB2 (mainframe implementation), 13, 36,
      44, 196, 292, 423, 427, 479, 481, 483,
      487, 497–498, 502, 507, 593
  DECLARE CURSOR and FETCH, 506–507
  DROP TABLE, 501
  EXEC SQL DELETE, 506
  EXEC SQL GRANT, 497
  EXEC SQL REVOKE, 497
  EXEC SQL SELECT, 479, 502, 504,
      507–508
  EXEC SQL UPDATE, 505
  host variables, 485, 495, 501–502, 504,
      506
  preprocessor, 443–444, 485, 495–497
  Query Manager, 450, 485–486, 493–494,
      497, 499, 504, 580, 594
  SQLCA, 496, 502, 509
  See also OS/2 EE Database Manager
START command, 167, 169, 234, 411, 450
STARTBR command, 233–235, 261
Storage control program, 37, 45, 129, 329,
      352
Storage violations, 129, 163, 352–354
Structured programming, 119, 144
Switching dump files, 329
Symbolic map, 33, 55, 77–82, 84–86, 89,
      116, 130–134, 136–137, 147–149, 449,
      480
  See also Basic mapping support (BMS)
SYNCPOINT command, 299, 302

Task
  definition of, 35
  task control area, 36–37, 355
Task control program, 37
Temporary storage
  browse (CEBR), 313, 316, 326, 475
  on VSAM file, 269
  selecting queue name, 269
  separate items, 272–273
  uses for, 268
TERMERR condition, 351
Terminal control program, 120, 123, 136,
      152
Terminal control table (TCT), 36–37, 45,
      155, 165, 286, 355
Terminal control table user area (TCTUA),
      165–166, 193, 355
Terminal I/O area (TIOA), 36, 79, 133, 148,
      401
Test plan, 304–306, 326
TIOAPFX, 79, 133, 401
TRACE command and trace table, 44, 327,
      330, 354–358, 419, 475, 592

Transaction
  definition of, 35
  IBM-supplied, 589–590, 592
  order of invoking, 75
Transaction routing, 423, 478
Transaction work area (TWA), 165, 355
Transaction, definition of, 35
Transient data queues, 174, 177, 287, 289,
      291–292, 410, 450, 466
Trigger fields, 76

UNLOCK command, 213

VS COBOL II, 593
  coding changes needed for, 119, 123–126
  SET ADDRESS statement, 126, 353
VSAM Access Method Services (IDCAMS)
  alternate index, 201, 261
  catalog, 199–200, 202–203, 207, 263
  control area, 36–37, 199–200, 207, 355
  control interval, 198–199, 207, 209, 213,
      265, 291
  DEFINE CLUSTER, 204–205, 213
  DELETE, 205
  LISTCAT, 204–205, 208, 265
  PRINT, 208
  REPRO, 204–205, 207–208, 265
VSAM dynamic access, 201
VSAM entry-sequenced data set (ESDS),
      201, 204, 207, 213
VSAM key-sequenced data set (KSDS),
      200–201, 203–204, 207–210, 212–213,
      261, 265–266
VSAM random access
  See READ command
VSAM relative byte address (RBA),
      200–201, 206, 211, 213
  highest allocated, 200
  highest used, 200
VSAM relative record data set (RRDS), 201,
      213
  relative record number, 211, 213
VSAM sequential access
  current record pointer, 234
  See also READNEXT command

WAIT JOURNAL command, 294–297
Working set, 432
  page fault, 432
WRITEQ TD command, 294
WRITEQ TS command, 270–271
  REWRITE, option, 271

XCTL command, 158